FUNDAMENTALS OF MARKETING

FUNDAMENTALS OF MARKETING

WILLIAM J. STANTON

Professor of Marketing
University of Colorado

SECOND EDITION

McGRAW-HILL BOOK COMPANY

New York   St. Louis   San Francisco   Toronto   London   Sydney

Fundamentals of Marketing

60846

456789 HDMM 109

To Kelly and Little Joe

PREFACE

While several changes have been made in this revision of *Fundamentals of Marketing,* those who are familiar with the first edition will find that the basic theme, approach, and organization have been retained. The central theme is that marketing is a *total system* of business action rather than a fragmented assortment of functions and institutions, as it has often been treated in marketing literature and in practice. More specifically, marketing is defined as a total system of interacting business activities designed to plan, price, promote, and distribute want-satisfying goods and services to household consumers and industrial users.

In this edition all material has been updated, and a chapter on the marketing of services has been added. The chapters on physical distribution and international marketing have been completely rewritten. In the section on the distribution structure, the chapters on selection of channels and competitive conflicts in channels have been rewritten, rearranged, and condensed from three to two chapters. Material on evaluation of salesmen's performances and evaluation of advertising effectiveness has been moved to the appropriate chapters in the section on the promotional program. Several other chapters have been rewritten to introduce recent developments and new concepts where appropriate.

For those not acquainted with the first edition, this is a basic textbook in the dynamic, complex field of marketing. While some attention is directed to the role of marketing in our socioeconomic system, the book is written largely from the viewpoint of management *in an individual firm*—either a manufacturer or a middleman. Emphasis is placed on the marketing problem solving and decision making required of a firm's executives. For the most part, the coverage is analytical and evaluative. At the same time, certainly some descriptive material is necessary in an introductory textbook. However, such material intentionally is limited to the amount needed by the student to undertake some intelligent analysis and evaluation.

Fundamentals of Marketing is intended for use in the introductory course in marketing, which may be offered in a school or college of business administration or in a liberal arts college. It is designed for students who plan to specialize in marketing and also for those who will be taking only one course in the field. Both of these groups are provided with a realistic treatment of marketing as it operates in American business today. The book may also be used in management training programs or for general reading by business executives.

The "systems" idea of marketing has become more meaningful in recent years with the acceptance and implementation of the marketing concept—a philosophy which stresses the need for marketing, rather than for production, orientation. A company's managerial planning and operations should be directed toward satisfying customers' wants and obtaining *profitable* sales volume. In short, marketing is becoming recognized as an all-pervasive part of the system of business management, and all managerial activity in a firm should be directed toward the goal of making the marketing process more effective.

This philosophy may be seen in the framework of the marketing process, which, to be effective, requires that a firm first identify, study, and measure its markets. Management then has four elements—its product, channels of distribution structure, price system, and promotional activities—which can be used to build a program to reach its markets. The firm is seeking to achieve the most effective marketing mix—that is, the best possible combination of the four ingredients. Throughout these four areas, especially in channel structure and promotion, management makes extensive use of another element—the human factor. Personnel or manpower considerations often are paramount in marketing decisions. At all stages in the marketing process, management uses quantitative and qualitative marketing research as an aid.

This framework of the marketing process is reflected generally in the organization of the book's content. The text is divided into eight parts. Part 1 serves as an introduction and includes a chapter on the role of the management process in marketing and one on marketing research. Marketing research is covered very early because frequent reference is made to this managerial tool for decision making. However, sufficient flexibility exists in the organization structure of the book so that an instructor may rearrange the order of some chapters to suit his preferences.

Part 2 is devoted to an analysis of the consumer and the industrial markets. Population, income, customer motivation, and buying patterns are analyzed as factors affecting the market for products.

Parts 3 through 6 deal with the development and operation of a marketing program, and each of these parts covers one of the above-mentioned four components of the marketing mix. In Part 3 various topics related to the product itself are discussed, including product planning and development, product-line policies and strategies, and several characteristics of a product such as branding and packaging. Part 4 covers the distribution structure. Retailing and wholesaling institutions are described and appraised. Consideration is given to the selection of channels of distribution, the selection of individual middlemen, and the ever-present conflict within and among marketing channels. The management of physical distribution, in which this activity is viewed as a system of product flow, is studied in a separate chapter. A firm's price system is the subject of Part 5 where we study pricing objectives, price determination in practice, and some major price policies and strategies. Part 6 is devoted to the total promotional program including the advertising and the personal selling programs.

The major portion of the book pertains to the *domestic* marketing of *manufactured goods*. In the interest of completeness, however, Part 7 is devoted to marketing fundamentals as they are applied in the special fields of agricultural marketing, international marketing, and the marketing of services.

Part 8 covers marketing planning and the analysis and evaluation of the marketing program. Included are such problem areas as sales forecasting and marketing-cost analysis. Chapter 29—the final chapter—is an appraisal of the role of marketing in the economy and a look to the future in this field.

Special attention has been devoted to the preparation of the discussion questions found at the end of each chapter. These questions generally cannot be answered "right out of the book." Instead, they are intended to be thought provoking and to serve as an aid in applying the material in the chapter. Some of the questions require outside field work, and thus have the merit of introducing the students to practical business applications of the textbook fundamentals.

Another feature of *Fundamentals of Marketing* is the inclusion of short cases at the end of each of the eight parts in the text. There are twenty-five cases (twelve new in this edition), and each one focuses on a specific issue related to a topic covered in the text. These cases serve as both a teaching tool and study guide. In line with the managerial approach in this book, the cases provide an opportunity for thorough problem analysis and decision making by the student.

Many people—businessmen, publishers, students, present and past colleagues, and other professors—have contributed greatly to this book. Many of these debts are acknowledged in footnotes and other references in the text. I particularly want to thank Professors Philip R. Cateora (University of Colorado), Charles L. Lapp (Washington University), and James U. McNeal (University of Georgia) for reviewing parts of the manuscript and offering several fine suggestions for its improvement. A review meeting with some of the marketing faculty from Kent State University was also most helpful. Professor John M. Hess of our faculty at the University of Colorado aided me by writing three of the cases, and his authorship is identified with each one.

WILLIAM J. STANTON

CONTENTS

xvi

FUNDAMENTALS OF MARKETING

PART ONE

MODERN MARKETING

1

MARKETING IN THE ECONOMY

Most of us probably consider ourselves rather well informed on the subject of marketing. After all, we watch television commercials and see how advertisers are trying to persuade us to buy; we purchase products on a self-service basis in a supermarket; we observe the quality of personal selling as we buy our clothes or gasoline. Many of us have friends who "can get it for us wholesale," or we ourselves may be shrewd shoppers who can ferret out bargains. Some of us have worked as salesclerks in retail stores. In short, everybody knows something about marketing. It is on this perilous base of a little knowledge that we begin our study.

NATURE AND SCOPE OF MARKETING

While most people probably do know a little something about marketing, the word itself has often been misunderstood and used loosely even by those in the field. When a salesman or sales manager speaks of marketing, he is actually talking about selling; an advertising account executive means advertising; and a department store manager means retailing or merchandising. Each of these people is talking about *one part* of the total marketing activity.

Narrow interpretation

The American Marketing Association Committee on Definitions says that marketing is "the performance of business activities that direct the flow of goods and services from producer to consumer or user."[1] In its comments, the committee suggests a somewhat broader meaning than this, and for the purpose of modern marketing, a broader definition is certainly needed. Marketing processes begin long before the goods go into production. Marketing decisions must be made regarding the product and its market, its pricing, and its promotion. Should the product even be made? How should it be designed, branded, packaged, and labeled? What is the precise composition and size of its potential market? Will advertising or personal selling be the main promotional tool? What will be the initial price? Just as marketing does not begin at the end of the production line, it does not end with the final sale. The customer must be satisfied if we expect his repeat business or if we want him to speak well of our company. Thus a product guarantee and considerable servicing may be required after the sale is made.

The American Marketing Association's narrow definition reflects the production orientation and thinking which have permeated so much of American business. Products have been designed by engineers, manufactured by production men, priced by accountants, and then given to sales managers to sell. This philosophy carries the theme that manufacturing sellers know what is good for the consumer.[2]

Broader concept

Possibly the most expressive, all-encompassing, yet short statement of modern marketing was made some years ago by Paul Mazur. He said that marketing is the delivery of a standard of living to society.[3] Prof. Malcolm McNair of

---

[1] Committee on Definitions, Ralph S. Alexander, Chairman, *Marketing Definitions: A Glossary of Marketing Terms*, American Marketing Association, Chicago, 1960, p. 15.

[2] For a report on one group of industries—forest products—which typically have placed too much emphasis on production and not enough on marketing what is produced, the result being overproduction, low prices, and loss of profits, see Charles J. Miller, "Progress toward Customer-oriented Marketing in the Forest Products Industry," *University of Washington Business Review*, April, 1963, pp. 37–50.

[3] See Paul Mazur, "Does Distribution Cost Enough?" *Fortune*, November, 1947, p. 138.

Harvard added an important concept when he amended Mazur's fine definition to read that marketing is the *creation* and delivery of a standard of living to society.

Just building a good product will not in itself result in a company's success, nor will it have much bearing on consumer welfare. The product must be marketed to consumers before its full value can be realized. Aggressive marketing policies and practices have been largely responsible for the high material standard of living in America. Today through mass low-cost marketing we enjoy products which were once considered luxuries and which are still so classified in many foreign countries.

Definition used in this book

This broad concept of marketing gives us a feel for the "big picture," but it is not precise enough. Consequently, the following definition will be used in this text. *Marketing* is a total system of interacting business activities designed to plan, price, promote, and distribute want-satisfying products and services to present and potential customers.

This concrete definition has several important implications. First, it is a managerial definition rather than a legalistic or economic one. Second, the entire system of business action should be market- or customer-oriented. Customers' wants must be recognized and satisfied effectively. Third, the definition suggests that marketing is a dynamic business process—a total, integrated process—rather than a fragmented assortment of institutions, functions, and products. Marketing is not any one activity, nor is it exactly the sum of several; rather, it is the result of the *interaction* of many activities. Fourth, the marketing program starts with the germ of a product idea and does not end until the customer's wants are completely satisfied, which may be some time after the sale is made. Furthermore, market programming should be done with a maximum of effectiveness and a minimum of cost. Finally, the definition implies that to be successful, marketing must maximize profitable sales *over the long run*. Thus, customers must be satisfied in order for a company to get the repeat business which ordinarily is so vital to success.

There is often some misunderstanding about the relationship between "marketing" and other terms, such as "merchandising," "selling," and "distribution." Marketing is the comprehensive term; the others are each only one part of the marketing system. *Merchandising* may be defined as product planning. It includes the internal planning needed to get the right product or service to the market at the right time, at the right price, and in the proper colors, quantities, and sizes. *Selling* is one method of promotion, and promotion is only a part of the total marketing program. The American Marketing Association recognizes that the term "distribution" is synonymous with the term "marketing." However, distribution is also used in connection with market coverage, and it carries a still different meaning in economics. Recently, *physical distribution* has received increasing attention from marketing executives. This concept refers to a narrower range of materials-flow activities such as transportation and warehousing. To avoid confusion, therefore, it is better not to use distribution as a synonym for marketing.

HISTORICAL DEVELOPMENT OF MARKETING

In a detailed historical study of marketing one could note, first, the causal factors in marketing changes; second, our present-day heritage from older marketing practices and institutions; and third, the relative stability of the system over the long run. In this brief review, we shall see how marketing is born and grows as a society moves from a home handicraft economy of self-sufficiency into a socioeconomic system which involves a division of labor, factory industrialization, and urbanization of the population. We shall see that marketing has developed in an evolutionary rather than a revolutionary fashion.

In a feudal, agrarian, or backwoods economy, the people are largely self-sufficient. They grow their own food, make their own clothes, and build their own houses and tools. There is very little specialization of labor and very little need for trade of any sort. As time passes, however, the concept of division of labor begins to evolve, and craftsmen concentrate on the production of the item in which they excel. This results in each man producing more than he needs of some items and less than he needs of others. Whenever a person makes more than he wants or wants more than he makes, the foundation is laid for *trade*, and trade is the heart of marketing.

As exchange begins to develop in agrarian economies, it is on a simple basis. Most businesses are small-scale endeavors with no specialization in management. They develop from home handicraft organizations, the emphasis is largely on production, and little or no attention is devoted to marketing. In fact, the general practice is to hand-make products to order.

In the next step in the historical evolution of marketing, small producers begin to manufacture their goods in larger quantities in anticipation of future orders. Further division of labor occurs as a type of businessman develops to help sell the increased output. This businessman—who acts as an intermediary between the producers and consumers—is the middleman. To facilitate communication and buying and selling, the various interested parties tend to assemble geographically; trading centers are thus formed. There are nations or parts of nations in the world today going through these various stages of economic development. We may conclude that advancement and refinements in marketing generally go hand in hand with advancements in a civilization.

Modern marketing in the United States was born with the Industrial Revolution. Concurrent with, or as a by-product of, the Industrial Revolution there was a growth of urban centers and a decline in rural population. Home handicraft operations moved into factories, and people came to the cities to work in the factories. Service industries grew to supply the daily needs of factory workers, who were no longer self-sufficient. Marketing remained an infant during the last half of the nineteenth century and the first two decades of the twentieth. Emphasis was on the growth of manufacturing enterprises because the market demand generally exceeded the available supply of products.

Actually, mass marketing was a prerequisite for successful mass production. Only with a system of mass marketing could factories operate at optimum rates of output and thus enjoy the economies of scale. As the factory economy developed and became more complex, the channels through which trade flowed became longer; better methods had to be devised to market the industrial output. The growth of specialists in marketing was a natural step in this evolutionary development.

PRESENT-DAY IMPORTANCE OF MARKETING

Modern marketing came of age after World War I, when the words "surplus" and "overproduction" became increasingly common in our economics vocabulary. Mass-production facilities in both industry and agriculture had developed in the 1800s; after 1920 we saw the growth of bigness in marketing. The importance of marketing in the United States as a whole has become more and more apparent as we have continued to rise above the subsistence economy of the pre-World War I period. Since about 1920, with the exception of war and immediate postwar periods, a strong buyers' market has existed in this country; that is, the available supply of products and services has far surpassed effective demand. There has been relatively little trouble in producing most of these goods; the real problem has been in marketing them.

Ordinarily there cannot be a high level of economic activity without a correspondingly high level of marketing activity. During recession or depression periods, people soon realize that it is a slowdown in marketing activity which is forcing cutbacks in production. (The deep social, economic, and political factors which cause the slowdown in marketing activities are outside the scope of this book.) It becomes evident that in our economy "nothing happens until somebody sells something," and there are urgent requests for increased marketing, not for increased production.

Importance of marketing in our socioeconomic system

Some quantitative measures may help to point up the importance of marketing in our socioeconomic system. The gross national product—the measure of the total goods and services produced in the United States—rose from about $285 billion in 1950 to approximately $765 billion in 1965. It has been marketing's monumental task to move the mountain of goods and nongovernmental services which constitute the bulk of the gross national product. Total retail, wholesale, and manufacturing sales increased from approximately $480 billion in 1950 to $945 billion in 1965. During the same period, retail sales alone doubled, from $144 billion to $284 billion. (The value of total sales exceeds the gross national product because a given unit of a product may be sold more than once before reaching the final customer.) Thus there has been a tremendous increase in the volume of goods and services produced and sold in the United States since World War II, even after allowing for the inflation of prices. Also, there is every evidence that the economy will continue to grow and will require even more effective marketing. Even under the most conservative assumptions, it is forecasted that the American economy will grow faster over the period 1965–1980 than at any time in the preceding fifty years.[4] Measured in constant purchasing power (1965 dollars), the gross national product is projected to grow from $675 billion in 1965 to $1 *trillion* in 1975 and to $1.2 trillion in 1980.

Another indication of the importance of marketing in the economy is the number of people employed in the field. Between one-fourth and one-third of the civilian labor force is engaged in marketing activities. This includes all employees in retailing, wholesaling, transportation, warehousing, and communications industries and all people employed in marketing departments of manufacturers and in marketing activities for financial, service, agricultural, mining, and other industries classified essentially as nonmarketing. Furthermore, over the past century jobs in marketing have increased at a much more rapid rate than jobs in production. Harold Barger pointed out that the number of people engaged in retailing and wholesaling activities increased more than twelve times from 1870 to 1950, as contrasted with a threefold increase in the number of production workers during the same period.[5] The great increase in marketing workers is a reflection of marketing's expanded role in the economy and the increased demand for marketing services.

A measure often used to indicate marketing's importance is its cost. On the average, about 50 cents out of the total retail dollar goes to cover marketing costs. Marketing *costs* should not be confused with marketing *profits,* however, nor should it be assumed that products and services would cost less if marketing activities were not performed.

An economy of abundance   A brief comparison of the American economy with economies found elsewhere in the world further demonstrates the importance of marketing. The type of economy we have largely explains why marketing as we know it is so much an American phenomenon, both in practice and as a field of study. Ours is not a raw-materials, "underdeveloped" economy, nor is it any longer a subsistence economy. It is not an economy of state capitalism, as is found in Russia, nor is it similar to the Western European economy of cartels and small shopkeepers. It most certainly is not the static, perfectly competitive economy of classical economic theory.

Instead, ours is an economy of abundance. This means that as a nation we produce far beyond our subsistence needs. We have an adequate national dis-

---

[4] "From Now to 1980: Amazing Growth," *Business Week,* Oct. 16, 1965, p. 56; forecasts prepared by McGraw-Hill Economics Department.

[5] Harold Barger, *Distribution's Place in the American Economy since 1869,* Princeton University Press, Princeton, N.J., 1955, pp. 4–5.

posable income and considerable discretionary purchasing power. We are under no necessary compulsion to consume all that is produced, but unless we do, a severe economic decline can set in. While marketing exists in every type of *modern* economy, it is an especially important foundation stone for successful business performance in a highly competitive economy of abundance.

American marketing activity has the huge task of encouraging the consumption of the vast output of goods and services of American business and industry. Successful marketing helps to deliver a high standard of living and to prevent a decreased level of economic activity. Although modern marketing has been successful to a reasonably high degree, it has not been greeted with equal joy in all quarters. There are still many scarce social and economic resources in our economy and a number of respected students of our social, economic, and political systems have raised serious questions with respect to the influence marketing activities have on the allocation of these resources. The question they raise is whether too much marketing is leading to a misallocation of these resources— is marketing accepting its responsibility for guiding our economic abundance into socially desirable channels? Possibly we may have been so successful in promoting the consumption of automobiles, fashionable dresses, and outboard motors that we have overlooked other more basic values such as education, savings, or metropolitan services—slum clearance, sewage disposal, and the elimination of air and stream pollution.

In *The Affluent Society*, Prof. John K. Galbraith raised the resource-allocation question in a slightly different fashion.[6] He said that we are investing too much in things and not enough in people, that we are producing too much of some things and not enough of others. This practice carries serious implications for the stability and integrity of our society. Galbraith also suggested that we decrease our emphasis on production and devote greater attention to a more rational use of what we produce. (This suggestion, it seems, would have the unfortunate effect of forcing us to relinquish greater economic growth only because we have not learned to use our abundance wisely.)

David M. Potter, then professor of history at Yale University, in his book *People of Plenty,* examined some of the influences which our economy of abundance has exerted upon the life, culture, and attitudes of the American people.[7] His analysis shows how the influence of abundance cuts across the fields of the behavioral sciences, history, and political science, how it has remade our social structure in the past thirty to forty years, and how it has made democracy in America different from democracy anywhere else in the world. He also points out that we have made mistakes in trying to get the American way of life adopted in foreign countries, largely because we do not understand how economic abundance has influenced our development. Truly the question of market-

[6] John K. Galbraith, *The Affluent Society*, Houghton Mifflin Company, Boston, 1958.

[7] David M. Potter, *People of Plenty*, The University of Chicago Press, Chicago, 1954.

ing and of its influence on the allocation of resources in an economy of abundance is a very important one.

Importance in the individual firm

The vital importance of marketing in the successful operation of an individual firm was suggested in our definition of marketing. Peter Drucker established the position of marketing in a firm and generally epitomized the idea that a business is a marketing organization when he pointed out that[8]

. . . marketing is the distinguishing, the unique function of the business. A business is set apart from all other human organizations by the fact that it markets a product or a service. Neither Church, nor Army, nor School, nor State does that. Any organization that fulfills itself through marketing a product or a service, is a business. Any organization in which marketing is either absent or incidental is *not* a business and should never be run as if it were one. [Italics supplied.]

Marketing considerations are today the most critical factors in business planning and decision making. The National Association of Manufacturers put this cogently when it said:[9]

In this exciting age of change, marketing is the beating heart of many operations. It must be considered a principal reason for corporate existence. The modern concept of marketing recognizes its role as a direct contributor to profits, as well as sales volume.

No longer can a company just figure out how many widgets it can produce and then go ahead and turn them out. To endure in this highly competitive change-infested market, a company must first determine what it can sell, how much it can sell, and what approaches must be used to entice the wary customer. The president cannot plan; the production manager cannot manage; the purchasing agent cannot purchase; the chief financial officer cannot budget, and the engineer and designer cannot design until the basic market determinations have been made.

Several economic forces are pushing marketing to the fore in American business and industry. Product lines are becoming more diversified; stiffer competition is coming both from substitute products and from directly comparable goods; production operations are growing more costly and complex. Markets are ever growing and rapidly changing. More and more money is needed to develop and support marketing programs. Thus risks are increased and the ability to make proper marketing decisions is at a premium.

[8] Peter Drucker, *The Practice of Management*, Harper & Row, Publishers, Incorporated, New York, 1954, pp. 37–38.

[9] As quoted in "An Historic Marketing Paper," *Sales Management*, Mar. 20, 1959, p. 7.

THE MARKETING CONCEPT

As business administrators increasingly recognize that marketing is vitally im-
̄ ̄ ̄ ̄ to the success of a firm and as they realize that a business is a marketing
new way of business thinking and business life is
̄ ̄ ̄ ̄ arketing concept, and it has developed as production-
firms have changed into market-oriented structures.
̄ ̄ pt is based on two fundamental beliefs. First, all com-
̄ ̄ ̄ nd operations should be oriented toward the customer;
̄ ̄ olume should be the goal of a firm. In its fullest sense,
̄ ̄ is a philosophy of business which states that the cus-
̄ ̄ is the economic and social justification of a company's
, all company activities in production, engineering, and
̄ ̄ arketing, must be devoted to, first, determining what
̄ ̄ e and, then, satisfying these wants while still making a

̄ ̄ utive at the General Electric Company, one of the first
̄ ̄ recognize and activate the marketing concept, expressed
when he said:[10]

̄ ̄ ing is a fundamental business philosophy. This definition
̄ ̄ s functions and methods of organizational structuring as
only the implementation of the philosophy. These things are not, in themselves,
the philosophy.

Fundamental to this philosophy is the recognition and acceptance of a
customer-oriented way of doing business. Under marketing the customer becomes the fulcrum, the pivot point about which the business moves in operating
for the balanced best interests of all concerned. . . .

The second fundamental on which the marketing philosophy rests is that it
is rooted in the profit concept, not the volume concept. (I am not eliminating
the use of volume as a rewarding way of obtaining profits from the efficiency
of the service rendered; rather, I am referring to the profitless volume or vol-
ume-for-the-sake-of-volume-alone concept.)

In another work, the marketing concept was defined as "a corporate state
of mind that insists on the integration and coordination of all marketing functions which, in turn, are welded with all other corporate functions, for the basic
objective of producing maximum long-range corporate profits."[11] The article

[10] Fred J. Borch, "The Marketing Philosophy as a Way of Business Life," *The
Marketing Concept: Its Meaning to Management*, American Management Association, Marketing Series, no. 99, New York, 1957, pp. 3–5. For an historical analysis
of the evolution of the marketing concept, starting with its developmental roots in
the 1920s, see Bernard J. LaLonde, "Evolution of the Marketing Concept," in Stephen
A. Greyser (ed.), *Toward Scientific Marketing*, American Marketing Association,
Chicago, 1964, pp. 333–343.

[11] Arthur P. Felton, "Making the Marketing Concept Work," *Harvard Business
Review*, July–August, 1959, p. 55.

also noted that the important ingredients in the concept are (1) a proper state of mind, (2) the actual coordination of all marketing functions, and (3) the use of professional and executive skill of a high order; and that common pitfalls in implementing the concept are (1) inexperienced executives, (2) unsound organizational structures, and (3) incomplete integration traceable to personality clashes, lack of executive teamwork, or one-man domination.

Distinction between the marketing concept and marketing

Administrators must recognize that there is a significant difference between the marketing concept and marketing itself. The marketing concept is a philosophy, an attitude, or a course of business *thinking,* while marketing is a process or a course of business *action.* Naturally the way of thinking determines the course of action.

MARKETING MANAGEMENT: THE APPLICATION OF THE MARKETING CONCEPT

For a business enterprise to realize the full fruits of the marketing concept, the philosophy must be translated into practice. This means that (1) the marketing activities in a firm must be better organized, coordinated, and managed, and (2) the chief marketing executive must be accorded a more important role in total company planning and policy making than has been generally true in the past. As these two changes take place, we see emerging in American business the idea of marketing management. *Marketing management* is the marketing concept in action.

Evolution of marketing management

Marketing management has been developing in American business since the Industrial Revolution. Roughly, it has gone through three stages of development, and a fourth is emerging. However, many small companies are still in one of the earlier stages of marketing organization. Only a few firms have the most developed form of marketing organization and the outlook and philosophy that go with it.

Early in the first period of development, company organization for marketing is simple. Manufacturers have sales departments headed by a sales manager whose major responsibility is to operate the sales force. Other marketing activities, such as market planning, advertising, and marketing research, are generally unknown; product planning and budgeting are the responsibilities of other departments. As markets expand, manufacturers are obliged to make more use of middlemen, thus lengthening the channels of distribution and increasing the complexity of marketing problems. A manufacturer then must devote more attention to reaching his final customers, and he has to work more closely with his middlemen.

COMPANY ORGANIZATION IN WHICH MARKETING ACTIVITIES ARE FRAGMENTED

fig. 1–1

*In the first stage of the evolution of marketing management, there is no marketing depart-
ment, and sales management consists only of operating a sales force. When managerial
responsibility for marketing is fragmented, consider the problems in planning, coordinating,
and directing such marketing activities as advertising, sales forecasting, product planning,
and personal selling.*

Market conditions which develop during this period force manufacturers to expand into specialized marketing activities such as research, advertising, and export sales. These functions are assigned to various executives. The department responsible for selling the company's output is called the sales department, and its chief executive typically still has the title "sales manager" or "director of sales." This type of organization is shown in Fig. 1-1. Planning the product and scheduling output are the responsibilities of the production manager.

In the United States this form of marketing organization predominated until about the start of World War II. There were some companies with a more sophisticated philosophy of marketing, but very few had consolidated marketing departments with their own marketing research bureaus, product-planning sections, and other staff services.

During the second stage, a better appreciation and understanding of the broad scope of sales management result in two important changes in the organizational structures of many firms (see Fig. 1-2). First, all marketing activities, such as advertising, marketing research, and sales promotion, are grouped under one marketing executive, although he is still typically called *sales* manager or vice-president of *sales*. Second, activities such as sales training, product servicing, and sales analysis, which were formerly in departments outside of sales or marketing, now are put under the marketing umbrella. While each of the several divisions (advertising, sales analysis, etc.) may have a separate manager, all report to the chief sales executive.

This type of organization was typical of the drive for increased sales which developed when backlog orders were exhausted during the decade after the close of World War II. The developmental stage extended well into the 1950s in most companies.

In the third stage of the evolutionary process, some companies have adopted the marketing concept and put it into action through the medium of fully integrated marketing management. The chief marketing executive in such a company is often called the marketing manager or has the title "vice-president of marketing." He is aligned with the top men in production and finance, and sometimes personnel, to work with the president as the company's top planning and policy-making group. After studying the changing role of the marketing function, Bund and Carroll stated that their research "lends substance to the position that the marketing plan is increasingly accepted as the cornerstone for a company's total planning effort. This does not mean that the marketing man need be supreme. It signifies only that marketing must be accorded a key role in company management."[12]

Furthermore, executives in production, finance, and engineering can all adopt the marketing concept in their thinking and yet not be involved *directly* in marketing departmental activities.

[12] Henry Bund and James W. Carroll, "The Changing Role of the Marketing Function," *Journal of Marketing*, January, 1957, p. 325.

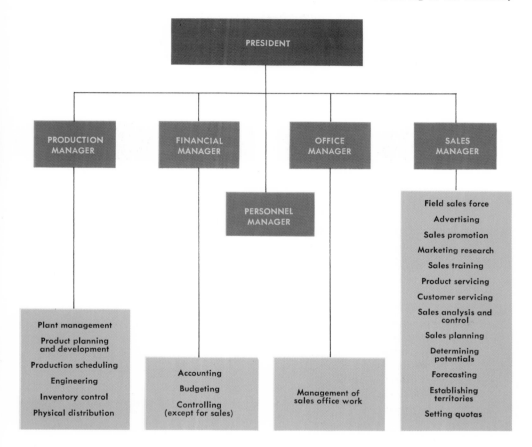

COMPANY ORGANIZATION IN WHICH MARKETING IS VIEWED MORE BROADLY

fig. 1–2

In this stage of the evolution of marketing management, most marketing activities are under the control of the sales manager. The personnel manager no longer handles sales training. But note that the production manager is still in charge of production scheduling, inventory control, and physical distribution, while the office manager still controls management of sales office work.

Under the concept of marketing management, several activities which traditionally are the province of the production manager, financial manager, or other executives become the responsibility of the marketing manager (see Fig. 1-3). For instance, inventory control, transportation, warehousing, and aspects of product planning are often turned over to the marketing manager. Obviously he must coordinate his efforts with those of the production manager and engineer and with the top financial executive, but in the final analysis the

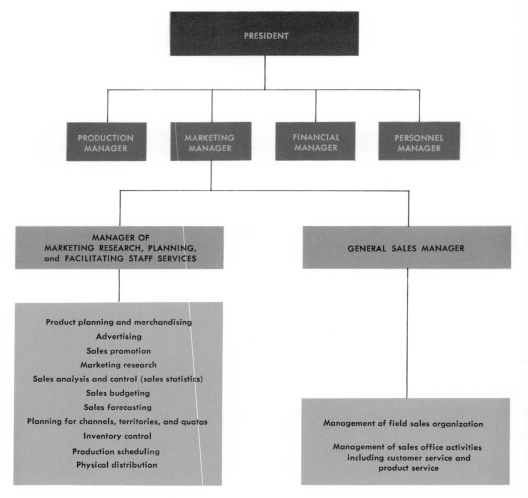

PRESIDENT

PRODUCTION MANAGER

MARKETING MANAGER

FINANCIAL MANAGER

PERSONNEL MANAGER

MANAGER OF
MARKETING RESEARCH, PLANNING,
and FACILITATING STAFF SERVICES

GENERAL SALES MANAGER

Product planning and merchandising
Advertising
Sales promotion
Marketing research
Sales analysis and control (sales statistics)
Sales budgeting
Sales forecasting
Planning for channels, territories, and quotas
Inventory control
Production scheduling
Physical distribution

Management of field sales organization

Management of sales office activities
including customer service and
product service

COMPANY ORGANIZATION APPLYING THE MARKETING CONCEPT

fig. 1–3

At this point all marketing activities have been integrated under a single marketing manager. Organizationally, the company has the "marketing concept."

marketing manager makes the decisions regarding packaging, labeling, design, color, and other product features. The position of the marketing manager is epitomized in General Electric's philosophy that he should be introduced at the *beginning* rather than at the *end* of the production cycle so that he can integrate marketing into each stage of the operations.

Historically, we are now living in this period of marketing organization.

Studies show that, to a large extent, the marketing concept has been adopted by both large- and medium-sized manufacturing companies.[13] How well they have actually implemented the concept, however, is still a moot question. Probably in many cases a company, while using the appropriately fashionable titles and other external trappings, is still paying little more than lip service to the concept. We know that market orientation can come in many forms and degrees.[14] Probably only a small percentage of firms, for example, have established a formal, written marketing program to achieve their marketing goals. The key to implementing the marketing concept successfully is a favorable attitude on the part of top management. As an executive of the Chase Manhattan Bank stated, "Marketing begins with top management. Only top management can provide the climate, the discipline, and the leadership required for a successful marketing program. Top management must know the customers and the prospects; it must set the objectives, establish the policies, develop the plans, and create the organization."[15]

Some companies are entering a fourth stage with respect to their marketing development. In this stage a company moves from the marketing concept to a philosophy in which the entire company becomes a marketing organization. It is not a development which can be represented in an organization chart. Rather, this stage is reached when the inner attitudes of all company executives change so that the whole firm functions to develop, manufacture, and sell a product from the marketing point of view. The president of the Burroughs Corporation caught the spirit of this when he said, "Any company is nothing but a marketing organization."[16] He meant, of course, that since this is true, the really progressive company will recognize that fact in both its organization and its operations. Marketing becomes the basic motivating force for the entire firm, and marketing increasingly conditions all short-term and long-range company policies. As the president of the Pepsi-Cola Company said, "Our business is the business of marketing."[17]

As a firm enters this fourth era it will become increasingly apparent that the marketing concept must permeate the entire company, starting with the board of directors and the president. These executives determine the nature of the business and are responsible for developing an overall program. Major marketing policy making should be the function of the board of directors, and

[13] See, for example, Richard T. Hise, "Have Manufacturing Firms Adopted the Marketing Concept?" *Journal of Marketing*, July, 1965, pp. 9–12.

[14] See Robert W. Lear, "No Easy Road to Market Orientation," *Harvard Business Review*, September–October, 1963, pp. 53–60.

[15] "The Marketing Executive: Industry's New Crown Prince," *News Front*, August 1963, p. 30; see also "Top Level Attitude Guides Change in Market Strategy," *Industrial Marketing*, October, 1964, p. 148.

[16] As quoted in "Burroughs Puts Sales under a Single Hat," *Business Week*, May 28, 1960, p. 62.

[17] As quoted in "Profit-squeeze Fighter: Who Is He?" *Printers' Ink*, Sept. 29, 1961, p. 27.

the president becomes the chief marketing executive. The vice-president of marketing at the International Minerals and Chemical Corporation summarized the organizational implications of the marketing concept when he said:[18]

> But a company cannot become customer conscious by edict. Since all organizations tend to emulate their leader, it is most important that the head of the business be thoroughly customer conscious. There can only be one marketing head in any business and that must be the president. He can develop a mood, an atmosphere, and an *esprit de corps* reflecting the pre-eminence of the customer that permeates every nook and corner of the company.

Figure 1-3 is generally representative of the organizational structure still typically found in firms which are in the fourth stage of marketing management's evolution. The conceptual differences existing during the second, third, and fourth stages are not reflected so much in the organizational structures illustrated in Figs. 1-2 and 1-3 as they are in the basic philosophies underlying each chart. No series of organization charts can fully illustrate the many marketing ideas that have evolved through the years. The philosophies underlying the organization charts shown here, however, can be stated briefly. Underlying Fig. 1-3 is the belief that management should be oriented toward the market. On the other hand, Figs. 1-1 and 1-2 depict structures based on the now-fading philosophy that management should be production-oriented and interested in sales volume, regardless of whether this is profitable.

Increased use of marketing management

The editors of *Sales Management* magazine, together with the Alexander Hamilton Institute, Inc., of New York City, undertook a survey to determine top management's attitudes and activities with respect to marketing organization. Questionnaires were mailed to the presidents of America's 500 leading corporations as ranked by *Fortune* magazine. About 80 per cent of the firms said they had adopted the marketing concept, while over one-half of the remaining presidents believed it was applicable to their companies. As Professor Lazo said, "Big business believes that, just as it applied scientific management to its production operations during the first half of the twentieth century, it must use this same approach to be geared for the second half, or the *marketing era*."[19]

As one might expect, the full implementation of the marketing concept will not be accomplished overnight. The inflexibilities and conservatism of business plus human opposition to change will create some time spread between

---

[18] Anthony E. Cascino, "Organizational Implications of the Marketing Concept," in William Lazer and Eugene J. Kelley (eds.), *Managerial Marketing: Perspectives and Viewpoints*, rev. ed., Richard D. Irwin, Inc., Homewood, Ill., 1962, p. 370.

[19] Hector Lazo, "Big Business Gives Big O.K. to Marketing Management," *Sales Management*, Nov. 21, 1958, p. 34. For a survey which reflects the increasing time being devoted to marketing activities by the chief executive, see "The Chief Executive's Role in Marketing," *Business Management Record*, May, 1963, pp. 23–28.

management's adoption of the concept and the fulfillment of all the consequent necessary organizational adjustments. General Electric executives have estimated that it took over five years to realign that corporation, once the decision was made to adopt the marketing concept.

A few examples from other companies will show that the marketing concept can be put to practical use in virtually every type of industry. The International Minerals and Chemical Corporation, the world's largest independent producer of fertilizers and agricultural chemicals, has applied the marketing concept to such unglamorous products as potash, phosphate, and nitrogen. The company's "full orbit" service program offers over forty marketing, financial, and other management services to wholesalers. IMC has also developed a regionally oriented selling program whereby company agronomists study the soil and then custom-mix the fertilizer best suited to the needs of specific crops grown by major farmers in the area.[20]

The Crown Zellerbach Company, the Westinghouse Electric Company, and the Pillsbury Company are only a few of the many firms which market both consumer and industrial products and which have adopted the marketing concept. A number of major airlines have switched to a marketing emphasis. At Eastern Airlines, for example, organized marketing planning was instituted, a scientific sales-force-management program was established, and the entire company orientation was directed toward customer satisfaction.[21] To an increasing extent marketing is being recognized as the key to success in other service industries such as insurance, telephones, banking, gas, and electricity.[22]

Perhaps a most unusual—but nevertheless highly successful—application of the marketing concept is found in the example of the New York Mets baseball team. While they may not win many ball games, they attract customers in droves. They have a sound marketing program based on analyzing their market, emphasizing the team's special pluses, cashing in on lapses of the competition (the New York Yankees), and going along with customer dictates.[23]

We have seen marketing emerge in its modern form—a total system of interacting business activity designed to satisfy consumers' wants. The marketing concept has been recognized as a philosophy of business, and firms have

[20] Jack B. Weiner, "They Make Things Grow at IMC," *Dun's Review and Modern Industry*, February, 1965, p. 32; for a report on the retail agricultural centers established by the Monsanto Company to provide localized feeding, weeding, and debugging service, see "Monsanto Moves into Farmers' Backyard," *Business Week*, Feb. 6, 1965, p. 60.

[21] "Eastern Takes Off," *Sales/Marketing Today*, April, 1965, p. 7; for a report on the shift to a marketing emphasis at United Airlines, see "United Charts a New Flight Plan," *Business Week*, Aug. 14, 1965, p. 128.

[22] Eugene M. Johnson, "Marketing Is Key to Success in Service Business," *Sales/Marketing Today*, November, 1964, p. 8; see also Martin R. Warshaw, "Effective Marketing—Key to Public Utility Growth," *Michigan Business Review,* November, 1962, pp. 16–20.

[23] "How to Make a Last-place Product a Banner Success," *Sales Management*, Apr. 16, 1965, p. 34.

moved to implement this concept. Organizational structures and management thinking have been reshaped. The marketing concept does not mean that marketing executives must run a company. The chief executive may come up through the ranks of production, accounting, or any other department, but he must be truly oriented toward the consumer.

QUESTIONS AND PROBLEMS

1   "From one point of view marketing may be defined as the revenue-generating activity in a company. Production men use these revenues and financial executives manage them. However, the main job of the marketing man is to generate a satisfactory revenue over a long period of time." Discuss the meaning and implications of this quotation. Is this revenue approach to marketing compatible with the marketing concept?

2   Marketing has been defined as the creation of time, place, and possession utilities. Explain the ideas involved in this definition.

3   What is the difference between marketing and selling?

4   One way of appraising and explaining the importance of marketing in our economy is to consider how we would live if there were no marketing facilities. Describe some of the ways in which your daily activities would be affected under such circumstances.

5   What are some ways in which a company's production manager can show that he is marketing-oriented? A financial manager?

6   "There is no such thing as overproduction in our economy; there is only under-consumption or underdemand." Explain.

7   How do you account for the fact that the number of workers engaged in wholesaling and retailing increased twelvefold between 1870 and 1950, as contrasted with only a threefold increase in production workers during the same period? Does this indicate growing wastes and inefficiencies in marketing?

8   What are the basic differences between the third and fourth stages in the evolution of marketing management?

9   What environmental factors have stimulated the development and implementation of the marketing concept?

10   How did the Industrial Revolution focus attention on marketing as a separate field of business activity?

11   Many financial institutions and public utility firms have no executive with the title "marketing manager," "vice-president of sales," or some similar title. Does this mean that these firms have no marketing problems? What companies or industries can you name which have no sales or marketing problems?

12   A sixty-five-year-old vice-president of a large midcontinent railroad was quoted as saying that in the railroad business, "marketing is just a new-fashioned idea of calling rates something different; really, marketing is nothing but determining rates." Do you agree? If not, how would you answer him?

13   One writer has stated that any business has only two functions—marketing and innovation. How would you explain this statement to a student majoring in production management, accounting, finance, or personnel management?

14 "The marketing concept is simply empire building on the part of the marketing people; it is an attempt to enlarge marketing's 'box' in a company's organization charts." Do you agree?

15 "The marketing concept does not imply that marketing executives will run the firm; the concept requires only that whoever is in top management be marketing-oriented." Explain and give examples of how a production manager, company treasurer, or personnel manager can be marketing-oriented.

16 The marketing concept seems to emphasize profit maximization as a goal of business. Is this an ethical goal? Is it in keeping with a firm's responsibility to society?

17 Cite examples in your college community of firms which in recent months or years have become more consumer-oriented. Explain specifically what these organizations have done in this matter. Prepare a similar list, with suitable explanations, of national firms.

2

MANAGEMENT'S ROLE IN MARKETING

What makes a business successful? The preceding chapter suggested that its marketing program is a major contributing factor. Then what is it that makes a marketing program successful? The answer is a marketing mix properly attuned to customers' wants, competition, social and legal controls, and other environmental forces. "Marketing mix" is the term used to describe the combination of the four elements which constitute the core of a company's marketing program. These elements are the *product*, the *channels of distribution*, the *pricing policies and practices*, and the *promotional methods*. Each element contains countless variables. A company may produce one product or several—related or unrelated; products may be branded or unbranded and packed in single or multiple units. They may be distributed through wholesalers or directly through retailers; they may be sold through one or many retailers in a single market. Ultimately, a marketing executive must select the marketing mix—the combination of all these variables—which will most improve his firm's profit position over the long run. Furthermore, his ability as an administrator may be judged by the results he gets from his arrangement of the marketing mix.[1]

We still have not identified the really basic factor in business success. If a proper marketing mix is influential in a firm's well-being, then who determines the nature and composition of this mix? The answer is the *management* of the firm. The fundamental determinant of a firm's long-run success is the caliber of its management. In many studies of business failure, poor management was identified as the primary factor. While poor marketing, inadequate financing, or ineffective production might have appeared as superficial reasons for the failure, each of these may be attributed to poor management.

NATURE OF MANAGEMENT

The "marketing" part of the term "marketing management" was defined in Chapter 1, but what about the "management" part? *Management* or *administration* (the terms are used synonymously here) may be defined as the process of planning, organizing, directing, and evaluating the efforts of a group of people toward a common goal. As a result of management, the combined group output surpasses the sum of individual outputs.

The management process is not limited to marketing or even to business in general. It may be found in any field of human endeavor where a group of individuals are seeking common objectives. Whether it is a political party, an athletic team, a military unit, or a governmental body, every group's efforts must be planned, organized, guided, and evaluated—that is, these efforts must be managed—if the group is to achieve its aims.

Management as a separate field

Management is a separate and distinct skill; it is an art (some people call it a science) in and of itself. As such, it should not be confused with technical operating skills. Managerial skills and operational abilities are not automatically interchangeable. A good salesman is not necessarily a good sales manager; one who excels at creating advertisements will not necessarily stand out as a fine manager of an advertising department. Conversely, an outstanding administrator may have had only modest success as a technical operator in his field, although some practical experience may be helpful.

Because administrative ability is a distinct skill, it is adaptable to various jobs. The ability to plan, direct, organize, and evaluate human efforts is equally usable whether the executive is working for an automobile manufacturer or an appliance maker. Military leaders have become business executives; business

---

[1] See Neil H. Borden, "The Concept of the Marketing Mix," *Journal of Advertising Research*, June, 1964, pp. 2–7.

executives have moved into college presidencies; college presidents have moved into administrative positions in other fields.[2]

Marketing executives as managers

A marketing executive is an administrator and, consequently, performs one or more of the usual management functions. This is true whether the person is working for a manufacturer, retailer, broker, wholesaler, or some other institution and regardless of whether he is in the top, middle, or lower echelon of management. The sales supervisor who is just above the rank of salesman is an administrator, and so is the vice-president in charge of marketing. The nature, scope, and significance of their administrative responsibilities may differ, but they both are managers.

THE MANAGEMENT PROCESS IN MARKETING

In the theory of management it is generally recognized that the management or administrative process is comprised of several major managerial functions. Although various authors assign different titles to these functions, there is an underlying agreement on what they are. In this book the management process will be interpreted as including the following managerial functions: (1) determining objectives, (2) planning, including the establishment of strategies and tactics, (3) organizing and coordinating, (4) staffing and assembling other resources, (5) operating and directing, (6) analyzing and evaluating. The following sections are devoted to the marketing application of the major functions of management.

Determining objectives

A firm's activity must be goal-directed to be effective. Since a firm's marketing objectives form the foundation of its marketing management, the first task of the marketing administrators is to determine their goals. These goals are an interpretation by management of its particular needs at a given time and place, and they guide the company's progress along the path to wherever management wishes the firm to be in the future.

Ordinarily a firm has different levels of marketing objectives ranging from its ultimate long-range goals to its specific short-run operational ones. The broad objective may be to market a volume of goods at a level of profit over the long run that will satisfy the interests of the stockholders, consumers, and labor unions and still meet all governmental regulations. Broadly stated goals,

---

[2] For a report on the growing number of marketing executives who are shuttling from one field to another—from TV sets to pots and pans, from pens to tractors, etc.—and who are demonstrating that marketing administrative skills can be applied successfully to almost any industry or product, see A. J. Vogl, "Marketing's New Breed: The Industry Switchers," *Sales Management*, Nov. 20, 1964, p. 25.

however, such as "maximize profits" or "capture the tape-recorder market," are too vague to guide management effectively. Management must develop more specific objectives. These goals should be so stated as to enable every decision-making unit in the company to coordinate its activities with those of the firm as a whole. A specific goal such as "sign up 300 new dealers next year" or "increase the sale of high-margin products by 20 per cent" then becomes a managerial tool for the guidance of executives in their day-to-day activities.

In marketing, as in other types of group effort, planning and operating decisions must be in line with the goals set up by management. For example, if the objective is to reach a mass market with a consumer product, then the company must attempt to get distribution through the maximum number of retail outlets. The decision to use only one retail outlet in each city would not be consistent with the goal and consequently would be a poor decision.

Planning

Once management has established its objectives, the next step in the administrative process is to determine the manner in which these goals will be reached. This managerial activity is called *planning*. Ordinarily planning involves the consideration of several alternative courses of action which could be taken to reach the objectives. Through problem-solving and decision-making processes, the administrators select the best of the alternatives. Without planning, a company's operations have no meaning and no direction; there can be no orderly procedure in management's pursuit of its goals.

Planning may be classified by the length of time for which it is done and by the relative breadth of the activities planned. Short-term planning usually covers a year or less; long-term planning, one to five or ten years. Plans may cover many areas of activity or one area.

The general management concept of planning has broad and countless applications in the field of marketing. Marketing executives are engaged in long-range and short-range planning regarding their markets, products, distribution systems, and promotional programs. The planning process may include laying plans for the introduction of a new car model or making sales forecasts. Marketing plans may be concerned with broad major programs, such as deciding when a large department store will open a new suburban branch, or with a specific situation, such as determining ways and means of promoting fresh produce in a supermarket on a weekend.

"Strategy" and "tactics" are essentially military terms, but they have achieved wide application in nonmilitary activities. In marketing terms, a *strategy* is the over-all plan of action to reach a predetermined marketing objective; *tactics* are the detailed methods and techniques employed to implement the strategy. As an illustration, assume that a garment manufacturer's goal is to enter the prestige, luxury, high-income market for clothes. His strategy regarding channels of distribution would be to sell his product through one high-quality clothing store in each market. The tactics of the situation would be the selection of the specific store, such as I. Magnin, Marshall Field and Company, or Saks Fifth Avenue. As promotional strategy, this manufacturer might plan an advertising campaign around a prestige appeal and nonprice competition. Promotional tactics would include using such media as *The New Yorker* and *Esquire* magazines and never mentioning price in the advertisements. The specific advertisements would feature social and business leaders— the "tastemakers"—wearing the clothes in nightclubs, country clubs, or expensive resorts.

Unless the objective in a given situation is specifically stated, there may be some confusion about what constitutes objectives, strategies, and tactics. In the above example of the garment manufacturer, some people might reason that the company's objective is to broaden its market. Then its strategy might be to capture the high-income market, and its tactics would consist of distribution in high-quality stores and a prestige-appeal promotional campaign. Other people might argue that the goal is to expand into the high-income market— which was the example as presented. The issue here concerns the *level* of the objectives, and the concepts of marketing strategies and tactics are meaningful only after the level of objectives is established. Thus, what is considered a specific goal by one executive may be interpreted by another as only a strategy helping to achieve a broader objective.[3]

Organizing and coordinating

Organizing is another major phase of the management process, and coordinating is a significant part of organizing. (Some authors regard the two as separate functions.) *Organizing* is the process of arranging activities and the people engaged in these activities in such a way as to achieve the maximum output with the highest possible degree of efficiency and coordination. This process begins after management determines the goals and establishes a plan of action. The end structure of the process is an organization. In a good organization, the people involved produce more effectively as a group than they could individually. Marketing management at all executive echelons and in all types of companies—manufacturers, wholesalers, and retailers—normally engages in the organizing process and is concerned with organizational structure.

Within the marketing department, activities in sales, advertising, marketing research, new-product development, customer service, and sales statistics all require careful coordination. Salesmen can help the advertising division and the advertising men can be of direct benefit to the sales force. All the divisions of the marketing department—both selling and sales-supporting—can be of value to one another. According to a top marketing executive at the Beatrice

---

[3] For a discussion by several marketing executives concerning practical methods of establishing marketing objectives and of developing marketing plans, see *The Development of Marketing Objectives and Plans*, National Industrial Conference Board, Inc., Experiences in Marketing Management, no. 3, New York, 1963.

Foods Company, one of the fastest-growing manufacturers of dairy, grocery, and candy products, his company's biggest challenge is to achieve "more effective coordination of the marketing efforts of our scattered and diverse operating divisions, tying these more closely to the overall corporate program."[4] A divisional director of marketing planning at the Pittsburgh Plate Glass Company anticipates increasing difficulty in achieving success in marketing unless the various functions of marketing are integrated by improved means.[5]

There are countless possible examples of *interdepartmental coordination.* Marketing can furnish sales estimates so the production department can better plan its work, or marketing can push items which are overstocked. Production can help marketing by manufacturing the proper quantity and quality of products at the right time; production can also provide product information for sales training and advertising programs. Marketing departmental budgets may be furnished for the finance department, and the two departments can cooperate in controlling selling costs.

Marketing executives must coordinate their activities with advertising agencies, transportation companies, and other *outside companies* which are helping the seller in his marketing program. Advertising agencies must plan their campaigns to coincide with the introduction of a new model. Transportation companies must have carrier facilities available when and where the product is to be loaded. The manufacturer can help by furnishing information regarding new products; middlemen can help by giving the product adequate promotion and good display space.

The marketing concept implies the coordination of all company activities which impinge on the consumer.[6] Yet the organizational proposals and changes made to achieve this coordination can result in organizational conflicts between the marketing department and other departments. Conflict occurs (1) because each department wishes to stress the importance of its own tasks (just as marketing stresses the consumer point of view) and (2) because each department defines its goals narrowly and in its own self-interest. Thus, engineering emphasizes functional features and few models with standard parts; marketing emphasizes sales features and many models with custom components. Finance wants set budgets and prices to cover costs; marketing wants flexible budgets and pricing to further market development. These conflicts will continue as long as each department is judged by the efficient performance of its own tasks, and not by its overall company contribution. In this light, top management should reduce any narrow interest in departmental efficiency and, instead, work toward interdepartmental policies designed to advance total company interests.

[4] "What's New in Marketing," *Sales Management,* Nov. 10, 1964, p. 159.

[5] *Ibid.*, p. 108. For a special report on the role of the marketing executive in formulating and directing *advertising* strategy, see "Controlling the Advertising Function," part 1, "Determining What to Do," *Sales Management*, July 3, 1964, pp. 69–92.

[6] This paragraph is adapted from Philip Kotler, "Diagnosing the Marketing Takeover," *Harvard Business Review*, November–December, 1965, pp. 70–72.

Staffing and assembling other resources

The most important function of management is staffing the organization—assembling the human resources. If management is the key to successful business operations, then staffing is the key to successful management. Many will prefer to nominate planning, motivating, or some other activity as the critical function of management. However, proper personnel selection—both executive and nonexecutive—will eliminate or substantially reduce many management problems. A marketing manager's job is made easier if he hires an excellent advertising manager, sales force manager, or director of marketing research. The sales force manager, in turn, has fewer problems with training, supervision, motivation, and compensation if he hires excellent salesmen.

Operating and directing

After the goals have been set, the planning accomplished, and the organization established and staffed, then the program must be executed. Thus operating, directing, and motivating become important phases of the management process. In the final analysis no plan is worth much unless it is carried out effectively. Particularly is this important in marketing, because success depends upon the way the business is operated. Management may develop excellent plans and strategies, but unless the sales force carries out its end of the task, success cannot be achieved. Here again we see the importance of staffing and selection. Good men may bring about successful results even if the original planning was mediocre. The management function of operating and directing includes operating a sales force, directing an advertising campaign, and working with middlemen. The selection, training, supervision, and motivation of the sales force are part of this management activity.

Analyzing and evaluating

The final stage of the management process consists of analyzing and evaluating the results of the company's plans and operations to determine whether or not they met expectations. There are at least four major areas of application of this managerial function with respect to the marketing program of an individual manufacturer or middleman. First, the executive may analyze net sales volume or marketing costs in total and also by territories, products, or customer groups. In many firms the bulk of the sales volume and net profits comes from a small percentage of the customers, products, or territories. Management is often unaware of this situation. Consequently, it misdirects its marketing efforts and costs by spreading them evenly over all territories, products, or customers even though these units do not produce equal returns to the company. Second, the performance and productivity of the individual salesmen may be evaluated. Third, both manufacturers and middlemen may evaluate the effectiveness of their advertising programs. Fourth, individual manufacturers may want to evaluate the performance of their middlemen. Manufacturers are interested in such things as a middleman's volume in the light of his quota, a middleman's adherence to the manufacturer's policies, and customers' reactions to middlemen.

THE ESTABLISHMENT OF MARKETING POLICIES

In order to guide executives in their decision making on recurring marketing problems, management should establish marketing policies covering every phase of its program. A *marketing policy* is a statement of a course of action which will be followed under a given set of circumstances. For example, after careful consideration the marketing executives in a manufacturing company may decide to place suggested retail prices on their products. Management may decide that it will pay half the cost of any retailer's advertisement which features the manufacturer's product. A retailer may decide to stay open until 9 P.M. on Monday, Wednesday, and Friday nights. Some policies are major ones, such as a manufacturer's decision to sell to only one retailer in a market or a retailer's decision to sell everything in the store at one price; others are less important. But they all serve the same essential purpose: they afford uniform executive action and uniform treatment of customers, and they save valuable executive time.

A policy is only as good as the study and research upon which it is based. Also, policies should be stable; if they are changed frequently, they cease to serve as guides. At the same time, a policy should be flexible; it should be reviewed periodically and revised when necessary. A flexible policy allows for some leeway in executive judgment and action. It is adaptable to a reasonable range of variations surrounding a given business situation.

PROBLEM SOLVING AND DECISION MAKING IN MARKETING

Marketing management consists in a never-ending process of recognizing marketing problems, analyzing them, and making decisions. In fact, relative abilities in the combined art of problem solving and decision making are the features which differentiate high-caliber executives from the less able ones. One reason marketing executives generally receive higher-than-average earnings is that problem solving is more difficult in marketing than in many other fields. It is difficult because much of it involves abstract reasoning and subjective analysis. Determining what high-fashion dresses to buy for the coming season or determining to what extent automobiles are symbols of social status is a decision which does not fully lend itself to mathematical analysis.

One hallmark of a good executive is his ability to make decisions and to make them promptly. Some managers evade the responsibility of making decisions by enveloping themselves in a cloak of anonymity called a committee;

some pass the buck to other executives. Many people find it difficult to make decisions. A student may ask his girl where she would like to go for the evening, rationalizing that he is being considerate. Actually he is refusing to make a decision. A businessman is really ducking the task of decision making when he says he "lets his wife run the house and raise the children without interference."

Some decision-evading executives issue progress reports, but never a final decision, saying that they need more information. This is often not a legitimate excuse. Ordinarily nobody has all the information needed or wanted, yet the situation will not wait; a decision must be made. This is as true in other walks of life as it is in business. The quarterback must call a play and execute it in less than twenty-five seconds, even though he would like more information, for example, what defense is being set up against him. Often all information needed will not be available until after the decision is made. After the team runs the play, the quarterback finds out what kind of defense was set up against him. After a company locates a branch on a given corner, the executives find out whether a sufficient number of customers are attracted.

Management ordinarily will never know if it made the best possible decision, even after it has been executed and the results are in. No matter how great the results are, an alternative decision might have turned out better. For example, if a quarterback with a ball on his own 15-yard line called a pass play and gained 60 yards, the move would be loudly acclaimed. But was that play the best one to call? No one knows; possibly an end run would have been good for 85 yards and a touchdown. A company which opens a store on a given corner may make $25,000 net profit the first year. Was this the best location? We do not know, and we never will know. If the store had been located across the street, it might have made $50,000 net profit, or it might have lost money.

Environmental factors affecting decision making

Marketing strategies, tactics, and policies are formulated within a framework of forces which constitute the firm's environment. Some of these forces are *external* factors generally not controllable by the executives in a firm. Other forces are *internal* to a company and thus are essentially controllable by management. An executive might paraphrase the words of one organization: "Grant me the strength to change the things I can change, the serenity to accept those I cannot, and the wisdom to know the difference." The ability and effectiveness of a decision-making executive may be measured by the creativity and skill with which he can (1) adjust to the external elements in his changing environment, (2) forecast the direction and intensity of these changes, and (3) use the controllable forces at his command in adapting to this external environment.

External, uncontrollable forces   Some of the major external factors which will influence an executive's decision making are the competition his firm faces, the nature of its market, various legal and social factors, and, finally, some aspects of the distribution structure.

COMPETITION   A firm usually faces competition from other firms in the same industry or from companies in other industries offering substitute products or services. Consequently, a marketing executive should understand a great deal about the economics of these industries. Regarding his own industry, he should understand its cost structure, pricing policies, general promotional practices, and any other competitive aspect which may influence his own planning and operation. For instance, in an industry where fixed costs are a large percentage of total costs, management may be willing to adopt flexible pricing practices so that it can cut its price below an announced level in order to make a sale. This willingness stems from the fact that in the short run management needs only to cover variable or out-of-pocket costs; any return above that level will help cover the huge fixed expense.

Management should be aware of the balance of power within its industry. The percentage of the total industry sales a company is getting in each geographical market and whether this share of the market is increasing or decreasing will influence policy decisions.

Management must also be constantly alert to the potential threat of industries marketing substitutable products or services. Steel manufacturers are feeling inroads from aluminum and plastics producers. Interindustry competition among companies making aluminum foil, plastic wrap, tin cans, and other types of containers has been heightened by the revolution in packaging.

MARKET DEMAND   The environmental influence of the market itself on marketing decisions was stressed in Chapter 1. This tremendously important factor is the subject of Part 2 (Chapters 4 to 7) and is pointed up frequently throughout the text. Both the quantitative and qualitative aspects of the market affect decision making by marketing management. The number of potential customers, their location, buying power, buying motives, and buying habits or patterns—all should be subjects of careful, detailed study.

LEGAL AND SOCIAL FORCES   To an increasing extent, management is becoming aware of the vital influence that legislation at the Federal, state, and local levels exercises in marketing decision making. Antitrust legislation, laws prohibiting price discrimination and unfair competition, and various restrictive measures pertaining to advertising, labeling, and packaging are only a few examples of public regulation which must be considered.

Marketing executives are also responding more and more to social influences. Management realizes the value of a good company image. Public disapproval of misleading advertising, poor product performance, hidden finance charges, and inadequate product information can indelibly hurt a business. In general, management knows that it must pay attention to its social responsibilities and that its decision making must be done within the framework of acceptable social practices if the company is to benefit in the long run.

DISTRIBUTION STRUCTURE   Several features of the distribution structure —the system by which goods flow physically and title is moved from producer to ultimate user—are beyond the control of executives who must use the structure. Facilities for handling and transporting the goods are largely external factors, for instance, as are the distribution institutions such as retailers and wholesalers.

Internal, controllable forces   Management has under its control three sets of internal forces which may serve both as effective forces in adjusting to the external environmental change and also as factors limiting the range of executive decision making: (1) the product itself; (2) the other components of the marketing mix—the price system, the promotional program, and some features of the distribution system; and (3) the company's resources in nonmarketing departments.

NATURE OF THE PRODUCT   Management may counteract, or capitalize on, the external environment by deciding to add to its group of products, to drop some, or to alter others. A company may also change its brand, package, or product design in order to adjust to outside forces. At the same time, the nature of the product will influence decisions on channels, advertising, and other areas of company policy making. To illustrate, the unit price, the frequency of purchase, and the postsale service needed are product factors influencing decisions on the marketing program. A staple product, slightly differentiated from competitive items, will require pricing, distribution, and advertising decisions different from those used for a highly distinctive product.

PRICING, DISTRIBUTION, AND PROMOTION   Price can be a powerful weapon to aid a marketing executive in adapting to his environment. Sound decisions on raising or lowering a price, for instance, may be a determining factor in whether a company increases or decreases its share of the market. Changing the mix of advertising and personal selling may be a way to counter a competitive threat, or a wise choice of advertising media (newspapers, TV, etc.) may help a company to improve its market position. Even though the distribution structure was noted above as an external factor, a marketing executive has considerable working latitude within that framework. He has a choice of channels through which he will distribute his products, for example, and the wisdom he uses in this selection may make the difference between a strong or a weak market position.

NONMARKETING RESOURCES   A firm's production and its financial and personnel capability, as well as its marketing structure, establish environmental limits on the marketing program. If a firm is considering the addition of a new product to its existing group, can existing facilities and experiences be used? If the new product requires a new plant or new machinery, then financial capability enters the picture. Some firms cannot enter new markets or embark upon marketing new products because of insufficient or inadequate personnel.

Problem-solving processes

A procedure for the solution of marketing problems is outlined below, but at this point three ideas should be considered. First, there is a growing need for empirical data and quantitative analytical tools as aids in problem solving. A facility with statistics and an understanding of the values of operations research, linear programming, and other mathematical concepts can be of the greatest assistance to a marketing executive today. Quantitative market analysis, transportation, warehousing, establishing channels of distribution, forecasting sales, establishing quotas and territories, and many other marketing tasks are performed more easily and decisions are apt to be more sound if quantitative analytical tools are used.

A second idea to ponder is the importance of the behavioral sciences as aids in decision making. For many years marketing men were oriented toward economics and political science. Today management is also beginning to capitalize on the potential contributions of psychology, sociology, and anthropology. These behavioral sciences can help in solving problems related to marketing organizational structures, product policies on branding and packaging, consumer motivation, attitudes, opinions, behavior, and so on.

The third point is really a note of caution and a corollary to the idea just stated. Marketing essentially presents a set of *human* problems because it involves the satisfaction of human wants. The temptation to consign decision making to mathematical devices, research gimmicks, and other contrivances should be avoided. Sometimes it becomes fashionable to adopt certain concepts. Management may leap so quickly or so far in its acceptance of new tools and concepts that they become almost a fetish.

One procedure for solving marketing problems will be explained briefly. No single approach is better than any other; basically, all are variations of a scientific method applied to marketing management problems.

In this approach, five steps are involved. (It is assumed that the executives already have a thorough understanding of their industry, product, and market and the other environmental forces which will influence their decision.)

1. Carefully and specifically define the problem.

2. Determine reasonable courses of action.

3. Identify the major issues, factors, or subproblems bearing on the main problem.

4. Analyze each major issue and come to a decision on each in light of the alternative courses of action.

5. Make a decision; that is, select the best alternative.

Before an executive can solve a marketing problem, he must recognize that one exists, and then he must be able to identify it clearly. This is no easy task. Sometimes a side issue is mistakenly interpreted as the main problem. In other instances, symptoms of a problem are mistaken for the problem itself. An analogy drawn from the medical field may sharpen this point. A person goes to a physician complaining of recurring headaches. Basically the headaches are only symptoms. The real problem may be emotional tension, eyestrain, or any one of several other factors. In any event, the physician must identify and clearly define the problem before he can hope to remedy it.

In a marketing situation a symptom is often diagnosed as the basic problem. A marketing executive may say that his big problem is that his sales have declined steadily for two years. Actually declining sales are only a symptom. The real problem may be noncompetitive pricing, poor service to middlemen or consumers, poorly packaged or designed products, poor advertising, or a combination of several weaknesses. Truly it may take some careful investigating to pinpoint the real problem. Often a physician or a marketing executive will treat a symptom for some time before finding out he has not yet found the real source of the trouble.

After an executive has decided what the main problem is, he should carefully define it in the form of a question. A question requires an answer. Instead of stating that the company's problem is its product packaging, the executive will ask: "From a marketing standpoint, what are the weaknesses in the product's packaging?" or "What packaging changes should be made to improve our product's marketability?" Questions should be specific. Broad questions, such as "What can the company do to increase its sales?" do not lend themselves to a good analysis.

The second step in the problem-solving process is to decide upon the alternative courses of action which seem reasonable under the circumstances. Normally this is not a difficult thing to do. Assume that a luggage manufacturer's problem is: "What channels of distribution should we use for our new line of airplane luggage?" Based on his understanding of the product, company, market, and other environmental factors, he may decide that the following channels might be used:

Manufacturer—retailers (department stores, large luggage stores, discount houses)—consumers

Manufacturer—leather goods wholesalers—retailers—consumers

Manufacturer—manufacturers' agents—retailers—consumers

Other *possible* alternatives, such as door-to-door selling, are not always *reasonable* ones.

In some problems there may be only two reasonable alternatives. Assume that a manufacturer of business machines such as Burroughs is trying to decide whether to add electric razors to its group of products. About the only major alternative courses of action are to add or not to add.

The third and fourth stages in problem solving are to identify the major issues which bear on the main problem, to analyze these issues, and finally to reach a decision on each one. The conclusions reached will have determining influences on the main decision. To illustrate, a manufacturer of electric office machines has posed the problem of whether to add a line of electric razors. The major issues bearing on this problem are as follows:

1.   Is there an adequate market demand for the proposed product?

2.   From a marketing standpoint, can the proposed product be handled through the company's existing channels of distribution, middlemen, sales organization, advertising program, and so forth?

3.   Does the product fit into the company's present production structure with respect to necessary labor skills, sources of materials, and product facilities?

4.   What are the profit possibilities for the proposed product?

5.   Does the new product pose any legal problems with respect to patent and antitrust regulations?

6.   Is the product in keeping with the company's overall image, self-concept, and objectives?

Thus, before it can make a sound decision on whether to add electric razors, management must first carefully analyze in great detail each of the above issues, or subproblems, and come to a decision on each one. Failure to recognize all the important issues may result in a very poor decision.

Management must consider the effect the subproblem decisions have on one another. Also, the major issues are not always equally important. An administrator cannot count up the number of "yes" and "no" decisions on the subproblems and from this make his final decision. In the above case, the decision on issues 2 to 6 may have favored adding the product to the line, but the decision on issue 1 may have been negative. This one negative decision—that there is not an adequate market demand—should override all the others, and the firm should not add the product. On the other hand, if there were a substantial demand and if the profit possibilities looked encouraging, the manufacturer might add the product even though it did not fit well into the existing marketing or production structure.

The final step is to make the decision regarding the main problem. This involves selecting the best alternative course of action in light of the analysis of the major issues or subproblems.

Problem solving and decision making are the heart of the management process. To aid in this activity, executives have at their disposal the important tool of marketing research, which is the subject of the next chapter.

QUESTIONS AND PROBLEMS

1   If administrative ability is a distinct skill and is transferable among various jobs, why do you think so many more top marketing executives come up through

the ranks of the sales force than through other divisions in marketing such as advertising or marketing research?

2   "The targets assigned to departmental operating executives should be consistent with company goals." Give some examples of sales department goals which might be in conflict with the goals assigned to production executives. To financial executives. To company engineers.

3   Explain how the marketing department can serve as a channel of communication between the top management in a firm and the company's market.

4   Suggest some strategies and tactics which might reasonably be employed to reach the following marketing goals:
    a. A furniture manufacturer wishes to market patio furniture as an addition to his present group of products.
    b. The Chrysler Corporation wishes to market successfully a compact model of its Chrysler car.
    c. A wholesaler of building materials wants to increase the average size of his sales; that is, he hopes to reduce the number of small orders.
    d. The cigar manufacturers' trade association wants to increase the market for cigars among male college students.

5   Based on your knowledge of the recent advertisements of the following companies, what do you think are their current marketing objectives?
    a. The Campbell Soup Company
    b. The Ford Motor Company
    c. The manufacturer of Crest toothpaste (Procter & Gamble)
    d. A leading department store in your college city or in the nearest large city
    e. The telephone company
    f. An office machines manufacturer such as IBM, Burroughs, or National Cash Register

6   Interview a few small, local retailers (barbershop or beauty shop, restaurant, shoe repair shop, hardware store, clothing store, etc.) located near your campus to determine what, if any, specific marketing objectives these firms have consciously established.

7   What department in a manufacturing firm should be responsible for each of the following activities?
    a. Credit management   d. Advertising
    b. Product development   e. Shipping
    c. Personnel selection   f. Public relations

8   How do you suggest that effective coordination might be secured between the department which includes the salesmen and each of the following departments?
    a. Advertising   d. Marketing research
    b. Production   e. Engineering
    c. Finance

9   In what ways might the implementation of the marketing concept change a company's organizational structure?

10   A manufacturer of small hand tools (hammers, saws, screwdrivers, etc.) frequently ran out of stock on some items while holding a five-year supply of other articles. Who was at fault for this badly balanced inventory situation?

11   Besides the inventory problem pointed out in question 10, give some examples of other problems which may arise in a manufacturing concern because of poor organization and coordination. Cite similar examples in a retail firm.

12   Suggest some specific ways that the salesmen and the advertising division within a marketing department can help each other. How can the advertising men specifically be of direct help to the sales force?

13   "The analysis-evaluation stage may be considered both the final and also the first stage of the management process; that is, this stage involves both a look backward and a look forward in managing a company." Explain.

14   Give some examples from your everyday life which show the need for making decisions and the difficulty of doing so.

15   What external environmental factors might be considered by management in each of the following firms in the course of formulating marketing policies? Be as specific as possible, building your answers around the factors of competition, nature of the market, and legal and social forces.
    a.   The Goodyear Tire and Rubber Company
    b.   The United States Gypsum Company
    c.   The Pepsi-Cola Company
    d.   The F. W. Woolworth Company
    e.   A small sporting goods store near your campus

3

MARKETING RESEARCH

The president of a perfume manufacturing company is wondering what women will want to smell like five years from now and how much they will be willing to spend to make themselves glamorous. An American luggage manufacturer, planning to market his product in Mexico, is wondering whether to license a Mexican company to make the products, establish a wholly owned subsidiary in Mexico, or enter into some form of joint ownership venture with a Mexican manufacturer. The owner-operator of a large cattle ranch in Wyoming is trying to decide whether he should sell his cattle at auction this year or contract in advance with buyers. The Florists' Telegraph Delivery Association (FTD) wants to find out more about consumers' attitudes toward floral gift giving, and what really constitutes flower-giving occasions. After a trial attempt to market instant coffee in bags, like tea, the manufacturers of Kleenex wanted to find out why women rejected the product. In all these seemingly unrelated marketing problems, there runs a common thread, namely, that marketing research is needed in the problem-solving and decision-making process.

NATURE AND IMPORTANCE OF MARKETING RESEARCH

The essence of what we mean by "marketing research" is contained in Richard Crisp's definition of the term. Crisp has called marketing research "the systematic, objective, and exhaustive search for and study of the facts relevant to any problem in the field of marketing."[1]

Marketing research has been formally identified only since about 1910, and its value and potential are still not fully appreciated. There is no universally accepted definition of the term, and, in fact, other terms, such as "market research," are sometimes used to describe the field. We shall use the American Marketing Association's interpretation:[2]

Marketing Research is the inclusive term which embraces all research activities carried on in connection with the management of marketing work. . . .

It (marketing research) includes various subsidiary types of research, such as (1) Market Analysis, which is a study of the size, location, nature, and characteristics of markets, (2) Sales Analysis (or Research) which is largely an analysis of sales data, (3) Consumer Research, of which Motivation Research is a type which is concerned chiefly with the discovery and analysis of consumer attitudes, reactions, and preferences, and (4) Advertising Research which is carried on chiefly as an aid to the management of advertising work. . . .

Marketing research in decision making

Marketing research is probably the key tool used by management in its problem solving and decision making in the field of marketing. As such, marketing research is an aid to sound executive judgment and not a substitute for it. The aim of marketing research is to furnish as many as possible of the necessary facts upon which to base decisions. It can also furnish substantive hypotheses or principles which can be carried over from one marketing situation to another and thus be useful in making predictions. It can, as well, supply analytical tools based on logic, mathematics, and statistics.

If marketing research is sufficiently broad in scope, it may serve as an integrating factor in marketing management. Administrators are becoming increasingly aware that they cannot isolate elements of a marketing situation. For example, if the cost of selling is rising, it is necessary to study the effective-

---

[1] Richard D. Crisp, *Marketing Research*, McGraw-Hill Book Company, New York, 1957, p. 3.

[2] Committee on Definitions, Ralph S. Alexander, Chairman, *Marketing Definitions: A Glossary of Marketing Terms*, American Marketing Association, Chicago, 1960, p. 17.

ness of the sales force, the advertising campaign, and the distribution system. Marketing research may also be used to integrate and coordinate marketing activities with those in production, engineering, finance, and other major areas in a firm.

Research and the scientific method

Although marketing itself is not a precise science—indeed it is more an art than a science—we do make extensive use of the scientific method and research. The *scientific method* is a systematic, orderly procedure for problem solving. *Research* is an accurate, critical, exhaustive, objective, and continuing investigation of a problem, an alternative course of action, or a hypothesis. Each of these adjectives is carefully chosen and each is important. Each one also raises certain difficulties in marketing research. Most of these difficulties can be traced to the fact that the field depends on human judgment and deals with people. Human beings conduct the research, and much of the research is done on human beings—the consumers. Thus, subjective elements enter the picture and make it difficult to establish a body of principles such as might be found in physics or chemistry.

Research is used as a basis of decision making in all walks of life—in business, government, athletics, the military, and personal affairs. Much of our everyday research is more scientific than we realize. Some of it is not scientific, but it is research. A football coach employs scouts to get facts concerning his opponents' strengths and weaknesses, and then he plans his strategy accordingly. A student does some research before deciding what college he will attend, what organizations he will join, and what job he will take upon graduation. A young woman will (or should) do considerable research before making a decision on whether or not to accept a proposal of marriage.

Scope of marketing research activities

It may be helpful in understanding the scope of marketing research if we outline some typical areas of research.[3] Very few (if any) companies, however, have one department which performs all the activities outlined below:

1. Research on products and services
    a. Determining customer acceptance of proposed new products
    b. Making comparative studies of competitive products
    c. Evaluating new competitive products
    d. Determining current or new uses of present products
    e. Evaluating and market testing proposed new products or services
    f. Determining sources of customer dissatisfaction with products

[3] Adapted from Richard D. Crisp, *Marketing Research Organization and Operation,* American Management Association, Research Study no. 35, New York, 1958, pp. 39–47.

    g. Simplifying product line

    h. Making packaging and design studies

2. Research on markets

    a. Analyzing size of market for existing products

    b. Estimating demand for new products

    c. Sales forecasting and general business forecasting

    d. Determining characteristics of markets for products

    e. Analyzing sales potentials and relative profitability of territories

    f. Studying trends in market size and composition

3. Research on sales methods and policies

    a. Establishing or revising sales territories

    b. Evaluating present and proposed sales methods

    c. Studying competitive pricing

    d. Analyzing salesmen's activities and effectiveness

    e. Setting sales quotas and developing salesmen's standards

    f. Studying distribution cost

    g. Establishing salesmen's compensation plans

4. Research on advertising

    a. Evaluating advertising effectiveness

    b. Analyzing competitive advertising and selling practices

    c. Selecting advertising media′

    d. Making motivational or qualitative studies

5. Research on miscellaneous activities

    a. Analyzing opinions of employees, public, or stockholders regarding the company, its product, or its policies

    b. Determining location of new stores or sales branches

    c. Studying current Federal, state, and local legislation and its possible impact on the company

Examples of the uses of marketing research

Some uses of marketing research will illustrate the scope of this managerial tool.[4]

Market analysis: quantitative and qualitative   As part of a project to develop the recreation resources of Alaska, the National Park Service wanted to know more about the economic aspects of the tourist industry in that state. In one phase of the project, marketing research was used to determine the characteristics of the Alaska summer visitor—where he came from, the purpose of his visit, what parts of Alaska he visited, what activities he participated in while in Alaska, the transportation methods and routes he used, the length of his stay, and how much money he spent in Alaska. In addition, the Park Service

---

[4] For some case examples of the use of marketing research by well-known companies, see *Marketing Research in Action*, National Industrial Conference Board, Inc., Studies in Business Policy, no. 84, New York, 1957.

wanted to know in some detail what the tourist liked and disliked about Alaska as a vacationland. This information was gathered from a sample of people leaving Alaska; persons were interviewed by questionnaire while on their airplanes or ships or while at the customs and immigration station at Tok Junction on the Alaska highway. Additional information was secured by mailing a questionnaire to a sample of vacation visitors. There was an extraordinarily high rate of return on the mail questionnaires—76 per cent. From an analysis of the questionnaire findings, the marketing researcher was able to furnish the National Park Service with considerable information.

Product research   A home appliance manufacturer was considering whether to add a vacuum cleaner to the company's product line. A marketing research firm was hired to find out something about consumer reactions and attitudes regarding the product. Consumers who were interviewed answered that what they wanted most in a vacuum cleaner was light weight, maneuverability, and easy storage. After investing $90,000 in manufacturing a prototype, the company took the model to a consumer panel for their reactions. The consumers promptly rejected the product on the grounds that it was too small and thus undoubtedly did not have enough power to do the cleaning job. Management scrapped the model and went back to design one with more mass, more apparent power, and hopefully more consumer appeal. Although the company had to write off $90,000, the loss would have been far greater if management had marketed the cleaner on a large-scale commercial basis without the marketing research.[5]

Research on pricing policies   A luggage manufacturer was trying to decide whether to establish a retail price on his product and insist by contract that the retailer maintain this price. (This price policy is called resale price maintenance or fair trade.) He knew that two national competitors, one located in Denver, Colorado, and another in Seattle, Washington, had employed the policy with a reasonably high degree of success. Here was a job for marketing research. All retailers currently handling the product were consulted. In addition, other dealers were asked if they would carry the brand if it had a set price which no one could undercut. On balance, the results showed that a policy of resale price maintenance would be a mistake for this manufacturer. Few new accounts would be picked up, and many established accounts, particularly the large ones, would be displeased. Consequently, the manufacturer discarded the idea.

Research on promotional policies   A supermarket chain, with stores in the Midwest and in Colorado, was concerned about the public's reaction to trading stamps. The chain had been offering stamps for a few years and wanted

[5] Cameron Day, "Consumer Testing: Mighty Power behind the Product," *Sales Management,* July 2, 1965, p. 20.

to know whether customers liked this or whether they would prefer a cash discount in lieu of stamps. In a few of the stores, each customer going through the check-out stand was offered the alternative of stamps or a 2 per cent cash discount. The researchers found that the customers split about fifty-fifty: half took the discount and half preferred the stamps. The percentage of customers selecting the discount, however, was much higher during evening hours and on Sundays. Many of these shoppers were not regular customers of this chain, and if they collected trading stamps, they were collecting a different brand. Regular customers, who did their shopping during the week, preferred the stamps. Consequently, after the period of trial the chain discontinued the discount offer.

Research on total marketing program   To study the past activities and to anticipate the future requirements of its total marketing program, the Edward Dalton Company, manufacturers of Metrecal, conducts marketing research on an organized and continuing basis. In these efforts the company uses its own marketing research department, its advertising agency, and four outside research firms. Each week Dalton's own field staff reports on competitive activity, price changes, and special deals at the retail level. The advertising agency keeps track of the advertisements and the advertising expenditures of competitors. Every two months, Dalton gets a report from one of the outside firms showing the retail store activity of Metrecal and its competitors. This report shows dollar and unit sales to consumers by territories and by size and type of store; inventory and display information is also reported. Each month, another outside firm surveys one hundred stores in sixteen key markets to measure the effects of various advertising and product tests. Four times a year, a third research service interviews a national sample of consumers to find out how many and what kind of consumers are using Metrecal and what their reaction to new marketing or advertising ideas or projected new products is. Twice a year, the fourth outside agency conducts a "marketing-opportunities study" of human wants in general, in order to discover new ways the Dalton Company might satisfy these wants.[6]

PROCEDURE IN A MARKETING RESEARCH PROJECT

In marketing research no two tasks are exactly alike, nor is there any single procedure that can be followed in all projects. The general procedure explained in this section, however, is applicable to most projects. Some of the steps listed here are interrelated, some overlap, and some are not needed in every project.

1.   Define the objectives of the project and define the problem.
2.   Conduct a situation analysis.
3.   Conduct an informal investigation.
4.   Plan and conduct a formal investigation.

[6] "Scouting the Trail for Marketers," *Business Week*, Apr. 18, 1964, p. 98.

    a.   Determine the sources of information.

    b.   Determine the methods for gathering primary data.

    c.   Prepare data-gathering forms.

    d.   Pretest the questionnaire or other forms.

    e.   Plan the sample.

    f.   Collect the data.

5.   Tabulate and analyze the data.

6.   Interpret the data and prepare recommendations.

7.   Prepare a written report.

8.   Follow up the study.

Define the objective and the problem

A researcher should have a reasonably clear idea of what he is trying to do in a research job. Usually this means defining a problem; however, the objective of a research job is not always to solve a problem. Often the purpose of a sales analysis is to determine whether the company has a problem and, if so, in what territory, product, or class of customer it lies. To illustrate, a manufacturer of commercial air-conditioning and refrigeration equipment had been enjoying a steady increase in sales volume over a period of years. For one reason or another, management decided to make a sales analysis, and this research project uncovered the fact that although the company's volume had been increasing, its share of the market had declined. In this instance, marketing research uncovered a problem which management did not know existed.

When marketing research ascertains that a problem does exist, then the objective of the project is to determine exactly what the problem is and to attempt to solve it. Normally, a company starts with a broad, tentative statement of its problem. Through investigation it is able to pinpoint the problem precisely. In the case of the refrigeration equipment manufacturer, the broad problem is, why has this company's share of the market decreased and how can it improve its position? To get this into manageable form, we can state the problem in parts. We can, for instance, ask: Have the company's product policies been the cause of its declining share of the market, or have weaknesses in the company's channel of distribution policies been the cause?

Early in the course of the project, management must determine whether it is able and willing to employ the personnel and spend the time and money necessary to solve the problem. Management must feel a real need to solve the problem; if it does not, any money or time spent on a partial solution will be wasted, and the reputation of marketing research in this particular company will be damaged.

The initial step of recognizing and defining a problem may be taken by the marketing research department or by some other department in the firm. The chief engineer or the production manager may suggest adding a product to the line and thus start a marketing research project. The marketing manager may propose shifting from intensive to selective distribution. The marketing research department may recommend a market test on a new product to get information regarding the brand, package, or color.

The case history of the Aurora Electronics Company (an actual company, but a fictitious name) may be used to illustrate the first three steps in a marketing research project, namely, problem definition, situation analysis, and informal investigation. The Aurora Company is a small electronics manufacturer, with the engineering department located in Chicago and the production plant and the president's office located in Phoenix, Arizona. Annual sales volume was $3 million, with 90 per cent of this coming from contracts with the Federal government. The other 10 per cent came almost entirely from sales of the electronic component part used in automatic garage-door openers. This component was sold directly to a large door manufacturer. Joseph Stacy, the president, was an engineer, and his company had an excellent reputation. The firm had no marketing department, no sales manager, and no salesmen. It had a fine engineering department; the entire company was heavily engineering-oriented. At the time of the case, the firm was interested in diversifying its product line and its market so as to reduce its heavy dependence on government contracts. The engineering department developed an FM auto radio—a tuner and amplifier unit which could be connected to the regular AM auto radio and could use the AM speaker.

The general problem, as presented to an outside marketing research firm, was to determine whether or not the company should add this product to its line. Breaking the problem down into parts which could be handled by research resulted in the following specific questions:

1. What is the market demand for such a product?

2. What product features are desired, such as push-button tuning or signal-seeking tuning?

3. What channels of distribution should be used for such a product?

4. What should its price be?

5. What changes or additions in the company's organizational structure would be required if the product were added?

With this tentative restatement of the problem, the researchers were ready for the next procedural step, the situation analysis.

Conduct situation analysis

The situation analysis involves getting acquainted with the company and its business environment by means of library research and extensive interviewing of company officials. The researchers try to get a "feel" for the situation surrounding the problem. They analyze the company, its market, its competition, and the industry in general.

In the situation analysis the researchers also try to define the problem more clearly and develop hypotheses for further testing. In research the establishment of hypotheses is a valuable step in problem solving. A *hypothesis* is a tentative supposition or a possible solution to a problem. It is something which is assumed or conceded merely for purposes of argument or action. In the Aurora Company problem, the situation analysis suggested the following hypotheses:

1. The company organization is inadequate to take on a consumer product.

2. The market for FM radios is limited geographically to a radius of 25 miles from FM stations. (This distance is the approximate sending or receiving limit for FM broadcasting.)

3. Marketing channels should be the same as those used for AM auto radios; distribution patterns for home radios are substantially different.

Conduct informal investigation

Having gotten a feel for the problem, the researchers are now ready to conduct an informal investigation; to some extent, this step overlaps the preceding one. The former involves getting background information from *within* the company or from a library. The latter consists of talking to people *outside* the company —middlemen, competitors, advertising agencies, customers, and men in the industry.

In the Aurora case, the researchers talked with many people. FM station owners and managers were of considerable help. Wholesalers and retailers of automobile radios were consulted, as were repairmen for auto radios. Long interviews were held with automobile dealers handling German FM auto radios —the Blau Punkt and the Becker. Consumers who had purchased these imports were interviewed. Helpful information was derived from talks with sales representatives of the Motorola Company. (This source was particularly valuable because there were rumors in the trade that Motorola had already engineered and produced models of an FM auto radio. As it turned out, the rumors were true, and a year later, Motorola introduced such a product to the market.) Advertising agencies were consulted regarding their possible future use of FM stations as an advertising medium—the idea being that an increase in their use of FM stations would in time increase the quantity of FM programming and thus make set ownership more attractive.

This important step in a research project will often determine whether further formal study is necessary. Decisions regarding the problem are frequently made after the informal investigation is completed. As a matter of fact, Aurora made its decision at this point. The decision is not divulged here because this problem appears in case form elsewhere in the book.

Plan and conduct formal investigation

After the problem is defined and the informal investigation shows that the project is economically feasible, the company determines what facts are needed.

The next step for the researcher is to plan how and where to get the desired data.

Determine sources of information   First the investigator must determine what sources of information he will use. He may use either primary or secondary data or both.

Primary data are those gathered specifically for the project at hand. *Secondary data* are those already available, originally having been collected for some other purpose. Thus, when a researcher stands in a supermarket and observes whether people use shopping lists and in what order they go to the various departments, he is collecting primary data. When he gets information from the Census of Population, a Ford Foundation report, or a library, he is using secondary sources.

One of the biggest mistakes made by many people in marketing research is rushing out to get primary data before exhausting the information already available in secondary sources. Ordinarily, secondary information can be gathered much faster and at far less expense than primary data.

On the other hand, secondary sources may be too outdated to be of maximum value. If quotas for salesmen in Florida or Arizona in 1967 are set on the basis of data found in the 1960 Census of Population or the 1963 Census of Business, the quotas will be understated because these are areas of rapid growth in market potential. Another problem is that the data may not be classified in such a way that the researcher can use it. He may want to make a study of college students and find that the secondary source classifies the data according to ages ten to nineteen and twenty to twenty-nine. A researcher may also find that definitions vary and that data are not comparable.

Another major limitation of secondary data is that the secondary source may not be reliable. In order to determine the validity of the data, the researcher may have to investigate the organization that collected the data and the methods it used in making its study.

SOURCES OF SECONDARY DATA   Several readily available, excellent sources of secondary information are at the disposal of a marketing research man.[7]

1.   Internal company records. The marketing executive or the marketing research department regularly maintains orderly records of salesmen's daily reports, call reports, sales orders, and customers' complaints. Companies usually keep sales records for each territory, product, and class of customer. When a problem must be solved, the first place a company should go for information is to its own files. In many cases, this source will furnish all the desired facts. It may well be the only place where the needed information can be found.

---

[7] For a good discussion of the major sources of secondary data, see Steuart H. Britt and Irwin Shapiro, "Where to Find Marketing Facts," *Harvard Business Review*, September–October, 1962, pp. 44ff.; and Harper W. Boyd, Jr., and Ralph Westfall, *Marketing Research*, rev. ed., Richard D. Irwin, Inc., Homewood, Ill., 1964, pp. 251–268.

2.   Government. The Federal government furnishes more marketing data than any other single source in the nation. These data are available at very low prices, even though there is a tremendous cost involved in collecting them. Also, the government has access under the law to types of information (company sales and profits, personal income, etc.) which is impossible for a private company to get. The decennial Census of Population, for example, published by the Department of Commerce in years ending in zero (1950, 1960), contains economic, market, and sociological data in addition to a count of people by state, county, city, metropolitan area, and census tract in big cities. The Census of Business is taken in years ending in 3 and 8 (1953, 1958, 1963). This census provides detailed information about the number of establishments, sales, expenses, employment activity, and other business indicators for retailing and wholesaling institutions and service trades. The Census of Manufactures, also taken in years ending in 3 and 8, furnishes an extremely detailed industrial classification, including the number of establishments, the value added by manufacturing, employment figures, etc., for each industry.

The Department of Commerce publishes various summaries of statistics. The most inclusive is the annual *Statistical Abstract of the United States*. The monthly *Survey of Current Business* furnishes data on a wide variety of topics. There is a regular annual supplement, and other special supplements are issued from time to time. The *County and City Data Book* is ordinarily published every three years and includes a variety of statistics for all counties and all cities with populations over 25,000. The *Minerals Yearbook* (Department of the Interior) is a comprehensive annual report on mining activities.

The U.S. Department of Agriculture is a fine source of information on agricultural activity. Reports issued regularly cover crop estimates, acreage yields, and acreage planted. At irregular intervals reports are issued on particular agricultural marketing problems. The Department of Agriculture also publishes many excellent studies and reports on marketing methods, channels, consumption patterns, prices, packaging, and the like. *Agricultural Statistics,* published annually, furnishes information on production, consumption, price, and trade of most agricultural products and minerals both in the United States and in many foreign countries.

The Department of Labor, particularly the Bureau of Labor Statistics, is another good source. Its *Monthly Labor Review* carries data on wages, employment, unemployment, and price indexes.

The *Monthly Catalog of United States Government Publications* lists all Federal government publications according to the agency or department which prepared them.

State and local governments provide a wide variety of sources of information, but normally they are not so well catalogued or easy to locate as the Federal sources. Data stemming from tax records, license applications, and other registration systems furnish much of the state and local information.

3.   Trade, professional, and business associations. Associations are excellent sources of information for their members. They also supply data for outside

groups, such as lobbyists or congressional committees. The National Association of Retail Druggists has been active in lobbying for resale price maintenance. The American Medical Association has quantities of information available for legislators interested in government-sponsored health plans and other medical matters. Through trade journals and periodic reports, members of associations can also keep up to date on activities in their given trades.

4.   Private business firms. Private marketing research firms, advertising agencies, and individual manufacturers or middlemen may be able to provide information needed by a researcher. Companies such as the A. C. Nielsen Company (the largest marketing research firm in the world) conduct various kinds of marketing research. Their findings are published and are available to persons who subscribe to the companies' publications. The Nielsen Company, for example, prepares a food-drug index giving information on a client's retail sales and his competitors' sales for particular products. Data regarding inventories, stock turnover, retail prices, and promotional activity at the retail level are also published. The Daniel Starch Company regularly measures readership of advertisements in various magazines and newspapers. The Market Research Corporation of America (MRCA) maintains a consumer panel of 7,500 families throughout the entire country. These families maintain diaries which record their purchases of food, drugs, and household products by item, price, and store. These records, when summarized, categorized, and cross-tabulated, can supply a wealth of marketing information.

Advertising agencies often furnish market data for their clients. Banks and insurance companies regularly issue reports containing material which may be of value to marketing men.

5.   Advertising media. Many magazines, newspapers, radio and television stations, and outdoor advertising companies publish information that marketing researchers may not find available elsewhere. *Sales Management* annually publishes its "Survey of Buying Power," which covers population, retail sales, income, and effective buying power for all states, counties, metropolitan areas, and cities with populations over 10,000. *Printers' Ink* publishes an annual "Advertisers' Guide to Marketing." Many media publish circulation data, station coverage maps, and statistics on their trading areas.

6.   University research organizations. Most large universities operate research bureaus and publish findings which are of value to the business community. Bureaus of business research play a leading role in this activity, although marketing men may also obtain useful reports from a bureau of agricultural research or social research.

7.   Foundations. Nonprofit research foundations and related groups carry out many kinds of research projects. Statistical analyses and reports on special topics are published by such groups as the National Industrial Conference Board, the American Management Association, and the Committee for Economic Development. While the Ford, Carnegie, Russell Sage, and similar foun-

dations are not limited to business research, many of their reports are of interest to marketing men.

8. Libraries. Lest the student forget, a good library is probably the best single, all-around location of secondary information. It will contain publications from practically all the sources mentioned here. The ability to use bibliographies, card indexes, and periodical indexes is virtually a prerequisite for anyone hoping to do any kind of research.

SOURCES OF PRIMARY DATA   After exhausting all reasonable secondary sources of information, the researcher may still lack sufficient data. Then he will turn to primary sources and gather the facts himself.

1. Company salesmen. Frequently a marketing analyst will interview salesmen in order to get pertinent market information, or he will ask the salesmen to interview middlemen, customers, or representatives from competitors. Salesmen can often supply information regarding conditions in their territories which will not be reported until several months later in secondary sources. Management should not, however, use expensive sales personnel in research capacities if this diverts them from their primary job of selling. Also, salesmen are not trained field researchers, and the information they collect may be biased.

2. Middlemen, consumers, and others. Manufacturers can seek information from their wholesalers and retailers; wholesalers, in turn, can use their retail customers as primary sources. Middlemen may be asked their opinion of, or reaction to, a given product, a company policy, or program. Sometimes middlemen can give a manufacturer a good indication of the feelings of the ultimate consumer or industrial user, but sellers may have to go directly to the household consumer or the industrial user to get the facts about attitudes, motives, and buying habits.

In some cases a firm's competitors may provide primary information. It may be gathered surreptitiously by having salesmen query the competitors' salesmen, or it may be gathered openly through the trade association. A firm may approach a competitor directly on matters of mutual interest. For instance, all supermarket operators or used-car dealers in a city may have a meeting to discuss the question of keeping their establishments open on Sundays. Noncompetitive businessmen also may supply helpful information.

Determine methods for gathering primary data   There are three widely used methods of gathering primary data: survey, observation, and experimentation. Normally, not all three are used on one project. A choice of method will be influenced by the availability of time, money, personnel, and facilities.

SURVEY METHOD   A *survey* consists of gathering data by interviewing a limited number of people (a sample) selected from a larger group. A survey has the advantage of getting to the original source of information. In fact, this may be the *only* way to find out the motives, opinions, or buying intentions of a group.

While the survey is still the most widely used method of collecting primary data, there may be a trend away from it. Not only have methods of observation and experimentation been improved and their value more fully realized, but the survey method contains certain inherent limitations. Surveys require careful planning, and there are opportunities for error in the construction of the questionnaire, in its editing, and in the interviewing process. Surveys may be very expensive, and they are time-consuming. Often the process is slow, and the researcher may need facts immediately. Another key weakness is that respondents often cannot or will not give correct answers. This is particularly destructive when a marketing analyst is searching for reasons underlying a respondent's behavior.

The interviewing or data gathering in a survey may be done by the researcher in person, by telephone, or by mail. These three types of interviews may be evaluated on the following bases: (1) flexibility, (2) amount of information to be obtained, (3) accuracy, and (4) speed, cost, and administration.[8]

*Personal interview*s are more flexible than the other two types because the interviewer can alter his questions to fit the situation as he sees it. He is able to probe more deeply if he is not satisfied with the answer. (Of course, there is a danger that a bias may be introduced into the survey if the original questions are altered.) Ordinarily, it is possible to obtain more information by personal interview than by telephone or mail. Virtually every subject lends itself to a personal interview. Also the interviewer can by observation obtain data regarding a respondent's socioeconomic status—his home, neighborhood, and apparent standard of living. Finally, a statistically sound sample is more easily obtainable by the personal interview.

The major limitations of this method of interviewing are its relatively high cost, the length of time needed to plan and execute the survey, and the opportunity to introduce errors in the interviewing process. When the personal interview method is used on a broad geographical basis, as in a national survey of magazine readership or shaving habits, the advantage of flexibility pretty much disappears. Interviewers in these situations ordinarily must follow an exactly prescribed procedure. Probing becomes difficult, questions should not be reworded, and very little is left to the interviewer's discretion.

In a *telephone survey* the respondent is approached by telephone and the interview is completed at that time. Telephone surveys can usually be conducted more rapidly and at less cost than either personal or mail surveys. Wide geographic areas can be covered without any traveling. Telephone surveys are less flexible than personal interviews but more flexible than mail surveys. Since a few interviewers can make any number of calls from a few central points, this method is quite easy to administer. Many of the problems involved in

[8] See Boyd and Westfall, *op. cit.*, pp. 164–179; and Richard D. Crisp, *Marketing Research*, McGraw-Hill Book Company, New York, 1957, pp. 192–198, for evaluations of the three methods.

the management of interviewers in personal surveys are not present here. Another significant advantage is that a telephone survey may be timely. For instance, people may be asked whether they are watching television at the moment and, if so, the name of the program and the sponsor.

One limitation of the telephone survey is that questionnaires must be short. Normally, lengthy interviews cannot be conducted satisfactorily over the phone. Also it is difficult to ascertain the socioeconomic characteristics of respondents. It is virtually impossible to get a complete cross section of the public because some people have no telephones, others have unlisted numbers, many are not at home when the interviewer calls, and some refuse to respond in this type of survey.

Interviewing by mail involves mailing a questionnaire to potential respondents and having them return the completed form by mail. Since no interviewers are involved, this type of survey is not hampered by interviewer bias and problems connected with the management of interviewers. Mailed questionnaires are more economical than personal interviews and are particularly useful in broad, national surveys. Respondents may answer the questions at their leisure, so the replies may be carefully thought out. Also, if the respondent remains anonymous, he will probably give true answers because he does not feel the need to impress the interviewer. Finally, it is easier to reach some groups by mail than by either of the other two methods.

A major problem with mail questionnaires is the compilation of a good mailing list, especially in a broad-scale survey. If the sample can be drawn from a limited list, such as property taxpayers in certain counties or subscribers to a certain magazine, the list presents no problem. Another significant limitation concerns the sample reliability of the questionnaire returns, particularly when the returns are anonymous. If the respondents have characteristics which definitely differentiate them from the nonrespondents, this factor would negate the validity of the survey results. A mail survey may lack timeliness; respondents are often slow about returning the questionnaire. Inflexibility is another problem; once the questionnaire is sent out, there is no opportunity to make changes. Furthermore, the questionnaire must be reasonably short and the questions very simple; there is no way to elaborate or explain a puzzling question. There is also no opportunity to get additional data by observing the respondent. Often the representativeness of the sample is quite doubtful because the rate of returns on mail questionnaires is so low.[9]

OBSERVATION METHOD   In this research method the data are collected by observing some action of the respondent. No interviews are involved, although an interview may be used as a kind of follow-up to get additional information. For example, a customer may be observed buying beer in cans instead of bottles, and then he may be asked why he preferred one form of packaging to another. The consumer is unaware that he is being observed,

---

[9] For a proposal to improve this situation, see Eugene E. Heaton, Jr., "Increasing Mail Questionnaire Returns with a Preliminary Letter," *Journal of Advertising Research*, December, 1965, pp. 36–38.

so presumably he acts in his usual fashion. This is a valuable research tool, but unfortunately it is often underrated in favor of the interview technique.

Information may be gathered by personal or mechanical observation. In one form of personal observation, the researcher poses as a customer in a store. This technique is useful in getting information about the caliber of the salesman or in determining what brands he pushes. In another situation, an observer may watch customers at a discreet distance and notice what motivates a purchase. One study was made to determine how people buy beer in a retail store. To some, price was important. ("What do you have on sale this weekend?" "What is a good low-priced beer?") Some had brand preferences. ("Give me a six-pack of ———.") Others needed help in selecting a brand. ("What brand do you recommend?") Suburban shopping centers have used the observation technique to determine where their customers come from. The investigators record the license numbers of cars in the parking lot, and the addresses of owners are then traced through license bureaus. Mechanical observation is illustrated by an electric cord stretched across a highway to count the traffic in a certain time period. Universities may post student workers at library exits and give them a mechanical counter to keep track of the number of people who leave the library. A mechanical recorder may be attached to a radio or television set; this device will record whether the set was on and to what station it was tuned. Hidden cameras are also useful in gathering data by observation.

The observation method has several merits. It can be highly accurate; often it removes all conjecture about what the consumer does in a given matter. If a researcher over a period of several weeks traces the license numbers of cars parked in a suburban shopping center, he has a pretty good idea of the area from which this center is drawing customers. The observation technique reduces interviewer bias, but the possibility of bias is not completely eliminated so long as field observers are used. Devices such as mechanical recorders or hidden cameras supply more detailed data than normally can be gathered by surveys. The Nielsen Audimeter (developed by the A. C. Nielsen Company) gives a minute-by-minute report regarding what, if any, television or radio station was tuned in.

A major drawback to the observation method, which has already been mentioned, is that field observer bias may creep in. However well trained an observer may be, mistakes are possible. A second disadvantage is that the technique is limited in its application. Observation tells *what* happened, but it cannot tell *why*; it cannot delve into motives, attitudes, beliefs, or opinions. Finally, this technique may be expensive. Observers must be posted at a given location for a certain period of time. During part of the time, however, they may be just waiting for a consumer to perform the act to be observed.

EXPERIMENTAL METHOD   This method of gathering primary data involves the establishment of a scale model or a controlled experiment which simulates the real-market situation as much as possible. The theory is that the small-scale experiment will furnish valuable information in designing a large-scale marketing program. This research method helps the marketing executive "work the bugs out" before venturing into the full market and thus increases his chances of success.

The experimental method may be used in several different ways and in countless situations. In one instance, a firm may manufacture a few units of a product and give them to employees or consumers to try out. Such field experimental tests aid considerably in product planning and development. Probably the major application of the experimental method has been in market testing. This technique consists of establishing a control market, in which all factors remain constant, and one or more test markets, in which one factor is varied. A firm may be trying to determine whether to change the color of its package. In city A, the product is marketed in its traditional color; in each of cities B, C, and D, a different color is used. All other factors presumably are kept constant. Thus, by measuring the sales in the four markets over a period of time, the manufacturer hopes to tell which color is best. Presumably the best color is the one in the market which had the largest percentage increase in sales over the period before the new colors were introduced.

The outstanding merit of the experimental method is its realism. It is the only one of the three methods of gathering primary data which affords actual market tests and simulates an actual market situation. In testing the relative values of different advertisements or the value of an entire advertising campaign, only the experimental method will tell which advertisement or campaign sold the most merchandise. Furthermore, this method holds great promise for the future as marketing research people improve their techniques. For instance, the method lends itself nicely to the use of mathematical models as a device for quantitative measurement.

Two big problems are encountered in market testing: selecting the control and test markets and controlling the variables. It is difficult—though necessary—to select markets that are identical in all significant socioeconomic factors; experimental models, which have recently been developed, may be helpful in solving this problem. Some variables are really uncontrollable, and these may upset the comparability of results. Competitors may get wind of the test and try to confuse the picture by suddenly increasing their advertising, for example. Company salesmen or retail dealers may act abnormally if they find out that a test is being run. Furthermore, the experimental method is expensive; it requires long, careful planning and administration. Tests frequently cover six months—two months during which activity in the test and control centers is measured before anything new is introduced, two months during which the variable being tested (new color, new price, new advertising) is placed in the market, and two more months to allow for sales which may have been motivated by the test variable but were not made until sometime after it was removed.

Prepare data-gathering forms Regardless of whether the interviewing or observation method is used to gather primary data, the researcher must prepare standard forms to record the information. All the fieldworkers should use identical data-gathering forms because comparable data can be recorded, tabulated, and analyzed faster, more easily, and more accurately with standardized forms. The importance of the questionnaire and the difficulty of preparing it cannot be overemphasized. In fact, most of the problems in data collection, whether by personal, mail, or telephone survey, center around the preparation of the questionnaire.[10] Marketing research textbooks devote whole chapters to this subject, and in at least one instance an entire book has been devoted to only part of the task.[11]

Pretest the questionnaire or other forms   No matter how good a researcher thinks his questionnaire is, it still should be pretested. This process is similar to field testing a product. Obviously, an engineer thinks a new model of his automobile is perfect; otherwise he would not have sent it away from the drawing board. But he knows from experience that the only way to test the automobile is to use it. The researcher must test in three areas. First, he wants to make sure that the questions are clear and are in proper order. Second, he wants to find out whether the instructions to the interviewers are adequate. Finally, he wants to uncover any problems which may arise in the course of editing, coding, and tabulating the questionnaires. The method used in pretesting consists simply in trying out the questionnaire on a small sample of people similar to those who will be interviewed. It is wise to let the research man himself do some interviewing. By observing the reaction of a few respondents, he may be able to catch a number of unforeseen problems.

Plan the sample   Normally it is unrealistic and unnecessary to survey or observe every possible person who could shed light on the research problem. Before the data can be gathered, therefore, the researcher must determine from whom he is going to seek the information. He must plan or establish a sample.

---

[10] For an explanation and appraisal of the standardized (structured) versus the nonstandardized (nonstructured) types of questionnaires, both when the objective of the questionnaire is clear to the respondent and when the objective is disguised, see Boyd and Westfall, *op. cit.*, pp. 157–164.

[11] Stanley L. Payne, *The Art of Asking Questions,* Princeton University Press, Princeton, N.J., 1951.

One procedure set forth by Boyd and Westfall, *op. cit.*, pp. 291–323, is as follows: (1) determine what information is wanted, for example, quantitative market characteristics (number, age, sex, income, geographic location) of people visiting Alaska for a vacation only; (2) determine the type of questionnaire to be used (mail, telephone, or personal interview); (3) determine the content and necessity of each question and try to determine whether the respondents can and will answer it; (4) determine the type of question to use—open-end ("What did you like about Alaska as a vacationland?") or multiple-choice or dichotomous ("Should the capital of Alaska be Juneau or Anchorage?"); (5) decide on wording of questions; (6) decide on sequence of questions; (7) determine physical form, layout, and method of reproduction; (8) prepare preliminary draft and pretest it; (9) revise questionnaire and prepare final draft.

As is true of research in general, sampling is no stranger to us, because we employ it frequently in our everyday activities. We often base our opinion of a person on only one or two conversations with him; we often take a bite of food before ordering a larger quantity.

Actually, the fundamental idea of sampling is that "if a small number of items or parts (called a sample) are chosen at random from a larger number of items or a whole (called a universe, or population) the sample will tend to have the same characteristics, and to have them in approximately the same proportion, as the universe."[12] In marketing research, sampling is another procedural step whose importance it is difficult to overestimate. Sampling is a source of errors in many survey results. In one study, an opinion on student government was derived from interviewing a sample of fraternity and sorority members. With no dormitory students, off-campus residents, and commuting students included, this was obviously a biased, nonrepresentative sample of student opinion.

One of the first questions asked regarding sampling is: How large should the sample be? To be statistically reliable, a sample must be large enough to be truly representative of the universe or population. There are other generalizations which a researcher should keep in mind, however. First, size is by no means the most important source of sampling errors. Second, huge increases in sample size are needed to produce small increases in the statistical reliability of the sample. Third, in the mathematical determination of statistical reliability the size of the universe is *not* a factor to consider. Finally, the size of the sample is often determined by such practical factors as the time and money available and the amount of cross-classification of data desired.

To be statistically reliable a sample must be proportionate. That is, all types of units found in the universe must be represented in the sample. Also, these units must appear in the sample in approximately the same proportion as they are found in the universe. Assume that a manufacturer of power lawn mowers wants to know what percentage of families in a certain metropolitan area own this product; further assume that in this market one-half of the families live in the central city and the other half in the suburbs. Relatively more families in the suburbs have power mowers than in the city. Now, if 80 per cent of the sample is made up of suburban dwellers, the percentage of families owning power mowers will be overstated because the sample lacks proportionality.

Innumerable sampling techniques may be used in marketing research; many of these are quite similar, and many are used only infrequently. We should be able to get a basic understanding of sampling by considering three types: (1) simple random samples, (2) area samples, and (3) quota samples. The first two are probability samples, and the third, a nonprobability sample.

In *simple random sampling*, the sample is selected in such a way that every

---

[12] Crisp, *Marketing Research*, p. 95.

unit in the predetermined universe has a known and equal chance of being selected. Thus, if we wished to use a random sample to determine department store preferences among people in Denver, Colorado, we would need an accurate and complete listing of all people within the city limits. If we wanted to use a random sample to determine feed and seed preferences among farmers in the Great Plains states, we would first decide what states to include and then get an up-to-date listing of all farmers in those states.

A variation of a simple random sample which is widely used is an *area sample*. Where it is not economically possible to prepare or obtain a full list of the universe, an area sample may be used. In the above example of a study covering department store preferences among Denver residents, one way to conduct an area sample would be to list all the blocks in the city and then select at random a sample of the blocks. Then every household or every other household on the sample blocks could be interviewed. In this sampling method, the researcher needs only a list of the city blocks, not a listing of all Denver residents.

A *quota sample* is not only a nonprobability sample but also a stratified sample. Randomness is lost because proportionality is "forced"; every element in the universe does *not* have a known chance of being selected. To select a quota sample, the researcher first must decide which characteristics will serve as the basis of the quota and then determine in what proportion these characteristics occur in the universe. Thus, in selecting a quota sample from among the people who went to Alaska for a vacation, the researcher may decide that the quota will be based upon the state of residence. In one study, it was found that 30 per cent of the tourists to Alaska came from California, 10 per cent from the state of Washington, and 15 per cent from the East North Central census region (Illinois, Indiana, Ohio, Michigan, Wisconsin). The sample was forced to the extent that it was stratified on a nonprobability basis according to the home state of the tourist. Consequently, of the people included in the final sample, 30 per cent were from California, 10 per cent were from Washington, and so forth. In some studies, as many as four or five quota characteristics, such as age, sex, income, education, geographic area, and city size, are established to delimit the sample.

Probability sampling has one big advantage: it is the only method where the reliability of the results can be measured with mathematical exactness. Furthermore, it does not require a considerable fund of detailed information regarding the universe. All that is needed is a knowledge of the total number of units in the universe and some method of listing or otherwise identifying them. On the other hand, probability sampling can be very expensive and time-consuming, particularly when there is wide geographic dispersion of the units in the sample. Adequate listings of units may not be available, and much skill in designing and selecting the sample is required. In simple random sampling these limitations are accentuated.

In quota sampling much reliance is placed on the judgment of those designing and selecting the samples; there is no mathematical way of measuring the accuracy of the results. Also, much depends on the field interviewer; if he is not well qualified to carry out his job, he may misrepresent his data in order to complete his allotted work on time.

Collect the data   The procedural stage during which the primary data are actually collected in the field, either by interviewing or by observation or both, normally constitutes the weakest link in the entire research process. Ordinarily, in all other steps reasonably well-qualified people are working very carefully to ensure the accuracy of the results. Great care goes into preparing the survey questionnaire or the forms used in an observational study; considerable thought and planning underlie the selection of the sample. Then the fruits of these and earlier labors may be entirely lost if the fieldworkers (data gatherers) are low-paid, uninterested, poorly selected, or inadequately trained and supervised. The management of fieldworkers is a difficult task because they are usually part-time workers with little job motivation, and their work is done where it cannot be observed, often at many widely separated locations.

A myriad of errors may creep into a research project at this point, and poor interviewers only increase this possibility.[13] Bias may be introduced because people in the sample are not at home, refuse to answer, or are not able to answer. Errors occur because the interviewers do not follow the prescribed sample. In some instances, fieldworkers are unable to establish rapport with respondents, or they revise the wording of a question and thus elicit untrue or inapplicable responses. Considerable error may be introduced by improper interpretation or recording of answers. Finally, some interviewers just plain cheat in one way or another.

Tabulate and analyze data

The next step is to tabulate the data that have been gathered and make the necessary statistical analysis. Although it is extremely important to consider this step when the questionnaire is being prepared, many researchers do not realize this until it is too late. The physical layout of the questionnaire, for example, may be planned in such a way as to facilitate tabulation. Whether the

---

[13] See Harper W. Boyd, Jr., and Ralph Westfall, "Interviewers as a Source of Errors in Surveys," *Journal of Marketing*, April, 1955, pp. 311–324. Ten years later, another survey of the subject was made by the same authors. They observed that some significant gains had been achieved in dealing with interviewer bias, but they also concluded that the same problems still exist to a major degree and that relatively little is being done to solve them; see Harper W. Boyd, Jr., and Ralph Westfall, "Interviewer Bias Revisited," *Journal of Marketing Research*, February, 1965, pp. 58–63.

forms are to be tabulated by hand or machine may play a big part in deciding the layout.

Interpret data and prepare recommendations

The researcher is now in a position to draw conclusions from the study and develop his recommendations. In effect, this stage is the end product; up to now we have dealt with the means to this end. Here is where the marketing executive gets the information needed in his decision making. The more sound the recommendations, the better will be the decisions.

Prepare written report

The recommendations, supported by a detailed analysis of the findings and a complete statement of the method used in the study, should be submitted in a written report. If time is an important factor an oral report may be made, but the report should be recorded in some fashion. It is helpful if an oral discussion can be held shortly after the written report has been submitted. Then the report can be clarified, expanded, or explained as the recipients raise questions. Whatever form is used for transmitting the recommendations, suffice it to say that the researcher has "a message for Garcia," and he should put it in such a form that Garcia will be sure to read and understand it.

Follow up the study

As a final step in an organized research project, the researcher should follow up his study to find out whether his recommendations are being implemented; if they are not, he should be interested in the reasons why. So often this step is omitted or played down. Actually the analyst's future relations with the company can be influenced seriously by this step, whether he is in the firm's own marketing research department or working for an outside agency. Unless there is a follow-up, the company may not pay much real attention to the report; it may be filed and forgotten. That is, it may be forgotten until the subject of marketing research arises again. Then an administrator will observe that the firm spent a considerable amount on an earlier research project and got little value out of it. The follow-up step is crucial when the recommendations are contrary to the executives' opinions or when executives fear that the proposal will encroach unduly on their administrative domain.

ORGANIZATIONAL STRUCTURE FOR MARKETING RESEARCH

When a firm wishes to carry out a project, there are two ways it can go about getting the job done. It can use the company's own personnel, or it can turn to an outside organization.

Within the company

In a small firm which does any of its own marketing research, the project will probably be carried out by the sales manager or even by the president. In medium and large enterprises marketing research may be done (1) in an over-all company research department which also does production and engineering research; (2) in the marketing department, where research is decentralized, with the advertising department and the sales department each covering its own field; or (3) in a separate marketing research department whose chief executive reports either to the marketing manager or to the company president.

Except in small companies, the trend is toward a separate marketing research department. From an organizational standpoint, the separate marketing research department is usually a centralized unit. The field sales force and branch personnel may be involved in data gathering—as in the "sales-force-composite" method of sales forecasting—but typically the analysis, interpretation, and action determination are accomplished in the central department. A case may be built, however, for decentralizing the research function to the extent that field sales management and personnel may perform certain organized research tasks in their respective territories. Strategic and tactical benefits are to be gained when branch managers can analyze their markets, make on-the-spot decisions, and adjust quickly to changing market and competitive conditions.[14]

When marketing research is done within the company, the researchers are well versed in company policy and procedures and know what information is available. Also, the firm is more apt to use its research facilities fully. On many problems, executives might not bother to call in an outside agency, while they might—if the firm had a research department—present the same problems to it. Using company manpower and facilities can be expensive, however, and unless the company has adequately qualified full-time personnel, needed research projects may be unavoidably delayed.

Outside the company

An interesting mark of maturity in marketing research is that despite the comparative youth of the field, it has already developed many institutions from which a company may seek help in marketing research problems. One group of organizations, which is regularly available for hire in research projects, includes advertising agencies, independent marketing consultants, and large marketing research or management consulting firms such as the A. C. Nielsen Company or McKinsey and Company. A second group includes firms such as railroads, public utilities, and advertising media which engage in marketing research in order to promote the services they are selling. A third type of outside organiza-

[14] Louis W. Stern and J. L. Heskett, "Grass Roots Market Research," *Harvard Business Review*, March–April, 1965, pp. 83–96.

tion includes trade associations, university bureaus of business research, and government agencies which conduct marketing research on common problems faced by a group of companies.

Some companies have in their normal setup the nucleus of a marketing research department which can on occasion work with an outside agency on problems calling for a larger staff and greater facilities than the companies themselves maintain.

These outside agencies employ highly qualified specialists in the marketing research field. Also, they have an objective, impartial approach. (Rarely does one hear of an actual case in which the agency seeks to retain its business by parroting what management wants to hear.) Finally, the agencies are experienced in their own right; they may bring to a given case the experiences of many other clients who had similar problems. Outside organizations do, of course, lack that intimate continuing knowledge of a firm which can come only from a permanent employee relationship.

STATUS OF MARKETING RESEARCH

American business is just beginning to realize the full potential of marketing research. Many firms have long since passed beyond the nose-counting, data-gathering stage—the stage where management was hindered by an insufficiency of information. Significant advances have been made in both quantitative and qualitative research methodology, to the point where researchers are making effective use of the behavioral sciences and mathematics. To dramatize the recent and rapid growth in the field, the president of the A. C. Nielsen Company estimated that more than two thousand United States companies had marketing research departments at the end of 1966. This is in contrast with the fact that only seventy companies had such departments thirty years earlier, and by 1957 the count was still under seven hundred.[15] Some three hundred firms in the United States specialize in marketing research. We realize, however, that far too many companies are still spending dollars on research for engineering and manufacturing their products, but only pennies, if anything, to determine the market opportunities and the marketing programs for these products.

Several factors account for this less-than-universal acceptance of marketing research. Unlike the results of a chemical experiment, the results of marketing research cannot always be measured quantitatively. The major areas of marketing research are qualitative. The research director cannot do a given job and then point to x per cent increase in sales. Also, because management is not yet convinced of the value of marketing research, it will not always spend the amount of money necessary to do a good job. Good research costs money. Executives may not realize that they cannot always get half as good a job for half the amount of money.

[15] Figures cited in *Printers' Ink*, Mar. 25, 1966, p. 3.

Another hindrance to the universal acceptance of marketing research is that it is far from perfect. We have noted several limitations of marketing research and several areas where major opportunities for error can occur—in sampling, field interviewing, etc. Even when marketing research is accurate, it is not a substitute for judgment. We cannot conduct a survey, feed the answers into a computer, and have it spew out a correct decision. Research gathers, analyzes, and interprets facts, but the executive himself must make the decision.

Marketing research cannot predict future behavior, and often that is what is expected of it. In fact, when dealing with consumer motivation or beliefs, the researcher is hard pressed to get the truth regarding present opinions or motives, much less those of next year.

Possibly a more fundamental reason for the modest status of marketing research has been the failure of researchers to communicate adequately with management.[16] These researchers, like many manufacturers, are often product-oriented when they should be market-oriented. Thus, they concentrate on research methods and techniques rather than on showing management how these methods can aid in making better marketing decisions. Executives are willing to invest heavily in technical research and development because they are convinced there is a "payout" in this activity. Management has not been similarly convinced of a return on its investment in marketing research. To communicate more effectively, the marketing researcher must let management know what he is doing for the company. He must take the initiative in communicating with management, talk their language, and be willing to make recommendations rather than straddle the fence on issues.

In management's relationship with marketing research today, another basic problem is the apparent inability or reluctance of management (1) to treat marketing research as a continuing process and (2) to relate marketing research and decision making in a more systematic fashion. Too often marketing research seems to be viewed in a fragmented, past-oriented, one-project-at-a-time manner; it is used only when management realizes it has a marketing problem. Possibly management's position here is, in part, an outgrowth of the inadequate communications mentioned above.

One study identified several possible reasons why many business executives have been unable to relate research and decision making more closely.[17] One impediment is the unfamiliarity of many business executives with modern concepts of decision-making processes and the informational sources available from related business and nonbusiness fields. Some executives resist the use of research because they fear it is a threat to their personal status; that is, research implies an evaluation of their effectiveness, and it may also invalidate many beliefs fondly held. Organizational defects such as the failure to identify clearly the company's goals and the lack of systematic marketing planning tend to limit

---

[16] Howard L. Gordon, "What Is the Next Breakthrough in Research?" *Journal of Marketing*, January, 1965, pp. 25–27.

[17] Joseph W. Newman, "Put Research into Marketing Decisions," *Harvard Business Review*, March–April, 1962, pp. 107–110.

the productive use of marketing research. Management furthermore tends to be unable to make effective use of specialists, particularly those from nonmarketing and nonbusiness disciplines. Finally, a marketing research department typically has low status in the organization, and its people are often isolated from key executives.

Regarding these basic problems, Newman observed:[18]

Reflecting executives' lack of understanding of research and its potential contribution to decision making is the fact that research departments have tended to be technical job shops to which operating people could bring requests if they chose to do so. The weakness of this system is that it depends on the initiative of executives who are unfamiliar with research and who typically are unable to identify their problems well enough to ask for the help they need.

Research departments which work only on requests brought to them tend to be occupied with routine, short-range operating problems. They are unlikely to be contributing to policy formulation, planning, and innovation. They cannot become an integral part of the decision-making process because line executives do not look to research for that sort of participation. Without a close relationship with the decision makers, research cannot play much of an educational role.

THE FUTURE: A MARKETING-INTELLIGENCE SYSTEM

As a possible solution to some of the fundamental problems confronting marketing research today, management in some firms is beginning to understand and adopt a relatively new systems concept in information—a concept called marketing intelligence or marketing-intelligence services. *Marketing intelligence* is a broad, centralized, continuing, future-oriented, systematic *processing* of information designed to guide business executives in the short-run and long-run management of their marketing programs. The concept of marketing intelligence, much like the marketing concept itself, is fundamentally a philosophy of business management. As such, marketing intelligence can be truly an aid to executives in their planning and decision making to an extent never reached by marketing research as it has generally been used.

As an information system, marketing intelligence is a broader and more inclusive activity than marketing research. It is the processing of information first gathered by marketing research, distribution cost analysis, or some other tool.[19] Marketing intelligence suggests a process, where marketing research is often a concern with techniques. Marketing intelligence is a systems concept,

---

[18] *Ibid.*, pp. 109–110. For a suggested procedure for bringing about the necessary interaction between researchers and decision makers, see Harper W. Boyd, Jr., and Steuart H. Britt, "Making Marketing Research More Effective by Using the Administrative Process," *Journal of Marketing Research*, February, 1965, pp. 13–19.

[19] Edward L. Brink, "The Current State of Marketing Intelligence in American Business," in L. George Smith (ed.), *Reflections on Progress in Marketing*, American Marketing Association, Chicago, 1965, pp. 367–370.

whereas marketing research usually deals with fragmented, unrelated research projects done to solve an existing problem identified by some executive. Thus, marketing intelligence is conducted on a continuing basis, serving as a prognosis as well as a diagnosis; it is preventive medicine as well as curative medicine for marketing.

Additional benefits should accrue from the introduction of a marketing-intelligence system in a company.[20] The system is future-oriented, whereas traditional marketing research, with some exceptions, has been concerned largely with explaining why something in the past happened as it did. It is true that we can learn from the past. We should study the past, however, not for its sake alone but only insofar as it can guide us in the future. The expansion of temporal horizons focuses management's attention on forecasting and long-range planning. The importance of this future orientation is summed up well in the statement: "To manage a business well is to manage its future; and to manage the future is to manage information."[21]

Today management is beset by an "information explosion" in which available data are increasing in geometric progression.[22] Most firms need a better system than they now have for filtering and refining the raw information into usable, meaningful form. This mass of information also tends to multiply the knowns and unknowns entering an executive's decision-making matrix, thus increasing its complexity. This further spotlights the limitations of traditional marketing research and emphasizes the need for a systems approach to the subject.

The "information explosion" will inevitably spawn specialists. However necessary they may be in today's business world, these specialists, left unattended, may produce uncoordinated, limited, and distorted results. Properly implemented, the marketing-intelligence concept envisions the employment of research generalists who can see the "big picture" and who will optimize the work of the specialists.[23]

As the philosophy of marketing intelligence is embraced in a firm and as the intelligence function becomes more important, we can expect some changes in the company's organizational structure.[24] We may see the establishment of a centralized department of intelligence services, which will include marketing

[20] Marion Harper, Jr., "A New Profession to Aid Management," *Journal of Marketing*, January, 1961, pp. 1–6.

[21] *Ibid.*, p. 1.

[22] For a report on the "knowledge revolution," where it is estimated that the "knowledge industry" accounts for one-third of the total United States output, engages one-fourth of the population, and contributes more to United States economic growth than physical capital, see "The Force of Intellect," *News Front*, April, 1964, pp. 14–19. See also Fritz Machlup, *Production and Distribution of Knowledge in the United States*, Princeton University Press, Princeton, N.J., 1962.

[23] For one summary of the responsibilities of the research generalist, see Newman, *op. cit.*, p. 111.

[24] William T. Kelley, "Marketing Intelligence for Top Management," *Journal of Marketing*, October, 1965, p. 21.

research along with economic research, market data, internal information, and administrative data. The director of intelligence services will surely occupy a higher place in the executive echelon than now is typically true of the director of marketing research.

To conclude, marketing intelligence today is truly on the threshold of a brilliant future. As an increasing number of firms put the marketing concept into practice and as top management more fully recognizes how important marketing is to the economic health of a company, there will be a growing appreciation of the value of marketing research as a management tool in problem solving and decision making. The scope of the field will be broadened, and marketing research will be applied in important new areas. One indication of the increasing maturity in the field has been the establishment of a code of ethics for marketing research and of a set of standards to guide the users of research.[25] As more and more firms—big and small, in all areas of the country, and in all types of industry—make increasing use of marketing intelligence, job opportunities in the field will expand considerably, and the vocation will become more attractive to a greater number of qualified people.

QUESTIONS AND PROBLEMS

1   Give some specific examples of how marketing research may serve as an *aid* in managerial decision making, but where executive judgment is still needed.

2   To refer to marketing research as a "science" or the application of the "scientific method" is sometimes considered a loose usage of terms by physicists or chemists. In what respects does marketing research differ from research in physics, chemistry, and similar disciplines? To what extent is research in marketing any more or less scientific than research in these other fields?

3   A large wholesaler of electrical supplies and equipment located in the Midwest wanted to learn as much as possible about the potential market for an electric milk cooler. This is essentially a chestlike container which will hold ten regular-sized farm milk cans.

Many small farmers now store their cans of fresh milk in cool well water. Before the cans are collected by a local dairy, processor, or shipper, the temperature of the water—and the milk—may fluctuate considerably. Heat tends to raise the bacteria count in milk. In some cities and states milk having more than a certain level of bacteria count cannot by law be processed for human consumption.

The manufacturer of the electric cooler approached the wholesaler with the hope that he would add the product to his line. Before making a decision, the wholesaler wanted to do some informal investigation of the product's market possibilities. What should this informal investigation consist of?

4   A group of wealthy businessmen regularly spent some time each winter at a popular ski resort—Aspen, Colorado, Sun Valley, Idaho, Snow Valley, Ver-

---

[25] Dik W. Twedt, "Why a Marketing Research Code of Ethics?" *Journal of Marketing*, October, 1963, pp. 48–50. See also *Criteria to Assist Users of Marketing Research*, American Marketing Association, Chicago, 1962.

mont, or Squaw Valley, California. These men were intrigued with the possibility of forming a corporation to develop and operate a large ski resort in the Colorado Rockies. This would be a totally new venture and would be on U.S. Forest Service land. It would be a complete resort with facilities appealing to middle- and upper-income markets. What types of information might they want to have before deciding whether to go ahead with the venture? What sources of information would be used?

5   Acquire the following information for the most recent year available, using secondary sources. In each case, cite your source of information and list alternative sources where the information is also available.

a. Tons of coal mined in Pennsylvania
b. Wholesale sales in Illinois
c. Value of cotton produced in California
d. Population of Dade County, Florida
e. Total number of new housing units started in the North-Central geographic region
f. Gross-margin percentage of the Johns-Manville Company
g. Total labor force in the United States—annual average
h. Number of shoe stores in Texas
i. Operating expense ratio for jewelry wholesalers
j. Consumer expenditures for personal services and for durable goods
k. Consumer price index—for any given month or the annual average

6   A manufacturer of a liquid glass cleaner competitive with Windex and Glass Wax wants to determine the amount of the product which he can expect to sell in various markets throughout the country. To help him in this project, prepare a report which shows the following information pertaining to your home state and also, if possible, your home city or county. Carefully identify the source you use for this information and also state other sources which carry this information.

a. Number of households or families
b. Income or buying power per family or per household
c. Total retail sales in the most recent year for which you can find reliable data
d. Total annual sales of food stores, hardware stores, and drugstores
e. The number of food stores

7   A wholesaler of air-conditioning and refrigeration equipment for both domestic and commercial use wants to analyze his marketing costs in each territory to determine the relative profitability of each district. Specifically, what types of internal data would he use in this study?

8   Evaluate surveys, observational techniques, and experimentation as methods of gathering primary data in the following projects:

a. A sporting goods retailer wants to determine college students' brand preferences for skis, tennis rackets, and golf clubs.
b. A supermarket chain wants to determine women shoppers' preferences for the physical layout of fixtures and traffic patterns, particularly around check-out stands.
c. A manufacturer of conveyor belts wants to know who makes buying decisions for this product among present and prospective users.

9   Carefully evaluate the relative merits of personal, telephone, and mail surveys on the bases of flexibility, amount of information obtained, accuracy, speed. cost, and ease of administration.

10   How would you plan or establish a sample in research projects designed to answer the following questions?

   a.   What brand of shoes is most popular among the female students on your campus?

   b.   Should the department stores in or near your hometown be open on Sundays?

   c.   What percentage of the business firms in the large city nearest your campus have automatic fire-sprinkler systems?

11   What criteria should a manufacturing firm use or what questions should its executives ask in selecting an outside research organization to aid in marketing research work?

12   Explain how the concept of a marketing-intelligence system is basically different from the marketing research function as traditionally performed.

13   "The marketing-intelligence executive—rather than an operating, decision-making executive—should be the one to identify marketing problems, delineate the area to be studied, and design the research projects." Do you agree? Explain.

14   Should the director of marketing intelligence report directly to the chief marketing executive or to the president?

case 1. AURORA ELECTRONICS COMPANY (A)

Introduction of the marketing concept into an engineering-oriented firm

The Aurora Electronics Company, a small manufacturer of a variety of electronic products, derives over 90 per cent of its sales volume from Federal government contracts acquired on a bid basis. In an attempt to reduce his virtually complete dependence on government contracts, the president, Joseph Stacy, is interested in expanding into nongovernment markets by means of product diversification. He has several new products in mind. Research and development work has been done on some of the products, and a few pilot models have been produced. One product which the company is considering is an FM auto radio which would play through the speaker system of an already installed regular AM set. Mr. Stacy has engaged a marketing consulting firm to determine the market potential for the product and to get advice on other marketing considerations which are involved in the decision of whether or not to add the FM auto radio to the company's line.

The firm was started by Joseph Stacy during World War II, and the business expanded until sales volume reached a peak of $5 million during the Korean War. Since then, sales to the government have declined, and the current annual sales volume is about $3 million. The engineering and production facilities were originally located about 7 miles apart in Chicago. A few years ago, the production facilities and the president's office were moved to Phoenix, Arizona, while the engineering research and development work continued in the original location. In spite of the decline in sales since the 1951 peak, the company has retained all its key engineering and production personnel, many of whom have been with the firm since its early days.

The auto radio is not the company's first venture into nongovernmental markets. Actually, the firm has had three earlier experiences, none of which were very successful. One involved a water purifier, priced at $75, which was connected directly to the waterline and which removed bacteria from the water. The product was favorably accepted by public health officials, and the company anticipated a large volume of sales in foreign countries where impure water is a serious problem. Another nonmilitary product was a beautiful console model of a TV–radio–hi-fi set which retailed for $995. The Aurora Company produced and/or assembled all the working parts and then placed them in wooden cabinets, designed and manufactured by a fine North Carolina furniture manufacturer. The sets were sold directly and on an exclusive franchise basis to a leading Chicago department store. Service problems and Aurora's failure to meet delivery commitments caused the retailer to discontinue its orders, and Aurora was left with fifty sets on hand. The third

Wednesday, May 13, 1970

YOU ARE CORDIALLY INVITED TO AN AFTERNOON OF

Leafletting & Canvassing for Peace

EVERYONE IS DESPERATELY NEEDED FOR A

City-Wide Canvass

WHEN: AT 10 AM FOR LEAFLETTING, AND AT 2 PM FOR CANVASSING. WE WILL
ASSEMBLE AT GRAHAM CHAPEL FOR ORIENTATION, MAPS, AND LITERATURE
ABOUT THE WAR. AFTERWARDS, WE WILL GO INTO ST. LOUIS.

WHERE: At Washington University's Graham Chapel

Phone VO3-0100
call ext. 4676 or 4682 for information

product was an electronic garage-door opener. This product is still being produced in small quantities and is sold directly to a large manufacturer of garage doors.

Early in the consultants' study, it became apparent to them that the key factor in the decision of whether to market the FM auto radio or, for that matter, any other product intended for a nongovernmental market really lay in the area of organizational emphasis. As is true of many electronics manufacturers, the Aurora Company is totally oriented toward engineering. There is no marketing department; there is not even a sales manager or a sales force. Mr. Stacy himself handles whatever marketing work is done. About a year ago, an ex-automobile salesman was hired as sales manager, but he lasted only six months. According to Mr. Stacy, this sales manager constantly sought approval to lower the prices.

Mr. Stacy, the president, is a fine engineer; he is careful, thoughtful, and thorough. His quiet, gracious manner sometimes conceals his tremendous energy and drive. Although he is technically oriented, his lack of success with nonmilitary products has opened his eyes to the need for marketing in his firm. As an administrator, Mr. Stacy maintains a tight centralized authority over his employees. Other executives can do nothing of any significance without his approval. In view of the geographical separation of facilities, this hesitancy to delegate authority often poses problems. The president does considerable traveling between Phoenix and Chicago, and the company's long-distance telephone bill is inordinately large.

Frank Sturgis, the executive vice-president, has his offices at the engineering center in Chicago. He, too, is an engineer. He seems to recognize that the extreme engineering orientation of the firm leaves much to be desired, and he cooperates completely with the marketing consultants. He manages the Chicago office competently, although he has to clear most decisions with Mr. Stacy.

The chief engineer, James Dickens, is the guiding technical spirit behind the FM auto radio project. It is his baby, so to speak, and he is convinced that there is a big market for a well-engineered product. He recognizes that Aurora's product still requires some technical improvement.

Martin Rast, a young man between twenty-five and thirty years of age, is the service manager; he has been with the company for over four years. Although his college training was in engineering, he is taking night-school courses in business administration. He has aspirations of becoming a sales manager (although he has had no experience in selling), and the other executives are considering him seriously for the job if they decide to market the FM auto radio.

George Rainero serves as controller and purchasing agent. He has impressed the consultants as a highly competent administrator, whose nontechnical orientation is much needed to balance—if only feebly—the concentration of engineering thinking in the firm. This concentration, however, and Mr. Stacy's unwillingness to delegate authority are discouraging, and Mr. Rainero has served notice that he is resigning in about a month. He is particularly bothered by the firm's hesitancy to produce in anticipation of orders. The company's long experience with government contract work has engendered the idea that it should first get firm orders and then go into production. This thinking is not compatible with the usual approach in selling to the consumer or nonmilitary industrial market.

QUESTIONS

1 What do you think should be done to make this firm more marketing-oriented?
2 What organizational changes do you recommend for this company to put it in a better position to sell to the nongovernmental market?

case 2. CHEYENNE CHEMICAL COMPANY

Organization for marketing research in a production-oriented company

In his new role as sales manager of the Cheyenne Chemical Company, Dr. Daniel Sadler is wondering whether the company should be doing some marketing research and, if so, what organizational arrangements would be most appropriate for conducting this work. Cheyenne Chemical Company is a medium-sized firm located in Colorado Springs, Colorado. It employs approximately sixty-five people, including a technical staff of fifteen graduate chemists and four graduate engineers. This highly trained technical staff, eleven of whom hold doctoral degrees, was carefully selected for diversity of background and talent. Their fields of academic specialization include inorganic chemistry, biological chemistry, chemical engineering, and organic chemistry.

The company was established by five men, all of whom are chemists or engineers, attended the University of Colorado, and knew one another as students. Dr. Sadler has said, "If Colorado Springs seems a strange place for a chemical company, our only excuse is that we like it here. Colorado Springs is a prosperous, stable community with a good growth rate, and it is becoming (along with Denver and Boulder, to the north) a major center for scientific research. We have found it easy to recruit top-notch professional personnel because Colorado Springs is recognized as an excellent city in which to live, play, and work."

The company's market niche is that of a moderately sized firm whose products complement rather than compete with those of other chemical companies. It is intended that the Cheyenne Chemical Company will remain modest in size, producing those chemicals of high price and small volume which are needed for pilot plant, experimental, or pharmaceutical purposes and which are not economically produced by larger companies. Sales have increased fairly steadily, from $12,000 in 1947 to a high of $2.6 million in 1966. Dr. Sadler expects that sales will pass the $3.0 million mark by 1970.

Cheyenne Chemical's products are sold to manufacturers of chemicals, pharmaceuticals, vitamins, estrogens, rubber, petroleum, and related products; to private medical and research institutions; to colleges and universities; and to governmental laboratories. While Cheyenne's market is world-wide, its main market is concentrated in the region east of the Mississippi and north of the Ohio Rivers.

New-product ideas come most often from customers or from Cheyenne's industrial distributors (wholesalers). In fact, the majority of Cheyenne Chemical's research projects are initiated by requests from customers. These requests are received in confidence, and an evaluation is made without charge or obligation to the customers.

During the company's early years, products were distributed to the domestic market through wholesalers, and all foreign sales were made through independent exporters. Now Cheyenne Chemical sells through a system of manufacturers' agents who are granted exclusive sales rights in their geographical markets. Domestic agents are maintained in New York, Chicago, Los Angeles, and San Francisco; foreign distributors are located in Italy, Switzerland, France, Great Britain, the Netherlands, Canada, Japan, Australia, and Mexico.

Physical distribution typically poses no great problems because freight costs are low in relation to the sales price to customers. Dr. Sadler has admitted, however, that the great distance from plant to market is at times a competitive disadvantage because of difficulty in maintaining personal contact with customers and because of occasional unavoidable delays of merchandise in transit.

In pricing a product, Dr. Sadler and the other executives undertake an evaluation of its cost and market possibilities. In this evaluation, they are concerned with the general nature and scope of the product in terms of quantity desired, possibility of repeat business, type of compound, general price range, and competitive situations. Other important factors considered are amount of material required, plant time, and direct labor costs. Catalogues and price lists are published.

Prior to the recent executive reorganization in the company, Dr. Sadler, who holds a Ph.D. in chemical engineering from Stanford University, was head of the new-product-development department. When he became sales manager, he incorporated his former research and development duties into his present position. As sales manager, Sadler is one of the most important executives in the company. He handles all sales and sales correspondence. Occasionally he travels in a missionary-salesman capacity to confer with customers and distributors. He is responsible for all advertising and sales-promotional activities. News releases are issued to trade publications such as *Chemical Engineering News* and *Drug Trade News*. Advertisements are sent to trade publications, and technical data sheets are prepared to answer inquiries.

Dr. Sadler has been with the Cheyenne Chemical Company only three years. Even though his background is in engineering, he has had an increasingly nagging concern that the company ought to be doing more in the way of studying the many facets of its marketing program. When he finally expressed his concern to two of the executive staff—both chemists—he got separate reactions. One, in effect, said, "We have been a successful company for over twenty years. Our sales and profits have increased almost every year. This year they will be the highest in our history. What evidence is there that we should be doing any type of research other than what we have always done?" The other executive said that the company's commitment to engineering and production research in chemistry, particularly in new products, were the research areas in which the company should continue to concentrate. He felt that a good research chemist was the key to corporate success in their industry.

Still not convinced and still not deterred, Sadler is somewhat stymied by not knowing exactly where to turn. He believes that the company should be engaging in marketing research, but he does not know in what way, nor is he certain about how much the company should spend for this activity.

He does feel that his first problem is to decide who should actually do the marketing research job for the firm. One possibility is to establish a one- or two-man marketing research department in the company. Another reasonable alternative is to farm out the research to an independent marketing research firm. Sadler has also thought of having the task assigned to the research and development men now working on product research.

QUESTIONS

1 Should this company be engaging in formal marketing research activities?

2 If so, what are some ways in which marketing research might be used? That is, what are some possible research projects?

3 Who should perform the marketing research job?

4 How much should be budgeted for the marketing research function?

PART TWO

THE MARKET

4

MARKETS, PEOPLE, AND MONEY

Today we read that we are experiencing a population explosion. We hear that the teen-age market or the baby market or the young-married market is a growing force in the economy. Political parties and businessmen alike are presently showering attention on the "geriatric set." We must adjust our marketing system to the concept of interurbia. Sellers are in a battle for the discretionary dollar. These and countless similar remarks are evidence of the attention being paid to markets and to the factors of people and money which, in turn, constitute these markets.

"THE CONSUMER IS KING"

A sound marketing program should start with a careful quantitative and qualitative analysis of the market demand for the product or service. Adam Smith and other economists and philosophers both before and after him stated the fundamental importance of consumption—it is the only social and economic justification for production. Yet, because of the scarcity of goods, the difficulty of understanding the consumer, and the ease of measuring machine output, most American economists devoted their attention to production rather than to consumption prior to the 1920s. This concentration on the study of production went on even longer in other countries.

In the United States, however, the output of the production system has been so great since the end of World War I that surpluses have developed. In this economy of abundance, the social and economic interest and emphasis have shifted from production to consumption. For several years now it has been considered axiomatic that "the consumer is king." The consumer is the basic determinant of what goods and services will be produced and of where, when, how, and at what price they will be sold. Up to the limits of his income, the consumer today is free to choose the amount and kind of want-satisfying goods and services which he buys.

From a realistic standpoint there are considerable limitations to consumer sovereignty. Possibly the principal ones are the consumer's lack of organization, his lack of a voice to make his edicts known, and his general apathy. If he is king, he maintains a strange palace court in which the subjects have to spend huge sums to try to find out what the vacillating, disorganized, fickle king wants and to proclaim loudly that they, over all other courtiers, have just what he wants.

Import restrictions also limit the consumer; in many instances they keep him from getting fine foreign products at reasonable prices. Interstate trade barriers reduce the free flow of some products from one state to another. Efforts of farm, labor, and business interests take price control out of the hands of consumers. Determination of product quality by the consumer is often difficult, if not impossible. These and other factors make one feel that "the consumer must be forgiven for thinking that he is today more a constitutional than an absolute monarch."[1]

WHAT IS A MARKET?

The concept of a market is sometimes confusing. There is a stock market and an automobile market, a retail and a wholesale market for furniture, and a local and a national market for building materials. One person may be going to the market; another may plan to market his product. Really, what is a market? Clearly, there are many usages of the term in economic theory, in business in general, and in marketing in particular. A market may be defined as a place or a geographical area where buyers and sellers meet and function, goods or services are offered for sale, and transfers of ownership of title occur. A market

---

[1] C. H. Grattan, "The Complex World of the Consumer," in William Lazer and Eugene J. Kelley (eds.), *Managerial Marketing: Perspectives and Viewpoints,* rev. ed., Richard D. Irwin, Inc., Homewood, Ill., 1962, p. 125.

also may be defined as an aggregate demand by potential buyers of a product or service. For example, there is a farm market for petroleum products. In economic theory a market implies a set of conditions and forces which determine prices. That is, the meeting of buyers and sellers, price determination, and transfer of title are activities essential to the existence of a market. The concept of a market also implies a *demand* for a product or service. In fact, the terms "market" and "demand" often are used interchangeably, and they also may be used jointly as "market demand."

The above definitions of a market still may not be sufficiently usable by a marketing executive in an individual firm. Consequently, in this book a *market* will be defined as people with needs to satisfy, the money to spend, and the willingness to spend it. Thus in the market demand for any given product or service, there are three factors to consider—people with needs, their purchasing power, and their buying behavior. We shall employ the dictionary definition of *needs*: A need is the lack of anything that is required, desired, or useful. We do not limit needs to the narrow physiological requirements of food, clothing, and shelter essential for survival. The potentially limitless number of needs offers unbounded opportunities for market growth. Satisfying wants may be interpreted as the first step toward satisfying needs. We want something that will answer our needs.

Market segmentation

Before a marketing executive attempts to analyze the market for his products, he should understand the value of market segmentation. *Market segmentation* consists of taking the total, heterogeneous market for a product and dividing it into several submarkets or segments, each of which tends to be homogeneous in all significant aspects. In terms familiar to an economist, we are developing several demand schedules—a separate one for each market segment—where only one schedule representing the total market existed previously. Thus, instead of speaking of a market for Bermuda shorts, we now segment this market into several submarkets—those for college men, college women, businessmen, housewives, and retired people. Still further segmentation might be based on geographic location; for example, we might speak of the Eastern college men's market or the Pacific Coast college women's market.

The total market for most types of products is too heterogeneous for marketing management to derive maximum value from an analysis of it as a whole. To speak of the market for industrial fuel oil, vitamin pills, electric razors, or tractors is to ignore the fact that within the total market for each of these products there exist submarkets which differ significantly from one another. This lack of homogeneity may be traced to differences in buying habits, ways in which the product is used, users' needs, motives for buying, or other factors. If markets are properly segmented by marketing management, the distribution, pricing, promotion, and other parts of the marketing program can be effectively tailored for these segments.

In some instances, a firm may sell the same product to different markets through the use of different advertising appeals. More often, however, market segmentation is accompanied by product differentiation—by developing a different product for each market segment. This relationship is discussed in Chapter 9, "Product-line Policies and Strategies."

Ultimate consumers and industrial users

One very important way of segmenting the entire American market is to divide it into ultimate consumers and industrial users, the sole criterion being the reason for buying. *Ultimate consumers* buy and/or use products or services for their own personal or household use. They are satisfying strictly nonbusiness wants, and they constitute what is called the "consumer market." A mother who buys food and clothing and the family members who eat the food and wear the clothes are all ultimate consumers.

Industrial users are business, industrial, or institutional organizations who buy products or services to use in their own businesses or in making other products. A manufacturer who buys chemicals with which to make fertilizer is an industrial user of these chemicals. The farmer who buys the fertilizer to use in commercial farming is an industrial user of the fertilizer. (If a homeowner buys fertilizer to use on his yard, he is an ultimate consumer because he buys it for household use.) A supermarket, hospital, bank, or paper manufacturer which buys accounting machines, pencils, and floor wax is an industrial user of these products because it uses them in a business or institution. Industrial users in total constitute the "industrial market."

The segmentation of all markets into two groups—consumer and industrial—is extremely significant from a marketing point of view because the two markets buy differently. Consequently, a seller's marketing program—his products, distribution, pricing, and promotion—will differ depending upon whether he is selling to the consumer or the industrial market.

CLASSIFICATION OF PRODUCTS

Just as it is necessary to segment markets for meaningful programming in marketing, so also is it helpful to separate products into homogeneous classifications. Here we shall divide all products into two groups—consumer goods and industrial goods—a classification that parallels our segmentation of the market. In later chapters we shall divide each of the two major product categories still further.

Consumer goods and industrial goods

Consumer goods include all products which are "destined for use by ultimate consumers or households and in such form that they can be used without (further) commercial processing." *Industrial goods* are those which are "destined to be sold primarily for use in producing other goods or rendering services as contrasted with goods destined to be sold primarily to the ultimate consumer."[2]

The fundamental basis for distinguishing between the two groups is the *ultimate* use for which the product is intended in its present form. A cash register purchased by a retailer for use in his store (the product renders a service in a business), a pair of overalls bought by a farmer to be worn while working (farming is his business), and materials or parts bought by a manufacturer for use in making his product—all are industrial goods.

A particular stage in a product's distribution has no effect upon its classification. Cornflakes or children's shoes would be classed as consumer products whether they were in the manufacturer's warehouse or on retailers' shelves because ultimately they will be used in their present form by household consumers. Cornflakes sold to restaurants and other institutions, however, are classed as industrial goods.

Often it is not possible to place a product definitely in one class or the other. A portable typewriter may be considered a consumer good if it is purchased by a student or a housewife for nonbusiness use, but if the typewriter is bought by a traveling salesman for use in his business, it is classed with industrial goods. The manufacturer of such a product recognizes that his product falls in both categories and therefore develops separate marketing programs for the different markets.

Marketing significance of product classification

The two-way product classification is a useful framework for programming marketing operations because each major class of products ultimately goes to a different market and requires different marketing methods. In the field of product planning, for example, branding, packaging, color, and fashion are generally far more significant for a consumer product than for an industrial good. Since the channels of distribution for consumer products are typically longer and involve more middlemen than those for industrial goods, distribution policies would vary. Advertising policies, too, would be affected. Manufacturers of consumer goods ordinarily use much more advertising than do manufacturers of industrial products.

POPULATION

According to our definition, population is one of the main components of a market. Therefore, a marketing man should study all aspects of the distribution

---

[2] Committee on Definitions, Ralph S. Alexander, Chairman, *Marketing Definitions: A Glossary of Marketing Terms*, American Marketing Association, Chicago, 1960, pp. 11, 14.

The American Marketing Association and some authors use the possessive term, "consumers." The adjective "consumer" is a more logical and parallel counterpart of "industrial."

and composition of the population. In the following sections we shall consider only those population factors which affect the consumer market. The industrial market is discussed in Chapter 7. In analyzing population, a marketing executive should first find out which characteristics of the population—such as age, education, or family size—substantially affect the composition of the market for his product or service. Then he should get the current quantitative measurement of each of these characteristics. Finally, he should determine the trends in the various data and understand the significance these hold for his marketing program.

Total population

A logical place to start is with an analysis of total population, and here the existence of a "population explosion" becomes evident. The population of the

fig. 4–1

Total population in the United States is projected at 275 million by 1985—an increase of 41 per cent over 1965 assuming the fertility rate remains at the 1960–1963 level. According to even the most conservative fertility estimate, however, the population should reach 248 million by 1985. Should a marketing man make definite plans based on these projections?

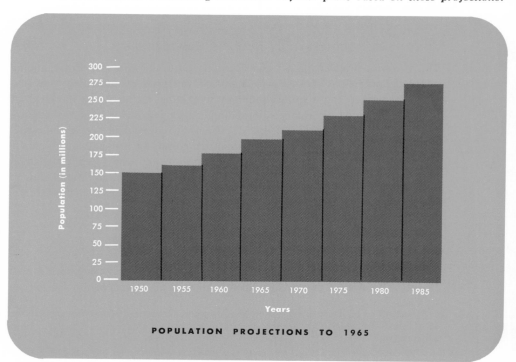

POPULATION PROJECTIONS TO 1965

United States did not reach 100 million until 1915. By 1950, the population had reached 150 million, and in 1965 it was about 195 million. The forecast for 1985 is from 250 to 275 million (depending upon which fertility rate is assumed); by the year 2000, we can expect that over 300 million people will be living in the United States (Fig. 4–1). This rate of growth is tremendous, and the marketing implications are staggering. The total spent for food, clothing, leisure-time goods and services, home furnishings, automobiles, and all the other products and services demanded by the population reaches an astronomical figure. This market is so large and so heterogeneous that it must be analyzed in segments.

Regional distribution

Table 4–1 shows the distribution of the 1965 population and the projected population growth by census regions in the United States. The biggest markets are still in the East and Midwest; the Middle Atlantic states represent about 19 per cent of the population, and the East North Central region accounts for 20 per cent. The largest rates of increase, however, are in the Pacific Coast and Mountain regions. Of course, this westward movement of population has been going on ever since the Eastern seaboard was first settled, and it shows no signs of abating. The forecast is that the Western part of the country will enjoy the

table   4–1

Regional distribution of population, 1965, and projected growth to 1975 and 1985

Although the Eastern census regions account for the largest part of our total population, the Western regions have a more rapid growth rate. The Pacific area is growing at the fastest rate. Movement of the population center of the United States is still generally westward.

		Projected growth	
Region	Regional distribution, 1965 (per cent)	1965–1975 (per cent)	1965–1985 (per cent)
New England	5.8	13.5	31.8
Middle Atlantic	18.7	12.0	26.4
East North Central	19.8	14.0	33.4
West North Central	8.2	8.1	22.5
South Atlantic	14.7	20.2	44.2
East South Central	6.5	11.0	23.8
West South Central	9.5	15.7	35.1
Mountain	4.1	27.0	56.4
Pacific	12.7	27.3	62.5
Total, U.S.	100.0	14.9	36.1

SOURCE: U.S. Bureau of the Census.

greatest *percentage* increases in the ten- and twenty-year periods following 1965. From 1965 to 1975, an increase of 15 per cent in the total population is forecasted (under one fertility assumption), while the population is expected to rise 27 per cent in both the Rocky Mountain and Pacific regions. These same two regions are the only ones in the country in which we anticipate a better than 50 per cent population increase from 1965 to 1985, as contrasted with 36 per cent for the nation as a whole. In fact, within the foreseeable future Los Angeles may pass New York as the leading consumer market in the nation.

The regional distribution of population is important to marketing men because sectional differences exist in the demand for many products. These differences are traceable to climate, religion, social mores and customs, and other factors. Bright, warm colors are preferred in Florida and the Southwest, while grays and cooler colors predominate in New England and the Midwest. Per capita consumption of soft drinks and cosmetics varies substantially among the regions of the country. People in the West are less formal than Easterners, and they spend more time outdoors. Consequently, as the Western population increases, there will be a larger market for such products as patio furniture, sports clothes, and barbecue equipment. To a marketing man, the fact that southern California, Florida, and Arizona are growing so rapidly means that there will be an increased demand for suntan lotion, swimsuits, backyard swimming pools, air-conditioners for homes and automobiles, and other warm-weather products.

Shifts and trends in the regional distribution of population may also influence policies regarding channels of distribution. As regional markets for a company's products grow, the firm may establish sales branches or expand its own sales force to cover markets which had previously been assigned to wholesalers or manufacturers' agents. Other companies may bypass former wholesalers and sell directly to retailers whose businesses have become large enough to make direct sales profitable.

Urban, rural, suburban, and interurban distribution

For many years in the United States there has been a relative and absolute decline in the farm population, and this decline is expected to continue. In 1940 about one out of four people lived on a farm; in 1950 it was about one out of six; and in 1965, one out of sixteen. The declining farm population has led some marketing people to underrate the rural market. Both as an industrial market for farm equipment and supplies and as a consumer market with increased buying power and a more urbanlike sophistication, the farm market is still a big one. Sociological patterns (family size and customs) among rural people differ significantly from those of city dwellers, and these patterns have considerable influence on buying behavior. Per capita consumption of cosmetics and other beauty aids, for example, is much lower in farm markets than in city markets.

While it is true that the farm population has been declining and the metropolitan areas growing, something new is also going on *within* the metropolitan areas. The central cities are growing very slowly, and in some cases, the older, established parts of the cities are actually losing population. The real growth is occurring in the fringe areas of the central cities or in the suburbs outside these cities. For the past twenty years, one of the most significant social and economic trends in the United States has been the shift of population to the suburbs.

The growth of the suburban population has striking implications for us. Since a great percentage of suburban people live in single-family residences, there is a vastly expanded market for lawn mowers, lawn furniture, home furnishings, and home repair supplies and equipment. The suburbanite is more likely to want two cars than is the city dweller. He is inclined to spend more of his leisure time at home, so there is a bigger market for items used in home entertainment and recreation.

In several places in the United States the metropolitan areas have expanded to the point where there is no rural space between them. This joining of metropolitan areas has been called "interurbia." Where two or more city markets once existed, there is today a single market. For example, there is virtually no space along the Atlantic coastline between Boston and Virginia which is not part of a standard metropolitan area. This is a 600-mile-long single market. The areas along the shores of the Great Lakes from Buffalo to Detroit, then across the lower part of Michigan to Gary, Chicago, and Milwaukee, constitute another series of interurban areas. Soon the coastal region from north of San Francisco to the Mexican border in California will be one great interurban market.[3]

For marketing men the concept of interurbia may mean the end of marketing on a metropolitan area basis. If so, sales territories will have to be radically revised. It will be difficult to isolate a test market in one city. Furthermore, as interurbia grows, it may not be economical for advertisers to seek true national distribution of their products. Instead, they may aim at interurban markets alone.

Number of families and size of family

The rate of household and family formation is a population factor of considerable significance to marketing men. A *household* is defined as one or more persons living in the same dwelling unit; a *family* is a group of two or more related persons living together.

Every new household or family is potentially a market for a dwelling place, furniture, appliances, and other home furnishings. Many firms direct

[3] See "Interurbia: Where It Stands Today, Where It's Going," *Sales Management,* Nov. 10, 1964, p. 69.

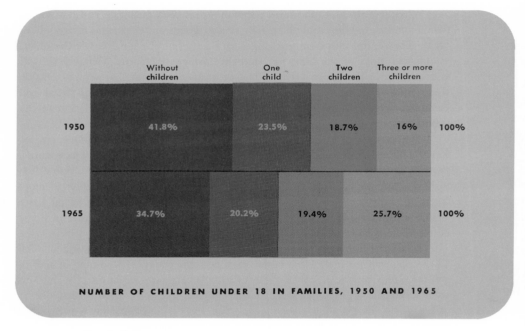

fig. 4–2

About 55 per cent of the families in the United States still have only one child or none at all. However, the average size of the family has been increasing since 1950. Assuming that the present size remains the same or increases, for what kinds of manufacturers is this important?

SOURCE: U.S. Bureau of the Census.

an entire segment of their promotional program to young married couples. For manufacturers of appliances and furniture, the *number* of families is often more important than the *size* of the family. A refrigerator manufacturer, for example, may hope to sell three refrigerators to three couples, whereas he could hope to sell only one to a family with six people in it.

The point developed in the preceding paragraph does not negate the fact that family size has significant marketing implications. After steadily declining for over one-half century, the average size of the American family began to increase in the 1950s. In 1965, 45 per cent of all families (where the head was under sixty-five years old) had two or more children; this compares with 35 per cent in 1950 (Fig. 4–2). The trend toward larger families will mean a continued demand for large cars and station wagons, large homes, some large appliances, and more clothing and furniture. In the late 1940s most homes were built with two bedrooms, but by 1960 three and four bedrooms were common, and very few homes were constructed with only two.

Age groups

The size of various age groups has a substantial effect on the market for certain products. The youth market (under twenty), for instance, constituted 34 per cent of the population in 1950, but is expected to reach 41 per cent of the total in 1975. In 1965, the under-ten age group was larger than America's total population 100 years ago. Developments in this market are upsetting traditional advertising appeals, are overloading traditional media, and are revising our previous understanding of how children think and buy.[4]

More and more, the teen-age market is being recognized as an important one.[5] Not only is the size of this market growing, but its members have an increasing amount of money to spend. They are good customers for records, automobiles, cosmetics, clothes, jewelry, and other products. In order to tap this market, many manufacturers are adopting new product and distribution policies. For instance, some clothing manufacturers are now designing junior ready-to-wear dresses which reflect the age and not merely the size of the teen-age girl. Bobbie Brooks, Inc., is also altering the distribution systems for its junior wardrobes. Many department stores have ready-to-wear departments labeled "college," "junior," or "miss," which handle similar or duplicate styles but different sizes. Furthermore, items such as skirts, sweaters, and blouses are sold in separate departments. The Bobbie Brooks firm feels this is "splintering" the market and consequently urges retailers to develop one "young adult" department which will carry all sizes and all items necessary for the complete wardrobe of girls from fifteen to twenty-four years old.

Entire promotional programs are geared to segments of the youth market. Children's television shows, for example, are sponsored by cereal manufacturers and other advertisers in an effort to develop brand preferences at an early age. Other manufacturers select as advertising media those magazines or radio programs which receive high ratings among teen-age audiences.[6]

At the other end of the age scale is another market segment which is not to be overlooked. The average age of the entire population today is a shade over thirty years, but the number of people over sixty-five is increasing both absolutely and as a percentage of the total. By 1975, there will be more than twenty-one million people age sixty-five or over, representing about 9 per cent of the total population.

[4] A. J. Vogl, "The Changing Face of the Children's Market," *Sales Management*, Dec. 18, 1964, p. 35.

[5] See Penelope Orth, "Teenager: What Kind of Consumer?" *Printers' Ink*, Sept. 20, 1963, p. 67; and Paul Gilkison, "What Influences the Buying Decisions of Teenagers?" *Journal of Retailing*, Fall, 1965, p. 33.

[6] For a cautionary analysis of the youth market in terms of six major problems it presents for marketing management, see Charles F. Adams, "Myths of the Youth Market," *Sales/Marketing Today*, December, 1965, pp. 8–11.

Manufacturers and middlemen alike are beginning to recognize that people in this age group are logical prospects for small, low-cost housing units (trailers, as well as more conventional types of housing), cruises and foreign tours, health products, and cosmetics developed especially for older people. Many firms are also developing promotional programs to appeal to the buying motives of this group and to cater to their buying habits.[7]

Sex

Another widely employed and very useful method of segmenting the American market is to divide it into two groups—men and women. The women's market is big, rich, and powerful. This market is well educated and is moving into better jobs. Furthermore, the number of women is increasing at a more rapid rate than the number of men, and they are living longer. It is little wonder that firms selling automobiles, liquors, stocks, outboard motors, insurance, and many other items usually considered men's products are now aiming promotional programs directly at women. Special efforts are being made to tailor advertising campaigns and to plan products so as to interest women.

From 1965 to 1975, the male population age twenty and over is expected to increase from 56 million to 66 million, or 18 per cent. The young adult age group (twenty to thirty-four) will increase by a whopping 40 per cent, while the number in the early middle years (thirty-five to forty-nine) will actually decline about 5 per cent. Manufacturers of such diverse products as cigars, guns and ammunition, men's wear, wristwatches, and injector-type razor blades are only a few examples of the kinds of companies which must pinpoint marketing programs for various age groups in the male population. A better understanding of the male market is resulting in reevaluation of product and advertising strategies. New promotional appeals, new packaging, and new advertising media are some of the phases of marketing programs affected by an awareness of the growing, changing, profitable men's market.

Other population factors

The market for some consumer products is influenced by such factors as education, occupation, race, national origin, and religion. With an increasing number of people attaining higher levels of education, for example, we can expect to see changes in product preferences and buyers with more discriminating taste

---

[7] One analysis of income and expenditure data concluded that (1) consumers over sixty-five are not becoming affluent (the increase in their average income since 1946 is far below that of younger age groups) and (2) for many products, the differences in expenditure patterns of older consumers, as compared with those of younger consumer units, are due almost entirely to their smaller-sized families and lower incomes, rather than to age. See John A. Reinecke, "The 'Older' Market: Fact or Fiction?" *Journal of Marketing*, January, 1964, pp. 60–64.

and higher incomes. With an increasing number of married women working, we have already seen a great expansion of the market for frozen foods, home appliances, and other labor-saving products and services.

To categorize a market in terms of religion, national origin, or race may seem farfetched, but from a realistic point of view these factors are highly influential. We know, for instance, that the per capita consumption of meat decreases considerably in some cities during Lent, largely because of the influence of the Roman Catholic market, and we know that there is a large market for Polish sausage in counties heavily populated with people of Polish descent. A statement in an article based on marketing research is even more true today than it was in 1960, when the article was published: "Controversy and emotionalism notwithstanding, there is a Negro market—a *big* market, with plenty of buying brawn, and some individualistic traits that demand the attention of every marketer!"[8]

CONSUMER INCOME

People alone do not make a market; they must have money to spend. Consequently, a detailed study of income, its distribution, and how it is spent is essential in any quantitative market analysis which an individual firm may make. The purpose of such an analysis is to interpret the marketing implications of the figures and trends revealed in the study.

Nature and scope of income

What is income? There are so many different concepts of income that it is well to review some definitions. The following outline is actually a mathematical equation:

National income: The total income from all sources including employee compensation, corporate profits, and other income
  Less corporate profits and social security contributions
  Plus dividends, government transfer payments to persons, and net interest paid by government, *equals*

Personal income: The income from wages, salaries, dividends, rent, interest, business and professions, social security and farming.
  Less all personal Federal, state, and local taxes and nontax payments, *equals*

Disposable personal income: The amount available for personal consumption expenditures and savings

---

[8] "Marketing to the Negro Consumer," *Sales Management,* Mar. 11, 1960, p. 36; see also "Burgeoning Middle Class Boosting Negro Buying Power," *Sales Management,* Nov. 20, 1964, p. 77; "A Little Richer and Better Educated," *Business Week,* Nov. 6, 1965, p. 136; "The Negro Market: Accent on Quality," *Media/scope,* part 1, April, 1964, p. 77, and part 2, May, 1964, p. 73.

Less (1) essential expenditures for food, clothing, household utilities, and local transportation, and (2) fixed expenditures for rent, house mortgage payments, insurance, and installment debt payments, *equals*

Discretionary income: The amount of disposable personal income over and above that which a person needs to maintain a standard of living equivalent to that which prevailed in the early years following World War II. It is an amount free of fixed commitments (debt repayments, homeowner taxes, tenant rent) and above that required for essential household needs. Consequently, as compared with personal income data, discretionary income is a better or more sensitive indicator of the consumer's ability to spend for nonessentials. (The definition and measurement of discretionary income are the works of the National Industrial Conference Board.)

In addition, a marketing man will hear and use the terms "money income," "real income," and "psychic income." *Money income* is the amount a person receives in actual cash or checks for wages, salaries, rents, interest, and dividends. *Real income* is what the money income will buy in goods and services; it is purchasing power. If a person's money income rises 5 per cent in one year, but the cost of what he buys increases 8 per cent on the average, then his real income decreases about 3 per cent. *Psychic income* is an intangible but highly important income factor imputed to climate, a satisfying neighborhood, enjoyment of one's job, etc. Some people prefer to take less money income and real income in order to live in a pleasant suburb or in a part of the country which features a fine climate and recreation opportunities.

On the basis of income, the American market has grown fantastically since the end of World War II. Personal income rose from $228 billion in

table   4–2

Personal, disposable, and discretionary income in United States: in billions of dollars

Briefly, personal income is gross income before taxes; disposable personal income is the money remaining after taxes; disposable personal income less expenditures to maintain a reasonable standard of living equals discretionary income—the amount which can be spent on nonessentials. See text for more precise definitions.

				Per cent increase in 1965	
	1950	*1960*	*1965*	*Over 1950*	*Over 1960*
Total personal income	$228	$401	$531	133	32
Disposable personal income	210	350	465	121	33
Discretionary income	78	121	157 (1964)	101	30

SOURCE: Personal and disposable income—*Survey of Current Business;* Discretionary income—National Industrial Conference Board, Inc.

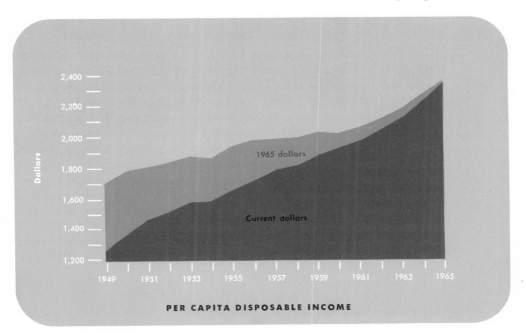

fig. 4–3

Even after adjusting for the inflationary effects of a rising price level, per capita disposable income has increased substantially over the past several years. Stated in constant (1965) dollars, per capita disposable income rose from $1,700 in 1949 to almost $2,400 in 1965.

SOURCE: *A Graphic Guide to Consumer Markets: 1966,* National Industrial Conference Board, Inc., New York, p. 26.

1950 to $531 billion in 1965, an increase of 133 per cent in only fifteen years. During the same period, disposable income increased 121 per cent ($210 billion to $465 billion), and discretionary income grew 101 per cent (Table 4–2). As large as these increases in discretionary income may seem, there is evidence that they are understated, because the classic definition of this income is arbitrary and limited. The quantitative measurement of discretionary income is affected by what is considered an essential purchase. Actually, there are many alternatives and choices on every level of spending, including the so-called "essential" areas.

Even after allowing for the rise in price level and the increase in total population, the advances in income are still very substantial. Some of these figures may be more meaningful when expressed on a per capita basis. Figure 4–3, for instance, shows per capita disposable income from 1949 to 1965. (These income figures are expressed both in 1965 dollars and in dollars which reflect the price levels of each specific year.) Thus, in terms of 1965 dollars, the per capita disposable income increased from about $1,700 in 1949 to almost $2,400 in 1965.

Income distribution

To get full value from an analysis of income, a marketing executive should carefully study the variations and trends in the distribution of income among regions and among population groups. Regional income data are particularly helpful in pinpointing the particular market to which a firm wishes to appeal. Income data on cities and even sections within cities may indicate the best locations for shopping centers and suburban branches of downtown stores.

In 1964, the highest total personal income was found in the Middle Atlantic and East North Central regions; each accounted for about 21 to 24 per cent of the nation's personal income, or together almost one-half of the total. The Pacific Coast states, however, topped the nation with respect to percentage growth in income during the period 1953–1964 (Fig. 4–4). This region doubled its personal income during that period.

On a per capita basis, the highest incomes are found in a cluster of states along the Atlantic seaboard (Connecticut, New York, New Jersey, Delaware),

fig. 4–4

The Middle Atlantic and East North Central regions together accounted for almost one-half of total personal income. The greatest growth rates occurred in the Far West, where personal income more than doubled in a decade.

source: *A Graphic Guide to Consumer Markets: 1966,* National Industrial Conference Board, Inc., New York, p. 26.

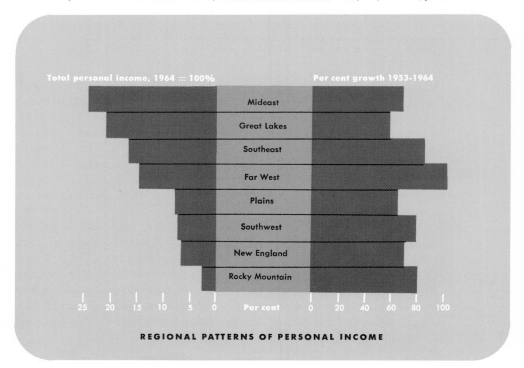

REGIONAL PATTERNS OF PERSONAL INCOME

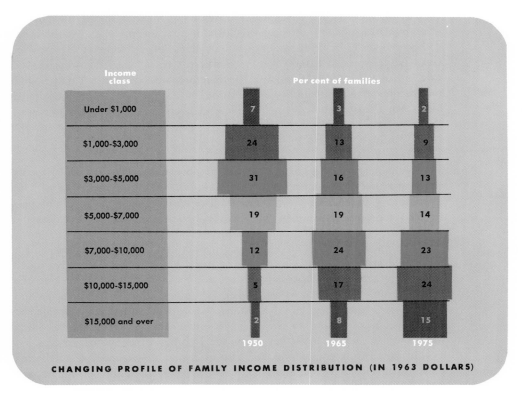

Income class	Per cent of families		
Under $1,000	7	3	2
$1,000-$3,000	24	13	9
$3,000-$5,000	31	16	13
$5,000-$7,000	19	19	14
$7,000-$10,000	12	24	23
$10,000-$15,000	5	17	24
$15,000 and over	2	8	15
	1950	1965	1975

CHANGING PROFILE OF FAMILY INCOME DISTRIBUTION (IN 1963 DOLLARS)

fig. 4–5

The income pyramid will be turned upside down in a twenty-five-year period. In 1965, 60 per cent of the families had incomes between $5,000 and $15,000. Families in the under-$3,000 class should decline from 31 to 11 per cent of the total. What are the marketing implications in the dramatic increase in the $10,000-and-over category?
SOURCE: National Industrial Conference Board projections using Department of Commerce data.

in Illinois, and in California. The marketing executive knows, however, that money alone—like population alone—does not make a market. Connecticut and Delaware have high per capita incomes, but their population is relatively small.

The income revolution which has been going on in the United States since the end of World War II may be seen in the changing profile of family income distribution, as pictorialized in Fig. 4–5. (These relationships are all expressed in constant purchasing power—1963 dollars—so the inflationary effects of rising prices are eliminated. We are seeing the changes in *real* income.) A major postwar development has been the tremendous growth of the middle-income market and a shrinking of the low-income groups. In 1965, 60 per cent of the families had incomes of $5,000 to $15,000, while in 1950 only 36 per cent were in that range. In 1950, almost one-third of the families earned less than $3,000—the government's cutoff figure defining the poverty level; by 1975, only 11 per cent should be in that income class. At the other end of the scale, by 1975 we expect that almost 40 per cent of the families will have incomes of $10,000 or more, whereas only 7 per cent were in that category in 1950. Since World War II, therefore, we have had not only a shift toward greater equality of income distribution among families in the United States, but also a substantial rise in the level of average family purchasing power.

Marketing significance of income data

The declining percentage of families in the poverty bracket, coupled with the sharp increases in the upper-income groups, presages an explosive growth in discretionary purchasing power. The level of discretionary income is of particular importance because as this type of income increases, so too does the demand for items which were once considered luxuries.

The middle-income market is a big market and a growing market, and it has forced many changes in marketing strategy. Manufacturers are using mass-marketing techniques—mass advertising, for example. They are seeking the widest possible distribution system which will appeal to the middle-income and not the low-income market. Many stores which once appealed to low-income groups are now "trading up" to the huge middle-income market by upgrading the quality of the products they carry and by offering additional services.

In spite of the considerable increase in disposable income and purchasing power since World War II, many households are still in the low-income bracket or find their higher incomes inadequate to fulfill all their wants. Consequently, consumers give certain wants priority, and the sellers of many different products must compete for every consumer dollar. Furthermore, many customers are willing to forego services in order to get lower prices. One consequence of this market feature has been the development of self-service retail outlets and discount houses.

The existence of a vast middle-income market should not blind a marketing man to the importance of the very high-income market. Although the "luxury market" is small, its purchasing power is impressive. The highest-income groups spend four times as much on food, five times as much on housing, and about eleven times as much on transportation and clothing as the lowest-income groups. The high-income market is an excellent one for good jewelry, furs, better housing, automobiles, and boats.[9]

EXPENDITURE PATTERNS

For most of the major categories of consumer products, there is a surprisingly high degree of similarity in the expenditure patterns of the nation's nonfarm

---

[9] See Thayer C. Taylor, "Pinpointed: The Most Promising Prospects in the Middle-wealthies," *Sales Management,* Apr. 3, 1964, p. 30; and "The Affable Affluents," *Sales Management,* Nov. 10, 1965, p. 58.

families. This point was ably developed from the information collected in a survey conducted by the Bureau of Labor Statistics of the U.S. Department of Labor. The findings represent average annual nonfarm family expenditures for 1960 and 1961. The National Industrial Conference Board, with the financial sponsorship of *Life* magazine, processed the survey data to make them available in a format which would be most useful in marketing research.[10]

Relation to population distribution

In Table 4–3, the nonfarm family expenditure patterns for nine categories of goods and services are tabulated in percentage form for (1) the four major geographic regions of the nation and (2) the metropolitan and nonmetropolitan area markets. In all families, regardless of region or urban-rural classification, 10 to 11 per cent of total expenditures went for clothing and accessories, 9 to 10 per cent was devoted to medical and personal care, and 5 to 6 per cent was spent on house furnishings and equipment. The greatest variations were found in the transportation and the housing–household operations categories. Central-city families devoted only 13 per cent of total spending to transportation, as contrasted with nonfarm rural families, where the figure was 17 per cent. Also, Northeastern families spent only 13 per cent on transportation, as against 16 per cent for families in other regions. Similar variations existed in expenditures for housing and household operations.

Other tables in the National Industrial Conference Board report support this impression of conformity in over-all spending habits. In most of the broad categories, the expenditure patterns for the professional and managerial occupations do not differ substantially from the spending behavior of families where the head is employed in clerical, sales, craftsman, or operative work. The findings are quite the same for families of different educational attainments and ages, and even for those in various stages of the life cycle.

The key question at this point is: Why should a marketing man study the population in such detail if there is considerable homogeneity among the various segments? Our answer has four parts. First, there is not complete homogeneity. Even among the broad categories in Table 4–3, for example, there are substantial regional differences in the food and transportation classifications. Second, the simple percentages shown in Table 4–3 may be misleading. Although a range of 5 to 6 per cent (as in house furnishings and equipment) is only one percentage point, this is, from another perspective, a variation of 20 per cent. Thus, for each product group in Table 4–3, the variation is considerable if the variation in percentage points between the areas with the highest and the lowest figures is expressed as a percentage of the lowest region's figure. To illustrate, families in central-city parts of the metropolitan areas devote

---

[10] See U.S. Department of Labor, Bureau of Labor Statistics, *Consumer Expenditures and Income: Total United States, Urban and Rural, 1960–61,* BLS Report no. 237–93, 1965; and *Expenditure Patterns of the American Family,* National Industrial Conference Board, Inc., New York, 1965.

table 4-3

Consumer expenditure patterns, 1960–1961: by geographic location

The regional differences in expenditures for food and transportation are significant. Families in large cities spent 25 per cent of their income on housing and household operations, while rural nonfarm families spent only 21 per cent on this class of products and services. Note the similarity in expenditure patterns in each of the other product categories. If so much similarity exists, why should we study population characteristics? The text cites four reasons.

| | | Geographic region | | | | Market location | | | | |
| | | | | | | Metropolitan areas | | | Outside metropolitan areas | |
Item	Total	North-east	North-central	South	West	Central cities	Urban fringe	Other areas	Urban	Rural
Per cent distribution of:										
All families	100	26.9	27.8	28.9	16.3	34.9	26.5	6.0	16.1	16.5
Total expenditures	100	30.1	27.2	24.8	18.0	34.8	32.4	6.6	14.0	12.2
Total expenditures	$5,152	$5,761	$5,028	$4,410	$5,677	$5,132	$6,303	$5,665	$4,482	$3,813
Per cent of total expenditures	100	100	100	100	100	100	100	100	100	100
Food, beverages, and tobacco	29	29	28	27	27	29	27	27	28	30
Housing and household operations	24	25	24	23	23	25	24	22	24	21
House furnishings and equipment	5	5	5	6	5	5	5	6	5	6
Clothing and accessories	10	11	10	10	10	10	10	10	10	9
Transportation	14	13	16	16	16	13	16	16	15	17
Medical and personal care	10	9	9	10	10	10	9	10	10	10
Recreation and equipment	4	4	4	4	5	4	4	4	4	4
Reading and education	2	2	2	2	2	2	2	2	2	1
Other goods and services	2	2	2	2	2	2	3	3	2	2

source: Adapted from *Expenditure Patterns of the American Family*, National Industrial Conference Board, Inc., New York, 1965, pp. 20–21.

19 per cent *more* of their total expenditures to housing and household operations than rural nonfarm families. Third, similarity exists only when we speak of the broad categories. A detailed breakdown of the product and service groups shows that often there are large internal variations. Finally, differences exist among population segments with respect to buying motives and habits. Separate regional groups or age groups may each spend the same share of their income on clothing, but they react favorably to entirely different selling appeals. Basically the same vitamin pills may be bought for consumers under ten or over sixty-five, but different appeals are used for the different age groups. It is essential, therefore, to study all aspects of population in detail and not be lulled by the superficial similarities.

Relation to income distribution

Marketing men can glean considerable information from an analysis of expenditure patterns of families in various income groups. For each income group, Table 4–4 shows the percentage distribution of family expenditures in 1960–1961 among nine major categories of goods and services. There is a surprisingly high degree of similarity in the expenditure patterns of the various income groups—especially the middle-income families earning from $5,000 to $15,000 a year. Within the three groups in this income range, all families tend to devote approximately the same percentages of their total expenditures to each major category except food and housing and household operations.

Despite the general similarity of expenditure patterns, significant differences are observable in some categories, and we can safely conclude that income distribution is a major determinant of these differences.

Some of the findings from the Department of Labor study are summarized below to suggest the type of information that an analysis of expenditure patterns by income groups might yield. A warning is in order, however, about the limited applicability of the generalizations. These studies compared the spending patterns of families in various income groups *during the same period of time*. They did not observe what happens in a household as its income changes *from one period to another*. There is the assumption, however, that the differences in spending patterns between families in two successive income groups do parallel the changes which occur as one family's income increases over a period of time. Thus these studies are useful if we wish to predict changes in spending behavior as a family moves from one income bracket to another. But the generalizations should *not* be used to predict changes in spending behavior which might result from short-term (even annual) shifts in total disposable income. With this warning in mind, then, we may make the following generalizations about the findings:

1.   There was a high degree of uniformity in expenditure patterns of *middle-income* spending units. As we shall learn in the next chapter, however, social-class structure is a much more meaningful criterion for determining expenditure patterns.

2. For each of the product categories shown in Table 4–4, there was a considerable *absolute* increase in dollars spent as income rose (or, more correctly, as we compared one income group with a higher-income group). In other words, people in a given income bracket spent significantly more *dollars* in each product category than their less well-off neighbors, even though the lower-income households devoted a larger *percentage* of their total expenditures to the given product class. A marketing man is probably more concerned with the total dollars available to him from each income group than with the percentage share of total expenditures.

3. In each successively higher-income group, the amount spent for food declined both as a percentage of disposable income and as a percentage of total expenditures.

table 4–4

Consumer expenditures, 1960–1961: by income groups

There is a marked similarity in the expenditure patterns of middle-income families ($5,000 to $15,000) except in the food and housing categories. But note the sharp differences in expenditure patterns that exist between the high-income and low-income families. How do you explain the fact that families in the $7,500-to-$10,000 bracket spend a lesser percentage of their incomes on food than families with lower incomes?

		Family income (before taxes)					
Item	*Total*	*Under $3,000*	*$3,000– $4,999*	*$5,000– $7,499*	*$7,500– $9,999*	*$10,000– $14,999*	*$15,000 and over*
Per cent distribution of:							
All families	100%	22.4	20.8	26.2	16.1	10.7	3.7
Total expenditures	100%	8.9	15.6	27.1	21.2	18.0	9.1
Total expenditures	$5,152	$2,043	$3,859	$5,315	$6,788	$8,679	$12,687
Per cent of total expenditures	100	100	100	100	100	100	100
Food, beverages, and tobacco	29	33	30	28	27	26	23
Housing and household operations	24	31	25	24	23	22	24
House furnishings and equipment	5	4	5	5	6	5	5
Clothing and accessories	10	7	9	10	11	11	12
Transportation	14	9	14	16	16	17	15
Medical and personal care	10	11	10	9	9	9	9
Recreation and equipment	4	2	4	4	4	6	5
Reading and education	2	1	1	2	2	2	3
Other goods and services	2	2	2	2	2	2	4

SOURCE: Adapted from *Expenditure Patterns of the American Family,* National Industrial Conference Board, Inc., New York, 1965, p. 18.

4.   The percentage of expenditures devoted to the total of housing, utilities, and home operation remained reasonably stable in the middle- and high-income brackets.

5.   Amounts spent for medical and personal care remained a reasonably constant percentage of total expenditures, regardless of income.

6.   The share of expenditures going for automotive products and services tended to increase as incomes increased in the low- through middle-income groups; the proportion leveled off or dropped a bit in the higher-income brackets.

7.   Regarding clothing, in each successively higher income group (with one exception), a greater share of total family expenditures went for clothing.

It is interesting to compare these generalizations on expenditure patterns with "Engel's laws." In 1857, Ernst Engel, a German statistician, published the results of his studies of spending patterns of workingmen's families. Later students of consumer spending behavior expanded on Engel's work, and the net result is a series of four statements regarding spending patterns in relation to various income levels. Engel's laws state that as family income increases:

1.   A smaller percentage of expenditures goes for food.

2.   Approximately the same percentage is devoted to clothing.

3.   The proportion of total spending allotted to housing and house operation remains the same.

4.   The share of total expenditures apportioned to other items (recreation, education, medical care, etc.) increases.

Based on what we have learned from recent empirical studies on spending patterns, we would have to restate Engel's laws somewhat to fit current conditions. The first and third generalizations (regarding food and housing and household operations) still hold true. The fourth is also still correct, with the exception of medical and personal-care items, which seem either to decline or to remain a constant share of total expenditures as income rises. The second generalization, regarding clothing, is *not* operative today; in successively higher-income levels, the percentage of income now allocated to clothing increases.

Generalizations such as these provide a broad background against which a marketing executive can analyze the market for his particular product or service. People with needs to satisfy and money to spend, however, must be willing to spend before we can say a market exists. Consequently, in the next two chapters we shall look into consumer motivation and buying patterns—the "willingness-to-buy" factor in our definition of a market.

QUESTIONS AND PROBLEMS

1   "The consumer is king." Do you agree? In support of your answer, go beyond the ideas developed in this chapter.

2   Give some examples of products, other than those cited in this chapter, which are both consumer and industrial goods. What determines the category in which a product will be placed?

3   Give some examples of consumer services. Of industrial services. Of services which may be found in both categories.

4   Can you name any products for which total population alone is an accurate indicator of the market demand—products for which it is not necessary to segment the market in any fashion?

5   For each of the following population factors, give several examples of products whose market demand would be particularly affected by the individual population factor:
   a. Regional distribution   d. Age
   b. Marital status   e. Urban, rural, and suburban
   c. Sex   distribution

6   For which of the following products is the *number* of families a more important determinant of demand than the *size* of the family?
   a. Residential housing   g. Outdoor barbecue grills
   b. Dresses   h. School supplies
   c. Lamps   i. Toys
   d. Refrigerators   j. Automobiles
   e. Men's shoes   k. Dishes
   f. Women's shoes   l. Toothpaste

7   Cite some sectional differences in product preferences caused by factors other than climate.

8   The average level of formal education attained by people in the United States has risen substantially over the past few decades. What influence does this factor have on buying habits? In what ways might this trend affect the demand for particular products and services?

9   List four or five of the major trends in population noted in this chapter—for instance, a growing segment of the population is over sixty-five years of age. Then carefully explain how each of the following types of retail stores might be influenced by each of the trends:
   a. Department store   d. Drugstore
   b. Supermarket   e. Restaurant
   c. Sporting goods store

10 Roger Carson, aged thirty-two, is married and has two children. The family income is $750 a month. If the family expenditures are average, approximately how much will the Carson family spend on the following items?
   a. Food   c. Automobile and its upkeep
   b. Clothing   d. Recreation

11 How will the expenditures in the Carson family compare with those of Paul Foster and his family? The families are the same size, but Paul's income is $425 a month.

12 What significant differences do you note between Engel's laws and the expenditure patterns uncovered in the Bureau of Labor Statistics study? How do you account for these differences?

13 In what ways do you think the rise in disposable personal income since 1950 has influenced the marketing programs of a department store? A supermarket? A furniture store?

14   Is psychic income a concept applicable to groups or only to an individual? Can psychic income be measured in a quantitative manner?

15   Give examples of products for which the demand is substantially influenced by fluctuations in discretionary income.

5

CONSUMER MOTIVATION AND BEHAVIOR

In the preceding chapter we observed that markets are people with money and the willingness to spend it. The willingness-to-buy factor in market demand involves a study of buying motives and of habits. Motives, the subject of this chapter, explain *why* we do something; habits, which we shall study in Chapter 6, relate to *how* we do it.

A *motive* may be defined as a drive or an urge for which an individual seeks satisfaction. It becomes a *buying* motive when the individual seeks satisfaction through the purchase of something. A motive is not an attribute of a product, nor is it part of an advertisement or a sales talk. It is in the individual's mind, and to the extent that it affects him it demands satisfaction. The seller does not create motives; he only channels the satisfaction urge toward his product.

IMPORTANCE OF UNDERSTANDING CONSUMER MOTIVATION

We know quite a bit about the *quantitative* aspects of markets: how many people live in each geographic region, how many own two cars, how many are high school graduates, and so forth. We also have reasonably adequate market information about income and its distribution. Quantitative market analyses have been made regarding how people buy, where they buy, who does the buying, and other aspects of overt purchasing behavior. We know relatively little, however, about the *qualitative* factor of *why* people act as they do in the market.

Marketing men are coming to realize that a quantitative analysis of the market is insufficient. Differences in age, education, income, and other demographic and economic factors do not satisfactorily explain differences in personal behavior. These factors cannot account for the differences between the woman who loves to cook and the one who does not, or for the differences between the man who prefers to wear sport shirts and the one who dresses in somber grays and muted blues. Much more study is needed, not only of individual market behavior, but of families and other groups—their structures, internal relationships, status, and attitudes.

One traditional view of the consumer held that he was a helpless, senseless, will-less puppet manipulated by unscrupulous, selfish men in the marketplace. Consequently, the facts concerning his income and demographic status were all we needed to know. As incomes increased, so also would total sales. As the number of babies, teen-agers, or other population segments increased, sales of products used by these groups would increase proportionately. Recent studies soundly disprove this thesis. Far from being at the mercy of hidden persuaders, the average consumer is a person with common sense and a high intelligence. Because he does, in general, know what he wants and because he has his own attitudes and values, his willingness to buy may decline even when his income and earning power are high. This is what happened during the 1960 recession.

An understanding of the reasons why people buy a given product (product motives) or shop at a certain store (patronage motives) is critical. If the seller does not appeal to the right motive, he will probably lose the sale. Attempting to sell decorative outdoor lighting to a buyer in an industrial plant who wants lighting solely for security purposes will probably get a salesman nowhere. A knowledge of the motives underlying the behavior of a large segment of the market helps the seller to select effective advertising appeals, plan personal selling activities, design his product, and develop other phases of his promotional program.

DIFFICULTY OF DETERMINING BUYING MOTIVES

The motives underlying the behavior of consumers are not always discernible to the seller or even to the buyer himself. Buying motives may be grouped on different levels depending upon the consumer's awareness of them and his willingness to divulge them. In the first group, the buyer recognizes, and is quite willing to talk about, his motives for buying certain products. In the second, he is aware of his reasons for buying but will not admit them to others. A man may buy a backyard swimming pool because he feels it adds to his social position in the neighborhood, or a woman may buy cosmetics to increase her attractiveness to men. But when questioned about their motives, they offer other reasons which they think will be more socially acceptable. Consequently, sellers who accept the direct answer to a direct question can be misled. The most difficult motives to uncover are those in the third group, where even the buyers themselves do not know the real factors motivating their buying actions. Often a buyer rationalizes a purchase for so long that he finally believes his rationalization is the real motive.

The difficulty of identifying buying motives is that usually many motives are involved. One study has uncovered over six hundred possible buying motives, including a host which may be termed biological, sociological, artistic, political, religious, intellectual, and economic. Rarely is a purchase the result of a single motive. Furthermore, various motives may conflict with one another. In buying a new dress a woman may want to please her husband, receive admiration (or possibly envy) as a fashion leader from other women in her social circle, show she is a shrewd shopper, and strive for economy. To do all this in one purchase is truly a difficult assignment. A man may want to buy a new outboard motor to enhance his enjoyment of fishing, but at the same time he wants to spend more of his leisure time with his children who are too young to go fishing.

Not only are a person's buying motives varied, hidden, and complex, but they also may change over a period of time. What a researcher found as a buying reason a few years ago may no longer be true. Changes in personal income, age, or stage in the life cycle often effect changes in behavior. Hence, a firm must constantly study buying behavior, even within the same group of people.

Consumers are separate individuals with unique personalities. Two people may react differently to the same motive, or they may react in the same way to different motives. Yet in the face of all this individuality, a seller must try to find reasonably similar behavior threads permeating a market segment so that he can appeal to a wide group with one marketing program.

THEORIES OF BUYING BEHAVIOR

Although many theories have been developed to explain consumer behavior, there still is no coordinated, cohesive body of knowledge which we can call "the theory of buying behavior." Advertising men, market researchers, and authorities in salesmanship have made fragmentary contributions. Economists have traditionally riveted their attention to problems of production, not of consumption. In fact, in classical theory the economists assumed that the consumer was a totally rational person operating with full market information. The study of any nonrational activity was considered the province of psychologists, and the psychologists typically paid little attention to problems of normal consumer behavior.

In recent years the situation has improved. Marketing executives have sought and received an increasing amount of assistance from psychologists, sociologists, cultural anthropologists, and other behavioral scientists. The continuing efforts and contributions of these scientists undoubtedly will result in new theories regarding buying behavior and will further refine the ideas and concepts already developed.[1]

At this point, we shall consider briefly some of the concepts and theories of behavior and see how they apply to the buying activity of consumers and industrial users.

Inherent versus learned motives

A study of behavior can begin with an understanding of motivation. *Motivation* may be defined as *"behavior that is instigated by needs within the individual and is directed toward goals that can satisfy these needs."*[2] Motivation thus involves a three-stage cycle. First there is a need, a drive, or a motive (here, the terms are considered synonymous). It may be a physiological need, such as hunger, or a learned motive, such as the desire for social approval. The need creates a tension which stimulates the individual toward the second stage of the cycle, instrumental behavior, or behavior which will reduce the tension and satisfy the need. The third stage is the attainment of the goal which satisfies the need. A person may have a need for an attractive front lawn (or he feels a tension which he identifies as a desire to have a lawn). His need stimulates behavior: planning the work and selecting the grass seed, fertilizer, and tools. He attains his goal by planting the seed and nurturing its growth.

An early theory of behavior held that human activity was based on instincts common to all human beings. It was popular to develop a list of inherent traits, and marketing men tried to determine which ones influenced the purchase of their products. This theory proved inadequate, for it could

[1] For an extensive inventory of basic research findings from the behavioral sciences, see Bernard R. Berelson and Gary A. Steiner, *Human Behavior: An Inventory of Scientific Findings,* Harcourt, Brace & World, Inc., New York, 1965.

For the contention that marketing research must not merely *borrow* from the behavioral sciences, but must actually *merge* with them whenever necessary, see Lawrence X. Tarpey, "Marketing Research and Behavioral Science," *Business Topics,* Winter, 1965, pp. 61–67. The author contends that a broad, social science view of marketing research is needed—that marketing research should be defined so as to include tools, concepts, and models from the behavioral sciences.

[2] Clifford T. Morgan, *Introduction to Psychology,* McGraw-Hill Book Company, New York, 1956, p. 56; see also the third edition, 1966, pp. 203–205.

not explain why two people or two groups reacted differently to given products, brands, advertisements, or stores. The inadequacies of this theory lay primarily in the fact that it ignored the influence that learning has on behavior.

For some years now, psychologists have recognized that human behavior is motivated by environmental or learned needs as well as by inherent physiological drives. To be sure, our physiological needs for food, drink, bodily comfort, sex, and self-preservation are strong, but, in addition, we have social needs, such as those for recognition, acceptance, companionship, status, prestige, and power. There is the social need to emulate others, to conform, or to be distinctive. Also, there are learned economic, political, and religious needs.

Another important consideration in motivation concerns the second stage of the cycle—instrumental behavior. Much of our instrumental behavior depends upon learning rather than instinct. To illustrate, a baby will cry when it is hungry. This is an unlearned pattern of activity. Later the baby learns that crying is instrumental to getting food, and thus crying becomes a learned behavior to satisfy a need. Later in life, how that person satisfies his hunger need is influenced by learning. His religious convictions (learned behavior) influence his consumption of meat or animal products. Learned religious beliefs or social values influence his choice of clothing and shelter and his sexual behavior. From the standpoint of the marketing executive, learned needs may be more important than physiological needs. Certainly there are far more learned needs than inherent ones. By the time a person is an adult, very few drives are satisfied in an inherent, unlearned manner. Marketing executives should attempt to determine how buying activity is affected by learned motives and learned instrumental behavior. To identify, categorize, and list all these motives would probably be impossible.

Emotional versus rational buying motives

In this history of marketing thought, it has been traditional to categorize buying motives into two camps—emotional and rational.[3] Emotional motives include hunger, thirst, desire for a mate, emulation, personal comfort, safety and security of loved ones, status, prestige, pride, and others. A food manufacturer advertises that leading athletes eat his brand of dry cereal. A cosmetic firm urges young girls to use its products in order to be socially acceptable. These are appeals to emotional buying motives. Examples of rational motives are economy of purchase price and considerations of usability, durability, utility, dependability, convenience, and efficiency. For example, the manufacturer of a compact car stresses its operating economy; a brand of gasoline guarantees dependable starting under freezing conditions.

The usual basis for classifying buying motives as emotional or rational

---

[3] This classification was formalized over forty years ago in the writings of Prof. Melvin T. Copeland. See his *Principles of Merchandising*, A. W. Shaw Company, Chicago, 1924, chap. 6.

is the amount of time and thought given to the purchase. Impulse buying is considered a response to emotional motives. Rational buying is said to involve a careful, formal reasoning process. Advertising which appeals to rational motives is sometimes called "reason-why" advertising.

Actually the nature and amount of thought involved in a given purchase are questionable bases for classifying motives. A well-informed, shrewd shopper may be able to make a buying decision very quickly, yet it may be a totally rational one. On the other hand, a person may ponder for some time the emotional purchase of a product, savoring and anticipating the full enjoyment, prestige, or comfort of the item. A better criterion for rational and emotional motives is the thought given to the net long-run cost of the product. If a person consciously seeks a product with a low net cost, he has rational buying motives. Here, cost includes considerations of dependability, quality, durability, etc., as well as of economy of the purchase price and operating cost.

A purchase may involve both emotional and rational motives. The decision to purchase a certain type of automobile may be emotional, but the decision regarding brand may be rational. Thus a man decides he wants a new car to "keep up with the Joneses." Any one of several brands may enable him to achieve his goal. Consequently, within this group of possibilities he rationally seeks the brand which will net him the lowest long-run cost. Having rational motives and "rationalizing a purchase" are complementary concepts. Rational motives are considered respectable and socially acceptable. A buyer often voices a rational motive to justify the purchase of an article which is bought for emotional reasons. Sellers know this type of behavior, and often their advertising offers rational reasons for buying and at the same time introduces emotional appeals. An advertisement for a Cadillac may picture the car in front of a swank hotel with a woman swathed in mink emerging from the driver's seat. Fine jewels may also appear in the ad. Accompanying copy may state that the cost of maintaining the car is moderate; trade-in values are high; and superior, dependable workmanship is used in its construction. Truly this ad offers a potential customer an opportunity to rationalize.

Marketing men should understand the shortcomings of emotional-rational classification. This two-way classification obscures the fact that behavior is almost always the result of multiple motivation. Surface appearances are often deceptive. The purchase of a new dress and a new car may seem to be made to keep up with the Joneses (emotional), but actually these items may be sound investments toward advancement in the social hierarchy of a company (rational). Even apparently rational behavior—using last year's models, buying with cash to avoid carrying charges—may really be prompted by emotional needs. Two people may act in opposite fashion but with similar motives —love for family, for example. One father may insist on buying his children the finest of everything, while another feels that low-priced clothing and inexpensive playthings are good enough. The second father's reasoning is that he wants to teach his children the value of a dollar and prepare them for the conditions they will face in adult life.

Consumer and product variables as behavior determinants

While all consumer behavior is motivated, the actual choices made are determined by two psychological variables—the personality of the buyer and the characteristics of the product.[4] Motivation per se may be a secondary consideration in specific purchases. To illustrate, a person may be motivated to eat because he is hungry or tense, or simply because it is time to eat. What he eats, however, is beyond this type of motivation. He may eat cereal for breakfast because of habit, because it is there (availability), because it is customary (social pressure), or because it has nutritional values which he needs (cognition). The reason cereal was purchased for the household or the reason a certain brand was bought may be found in habit, impulse, cognition, or a social motive, such as a desire to please the children.

Differences in consumers' habits, their cognitive structures, and their motives cause them to behave differently when buying. Although an individual does not act the same way in all situations, people tend to act consistently. Consequently, we may identify six groups of consumers by their buying behavior:

1. A habit-determined group of brand-loyal consumers who tend to be satisfied with the product or brand last purchased.

2. A cognitive group of consumers who are sensitive to rational claims.

3. A price-cognitive group of consumers who decide principally upon the basis of price or economy comparison.

4. An impulse group of consumers who buy on the basis of physical appeal and are relatively insensitive to brand name.

5. A group of emotional reactors who respond to product symbols and are heavily swayed by images.

6. A group of new consumers who have not yet stabilized the psychological dimensions of their behavior.

Particular characteristics of some products have a psychological influence on buying behavior. Six classes of products may be identified by their psychological appeal:

1. *Prestige* products are those which become symbols. They not only represent some image or personality attribute, but become identified with that attribute. Ownership of a prestige-laden automobile is not only a symbol of success but is evidence of success. Expensive homes, *haute couture* clothing, period furniture, art objects, and certain magazines fall into this category.

2. *Maturity* products are those which are typically withheld from younger people because of social customs. Consequently, the initial use of such products suggests that the consumer has achieved a certain stage of maturity. Products in this category include cigarettes, cosmetics, coffee, beer, and liquor.

---

[4] Much of this section is based on Walter A. Woods, "Psychological Dimensions of Consumer Decision," *Journal of Marketing*, January, 1960, pp. 15–19.

3. *Status* products are those which impute class membership to their users. Particular brands are selected because consumers believe these brands impute success, substance, quality, or other attributes to the user. We may say that prestige products denote leadership, while status products denote membership.

4. *Anxiety* products are those which are used to alleviate a personal or social threat. This category would include soaps, dentifrices, perfumes, and razors. These products involve ego-defense, whereas the three preceding classes of products are concerned with ego-enhancement.

5. *Hedonic* products are those which depend highly upon their appeal to the senses. Their appeal is immediate and frequently results in impulse purchases. Included in this category are snack items, many types of clothing, presweetened cereals, and visual style features, such as design and color.

6. *Functional* products are those to which little cultural or social meaning has been imputed. Most staple food items, fruits and vegetables, and many building products fall into this group.

In competitive marketing, product classification may determine many company policies. Where ego-involvement is present or can be developed, consumer interest in a brand can be built on the basis of the product image. This, in turn, means that the market is highly susceptible to other brands. Buyers are not habit-bound; they will switch brands easily. Where ego-involvement exists, sellers must depend heavily on motivational selling.

If ego-involvement is low, product image is not important; brand loyalty is established through product identity and familiarity. Once brand loyalties are established, they are very strong. It is much more difficult and costly to break down brand loyalties than to build up ego-involving motives. "Other brands" must rely heavily on rational, cognitive appeals to reach a habit-bound audience.

The self-image as a behavior determinant

Another useful approach in analyzing and interpreting consumer behavior is through the concept of the self-image. The self-image is the way a person sees himself, and at the same time, it is the picture which he thinks others have of him. To some extent, the self-image theory is a reflection of other psychological and sociological concepts discussed in this section. A person's self-image is influenced, for instance, by innate and learned physiological, psychological, and social needs; it is conditioned also by economic factors, demographic factors, and social-group influences.

Consumers' self-images are not easy to identify, nor do they fall into sharply defined categories. A person's self-image is a complex thing and often consists of conflicting elements. A secretary may see herself as a coolly efficient, highly effective, and valuable asset in a business organization, while at the same time considering herself an attractive, well-dressed, desirable woman. Furthermore, various groups will have different self-images.

Human behavior is ordinarily goal-oriented. As marketing people, we want to know, or be able to identify, those goals because they influence consumers' behavior in the marketplace. In many situations, we can determine those goals if we know what a person's self-image is. We must note, however, that a person's self-image tells us only *what* his goals are. This does not tell us *why* his self-image is as it is, nor does it explain why different people have different self-images. It is helpful just to understand that people *do* have different pictures of themselves. Our job is to determine what a person's self-image is. Then we can predict what his goals are and what his behavior is apt to be in the marketplace.[5]

Group influences

Throughout our discussion of learned needs and emotional motives, frequent mention was made of *social* drives, such as the need for recognition or the desire to conform. We spoke of learned instrumental behavior which was socially acceptable. The recurrence of the word "social" suggests that the consumer's behavior is tempered considerably by his relationships with other people. Human beings are social animals and normally do not live in isolation. Consequently, social groups exert considerable influences on buying behavior.

In effect, we are concerned here with reference-group theory or "frames of reference," as this concept applies to consumer buying behavior. The concept is a simple one which has long been recognized by social scientists and others concerned with human behavior. Basically, the idea is that a person's behavior is influenced by a reference group to which he belongs (with which he identifies) or would like to belong. The group norm becomes a frame of reference which he seeks to emulate and against which he evaluates his own performance. Before making a decision, he considers what the group would do under the circumstances or what the group will think of him for making one move rather than another.

Thus, marketing administrators should understand something about the influence which both small reference groups and large social classes have on consumer buying behavior.

Small groups   Virtually all consumers belong to one or more small groups: families, fraternal organizations, social clubs, church groups, or a circle of friends or neighbors. This is part of a consumer's social environment; it influences his learning processes and thus his behavior. Knowledge of how information and influence permeate a small group can be used in shaping a firm's product-planning and advertising program. Small-group theory provides

[5] For a brief description of some other possibly useful psychological theories—newer concepts which might replace the "motive construct," or theory of motivation as a basis for explaining and predicting consumer behavior—see James U. McNeal, "The Disappearing Motive in Motivation Research," *Business Topics,* Autumn, 1964, pp. 30–36.

especially useful insights into understanding, explaining, and predicting the adoption and diffusion of new products.[6]

The key problems here, perhaps obviously, are (1) to identify the relevant reference group likely to be used by a consumer in a given buying situation and (2) to measure the extent of the group's influence on this consumer.[7] To maximize the chances for the successful introduction of a new product or fashion, marketing strategy should focus on identifying and communicating with two key people in the group—the innovator (early buyer) and the influential person (opinion leader). Each group has a leader—a tastemaker, or opinion leader—who influences the decision making of others in the group. The key here is for the seller to convince that person of the value of his product or service. The opinion leader in one group may be an opinion follower in another. The mother of a family may be influential in matters concerning food, whereas unmarried girls are more apt to influence fashions in clothing and makeup.[8]

For years marketing men have operated in conformity with the "snob appeal" theory—the idea that if they could get social leaders and high-income groups to buy and use their products, the mass market would also buy these products. The assumption has been that influence in a group follows a *vertical* path starting at levels of high status or prestige and moving downward through the group. Contrary to this popular assumption, studies by Katz and Lazarsfeld have pointed up the *horizontal* nature of opinion leadership. Influence emerges on each level of the socioeconomic scale and permeates a given area wherein the opinion leader is dealing with his peers.[9]

[6] See Steven J. Shaw, "Behavioral Science Offers Fresh Insights on New Product Acceptance," *Journal of Marketing*, January, 1965, pp. 9–13.

[7] For a summary of some of the methodological approaches generally available for identifying reference groups, see *Group Influence in Marketing and Public Relations*, Foundation for Research on Human Behavior, Ann Arbor, Mich., 1956, pp. 17–28.

[8] See *The Adoption of New Products: Process and Influence*, Foundation for Research on Human Behavior, Ann Arbor, Mich., 1959; Charles W. King, "The Innovator in the Fashion Process," in L. George Smith (ed.), *Reflections on Progress in Marketing*, American Marketing Association, Chicago, 1965, pp. 324–339; William E. Bell, "Consumer Innovators: A Unique Market for Newness," in Stephen A. Greyser (ed.), *Toward Scientific Marketing*, American Marketing Association, Chicago, 1964, pp. 85–95; Charles W. King, "Communicating with the Innovator in the Fashion Adoption Process," in Peter D. Bennett (ed.), *Marketing and Economic Development*, American Marketing Association, Chicago, 1965, pp. 425–439; and James H. Myers, "A Competitive Edge in Marketing Communications," in Taylor W. Meloan and Charles M. Whitlo (eds.), *Competition in Marketing*, University of Southern California Press, Los Angeles, 1964, pp. 23–33.

[9] Elihu Katz and Paul Lazarsfeld, *Personal Influence*, The Free Press of Glencoe, New York, 1955, p. 325; see also Elihu Katz, "The Two-step Flow of Communications: An Up-to-date Report on an Hypothesis," *Public Opinion Quarterly*, Spring, 1957, pp. 61–78. For later empirical data supporting the horizontal-flow hypothesis ("trickle across"), see Charles W. King, "Fashion Adoption: A Rebuttal to the 'Trickle Down' Theory," in Stephen A. Greyser (ed.), *Toward Scientific Marketing*, American Marketing Association, Chicago, 1964, pp. 108–125.

Social class   In recent years, marketing men have come to realize that the concept of social class provides a greater depth of understanding and a better basis for interpreting consumer buying behavior than does income alone. Social classes do exist in the United States, and a person's buying behavior is more strongly influenced by the class to which he belongs, or to which he aspires, than by his income alone. The idea of a social-class structure and the terms "upper," "middle," and "lower class" may be repugnant to many Americans, but the sociologists who identified the class structure and the marketing men who use it do not impute value judgments to it. We do not claim that the so-called "upper class" is superior to, or happier and better off than, the "middle class." Our use of the sociologists' findings, however, once again points up the value of the contributions made by behavioral scientists to the advancement of knowledge in the field of marketing.[10]

Some years ago W. Lloyd Warner and Paul Lunt directed a study which identified a six-class system within the social structure of a small town.[11] A person's placement in the structure was based on his *type*, not amount, of income and on his occupation, type of house, and area of residence within the community. The research division of the *Chicago Tribune* has also conducted several studies of the relationships among social class, buying behavior, and consumers' perception of various products and types of stores.

One of the *Tribune* studies in particular was a giant stride forward in this area. Done under Warner's guidance, the study was made in Chicago to determine whether his own analysis of social-class structure—developed from studies of small towns—also applied to a large metropolitan center.[12] To classify individuals, a weighted index was constructed based on occupation, sources of income, and housing type. Descriptions of the five classes which the study used and the percentage of the population falling into each are given below.

The first two classes constitute the "quality market," and yet they include only 8.1 per cent of the population. Also, we should note that although we speak of America as a middle-class society, two-thirds of our society is not middle class under this classification system.

1.   The upper class, 0.9 per cent, includes the old families and the socially prominent newly rich. These have been the traditional leaders in the American

[10] For a concise review of the theory of social classes as developed in both sociology and marketing research, plus a report on some findings on the measurement of this concept, see James M. Carman, *The Application of Social Class in Market Segmentation*, University of California Press, Berkeley, Calif., 1965.

[11] W. Lloyd Warner and Paul Lunt, *The Social Life of a Modern Community*, Yale University Press, New Haven, Conn., 1941; W. Lloyd Warner, Marchia Meeker, and Kenneth Eells, *Social Class in America*, Science Research Associates, Chicago, 1949.

[12] See Pierre D. Martineau, "Social Classes and Spending Behavior," *Journal of Marketing*, October, 1958, pp. 121–130. Several studies of buying motivation and their applicability to advertising and marketing are found in Pierre D. Martineau, *Motivation in Advertising*, McGraw-Hill Book Company, New York, 1957. Much of the discussion in this section is based on these two sources.

community. Most manufacturers and top advertising agency executives also belong to this group. (Warner's original study divided this group into upper-upper and lower-upper.)

2.   The upper-middle class, 7.2 per cent, includes successful businessmen, professionals, and the best salesmen.

3.   The lower-middle class, 28.6 per cent, is the white-collar class. It includes small tradesmen, office workers, and most salesmen. It is the source of America's moral code and aspirational system and is the most conforming, churchgoing, and morally serious part of the society.

4.   The upper-lower class, 44 per cent, includes factory workers, union labor groups, skilled workers, and the politicians and union leaders who would lose their power if they moved out of this class.

5.   The lower-lower class, 19.5 per cent, includes unskilled laborers, racial immigrants from other parts of the country, and people in nonrespectable occupations.

Three basic conclusions, highly significant for marketing, come out of the *Chicago Tribune* study. First, a social-class system is operative in large metropolitan markets and can be delineated. Substantial differences exist among classes with respect to their spending-saving behavior, the stores they patronize, the products they buy, and the brands they prefer. Furthermore, there is relatively little interclass movement. Although our history is replete with examples of people rising to the heights from humble beginnings, and although hard-and-fast barriers between classes do not exist, marketing men should recognize

table   5–1

Psychological differences between two social classes

There are many exceptions to this picture of class attitudes. For instance, can you think of a lower-class person (in terms of income and social status) who has middle-class attitudes? Are there enough exceptions to these patterns to render them invalid in planning marketing campaigns?

Middle class	*Lower class*
1. Pointed to the future	1. Pointed to the present and past
2. Viewpoint embraces a long expanse in time	2. Lives and thinks in a short expanse of time
3. More urban in identification	3. More rural in identification
4. Stresses rationality	4. Nonrational essentially
5. Has a well-structured sense of the universe	5. Has vague, unclear, and unstructured sense of the world
6. Horizons vastly extended or not limited	6. Horizons sharply defined and limited
7. Greater sense of choice making	7. Limited sense of choice making
8. Self-confident, willing to take risks	8. Very much concerned with security
9. Immaterial and abstract in his thinking	9. Concrete and perceptive in his thinking
10. Sees himself tied to national happenings	10. World revolves around family and self

SOURCE: Pierre D. Martineau, "Social Classes and Spending Behavior," *Journal of Marketing*, October, 1958, p. 129.

that the vast majority of people always remain within the boundaries of their own class tastes. In the *Tribune* study, only some 15 per cent of the families tried to break their class ties and move upward, and most of these people started out in the middle class.

The second conclusion to which we must pay heed is that there are far-reaching psychological differences between classes. Some of the contrasting characteristics of middle and lower groups are listed in Table 5–1. The classes do not think in the same way; thus they respond differently to a seller's marketing program, particularly his advertising. The supersophisticated, clever advertising in *The New Yorker* and *Esquire* is almost meaningless to lower-status people. They do not comprehend the subtle humor and are baffled by the bizarre art. This does not mean that they lack intelligence or wit, but only that they have different symbols for humor or art. Advertising must be believable by the class at which it is aimed; the reader must be able to identify himself with the people and the setting in the advertisement.

The third conclusion is that consumption patterns are symbols of class membership, and class membership is a more significant determinant of economic behavior than is the amount of income.[13] Traditionally, marketing men have relied on income as an index to buying behavior. With what we now know about social class, however, we question the accuracy of this index. Today the bulk of the population falls in the middle-income group. This group comprises not only white-collar workers—traditional members of the middle class —but also skilled and semiskilled blue-collar workers. These people are poles apart in their behavior, tastes, spending patterns, and aspirations. There is an old saying that a rich man is just a poor man with money and that given the same amount of money a poor man would behave exactly like a rich man. Studies of social-class structure have proved that this statement is just not true. Certainly a rough correlation exists between income and social class, but social class provides a much more accurate means of explaining behavior.

The concept of social class is most useful in interpreting buying behavior only when the concept is applied in a sophisticated, realistic, and sometimes subtle fashion.[14] There is a risk that the concept may be misunderstood or oversimplified, and thus misused. It does not possess universal applicability. Consequently, a marketing executive needs to understand when and in what ways a social-class stratification is significant in marketing and, conversely, what its limitations of application are. Some products—air conditioners and children's playclothes, for instance—are classless; that is, social class is relevant only to the extent that it is correlated with income. Furthermore, the

[13] For further evidence that a product's meaning (symbolism) varies from one social class to another, see Montrose S. Sommers, "Product Symbolism and the Perception of Social Strata," in Stephen A. Greyser (ed.), *Toward Scientific Marketing,* American Marketing Association, Chicago, 1964, pp. 200–216.

[14] This paragraph is adapted from Richard P. Coleman, "The Significance of Social Stratification in Selling," in Martin L. Bell (ed.), *Marketing: A Maturing Discipline,* American Marketing Association, Chicago, 1961, pp. 171–184.

structure is a dynamic one; the membership in each class, their goals, and their way of life are in a constant state of flux.

CONSUMER PATRONAGE MOTIVES

Marketing men also want to know what motivates consumers to buy at certain stores. While many sellers are interested in the patronage motives of industrial buyers, our attention here will be directed to the motives of ultimate consumers. A knowledge of these motives is extremely valuable to both retailers and manufacturers. A producer who appeals to prestige and status motives in the sale of his product ordinarily would not want it distributed to retail stores which feature low-priced merchandise and no services.

A consumer, of course, prefers to patronize stores where she perceives she is maximizing money, service, and product benefits while minimizing her risks as perceived in terms of product price, acceptability of product offerings, and required expenditure of time and effort. Customers' perceptions of the maximum-benefit, minimum-risk mix will vary according to their social class.[15]

Patronage motives, like product motives, are multiple and sometimes conflicting. Obviously a retailer cannot be all things to all people. He should not stress his many services and luxurious furnishings while trying to build up a low-priced, economy-appeal store image.

Some of the most important consumer patronage motives are as follows:

1. Convenience of location, rapidity of service, ease of locating merchandise, and uncrowded conditions

2. Price

3. Assortment of merchandise

4. Services offered

5. Attractive store appearance

6. Caliber of sales personnel.

The several motives to which a store appeals can be used to describe the store's image, reputation, or personality. Truly every store has an image, and the store's advertising is largely responsible for creating it. Women shoppers are acutely sensitive to cues in store advertising. They can accurately identify the characteristics of a store from its advertising alone. The findings from one study of a leading store in Kansas City illustrate this point (Fig. 5-1). Women in two cities, Kansas City and Atlanta, were asked to evaluate the store's newspaper ads. The evaluations made by women who did not know the store's identity and who were judging solely by the physical appearance of the advertisements almost perfectly matched those made by shoppers who knew the store personally.

The marketing implications in this advertising-store image relationship

---

[15] F. E. Brown and George Fisk, "Department Stores and Discount Houses: Who Dies Next?" *Journal of Retailing*, Fall, 1965, pp. 15–27; see also Wesley C. Bender, "Consumer Purchase-costs: Do Retailers Recognize Them?" *Journal of Retailing*, Spring, 1964, pp. 1–8ff.

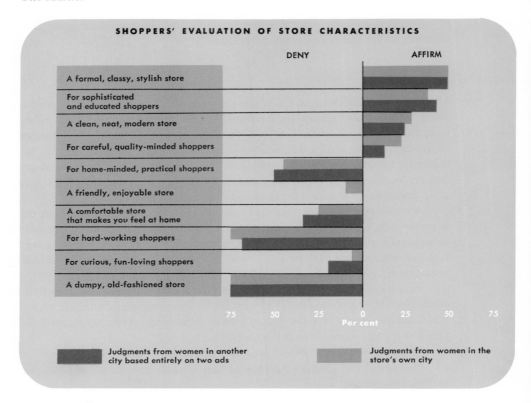

SHOPPERS' EVALUATION OF STORE CHARACTERISTICS

fig. 5–1

Shoppers often identify a store's "social status," without ever having been in the store, by reading its advertising. The judgments of women who read a store's advertising but had never been inside it were almost identical to those of people who knew the store. For instance, nearly 75 per cent of both groups agreed that the store in this study was for "sophisticated and educated shoppers." Almost everyone in both groups denied that the store was for "hardworking shoppers."

SOURCE: Pierre D. Martineau, *Motivation in Advertising*, McGraw-Hill Book Company, New York, 1957.

make it imperative, from the beginning, that management plan its advertising program so as to accomplish the store's intended purposes. The store's image preselects its customers and thus determines the composition of its market. It is possible to change a store's image, but this can be done only gradually over a period of time.[16]

[16] For a report on how downtown and suburban department stores differ in their respective images, see Stuart U. Rich and Bernard D. Portis, "The 'Imageries' of Department Stores," *Journal of Marketing*, April, 1964, pp. 10–15. After analyzing the images of three groups of department stores (high-fashion appeal, price appeal, and broad appeal), it was concluded that store images are weaker and less distinctive in the suburbs—that policies established in the move to the suburbs have resulted in a fairly high degree of sameness among the suburban branches of *different* types of downtown stores.

Patronage motives, choice of stores, and store clientele are related to the concept of social structure described earlier in this chapter. The *Chicago Tribune* study of social class in Chicago showed definitely that people match their own values and expectations with the status of the store. Not all people want to shop at glamorous, high-status stores. A lower-status woman knows that she will be punished in subtle ways by the clerks and other customers if she goes into an exclusive department store. "The clerks treat you like a crumb," was one response. A clerk loftily told another customer, "We thought you were a clerk," after the shopper had tried to be waited on. Because social-class membership and choice of store are closely related, an important function of retail advertising today is to help a shopper make the necessary social-class identification. The shopper does not want to go to a store where she does not fit, and if she has any doubts she is apt to stay away from a store whose advertising appeal is not clear-cut. Usually a retailer must select his desired niche in the social structure and then set up his marketing and advertising accordingly. Normally, a store—even a large department store with a bargain basement as well as exclusive salon departments—cannot appeal strongly to all classes. Even as mundane a store as a supermarket may project a certain image. The *Chicago Tribune* study showed that two grocery chains offering essentially the same products, services, and prices in the same neighborhood still appealed to two different social classes.

MOTIVATION RESEARCH

"Motivation research" is the currently popular term used to describe the application of "psychiatric and psychological techniques to obtain a better understanding of why people respond as they do to products, advertisements, and various other marketing situations."[17] It attempts to determine and explain the "why" of buying behavior, especially in situations where the buyer himself does not know the real reason or, if he does, is not willing to state it openly. For years marketing men have attempted to interpret and predict buying behavior; only the methods and techniques of motivation research are new to marketing. Scientists in several fields have long been concerned with studies in human behavior, and each group has developed its own set of techniques. Marketing men have adopted these tools and in some cases have also borrowed scientists from these fields to study consumer behavior in the market.

Motivation research techniques

Marketing researchers have always asked people why they bought a particular product or brand, why they patronized a given store, and what they liked or disliked about certain articles. The traditional technique, a structured question-

[17] Lawrence C. Lockley, *Use of Motivation Research in Marketing*, National Industrial Conference Board, Inc., Studies in Business Policy, no. 97, New York, 1960, p. 7.

naire not particularly disguised in any way, still has considerable value in motivation research. For instance, the large, controlled sample can be used to validate results from studies made with small, statistically unreliable samples. At the same time, we should recognize some of the borrowed techniques now generally associated with motivation research.[18]

Depth interview   This technique involves a long unstructured interview during which the interviewer gets the respondent to talk freely about the subject without inhibitions or fear of disapproval. A relaxed atmosphere is established. The interviewer is primarily a listener and a recorder, interrupting only to keep the interview from rambling too far afield or to encourage the respondent to continue talking. A few probing questions may be necessary to bring out important comments from the respondent. Actually this technique requires highly skilled interviewers and analysts.

Projective technique   The various types of projective techniques used in motivation research have essentially the same purpose. The idea is to get a respondent to project his thoughts into a completely innocuous situation or to place himself in another person's position and express what he thinks the other person is doing or saying. In this way it is expected that the respondent will reveal his own true feelings, motives, and beliefs. One such technique is the *word-association* test, in which the researcher mentions a word and the respondent tells the first word or first few words that come to his mind when he hears the test word. A variation of the word-association technique is the *incomplete-sentence* test. The respondent is asked to complete with the first thought that comes into his mind a sentence such as, "I use brand A because . . ." or "I think the average person would prefer brand A because. . . ." Another extensively used projective technique is the Thematic Apperception Test (TAT). Respondents are shown one or more vague or ambiguous pictures and are asked to tell a story about the pictures or to tell what is happening in them. Again the intent is that the respondent will reveal his own feelings by projecting himself into the situation. The *cartoon* test is a variation of the TAT. A respondent is shown a cartoon and alternative captions and is asked to select the caption he feels best suits the situation. In another type of cartoon test, two people are pictured, and the comment made by one of them is shown. The respondent is supposed to fill in the remark that he thinks the second person is making.

Controversies and outlook

If motivation research has been one of the fastest-growing phenomena in marketing in the past two decades, it has also been one of the most controversial. A major argument has been raised over the validity and reliability of motiva-

---

[18] For a summary of interviewing and projective techniques in motivation research, see George H. Smith, *Motivation Research in Advertising and Marketing*, McGraw-Hill Book Company, New York, 1954, pp. 29–72, 75–172.

tion research samples. Typically in such a study the researchers work with very small samples, sometimes with only 50 respondents and often with only 100 to 200. Opponents of motivation research object to the broad market generalizations drawn from the small sample and the uses to which the findings are put. It is questionable whether results based on psychological clinical procedures can be quantified and projected to represent mass market motivations. These studies can, however, develop generalizations which in turn should lead to further quantitative marketing studies. Opponents point out that to be effective, the type of research done in motivation research should be conducted by trained scientists.

On the other hand, applying motivation research techniques to a small sample of people permits a *complete* response from a few individuals rather than *superficial* answers from many. We should remember that so-called "conventional marketing research" has been influenced through the years by statisticians who usually prefer that research findings be numerically strong. Today many marketing questions arise where the votes of a multitude are of little help. Motivation research is offering many contributions in matters where ideas, innovations, differentiations, and ingenuity are important, as in packaging, product development, and advertising themes.

On balance, however, there is no doubt that motivation research represents a real scientific breakthrough in the field of marketing research. Despite present controversies, or perhaps because of them, substantial progress has been made in the use of motivation research and in the refinement of its concepts.

QUESTIONS AND PROBLEMS

1 "If a company can get a highly accurate, detailed picture of consumer buying habits, for example, *when* and *where* consumers buy and *who* makes the buying decisions, then this firm does not need to devote much time and effort to determining *why* its consumers act as they do." Comment on this idea.

2 Name some products which you recently purchased where more than one motive was involved. Identify the motives.

3 Have your buying motives changed toward any products over a period of years? Name some products and trace the motivation changes, identifying the motives and explaining the reasons for the changes.

4 What is the relationship between buying motives and appeals used in advertisements?

5 Carefully distinguish between inherent and learned motives and give examples of each.

6 Select two advertisements which you believe appeal entirely to emotional buying motives. Identify the motives.

7 Select two advertisements which you feel offer rationalizations to cover up emotional buying motives. What rationalizations and what emotional motives are included in each ad?

8 Describe the differences you would expect to find in the self-images of an insurance salesman and a man working on the assembly line in an automobile

plant. Give some examples of resultant buying behavior. Assume that each has the same income.

9   Explain some practical marketing applications of the self-image theory.

10   Name several of the small groups to which you belong, identify the opinion leader in the group, and explain how each group affects your buying behavior.

11   Who are the tastemakers, or opinion leaders, on your campus? With regard to what products, services, or activities is each leader influential?

12   What is the marketing significance of small-group influences on behavior?

13   Based on your study of Chapters 4 and 5, describe in detail the characteristics of the typical consumer who offers the best potential market for each of the following products:

    a.   Stereophonic record player in   c.   Power lawn mower
       console size   d.   TV dinners
    b.   Sports car

14   What phases of a company's marketing program are most apt to be affected by an understanding of the social-class structure in the firm's market?

15   Which of the five social classes do you identify with each of the following products or activities? In some cases more than one class may be listed, but try to associate each item with only one of the five classes.

    a.   Debutante parties
    b.   A cocktail before dinner
    c.   Wine and liqueurs with dinner
    d.   Beer with dinner
    e.   A Cadillac
    f.   *The New Yorker* magazine
    g.   Boats
    h.   Sitting on the front porch in warm weather in an undershirt
    i.   Shopping at a credit jeweler
    j.   Borrowing at a bank
    k.   Borrowing from a pawnbroker

16   What patronage motives influence your choice of the following?

    a.   Restaurant   d.   Sporting goods store
    b.   Movie theater   e.   Shoe store
    c.   Department store

17   Following is a series of headlines or slogans taken from advertisements of various retailers. To what patronage motive does each appeal?

    a.   "Factory trained mechanics at your service."
    b.   "We never close."
    c.   "Nobody but nobody undersells Gimbels."
    d.   "Where Denver shops with confidence."
    e.   "We never have missed paying a semiannual dividend since we opened." (Savings and loan association.)
    f.   "One dollar down, no payments until the steel strike is over."
    g.   "Most complete department store west of the Mississippi."

18   In what ways can retail stores make profitable use of the findings on social-class structure? If possible, use specific stores to illustrate your points.

6

CONSUMER BUYING PATTERNS AND GOODS

The supermarkets in a suburb announced that they would remain open every weekday night until 8 P.M. and all day Sunday until 6 P.M. A manufacturer of children's clothing announced that he would sponsor a thirty-minute cartoon show on television. Stores in a suburban shopping center jointly announced that they would start cashing checks, and the supermarket in this center set up a comic-book corner for children to play in while their mothers did their grocery shopping. During the Christmas shopping season a department store announced a stag night during which only men customers would be allowed in the store.

All these manufacturers or middlemen are trying to attract consumers by catering to their buying habits. In addition to understanding consumers' buying motives—that is, *why* they buy or behave as they do—a marketing executive also must understand *when, where,* and *how* consumers buy and *who* does the buying. These topics carry the executive into the realm of consumer buying habits or, as they are often called, patterns of overt buying behavior.

BUYING PATTERNS AND THEIR MARKETING SIGNIFICANCE

A marketing executive should be able to answer at least three questions about *when* people buy his products or service—the season, the day of the week, and the time of the day. If seasonal buying patterns exist, he should try to extend the buying season. He may find that a change in his product or in his promotional program will smooth out seasonal fluctuations. There is obviously little opportunity for extending the season on Easter bunnies, valentines, or Christmas tree ornaments, but the season for vacations has been shifted to such an extent that winter or other "off-season" vacations are now quite popular.[1] This shift has important implications for the marketing of clothes, sporting equipment, and other products. The season for lemons likewise has been extended beyond summer (when lemons are used in cold drinks) by promotional programs advocating that lemons be used as a cold remedy, food product, and mild laxative.

When people buy may influence the product-planning, pricing, or promotional phases of a firm's marketing program. After-shave lotion, cigarettes, and alcoholic beverages are distinctively packaged at Christmastime because they are purchased for gifts. In order to smooth the seasonal peaks and valleys in his production schedule, a doll manufacturer may want retailers to buy well in advance of the Christmas season, the season when the majority of dolls are sold. To get the retailers to do this, the manufacturer may offer them "seasonal datings," a pricing policy whereby retailers take delivery in September but do not have to pay until December. If people do most of their grocery shopping on Fridays and Saturdays, then retailers must plan to do their major advertising on Thursday nights or Friday mornings.

Where consumers buy

A firm should consider two factors with respect to *where* people buy—where the buying decision is made and where the actual purchase occurs. For many products and services the decision to buy is made at home. Examples include insurance, automobiles, furniture, appliances, and many articles of clothing. On the other hand, the decision is often made in whole or in part right at the point of purchase. A person may be shopping in a sporting goods store for golf clubs when he sees some tennis balls on sale, knows he needs some, and decides on

[1] There is growing evidence, however, that the Christmas season *is* being extended in that Christmas buying by some consumers starts as early as September; see "When Does Santa Claus Start His Christmas Shopping?" *Sales Management*, Oct. 16, 1964, p. 45.

the spot to buy them. A husband may decide at home that he wants to buy a birthday gift for his wife, but he waits until he gets to the store before deciding whether it will be jewelry, candy, or lingerie.

A company's entire promotional program, and in many cases its product planning, must be geared to carry the greatest impact at the place where the buying decision is made. If the decision to buy is made in the store, then attention must be devoted to packaging and other point-of-purchase display materials, particularly if the store is operating on a self-service basis. A shopper may decide at home to buy some cold cereal, but the key decision regarding which type and which brand may be made at the store. Of course, some advertising effort must be directed to the consumer in his home because a totally unknown brand, no matter how attractively packaged, will usually be rejected in favor of a known brand.

If the primary decision to buy is made at home, substantial promotional effort must be devoted to such advertising media as newspapers, magazines, and television. Insurance salesmen and automobile salesmen often call at a prospect's home in order to influence buying decisions at that location.

The place of purchase influences a manufacturer's choice of distribution channels and a retailer's choice of products. Problems may occur for manufacturers and middlemen alike when customers develop new buying patterns in which they seek certain products in locations beyond the traditional outlets. Although manufacturers are often pressured by retailers to use only the traditional outlets, manufacturers stand to lose much business if they fail to follow newly emerging consumer buying patterns. Some manufacturers, for example, refused to sell through discount houses because of objections from older, established outlets. These producers lost a considerable amount of business simply because many customers had formed the habit of shopping in discount houses.

How consumers buy

The "how" part of consumers' buying habits encompasses several areas of behavior. It has considerable marketing significance for both retailers and manufacturers; it affects product and pricing policies, promotional programs, and other management decisions. Price, service, and brand relationships, for example, affect consumer preferences. Some people are highly price-conscious and will select the lowest-priced item regardless of brand; others will buy the lowest-priced product just as long as it is a known brand. Some people willingly pay a higher price to get the service they desire.

Long ago many firms found that consumers preferred to buy such products as pickles, cookies, and butter already packaged. The advantages of cleanliness and ease of handling offset the higher unit price. If the consumers buy a manufacturer's product primarily in self-service stores, increased importance is placed on developing an attractive package and label. When deciding to use packages, manufacturers and middlemen should be aware of consumer preferences with respect to quantity. If a soap manufacturer packages all his soap in lots of three bars in an attempt to stimulate buying, much business will be lost if customers typically buy only one bar at a time.

The trend toward one-stop shopping has encouraged retailers to add related and even unrelated lines of merchandise to their basic groups of products. Self-service stores have found, however, that the addition of certain products to their lines does not materially increase sales. For example, many people prefer to buy groceries and drug items on a serve-yourself basis, but they will not buy clothing, carpets, or furniture on this basis.

Some people always pay cash, whereas others prefer to buy on credit. A firm may have to abandon its cash-and-carry policy if there is considerable demand for credit buying. Services such as delivery, installation, and even credit may be priced separately and offered on an optional basis.

Management decisions regarding store location and layout may be affected by how people buy. In the suburbs, where mothers bring the children to the store and where one-stop shopping is preferred, a store owner may set up a "kiddy corner" where children can amuse themselves while mothers shop. The planned suburban shopping center itself is the suburban counterpart of the downtown area, where the stores are clustered for the sake of consumer convenience.

Who does the family buying

When determining buying habits with respect to *who* does the family purchasing, there are three important areas for consideration—who makes the physical purchase, who makes the buying decision, and who actually uses the product.

For many years women have done most of the family buying. They still exert substantial influence in buying decisions and do a considerable amount of the actual purchasing, but men have increasingly entered the family buying picture. Self-service stores are especially appealing to men; night and Sunday openings in suburban shopping centers also encourage men to play a bigger role in family purchasing. The fact that durable goods such as automobiles account for a larger percentage of the total family expenditures today than they did twenty-five or fifty years ago also adds meaning to the man's role in buying.

In recent years teen-agers and young children have become decision makers in family buying as well as actual purchasers. The amount of money teen-agers now have is substantial enough to be considered in the marketing plans of many manufacturers and middlemen. Even very young children are an influence in buying decisions today because they watch television programs or shop with their parents. Thus they are exposed to more products than were their counterparts of one or more generations ago.

Purchasing decisions are often made jointly by husband and wife (sometimes even the children are included). One study of this problem suggested that age is a factor in joint decisions.[2] That is, young married people were much more apt to make buying decisions on a joint basis than were older couples. Apparently the longer a husband and wife live together, the more they feel they can trust each other to act unilaterally. In many cases, decisions regarding savings, life insurance, vacations, housing, food, and the handling of money and bills are made jointly.

Who buys a product will influence a firm's marketing policies regarding its product, channels of distribution, and promotion. If children are the key decision makers, as is often the case in cereals, for instance, then a manufacturer may include some type of cutout toy or other premium with the product. The product may be colored differently depending upon whether the manufacturer is appealing to men or women. If women are the main shoppers in a store, management must pay more attention to interior decorations. In a department store—traditionally considered a woman's store—the men's furnishings department is often located on the street floor near a door. Then the man can enter, shop, and leave the store without having to plow through crowds of women shoppers.

"Free" services, such as bridal information, knitting lessons, or baby-sitting, may be necessary if women are the main customers; a jukebox is an attraction to teen-agers. The entire advertising campaign—media, appeals, copy, radio and television programming, and so forth—is affected by whether the target is men, women, or children. If women are the target, the advertiser is more apt to use *Ladies' Home Journal* or *Glamour* than *Business Week* or *Field and Stream.* He will select daytime radio or television hours for his program, and this program is more apt to be a soap opera or a cooking school than a baseball game or cartoons.

BEHAVIORAL CHANGES AND THEIR INFLUENCE ON MARKETING

In Chapter 5 it was noted that buying motives not only are complex but also are constantly in a state of flux. This dynamic feature of buying motives has a profound influence on consumer buying patterns; it means that these patterns or habits also change *over a period of time.*

A paradox may seem to exist with respect to buying habits. A habit suggests a relatively unchangeable behavior pattern, yet we speak of shifts and changes in these patterns. The answer to this apparent inconsistency lies in the time factor. In the short run, buying habits are reasonably stable. It is a

---

[2] See Elizabeth H. Wolgast, "Do Husbands or Wives Make the Purchase Decisions?" *Journal of Marketing,* October, 1958, pp. 151–158; and Harry Sharp and Paul Mott, "Consumer Decisions in the Metropolitan Family," *Journal of Marketing,* October, 1956, pp. 149–156. These studies support the idea that the husband is the dominant factor in the purchase of an automobile. Sharp and Mott's study showed that in a surprisingly high 42 per cent of the cases, the decision regarding what house or apartment to take was made by the husband *or* the wife; it was not a joint decision.

human trait to develop routine ways of carrying on everyday activities. Every time we want to buy golf balls, gasoline, or butter, we do not want to make a major project out of the incident. We have made the decision that store A is where we buy our staple foods and that we go to store B for athletic supplies. Incidentally, we probably take the same route every time we go to a particular store.

However, over the long run, old patterns gradually give way to new. Some of these shifting buying patterns have already been mentioned in this chapter. Others are noted in the following paragraphs.

Impulse buying

In recent years there has been a significant increase in impulse buying, that is, purchases made without very much advance planning.[3] A housewife may go to the grocery store with a mental note to buy meat and fruit. In the store she selects some fresh peaches because they look more appealing or are priced more attractively than the other kinds of fruit on display. She sees some cleansing tissue on the shelf and is reminded that she is running low on this item, so she buys two boxes. These are impulse purchases.

In contrast to the patterns of many years ago, substantially more people embark on supermarket shopping trips today without a shopping list of specific items. They simply walk through every aisle, looking at all types of products and hoping to be reminded of what they need.

Many items of clothing, drugs, cosmetics, toys, records, sports equipment, and other products are also bought on impulse. Increases in disposable income and discretionary income have been major contributing factors to this trend. The self-service method of retailing has been both a cause and an effect of this behavior pattern.

A key point for marketing men to understand is that impulse buying is often done on a very rational basis.[4] Self-service, open-display selling has brought about a marketing situation wherein planning may be postponed until the buyer reaches the retail outlet.

Because of the trend toward impulse buying, greater emphasis must be placed on promotional programs to get people into a store. Displays must be more appealing because the manufacturer's package must serve as a silent salesman. Manufacturers prefer distribution outlets which offer a consumer

[3] For a useful four-way classification of types of impulse buying and an analysis of nine factors which influence impulse buying, see Hawkins Stern, "The Significance of Impulse Buying Today," *Journal of Marketing*, April, 1962, pp. 59–62.

[4] For a study which suggests that impulse buying is *not* simply a rudimentary cognitive process, but instead may be a complex form of purchasing behavior, involving true decisions and subject to a wide variety of purchasing influences, see Ronald P. Willet and David T. Kollat, "Impulse Purchasing as a Special Case of Customer Decision Making," in L. George Smith (ed.), *Reflections on Progress in Marketing*, American Marketing Association, Chicago, 1965, pp. 212–228.

an opportunity to buy on impulse. Retailers, in turn, have shifted to self-service operation to take advantage of this behavior pattern.

Desire for conformity

Slowly but surely over the past century we have evolved from a nation of "rugged individualists" to one of conformists. In the post-World War II era this trend has been accelerated by several factors. One has been the tremendous growth in suburban living, with its many look-alike housing developments. Another factor has been the rise of a managerial class working in lower and middle management for large corporations. These executives seem to strive to dress alike, drink alike, and otherwise follow the prescribed pattern of the "organization man." The fact that most families can afford national mass-communication media such as television and magazines is still another impetus toward conformity.

The preceding chapter included a consideration of some of the motivational aspects of group influences on consumer buying behavior. In short, there is an overpowering drive to be accepted by the group and to be like others. This desire is seen among grade school children and high school and college-age consumers. At the same time, no group remains static in its wants; all are constantly shifting. The key is to find out who or what makes them shift. Here we encounter the concept of the group leaders—the "tastemakers," or opinion leaders.

Importance of time

A frequently heard complaint in our society today is that "I don't have time" to do this or that. In our fast-paced way of living, time is becoming an increasingly precious commodity. This passion for time is coupled with an increasing consumer affluence which is taking some of the glitter from forms of ownership directed more to status than to use.[5] The net result of this combination is a change in shopping patterns and the opening of vast new markets for personal services, disposable goods, and rented products. That is, the trend is to rent a product or buy a disposable one, rather than to own an article which requires our time for maintenance. The consumer's acceptance of time-oriented value systems is bound to have implications for many aspects of a company's marketing program.

Increased leisure time

American families are acquiring an increasing amount of leisure time from a shorter workweek, paid vacations, laborsaving devices in the home, and more

[5] Phyllis Daignault, "New Markets in Time," *Sales Management*, June 18, 1965, p. 30.

rapid commuter transportation. This trend has created a large market for goods and services such as travel, boating, photography, home swimming pools, musical instruments, outdoor furniture, commercial entertainment, and radio, television, and phonograph sets.[6]

Leisure-market spending shows no sign of abating. One note of alarm might be sounded in this connection: in the American economy it is not possible to continue increasing leisure time unless we have a corresponding increase in productivity. Otherwise there will be a decrease in disposable income and discretionary income.

Marketing men should recognize that leisure time is interrelated with and an influence on how, when, and where people buy. As Marion Harper, Jr., chairman of the board of McCann-Erickson—one of the nation's largest advertising agencies—said, "It is a dynamic influence in the character of today's living." It "is not simply an attribute of modern life—it is a pervasive force in shaping it. Leisure is a cause."[7] A five-day workweek, for example, permitted Americans to move to the suburbs, and we have already noted some of the influence of this population shift.

As a consequence of the increased leisure-time market, many companies, such as camera manufacturers and boat producers, have added greatly to the number and variety of their products. Product design and styling have been influenced by the "do-it-yourself" enthusiasts and by the expanded participation of amateurs in sports activities. Channels of distribution also have been altered to reach the leisure market.

Desire for convenience

As an outgrowth of the increase in discretionary purchasing power and the importance of time, there has been a substantial increase in the consumer's desire for convenience. Several years ago, Charles G. Mortimer (then president and later chairman of the board of directors of the General Foods Corporation) pointed out the following ten kinds of convenience to be reckoned with in marketing:[8]

1. Form. Products must be available in a wide variety of forms. Thus drug products, for example, come in liquid, paste, syrup, powder, pill, or inhalant form.

---

[6] See, for example, Robert L. Brown, "The Hunting Market: A Sporting $1.5 Billion Target," *Sales Management,* Nov. 6, 1964, p. 31.

[7] As quoted in "Harper Probes Leisure Market as a 'Cause,'" *Printers' Ink,* Mar. 25, 1960, p. 15.

[8] Charles G. Mortimer, *The Creative Factor in Marketing,* General Foods Corporation, White Plains, N.Y., 1959, pp. 10–16. This is a reprint of the 1959 Parlin Memorial Lecture, an annual event sponsored by the Philadelphia chapter of the American Marketing Association.

2. Quantity or units. Goods must be offered in all sizes, quantities, or units desired by the consumers.

3. Time. Products must be available at any time the consumer wants them. This factor has stimulated the success of convenience stores (7-Eleven, Li'l General, Lawson, Circle K, Speedee Mart, UtoteM, and others) which carry household necessities and which do most of their business when the super-market is closed.[9]

4. Place. Sellers must offer opportunities for consumers to shop in the most convenient locations possible. Historically, cities and other trading centers rose, in part at least, to satisfy this demand for convenience. Today the retail structure of cities is intertwined with consumer convenience. One student of the subject perceptibly sharpened the focus on place convenience by pointing out that when consumers make shopping decisions, they do so by balancing commodity costs and convenience.[10] *Commodity costs* are defined as the amount of money paid to the seller for the goods or services purchased. *Convenience costs* include expenditures of time, physical and nervous energy, and money (gasoline, parking, phone calls, carfare) necessary to obtain the goods or services. Furthermore, convenience costs are becoming an increasingly significant factor in determining where people will shop.

5. Packaging. Packages must be easy to find, open, use, and store.

6. Combination. Combination, or "packaging," convenience is also found in service industries. For example, insurance firms offer homeowners' combination policies, the travel industry sells "packaged" tours, and the dry-cleaning people sell a combination which includes cleaning, repairing, and storage.

7. Automation. Many consumers dream of a push-button home.

8. Credit. One of the most significant marketing developments since World War II has been the tremendous increase in consumer credit. Before the war, installment credit purchases were limited largely to homes, cars, furniture, and appliances. Also, many people had charge accounts payable at the beginning of the month. In general, however, our Puritan heritage and the vivid memories of the Great Depression tended to place considerable emphasis on thrift. In recent years, during which incomes have risen and jobs have increased, a new psychology has enveloped the consumer: he wants to buy all kinds of products and services *now* and pay for them out of future income.

9. Selection. A seller must offer his products or services at convenient prices and in an assortment of colors, materials, or flavors.

10. Readiness. Virtually everything we buy today must be ready and easy to use.

---

[9] "Snaring Sales while Others Sleep," *Business Week*, Nov. 6, 1965, p. 130.
[10] Eugene J. Kelley, "The Importance of Convenience in Consumer Purchasing," *Journal of Marketing*, July, 1958, pp. 34–38.

Every major phase of a company's marketing program is affected by this "tidal wave" of craving for convenience. Product planning and development are influenced by the need for convenience in packaging, quantity, readiness, and selection. Pricing policies must be established in conformity with the demand for credit and with the costs of providing the various kinds of convenience. Advertising, display, and personal selling play a role in practically every phase.

Upgraded tastes and desire for elegance

For some years we have been in the midst of a "cultural explosion" which is having a significant influence on marketing.[11] This upgrading of living habits is being fostered by both economic forces (increased incomes) and social forces (improved education, extensive travel, and the influence of mass communications media). This new age of elegance, improved tastes, and gracious living is reflected in changing patterns of consumption and behavior on the part of consumers. There is an ever-growing appreciation of art, music, literature, and drama; demand is increasing for gourmet foods, vintage wines, two homes, month-long vacations, period furniture, and art collections. The upgrading of tastes and income also means that consumers now crave the kind of attention that only the "carriage trade" used to get. Alert retailers are already responding to this new behavioral pattern.[12]

CLASSIFICATION OF CONSUMER PRODUCTS

Although the marketing differences between consumer and industrial goods make a two-part classification of products valuable, the category of consumer goods is still too broad for a marketing manager. Consequently, consumer products are further classified as convenience goods, shopping goods, and specialty goods (see Table 6–1). This classification was first suggested many years ago by one of the pioneers in, and major contributors to, the field of marketing, Prof. Melvin T. Copeland of Harvard University.[13] This is the traditional classification and, while it raises objections in some quarters, it is still better understood and more generally followed by businessmen than any of the alternatives yet suggested. It is important to note that this three-way subdivision is based on consumer *buying habits* rather than on consumer *products*. Specifically the two criteria used as bases for classifying consumer products are (1) the degree to which the consumer is aware of the exact nature of the

---

[11] Robert L. Brown, "A Compelling New Age of Elegance," *Sales Management*, Feb. 19, 1965, p. 25; see also Russell Lynes, "How High Is the American Brow?" Papers from American Association of Advertising Agencies, 1963 annual meeting.

[12] "Tender, Loving Care for the Masses," *Business Week*, Mar. 5, 1966, p. 84.

[13] See Melvin T. Copeland, *Principles of Merchandising*, A. W. Shaw Company, Chicago, 1924, chaps. 2–4.

table 6—1

Characteristics of classes of consumer goods and some marketing considerations

Characteristics and marketing considerations	Type of product		
	Convenience	Shopping	Specialty
Characteristics:			
1. Time and effort devoted by consumer to shopping	Very little	Considerable	Cannot generalize. May go to nearby store and exert minimum effort, or may have to go to distant store and spend much time
2. Time spent planning the purchase	Very little	Considerable	Considerable
3. How soon want is satisfied after it arises	Immediately	Relatively long time	Relatively long time
4. Are price and quality compared?	No	Yes	No
5. Price	Low	High	High
6. Frequency of purchase	Usually frequent	Infrequent	Infrequent
7. Importance	Unimportant	Often very important	Cannot generalize
Marketing considerations:			
1. Length of channel	Long	Short	Short to very short
2. Importance of retailer	Any single store is relatively unimportant	Important	Very important
3. Number of outlets	As many as possible	Few	Few; often only one in a market
4. Stock turnover	High	Lower	Lower
5. Gross margin	Low	High	High
6. Responsibility for advertising	Manufacturers'	Retailers'	Joint responsibility
7. Importance of point-of-purchase display	Very important	Less important	Less important
8. Advertising used	Manufacturers'	Retailers'	Both
9. Brand or store name important	Brand name	Store name	Both
10. Importance of packaging	Very important	Less important	Less important

product *before* he starts on his shopping trip and (2) the satisfaction received from searching for and comparing products weighed against the time and effort required for this task.[14]

It is helpful if an administrator can determine whether his product is a convenience, shopping, or specialty good because such a classification, based on consumer buying habits, has a strong influence on the company's distribution and promotional programs.[15]

Convenience goods

The significant characteristics of convenience goods are that the consumer has complete knowledge of the particular product (or its substitutes) which he wants *before* going out to buy it and that it is purchased with a minimum of effort on his part. Normally the gain resulting from shopping around to compare price and quality is not considered worth the extra time, money, and effort required. The consumer is willing to accept any of several substitutes, and thus he will buy the one which is most accessible.[16] For most buyers this subclass of goods includes groceries, tobacco products, inexpensive candy, chewing gum, magazines, drug sundries such as toothpaste and shaving accessories, and staple hardware items such as light bulbs, nails, and flashlight batteries. When the need for this type of good arises, the consumer wants to make his purchase as rapidly and as easily as possible. Consequently, this type of product must be readily accessible in neighborhood stores or shopping centers. Stores located in central downtown shopping districts also carry convenience goods for people working or shopping in the downtown area.

Convenience goods typically have a low unit price, are not bulky, and are not greatly affected by fad and fashion. Among the well-known brands, one is not usually strongly preferred or demanded over another. Convenience goods are purchased frequently, although this is not a differentiating characteristic. Items such as Christmas tree lights, birthday cards, or window cleaner

---

[14] The first of these criteria is a concept which was expressed by Professor Copeland but has sometimes been overlooked through the years. It is recalled and developed nicely in Louis P. Bucklin, "Retail Strategy and the Classification of Consumer Goods," *Journal of Marketing*, January, 1963, pp. 50–55.

[15] For an analysis of the marketing implications in the relationships among distribution, promotion, and classification of products, see Leo V. Aspinwall, "Parallel Systems of Promotion and Distribution," *Cost and Profit Outlook*, October, 1965.

For a refinement and broadening of Aspinwall's "characteristics of goods" theory, in which the author extends the concept to include product planning and pricing, see Gordon E. Miracle, "Product Characteristics and Marketing Strategy," *Journal of Marketing*, January, 1965, pp. 18–24. In his conceptual model, Professor Miracle uses a series of nine characteristics as the bases for dividing products into five groups.

[16] For an excellent development of this point, plus a careful analysis of the three types of consumer products, see Richard H. Holton, "The Distinction between Convenience Goods, Shopping Goods, and Specialty Goods," *Journal of Marketing*, July, 1958, pp. 55–56.

are convenience goods for most people, even though they may be bought only once a year.

Convenience goods are sometimes further subdivided into staple goods and impulse goods. Staple convenience products are those which the consumer knows he wants before he sees them in the store and which he plans to buy as soon as possible and with a minimum of effort. When a light bulb burns out, for example, the housewife makes a written or mental note to buy a new supply on the next trip to the store. An impulse convenience product is one for which the want arises only after the consumer sees the item in the store; following his impulse he buys it immediately.

Marketing considerations   Since a product must be readily accessible when the consumer's demand arises, a manufacturer must secure wide distribution. But since most retail stores sell only a small volume of a manufacturer's output, it is not economical for him to sell directly to all retail outlets. Instead, he relies on wholesalers to reach part of the retail market.

The promotional policies of both the manufacturers and the middlemen, especially the retailing middlemen, are involved here. A retailer typically carries several brands of a convenience item, such as shaving cream or dry cereal, so he is not able to promote any single brand. He is not interested in doing much advertising of these articles because many other stores carry them, and any advertising he does may help a competitor. Furthermore, quality and price of competitive products are reasonably similar, the product requires little or no explanation or sales talk, and the retailer normally has no incentive to push one brand over another. Therefore many retailers of convenience goods have adopted a self-service marketing technique. As a result, virtually the entire promotional burden is shifted to the manufacturer. He must advertise extensively to develop a recognition of, and a preference for, his brand. As a consequence of this fact, the gross margins available to the retailer are typically very small. This, in turn, decreases his interest in applying selling effort, providing display space, and paying for advertising. Self-service in retailing places great importance on point-of-purchase displays and packaging because these tools have considerable influence on impulse buying. Usually the manufacturer must supply the materials and ideas for displays if he hopes to have the retailers provide the space.

Shopping goods

Shopping goods are products for which a customer usually wishes to compare quality, price, and style in several stores before purchasing. A key identifying characteristic, and the one which separates shopping goods from convenience goods, is that for shopping goods the consumer lacks full knowledge of pertinent product features before embarking upon the shopping trip. Thus, on the trip he not only purchases the article, but he first must search for the information needed to assess the relative suitability of alternative products. This search will continue only as long as the customer believes that the gain from comparing product features offsets the additional time and effort required. Examples of shopping goods typically include women's apparel, furniture and other durable goods, jewelry, piece goods, and, to some extent, men's ready-to-wear and shoes. In general, shopping goods are larger in unit value and are purchased less frequently than convenience goods.

The demand for a shopping good is not often sharply aroused. It does not require immediate satisfaction, and the source of this want satisfaction is not clearly defined. To illustrate, a college girl knows a big dance is coming up in a month or so. She thinks she ought to get a new formal gown for the occasion, but she does not rush out the next day to buy one. She has no particular store or brand of dress in mind. She just generally has a demand for a new formal and knows that someday pretty soon she ought to go shopping around for it.

Marketing considerations   The buying habits associated with shopping goods affect the distribution and promotion strategy of both manufacturers and middlemen. A manufacturer of a shopping good requires fewer retail outlets because the consumer is willing to look around a little for what he wants, purchases are usually made infrequently, and the want does not require immediate satisfaction. In order to increase the convenience of comparison shopping, a manufacturer tries to place his product in a store located near other stores carrying competing items. Similarly, department stores and other retailers who carry shopping goods primarily want to be bunched together. A women's dress shop ordinarily will not be located away from similar stores because a shopper does not wish to look in only one store for a dress or a coat, nor does she wish to go to a district which has only one dress shop and then travel some distance to look at other stores.

Manufacturers usually work closely with retailers in the marketing of shopping goods. Since a manufacturer uses fewer retail outlets, he is more particular in his selection and more dependent upon those he selects. Retail stores typically buy shopping goods in large quantities. Thus there is less use of wholesalers than there is with convenience goods; distribution direct from manufacturer to retailer is common in shopping goods. Finally, the store name is often more important to the buyer of a shopping good than is the brand name or the manufacturer's name.

This last point carries significant promotional implications. The retailer is quite willing to assume a good part of the advertising, displaying, and selling costs, particularly for items such as wearing apparel, where the average customer does not know or care who made the product. The manufacturer's advertising to consumers is then less important and may even be nonexistent.

Specialty goods

Specialty goods have been defined as those with "unique characteristics and/or brand identification for which a significant group of buyers are habitually willing to make a special purchasing effort."[17] In the case of specialty goods, as with convenience goods but unlike shopping goods, the buyer has complete knowledge of the particular product he wants before going on his buying trip. The distinctive feature of specialty goods is that the buyer will accept only one brand. He is willing to forego more accessible substitutes in order to procure the wanted brand, even though this may require a significant expenditure of time and effort. Examples of products usually classified as specialty goods include expensive men's ready-to-wear, fancy groceries, health foods, hi-fi components, photographic equipment, and, for many people, automobiles and certain home appliances. Ordinarily, only certain *brands* of these products fall into the specialty goods classification. For many men, a Kuppenheimer suit would be considered a specialty good—they insist on that brand and will accept no other—but men's suits in general would not be so classified.

The consumer's *insistence* on a certain brand is the key characteristic of specialty goods. Retailers ordinarily cannot effectively substitute other brands if they are out of the one asked for. Since the consumer insists on a certain brand, he is willing to expend considerable effort to find it. Consequently, manufacturers can afford to use fewer outlets. With the insistence on a given brand and with few outlets, the consumer *must* make a special effort. Thus the *willingness* to exert extra effort becomes a *need* to do so.[18]

Marketing considerations The ultimate goal of a manufacturer, of course, is to turn out a product that customers will insist upon buying. Having his product in a specialty goods category is often a fleeting luxury, however, and seldom will a majority of customers treat any product as a specialty good. A man may insist on a particular shirt today, but tomorrow he may decide to try something new he has heard about. Consequently, the manufacturer must strive to reach the pinnacle called "specialty goods," and once there, he must remain deserving lest he be thrown into the struggling competitiveness of convenience or shopping goods.

Usually only one outlet is used in a given area or market. Ordinarily, the manufacturer deals directly with his chosen retailers. The retailers are ex-

---

[17] Committee on Definitions, Ralph S. Alexander, Chairman, *Marketing Definitions: A Glossary of Marketing Terms*, American Marketing Association, Chicago, 1960, p. 22.

[18] Holton, *op. cit.* For a statement of disagreement and a subsequent rebuttal, see David J. Luck, "On the Nature of Specialty Goods," *Journal of Marketing,* July 1959, pp. 61–64; and Richard H. Holton, "What Is Really Meant by 'Specialty Goods'?" *Journal of Marketing,* July, 1959, pp. 64–66.

tremely important, particularly if the manufacturer is using only one in each area. Where the franchise to handle the product is a valuable one, the retailer may become quite dependent upon the producer. Actually they are interdependent; the success of one is closely tied to the success of the other.

Because brand is important and because only a few outlets are used, both the manufacturer and the retailer advertise the product extensively. Often the manufacturer pays some portion of the retailer's advertising costs, and the retailer's name frequently appears in the manufacturer's advertisement.

Criticism of product classification

Although we continue to use the convenience-shopping-specialty categorization, we cannot ignore its shortcomings. One of the quarrels with the traditional classification is that we really are not classifying consumer products at all; instead, we are grouping consumer buying patterns. We are talking about convenience buying habits, not convenience products. The critics point out, and with justification, that buying habits may be categorized in this manner but that products cannot. When we attempt to establish the three-way classification, we find that given products shift in and out of one or more of the groups. Automobiles furnish a good illustration. When a person first buys a car, he may shop extensively. He finally buys a Ford and is quite satisfied. When he needs a replacement, he goes straight to a Ford agency without any shopping around; to him a car has shifted from a shopping to a specialty good. Later, for one reason or another, he becomes disenchanted with his Ford. Then when car-buying time comes around a third time, he will revert to shopping.

An adjunct to this first basic criticism is that the attempt to classify products by systems that were really designed to sort out buying habits results in considerable overlapping of the product groups. Not all consumers react in the same way to a given product. Cigars may be a convenience good to one person and a specialty good to another. In fact, some items may fall in all three classes, depending upon the consumers.

A second objection to the classification is that it suggests sharp, rigid demarcations, when in fact none exist. Actually this criticism should not worry a marketing man. He should have long since realized that marketing does not lend itself to black-and-white, night-and-day categorizations. Instead, the marketing man deals constantly with gray areas and twilight zones where imperceptible shadings often occur.[19] In reality, the distinction between staple and impulse

---

[19] The idea of imperceptible shadings suggests a color spectrum wherein the products would be arrayed as colors are. There would be no sharp breaks between divisions. Rather, we would start with various convenience goods at one end and find specialty products occupying positions near the other end. See Leo V. Aspinwall, "The Marketing Characteristics of Goods," *Cost and Profit Outlook*, September, 1956, p. 1.

The idea of using a spectrum to represent consumer buying intent as a continuum

convenience products, and between convenience and shopping goods, is based on degrees of effort expended. The differences are better illustrated by a slope than by a series of steps.

Another criticism concerns the confusion surrounding the concept of specialty goods. The term "specialty" itself is used in conjunction with several other phases of marketing—specialty salesmen and specialty stores, for example —and these have no connection with specialty products. In fact, many specialty stores sell shopping goods and many specialty salesmen carry convenience products. Furthermore, because a brand's stay in the specialty goods category may be so short and because there is so much shifting back and forth between shopping goods and specialty goods, many people wonder if there is any valid or useful reason for continuing to use the classification of specialty goods.

QUESTIONS AND PROBLEMS

1   Explain how the factors of when and where people buy might affect the marketing program for each of the following products:

    a.   Water skis   d.   Outboard motors

    b.   House paint   e.   Room air conditioners

    c.   High-quality sunglasses

2   Identify the sponsors of three television programs designed to reach a children's audience and also three programs appealing to the women's audience during the daytime. In light of the factors explained in this chapter, do you think this is a wise expenditure of advertising funds by each of the sponsoring companies?

3   From your personal experience, give some examples of changes in operating policies and procedures in specific retail stores which were in response to consumer buying patterns.

4   Cite examples of manufacturers or retailers who are recognizing the emergence of teen-agers as decision makers in family buying and as actual purchasers.

5   Surveys indicate that women constitute an increasing proportion of gasoline service station customers and that they account for a growing share of service stations sales. What changes should these retailers make to take advantage of these trends in consumer buying patterns?

6   "Within a few years all retailers in the suburban areas surrounding large cities will be open six or seven days a week from noon until 9 P.M." In light of consumer buying habits, analyze this statement, pointing out the extent to which you believe it is an accurate forecast. Will there be any major exceptions? If so, in what fields?

7   Cite a few examples of products where the same person normally makes the buying decisions and the physical purchase and also uses the product. Then

is also advocated in Leonard Groeneveld, "A New Theory of Consumer Buying Intent," *Journal of Marketing*, July, 1964, pp. 23–28; products are placed in a spectrum according to the degree of prethought involved in their purchase. Five criteria were established to differentiate quantitatively the amount of prethought in the purchasing decision and act.

give some examples in which two or three different people are involved in these processes. Explain how a firm's marketing program may be affected by the number of people involved in the deciding, buying, and using processes.

8   What factors account for changes in a person's buying habits?

9   "Impulse buying is not rational buying." Do you agree? Discuss.

10   How do you account for the increase in impulse buying?

11   In what ways may our desire for conformity increase the efficiency of marketing?

12   Give some examples of specific companies whose marketing programs reflect an attempt to satisfy consumers' desires for the following kinds of convenience:
     a. Form   d. Quantity
     b. Time   e. Automation
     c. Readiness

13   After being recognized favorably by the American Dental Association, Crest toothpaste increased its sales substantially. Many products do not experience this type of sales increase when they receive a seal of approval from a rating agency. How do you account for these differences in consumers' reactions? Do you believe the typical consumer relies upon seals of approval from such organizations as Good Housekeeping or the American Medical Association?

14   What are some brands or types of products which are specialty goods so far as your personal buying patterns are concerned? In each instance do you believe that most consumers would classify the article as a specialty product? If not, how do you explain your own rating?

15   "As brand preferences are established by women with regard to women's shoes and ready-to-wear, these items, which traditionally have been considered shopping goods, will move into the specialty goods category. At the same time, women's clothing is moving into supermarkets and variety stores, thus indicating that some articles are convenience goods." Explain the reasoning involved here. Do you agree that women's clothing is shifting away from the shopping goods classification? Explain.

16   In what way is the responsibility for advertising a convenience good distributed between the manufacturer and the retailers? A shopping good? A specialty good?

17   Compare a manufacturer's marketing mix for a convenience good with the mix for a specialty good.

18   To what extent is the marketing mix for a shopping good similar to the mix for a specialty good?

7

THE INDUSTRIAL MARKET

Besides the consumer market there is another market—a big, rich, and widely diversified one, requiring the efforts of millions of workers in thousands of different jobs. This market is not criticized for extreme claims in selling or advertising; it is not accused of costing too much, of offering duplicate brands, or of paying middlemen exorbitant profits. It is not a target for widespread complaint because it is largely unknown to the public. The market of which we speak is the industrial market.

NATURE AND IMPORTANCE OF THE INDUSTRIAL MARKET

In Chapter 4 *industrial users* were defined as business or institutional organizations that buy products and services either to use in making other goods and services or to use in their own business. *Industrial goods* were differentiated from consumer goods on the basis of their ultimate use. Industrial goods are those intended for use in making other products or for rendering a service in the operation of a business or institutional enterprise. *Industrial marketing*, then, is the marketing of industrial goods and services to industrial users.

Because the industrial market is largely an unknown quantity to the average consumer he is apt to underrate its significance. Actually this market is a huge one in terms of its total sales volume and the number of firms involved in it. It is estimated that about 50 per cent of all manufactured goods are sold to the industrial market. In 1965, this volume of manufactured industrial goods was close to $250 billion.

As large as these figures are, they by no means give the complete picture of the industrial market. They are for *manufactured* products only. In addition to manufactured products, about 80 per cent of all farm products and virtually all minerals and forest and sea products are industrial goods. They are sold to firms for further processing. Industrial farm products and minerals alone would add another $54 billion to the volume of industrial goods marketed.[1]

The magnitude and complexity of the industrial market may also be shown by the many transactions required in producing and marketing a product. Consider the number of industrial marketing transactions and the total sales volume involved in getting a pair of cowhide work shoes to a consumer. First, the cattle must go through one or two middlemen before reaching a meat-packer. Then the hides are sold to a tanner, who in turn sells the leather to a shoe manufacturer. The shoe manufacturer may sell to a shoe wholesaler, who will market his products to factories which supply shoes for their workers. Each time the cow, leather, and shoes are sold, it is an industrial marketing transaction.

In addition to the leather, the manufacturer must buy metal eyelets, laces, thread, steel safety toe plates, rubber or composition heels and/or soles, and shoe polish. He does not make any of these products himself. Although he may buy shoestring material in large quantities, cut it to the desired length, and add the metal tips, other industrial firms must first buy the raw cotton and then spin, weave, dye, and cut it so that it becomes shoestring material. All the manufacturers involved have plants and offices with furniture, machinery, and other equipment—industrial goods which have their own marketing patterns and problems. The factories themselves are industrial products, as are the heating and maintenance equipment and supplies. In short, a myriad of industrial products and industrial marketing situations come into play before almost any product, whether it is a consumer or industrial good, reaches its final destination.

---

[1] Total sales volume of manufactured goods from *Survey of Current Business*, February, 1966, back cover. Sales volume of minerals produced in the United States in 1964 was about $20 billion, according to *Minerals Yearbook: 1964*, U.S. Government Printing Office, Washington, D.C., 1965, p. 3. Cash farm income in 1965 was estimated at $43 billion; 80 per cent of this (industrial farm products) is about $34 billion.

Another indication of the scope and importance of the industrial market may be seen in the following industry classifications which make up this market:

1. Agriculture, forestry, and fishing

2. Mining and quarrying

3. Contract construction

4. Manufacturing

5. Transportation, communication, and other public utilities

6. Wholesale trade

7. Retail trade

8. Finance, insurance, and real estate

9. Services

10. Government—Federal, state, and local

Every retail store and wholesaling establishment is an industrial user. Every bus company, airline, and railroad is part of this market, as are all gas, electric, and telephone companies. Every contractor is part of the industrial market, as is every hotel, restaurant, bank, insurance company, hospital, theater, garage, and so on. In addition, there are thousands of Federal, state, and local governmental units buying for countless governmental institutions, such as schools, offices, and military bases. In total, there are close to ten million industrial users in the United States. While this is far short of the approximately two hundred million consumers, the total sales volume in the industrial market far surpasses total sales to consumers. This differential occurs because there are so very many industrial marketing transactions involved before a final product is sold to its ultimate user.

CLASSIFICATION OF INDUSTRIAL PRODUCTS

Separating all products into consumer and industrial goods is a valuable aid to marketing executives. The general category of industrial products is still too broad, however, because marketing practices for various products are different. Consequently, some subdivision is necessary. The classification used here separates industrial goods into five categories: raw materials, fabricating materials and parts, installations, accessory equipment, and operating supplies. This classification is based on the broad *uses* of the product, in contrast to the classification of consumer products on the basis of buying habits.

Parenthetically, it may be noted that the consumer goods classification of convenience-shopping-specialty products is also applicable in part to industrial goods. Items such as postage stamps, scratch pads, light bulbs, erasers, and dust mops are the "convenience goods" of the industrial market. They are purchased with a minimum of effort and searching time. For other products, such as office machines or replacement motors for production machines, a purchasing agent for a manufacturer will shop carefully. He will compare price, quality, features, and service given by the sellers, thus placing these products in the shopping goods category. Industrial products fall into the specialty goods category when, for example, a food manufacturer insists on a Falcon automobile for his sales force, a coal mining firm insists on Goodyear conveyor belts, or a steel mill insists on safety goggles made by the American Optical Company.

Raw materials

Raw materials are industrial goods which will become a part of another physical product and which have received no processing at all other than that necessary for economy or protection in physical handling. Raw materials include (1) goods found in their natural state, such as minerals, land, and products of the forests and the seas, and (2) agricultural products, such as wheat, corn, cotton, tobacco, fruits, vegetables, livestock, and animal products—eggs and raw milk. As will be seen, these two groups of raw materials are marketed quite differently.

Marketing considerations   The marketing of raw materials found in their natural state is influenced by several factors. The supply of these products is limited and cannot be substantially increased. Usually only a few large producers are involved. The product must be carefully graded and, consequently, is highly standardized. Because of their great bulk, their low unit value, and the long distance between producer and industrial user, transportation is an important consideration.

These factors necessitate short channels of distribution and a minimum of physical handling. Frequently marketing is direct from producer to industrial user; at most, one middleman may be used. The limited supply forces users to assure themselves of adequate quantities. Often this is done either by contracting in advance to buy a season's supply of the product or by vertical integration. Advertising and other forms of demand stimulation are used very little. Because there is little brand or other product differentiation, competition is built around price and the assurance that a producer can deliver the prescribed quantity of the product in the exact quality specified.

The marketing of agricultural products is covered in Chapter 25, so only a few remarks are necessary here. Agricultural products used as industrial raw materials are supplied by many small producers located some distance from the markets. The supply is largely controllable by man, but it cannot be increased or decreased rapidly. The product is perishable and is not produced at a uniform rate throughout the year. Close attention must be given to transportation and warehousing. Transportation costs are high relative to unit value, and standardization and grading are very important.

Because producers are small and numerous, many middlemen and long channels of distribution are needed. Very little promotional or demand-creation activity is involved, and branding is unimportant.

Fabricating materials and parts

Fabricating materials and parts are industrial goods which become an actual part of the finished product. They have already been processed to some extent (in contrast to raw materials). Fabricating *materials* will undergo further processing. Examples include pig iron going into steel, gray goods becoming a part of finished printed cloth, yarn being woven into cloth, and flour becoming a part of bread. Fabricating parts will be assembled with no further change in form. They include such products as spark plugs, tires, and fan belts in an automobile; the barrel and stock of a rifle; and the buttons on a suit or dress.

Marketing considerations   Fabricating materials and parts are usually purchased in large quantities. To ensure an adequate, timely supply, a buyer may place his order a year or more in advance, with the guarantee that he will be given the advantage of price reductions. Because of these buying habits, most fabricating products are marketed on a direct-sale basis between producer and user. Individual industries, such as textiles, may provide exceptions to this rule.

Middlemen are used most often where the buyers are small or are placing small fill-in orders on a rapid-delivery basis. Normally, buying decisions are based on price and service provided by the seller. Branding is generally unimportant, although some firms have made successful attempts to pull their products out of obscurity by identifying them with a brand. Botany Woolen Mills, Timken Roller Bearing Company, and Burlington Mills are notable examples.

Installations

Installations are manufactured industrial products—the long-lived, expensive major machinery and equipment of an industrial user. Examples would include large generators in a dam, a factory building, diesel engines for a railroad, coke ovens and blast furnaces for a steel mill, computers for a missile manufacturer, and jet airplanes for an airline. The differentiating characteristic of installations is that they set the scale of operation in a firm. Adding twelve new typewriters or office desks will not affect the scale of operation at Eastern Airlines, but adding twelve new jet airplanes certainly will.

Marketing considerations   Marketing of installations presents a real challenge to management because every single sale is important. Usually no middlemen are involved; the channel is direct from producer to industrial user. Typically the unit sale is large, and often the product is made to detailed specifications. There may be a long negotiation period before the transaction is consummated. Much presale and postsale servicing is needed. High-caliber salesmen are needed to market installations, and often sales engineers are used. Promotional emphasis is on personal selling rather than advertising, although some advertising is used.

While direct sale is most common, middlemen agents or wholesalers are often used to sell less expensive, standardized installations. Middlemen are also relied upon to reach small buyers and to sell supplies and replacement parts used with large installations.

Accessory equipment

Accessory equipment is a class of industrial products used to aid and implement the production operations of an industrial user, but it does not have a significant influence on the scale of operations in a firm. Accessory equipment does not become an actual part of the finished product. The life of accessory equipment is shorter than that of installations and longer than that of operating supplies. Examples would include office equipment, office machines, cash registers in a retail store, small power tools, and forklift trucks.

Marketing considerations It is difficult to generalize on the distribution policies of firms marketing accessory equipment. In some cases direct sale is used, particularly where the order is for several units of the product or where the product is of relatively high unit value. A firm like the Hyster Company in Portland, Oregon, manufacturing forklift trucks, may sell directly because the price of a single unit is large enough to make this distribution policy profitable. In the main, however, manufacturers of accessory equipment use middlemen because the market is geographically dispersed, there are many different types of potential users, and individual orders may be relatively small.

Accessory equipment is not generally made to specification, so the products of a given manufacturer are ordinarily standardized. Also, the goods are not highly technical. For these reasons, manufacturers can use advertising effectively in a promotional program.

Operating supplies

Operating supplies are the "convenience goods" of the industrial field; they are short-lived, low-priced items usually purchased with a minimum of effort. They aid in a firm's operations but do not become a part of the finished product. Illustrations are floor wax, lubricating oils, pencils and stationery, registration supplies in a university, heating fuel, and washroom supplies.

Marketing considerations As with consumer convenience products, industrial operating supplies necessitate broad distribution. A firm will make extensive use of wholesaling middlemen because the product is low in unit value, is bought in small quantities, and goes to many users. Price competition is heavy because competitive products are quite standardized and brand insistence is low.

CHARACTERISTICS OF INDUSTRIAL MARKET DEMAND

Four general demand characteristics help to differentiate the industrial market from the consumer market.

Demand is derived

Since industry has no purpose except to supply the wants of the consumer market, the amount of goods which can be sold to an industrial user is dependent upon the behavior of the ultimate consumer. That is, the demand for industrial goods is derived from the demand for consumer products which the industrial items play a part in making. The demand for steel is partially dependent upon the consumer demand for automobiles and refrigerators, for example. The demand for steel is also dependent upon the demand for butter, baseball gloves, and bongo drums because the tools, machines, and other equipment involved in making these items are made of steel. Thus as the demand for baseball gloves increases, the glove manufacturers may buy more steel sewing machines, steel filing cabinets, or adding machines.

We should note, however, that the factor of derived demand is often operative only over the long run. In the short run, the derived demand is most noticeable in those products which are used directly in the production of consumer goods, for instance, steel used to make automobiles. This would exclude the large number of goods (often called producers' durables) whose demand is so indirectly dependent on consumer demand that it is hardly amenable to treatment as derived demand at all. Their demand is largely dependent on other variables, such as changes in the cost of labor, in technology, and in the availability of capital.

There are several important marketing implications in the fact that industrial market demand is a derived demand. The producer of an industrial product may direct a considerable share of his promotional program to the ultimate consumer. Thus steel manufacturers, through consumer media such as television and magazines, have urged consumers to have a "white Christmas" by buying new refrigerators and stoves or by furnishing their kitchens with all-steel cabinets. The Du Pont Company has advertised to the consumer the advantages of clothing made of Dacron (a Du Pont-branded fiber).

Accurate long-range market planning and forecasting of consumers' needs are of vital importance to producers of industrial goods. Telephone, gas, and electric companies must forecast consumer population movements years in advance so that pipelines, cables, and other equipment can be installed underground.

Demand is inelastic

Another significant characteristic of the industrial market, and one related to the derived-demand feature, is that the demand for many industrial products is inelastic. That, is the demand for the product will respond very little to changes in its price. If the price of buttons for men's shirts and jackets should suddenly rise or fall considerably, there would probably be no appreciable change in demand. If there were a radical increase in price, manufacturers might put fewer buttons on coat sleeves; or if prices were to drop substantially, some firms might stockpile a supply. On balance, however, there would be very little shift in demand.

A basic reason for the general inelasticity of demand for industrial goods is that the cost of a single part or material is ordinarily an inconsequential portion of the total cost of the finished product. The cost of the chemicals in paint is a small part of the price that a consumer pays for a gallon of enamel; the cost of enamel on a refrigerator or automobile is a small part of the price of the product to the consumer. Even the cost of expensive capital equipment (installations), when distributed over thousands of units of a product, becomes a very small part of the total unit cost. As a result, when the price of the industrial product shifts, there is very little change in demand for the ultimate consumer product, even when the effect of the price shift is passed on to the consumer. If there is no appreciable shift in the demand for the consumer good, then by virtue of the derived-demand feature, there is no change in the demand for the industrial product going into the consumer good.

From a marketing point of view, there are three factors to consider regarding the inelasticity of industrial market demand. The first is the position of an entire industry as contrasted with that of an individual firm. An industry-wide cut in the price of nylon cord used in tires will have a negligible effect on the demand for automobile tires, and consequently there will be a negligible change in the total demand for nylon cord. The pricing policy of an individual firm, however, can substantially alter the demand schedule facing this firm. If one supplier significantly cuts the price of nylon tire cord, he may draw a great deal of business away from his competitors. His advantage, of course, will be temporary because his competitors will undoubtedly retaliate in some way in order to recapture their lost business. Nevertheless, in the short run, the demand curve facing a single firm is much more elastic than is the industry's curve.

Another marketing factor involved here is time. Much of what has been said refers to short-run situations. Over the long run, the demand for a given industrial product is more elastic. If the price of cloth for men's suits is raised, there probably will be no immediate shift in the price of the finished garment or in the demand for it. The increase in cost of materials may be reflected in a $5 rise in suit prices for next year and may influence the demand for suits, and thus for cloth, over a period of a year or more.

One further aspect of this point is the relative importance of a specific industrial product in the cost structure of a finished good. We may generalize to this extent: the more significant the cost of an industrial product as a percentage of the total price of the finished good, the greater the elasticity of demand for this industrial item.

Demand is widely fluctuating

The market demand for most classes of industrial goods fluctuates considerably more than the demand for consumer products. Fluctuations in the demand for installations—major plant equipment, factories, large generators, etc.—are especially great. Substantial fluctuations also exist in the market for accessory equipment—office furniture and machinery, minor plant equipment, delivery trucks, and similar products. These are reflected in, and tend to accentuate the swings in, the demand for industrial raw materials, such as metals and other minerals. One exception to this generalization is found in agricultural products intended for processing. There is a reasonably consistent demand for animals intended for meat products, for fruits and vegetables which will be canned or frozen, and for grains and dairy products.

Fluctuations in market demand for industrial products can influence all phases of a firm's marketing program. In product planning and development, they may stimulate a firm to diversify—to go into other product lines, even into consumer products—in order to ease production and marketing problems. Distribution policies may be affected. Rather than use a sales force, which must be either trimmed back or maintained at full strength (but at a loss) when demand declines, a seller may decide to make greater use of manufacturers' agents or wholesalers to reach his market. Pricing policies and practices may be involved; management may attempt to stem a decline in sales by cutting prices and thus attracting the business of competing firms. Marketing management is hard pressed to know how to budget for its advertising program. When demand declines, the inclination is to cut back in advertising. Yet at the same time, a firm wants to keep its name before its potential market and also be in there promoting when the market starts to pick up again.

Market is knowledgeable

Unlike the ultimate consumer, the typical industrial buyer is usually well informed about what he is buying. He knows the relative merits of alternative sources of supply and of competitive products. A purchasing agent's advancement in the firm, often his very job, depends upon how well he performs; naturally he will do all he can to ensure that what he orders is a combination of the lowest cost, best quality, and most service from the seller.

In marketing its product, an industrial goods firm places greater importance on its personal selling program than does a firm selling consumer goods. Industrial salesmen must be carefully selected, properly trained, and adequately compensated; they must give the most effective sales presentation possible and furnish satisfactory service both before and after the sale is made.

DETERMINANTS OF INDUSTRIAL MARKET DEMAND

To make a detailed analysis of market demand, a firm selling to *consumer* markets would make a quantitative analysis of the distribution and composition of population and income and a qualitative analysis of consumer motivation and buying patterns. Essentially the same basis of analysis can be used by a firm selling to the *industrial* market. The factors affecting the market for industrial products are the number of potential industrial users and their purchasing power, buying motives, and buying habits. Since the quantitative and qualitative aspects of the industrial market are examined from the point of view of an individual seller, it will be possible to bring out additional differentiating characteristics of this market and to observe many specific differences between consumers and industrial users.

Number and types of industrial users

Total market   Analysis of the industrial market shows that it contains relatively few buying units when compared with the consumer market—approximately ten million industrial users, in contrast to over two hundred million consumers divided into more than sixty million households. The industrial market will seem particularly limited to most companies because they sell to only a segment of the total. A firm selling to manufacturers of metal cans in 1963, for example, had only 205 customer plants with twenty or more employees. In that same employment-size class, the Bureau of the Census listed only 219 establishments manufacturing textile machinery and 993 meat-packing plants.[2] Consequently, marketing executives should try to pinpoint their market carefully by type of industry and geographic location. A firm marketing hard-rock mining equipment is not interested in the total industrial market or even in all 40,000 firms engaged in mining and quarrying. This seller is interested in information which will help him identify the market for his particular products.

One very useful information source developed by the Federal government is the Standard Industrial Classification system (S.I.C.), which enables a company to identify relatively small segments of its industrial market.[3] All types of businesses in the United States are divided into ten groups, and a range of two-digit classification code numbers is assigned to each group as follows:

01–09	Agriculture, forestry, fishing
10–14	Mining
15–18	Contract construction
19–39	Manufacturing
40–49	Transportation and other public utilities
50–59	Wholesale and retail trade
60–67	Finance, insurance, and real estate
70–89	Services
90–93	Government—Federal, state, local, and international
99	Others

A separate two-digit number is assigned to each major industry within each of the above groups; then, three- and four-digit classification numbers are used to subdivide each major industry into finer segments. To illustrate, within the

---

[2] U.S. Census of Manufactures: 1963, Summary Series, MC 63(P)-3.

[3] For a description of the Standard Industrial Classification system and a complete listing of all S.I.C. numbers and classifications, see *Standard Industrial Classification Manual,* U.S. Government Printing Office, Washington, D.C., 1957; supplement published in 1963.

broad category of manufacturing, "apparel and related products" carries S.I.C. #23. Some of the subclassifications are as follows:

S.I.C. code	Industry group
231	Men's and boys' suits and coats
232	Men's and boys' furnishings
2321	Men's dress shirts and nightwear
2322	Men's, youths', and boys' underwear

Size of industrial users   While the market may be limited in the total number of buyers, it is large in purchasing power. As one might expect, industrial users range in size from very small companies with less than five employees to firms with over 2,500 workers. A relatively small percentage of firms account for the greatest share of the value added by a given industry. As an example taken from the 1958 Census of Manufactures, 2 per cent of the firms—those with 500 or more employees—accounted for about 50 per cent of the total dollar value added by manufacturing. The firms with less than fifty employees accounted for 90 per cent of all manufacturing establishments but produced only 22 per cent of the value added by manufacturing (see Table 7–1).

The marketing significance in these facts is that the buying power in the industrial market is highly concentrated in a relatively few firms. This market

table   7–1

Size distribution of manufacturing establishments in United States, 1958: by number of employees

This table shows that buying power in the industrial market is highly concentrated among relatively few firms. Less than 4 per cent of the companies—those with 250 or more employees—accounted for 62 per cent of the value added by manufacturing. How might this market concentration influence a seller's marketing program?

Number of employees	Number of establishments	Value added by manufacturing ($000,000)	Per cent of firms	Per cent value added	Per cent of employees
1–4	105,641	$ 1,832	35.4	1.3	1.4
5–9	50,660	2,544	17.0	1.8	2.2
10–19	46,820	4,838	15.7	3.4	4.2
20–49	46,307	11,089	15.5	7.8	9.4
50–99	21,764	12,024	7.3	8.5	9.8
100–249	16,132	21,162	5.4	15.0	16.2
250–499	6,240	19,291	2.1	13.7	14.0
500–999	2,757	18,103	0.9	12.8	12.3
1,000–2,499	1,363	21,449	0.5	15.2	13.3
2,500 or more	498	28,938	0.2	20.5	17.2
Total	298,182	$141,270	100.0	100.0	100.0

SOURCE: U.S. Census of Manufactures: 1958, vol. I, p. 2–2.

concentration has considerable influence on a seller's policies regarding his channels of distribution. He has greater opportunity to deal directly with the industrial users; middlemen are not so essential as in the consumer market.

Regional distribution of industrial users   There is a substantial regional concentration of several of the major industries and of industrial users as a whole. A firm selling products usable in oil fields will find the bulk of its market in Texas, Oklahoma, Louisiana, and southern California; another segment is found in parts of North Dakota and Montana and in the "four corners" region, where the states of Colorado, New Mexico, Arizona, and Utah are joined. Hat manufacturers are located mostly in New England, shoes are produced chiefly in New England and St. Louis, and a substantial share of the nation's garment manufacturers are located in Chicago, New York, and southern California. There is a similar regional concentration in the farm market.

The eight states comprising the Middle Atlantic and East North Central census regions accounted for fifty-two per cent of the total value added by manufacturing in 1963, according to the Census of Manufactures. Firms which are selling to the industrial market, and particularly those selling to manufacturers, should be aware of the expansion now being experienced in the South, Southwest, and Pacific Coast regions.

While a large part of a firm's market may be concentrated in limited geographic areas, a good portion may lie outside these areas. Consequently, a distribution policy must be developed which will enable a firm to deal directly with the concentrated market and also to employ middlemen (or a company sales force at great expense) to reach the outlying markets.

Vertical and horizontal industrial markets   A marketing executive who is analyzing his industrial market should determine whether this market is vertical or horizontal. If his product is usable by virtually all firms in only one or two industries, he has a *vertical* market. Some precision instruments are intended only for the marine market, but every boatbuilder or shipbuilder is a potential customer. Many types of agricultural equipment may have no market outside the farm market, but every operating farm is a potential user. If his product is usable by many industries, his market is said to be broad or *horizontal*. Industrial supplies, such as lubricating oils and greases, small tools, small motors, and some paper products, may be sold to a wide variety of industries.

This analysis of the market will influence a firm's marketing policies. In a vertical market a product can be tailor-made to meet the specific needs of one industry. In a horizontal market the product must be developed as an all-purpose item. Middlemen are more apt to be used in the marketing program for horizontal markets, although some vertical markets do employ middlemen simply because their orders are too small to warrant the cost of using company salesmen. Advertising and personal selling programs can be more pinpointed in vertical marketing situations, and industrial journals in specific fields can be used as advertising media.

Buying power of industrial users

Another determinant of industrial market demand, and thus a factor to be analyzed carefully by marketing executives, is the purchasing power of industrial users. This can be measured either by the expenditures of industrial users or by their sales volume. Many times, however, expenditures or sales volume data are not available or are very difficult to estimate. In such cases it is more feasible to use an activity indicator, or market factor, which is related to income generation and expenditure. Sometimes an activity indicator is a combined indicator of purchasing power and the number of industrial users. Following are examples of activity indicators which might be used to estimate purchasing power of industrial users.[4]

Measured by manufacturing activity   Firms selling to manufacturers might use as market indicators such factors as the number of employees, the number of plants, and the dollar value added by manufacturing. A firm selling work gloves used the number of employees in manufacturing establishments to determine the market trend and the relative values of various geographical markets. A company which sold a product to control stream pollution used two indicators—the number of firms processing wood products (paper mills, wood pulp processors, plywood mills, and so forth) and the manufacturing value added by these firms.

Measured by mining activity   The number of mines operating, the volume of their output, and the dollar value of the product as it leaves the mine all may indicate purchasing power of mines and thus may be used by any firm marketing industrial products to mine operators.

Measured by agricultural activity   A company marketing fertilizer, seed, feed, or agricultural equipment can estimate the buying power of its market by studying such indicators as cash farm income, acreage planted, crop estimates and yields, and number of farms with electricity. The chemical producer who sells to a fertilizer manufacturer might study the same indices because the demand for chemicals in this case is derived from the demand for fertilizer.

Measured by construction activity   If an enterprise is marketing building materials or supplies, such as lumber, plywood, brick, gypsum products, or builders' hardware, its market is dependent upon construction activity. This may be indicated by the number or value of building permits issued or by the number of construction starts by type of housing (single-family residence,

---

[4] In some instances the consumer market also must be measured by activity data rather than by direct counts of consumers and their income. For instance, the consumer market for automobile tires or gasoline is a function of automotive activity, such as the number of cars on the road, the number of each year's models, and the average miles driven.

apartment, commercial). A seller must select the appropriate indicator. A firm producing residential builders' hardware (door locks, window catches, and kitchen cabinet hardware) should not use an index which includes industrial and commercial construction.

Buying motives of industrial users

An analysis of buying motives as a factor affecting market demand is as important in the industrial market as it is in the consumer market. Industrial buying motives are quite different from consumer buying motives. Some businessmen feel that consumer motives are far more complex and difficult to determine. For the most part, industrial buying motives are rational, and an industrial purchase is normally a methodical, objective, preplanned undertaking.

The industrial buyer is motivated primarily by a desire to maximize his profit. To this extent, motivation of industrial users is less complex than that of ultimate consumers. Most firms attempt to maximize their gains over the long run, although a few—usually unethical or just plain shortsighted—companies strive for a profit only in the short run.

To achieve an optimum profit position, industrial users may be motivated by one or more of several specific factors. Of course, one basic motive is that they want to buy a product at the lowest possible price consistent with the quality, quantity, and service required. A buyer must be assured, however, of an adequate supply, dependable in both quantity and quality.

Another specific motive may be that the company prefers to buy goods that will help to sell its end product. Thus a shoe manufacturer may buy a well-known brand of heels, or a garment manufacturer may buy a branded material, in the hope that the branded parts or materials will make the final product more salable. A compelling reason behind many purchases is the buyer's desire for adequate service, both before and after the purchase.

With all the attention devoted to the rationality and objectivity in industrial buying, one might get the idea that emotional buying is totally absent. This is not the case at all, for we are still dealing with people. A buyer can be appealed to through his ego, whether he is acting as his firm's purchasing agent or as a consumer. Particularly is this possible when two or more competing sellers are offering essentially the same products or services. The salesman whom the buyer likes best will get the order. And why does the buyer like him? Perhaps they came from the same school, or the salesman flattered the buyer's wife, or the buyer was properly entertained.[5]

[5] For a study of the motivation and behavior of industrial purchasing agents, including an identification of the in-company and outside-the-company forces influencing this behavior, see Delbert J. Duncan, *Some Basic Determinants of Behavior in Industrial Purchasing*, University of California, Institute of Business and Economic Research, Berkeley, Calif., 1965, reprinted from *Pacific Purchasor*, May, June, July, August, 1965.

As in the consumer market, a seller in the industrial market should understand how, when, and where his customers buy, and who does the purchasing or makes the purchasing decisions. Buying patterns in the two markets differ in a number of ways.

Length of negotiation period   The period of negotiation in an industrial sale is usually much longer than in a consumer market sale. Some of the usual reasons for the extended negotiations are (1) several executives are involved in the buying decision, (2) the size of the sale is often large, (3) the industrial product is made-to-order, and considerable discussion is involved in establishing the exact specifications, and (4) bids are often involved (as in construction work) and the seller needs time to prepare careful estimates.

Frequency of purchase   In the industrial market, firms buy certain products very infrequently. Large installations are purchased only once in many years. Smaller parts and materials to be used in the manufacture of a product may be ordered on long-term contracts so that an actual selling opportunity exists only once every year or once in several years. Even standardized operating supplies, such as office supplies or cleaning products, may be bought only once a month.

Because of this buying pattern, a great burden is placed on the advertising and personal selling programs of industrial sellers. Their advertising must keep the company's name constantly before the market so that when a buyer is in the market, he will be acquainted with the selling firm. The salesmen must call on potential customers often enough to know when a customer is considering a purchase. In this instance, patterns of infrequent sales and lengthy negotiation periods are closely related. A salesman for Burroughs or the National Cash Register Company may find out, through a regular call, that a hospital is considering the installation of a machine accounting system. The sale may not be consummated for a year or more. Nevertheless, the seller would have lost all opportunity for the sale if his representative had not called when the prospective customer was first contemplating the changeover.

Size of order   The average industrial order is considerably larger than its counterpart in the consumer market. This fact, coupled with the infrequency of purchase, means that an industrial seller cannot afford to lose sales or alienate customers because of a weakness such as poor salesmanship, noncompetitive pricing, uncertain delivery, or imperfect products.

Many sellers in the industrial market are plagued by firms that buy in small, hand-to-mouth quantities. A small order is unprofitable for most sellers, who are constantly combating this problem through buyer education and changes in their pricing and distribution policies.

Direct purchase   Direct sale from the producer to the ultimate consumer is rare. In the industrial market, however, direct marketing from the producer to the industrial user is quite common, especially when the order is large and much technical assistance is needed by the buyer both before and after the sale is made. From a seller's point of view, also, direct marketing is reasonable because there are relatively few potential buyers, these are big buyers, and they are geographically concentrated. Nevertheless, some products, such as small hand or power tools, office supplies, and many manufacturing supplies, are marketed through middlemen, as are most industrial agricultural products.

When a seller deals directly with industrial users, he must organize and operate a high-caliber sales force. If a firm cannot build up a topnotch sales force, middlemen may have to be used in spite of the advantages of direct selling.

Multiple influence on purchases   In the industrial market, the purchasing decision is frequently influenced by more than one person, particularly in medium- and large-sized firms. Even in small firms where the owner-manager makes all major decisions, he will probably consult with someone in the office or factory before making certain purchases. In firms large enough to have a separate purchasing agent or purchasing department, a seller may be misled into thinking that the real purchasing power in the firm lies in one man or one department. We must distinguish among (1) making a decision to buy, (2) selecting a supplier, and (3) actually placing a purchase order. Typically the purchasing department places the orders. In many instances the purchasing agent also selects the individual supplier, but he must select one who carries the item or brand agreed upon by others in the firm. It is not at all unusual to have as many as five executives involved in a buying decision.[6]

This buying pattern tends to lengthen the negotiation period, and it requires salesmen who are capable of determining who influences the buying decisions. Very often a salesman will call on the wrong executive. Even after he finds out who the decision makers are in the buying firm, it may be very difficult to reach them.

Reciprocity arrangements   A highly controversial industrial buying habit is the practice of reciprocity, the policy of "I'll buy from you if you'll buy from me." In some instances, reciprocity arrangements may be triangular: company A pressures company B to buy from firm C, who is a customer of A. Traditionally, reciprocal selling was found in several of the basic industries, such as oil, steel, rubber, chemicals, and machinery. Today it touches virtually all industries. An investigation by the editors of *Sales Management* showed that "a

---

[6] The findings of a study of purchasing influence are reported in "Who Makes the Decision to Buy in Business?" *Management Methods*, October, 1960, p. 48. See also Ralph S. Alexander, James S. Cross, and Ross Cunningham, *Industrial Marketing*, rev. ed., Richard D. Irwin, Inc., Homewood, Ill., 1961, pp. 46–51, for studies of purchasing influence in different industries.

record number of companies are employing reciprocal selling as a tool for increasing sales, acquiring new customers, expanding share of market."[7]

Several firms have "trade relations" departments and are methodically collecting the sales records and other data needed to make the most effective use of this powerful selling tool.[8]

Some reasons are suggested for the increased use of reciprocity arrangements. First, a tightening in general economic conditions may stimulate some firms to adopt reciprocity as a countermeasure to declining sales volume; after economic conditions improve, the companies are hesitant to give up their new policy. Second, the trend toward product diversification opens additional avenues and opportunities for reciprocity dealings. Also, increased foreign and domestic competition encourages sellers to try to control markets through reciprocity. Finally, most products today are of such acceptable and standardized quality that a given item made by any one of several manufacturers normally will satisfy a buyer's need for that type of product.

On the other hand, reciprocity has several built-in "powder kegs." Small firms can become engulfed by, and lose control to, a large company. The large company is more in the public eye, and is thus vulnerable to attack from the public or from the government. A firm engaging in reciprocity runs the risk of serious loss of morale in its sales force. Similarly, unless a clear policy statement is written regarding the practice, the morale and efficiency of the purchasing department may suffer. Under any circumstances it is difficult to justify purchasing from customers unless the purchases are voluntary acts and unless the buyer is getting competitive prices, quality, and service from the reciprocating seller.

Catalogue buying and selling   Catalogue buying is quite prevalent among industrial users, particularly in connection with standardized, short-lived, and relatively low-priced products. Many wholesalers depend heavily upon their catalogue when selling to retailers.

From a marketing standpoint, catalogue buying relieves a sales force of some pressure but adds considerable importance to the preparation of the printed sales messages. In some cases, printed aids do virtually the entire selling job; salesmen call infrequently or not at all. In other instances, a salesman always calls but depends heavily on his catalogue. A firm selling to catalogue buyers has two general choices regarding the distribution of its printed mate-

---

[7] "Reciprocity: Dangerous Selling Tool Winning New Users!" *Sales Management,* May 20, 1960, p. 40. See also *Trade Relations Defined: The Concept, Legal Aspects, Ethical Problems,* American Management Association, Management Bulletin no. 19, New York, 1962.

[8] For a discussion of the trade relations director—his rise, place in the organization, and responsibilities and the typical services he performs—see Velma A. Adams, "The Rise of the Trade Relations Directors," *Dun's Review and Modern Industry,* December, 1964, p. 35; "The Trade Relations Director," *Sales/Marketing Today,* April, 1965, p. 10; and Edward McCreary, Jr., and Walter Guzzardi, Jr., "A Customer Is a Company's Best Friend," *Fortune,* June, 1965, p. 180.

rials: it may send its own catalogue to each buyer, regardless of what its competitors are doing, or it may contribute its printed information to a common catalogue which will include material furnished by competitive firms and firms selling related products. *Thomas's Register of Manufacturers* is an example of a widely used common catalogue.

Demand for product servicing   The user's desire for excellent service is a strong industrial buying motive and may determine buying patterns. Consequently, sellers appeal for sales on the basis that they furnish better service than competitors. Frequently a firm's only attraction is its service; the product itself is so standardized that it can be purchased from any number of companies.

Sellers must stand ready to furnish services to both potential and actual buyers. In fact, an order may be signed because of a service supplied in advance of the sale. A manufacturer of office machines may study a firm's accounting operation and suggest a more effective, lower-cost system which, incidentally, involves using the seller's machines. He will also arrange to retrain the present office staff. He may even assume the responsibility of selecting and training additional machine operators. After the machines are installed, other services, such as repairs, may be necessary; buyers want to know that the seller will handle these matters promptly.

Quality and supply requirements   Another industrial buying motive which is reflected in buying patterns is the industrial user's insistence upon an adequate quantity of uniform-quality products. Variations in the quality of materials and parts going into his finished product can cause considerable trouble for a manufacturer. He may be faced with costly shutdowns and other disruptions in his production processes if the imperfections exceed quality-control limits. Adequate quantities are as important as good quality. A work stoppage caused by an insufficient quantity of material is just as costly as one caused by an inferior quality of material.

Meeting these supply requirements is in large part the responsibility of the production department. But the marketing people are not completely absolved of responsibility because they must furnish forecasts of what quantity and quality will be needed and when it must be available.

Adequacy of supply is an especially big problem for sellers and users of industrial raw materials such as agricultural products, metal ores, or forest products. Climatic conditions may disrupt the normal flow of goods; for example when logging camps or mining operations become snowbound, or when agricultural products fluctuate in quality and quantity from one growing season to another. These "acts of God" create additional managerial problems for both buyers and sellers with respect to their warehousing, standardization, and grading activities.

Leasing instead of buying   A growing behavioral pattern in the industrial market is for firms to lease industrial products instead of buying them outright.

In the past, this practice was limited to large equipment. Examples of products which have traditionally been leased are shoe manufacturing equipment (The United Shoe Machinery Company), data-processing machines (IBM), packaging equipment (American Can Company), postage meters, heavy construction equipment, and textile machinery. Even some freight cars and locomotives are owned by life insurance companies and leased to railroads. Today, industrial suppliers and users are expanding leasing arrangements to include delivery trucks, salesmen's automobiles, machine tools, agricultural feed mills, storage bins, and other items generally less expensive than big installations.[9]

Leasing has several merits. For the firm leasing out its equipment, total net income, after charging off pertinent repair and maintenance expenses, is often higher than it would be if the unit were sold outright. Also, the market may be expanded to include users who could not afford to buy the product, especially if it is large installation type of equipment, such as that leased by IBM and the can manufacturers. Leasing offers an effective method of getting distribution for a new product. Potential users may be more willing to rent a product than to buy it. If they are not satisfied, their expenditures are limited to a few monthly payments. Another advantage to the lessor is that he may be able to sell supplies for use with the machine (although he can no longer *require* the renter to buy his supplies).

From the lessee's point of view, some of the benefits may be summarized as follows:

1. Leasing allows the user to keep his investment capital free for other purposes.

2. There may be significant tax advantages; rental payments are totally tax deductible and they are usually larger than corresponding depreciation charges on owned products.

3. Leasing costs are ordinarily considered current operating expenses; therefore the advantage of using the equipment can be enjoyed sooner and the disadvantages of major capital expenses avoided if the equipment is rented rather than purchased.

4. New firms can enter a business with less capital outlay than would be necessary if they had to buy the equipment outright. This may not be an unmixed blessing, however. While ease of entry increases competition, it can also lead to an overcrowding of the field.

5. The user has available to him the newest products developed by the lessor.

6. Rented products are usually serviced by the lessor; this eliminates one headache associated with ownership.

---

[9] For an analysis of the feasibility of leasing automobiles for a sales force, see William J. Stanton and Richard H. Buskirk, *Management of the Sales Force*, rev. ed., Richard D. Irwin, Inc., Homewood, Ill., 1964, pp. 429–432. See also Henry G. Hamel and G. Clark Thompson, "Another Look at Leasing," *Business Management Record*, Nov. 1963, pp. 47–52.

7.   Leasing is particularly attractive to users who need the equipment seasonally or sporadically, as in food canning or construction.

On the foundation of a careful market analysis an industrial goods manufacturer or middleman can develop policies and strategies with respect to various parts of his marketing mix. In the following three chapters we shall consider some of the programming done in connection with one ingredient in the marketing mix—the product.

QUESTIONS AND PROBLEMS

1   "About 80 per cent of all farm products are industrial goods." Give some examples of farm products which are *consumer* goods.

2   Some industrial products may be included in more than one of the industrial goods classifications, depending upon the potential customers. Explain how this multiple listing may occur, giving examples of products in more than one group.

3   What are the fundamental differences between industrial and consumer goods? Between industrial and consumer markets?

4   In which of the five subclassifications of industrial goods should each of the following be included? Explain your choice in each case, noting especially the products which may belong in more than one category.

a.	Typewriters	g.	Automobile wax
b.	Central air conditioners	h.	Land
c.	Aluminum ingots	i.	Cotton cloth
d.	Nuts and bolts	j.	Printing presses
e.	Plywood	k.	Copper wire
f.	Dental chairs	l.	Trucks

5   Give some examples of industrial products where the factor of derived demand is operative mainly in the long run. In the short run. From a marketing standpoint, what difference does it make whether the derived-demand characteristic is effective in the long run or the short run?

6   If the demand for most industrial goods is inelastic, why is it that sellers do not raise their prices to maximize their revenues?

7   Why is the demand for industrial goods usually less elastic (more inelastic) than the demand for consumer products?

8   Why do industrial goods usually fluctuate more widely in demand than consumer goods?

9   What are some marketing implications in the fact that the demand for industrial goods:
   a.   Fluctuates widely
   b.   Is inelastic
   c.   Is derived

10   Which characteristics of industrial market demand accentuate the need for accurate sales forecasting?

11   "Economic recessions decrease the market demand for industrial goods more than for consumer goods." Do you agree? Explain.

12   What are the marketing implications for a seller in the fact that his customers are geographically concentrated and limited in number?

13   What differences would you expect to find in the marketing program of a company selling to horizontal industrial markets and that of a company selling to vertical industrial markets?

14   Select three advertisements of industrial products and identify the buying motives stressed in the ads.

15   "The buying motives of a given consumer usually will change over a period of time; however, the buying motives of industrial purchasers do not change as regards a given product." Do you agree?

16   National Cash Register, IBM, Burroughs, and other manufacturers of office machines make a substantial proportion of their sales directly to industrial users. At the same time, wholesalers of office equipment are thriving. Are these two market situations inconsistent? Explain.

17   What suggestions do you have for industrial sellers to help them determine who influences the buying decisions among industrial users?

18   What are the marketing implications for both buyers and sellers in the fact that a multiple purchasing influence often exists in industrial marketing?

case 3. AURORA ELECTRONICS COMPANY (B)
Analysis of consumer market for FM auto radio

In considering the addition of an FM auto radio to their line of products, executives of the Aurora Electronics Company want to determine whether an adequate potential market exists for this product and to identify this market in as much detail as possible. They particularly want to know the motivation and buying patterns of potential consumers. The company is heavily dependent upon contracts with military agencies in the Federal government. Consequently, management is seeking ways to diversify the product line and thus enter nongovernmental markets. Company engineers have developed an FM auto radio— a three-piece unit which would play through the speaker system of any AM radio already in a car. The FM set would retail for about $125 to $145, installed.

Because the company has no marketing organization of its own, it has retained a firm of marketing consultants to do the preliminary market studies and to conduct some informal investigations in the Chicago area. Interviews with executives in nine FM stations in Chicago and its suburbs have called forth highly enthusiastic responses to the idea of an FM auto radio. These stations, of course, would normally want to encourage anything that increased the ownership and use of FM radios. Several station executives, however, have offered to stock and sell these sets. Others have offered advertising time, either free or at reduced rates.

Interviews with operators of automobile radio stores and repair shops have uncovered mixed reactions. Some are strongly in favor of the product, while others have questioned the merits of a separate FM set. They feel that consumers do not want a separate dial and tuning device hanging under the dashboard or in some other conspicuous spot. These retailers would prefer a combined AM-FM set, and they consider models of the proposed FM set unattractive.

The reception range for FM radios (home or automobile) under usual circumstances is limited to about 25 to 30 miles from the FM station. This means that the market normally would be limited to metropolitan centers having one or more FM stations. The Aurora Company engineer responsible for developing the product feels that its strongest selling features are its fine tone and the absence of sound interference from passing automobiles, overhead wires, and tall buildings. Product-use tests show that he has been a bit strong in his claims. Actually, passing cars do inject some interfering noise into the set.

Consumers who now own and listen to FM sets in their homes are considered prime prospects for the proposed product. These people are also considered a good measure of the potential market. Pulse, Inc., a national marketing research firm which measures audience response to radio and television programs, has made some studies of FM listenership in Chicago, San Diego, and Los Angeles. One of these studies showed that 40 per cent of the Chicago-area homes have AM-FM radios. This constitutes a market of about 800,000 FM homes. Another report showed that 42 per cent of the Chicago homes which have such sets listen to FM radio programs. In Los Angeles, 70 per cent of the FM homes listen to these programs. Market analyses in San Diego reported the following income distribution of families with FM sets:

Family income	Percentage of FM families in each income bracket
Under $4,000	8
$4,000–$7,000	43
$7,000–$10,000	31
Over $10,000	18

In the same study, the reasons given for listening to FM radio were as follows. The figures represent the percentage of people surveyed who mentioned the particular reason.

Reasons	Percentage
Liked the music	51
Limited commercials	31
Better programming than AM stations	15
Better sound than AM stations	14
Relaxation	12
Little talking by announcer	7

Incidentally, 24 per cent of the audience of one San Diego FM station listens only to FM programs.

In general, the executives of the Aurora Company feel that FM would appeal to a broad market of people over twenty-five years of age. The programs feature classical music and have few interruptions. Commercials are limited and are in good taste. With AM radio featuring rock-and-roll music, adults are attracted to FM stations. Consequently, the market for the FM radio seems to have a bright future.

The vice-president of the Aurora Company has brought out the point that home habits regarding FM listenership are not necessarily indicative of the market for FM auto sets. He feels that a person who never listens to FM at home could be an ardent FM fan in the car. While driving, he would prefer the relaxing type of programming found on FM stations.

Another of the company's officers has studied, and been impressed by, the research work done by the *Chicago Tribune* in collaboration with W. Lloyd Warner in the area of social-class structure. This administrator is wondering whether social-class structure or small-group behavior has any potential influence on the market for the FM auto radio. He is interested in identifying groups where the opinion leaders might be prime market targets for this product.

QUESTIONS

1 What characteristics do you think a potential customer for an FM auto radio would have? Consider such things as his age, sex, income, and occupation; whether he has an FM set at home; and any other market factors which you feel are important.

2 Who do you think will make the family buying decision for this product? Who do you think will make the actual purchase?

3 What product features should be used as the main appeals in the company's promotional program?

4 Do you think social-class patterns play a significant role in this case? If so, which of Warner's social classes seem to offer the best potential market?

5 Which small groups do you feel offer the best potential market for this product? What type of opinion leader do you feel exists in these groups?

case 4. CONTINENTAL GYPSUM COMPANY (A)

Analysis of market for an industrial product

The Continental Gypsum Company has recently acquired mineral rights to a vast deposit of extraordinarily high-quality gypsum—a deposit large enough to guarantee a supply for many, many years to come. The company is planning to build processing and finishing plants for gypsum products near the site of the mineral deposits. The exact location of the plant will depend upon transportation arrangements and freight rates, which are to be negotiated with one of the railroads servicing the area. Executives in the Continental Company are trying to find out all they can about the marketing of gypsum products. One particular area of their marketing interest involves the characteristics of the market for these products.

For Continental's purposes, all gypsum products may be divided into three groups: (1) uncalcined products (cement retarders, agricultural gypsums, etc.); (2) industrial plasters used in pottery, dental, art, molding, and casting work; and (3) products used for building purposes (wallboard, lath, and building plaster). According to the *Minerals Year-book,* published annually by the U.S. Department of Commerce, the relative importance of these products, both in tonnage and in dollar sales volume, has been approximately as follows for the past several years:

Product group	Tonnage sold, per cent		Dollar sales volume, per cent	
Uncalcined products		25		6
Industrial products				
Building products		75		94
Wallboard	33		55	
Lath	15		20	
Building plaster	22		16	
Others	5		3	
Total		100		100

From the above figures, it is apparent that as housing goes, so goes the market for gypsum products. Continental is especially interested in learning more about the users of gypsum lath and wallboard. The main users of these products are building contractors and construction specialists, called "applicators," who install gypsum wallboard and lath. Applicators tape the wallboard junction spots and then feather the edges, leaving a smooth wallboard surface which is ready for painting or wallpapering. Architects are also influential in determining the extent to which gypsum building products will be used in construction projects.

Building contractors and applicators almost always buy wallboard and lath from lumber and building materials dealers, who in turn buy directly from manufacturers in carload quantities. Wholesalers are rarely used because dealers can buy in large amounts. Warehousing at the wholesale level is not necessary unless the product is shipped by water. Also, contractors rarely buy directly from manufacturers. One reason for the low incidence of direct sales is that retail lumberyards take such a low markup—up to 15 per cent—that it does not pay the contractors to buy directly. Users do not stockpile or carry inventories of wallboard and lath. They wait until they need some on a construction project and then place their orders with a dealer. It is quite common for a contractor to place several orders for a single construction job. The builder or applicator usually wants immediate delivery of his order.

Users ordinarily do not specify any brand preference. The product—gypsum wallboard and lath—is highly standardized among the major producers, such as the United States Gypsum Co., the National Gypsum Co., Fibreboard Products (Pabco), and the Kaiser Gypsum Co. All producers offer similar services to dealers and users. Because of these market conditions, the same delivered price is usually quoted by all producers selling in a given geographical market. Some producers enjoy advantageous freight differentials to their location, and these may be reflected in their quoted prices.

Building materials dealers exhibit a high degree of loyalty to their suppliers. The producers who generally were fair with their dealers in the days when wallboard was in extremely short supply now have the loyal support of these retailers. In an industry where a nondifferentiated product is sold, where brand is not very important, and where all producers sell at the same price in a given market, the factor of dealer loyalty is important. This factor also makes it difficult for a new firm to enter a market.

To break through this situation and get new accounts, a manufacturer's salesmen may approach contractors and applicators directly, getting these users to specify the manufacturer's brand when buying from the local dealer.

QUESTIONS

1. What marketing implications are involved in the above analysis of the market for gypsum lath and wallboard?
2. From the above analysis of industrial users, what marketing problems are faced by the Continental Gypsum Company?
3. Suggest some tactics which a firm might use to enter a geographical market where the company has not previously been represented.

case 5. PARK MANOR CONDOMINIUM*
Analysis of social and psychological market factors

Park Manor is a condominium apartment community located twenty-five minutes from downtown Milwaukee, Wisconsin. (A condominium is a building in which individuals

* Case written by Prof. John M. Hess, University of Colorado.

own separate apartments, but share the ownership and maintenance of common facilities such as halls, roofs, heating systems and outdoor area.) Park Manor was developed especially for individuals who have passed their forty-eighth birthday. In the first five years of its development, the 200-acre development has sold nearly four hundred apartments priced from $18,000 to $27,000, with an aggregate value of some $9 million.

Park Manor differs from the retirement communities which have been so successful on the West Coast and in Florida in that it tries to attract both retired and working individuals. It has succeeded in this attempt, and over two-thirds of the residents are regularly employed. Further, Park Manor has been designed to serve and draw from a local, rather than a national, market. It also differs from the "family" condominiums which have sprouted in most large cities and which abound with children. No one with children under sixteen may live at Park Manor. In other respects, however, Park Manor is similar to the other types of condominium communities. It is attractive, well built, and located on spacious grounds with rapid access to the central city. Numerous recreational and personal-achievement activity opportunities are available. The chief rationale for Park Manor is that it provides "elegant but economical living in a maintenance-free, parklike atmosphere."

Troubled by a significant decline in sales in recent months, the developers, Herbert Klein, Hilton Howard, and Lloyd Franklin, have debated whether they have curtailed the market too severely by their age and no-children barriers. Mr. Howard believes they have already exhausted the "over-forty-eight" market and should lower the minimum age limit. Most present residents, however, view the peaceful, childless atmosphere as a major advantage and would fight such a change. Mr. Franklin contends that the market is hardly touched but that they have drawn too heavily on retired individuals and have not spent enough of their energies attracting working people whose children have left home and who no longer desire a large house with its attendant maintenance problems. Mr. Klein thinks that they have taken the wrong track entirely in terms of their geographic market. Rather than limiting their efforts to the local area, he suggests that Park Manor should attempt to draw retirees from a regional, or even a national, market. He points out that the Chicago area alone has some 200,000 eligible retirees, with an additional 20,000 persons retiring each year: "Just give me 1 per cent of the Chicago retirement market, and I'll be happy."

A recent market study conducted for Park Manor has revealed some public misconceptions and prejudices. There has been a tendency to shift promotional emphasis entirely each time one of the three partners perceives a new market segment which might be approached. This, in turn, has contributed to the public's confusion. A summary statement from the market study report reads as follows:

In review, the chief objections to Park Manor are:

1. Age. Most respondents view Park Manor as an old-people's home. It is clearly identified with the retirement, perhaps even the nursing-home market. Most people, regardless of their age, just do not think they are old enough to move there *yet*.

2. Income. The majority of the respondents identify Park Manor as an expensive, high-income, high-cost place to live. They frequently parroted words from Park Manor's advertising such as "exclusive," "luxurious," and "country-club atmosphere." Another group has taken the economy advertising seriously and sees Park Manor as low-cost housing.

3. Institutionalization. People feel that they would lose their freedom if they moved to Park Manor. They associate the many activities and facilities with regimentation and institutionalism.

4. Not quite respectable. Many respondents perceive Park Manor as being not quite respectable. They suggested that the residents were probably rather shiftless and hedonistic. Words such as "playground," "leisure living," "pleasure," and "fun" were apparently drawn directly from advertising copy by such respondents.

5. Apartment living. Homeowners do not like the idea of living in an apartment, and apartment dwellers do not wish to invest or tie up funds in their residences.

It appears that each segment of the market reads or hears only that portion of the advertising which confirms his feelings that Park Manor is for someone else.

The development company has learned that buying a home and moving are emotion-laden activities and that each segment of the market has substantially different motives for changing residences. Unfortunately, it also appears that the motives of various segments are often at cross-purposes, so appeals to one segment may well alienate other segments. Park Manor, however, can no longer prosper by appealing to one segment of the market, so it must identify and select those market elements which are most compatible.

QUESTIONS

1   Which market should be the prime target for Park Manor?

2   Identify other logical submarkets for Park Manor and indicate which might be approached without alienating other submarkets.

3   What psychological or sociological factors are at work in limiting the market for Park Manor condominium apartments?

PART THREE

THE PRODUCT

8

PRODUCT PLANNING AND DEVELOPMENT

After a careful study and analysis of his market, a marketing manager is in a position to develop a sound total marketing program designed to capture his desired share of the market. He has four "tools" with which to work: his product, distribution structure, price system, and promotional activities. Each of the next four parts of this book (Parts 3 to 6) is devoted to an analysis of one of these tools.

IMPORTANCE OF PRODUCT INNOVATION

Sooner or later, practically every product either is replaced by another one or degenerates into profitless price competition. Most new products are failures! Even among a group of prominent, well-managed companies, the success rate for products which reached the market—while improved—was still only two out of three.[1] Other estimates

[1] *Management of New Products,* 4th ed., Booz, Allen & Hamilton, Inc., New York, 1964, pp. 2, 11–12. A similar study in 1960 by this well-known management consulting firm placed the success rate at one out of two.

covering a broader range of companies place the product failure rate at 80 to 90 per cent or higher.[2] These sobering thoughts should awaken an executive to the necessity and importance of a careful program for planning and developing his products.

Justification of a firm's existence

Fundamentally, the social and economic justification for the existence of a business is its ability to serve and satisfy its customers, whether they are industrial users or ultimate household consumers. A company meets its basic responsibility to society through the medium of its product (using the term broadly here to include nontangible "goods," usually called "services"). Unless it fulfills this mission, a firm should not exist, and normally the competitive forces in our socioeconomic system do not permit its continuation, at least not for long. This is particularly true in a buyers' market, where competition among sellers is fierce.

Here an implicit and corollary social responsibility of business is to make effective use of its resources—particularly to minimize the waste of scarce human resources such as scientific and technical talent. Yet even in leading industrial firms, it is estimated that about 70 per cent of new-product expenditures is on products that never become commercial successes. Of the moneys spent in the scientific and engineering development stage, 80 per cent goes into the development of products that fail.[3]

Marketing programming starts with the product

It has been said that nothing happens until somebody sells something. This is not entirely so. First, there must be something to sell—a product, a service, or an idea. Product planning is the starting point for the entire marketing program in a firm. From inside or outside the firm must come the germ of a product idea. In the latter case, an express demand may come from the market. That is, the question may be asked: Why don't they make a _____? The next step is to get the firm's marketing department to determine whether there is an adequate market for the product and to decide how the product should be planned.

Product is basic profit determinant

Good executive judgment elsewhere cannot offset weaknesses in product planning. A company cannot successfully sell a poor product over the long run. Often it is easy to create a demand for initial sales, but a company needs a good

---

[2] There are some notable exceptions. For a case history of a firm with an especially successful history in new-product marketing, see Lawrence M. Hughes, "The Midas Touch at Johnson's Wax," *Sales Management*, May 18, 1962, p. 37; see also "Sunbeam's 'In' Is Innovation," *Sales Management*, Sept. 4, 1964, p. 36.

[3] *Management of New Products*, pp. 10–11, 24.

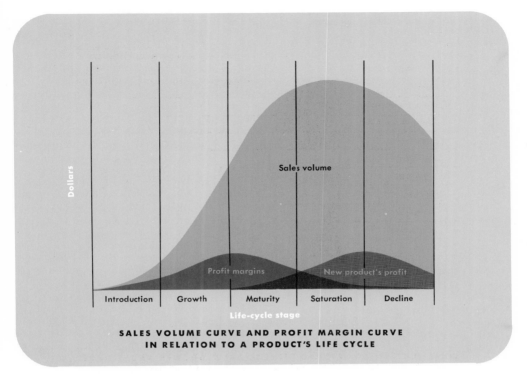

Dollars

Sales volume

Profit margins

New product's profit

| Introduction | Growth | Maturity | Saturation | Decline |

Life-cycle stage

**SALES VOLUME CURVE AND PROFIT MARGIN CURVE
IN RELATION TO A PRODUCT'S LIFE CYCLE**

fig. 8-1

Profit margin usually starts to decline while a product's sales volume is still increasing. How does the relationship between these curves influence the time at which additional new products are introduced?
source: Booz, Allen & Hamilton, Inc.

product to get repeat sales, and repeat sales are needed to stay in business. Problems with channels of distribution are magnified by a poor product. Tactical and strategic skill in pricing is largely wasted on poor products.

New-product planning is essential for sustaining a company's expected rate of profit. Figure 8-1 illustrates a typical relationship between the sales volume curve and the profit margin curve through the life cycle of new products. While similar in shape, the two curves have different timing. The profit curve starts to decline while the volume sales curve is still ascending. Often the sales curve has been the basis for marketing planning. The action of the profit curve, however, suggests that management should gear its product strategy to this curve rather than to the sales curve.

New products are essential to growth

The watchword for management must often be "innovate or die," and this innovating attitude can become a philosophy almost paralleling that of the market-

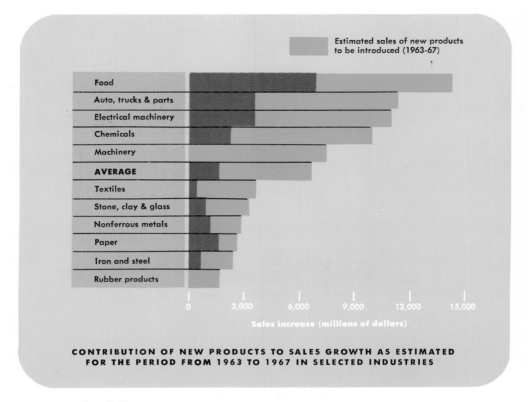

Estimated sales of new products
to be introduced (1963-67)

Food
Auto, trucks & parts
Electrical machinery
Chemicals
Machinery
AVERAGE
Textiles
Stone, clay & glass
Nonferrous metals
Paper
Iron and steel
Rubber products

0   3,000   6,000   9,000   12,000   15,000

Sales increase (millions of dollars)

**CONTRIBUTION OF NEW PRODUCTS TO SALES GROWTH AS ESTIMATED
FOR THE PERIOD FROM 1963 TO 1967 IN SELECTED INDUSTRIES**

fig. 8–2

In an expanding economy, new products contribute substantially to sales growth. For instance, a careful estimate shows that 70 per cent of the sales increase in the electrical machinery industry in the period from 1963–1967 came from products first introduced during that same period.

SOURCE: Booz, Allen & Hamilton, Inc., from Federal Trade Commission and McGraw-Hill data.

ing concept. Peter Drucker recognized the coimportance of the two concepts when he said, "Because it is its purpose to create a customer, any business enterprise has two—and only these two—basic functions: marketing and innovation."[4]

Many companies will get a substantial percentage of their sales volume and net profits this year from products which did not exist five to ten years ago, and this situation undoubtedly will continue. Even in short-term plans, new products are a major factor in company growth. Figure 8–2 shows the dollar sales increase estimated (in 1964) for the period 1963–1967 in eleven industries

[4] Peter Drucker, *The Practice of Management*, Harper & Row, Publishers, Incorporated, New York, 1954, p. 37.

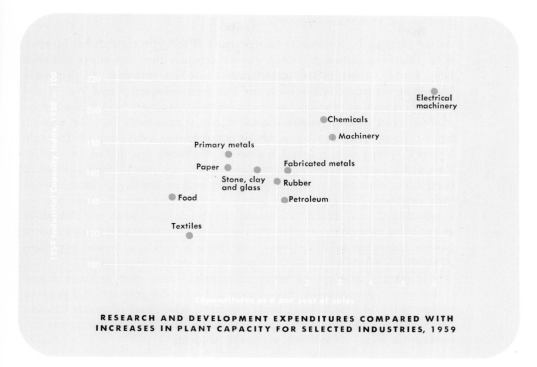

RESEARCH AND DEVELOPMENT EXPENDITURES COMPARED WITH
INCREASES IN PLANT CAPACITY FOR SELECTED INDUSTRIES, 1959

fig. 8–3

*There is usually a close relationship between the amount of research and development
expenditures and increases in plant capacity in a given industry. Growth industries are
typically new-product oriented and spend a great deal on research and development. Compare the electrical machinery and textiles industries.*
SOURCE: Booz, Allen & Hamilton, Inc.

and the share of this growth which was expected from new products. From 46
per cent (for paper products) to 100 per cent (for rubber goods) of the sales
increase was anticipated from new products; the eleven-industry average was
75 per cent.[5]

Using historical perspective, the Booz, Allen & Hamilton studies note the
fact that growth industries are new-product-oriented. Figure 8–3 shows a comparison between research and development expenditures of, and growth rates
in, selected industries from 1950 to 1959. Expenditures for research and development are assumed to be a reasonable indication of new-product effort. Figure
8-3 shows generally that the industries spending the most for new-product development have enjoyed the greatest rates of growth.

[5] *Management of New Products*, p. 6.

As the years go by, consumers become more selective in their choice of products. This point, although probably more nebulous than the others discussed here, further attests to the importance of product planning. As disposable income in the hands of the consumer has increased since World War II and as an abundance of products has been available, consumers have fulfilled many of their wants. The big middle-income market is reasonably well fed, clothed, housed, transported, and equipped. In our economy today, one of Thorstein Veblen's theories may be found in practice. His theory was that as members of a social class attain means to accumulate wealth, they pass through a period of conspicuous consumption, during which they acquire worldly goods to impress their neighbors. When they have proven to themselves that they can pay for a large house, a trip abroad, or a second car, these people switch to a philosophy and practice of conspicuous *underconsumption*. They buy small foreign cars or compact American cars. They need not continue to buy additional mountains of goods to impress people because people are already impressed.

If market satiation—in terms of quantity—does exist to some extent, it follows that the consumer may be more critical in his appraisal of a product, more selective in what he buys, better informed, more aware of quality differentials, and more responsive to improved labeling. It is possible that a case can be made for rising, albeit slowly, consumer standards.

MEANING OF THE "PRODUCT"

In a very narrow sense, a product is simply a set of tangible physical and chemical attributes or characteristics assembled in an identifiable and readily recognizable form. Each different product category carries a commonly understood descriptive name, such as apples, steel, shoes, or baseball bats. Product attributes appealing to consumer motivation or buying patterns play no part in the definition. A Sunbeam Shavemaster and a Remington Rollectric are one and the same product—an electric shaver.

A broader interpretation recognizes each separate brand as a separate product. In this sense a Kuppenheimer man's suit and a Hickey-Freeman man's suit are two different products. So too, Squibb's aspirin and Bayer aspirin are separate products, even though the only physical or chemical difference may be the imprint of the brand name on the aspirin tablet. The brand name suggests a product difference to the consumer. Thus the concept of consumer want satisfaction begins to enter the picture.

Carrying the analysis further, we can see that an RCA television set bought in a discount house on a cash-and-carry, no-service-guarantee basis is a different product from the identical model purchased in a department store, where the customer buys the set for a higher price but gets it on credit, has it delivered free of extra charge, and avails himself of other store services. Again the interpretation of "product" is broadened, and we come nearer to a definition valuable to marketing men.

Our definition is as follows: a *product* is a complex of tangible and intangible attributes, including packaging, color, price, manufacturer's prestige, retailer's prestige, and manufacturer's and retailer's services, which the buyer may accept as offering satisfaction of wants or needs.

Any change in a physical feature (design, color, size, packaging, etc.), however minor it may be, creates, in effect, a new product. The seller has an opportunity to use a new set of appeals to reach what may be essentially a new market. When the manufacturers of Marlboro and Philip Morris cigarettes came out with the flip-top boxes, this packaging change created a new product. Schlitz beer in a 12-ounce can is a different product from Schlitz beer in a 12-ounce bottle. The economy-size tube of Pepsodent is not the same product as the giant or family-size tube. Mennen's shave cream, Rise, became three products when ingredients in the basic item were modified to create Rise with Lanolin, Rise with Menthol, and Rise Regular.

The key idea in our definition of a product is that the consumer is buying more than a set of chemical and physical attributes. Fundamentally he is buying want satisfaction. A wise firm sells product *benefits* rather than just the product. As Elmer Wheeler, an author and well-known sales training consultant says, "Don't sell the steak, sell the sizzle." A travel agency should not sell a two-week Caribbean cruise; rather, it should sell romance, glamour, rest, a chance to meet people, and the opportunity for education.

Manufacturers sell symbols as well as products. "People buy things not only for what they can do, but also for what they mean."[6] Goods are psychological symbols of personal attributes, goals, and social patterns. As was suggested in Chapter 5, "Consumer Motivation and Behavior," we buy products which reinforce our self-image or self-concept, and people are shrewd judges of symbols.

In summary, any combination of these tangible and intangible attributes can constitute a separate product because each combination can result in a different set of product benefits or consumer want satisfactions. Thus the opportunity to differentiate products is seemingly limitless.

RELATED TERMS

In addition to "product" and "product policies," one will hear such terms as "product planning," "product development," and "merchandising" and may wonder what they mean and how they are related. *Product* is the key concept

---

[6] Sidney J. Levy, "Symbols for Sale," *Harvard Business Review*, July–August, 1959, p. 118.

here. *Product policies* are managerial guides regarding what products will be made or sold and what attributes these products will have.

Product planning and product development

Product planning embraces all activities which enable producers and middle-men to determine what should constitute a company's line of products. Ideally, product planning will ensure that the full complement of a firm's products are logically related, individually justifiable items, designed to strengthen the company's competitive and profit position. It requires an estimate of the industry's market potential, the company's sales potential, the cost requirements, and the profit possibilities of products to determine whether product development is feasible. "Product development," a more limited term, encompasses the technical activities of product research, engineering, and design. Here we are concerned with product innovation or improvement and are working with production, research, and engineering departments.

More specifically, the scope of product-planning and product-development activities includes decision making and programming in the following areas:

1.   Which products should the firm make and which should it buy?

2.   Should the company expand or simplify its line?

3.   What new uses are there for each item?

4.   Is the quality right for the intended use and market?

5.   What brand, package, and label should be used for each product?

6.   How should the product be styled and designed, and in what sizes, colors, and materials should it be produced?

7.   In what quantities should each item be produced, and what inventory controls should be established?

8.   How should the product be priced? (Part 5 is devoted entirely to the price system.)

Merchandising

"Merchandising" is probably one of the two most loosely used terms in the marketing vocabulary. (The other, "sales promotion," is discussed in Part 6.) Merchandising means many things to many people. To some it is synonymous with marketing; to others it is the all-inclusive term, and marketing is only a part of merchandising. Retailers make particularly heavy use of the word as a verb, noun, or adjective. A clothing buyer may be complimented for having "merchandised" a new sports shirt very well this season. Another executive may claim that sound merchandising is the foundation of a store's success. A third may note that the merchandising plans for next season are completed. One of the high-level executives in a department store is the merchandising manager, and normally retail stores have no one with the title "marketing manager" or "sales manager."

In this book, merchandising is synonymous with product planning. That is, merchandising includes all planning activities of manufacturers and middlemen designed to adapt or adjust their products to the market demand.

Merchandising by manufacturers versus merchandising by middlemen

While it is true that most manufacturers are concerned with what to *make* and most middlemen are concerned with what to *buy*, one thing that is even more fundamental is that both groups are concerned with what to *sell*. The goals of product planning by manufacturers and middlemen are similar. Both want their merchandising to be market-oriented—to please a consumer by satisfying his wants. In fact, manufacturers and middlemen often work jointly or cooperatively to reach this goal. For instance, some high-quality furniture stores take a customer's order for an individually tailored bedspread or for a sofa covered with individually selected fabrics and then relay the order to a prearranged manufacturer. Very often retailers or wholesalers provide ideas which result in new mass-produced articles or refinements on established products.

THE DECISION TO MAKE OR BUY

One of the first product problems calling for a decision is whether to make a product or buy it. All manufacturers must wrestle with this problem, while most retailers and wholesalers automatically think in terms of buying. Some large retail food chains, variety chains, and department stores, however, do make their own bakery goods and candy. Other firms, such as Sears, Roebuck and Company, establish such rigid product specifications, work so closely with the product department of a manufacturer, and take such a large percentage of the firm's output that for all practical purposes they are making rather than buying.

A firm may solve its make-or-buy problem at some in-between point. For example, it may decide simply to assemble a series of premanufactured and prefitted parts. Other firms may decide to make some parts and buy others and then assemble them. Furniture manufacturers usually follow this approach. In still another situation, an enterprise may assemble premanufactured parts and then paint, polish, or otherwise finish the end product. Automobiles, generally, are a case in point. Often many of the final parts, such as engines, call for make-or-buy decisions with respect to the components of the part. That is, an automobile manufacturer must decide whether to make or buy spark plugs, gaskets, valves, engine blocks, and other units making up the completed engines.

There are no pat solutions: one firm may be moving toward making, while another may be moving away. As in so many other phases of marketing, the answer is, "It depends." Whether to make or buy a product depends upon the outcome of management's careful analysis of several issues, such as the following:[7]

1.   Relative costs of making or buying.

2.   Extent to which specialized machinery, techniques, and production resources are needed.

3.   Availability of production capacity.

4.   Managerial time and talents required—the amount of production supervision needed.

5.   Secrecy of design, style, and materials—the extent to which the company wants its processing methods kept secret. Because of a patent situation, what the firm wants may be available only through buying.

6.   The attractiveness of the investment necessary to make a product.

7.   Willingness to accept seasonal, cyclical, and other market risks. If a company decides to buy, the supplier can still shift some of these risks to the purchasing manufacturer by requiring a contract guaranteeing acceptance of a certain quantity of the product.

8.   Risk of depending upon outside sources—will they raise price, cut off relationships, etc.?

9.   Extent of reciprocity present—is the supplier of the item also a customer for the firm's other products?

This make-or-buy analysis has been centered on items which will be resold. Manufacturers also face a make-or-buy decision with respect to the machinery, supplies, and equipment used in their production processes, office work, and marketing activities. A manufacturer of refrigerators must decide whether to make or buy not only the parts in the refrigerator, but also the presses, motors, conveyor belts, office chairs, salesmen's demonstration kits, and so on.

ORGANIZING FOR PRODUCT INNOVATION

Product innovation is a top-management responsibility; the major problems in the management of a new-product program require the attention of the top executives in a company. These conclusions have been reached in several studies of programs for product planning and development. To be effectively managed, these programs must be effectively organized and controlled. In one study of major problems encountered in new-product programs, more than four out of five (81 per cent) of the companies—and these were experienced, well-managed firms with relative success in new products—identified some kind of problem

---

[7] See Carter C. Higgins, "Make-or-Buy Re-examined," *Harvard Business Review*, March–April, 1954, pp. 109–119. For an earlier analysis, see James W. Culliton, *Make or Buy*, Harvard University Bureau of Business Research, Business Research Studies, no. 27, Boston, 1942. Culliton's general, but qualified, recommendation points up the difficulty of the decision.

relating to organization. Organizational problems constituted over one-half (55 per cent) of all those mentioned by the reporting firms.[8]

Even in face of the generally recognized importance of new products, most companies have no organization for product planning and development. After examining several studies, one authority concluded that formal organization for this activity exists in something less than one-third (25 to 30 per cent) of American manufacturing firms.[9] Furthermore, in most of these cases, product planning and development is a new managerial activity; a formal organization dates back only a few years and is often in a state of flux.

Need for constructive, innovating attitude

While it is helpful to have a well-designed organizational framework within which to carry on the product-planning and product-development functions, a more important key to success is the *attitude* which the entire company has toward planning and developing products. The right attitude toward planning and developing products must permeate all levels of managerial thinking. This "right" attitude is one that constructively encourages—in fact, thrives on—innovation.

Management should have a critical attitude, but its criticism must be constructive, not destructive. When management reacts to new-product ideas with the philosophy, "We have been doing it this way for twenty years, why do you want to change it?" or "You will have to convince me that this product will be successful before I will approve it," management is an impediment to growth. Some managers can test a new product to death. They are forever wanting to run another product or market test and then wait for the findings, with the result that the item never does reach the stage of a full-scale marketing program.

Potential problems in organization

In some organizations—the Jell-O division of General Foods, for example—the responsibility for new-product development is separated from product-planning activities (such as finding new uses for a product and making package or color changes) which are related to the improvement or modification of established products. This kind of situation, where the division of responsibility is not always sharply demarcated, can create real managerial problems, and careful administrative coordination is an absolute requirement. Effectiveness is greatly reduced if the two separate organizational units strongly disagree over whether a given item is a brand-new product and thus should be developed

[8] *Management of New Products*, pp. 16–17.
[9] Hector Lazo, "New Products: Are We Organized for Them?" *Industrial Marketing*, December, 1963, p. 82.

by department A or whether it is an improvement on an already existing product and thus should be assigned to department B.

Regardless of the organizational setup, there may be a shift in responsibility as the product moves through the various stages from the inception of the idea to a full-scale marketing program. A new-product development manager may be responsible for the initial development and market testing. Then at an appropriate time, responsibility may be handed over to a product manager, who carries the product to its fulfillment as a nationally marketed item. If the product manager is already satisfied with the growth rate and profit results in his department, however, he may not want to take on a new, untried product which will cause disruption in his scheduled routine. The many possibilities for a breakdown in communications and operations are apparent. Also, the vital importance of a proper innovating attitude is once again pointed up.

Types of organization

At the outset, it should be emphasized that there is no "one best type" of organizational structure for new-product planning and development, nor does any one type seem to be selected by a large majority of manufacturers. The type which is most effective for any given firm will depend upon the company's size, products, and managerial abilities and philosophies and upon other circumstances.

As one criterion, an organizational structure may be considered useful for product innovation if it enables management to implement effectively the processes of specialization and coordination. While these are basic processes in any organization, they are especially key ingredients in a company's organizational mix pertaining to new-product planning and development. As specialists in the research, production, and sales area all work on product innovation, they typically develop different viewpoints and work better in different organizational structures. While these specializations and differences may improve the innovative research and development, they may also contribute to disagreements which can impede product innovation. At this point in the innovative process, a company must depend upon its organization structure to provide a counterbalancing provision for coordination so that the executives with diverse points of view can resolve their differences of opinion and progress with a unity of effort.[10] The effective coordination of the specialized processes can do much to forestall some potential organization problems such as those observed in the preceding section.

In medium- and large-sized companies which have enjoyed relative success in new-product marketing, apparently the popular trend is to locate the organizational responsibility for product planning and development in one of the

---

[10] Jay W. Lorsch and Paul R. Lawrence, "Organizing for Product Innovation," *Harvard Business Review*, January–February, 1965, pp. 109–122.

following: (1) product-planning committee or team, (2) new-product department, or (3) product managers. Historically, the responsibility for developing new products was usually placed in the production-oriented departments, such as engineering or product research. This location may still be justified if the product planning is not complex and the product line is limited to a few items, such as large installations.

In a small company, the president is usually directly responsible for product planning. While his decisions probably create very little friction or jealousy within the firm, at the same time he is often too busy to give much attention to this important activity. It may surprise some marketing men to find out that only a very small proportion—something like 10 per cent—of all companies, large or small, assign product-planning and product-development responsibilities to the marketing department.[11] Product-planning executives usually report directly to the president, to an executive vice-president, or to the vice-president of some department other than marketing—usually production or research and development.

In the years immediately ahead, it is expected that an increasing number of companies will establish a separate organizational unit to handle new-product development. Today's highly competitive market forces companies to recognize this activity as a full-time administrative responsibility. In parallel action, management is realizing that full-time administration is also required to maintain and expand markets for existing products.

Product-planning committee   Today the most widely used organizational structure for new-product planning and development is probably the committee, with heavy representation from top management. The firm's president and men from the marketing, production, engineering, research, and finance departments usually are involved.

In a committee, the ideas and wisdom of several executives can be pooled; any new product which results is likely to win the approval of the administrators who took part in its planning and development. On the other hand, committee activity takes much valuable executive time and slows the decision-making process. Also, the committee structure makes it difficult to place responsibility for managerial actions and may even serve as a "buck-passing" device.

Many companies which use a new-product development committee also have a product manager who is responsible for marketing the item after it has successfully passed through the necessary testing and other introductory stages of development. In other instances, a new-product department has evolved as the next step beyond a product-planning committee, but the company will still retain the committee as an advisory group to evaluate new-product ideas and development plans. Some companies establish a new-product team— a close relative of the committee—to guide the planning, development, and

[11] Lazo, *op. cit.*, pp. 84–85.

marketing of a new item. In fact, such a team may later constitute the nucleus of a formal department responsible for commercially marketing the product.

New-product department   In recent years a separate and formally organized department devoted to new-product planning and development has been created in an increasing number of America's large, best-known manufacturing firms. In the 1964 Booz, Allen & Hamilton study, 86 per cent of the companies surveyed had established new-product departments, in contrast to 56 per cent in the 1960 study and only 22 per cent in 1956.[12] As suggested earlier, these departments have often evolved as the next logical step beyond a product-planning committee. Although there are some exceptions, generally the departments are relatively small, containing no more than four or five people, and frequently these are one-man departments. Usually the head of this department reports to the president, or the department itself may be one division of a staff unit directly serving the president. Typically these departments have administrative responsibility for such new-product tasks as determining objectives and programs, recommending new projects, planning the activities, generating and screening ideas, guiding the new products through the various developmental stages, and coordinating the new-product activities involving other departments. When a product is ready for full-scale commercial marketing, it is turned over to the appropriate operating department.

This organizational pattern has the advantage of making new-product development a full-time activity, so there is less risk that it will become a stepchild in a department which is more concerned with day-to-day, short-range problems. The Booz, Allen & Hamilton studies identify two operating weaknesses sometimes found in new-product departments. One is the failure to plan thoroughly just how the department will operate; the other is the failure to staff the department with a man who has the background and prestige to gain from other executives the cooperation and support necessary for success.

Product manager   The structure which activates the concept of the product manager is another widely used form of organization for product planning and development. Normally, however, a product manager's responsibility is *not* limited to new products. This executive is ordinarily an administrator in the marketing department who reports to the chief marketing executive. The scope of his activities and responsibilities varies widely among different companies, which is probably as it should be in that businesses differ in their product and market requirements. In companies at one end of the spectrum, the product manager's activities may be limited essentially to selling and sales-promotional work; or, as in one grocery products manufacturing company,

[12] *Management of New Products*, p. 20.

his efforts may be devoted primarily to packaging, advertising, and sales promotion.[13]

For effective product planning and development, other firms—the National Biscuit Company, Pillsbury, Kimberly-Clark (Kleenex), Colgate-Palmolive, and Procter & Gamble, for example—find it more useful to view the product manager's job as involving a much broader and more complex group of activities.[14] In such cases, this executive, sometimes called a "brand manager," is responsible for planning the complete marketing program for his brand or group of products. Thus, he may be concerned with new-product development as well as the improvement of existing goods. His responsibilities may encompass such activities as setting marketing goals and planning marketing strategies, pricing, developing advertising and sales-promotional plans, preparing budgets, and helping field sales managers and salesmen to do a more effective selling job.

As an organizational structure, product management seems to be a preferred alternative when the company is a multiproduct business but when it is *not* practical to have physically separated sales forces, advertising departments, or other marketing groups. Use of a product manager in these cases means that individual attention can be paid to each product without separating the line operating divisions by products.

Probably the biggest single problem most companies face in the use of a product manager is that they saddle him with great responsibility and yet refuse to give him the corresponding authority. Outside his own department, the product manager has no line authority in the classical organizational sense. He cannot, for example, order the salesmen or sales managers to do something. Even though advertising may be critical to the success of his plans, the product manager does not select the advertising agency. Perhaps the most burdensome aspect of the product manager's responsibility is that he is made accountable for the profitability of his brand and yet is often denied any control over production costs, setting of prices, or determination of advertising budgets.[15]

PRODUCT INNOVATION IN MATURE AND GROWTH INDUSTRIES

While a sound product-planning and product-development program is essential to the competitive success of a business, innovation alone is not the *sole* de-

[13] See B. Charles Ames, "Payoff from Product Management," *Harvard Business Review*, November–December, 1963, pp. 141–152.

[14] See Robert M. Fulmer, "Product Management: Panacea or Pandora's Box?" *California Management Review*, Summer, 1965, pp. 63–74.

[15] For a review of additional constraints placed on the product manager and for a six-point program to improve the effectiveness of this type of organization, see David J. Luck and Theodore Nowak, "Product Management: Vision Unfulfilled," *Harvard Business Review*, May–June, 1965, pp. 143–154.

terminant of a firm's growth. After new products have been developed, they must be effectively financed and produced, properly priced and channeled to the market, and finally sold and delivered.

The stress on product innovation may also make us forget that the advantages of a new product are usually temporary. This is true whether the firm is in a "growth" industry, where the annual rate of growth is large, or in a "mature" industry, where growth rate is small. In either type of industry, it is extremely difficult to achieve effective patent protection for any period of time. If a firm develops, patents, and markets a new item which appears to have a large market, a competitor will soon come out with a product which does not infringe on the first company's patents but which is so similar that consumers' wants can be satisfied with either item. Sometimes in a rapid-growth industry, such as plastics, electronics, or some of the miracle drugs, a firm cannot even recoup its product-development costs before a competitive firm makes the first product virtually obsolete.

In more mature industries a similar situation exists. A manufacturer who markets a Dacron suit or an Acrilan shirt is soon copied. The first washing machine manufacturer to market an effective low-cost machine which cleans clothes electronically without soap or water will find that many of his competitors have a reasonably comparable item. Furthermore, in mature industries a "new product" is usually only a modification of an existing item. Relatively minor changes, such as sugarcoating the cornflakes or adding a lint collector to a washing machine, are rapidly and easily copied. Consequently, sound marketing and general business management are needed in addition to product innovation if a firm is to achieve competitive market success over the long run.

DEVELOPMENT OF NEW PRODUCTS

As a new product is developed and produced, it progresses from the idea stage to the production and marketing stage. Although it may seem to follow no particular pattern, we may say that, in general, it follows the steps outlined below. Since several of the steps are taken concurrently, proper managerial coordination and timing are essential.[16]

1. Generation of new-product ideas. New-product development starts with an idea. Excellent ideas may come from salesmen or servicemen, nonmarketing employees, consumers or industrial users, middlemen, governmental agencies, competitive products, trade associations, private research organizations, and inventors. The particular source of ideas is not nearly so important as is the company's system for stimulating new ideas and then acknowledging and reviewing them promptly.

---

[16] For a more detailed outline of activities involved in each of the six stages, see *Management of New Products*, pp. 26–28.

2.   Screening of ideas. Determine which ideas warrant further study. This is only the first of several screening reviews the product will receive.

3.   Business analysis. The idea is expanded into a concrete business proposal in which management (1) identifies product features, (2) estimates market demand and product's profitability, (3) establishes a program to develop the product, and (4) assigns responsibility for further study of the product's feasibility.[17]

4.   Product development. Convert the idea-on-paper into a physical product. Manufacture pilot models or small quantities to designated specifications. Conduct laboratory tests and other technical evaluations necessary to determine the engineering and production feasibility of the article.

5.   Test marketing. Plan and conduct market tests, in-use tests, and other commercial experiments in limited geographical areas in order to ascertain the feasibility of the full marketing program. In this stage, design and production factors may have to be adjusted as a result of test findings. At this point management must make a final decision regarding whether to market the product commercially.

6.   Commercialization. Plan full-scale production and marketing programs and then launch the product.[18] Up to this point in the development process, management has virtually complete control over the product. Once the product is "born," however, and enters its life cycle (as discussed later), the external competitive environment becomes a major determinant of the product's destiny.

In reviewing the six-step evolution, management should realize that the first three stages—the idea or concept stages—are the critical ones. Not only are they less expensive—each stage becomes progressively more expensive in dollars and scarce manpower—but, more importantly, experiences of companies indicate that most products fail because either the idea or the timing was wrong, and not because the company lacked the production or marketing know-how. Studies also indicate, fortunately, that companies in general are doing a better job of eliminating product ideas of limited potential before they reach the more expensive stages of development. However, wide variations do exist in the effectiveness of companies' development programs.

To improve the effectiveness of their new-product-development programs, an increasing number of companies are employing PERT (Program Evaluation and Review Technique) as a managerial tool to aid in the planning and

[17] For a profit-analysis methodology which illustrates how different combinations of price, advertising, and personal selling will yield different estimates of profit potential, see Philip Kotler, "Marketing Mix Decisions for New Products," *Journal of Marketing Research*, February, 1964, pp. 43–48.

[18] For case histories of six new-product successes which illustrate how the launching risks were overcome by careful consideration of timing, market conditions, competition, and other factors critical in a product's introduction, see "Why Certain New Products Survive," *Printers' Ink*, Feb. 8, 1963, p. 21.

control of the programs. Introduced originally for use in the aerospace industry, it is claimed that the successful application of PERT enabled the Navy to launch the Polaris missile two years ahead of schedule. The use of PERT can aid tremendously in surmounting problems in coordinating, timing, and scheduling the many activities in the new-product-development process.[19]

Manufacturers' criteria for new products

Insofar as possible, a manufacturer should establish objective bench marks against which he can measure a prospective addition to his product line:[20]

1. There should be an adequate market demand. This is the first and by far the most important criterion to apply to a proposed product. Too often management begins with a question such as, "Can we use our present sales force?" or "Will the new item fit into our production system?" The basic question is: Do enough people really want our product? Administrators should try to get quantitative measures of the size and location of the potential market.

2. The product should fit into the company's present marketing structure. The general marketing experience and management of the company are important here. The Sunbeam Corporation would probably find it easy to add another kitchen appliance to its line, whereas a paint manufacturer would find it quite difficult to add margarine to his. Certainly the Armour Company would have had an easier (although hardly more successful) marketing job several years ago if it had added a line of frozen meats instead of getting into the fiercely competitive soap field with its product Dial. Sometimes the general marketing relationship may not be apparent at first. Many people questioned the wisdom of Procter & Gamble's move in adding Gleem toothpaste to its list of products. On closer observation, however, it can be seen that the marketing of Gleem is similar in many respects to the marketing of Tide, Ivory, and other Procter & Gamble soap products. Gleem is a consumer convenience product which will be distributed, priced, and promoted in much the same manner as consumer soaps and detergents.

More specific questions may also be asked regarding the marketing fit of new products: Can the existing sales force be used? Do the salesmen have the time and ability to sell the new product? Can the present middlemen and channels of distribution be used? If the company has a service organization,

---

[19] See also Yung Wong, "Critical Path Analysis for New Product Planning," *Journal of Marketing*, October, 1964, pp. 53–59.

[20] For an example of a system for evaluating new products, see John T. O'Meara, Jr., "Selecting Profitable Products," *Harvard Business Review*, January–February, 1961, pp. 83–89; for an evaluation matrix which quantifies in a systematic and structured manner some of the qualitative considerations involved in selecting new products, see Barry M. Richman, "A Rating Scale for Product Innovation," *Business Horizons*, Summer, 1962, pp. 37–44.

can it handle the new product, or must a new structure be established? Will the new product compete or conflict with other products in the company's line?

3. The product should fit into the company's present production structure. A new-product idea will be more favorably received if the item fits in with existing production facilities, manpower, and management.

4. The product should fit from a financial standpoint. With regard to the financial criteria for a new product, at least three questions should be asked: Is adequate financing available and feasible? Will the new item increase seasonal and cyclical stability in the firm? Are the profit possibilities worthwhile? Here again some objective criteria are needed to decide what a "worthwhile" profit is. Some products must cover the total costs their production incurs, while others may be considered satisfactory if they cover only their variable costs and contribute something to overhead. The latter type may be acceptable when they are added only to satisfy middlemen who want a full line from a manufacturer.

5. Legal considerations should be satisfactory. Before accepting a new product, management should make certain that there are no legal objections. Patents must be registered or applied for, labeling and packaging must observe all pertinent regulations, and so on.

6. Management of adequate ability should be available. It is important that the executives in the company have the necessary time and ability to handle the proposed new product.

7. The product should be in keeping with the company's overall image, self-concept, and objectives. Caution should be exercised to ensure that the proposed product does not run counter to the company's goals. A firm stressing low-priced, low-margin, high-turnover products normally should not add an item which shouts prestige or status.

Middlemen's criteria for new products

A middleman who is trying to determine whether to add a new product to his line must consider all the criteria that a manufacturer would, except those related to production. He has, in addition, two further points to consider:

1. Relations with manufacturer. Before accepting a new product, a middleman in wholesaling or retailing should consider the reputation of the manufacturer. A middleman should examine the possibility of acquiring exclusive sales rights in a given geographic territory. He must be sure that he can get an adequate supply. In the ready-to-wear fields, a retailer often will not place an original order unless he is guaranteed delivery of reorders within a certain number of days after placing them. A retailer should also consider the nature and amount of promotional help given by the manufacturer.

2. In-store policies and practices. A retailer has to study the type of selling effort a new product will require. He must consider how the proposed product fits in with in-store policies and practices regarding mechanical service, clothing alteration, credit, and delivery. Stores using self-service ordinarily do not want to add items requiring extensive demonstration and personal selling; for this reason, supermarkets tend to carry very little in the way of clothing and appliances. Some food chains have experimented with large appliances, such as television sets and refrigerators, however, and their experience may prove that the type of selling used in a store does not necessarily prohibit the addition of such items.

Importance of timing

An analysis of case histories will show that new-product development is considerably more time-consuming than many marketing executives realize.[21] As a result of underestimating the time needed for orderly development, management may take shortcuts in some of the developmental stages, the result frequently being product failure. In many cases, five, ten, or more years (television took fifty-five years, and Talon zippers took thirty years) have elapsed between the time the new-product idea was born, or development was started, and the date the product was introduced in test markets. This means that a company should have several new products in the development hopper at any given time.

Proper timing is of the utmost importance in every stage leading to the introduction of a new product. Managerial decisions involving time generally start with a determination of when to offer the product for sale. If the product has an annual model change or if it is intended primarily for a special occasion or given season, the decision is reasonably easy. If the product is to be sold to the industrial market, or if it affects the use of other products now in the hands of retailers and wholesalers, timing can create many problems for management.

After deciding when the product will be offered for sale to the ultimate consumer or industrial user, the producer must determine when the product will be sold to the wholesalers and retailers. Arrangements must be made to reduce inventories of the old product and build up stocks of the new. The physical distribution of the product must be dovetailed with the promotional program so that supplies will be on hand when advertising is released and the personal salesmen start selling.

CONCEPT OF THE PRODUCT LIFE CYCLE

Products, like people, have life cycles. From its birth to its death, a product exists in different stages and in different competitive environments. Its adjust-

---

[21] Lee Adler, "Time Lag in New Product Development," *Journal of Marketing,* January, 1966, pp. 17–21.

ment to these environments determines to a great degree just how successful its life will be. One set of product strategies employed by many firms is built around the understanding and management of the life cycles of their products.[22] To better manage the cycle, it is useful to divide a product's life into six stages —introduction, growth, maturity, saturation, decline, and abandonment.

The length of the life cycle will vary as between products, ranging from a few weeks or a short season (a fad or an apparel fashion) to several decades (autos, telephones). The shape of the sales and profit curves may vary somewhat among products, although the basic shape and the relationship between the two curves is usually about the same as pictured in Fig. 8–1. Even the duration of each stage may be different among products; some take years to pass through the introductory stage, while others are accepted in a few weeks. Certainly not all companies' products go through all stages; some may fail in the introductory stage, and other firms may not enter with their brand until the market is in the growth or maturity stage. In virtually all cases, however, decline and possible abandonment are inevitable because (1) the need for the product disappears (as when frozen orange juice generally replaced juice squeezers), (2) a better or less expensive product is developed to fill the same need (plastics are replacing wood, metal, and paper in many products), or (3) a competitor does a superior marketing job.[23]

Marketing and environmental characteristics of each stage

It is quite important that management recognize what part of the life cycle its product is in at any given time, because the competitive environment and the resultant marketing strategies and programs will ordinarily differ depending upon the stage. A brief summary of the competitive environment and some of the marketing reactions which typify each stage may be useful here.[24]

Introduction   During the first stage of a product's life cycle, it is launched into the market in a full-scale production and marketing program. It has gone through the embryonic stages of idea screening, pilot models, and test marketing. The entire product may be new, as in the case of a machine which cleans clothes electronically without using any water, or the basic product may be well known, but a new feature or accessory is in the introductory stage—a gas turbine engine in an automobile, for example. In still another situation, a product may be well accepted in some market segments, but be in the pioneer-

[22] See, for example, Theodore Levitt, "Exploit the Product Life Cycle," *Harvard Business Review*, November–December, 1965, pp. 81–94.

[23] Donald K. Clifford, Jr., "Leverage in the Product Life Cycle," *Dun's Review and Modern Industry*, May, 1965, p. 62.

[24] For an excellent and more detailed analysis of the characteristics of each stage, see Thomas A. Staudt and Donald A. Taylor, *A Managerial Introduction to Marketing*, Prentice-Hall, Inc., Englewood Cliffs, N.J., 1965, chap. 8.

ing stage in other markets. Introductory promotion was needed (and in many cases still is) to sell automatic dishwashers to housewives, air travel to old folks, and home freezers to consumers long after these products and services were well accepted in some markets.

In many respects, the pioneering stage is the most risky and expensive one, as witness the high percentage of product failures in this period, even among firms with a reasonably successful history of new-product introductions. Operations in the introductory period are characterized by high costs, low sales volume, and limited distribution. For really new products, there is very little direct competition. The promotional program stimulates primary, rather than secondary, demand; that is, the type of product rather than the seller's brand is emphasized.

Growth   In the growth, or market-acceptance, stage, both the sales and the profit curves rise, often at a rapid rate. Competitors enter the market, and in large numbers if the profit outlook is particularly attractive. Sellers shift to "buy-my-brand" rather than "try-my-product" promotional strategy. The number of distribution outlets increases, economies of scale are introduced, and prices may come down a bit.

Maturity and saturation   Sometimes it is difficult to tell whether we are dealing with two separate stages or simply separate parts of one stage. During the first part of the period, we see sales still increasing but at a decreasing rate. While the sales curve is leveling off, the profits of both the manufacturer and the retailers are starting to decline. Marginal producers are forced to drop out of the market. Price competition becomes increasingly severe, and the producer assumes a greater share of the total promotional effort as he fights to retain his dealers and the shelf space in their stores. New models are introduced as manufacturers broaden their line, and trade-in sales become significant.

As the market reaches the saturation stage, each of the characteristics in the preceding paragraph is intensified. Replacement sales become a major factor, and the sales curve will react to changes in economic conditions. Good middlemen become particularly important.

Decline and possible abandonment   For virtually all products, obsolescence sets in inevitably as new products start their own life cycle and replace the old ones. Cost control becomes increasingly important as demand drops. Advertising declines, and a number of competitors withdraw from the market. Whether the product has to be abandoned or the surviving sellers can continue on a profitable basis in a specialized, limited market often depends upon management's abilities.

Management of the product life cycle

The shape of a product's sales and profit curves is not inevitable in a company; to a surprising extent, the shape can be controlled, or managed. One key to life-cycle management is to forecast the profile of the proposed product's cycle even before it is introduced. Then at each stage management should anticipate the marketing requirements of the following stage.[25] The introductory period, for instance, may be shortened by concentrating on broadening the distribution or by increasing the promotional effort. A product's life can be extended in the maturity and saturation stages by revitalizing it through new packaging, repricing, or product modifications. The makers of nylon, Jell-O, and Scotch tape—as an illustration—all have employed four different strategies to expand sales: (1) increase frequency of the product's use, (2) develop more varied use of the product, (3) attract new users, and (4) find new uses for the product.

Perhaps it is in the sales-decline stage that a company finds its greatest challenges in life-cycle management. At some point in the product's life, management may well have to consider whether to abandon it. The costs of carrying profitless products go beyond the uncovered direct or indirect expenses which are found on financial statements. The real burdens are the insidious costs accruing from the managerial time and marketing effort which are diverted to sick products instead of being applied to the healthy ones. Unfortunately, management often seems reluctant to discard a product, either for emotional and sentimental reasons or because they rationalize that they need the item to round out the product line or that the decline is temporary and they will soon hit the jackpot.

When sales are declining, management has these alternatives:

1. Improve the product in a functional sense or revitalize it in some manner.

2. Review the marketing and production programs to make sure they are as efficient as possible.

3. Streamline the product assortment by pruning out unprofitable sizes, styles, colors, and models. Frequently, this tactic will *decrease* sales and *increase* profits.

4. "Run out" the product; that is, cut all costs to the bare-minimum level that will optimize profitability over the limited remaining life of the product.[26]

5. Abandon the product.

Knowing when and how to abandon products successfully may be as important as knowing when and how to introduce new ones. Certainly management should develop a systematic procedure for identifying and then phasing out its weak products.[27]

---

[25] Levitt, *op. cit.*, pp. 84–93.

[26] For a report on the run-out process in two companies (matches and auto accessories) and an analysis of alternative choices within the run-out process, see Walter J. Talley, Jr., "Profiting from the Declining Product," *Business Horizons,* Spring, 1964, pp. 77–84.

[27] For three approaches to the pruning-out process, see R. S. Alexander, "The Death and Burial of 'Sick' Products," *Journal of Marketing*, April, 1964, pp. 1–7; Conrad Berenson, "Pruning the Product Line," *Business Horizons*, Summer, 1963, pp. 63–70; and Philip Kotler, "Phasing out Weak Products," *Harvard Business Review*, March–April, 1965, pp. 107–118.

WHY NEW PRODUCTS FAIL: A SUMMARY

"Failure is not only the price of new-product introduction, it is also an important part of the learning process that ultimately leads to success."[28] As a conclusion to this chapter, the first of three on product planning and development, it might be useful to summarize the results of one study on why new products fail and to outline for management a positive program of corrective action. The National Industrial Conference Board surveyed eighty-seven companies which were considered highly successful product innovators. Even these successful marketers experienced a failure rate of three out of ten among products which had been fully researched, developed, and commercialized during the preceding five years. Following are the eight major reasons given for new-product failure, in order of frequency of mention:

1. Inadequate market analysis. Includes inaccurate quantitative measurement of the market, inability to determine buying motives and habits, misjudgment of what products the market wanted, and failure to provide a sufficiently new and different product.[29]

2. Product defects. Lack of durability, poor design, and inadequate quality control were cited here.

3. Higher costs than anticipated. This sometimes resulted in higher prices, which in turn led to smaller sales volume than anticipated.

4. Poor timing. Some products became technically obsolescent between the conception of the idea and the commercialization of the product.

5. Competition. Price reductions by competitors undercut the market entry of some new products.

6. Insufficient marketing effort. Failure to commit the resources needed for intensive marketing effort hurt some firms.

7. Inadequate sales force. Salesmen were insufficiently trained or motivated to do the necessary job.

8. Weaknesses in distribution. Some firms failed to select proper trade channels or did a poor job in promoting the product to the wholesalers and retailers.

An analysis of the above eight factors points up two observations sharply. As one executive said, "Painful though it may be to admit, the principal factors that caused our failure were within our control." The other conclusion is that about two-thirds of the causes of failure were marketing shortcomings, while all other functions of business combined (production, finance, purchasing, etc.) accounted for only one-third.[30]

The NICB study indicated that most companies have taken positive steps

[28] "Why New Products Fail," *Conference Record*, October, 1964, pp. 11–18; quotation on p. 18.

[29] See Walter Joyce, "Why So Few Really New Products?" *Printers' Ink*, Feb. 1, 1963, p. 25.

[30] Hector Lazo, "Finding a Key to Success in New Product Failures," *Industrial Marketing*, November, 1965, pp. 74–75.

to remedy the deficiencies in their programs for planning and developing new products. This corrective action may be summarized as follows:

1. Improved screening and evaluation of ideas and products
2. Organization changes
3. Changes in procedures and communications
4. Strengthening research and development efforts
5. Improvements in production and quality control
6. Improved caliber of personnel working on new-product programs

If the first commandment in marketing is, "Know thy customer," then the second is, "Know thy product." The products or services sold by a firm are prime determinants of the company's rate of growth, rate of profit, and total marketing program. Policies and strategies with respect to the full complement of a firm's products are considered in the following chapter.

QUESTIONS AND PROBLEMS

1   Why do so many new products turn out to be market failures?

2   Name some companies which have not added new products in the past few years. Name some products which have not been changed in the past three years.

3   What factors account for the growing importance of product planning?

4   In what respects, if any, are the products different in each of the following cases?
   a. An Arrow shirt sold by a local men's clothing store and a similar shirt sold by Sears, Roebuck and Company under the retailer's brand name. Assume that the same manufacturer makes both shirts.
   b. A Sunbeam Mixmaster sold by a leading department store and the same model sold by a discount house.

5   Bring to class three advertisements which stress product benefits. Bring three which stress some part of the product rather than the benefits to be derived from this product.

6   In what respects does product planning done by a consumer goods manufacturer differ from that done by a firm producing industrial products?

7   Compare and contrast the product-planning activities of a manufacturer and a retailer.

8   Interview the executives of a nearby manufacturing concern which is buying some of the components of its finished product. Analyze the company in order to determine if its decision to buy rather than make these components was a sound one.

9   List the factors which influence the type of organizational structure selected for new-product development. Explain how each of these factors might affect the choice of structure.

10   This chapter mentioned two organizational situations in new-product development which potentially pose problems. What recommendations can you offer to management as possible means of avoiding or solving these problems?

The Product

11   Under what conditions might a firm profitably use a separate department for new-product development?

12   What are some of the problems typically connected with the "product-manager" type of organizational structure for new-product development?

13   What are some of the questions which management is likely to want answered during the "business-analysis" stage of new-product development?

14   Assume that the following additions to their product lines are being considered by the stated companies. What is your initial recommendation, based upon general information which you may already have relating to the criteria set forth in this chapter?

      a.   Automobile manufacturer—outboard motors
      b.   Firm such as National Cash Register—office dictating machines
      c.   Discount house—medium-priced copies of current fashions in women's ready-to-wear
      d.   Supermarket—wallpaper
      e.   Manufacturer of electronic parts and equipment—automatic garage-door opener
      f.   Department store—well-known brand of compact cars

15   Name some products which you believe are in the introductory stage of their life cycles. Be sure to identify the market which considers your examples to be new products.

16   Give examples of products which are in the stage of market decline. In each case, point out whether you think the decline is permanent. If you think the decline is not permanent, what recommendations do you have for rejuvenating the demand for the article?

17   How might a company's pricing strategies differ depending upon whether a product is in the pioneering stage or maturity stage of its life cycle?

18   What advertising strategies are apt to be used when a product is in the growth stage?

9

PRODUCT-LINE POLICIES AND STRATEGIES

The Columbia Broadcasting Company acquired controlling interest in the New York Yankees baseball team. An appliance manufacturer eliminated a number of models of refrigerators, kitchen ranges, and air conditioners. The Ford Motor Company dropped the Edsel and later added the Mustang. The makers of Philip Morris and Marlboro cigarettes have diversified into shaving tools, adhesives, packaging materials, electronic parts, and other nontobacco products. A producer of industrial materials-handling and construction equipment has expanded into hydraulic pumps, motors, and valves. Several large American department stores regularly shop for the latest European fashion creations and then adapt these to the mass market. All these cases have one thing in common: they involve managerial strategies and policy making with respect to the firm's line of products and services.

PRODUCT LINE AND PRODUCT MIX

A broad group of products, intended for essentially similar uses and possessing reasonably similar physical characteristics, constitutes a *product line*. Wearing apparel is one example of a product line. But in a different context, say, in a small specialty shop, men's furnishings (shirts, ties, and underwear) and men's ready-to-wear (suits, sport jackets, topcoats, and slacks) would each constitute a line. In another context, men's apparel is one line as contrasted with women's apparel, furniture, or sporting goods.

The *product mix* is the full list of all products offered for sale by a company. The structure of the product mix has dimensions of both breadth and depth. Its breadth is measured by the number of product lines carried; its depth, by the assortment of sizes, colors, models, prices, and quality offered within each product line.

MAJOR PRODUCT-LINE STRATEGIES

Several major product-line strategies are used by manufacturers and middlemen in marketing either industrial or consumer products. Most of these strategies involve a change in the product mix; however, some involve an expansion of the market by means of new uses for the product but with no alterations in the mix. A discussion of planned obsolescence as a product strategy, and of fashion as an influence on the product mix, is deferred until later in the chapter.

Expansion of product mix

A firm may elect to expand its present product mix by increasing the number of lines and/or the depth within a line. New lines may be related or unrelated to the present products. The SCM Corporation (formerly Smith-Corona-Marchant) added a line of electrostatic office copiers and peripheral data-processing equipment to complement its typewriters and calculators. The 3M Company (Minnesota Mining and Mfg. Co.), manufacturers of Scotch tape, also markets the Thermo-Fax office copier and the Cantata 700, a background music system including transmitting unit and tape. The Green Giant Company increased the depth of its line by adding a series of frozen vegetables to its highly successful canned peas and corn. A company may expand in both breadth and depth. For example, food chains have added lines of drug sundries and housewares (breadth) while at the same time increasing their assortments of dry cereals and cleaning products (depth).

Contraction of product mix

A manufacturer or middleman may contract his product mix either by eliminating lines or by the more usual practice of simplifying the assortment within a line. A number of years ago the Hunt Food Company pruned its line of canned food products until only tomato products, fruit cocktail, and peaches remained. Some appliance retailers who used to carry several brands now carry only one manufacturer's line.

Alteration of existing products

As an alternative to developing a new product, management should be encouraged to take a fresh look at the company's existing products. Often improving and revitalizing an established product can be more profitable and less risky than developing and introducing a new one.[1] This alternative strategy should be followed regardless of the breadth and depth of the product mix and regardless of whether management is committed to a policy of expansion or contraction of the mix.

For industrial goods, especially, a *redesigning* of the product is often the key to that product's renaissance.[2] Not only did a redesigned pressure switch cost 52 per cent less than the model it replaced, but the new one also was easier to install and performed better. The market for a hospital centrifuge was expanded by redesigning it so that it harmonized architecturally with modern cabinetry. *Packaging* has been a very popular area for product alteration, particularly in consumer products. Even something as mundane as thread, glue, or cheesecloth can be made more attractive by creative packaging and display. The *use of new materials* has also been popular. In place of cotton and wool, clothing manufacturers have substituted materials of branded synthetic fibers. Industrial rubber companies have mixed synthetic with natural rubber and have used nylon instead of rayon cord in their advertising appeals.

Sometimes the alteration is only in the advertising appeal—the product remains unchanged—as when the advertising for Welch's grape juice ceased to be *against* fat and *in favor of* refreshment and energy production. It should also be beneficial if management would analyze the qualities which have contributed to the long-lived, seemingly indestructible success of such products as 20 Mule Team borax, Hershey chocolate, Vaseline petroleum jelly, and Arm & Hammer baking soda.[3]

Development of new uses for existing products

Another major product strategy used by several manufacturers is to search for new uses for their products. Although a company probably cannot rely on this strategy alone to increase sales volume and profits, we should not under-

[1] See Ralph Freas, "Take a Fresh Look at Your Old Products," *Sales Management*, Jan. 1, 1965, pp. 21–23.

[2] Kenneth Van Dyck, "New Products from Old: Short-cut to Profits," *Industrial Marketing*, November, 1965, pp. 85–87.

[3] See "Why the Old Products Last," *Dun's Review and Modern Industry*, April, 1965, p. 46.

estimate the effectiveness of this strategy in tapping new markets. The 3M Company has followed this approach successfully with its product Scotch tape. Several years ago, the manufacturers of the soap product Duz offered a weekly prize to the consumer coming up with the best new use for the product.

Trading up and trading down

Trading up and trading down involve, essentially, an expansion of the product line, but they are also used as a promotional strategy. Normally, with regard to line expansion, a given firm will trade up or down, *not* both.

Trading up means that a manufacturer or middleman adds a higher-priced, prestige product to his line in the hope of increasing his sales of an existing lower-priced product. In the automobile industry, Ford Motor Company introduced the Thunderbird, and the Chevrolet division of General Motors marketed the Corvette. Both companies expected their lower-priced, established cars to benefit from the reflected prestige of the new ones.

When a company embarks upon a policy of trading up, at least two avenues are open with respect to promotional emphasis: (1) usually the seller continues to depend upon the older, lower-priced product for the bulk of the sales volume, and (2) eventually he may shift the promotional emphasis to the new product and expect it to produce the major share of volume. In fact, the lower-priced line may be dropped altogether after a transition period. Many department stores have followed this policy over the past twenty years as they have traded up from their target of the low-income market to a new, larger middle-income market.

A company is said to be trading down when it adds a lower-priced item to its line of prestige products in the hope that people who cannot afford the original product will want to buy the new one because it carries some of the status of the higher-priced good. Several years ago Buick attempted to broaden its market by introducing four series of cars in an attempt to compete at all price levels. Packard, once a fine name in fine cars, traded down by bringing out the lower-priced Packard Clipper.

Trading up and trading down are perilous strategies because the intended goal may not materialize. The new product may simply confuse buyers, so that the net gain is negligible. Nor is any useful purpose served if sales in the new line are generated at the expense of the older product. Trading up or trading down cannot be considered successful unless sales increase in total or the company retains business that would otherwise go to competitive products.

When trading down, the new article may permanently hurt the firm's reputation and its established high-quality product; in fact, it is generally agreed that this is exactly what happened in the Packard case. This situation may be avoided or minimized by using differentiating brands, channels of distribution, promotional programs, or product design.

When trading up, the seller's major problem is to change his image enough so that the market will accept his new, higher-priced, higher-quality product. To illustrate, many women will never believe that they can buy good-quality, high-fashion clothing in a chain department store or in women's ready-to-wear chain stores. Through the years these stores have projected a corporate image or personality which connotes low-priced merchandise. Attempts at trading up will be unsuccessful, no matter how good the products may really be, until that image is changed.

Product differentiation and market segmentation

Product differentiation and market segmentation are two related product strategies which may be employed by firms who wish to engage in nonprice competition in markets characterized by imperfect or monopolistic competition.[4] These strategies usually require a considerable amount of advertising and other kinds of promotional effort. Consequently, they are often regarded as both promotional and product-planning strategies.

As a product strategy, *product differentiation* involves developing and promoting an awareness of differences between the advertiser's product and the products of competitors. The strategy is used to enable a business to remove itself from price competition so that it can compete on the nonprice basis that its product is different from, and better than, competitive models. Sometimes a company will differentiate the quality or design of the product, or the only differentiation may be in the brand or packaging. Frequently two products are virtually identical in a physical and chemical sense; the difference between them is trivial and sometimes only psychological. This strategy is frequently used by companies selling reasonably standardized products, such as soaps, cigarettes, and gasoline, to a broad horizontal market which is fairly homogeneous in its wants for the given item.

In terms familiar in economic theory, the seller assumes in a general sense that there is a single demand curve for his product. Any variations in the wants of individual consumers will be minimized by extensive advertising and sales promotion emphasizing the product's broad market appeal. Essentially, as Wendell R. Smith has said, ". . . *product differentiation* is concerned with the bending of demand to the will of supply."

Inexorable market pressures are working against the seller who attempts to expand his market by using the strategy of product differentiation. The broader the market, the more difficult it becomes to fit all consumers' wants to the single product. Competition is felt to an increasing extent; any one of these alternative products is apt to satisfy more precisely the wants of some group in this broadening range of consumers. Our seller must resort to increased promotional expenditures or reduced prices, or both, in his attempts to offset

---

[4] Much of this section is based on a penetrating analysis of these strategies by Wendell R. Smith. See his "Product Differentiation and Market Segmentation as Alternative Marketing Strategies," *Journal of Marketing*, July, 1956, pp. 3–8.

the variations in consumer preference, that is, in his attempts to fit more consumers in that single demand curve.

In employing the strategy of *market segmentation*, a seller recognizes that his total heterogeneous market is made up of many, smaller homogeneous units. Each of these smaller units has a different set of wants, motivations, and other characteristics. He sees his market as a *series* of demand curves rather than the *single* curve considered above in product differentiation. The seller then attempts to develop different products, each one specifically for one or more of these market units. Tailor-made or custom-made products are extreme examples of this strategy in action. Market segmentation is related to the strategy of expanding the product mix, since additional products are developed to better pinpoint the segmented markets. Appropriate advertising and other promotional efforts are still needed in order to inform each market segment of the ways in which the product particularly satisfies its wants.

Market segmentation has been employed for years in the field of industrial products, where it is quite common to make products according to buyers' specifications. The strategy is also being used to an increasing extent in the consumer market. As useful bases for segmenting a market, a seller may consider some of the market characteristics identified in Chapter 4—geographic, demographic, or income factors, for instance. Clothing manufacturers design one set of products for the New England climate and a different set for Florida or Arizona. With different price lines, these same manufacturers may segment the market on an income basis. Product use may be the basis of segmentation —one kind of ski is made for the slalom and another for downhill racing. Manufacturers of outboard motors recognize that inland lake fishing, water-skiing, and deep-sea fishing entail different uses of motors and thus represent different markets. Sociologists suggest that we categorize markets in line with psychological or sociological profiles, recognizing some of the factors discussed in Chapter 5, for example.

Market segmentation attempts to penetrate a limited market in *depth*, whereas product differentiation seeks *breadth* in a more generalized market. Smith says, "The differentiator seeks to secure a layer of the market cake, whereas one who employs market segmentation strives to secure one or more wedge-shaped pieces."

A firm may first employ the strategy of market segmentation, but soon be forced by competition to switch to product differentiation. A firm that makes electric razors may divide the market into two groups—men and women— and then develop separate products to meet the specific wants of each group. Eventually the women's market will be recognized as a separate market by many firms, each of which will bring out an electric razor for women. Soon all these sellers will resort to differentiation to maintain a separate identity. Thus any given segmentation of markets is a transitory phenomenon, and competitive conditions force a seller constantly to seek new ways of segmenting his market.

Some of the reasons for the emergence of market segmentation as a formally recognized strategy follow:

1.   There has been a decrease in the minimum size of the efficient manufacturing unit for many products; thus production runs of identical items need not be so long as in the past.

2.   Self-service and similar cost-cutting techniques require that products be better adjusted to demand.

3.   Increases in discretionary purchasing power result in more careful shopping; the customer is willing to pay a little more to get just what he wants.

4.   An expanded variety of goods are competing for the customer's dollar.

5.   Market segmentation becomes necessary for growth after promotion on a generalized basis to a broad market reaches a point of diminishing returns.[5]

FACTORS INFLUENCING CHANGES IN PRODUCT MIX

A marketing executive who wishes to use his product mix strategically in the competitive market battle should understand the main factors underlying a company's desire to expand or simplify its line.

The following considerations are pertinent to manufacturers of both industrial and consumer goods. Many are also relevant to middlemen. Usually a firm's decision to change its product mix is based on several factors.

Changes in market demand

Consumer population and industrial users   A major change in a component of population may induce a firm to change its product mix. As birthrates declined in the 1960s, the Gerber Products Company—producer of baby foods —added a line of other baby products (bibs, crib sheets, socks, shirts, and waterproof pants) for distribution through supermarkets, along with its food

---

[5] For a suggestion that the concept of market segmentation may need further refinement and interpretation—that a product policy based on *variety* may be more realistic than one based on *market segmentation*—see William H. Reynolds, "More Sense about Market Segmentation," *Harvard Business Review*, September–October, 1965, pp. 107–114. Reynolds contends that much (not all, of course) of what passes for market segmentation is, in reality, better termed a "variety" strategy. This strategy looks on the market as relatively uniform—people are pretty much the same across the country. Two of their many common characteristics are (1) they shift from brand to brand frequently, and (2) they tend to be attracted to new brands and products.

For another analysis which contends that demography is not the only or the best way to segment markets, see Daniel Yankelovich, "New Criteria for Market Segmentation," *Harvard Business Review*, March–April, 1964, pp. 83–90. The author states that more valuable segmentation criteria are buyers' attitudes, motivations, values, patterns of usage, aesthetic preferences, and degree of susceptibility.

lines.[6] The growth in suburban population has led furniture manufacturers to expand into patio and lawn furniture and has encouraged other businesses to develop residential-sized power lawn mowers. After World War II, a chain of photographic studios closed a number of its retail outlets located on or near military bases and dropped from its line a series of photographs and frames intended for members of the military forces.

In the industrial market, the mobility of customers may force a manufacturer or wholesaler to drop some lines and add others to take up the slack. Many plants have moved from New England to the South. Industries formerly serving these New England factories cannot continue to do so, in part because excessive transportation rates give Southern suppliers a favorable cost differential. Hence the New England firms must look for new products and new markets.

Buying power Increases in purchasing power have played a significant role in leading several firms to raise the quality of their merchandise. No doubt this is one reason Evinrude and other manufacturers of outboard motors are adding larger motors to their lines.

Oddly enough, products are sometimes dropped because of increase in purchasing power. In the past two decades, people have become able to afford better merchandise, and the market for low-priced, low-quality goods has declined considerably.

Customer behavior Several situations involving customer motivation, attitudes, preferences, and buying habits will encourage a marketing executive to expand or contract his product mix. In the first place, he will add products in order to satisfy ultimate consumers or industrial users who want a more complete line. As household consumers have made it evident that they prefer the convenience of one-stop shopping, supermarkets have broadened their mix by adding magazines, health and beauty aids, small housewares, staple clothing, and many other nonfood lines.

Sometimes the impetus for a change in product mix comes from middlemen who prefer a more complete line, for competitive, cost, or promotional reasons. A Colorado manufacturer of a glass-cleaning compound found that when he added other cleaning and polishing products to his line, wholesalers were much more eager to work with him.

The increase in the leisure-time market was undoubtedly a major factor in prompting the Chrysler Corporation to add a line of small pleasure boats and later to add the Volvo inboard-outboard drive engine. Growth in the entertainment market has prompted four jukebox manufacturers (including Seeburg and Wurlitzer) to sell complete and automated discotheque packages which include jukebox records, speakers, prefabricated dance floor, phospho-

[6] "How to Feed Profits as Well as Babies," *Business Week,* Jan. 8, 1966, p. 64.

rescent wall panels, and advertising materials.[7] The consumer's demand for convenience helped to spark the market for battery-powered, cordless electric appliances such as razors, carving knives, mixers, and vacuum cleaners.

In the industrial market, product alterations may result from changing requirements in customers' industries. A supplier who sells to industries which are subject to annual model or design changes—autos, for example—must add new products annually to meet his customers' needs.

Competitive actions and reactions

In order to meet competition more effectively, a firm may want to differentiate its product line so that price comparisons will not be possible. In other instances a manufacturer may want to diversify his product line so as to free himself somewhat from a bitterly competitive situation in which his profit margins are dangerously low. The plywood industry is a good example of one in which price competition is prevalent and differentiation of the basic product is difficult. Some of the larger firms—United States Plywood Company, for instance—have added other products to their mix such as a variety of finished interior paneling and adhesives. In the same industry and for the same reasons, the Weyerhaeuser Company has diversified into many fields including packaging products, paper, and molded fiber doors.[8] The makers of Bardahl additives for oil and gasoline changed their product radically—the formula, pricing, packaging, and advertising—to meet more effectively the growing competition from additives marketed by big oil companies and automobile manufacturers.[9]

A "follow-the-leader" policy often seems to prevail in industry. It is difficult to know whether this "me-tooism" is based on sound economic and marketing analysis or whether it stems from a belief that "if those other fellows are doing it, maybe we should try it too; they usually know what they are doing." Of course, if one firm enters a market with a new or improved product that holds promise of being successful, other companies are almost forced to meet this competition. After the success enjoyed by early manufacturers of metal skis, many competitive firms felt they had to add this product to their lines.[10]

Sometimes new competitive products enter the market within a few months of each other. The buttered pancake syrup battle between Lever Brothers and General Foods is a classic example of a competitor moving in rapidly when it is apparent that a new product is filling a need. Supposedly, Lever Brothers

---

[7] See "Instant Discotheque: Just Add Dancers," *Business Week*, Feb. 27, 1965, p. 108.

[8] Steve Blickstein, "The Weyerhaeuser Way: It All Starts with the Log," *Sales Management*, Dec. 17, 1965, p. 25.

[9] "When to Change a Winner," *Sales Management*, Nov. 10, 1964, p. 142.

[10] For a brief article on the planning, development, and current marketing of Head skis, see Phyllis Daignault, "A Man, an Obsession, and Sweet Success," *Sales Management*, Feb. 5, 1965, p. 30.

was first in the market with its Mrs. Butterworth brand. General Foods, how-ever, took an old buttered syrup product from its institutional line and intro-duced it so quickly that it actually beat Lever into some markets.

Marketing influences

Two major reasons for adding products are (1) to increase sales by tap-ping new markets or expanding present ones and (2) to use the firm's market-ing capacity more efficiently by a better use of salesmen, branch offices, or warehouses. Adding 10 per cent more products usually results in less than a 10 per cent increase in salesmen's salaries and traveling expenses, marketing research expenses, marketing administrative overhead, and other marketing costs.

Of course, in some cases a firm can increase its marketing effectiveness by simplifying its line. The salesmen may be spreading themselves too thinly over the market, or warehouse space may be taken up by slow-moving, obsolete items. With the elimination of some products, salesmen can concentrate on fewer items and really sell them properly.

Production influences

A manufacturer often wishes to change his product mix in order to use his manufacturing capacity more effectively and thus lower his net production costs. Here it is assumed that the firm is producing at a level of output such that if there were an increase in output, using the present facilities, the result would be a reduction in unit cost. Product additions also occur when a firm wishes to use an item whose manufacture elsewhere has been discontinued.

Product mix may be expanded in order to put by-products or waste prod-ucts to better use. A classic example is found in the meat-packing industry, where by-products have resulted in the production of fertilizer, glue, soap, leather products, and many other items. Several firms have developed new products by using wood scraps.

Financial influences

There are several financial reasons why a business enterprise may wish to change its product mix. One is to enable the firm to use its finances more effectively by generally diversifying its risks. Any one of several factors, such as a new competitive product or a change in a component of demand, can rapidly ob-solete a given product. Hence from a financial standpoint, it is wise to spread risks among several products.

Expanding the product mix can help to increase a firm's profitable sales volume. Supermarkets, for example, have added several nonfood items to their lines; these items ordinarily bring a significantly higher margin than the 15 to 18 per cent typical gross margin for the store as a whole. A full line can also help smooth out the seasonal fluctuations in sales volume. The classic example in days gone by was the iceman who added coal to his product mix in the winter.

A full line of products can make a manufacturer's product-servicing organization financially feasible. It is not economical to maintain a service organization, as many appliance manufacturers do, unless there are several products over which the costs can be spread.

A firm may hope to cushion depressions or recessions by product diversification. A company with one major product or one major market is like a town with one industry. Manufacturers who sell all or virtually all of their output to the government or to a firm with government contracts are particularly susceptible to losses caused by canceled or unrenewed contracts.

Financial considerations may encourage a company to simplify its line. Sometimes a few items require so much capital investment in production or inventory facilities that the value of these products to the company can be questioned. By dropping slow-moving items, such as extremely large or extremely small shoe sizes, a manufacturer or middleman may experience a small decline in sales but a substantial decrease in cost. Such a change might result in longer and thus lower-cost production runs, less chance of mistakes in filling and shipping orders, lower insurance and investment costs on inventory, and curtailed losses from obsolescence.

Desire to change company image

Changing the product mix in an attempt to alter the firm's image is related to the strategy of trading up or trading down. So many variety chains have added higher-quality, higher-priced, non-variety-store items to their mix that today they are almost small department stores, a far cry from the "five-and-ten-cent store." Of course, the desire to upgrade a store's image involves more than the emotional factor of management's own self-concept. There are sound, rational business reasons at play: the low-income market is not so big today as it was twenty-five years ago, but the middle-income group is a prime target.

PLANNED OBSOLESCENCE AND FASHION

The preceding sections of this chapter established the fact that in today's economy manufacturers and middlemen are engaging in the expansion and diversification of their product lines. In fact, the competitive situation is such that product change is often necessary if a company wants its products to maintain an aura or halo of "dynamic progressiveness."

As one student of marketing observed, obsolescence as a marketing device has not lost its place in our economy.[11] He noted that if the ten-year Depression of the 1930s did not dislodge our love of the "new," then it is doubtful that

[11] Martin Mayer, "Planned Obsolescence: Rx for Tired Markets?" *Dun's Review and Modern Industry*, February, 1959, p. 80.

anything can. Apparently, the roots of our quest for the new lie deep in our desire to escape boredom, the psychology of a highly mobile population, our love of the frontier, and our belief in progress. Changes cannot be radical, however. The market wants newness, but still it wants to be moved gently out of its habitual patterns, not shocked out of them. Consequently, many manufacturers have developed the product strategy of planned obsolescence.

Nature of planned obsolescence

The economic and social aspects of planned obsolescence have been discussed at length and usually with much emotion. Although there is often no clear agreement on what planned obsolescence involves or how it should be defined, there does seem to be general agreement on its object. It is intended to make a product out-of-date and thus to increase the replacement market.

Planned obsolescence has been interpreted in a number of ways:

1. Technological, or functional, obsolescence. Under this interpretation, there is true innovation; significant improvements as measured by technical standards have been made. When an automobile manufacturer installed power steering equipment and automatic transmissions, these changes created functional, or technological, obsolescence with respect to earlier models.

2. Postponed obsolescence. Technological improvements are not introduced until the market demand for present models decreases and a new market stimulus is needed.

3. Intentionally designed physical obsolescence. In this instance, a product is designed to wear out physically within a reasonably short period of time. Obviously this is a dangerous strategy because a firm may acquire a reputation for shoddy merchandise. Durability is still a significant buying motive.

4. Style obsolescence. This is sometimes called "psychological" or "fashion" obsolescence. The intent is to make a person feel out-of-date if he continues to use an old model. Stated another way, this is "the alteration of superficial characteristics of a product to create an easily discernible difference between model years."[12]

When a person criticizes planned obsolescence, he is usually referring to this last interpretation—style obsolescence. In our discussion, planned obsolescence will mean style obsolescence only, unless otherwise stated.

Nature and importance of style and fashion

Although style and fashion are often used interchangeably with respect to planned obsolescence, there is a clear distinction between the two, and it should be noted. *Webster's New Collegiate Dictionary* defines a *style* as a "distinctive or characteristic mode of presentation, construction, or execution in any art, employment, or product, especially in any fine art; also, distinctive manner or

[12] "Planned Obsolescence Starts to Slip," *Sales Management*, Jan. 15, 1960, p. 17.

mode of singing, playing, behaving, etc."[13] Thus we can have several styles in many different products. There are styles in automobiles (sedans, convertibles, station wagons) and in bathing suits (one-piece suits, swimming trunks, bikinis). Early American and French Provincial are furniture styles, and Gothic and Italian Renaissance are architectural styles.

A *fashion* is any style which is popularly accepted and purchased by several successive groups of people over a reasonably long period of time. "A fashion is always based on some particular style. But not every style is a fashion. . . . A style does not become a fashion until it gains some popular use, and it remains a fashion only so long as it is so accepted."[14]

A *fad* normally does not remain popular so long as a fashion, and it is based on some novelty feature.

A student of fashion should recognize its separate identity, its importance, and its pervasiveness in all societies. Fashion is really a field by itself. It is not simply a factor affecting buying patterns in the consumer market, and it is not merely a product strategy. Fashion is "the pursuit of novelty for its own sake."[15] While basic styles never change, fashion is always changing. Fashion is the behavioral complex underlying all stylistic innovations, that is, all design changes which are not purely the result of engineering advances. Furthermore, if fashion influences a market, that market is subject to a compelling need for never-ending change in the styling of its products.

Style obsolescence is not limited to the fields of women's ready-to-wear and automobiles; it is planned in countless commodities, including small and large appliances, motor boats, and bathroom scales. It is also apparent in such vastly different fields as architecture, pedigreed dogs, and music. Fashion is found in all societies, whether they are primitive groups, the great Oriental cultures, or the societies of ancient and medieval Europe. Essentially the only difference between these cultures and our own is that fashions change more rapidly in our society.

The Industrial Revolution and the rise of the common people are the two basic factors which account for the accelerated rate of change in our socioeconomic system. Industrialization increased the ease with which fashions could be produced and distributed, and the rise of the common people increased the size of the potential market. The power behind fashion shifted from "the aristocracy of rank to the aristocracy of wealth."[16]

[13] In Paul H. Nystrom, *Economics of Fashion*, The Ronald Press Company, New York, 1928, p. 3, style is defined as a "characteristic or distinctive mode or method of expression, presentation or conception in the field of some art."

[14] Paul H. Nystrom, *Fashion Merchandising*, The Ronald Press Company, New York, 1932, p. 33.

[15] Dwight E. Robinson, "Fashion Theory and Product Design," *Harvard Business Review*, November–December, 1958, pp. 121–138.

[16] Edward Sapir, "Fashion," *The Encyclopedia of Social Sciences*, The Macmillan Company, New York, 1931, vol. VI, pp. 139–144. Much of the following section on the origin of fashion is drawn from this article.

Origin of fashion

Understanding the origin of fashion helps to explain its course or movements. Sapir has said that "fashion is emphatically a historical concept." Bare legs among modern women in the summer do not have the same fashion meanings as bare legs and feet among primitive groups in the tropics. A fashion must be studied within its historical context and related to prevailing cultures and social norms.

Fashion is also rooted in sociological and psychological factors. Basically, people are conformists; they follow rather strictly the patterns and standards established by the opinion leaders, or tastemakers, in their groups. At the same time, people yearn to look, act, and be a little different from others. They are not in revolt against custom; they simply wish to deviate a bit and still not be accused of bad taste or insensitiveness to the code. Fashion discreetly furnishes them the opportunity for self-expression because "fashion is custom in the guise of departure from custom."

Stanley Marcus, president of Neiman-Marcus, the nationally known high-fashion women's store in Dallas, Texas, observed:[17]

If, for example, a dictator decreed feminine clothes to be illegal and that all women should wear barrels, it would not result in an era of uniformity, in my opinion. Very shortly, I think you'd find that one ingenious woman would color her barrel with a lipstick, another would pin paper lace doilies on the front of hers, and still another would decorate hers with thumb-tacks. Other women would emulate the examples they liked the best until a bare barrel would be unique. *This is a strange human urge toward conformity, but a dislike for complete uniformity.* [Italics supplied.]

Another sociopsychological factor underlying the growth of fashion in sophisticated societies such as ours is boredom. This is fostered by leisure time and highly specialized forms of activity, and it leads to restlessness and curiosity. In an attempt to break the monotony, people seek change.

Along with the desire to break a little from a regularized conforming existence, there is a corollary factor involving a person's ego. Most people want to add to their personal attractiveness, or to any object of their love or friendship. This ego-building consideration is also expressed in the desire to attract favorable attention and in the desire for prestige or even notoriety.

In the evolutionary development of fashion, the focal point of fashion expression has shifted from men to women. As one writer said:[18]

Fashions for women show greater variability than fashions for men in contemporary civilization. Not only do women's fashions change more rapidly and

---

[17] Stanley Marcus, "Fashion Merchandising," a Tobé lecture on retail distribution delivered at the Harvard Graduate School of Business Administration, Cambridge, Mass., Mar. 10, 1959, pp. 4–5.

[18] Sapir, *op. cit.*, p. 142.

completely but the total gamut of allowed forms is greater for women than for men. In times past and in other cultures, however, men's fashions show a greater exuberance than women's. Much that used to be ascribed to woman as female is really due to woman as a sociologically and economically defined class. Woman as a distinctive theme for fashion may be explained in terms of the social psychology of the present civilization. She is the one who pleases by being what she is and looking as she does rather than by doing what she does. Whether biology or history is primarily responsible for this need not be decided. Woman has been the kept partner in marriage and has had to prove her desirability by ceaselessly reaffirming her attractiveness as symbolized by novelty of fashion. Among the wealthier classes and by imitation also among the less wealthy, woman has come to be looked upon as an expensive luxury on whom one spends extravagantly. She is thus a symbol of the social and economic status of her husband. Whether with the increasingly marked change of woman's place in society the factors which emphasize extravagance in women's fashions will entirely fall away it is impossible to say at the present time.

Fashion-adoption process

As was pointed out in Chapter 5 in the discussion of large-group and small-group influences on consumer buying behavior, people usually seek to emulate others in the same social or economic stratum or those on the next higher level. Consequently, in fashion adoption the scene is set for successive waves of purchases, as a given style is popularly accepted throughout a group until it finally falls out of fashion. This wavelike movement, representing the introduction, rise, popular culmination, and decline of the market's acceptance of a style, is referred to as the "fashion cycle."[19] Like an ocean wave, the fashion cycle builds up slowly, but declines rapidly once its crest is reached.

Somewhat conflicting theories exist regarding whether a given fashion cycle flows *vertically* through several socioeconomic strata or moves *horizontally* and *simultaneously* within several strata. These theories of fashion adoption have been called, respectively, the "trickle-down" and the "trickle-across" processes.

Historically and traditionally, the trickle-down theory has been used as the basic model to explain the fashion-adoption process. For example, designers of women's apparel first introduce a style to the leaders in a group—the taste-makers. Usually these people are social leaders and are in the upper-income brackets. They adopt a style as a symbol of newness, distinctiveness, and exclusiveness. If they accept the style, it will quickly appear in leading fashion stores. Soon the middle-income and then the lower-income markets will want to emulate

---

[19] As Nystrom observed, *Economics of Fashion*, p. 18, "The popular use of the term [fashion cycle] unfortunately may be both confusing and misleading. Cycle literally means circle and as applied to fashion suggests starting with some style, moving away from it and finally coming back to the same style again. Nothing like this is meant by the term 'fashion cycle' here. . . . The fashion cycle is simply the forward wavelike movement completed and involves no necessary repetition of the style."

the leaders, and the product will be mass-marketed. As its popularity wanes, the style will appear in bargain-price stores and finally will no longer be considered fashionable. Once a style reaches some lower level of adoption, its fashion decline is rapid, because by then the original leaders no longer want to be associated with it. They are seeking a new style to "fashionize," and another cycle will start.

To illustrate the trickle-across fashion-adoption process, let us again use the example of women's apparel. Within a few days, or a few weeks at the most, at the beginning of the fall season the same style of dresses will appear (1) in small, exclusive dress shops appealing to the upper social class, (2) in large department stores appealing to the middle social class, and (3) in discount houses and low-priced women's ready-to-wear chain stores, where the appeal is to the upper-lower social class. Price, quality, and materials mark the differences in the dresses sold on the three levels—the style is basically the same. Within each class the dresses are purchased early in the season by the opinion leaders—the innovators. If the style is accepted, its sales curve will rise as it becomes popular with the early adopters, then followed by the late adopters. Eventually the sales decline as the style ceases to be popular. This cycle or flow of fashion information, adoption, acceptance, and decline is a horizontal movement occurring virtually simultaneously within each of several social strata.

Students of fashion marketing are beginning to question whether the trickle-down theory accurately reflects the contemporary adoption process.[20] While granting the existence of some vertical flow, they hypothesize that several market factors today would seem to impede the trickle-down adoption process while at the same time fostering a horizontal flow. Our modern social and economic environment, for instance, is such that today a much larger segment of the total population can afford to purchase fashion merchandise. By means of modern production processes, communications systems, and transportation methods, we can disseminate style information and products so rapidly and completely that all social strata can be reached about the same time, thus short-circuiting the traditional vertical flow of influence among classes. In the apparel field, particularly, the fashion industry's manufacturing and marketing programs also tend to foster the horizontal movement of the fashion cycle. Manufacturers produce a wide *variety* of essentially one style; they also produce various *qualities* of the same basic style so as to appeal to different income groups simultaneously. Retailers, in turn, introduce that same basic style simultaneously at different price levels, thus reaching several social strata concurrently. When an

---

[20] See, for example, Charles W. King, "Fashion Adoption: A Rebuttal to the 'Trickle Down' Theory," in Stephen A. Greyser (ed.), *Toward Scientific Marketing*, American Marketing Association, Chicago, 1964, pp. 108–125; in this study the empirical research was done in the product category of women's millinery. The trickle-across theory is also compatible with the small-group research findings of Katz and Lazarsfeld, as noted in Chapter 5, where the *horizontal* nature of opinion leadership was identified.

entire cycle may last only one short season, a seller cannot afford to wait for the style acceptance to trickle down; he must introduce it into many social levels as soon as possible.

The length of the fashion-adoption cycle may vary considerably from one product to another, although in general the cycle for any given product is considerably shorter today than it was years ago. A style in houses or furniture may remain fashionable for many years, whereas styles in women's hats or shoes may be in fashion for only one season. This does not mean that all parts of the national market accept and adopt a style with the same rapidity and eagerness. It may reach a given point in its fashion cycle a year later in Denver than in New York, and it may never be accepted as a fashion in rural communities.

Three basic elements in fashion theory may help to explain why fashions move as they do.[21] First, all styles build up to a point of excess. The overriding responsibility of a fashion designer is the unending provision of novelty. He must keep adding various frills to a basic style in order to give it a continuing semblance of newness so that it will appeal to the market. Thus in the Victorian era so much gingerbread was added to houses and furniture that they became style monstrosities, and the market rebelled. The styles which took over were noted for their stark, functional simplicity. In the early 1960s there were indications that some people were preferring a little more decoration and adornment on their furniture and houses. Thus the currently fashionable styles in housing and furniture are already moving from the stage of simplicity toward their inevitable end of complexity and excess.

The second basic consideration in fashion theory is that the designer must shift the consumers' attention from one feature of a style to another as the style is running its fashion course. Thus as the "new look" (perhaps the only really successful style development in women's apparel since World War II) progressed through its fashion cycle, attention was drawn in one year to hemlines, while the waistline, neckline, or silhouette was emphasized in other years.

The third principle of fashion concerns the rapid demise of a given cycle. "A fashion can never retreat gradually and in good order. Like a dictator it must always expand its aggressions—or collapse. Old fashions never just fade away—they die suddenly and arbitrarily."[22] Fashion cannot stand to repeat a recently outmoded style. Once a style is sold at low prices and in large quantities (the economic emulation stage of the fashion cycle), it no longer appeals to fashion leaders who desire distinctiveness. Once the tastemakers begin to seek another style, the emulators rebel against the first, and it collapses as a fashion.

Marketing considerations in fashion

Manufacturers and middlemen should be able to recognize the stage a fashion cycle is in at any particular time. They must decide at what market they are

---

[21] Robinson, *op. cit.*, p. 127.

[22] *Ibid.*, p. 128.

aiming, at what point they want to get into the cycle, and when they should get out. Ordinarily, a retailer cannot successfully appeal to several income markets or participate in all stages of the fashion cycle at the same time. A high-grade specialty store in women's apparel—whose stocks are displayed discreetly in limited numbers without price tags—will want to get in at the start of a fashion trend. A department or specialty store appealing to the middle-income market will plan to enter the cycle in time to mass-market the style as it is climbing to its peak of popularity.

A seller—manufacturer or retailer—who typically enters a fashion cycle at its beginning will find that his ability to identify and communicate with the fashion innovators or early buyers in any group is one major key to successful fashion marketing. This is true regardless of whether the fashion cycle for that product is a trickle-down or a trickle-across adoption process. These innovators are often quite influential, serving as opinion leaders, in their social structure. Recent empirical studies point out that these acceptors of newness do constitute a unique market segment which can be differentiated from other segments.[23] The evidence suggests that the type of people who accept newness will depend upon the type of innovation being offered; that is, different types of people accept different types of innovation.

A manufacturer's product and distribution channel policies will also be related to the fashion cycle. If he wishes to project an image of distinctiveness, he will produce only a few units of each model; they will be relatively expensive and will be distributed through a limited number of high-grade stores. If he produces low-cost products with inexpensive materials, he must market them through low-quality stores active in the declining stage of the cycle.

To a great extent, success in fashion merchandising lies in the keen sense of timing of the marketing man. He must not enter the cycle too early or leave it too late. For example, in a mass fashion market, a manufacturer or a middleman who waits until the style reaches its peak of popularity, and then produces or stocks it, is apt to be left with a large quantity on hand after the downswing starts.

Accurate forecasting, therefore, is of inestimable value in achieving success in fashion merchandising. This is an extremely difficult task, however, because the forecaster is often dealing with complex sociological and psychological factors. Frequently a retailer or a manufacturer operates largely on intuition,

[23] See William E. Bell, "Consumer Acceptance of Product Innovations," *Houston Business Review*, Summer, 1964, pp. 27–49; highlights of the same study appear in Stephen A. Greyser (ed.), *Toward Scientific Marketing*, American Marketing Association, Chicago, 1964, pp. 85–95. See also Charles W. King, "The Innovator in the Fashion Process," in L. George Smith, (ed.), *Reflections on Progress in Marketing*, American Marketing Association, Chicago, 1965, pp. 324–339; and Charles W. King, "Communicating with the Innovator in the Fashion Adoption Process," in Peter D. Bennett (ed.), *Marketing and Economic Development*, American Marketing Association, Chicago, 1965, pp. 425–439.

inspiration, and his own sensitivities, tempered by considerable experience. Of course, the earlier the stage of the fashion cycle in which a firm participates, the tougher the forecasting job.[24]

Future of planned obsolescence

If someone asks whether obsolescence of any kind is losing its hold on the American market, the answer is a definite "no." Our interest in something new is still strong, and the economy thrives on replacement demand. If the question is whether planned or style obsolescence is diminishing in favor, however, the answer is a qualified "yes." For instance, planned obsolescence seems to be decreasing in popularity in both the automobile and major appliance industries. On several makes of automobiles, major design changes are no longer introduced every year or even every second or third year.

If planned obsolescence is declining in some fields, then what will take its place? The answer seems to be that technological change will become increasingly important. Increased leisure time, higher discretionary income, and improved communications have opened up new fields to consumers. They still want newness, and they still have the psychological drives that lead to fashion changes. The difference is that they now seek new kinds of products rather than style or model variations of the same product. They can better satisfy their egoistic demands with a new boat or swimming pool (new product) than with a new car (new model of old product). The consumer is also more discriminating. He is buying more and more imported products. Finally, people have accumulated considerable quantities of tangible goods, thus socially establishing their ability to buy. As former status symbols lose their prestige, consumers find it fashionable to spend money for travel, the arts, and other educational and cultural pursuits.

Of course, as technological obsolescence supersedes the emphasis on style and fashion, several marketing problems will arise. Technological obsolescence is expensive and difficult to plan. Product-research and product-development costs will increase, and greater burdens will be thrust on marketing research to ensure that the company is making sound marketing decisions. Designers cannot be ordered to "invent on schedule." This means that there may be years when a firm has nothing really new to sell. Even though increased expenditures for product research may encourage management to cut back on product pro-

[24] For a report on the increasing extent to which the apparel industry—immersed in fashion, yet traditionally backward in the marketing techniques which have stimulated profitable growth in other consumer goods fields—is adopting modern marketing practices in its product planning, distribution, and promotion, see Ann R. Lyon, "Marketing: Latest Thing in Fashions," *Printers' Ink*, Apr. 26, 1963, p. 25. The marketing push is coming both from large firms (Jonathan Logan, Bobbie Brooks) within the apparel industry and from fiber manufacturers (Du Pont, Chemstrand, Celanese) outside the industry.

motion, technological change may require more advertising than style change. Technological improvements often are difficult to explain, and they will require new thinking in the advertising and personal selling fields.

Evaluation of planned obsolescence

Style obsolescence is one of the most controversial aspects of modern marketing. As is true of most social complaints against marketing, much of the criticism of style obsolescence is neither all true nor all false. One criticism is that fashion designers are dictators (especially in women's ready-to-wear) and people voluntarily follow like sheep to buy whatever the designers decree will be fashionable. This is true only in a very superficial sense; the designers themselves obey many masters. First and foremost, the designs must be profitable to the manufacturers. Thus, behind the psychological determinants of fashion, there is the necessity of considering manufacturing processes and the cost and availability of materials. Also, the designer is guided and controlled by established custom; he cannot depart too far from it. Actually, what he tries to do is to anticipate intuitively what the customers want even before they themselves know. That is, rather than impose fashion, the designer seeks to coax people into accepting what they themselves have unconsciously suggested. Furthermore, a designer just cannot combat a fashion trend established by the social psychology factors noted earlier. No matter how aesthetically pleasing a style may be in the abstract, if it does not fit in with a trend it will be a failure.

Professor Sapir, along with other writers, has noted that throughout history there has been both a social and an economic criticism of fashion. Social critics object to fashion—particularly women's ready-to-wear—because it calls attention to the human body. Actually, the criticism is true; women's apparel generally is intended to draw attention to the human form. This fits in with human psychology. People want to be as expressive—even as immodest, perhaps—as society will allow. Fashion helps them to achieve this objective. Regarding the factor of economic waste, whether the criticism is justified or not seems to be somewhat beside the point. "Waste seems to be of no concern where values are to be considered, particularly when these values are both egoistic and unconscious."[25] A corollary criticism is that fashion makes everyone dress alike. This does not seem to be a warranted criticism either, because the individual in society is rarely individualistically expressive. Again, to a great extent, most people want to conform.

Supporters of the strategy of style obsolescence and annual model changes point out that it satisfies the consumers' desire to have something new. It also maintains our economy at a higher level than would be possible if consumers used a product until it wore out physically. Furthermore, people who cannot afford to buy new automobiles or appliances have an opportunity to satisfy

[25] Sapir, *op. cit.*, p. 143.

their wants for these products by purchasing used models. These would not be available if other consumers had not traded in their older models in order to acquire the latest ones. Many manufacturers and middlemen like the strategy because it enables them to promote a product on the basis of new, differentiated features; it offers them ample opportunity for nonprice competition.

Frequently it is difficult to distinguish between technological obsolescence and style obsolescence. Small functional improvements each year may add up to a substantial change over a period of years, but no single change might be said to have created technological obsolescence.

It should be noted that planned obsolescence—both functional and style —is a characteristic of a free and expanding economy. In an economy which is controlled by the state or by cartels, product obsolescence and innovation are apt to take place slowly. In a free economy, in the long run, the consumers' marketplace vote is the controlling factor which determines whether a product stays on the market. As American consumers continue to desire new products and can afford them, and as manufacturers are willing and free to supply them, the result is a flow of new products, which inevitably tends to make obsolete many existing goods.[26]

No matter how marketing people try to answer the social and economic criticisms—and some of the typical answers have been noted above—many people, including businessmen, have a nagging conscience about style obsolescence, and these answers are not sufficiently quieting. Two basic issues seem to keep arising. First, does our prevailing system of style obsolescence make sensible use of our resources and productive capacity? Certainly, antifunctionalism is materialism at its worst. When management is engaged in a policy of style obsolescence, often it has no choice but to make a slight model change in order to make the differentiation apparent to the consumer, even though this is done at the cost of a postponed functional or technological innovation. Frequent model changes increase the manufacturers' production costs and the middlemen's investment in inventory. The second, and related, issue is, does the system of planned obsolescence create an artificially short life for the products which are produced, thus creating some sort of disutility? One cannot help asking why marketing men cannot be just as aggressive with worthwhile appeals and functional innovation as they are with superficial styling and prestige appeals.

To determine the thinking of businessmen regarding the above two issues, a questionnaire survey was conducted among business executives, including some nationally known leaders. The survey sought their reactions to such questions as: (1) Is the stream of products that flows daily from American factories taking our nation where we want to go? (2) Are we wandering off course by allowing a substantial proportion of production and sales to be based upon trivial and superficial product obsolescence? (3) Can businessmen legitimately

[26] Lippincott and Margulies, Inc., "Obsolescence: Vice or Virtue?" in J. H. Westing and Gerald Albaum (eds.), *Modern Marketing Thought*, The Macmillan Company, New York, 1964, pp. 184–188.

absolve themselves from all responsibility for guidance by replying that the consumer is king—we only make what he wants? (4) If so, what happens when the businessmen become so effective at persuasion that they can shape what the consumer-king wants? In this survey, 64 per cent of the respondents agreed that for the long-run benefit of the United States, too great a part of our present economy is based on superficial product obsolescence, inducing people to buy new models before their old ones are worn out.[27]

Sixty-eight per cent of the businessmen felt that, to a large extent, advertising and other selling activities have encouraged consumers to spend their money for new models they really do not need. Another 20 per cent said that advertising and other selling activities are wholly or *almost* wholly responsible for this consumer behavior. In total, about 90 per cent felt that advertising and other selling activities played either a large part or the entire part in encouraging consumers to spend their money in this fashion. The survey also asked: If businessmen continue to spend more money on promotional activities and to develop still more effective means of influencing consumers, will business eventually become the most important influence in shaping consumers' wants? To this question, 70 per cent of the respondents replied that business already is the most important influence, and another 20 per cent said that it would become the most important influence.

In general, the question of the ultimate desirability of planned obsolescence probably goes unanswered, although there is genuine interest in seeking alternative methods of stimulating consumer demand. For some firms the problems surrounding the strategy of planned obsolescence occupy much of the executives' time.

After basic decisions have been made concerning the product line and product mix in a company, management may turn its attention to questions of branding, packaging, labeling, color, sizes, and other attributes or characteristics of the products. These topics are covered in the following chapter.

QUESTIONS AND PROBLEMS

1   "It is inconsistent for management to follow concurrently the product-line strategies of *expanding* its product mix and *contracting* its product mix." Discuss.

2   Cite examples of firms that have simplified or contracted their product mix in recent years.

3   Name some companies outside the automobile industry which have traded up or traded down.

4   "Trading up and trading down are product strategies closely related to the business cycle. Firms trade up during periods of prosperity and trade down during depressions or recessions." Do you agree?

[27] John B. Stewart, "Planned Obsolescence," *Harvard Business Review*, September–October, 1959, pp. 14ff.

5   Carefully distinguish between market segmentation and product differentiation as product-line strategies.

6   How might the manufacturers of each of the following articles implement the product strategy of market segmentation? Of product differentiation?
a. Shoes   c. Tape recorders
b. Paint   d. Typewriters

7   Select two of the population trends discussed in Chapter 4 and describe how these two might influence the product mix of consumer goods manufacturers.

8   "Marketing departments encourage the strategy of product diversification, whereas production departments try to simplify and streamline their operations." Discuss all aspects of this statement.

9   "If management in a retail store did a perfect job of product planning, there would be no need for clearance sales in which merchandise is marked down in price." Discuss.

10 "Between technological obsolescence (which is generally considered desirable) and style obsolescence, there is really a shadow zone rather than a sharp line. What one person considers functional obsolescence, another may class as style obsolescence." Give examples of product changes which may fall in this shadow zone.

11 Carefully distinguish between "style" and "fashion," using examples other than the ones (automobiles, swimsuits, furniture, and architecture) cited in this chapter.

12 What products, other than wearing apparel and automobiles, stress fashion and style in marketing? Do styles exist among industrial products?

13 "Emphasis on fashion and style is found only in an economy of abundance and in an economy of free enterprise." Do you agree?

14 Select a product and trace its marketing as it moves through a complete fashion cycle. Particularly note and explain the changes in the distribution, pricing, and promotion of the product in the various stages of the cycle.

15 What is the relation between fashion and the small-group influence on buying behavior explained in Chapter 5?

16 How is the concept of social-class structure (discussed in Chapter 5) related to fashion?

17 Is the trickle-across theory applicable in describing the fashion-adoption process in product lines other than women's apparel? Explain, using examples.

18 "The trickle-down theory no longer accurately reflects the fashion-adoption process." Do you agree?

19 Do you believe that clothing designers lead women to buy articles they do not like or want simply because the articles are fashionable?

20 Planned obsolescence is criticized as a social and economic waste because we are urged to buy things we do not like and do not need. What is your opinion in this matter? If you object to planned obsolescence, what are your recommendations for correcting the situation?

10

BRANDS, PACKAGING, AND OTHER PRODUCT CHARACTERISTICS

Have you ever stopped to think why you selected some of the products you are now using? Many industrial plant superintendents insist on Texaco lubricating oils and greases, while others prefer lubricants made by one of the Standard Oil companies. Some women choose Del Monte peaches; others buy Libby's. Yet many people contend that there are no significant physical or chemical differences among the well-known brands of lubricants, canned peaches, and so on. The buyer's choice may have been influenced by the guarantee offered or by an attractive package. Frequently the brand, the package, the color and design, and other product characteristics combine to project an image of the product to the prospective consumer. Then his choice is based on whether or not this image is favorable.

INFLUENCES OF PRODUCT CHARACTERISTICS ON BUSINESS FUNCTIONS

Branding, packaging, and the other product characteristics analyzed in this chapter are interrelated with the production and financial functions of a firm as well as with other marketing activities. With regard to production, the decision made concerning the product characteristics can affect unit production costs, length of production runs, and production planning and scheduling. Production runs will be shorter and thus more costly if goods are manufactured in six colors instead of one. A product made in small units and packaged in an attractive wrapper is ordinarily more costly than one put up in large, bulk-packaged units.

Financial risks increase as the variety of sizes and colors stocked or produced is increased. Packaging products in special Christmas containers exposes a company to a financial loss on merchandise unsold on December 26. A business which offers a generous warranty—double your money back if not entirely satisfied or free servicing for one year—has greater financial risks than a firm which says "all sales are final" and gives no allowances for servicing.

A multitude of interrelationships exist among the various product characteristics and the marketing policies regarding distribution, pricing, and promotion. A few examples will illustrate this point. A firm manufacturing products which will be sold by retailers on a self-service basis must devote special attention to packaging and labeling in order to attract the customer at the point of purchase. Normally, branding increases price rigidity. At the same time, however, well-known brands are most likely to have their prices cut below the usual level to attract customers to the seller's establishment. In some cases a company's label or brand has been redesigned for more effective display on television. Distinctive packaging may be the only differentiating feature of a product and thus may be the basis of an advertising campaign.

BRANDS

The word "brand" is a comprehensive term, and in one way or another it includes other, more particularized terms. A *brand* is "a name, term, symbol, or design, or a combination of them which is intended to identify the goods or services of one seller or group of sellers and to differentiate them from those of competitors."[1] A brand *name* consists of words, letters, and/or numbers which may be *vocalized*. A brand *mark* is the part of the brand which appears in the form of a symbol, design, or distinctive coloring or lettering. It is recognized by sight but is not expressed when a person pronounces the brand. Tide,

[1] Committee on Definitions, Ralph S. Alexander, Chairman, *Marketing Definitions: A Glossary of Marketing Terms*, American Marketing Association, Chicago, 1960, p. 8.

Cadillac, and Monsanto are examples of brand names. Brand marks are illustrated by the colonial gentleman on Quaker Oats products and the red star of Texaco petroleum products.

The American Marketing Association defines a *trademark* as a brand which is given legal protection because under the law it has been appropriated exclusively by one seller. Thus "trademark" is essentially a legal term. All trademarks are brands and thus include the words, letters, or numbers which may be pronounced; they may also include a pictorial design. Some people erroneously believe that the trademark is only the pictorial part of the brand. To repeat, "brand" is the comprehensive term.

One major method of classifying brands is on the basis of who owns them —producers or middlemen. Chemstrand, Burroughs, Squibb, and Canada Dry are producers' brands, while A & P, Monarch (foods), Shurfine, Penncrest, Coldspot, and Kenmore are middlemen's brands.

Although the terms "national" and "private" brands have been used to describe producer and middleman ownership, respectively, marketing people prefer the producer-middleman terminology. To say that the brand of a small manufacturer of poultry feed in Birmingham, Alabama, who markets in three states is a national brand, while the brands of A & P or Sears, Roebuck and Company are private brands, seems to be stretching the meaning of the terms "national" and "private."

Importance to the customer

A brand can be of considerable help to the consumer or industrial user. Brands are an easy way for a purchaser to identify the product or service he desires. Furthermore, the individual units of a branded item maintain a consistency of quality that buyers can depend upon. A brand also offers some protection to the consumer: it identifies the firm behind the product. A customer may have purchased a fan belt or a few yards of woolen plaid piece goods with which he was greatly pleased. When replacement parts or additional material is needed and the customer wants to get the same product, he can be assured of doing so only if the item is branded. Branding is an insurance of merchandise comparability when the buyer uses more than one source of supply. Westinghouse light bulbs are Westinghouse light bulbs, and Whitman's chocolates are Whitman's chocolates, regardless of where purchased.

Branded products tend to improve in quality over the years. Competition forces this improvement, because brand owners are constantly seeking new ways to differentiate their products in order to secure a stronger market position. In the constant search for more profitable sales volume, product improvements have frequently been the key to success. Improvements may not be perceptible on a year-to-year basis, but a 1968 Sylvania fluorescent light bulb is noticeably better than one made in 1958.

Importance to the seller

Branding can be used to achieve several of the typical marketing objectives of both manufacturers and middlemen.

To aid in advertising and display programs   Having a brand gives a seller something to advertise—something around which to build a company image. The brand is often of greater help in demand stimulation than is the company name or the technical aspects of the product. Not only can brand names or marks denote more to a customer than several lines of advertising copy, but the brand itself can also do it more rapidly. In the case of many manufacturers' brands, the consumer probably does not even know the name of the producer. A company must find some short, quick method of attracting the consumer's attention and registering an impression which will motivate him to buying action.

A firm whose product is sold on a self-service basis ordinarily must rely heavily on brand appeal. The product must be presold through advertising so that it will be immediately recognized and selected by the customer as he walks by the mass of products displayed on shelves and counters.

To help increase control and share of market   A firm which sells unbranded canned tomato juice and advertises and promotes the generic product is helping the whole industry, but it is not necessarily increasing its share of the market. By the same token, a retailer who advertises a manufacturer's brand, such as Dutch Boy paints, may stimulate a customer to buy this brand but to buy it in a competitive outlet. Only when a manufacturer or middleman puts his own brand on a product can he be assured of some control over the market.

Branding also helps the brand owner to stimulate repeat sales and to protect himself from product substitution. This is closely related to the manufacturer's desire to produce specialty goods. Unless the product has a brand identification, company A has no assurance that a retailer will not substitute a product made by another firm and tell the customer it was made by the company A.

In order to increase his sales volume, a seller may offer to service a product or he may guarantee its satisfactory performance. These promises are obviously worthless as a promotional device or sales stimulant unless the buyer can identify the firm behind the guarantee.

To reduce price comparisons and help stabilize prices   A brand in itself differentiates a product and enables the brand owner to establish a price for his product which cannot easily be compared with prices for competing goods. The mere act of branding may create a marketing difference between two items.

At the retail level, a store can prevent customers from price comparison shopping by the expedient of putting its own brand on products instead of using manufacturers' brands. A customer can compare prices on RCA Whirlpool washing machines at several department and appliance stores. Sears, Roebuck avoids this type of competition by placing the Sears' Kenmore brand on its washing machines.

There is little doubt that branding increases a firm's independence in pricing activities. The less desirable alternative for the individual firm is to expose itself to the unrelenting mercies of the market for the determination of its prices. Competition on the basis of price alone may be desirable from a consumer's standpoint, but a seller usually prefers to compete on a nonprice basis. Branding enables the seller to do this to some extent. Price competition is never completely eliminated, of course.

Branding also reduces price flexibility. Several studies have shown that prices of well-known brands tend to fluctuate less than those of nonbranded items or obscure brands. Whether price rigidity is desirable for society in general or for the individual firms involved is open to question.

To facilitate expansion of product mix   If a firm has one or more lines of branded goods, it can add a new item to its product mix much more easily than can a company selling unbranded merchandise. If the new item is similar to established products and the same brand name or mark can be attached, introduction of the new item is facilitated. Even when a new brand must be affixed, however, it certainly helps to be able to say, "The new product, brand A, is made by the ABC Company, manufacturers of brand Z and other fine products for over fifty years."

Reasons for not branding

Many firms do not brand their products because they are either unable or unwilling to assume the two major responsibilities inherent in brand ownership: the responsibility for demand stimulation through advertising, personal selling, and other forms of promotion, and the responsibility of maintaining a consistent and adequate quality of output.

Company considerations   Customer dissatisfaction with the quality of the product purchased will reflect unfavorably on the brand owner. If it is a manufacturer's brand, the customer may seek an immediate remedy from the middleman who sold the item, but the long-run harmful effects are felt by the manufacturer-owner. The customer will hesitate to repurchase not only the item that once proved unsatisfactory but any other product carrying the same brand.

Nature of product   Some items are not branded because of the difficulty of differentiating the products of one firm from those of another. Clothespins, safety pins, nails, and industrial raw materials (coal, cotton, wheat) are examples of goods for which product differentiation is generally unknown. The physical nature of some items, such as fresh fruits and vegetables, may discourage branding, although now that producers or middlemen are packaging these goods in typically purchased quantities, the brand can be applied to the package. Producers frequently do not brand that part of their output which is below their regular quality. Products graded as seconds or imperfects are sold at a cut price and are often distributed through channels different from those used for the regular goods.

Selecting a good brand

Selecting a good brand name is one of the most difficult tasks facing marketing management. In spite of the acknowledged importance of a brand, it is surprising how few really good brand names there are. In a study made many years ago, it was found that only 12 per cent of the names helped sell the product; 36 per cent actually hurt sales, and 52 per cent were "nonentities—contributing nothing to the sales appeal of the product."[2] There is no reason to believe that the situation has improved materially since this study was made.

Characteristics of a good brand   Most marketing men would agree that a good brand should possess as many of the characteristics noted below as possible. It is extremely difficult, however, to find a brand which possesses all of them.

In the first place, a good brand should suggest something about a product's benefits—its use, characteristics, quality, and action. Furthermore, the name must achieve these objectives without legally being considered descriptive (unfairly appropriating ordinary English words) or deceptive. Examples of names suggesting desirable benefits include Coldspot, Frigidaire (refrigerators and home freezers), Beautyrest, Twindow, and Craftsman (tools). Product action is suggested by Minute Rice, Thermopane, Spic and Span, Duz, Ditto, and Reddi-Wip. The name should be easy to pronounce, spell, remember, and recognize. Simple, short, crisp, one-syllable names are helpful. Pard, Tide, Gleem, Mum, and Crest fulfill these requirements. A brand name should also be distinctive. Many brands fail on this point. Countless products carry the name Acme, National, Star, Ideal, Standard, or Universal.

A brand should be sufficiently versatile to be applicable to new products which may be added to the product line. An innocuous name, such as Burroughs, Campbell, or Heinz, may serve the purpose better than a highly distinctive name suggestive of product benefits. Frigidaire is an excellent name for a

[2] "Brand Name Bugaboos," *Business Week*, May 14, 1949, p. 67; see also J. Gordon Knapp, "What's Wrong (and Right) with Today's Trademarks?" *Industrial Marketing*, July, 1963, p. 101; and "Name of the Game: The Name," *Newsweek*, Oct. 25, 1965, p. 89.

refrigerator, air conditioner, and other cold-image products, but when General Motors expanded its line of home appliances and added Frigidaire kitchen ranges, the name lost some of its sales appeal. Management should select a brand name and a mark which are adaptable to any advertising medium. In recent years many firms—Dutch Cleanser and Citgo (Cities Service Oil Co.), for example—have redesigned their brands in order to meet this requirement more effectively. Finally, the brand selected by a firm should be capable of being registered and protected legally under the Lanham Act and other statutory or common laws.[3]

Generic usage of brand name   Over a period of years some trademarks become so accepted that the brand name is substituted for the generic or descriptive name of the particular product. People associate the name with the product and not with the producer-owner of the brand. Examples of brand names which legally have become generic are linoleum, aspirin, celluloid, cellophane, kerosene, shredded wheat, and nylon. Originally these were trademarks limited to use by the owner, but they have long since lost their distinctiveness and are in the public domain. Any firm may use them.

A brand name may become generic in several ways. Sometimes a patent expires and there is no other practicable name available to the public. This happened with shredded wheat, nylon, and cellophane. Sometimes a firm just does too good an advertising and selling job with an outstanding brand name. While not yet legally generic, names such as Band-Aid, Frigidaire, and Kleenex are on the border line. They are outstanding brand names for the original product and have been promoted so well that many people use them generically. Ideally a firm wants its brand to be preferred and even insisted upon by consumers, but it does not want its brand name to become generic. This is a neat tightrope to walk.

There are several general strategies which marketing management may adopt to prevent the generic use of its brand.[4] One is to use two names—the brand name in conjunction with the company name or the brand name together with the generic name. Eastman Kodak Company advertises, "If it isn't an Eastman, it isn't a Kodak," thus fighting the tendency of the brand Kodak to become generic. Manufacturers of Vigoro, Formica, and Band-Aids have followed a similar policy. A third alternative is to give actual notice to the public that the brand has been copyrighted. This is accomplished by enclosing the letter R in a circle next to the brand name or by adding the abbreviation Reg. U.S. Pat. Off. (Registered in the United States Patent Office). Additional preventive strategies include displaying the brand in some distinctive typographical

---

[3] See "Trademark Talk," *Sales Management*, Oct. 15, 1965, p. 70.

[4] For an excellent discussion showing why trademarks become generic and a description of several methods which may be used singly or in combination to avoid this result, see Sidney A. Diamond, "Protect Your Trademark by Proper Usage," *Journal of Marketing*, July, 1962, pp. 17–22.

fashion, or avoiding the use of the trademark in a wrong grammatical form or in any altered form. Talon (zippers), Sunbeam Corporation, and Sunkist are examples of companies which have adopted the drastic alternative which involves changing the company's name to coincide with that of the brand.

Brand policies and strategies

Manufacturers' strategies   A manufacturer's decision must be based on a recognition of the values of branding and the responsibilities of brand ownership. He must decide whether to brand his product and whether to sell any or all of his output under a middleman's brand.

MARKET ENTIRE OUTPUT UNDER MANUFACTURER'S OWN BRAND   Many of the reasons for following this policy have already been covered in the section on the importance of branding to the seller. In addition, middlemen often prefer to handle manufacturers' brands, especially when the brands have high consumer acceptance. Of course, manufacturers' brands are virtually imperative for middlemen who are unable to establish their own.

Besides the earlier-mentioned responsibilities of brand ownership—the need to promote the brand and stand behind the product's quality—manufacturers face other problems when they use brands. Large retailers who want to use their own brands often will not buy products which carry the producer's brand. Also, many retailers chronically complain that manufacturers' brands provide inadequate gross margins and too little middleman control over the pricing.

BRANDING OF FABRICATING PARTS AND MATERIALS   A corollary to the above strategy is one in which producers of industrial fabricating materials and parts (products used in the further manufacturing of other goods) decide to brand their products. This strategy is used in the case of Botany Woolen Mills, Dan River cottons, Goodyear's Neolite soles and heels, Acrilan fabrics, and many automotive parts—spark plugs, batteries, oil filters, and so on.

Underlying this strategy is the seller's desire to develop a market preference for his branded part or material; he wants consumers and industrial users to specify that they want his item in the finished product. For instance, the Du Pont Company wants to build a market situation where customers will insist on a shirt or a suit made with Dacron. In addition, the parts manufacturer wants to persuade the producer of the ultimate finished item that using the branded parts or materials will help sell the end product. That is, the Du Pont Company hopes to convince the manufacturers of Manhattan or Van Heusen shirts that their sales will increase if their shirts are made with Dacron (the Du Pont Company's branded material).

From the standpoint of a purchaser, this can be an effective strategy for a manufacturer who wishes to capitalize on the reputation of these brands when he is selling his finished product. By building in highly promotable components and materials during the earliest phases of product planning, the seller may be able to keep customer interest alive long after the new-product promotional activities have ceased to be effective.[5]

Certain product characteristics are particularly conducive to the effective employment of this strategy. First, it helps if the product is also a consumer good bought for replacement purposes. If the customer must replace the oil filter or spark plugs in his car, this encourages the branding of Champion or A.C. spark plugs and Fram or Purolator oil filters. The seller's situation is improved in a second way if the part is of high unit value and is a major part of the finished product—a television picture tube, for example. In the third place, if the material or part is easily distinguished or frequently replaceable, it is apt to be branded. Here an interesting comparison arises between parts in the hard-goods industries and materials in soft goods. Hard goods parts, in automobiles, for example, are not replaced often, but they stand out clearly. In textiles, the material may not be easily distinguished or visibly labeled, but the brand is brought to the fore because the item is replaced more often.

MARKETING UNDER MIDDLEMAN'S BRAND   By selling part or all of his output under the brands of one or more middlemen, a manufacturer may utilize more effectively his production resources, including his plant capacity. Furthermore, refusing to sell under a retailer's brand will not eliminate competition from this source. Many middlemen want to market under their own brands, and if one firm refuses their business, they will go to another. In many cases, manufacturers are too small, are inadequately financed, or lack the marketing know-how to warrant the use of their own brands.

Probably the most serious limitation to marketing under a middleman's brand is that the manufacturer is at the mercy of the middleman. This disadvantage increases as the proportion of his output going to the middleman's brand increases. A manufacturer may find that he is competing on a price basis only; he can keep the business only so long as no competitor offers the retailer a lower price. Furthermore, the manufacturer has no assurance of continuity of orders, and often the profit is lower on volume sold under the middleman's brand. Another drawback is that the manufacturer's goodwill may suffer if the public becomes aware of his dual role of selling under his own and a middleman's brand, particularly if the latter is priced significantly lower than his own.

Middlemen's strategies   The question of whether "to brand or not to brand" must also be answered by middlemen.

CARRY ONLY MANUFACTURERS' BRANDS   Most retailers and wholesalers follow this policy because they are in no position to take on the dual burdens of promoting a brand and being responsible for maintaining its quality. Manufacturers' products afford a more ready source of supply. Even though they

[5] "New-product 'Middle Age': The Dangerous Years," *Sales Management*, Nov. 2, 1962, p. 37.

usually carry lower gross margins, manufacturers' brands often have a higher rate of turnover and a better profit possibility.

CARRY MIDDLEMEN'S BRANDS IN CONJUNCTION WITH MANUFACTURERS' BRANDS   Many large retailers and some large wholesalers have their own brands. In a given line, a retailer may use only middlemen's brands, or he may carry one or more manufacturers' brands in direct competition with his own. To establish and market his own brand successfully, a retailer must have earned the confidence of his customers, and he must carefully maintain a high level of quality control over the items which he selects to sell under this brand. He should also have a very large sales volume because no other firm will help him sell this brand.

Large middlemen, retailers particularly, incur the ill will and antagonism of manufacturers if they decide to use their own brands in direct competition with strong, established manufacturers' brands. For many reasons, however, a middleman may feel that it is advantageous to market his own brand. In the first place, it increases his control over his market. If a customer prefers a middleman's brand, he can get it only at the middleman's store.

By using his own brand a middleman can reap the full benefit of his promotional efforts and any customer goodwill attached to the brand. Salesclerks in the store can even use the sales argument that "our brand is the same as the widely advertised brand A which is selling for a 20 per cent higher price." Furthermore, where self-service is employed as a selling technique, the retailer has learned that by putting his own brand at eye level and a manufacturer's brand above or below this level, he can improve the sales picture of his own brand considerably.

If a middleman decides to adopt his own brand, he can usually sell it at a price below that of the manufacturers' brands and still get a higher gross margin. This is possible because he can buy at a lower cost. The cost may be lower because the manufacturer does not include a share of his advertising and selling costs in the price or because he is anxious to get the extra business in order to keep his plant running in slack seasons.

Middlemen have more freedom and flexibility in pricing products sold under their own labels. Some manufacturers give a retailer no price flexibility, even to meet local competition. From the 1930s to the 1950s, many manufacturers fixed their prices under the resale-price-maintenance (fair-trade) laws. Some manufacturers still adhere to this pricing policy. At the other extreme, some manufacturers' brands are used as a price football; the price is cut indiscriminately by competing stores to a point where a retailer may lose money on every sale. When a middleman has his own brand, it becomes a differentiated product, and this hinders price comparisons which might be unfavorable to the store.

Middlemen may be able to control their own branded product and its supply more than they can a manufacturer's brand. A middleman who has his own brand need not fear that manufacturers will either withdraw their brand or not sell to him in the first place. He may avoid problems caused by frequent model changes which leave him with large inventories of obsolete merchandise. Also, a retailer or wholesaler who decides to use his own brand can establish specifications under which his brand is to be produced.

Some middlemen decide to use their own brands because they can hitch-hike on the established reputation of manufacturers whose branded parts or materials are used in the middlemen's products. For example, the J. C. Penney Company will sell its own brand of shirts but advertise that they are Sanforized or made of Dacron material.

Strategies common to manufacturers and middlemen   Manufacturers and middlemen alike must adopt some strategy with respect to branding a line of products and also with respect to branding for market saturation.

BRANDING A LINE OF PRODUCTS   At least four different strategies are widely used by firms which have more than one product. (1) The same "family" or "blanket" brand may be placed on all products. This policy is followed by Heinz, Campbell, Libby, and others in the food field, as well as by Squibb and General Electric. (2) A separate name may be used for each product. This strategy is employed by International Shoe Company, Procter & Gamble, and Lever Brothers. (3) A separate family brand may be applied to each grade of product or to each group of similar products. Sears, Roebuck and Company groups its baby items under the Honeysuckle brand, its women's clothes under Kerrybrook, its major home installations (furnaces, building materials) under Homart, and so on. (4) The company's trade name may be combined with an individual name for the product. Thus there is Johnson's Pride and Johnson's Glo-Coat, and Kellogg's Rice Krispies and Kellogg's Sugar Corn Pops.

A family brand is best suited for a marketing situation where the products are related in quality, in use, or in some other manner. Swift's does not associate its Premium ham brand with Vigoro, its fertilizer.

When used wisely, a family-brand strategy has considerable merit. It is much simpler and less expensive to introduce new related products to a line. Also, the general prestige of a brand can be spread more easily if it appears on several products rather than on one.

On the other hand, the use of family brands places a greater burden on the owner to maintain adequate and consistent quality among all products. One bad item can reflect unfavorably, and conceivably even disastrously, on all other goods carrying the same brand. Another drawback to family brands is that each individual item under the brand usually gets less aggressive promotional effort than it would if each product were separately distinguished. Also, just because one product under the family brand has considerable consumer acceptance does not mean that all other similarly branded products will rate as high in consumer esteem.

BRANDING FOR MARKET SATURATION Frequently, in order to achieve a greater degree of market saturation, a firm will employ a multiple-brand strategy. Various brands may be used for identical products, for the same general type of product, or for different qualities or grades of the same product. Often one type of sales appeal is built around a given brand. To reach another segment of the market, the company must use other appeals. Procter & Gamble's two detergents, Tide and Dreft, illustrate this point. Some people feel that if Tide is strong enough to clean dirty, greasy work clothes, it cannot be used on lingerie and other fine clothing or on dishes because it would be too strong for their hands. For these people, Procter & Gamble has marketed Dreft, still a detergent, but one whose image is more gentle than that of Tide.

Sometimes a producer wants to expand the number of retail outlets in a given geographic market. Possibly he has granted an exclusive territory to one retailer, and now that the market has enlarged enough to support two or three retailers, the original store does not want to have the brand distributed to its competitors. Rather than antagonize his original dealer, the manufacturer may market the identical product in other outlets but under another brand.

The use of multiple brands on the same or similar products affords the seller some flexibility in his pricing. A competitor may have an attractively priced item, and rather than cut the price on his known brand, a manufacturer or middleman may come out with another "fighting brand" priced to beat that of the competitor and still leave the price image of the original brand unscathed. Sometimes even different channels are used by manufacturers marketing a fighting brand in order to further dissociate it from their regular product.

As a rule, it is a sound strategy to use separate brands on different qualities of the same general type of product. Obviously, to run counter to this policy—that is, to market different qualities under the same brand—is risky. It violates a fundamental thesis in branding, namely, that all units of a given brand should be reasonably consistent in quality. Several manufacturers of sheets, towels, and pillowcases do market various levels of quality under the same general brand, but with additional differentiating labels.

The battle of the brands

Middlemen's brands have proved to be eminently successful in competing with manufacturers' brands. However, in their brand strategies as discussed above, neither group has demonstrated a convincing competitive superiority over the other in the marketplace. Consequently, the "battle of the brands," which has been one of the significant marketing developments of the past decade, shows every indication of continuing and becoming more intense.[6] In some of the larger department stores, 10 per cent of the sales volume is in the store's brand;

[6] Leon Morse, "The Battle of the Brands," *Dun's Review and Modern Industry*, May, 1964, p. 53. Some of the points in this section are adapted from this article.

in the A & P Company, the store-brand volume is 25 per cent of total volume, and Montgomery Ward is intending that 80 per cent of its total volume will be in the company's own brand.

Historically, middlemen's brands emerged generally in the 1920s, became of some significance during the Depression of the 1930s, and with a few exceptions almost disappeared during World War II. Several factors have accounted for the highly successful resurgence of these brands. The thin profit margins on manufacturers' brands in particular, and on total volume in general, have encouraged retailers to establish and promote their own labels. The consumer himself has become more sophisticated in his buying, and his brand loyalty has declined, so he will consider many alternative brands. The improved and dependable quality of retailers' brands has boosted their sales. Finally, it is quite generally known that middlemen's brands are usually produced by large, well-known manufacturers.

In this battle, the manufacturers are vocal in their point of view. A few— not many—refuse to produce store-branded merchandise. Manufacturers charge retailers with accepting funds for cooperative advertising of manufacturers' products and then diverting these funds for the advertising of the stores' brands. Furthermore, retailers generally have not contributed much to product innovation. Certainly store brands would be apt to suffer considerably if they did not have manufacturers' advertised brands to use for price and quality comparisons.

PACKAGING

Packaging may be defined as the general group of activities in product planning which involve designing and producing the container or wrapper for a product. Packaging obviously is closely related to labeling and branding, two other product-planning activities, because the label often appears on the package and the brand is typically on the label.

There are three reasons for packaging:

1. A utilitarian as well as a marketing reason for packaging a product is to protect it on its route from the manufacturer to the consumer or industrial user, and in some cases even during its life with the customer. Compared with bulk items, packaged goods generally are more convenient, cleaner, and less susceptible to losses from evaporation, spilling, and spoilage. Packaging helps to identify a product and thus may prevent substitution of competitive goods.

2. Packaging also may implement a company's promotional program. A package may be the only significant way in which a firm can differentiate its product. Of the many products, particularly convenience goods or industrial operating supplies, most buyers feel that among the well-known brands one is about as good as another. Also, changing a package is an inexpensive way to give the impression that the product itself has been changed. Packaging can be used

effectively to help introduce a new product or to help increase or maintain the market for existing products.[7] Sometimes a packaging change can rejuvenate an old product by giving it a new image.

The utilitarian reasons for packaging—protection, identification, and convenience—may in themselves be exploited in advertising or personal selling. Some features of the package may serve as a sales appeal, for example, a no-drip spout, a self-applicator, an aerosol spray dispenser, or a reusable jar. Furthermore, the package advertising copy will last as long as the product is being used in its packaged form. Every time the housewife takes down a jar of peanut butter, she is exposed to the message on the label. At the point of purchase, the package serves as a silent salesman encouraging impulse buying; in the customer's possession, it is a constant suggestion that she reorder the same brand.

3. Management may package its products in such a way as to increase profit possibilities. A package may be so attractive that customers will pay more just to get the special package—even though the increase in price exceeds the additional cost of the package. Also, an increase in ease of handling or a reduction in losses due to damage will cut marketing costs.

Growing importance of packaging

Most companies recognize that packaging is important for purposes of protection and convenience. The activity has been production-oriented in most firms, however, and marketing and sales values have been ignored. This attitude still exists in companies where packaging has little or no impact on sales. But in other firms, producers of both consumer and industrial goods, the marketing significance of packaging is now recognized.[8]

The increased use of branding and the public's generally rising standards of health, cleanliness, and sanitation have undoubtedly contributed to the growth of packaging. The major factor, however, is the importance of packaging as a real competitive force in today's struggle for markets. The widespread use of self-service, automatic vending, and other self-selection methods of retail selling means that the package must do the selling job at the point of purchase. It is no simple task for a manufacturer even to get his product placed on display in a retail outlet. Shelf space is at a premium, and retailers are inclined to cater to producers who have problems at the store level and who then, wherever possible, have used better packaging to solve these problems.[9]

Packaging today is a major business activity. Four cents out of every

---

[7] See Penelope Orth, "Can the Package Work Harder Still?" *Printers' Ink*, May 29, 1964, p. 182 (a special issue devoted to new-product marketing).

[8] For a comprehensive special report on various aspects of packaging, see "The Power of Proper Packaging," *Business Week,* Feb. 20, 1965, p. 90.

[9] See Walter B. Bruce, "How It Batters down Barriers," *Printers' Ink*, May 29, 1964, p. 184.

dollar spent for goods and services goes into packaging. At General Electric, for example, packaging materials are third on the list (behind copper and sheet steel) of all materials purchased by the company.[10] A leading business journal, *Dun's Review and Modern Industry*, has for several years devoted an entire supplement to packaging problems and developments in its November or December issue.

As products face murderous visual competition from all sides, the pace of packaging development has left industry the victim of unplanned obsolescence. These new developments, occurring rapidly and in a seemingly endless flow, require management's constant attention in order that the marketing opportunities presented by these features can be optimized. We see new packaging materials replacing the traditional ones, exotic new shapes and sizes, new closures (flip-top, pull-tab, rip-cap), and other new features (measured portions, fractional packages, metered flow)—all making for increased convenience for consumers and additional selling points for marketers.[11]

The growing importance of packaging makes it evident that responsibility for this activity should rest on the shoulders of top management. To an increasing extent, packaging decisions are being centralized at the vice-presidential and even the presidential level. Major companies—General Foods and the National Biscuit Company, for instance—have established separate corporate packaging staffs; at Nabisco, the head of this division is a vice-president.[12]

Policies and strategies of packaging

Companies that realize the potential marketing value of good packaging strive to develop a packaging policy that gives them considerable flexibility in pursuing various packaging strategies.

Changing the package Whether to change a package and, if so, when to make the change are related problems. The trend today is in favor of change, and there is every indication that this trend is gaining momentum. In general, management has two reasons for considering package innovation: a decrease in sales or a desire to expand a market by attracting new groups of customers.

More specifically, a firm may want to correct a bad feature in the existing container. The box may leak after being opened, or it may not be sufficiently airtight. A company may want to take advantage of new materials or ideas. Adopting the flip-top box for cigarettes, placing plastic liners in paper con-

---

[10] "Packaging: Order from Chaos," *Dun's Review and Modern Industry*, November, 1962, p. 52 (a five-part report).

[11] See Phyllis Daignault, "New Dimensions in Convenience Packaging," *Sales Management*, Jan. 17, 1964, p. 25.

[12] See Ted Sanchagrin, "The New Power of Packaging: Management Takes Control," *Printers' Ink*, June 11, 1965, p. 13; and Phyllis Daignault, "Packaging's 'Sell' Gets Organized," *Sales Management*, Mar. 19, 1965, p. 59.

tainers, and using new printing processes are examples. Some companies change their containers to aid in the firm's promotional program. The new package may be used as a major appeal in the advertising copy, or the old containers may be modified because they do not show up well in advertisements.

Packaging product line   A company must decide whether or not to develop a family resemblance in the packaging of its several products. *Family packaging* involves making the entire package identical for all products or using some common feature on all the packages. For example, both Heinz and Campbell soups use virtually identical packaging on all their soup products. Management's evaluation of family packaging parallels, to some extent, its evaluation of family branding. When new products are added to a line, promotional values associated with old products extend to the new ones. On the other hand, this strategy should be used only when the products are related in use and are of similar quality. Extensive family packaging can give a middleman the impression that he is overstocked on the brand; it can make a customer wonder if the retailer's stock is limited to a single company's products.

Reuse packaging   Another strategy to be considered is reuse packaging. Shall the company design and promote a package which can serve other purposes after the original contents are consumed? Glasses containing cheese can later be used for fruit juices. Peanut butter, jelly, and pickle jars can make good containers for leftovers or can be used for home canning purposes. This strategy should be employed only when it is possible to leave an impression with the customer that he is getting something in return for the increased price of the product. Reuse packaging should stimulate repeat purchases. If a person purchases a certain brand of peanut butter in order to collect a set of drinking glasses and, once he has them, switches to another brand, the dual-use packaging strategy has been of little help to the peanut butter manufacturer.

Multiple packaging   For many years there has been a trend toward *multiple packaging*, or the practice of placing several units in one container. Dehydrated soups, dog food, motor oil, beer, golf balls, soap, building hardware, candy bars, towels, sheets, and countless other products are packaged in multiple units. Test after test has proved that multiple packaging increases total sales as well as unit sales of a product. Multiple packaging can also help introduce new products and win consumer acceptance of a new idea or concept. Although a user may not particularly like the different taste of a new product the first time he tries it, by the time he has finished the third box that came in the multiple package he may be impressed favorably. In other instances, multiple packaging is convenient for special price offers and for the sale of small items. Retailers like this method of packaging because it cuts unit-handling and price-marking costs. On the other hand, if a product is used infrequently or if it lasts a long time, quantity packaging is not advantageous.

LABELING

Labeling is another product characteristic which requires managerial attention. The *label* is that part of a product which carries verbal information about the product or the seller (manufacturer or middleman). A label may be part of a package, or it may be a tag attached directly to the product. Obviously there is a close relationship between labeling and packaging, and between labeling and branding.

Labeling also has considerable social significance. Several of the public's criticisms of marketing have centered around charges of false, misleading, or deceptive labeling. In the textile field, this has led to Federal legislation on the labeling of furs, wool products, and other textiles. Historically, inadequate labeling hastened the passage of the Federal Food, Drug, and Cosmetic Act.

Although there has been immeasurable improvement in labeling practices over the past twenty-five years, legislation alone cannot do the job. Many products are still inadequately labeled from a marketing standpoint. Further improvement is needed, and it will come as additional firms begin to realize the marketing advantages of good labeling. Nevertheless, it will not be easy to develop a labeling system which will enable consumers to determine quality and compare competitive products. Standards must be developed so that comparisons can be made. Then the customers will have to be taught the meaning of the standards and the importance of reading the information on the labels.

Types of labels

Typically, labels are classed as brand, grade, descriptive, and informative. A *brand label* is simply the brand alone applied to the product or to the package; thus some oranges are brand-labeled Sunkist or Blue Goose, and some clothes carry the brand label Sanforized. A *grade label* identifies the quality by a letter, number, or word. Canned peaches are grade-labeled A, B, and C, and corn and wheat are grade-labeled number 1 and 2. Some stores grade their products "good," "better," and "best." In this book, *descriptive labels* and *informative labels* are grouped together and used synonymously. There are labels which give written or illustrative objective information about the characteristics, use, construction, care, performance, or other features of the product. On a descriptive-informative label for a can of corn there will be statements concerning the type of corn (golden sweet), style (creamed or in niblet kernels), can size, number of servings, and net contents. A descriptive-informative label on a suit, on sheets, or on an electric blanket will give details concerning (1) what the item is made of, (2) how it is made (worsted or flannel; weave; thread count), (3) how it should be cared for (dry cleaning only), (4) how it should be used (AC current only), (5) how it will perform (water-repellent, wrinkle-free), and (6) the name and address of the manufacturer or middleman.

Relative merit   Brand labeling creates very little stir among critics. While it is an acceptable form of labeling, its severe limitation is that it does not supply sufficient information to a buyer. The real fight centers around grade versus descriptive labeling, and whether grade labeling should be made mandatory. Historically, consumer organizations have been in favor of grade labeling, and businessmen have advocated descriptive-informative labeling. Some of the arguments on both sides are noted here, but on balance it seems that no one type of labeling is best for all products.

The proponents of grade labeling argue that it is simple, definite, and easy to use. They also point out that if grade labels were used, prices would be more related to quality, although grade labeling would not stifle competition. In fact, they believe that grade labeling might increase competition because consumers would be able to judge products on the basis of both price and known quality. The cost of grade labeling is very low, so it would not place a great burden on the manufacturer. Grade labeling would in no way do away with brand names. Many firms already using grade labeling have tied in the grade with their promotional programs.

Those who object to grade labeling point out that it is not possible to grade differences in flavor and taste or in style and fashion. A very low score on one grading characteristic can be offset by very high scores on several other factors. Companies selling products which score high within a given quality bracket would be hurt by grade labeling. It would not be possible for these companies to justify a higher price than that charged for another Grade A product which scored very low in the Grade A quality range. Some people feel that grades are an inaccurate guide for consumer buying because the characteristics selected for grading, the weights assigned to them, and the means of measuring them are all established on an arbitrary basis.

Statutory labeling requirements

The importance of labeling and many of its problems are evidenced to some extent by the large number of Federal laws regulating this marketing activity. Several states also have labeling statutes. At the Federal level, concern for this activity comes within the province of at least four agencies—the Federal Trade Commission, the Food and Drug Administration, the Department of Agriculture, and the Treasury Department. The Federal Trade Commission Act of 1914 and the Wheeler-Lea amendment (1938) state that unfair competition is illegal if it may injure a competitor or the consumer. Although the law does not give explicit examples of unfair-trade practices, a false, misleading, or deceptive label or package would provide a specific instance of unfair competition.

In the past, the labeling of clothing, furs, and piece goods was often confusing and misleading to the consumer, and existing laws were apparently inadequate. As a result, three important labeling laws have been passed. The Wool Products Labeling Act (1941) provides that a clothing product which contains any wool must be labeled to explain clearly what kind of wool is used (virgin, reused, reprocessed, etc.) and what percentage by weight of each type is included in the product. Label legislation was expanded in 1952 with the passage of the Fur Products Labeling Act. This law provides that in identifying a fur garment, the label must state the usual or natural name of the fur and its country of origin. The Textile Fiber Products Identification Act (1960) provides that clothing garments and household textiles, including rugs, must carry the generic or chemical description of the fiber content. It is insufficient to give only the fiber maker's brand name or to use only such descriptive terms as "wash and wear." Also, the label must state the percentages (by weight) of all fibers present in amounts over 5 per cent, the name of the manufacturer of the article, and the name of the country where the product was manufactured if it was imported.

The Food and Drug Act of 1906 and its 1938 amendment, the Food, Drug, and Cosmetic Act, are administered by the Food and Drug Administration. These laws provide explicit regulations for labeling drugs, foods, cosmetics (except toilet soaps), and therapeutic devices. If artificial coloring or preservatives are used, the label must note this fact. Any conditions for safe use must be included on the label, and items with poisonous content must be so labeled.

In an effort to bring safety and quality controls into line with the swift pace and modern methods found in the drug industry, Congress passed in 1962 a bill establishing considerably tighter controls over the manufacture and marketing of ethical pharmaceuticals. One section of the new law (which also is administered by the Food and Drug Administration) pertains to labeling. Labels and advertising are now required to display prominently the generic name of the drug in addition to the brand name.

The U.S. Department of Agriculture has established standards for A, B, and C grades of canned food products, but a producer is not obliged to have his products so graded. There are mandatory provisions for inspecting and labeling as "U.S. Inspected" any fresh meats sold in interstate commerce. Finally, the Treasury Department is responsible for seeing that appropriate tax stamps and labels are affixed to alcoholic beverages, tobacco products, and playing cards.

OTHER IMAGE-BUILDING CHARACTERISTICS

A company cannot assert that it has a well-rounded program for product planning and development until it has made decisions and instituted a company policy on several additional product attributes: product design, color, sizes, product quality, and guarantee and servicing.

Product design

One way to build an image of a product is through its design. In fact, a distinctive design may be the only significantly differentiating feature of a product.

For the past several years, many firms have felt that there is considerable glamour, romance, and general promotional appeal in product design and the designer's name. It is not at all unusual to see in an advertisement that a product or package was designed by Raymond Loewy, Henry Dreyfuss, or Walter Teague. In the field of industrial products, engineering design has long been recognized as extremely important, but today there is a growing realization of the marketing value of appearance design as well. Office machines and office furniture and fixtures are examples of industrial products where conscious attention has been given to product design, and usually with good sales results. The marketing significance of design has been recognized for years in the field of consumer products, whether they are big items like automobiles and refrigerators or small products like fountain pens, packaged goods, and apparel. Design has been an important contributor to planned obsolescence in automobiles and clothing.

Product materials and product performance are related to design. New developments in plastics, synthetic fibers, lightweight metals, and other materials have broadened the designer's horizon considerably. Of course, the marketing opportunities presented by new materials must not completely obscure production and financial considerations. Regarding product performance, the designer must know the answers to the following questions: What will the product be used for? What does the buyer expect? What is the cost of building in the various levels of performance?

Good design can improve the marketability of a product in many ways. It can make the product easier to operate; it can upgrade the product's quality or durability; it can improve product appearance and lower manufacturing costs. Good design can also generate new uses for a product or make it adaptable for initial use by new customers.[13]

Visual design may be viewed as a separate marketing strategy or as a method of implementing the strategies of market segmentation and planned obsolescence. "By offering a variety of design, the marketer abets the consumer in exercising his sense of discrimination and fulfilling his inherent need of change and novelty."[14]

Color

People seem to be more conscious of color today than in the past. It is often the determining factor in a customer's acceptance or rejection of a product, whether it is a dress, a table, or an automobile. Even in industrial products, color is an important aspect of design.

Color by itself, however, is no selling advantage because many competing firms offer products in color. The marketing advantage comes in knowing the

[13] See Henry Dreyfuss, "Where Function Weds Esthetics," *Printers' Ink,* May 29, 1964, p. 165 (a special issue devoted to new-product marketing).

[14] John E. Mertes, "Product Planning and Visual Design Policies," *Business Topics,* Summer, 1962, p. 66.

right color, how many colors to use, and when to change colors. If a garment manufacturer or a retail store's fashion coordinator guesses wrong on what will be the fashionable color in women's clothing, it can be disastrous. There is an increasing need for thorough research and expert help on the subject; many firms employ the services of color stylists today.

A marketing man must reckon with color as both a psychological and a sociological force. Its careful use can increase sales, increase worker productivity, reduce eyestrain, and generally affect emotional reactions. Some colors have different meanings to various ethnic groups, and there are geographic preferences in color.

Sizes

The assortment of sizes in which goods are produced by a manufacturer or stocked by middlemen can have a substantial bearing on the marketing success of a firm. It is simply lost business when an industrial distributor does not have a desired size of valve or rubber belting in stock, or when a clothing store does not have the right shirt or blouse size.

Manufacturers and middlemen alike are pressured to increase the number of sizes they market and to carry something for everybody. On the other hand, middlemen know that their shelf space is at a premium and that the little-called-for sizes often end up being sold at a considerable markdown. Manufacturers may fight the pressure because they too fear economic losses inherent in slow-moving sizes.

It is difficult to detect whether there is a trend toward larger or smaller package sizes; possibly there is significant movement in both directions.[15] Coca-Cola added a 12-ounce bottle to the traditional 6-ounce size. Jell-O added a larger package size, and several brewers have come out with 16-ounce containers for beer. On the other hand, Coors now markets some of its beer in 7-ounce aluminum cans, and some brands of coffee appear in ½-pound tins. Large packages offer economy, and small ones offer convenience.

There is often an important relationship between price and package size. Sometimes the package size is reduced slightly and the price remains the same. One wonders whether the vast number of package sizes is not misleading, as well as confusing, to a buyer. If so, one may well question the social responsibility of companies employing such strategies and tactics.

Product quality

The quality of a good is extremely important, but it is probably the most difficult of all the image-building features to define. Users frequently disagree on

[15] The results of an A. C. Nielsen Co. study covering leading brands in five categories of food and household products sold in supermarkets indicated a definite trend to packaging in larger sizes. See "A Continuing Trend: Large Package Sizes," *Printers' Ink*, Feb. 12, 1965, p. 60.

what constitutes quality in an item, whether it is a cut of meat, a piece of music, an article of clothing, or an automobile. Personal tastes are deeply involved. Nevertheless, a marketing executive must make several decisions about product quality. First, the product should reach only a level of quality compatible with the intended use of the item; it need not be any better. In fact, "good" and "poor" are misleading terms. "Correct" and "incorrect" would be much more appropriate. If a housewife is making peach cobbler, Grade B or C peaches are the correct quality; they are not necessarily the best quality, but they are right for the intended use. It is not necessary to pay Grade A prices for large, well-formed peaches when these features will not be seen in the cobbler. In the industrial field, if a manufacturer is going to use certain tools and dies for one season only, he does not need to buy high-quality items that are guaranteed to last five years.[16]

Next, a marketing administrator should insist that all units of output maintain as consistent a degree of quality as is reasonably possible. Furthermore, all the components of a given product should be similar in quality; like the parts of the "one-hoss shay," ideally all parts will perform equally well and cease performing simultaneously.

Guarantee and servicing

Management must determine what kind of guarantee it will offer with the product and what servicing it will provide both before and after the sale. The general purpose of a guarantee is to give the buyer some assurance that he will be protected in case the product is not up to reasonable expectations.[17] More specifically, there are several situations in which a guarantee may be an essential ingredient for marketing success. If guarantees are common practice in the trade, then all companies will probably have to comply. When the unit price is high, a guarantee is often necessary. It is difficult to sell a new type of product without written assurance that the seller will stand behind the item. Selling methods may influence the use of guarantees. They are essential in direct-mail selling, especially when the customer pays in advance. Also, middlemen may not handle a product unless the manufacturer offers a guarantee.

The nature of the product itself may necessitate a guarantee. When the customer cannot judge the quality of an item by inspecting it or when quality may deteriorate during shipping or while the product is on a shelf, guarantees

[16] For some new methods of matching product features with consumers' wishes and of measuring consumers' ability to recognize differences among products, see Alfred A. Kuehn and Ralph L. Day, "Strategy of Product Quality," *Harvard Business Review*, November–December, 1962, pp. 100–110.

[17] For a report on a rapidly expanding legal trend which indicates that a manufacturer is liable for product-caused consumer injuries, even when the company is *not* proved negligent in the product's manufacture, see "New Peril in Product Liability," *Sales Management*, Dec. 17, 1965, p. 21; and Arthur F. Southwick, Jr., "Mass Marketing and Warranty Liability," *Journal of Marketing*, April, 1963, pp. 6–12.

are vital. If a complex installation is required, the customer wants specific assurance that the seller will correct any deficiencies.

For some products, marketing success requires the manufacturer or middleman to service the goods. This may involve simply installing the product or explaining its operation. On the other hand, servicing may be an extensive, time-consuming process, especially for certain industrial equipment.

QUESTIONS AND PROBLEMS

1   What is the difference between a brand and a trademark?

2   List five brand names which you think are good ones and five which are poor. Explain the reasoning behind your choices.

3   Evaluate each of the following brand names in light of the characteristics of a good brand, indicating the strong and weak points of each name:

a.   Xerox (office copier)   d.   Hush Puppies (shoes)
b.   IBM (business machines)   e.   A-1 (steak sauce)
c.   Mustang (automobiles)   f.   Hotpoint (appliances)

4   Can you name some products which are sold unbranded? In each case, why do you think that neither the producer nor the middlemen branded the article?

5   A Senate committee was investigating pricing practices in the drug industry. Some of the legislators objected to the practice of several manufacturers' producing chemically identical products and then differentiating the products by the use of brand names. One senatorial recommendation was to pass a law requiring that all drug products be identified by their generic names rather than by brand names. What is your opinion? Are there other products which you feel should be sold only under their generic names?

6   Advocates of branding point out that it aids in price stabilization. Critics claim that "stabilization" is just a nice word for price-fixing. What is your opinion?

7   Suggest some brands which are on the verge of becoming generic. What course of action should a company take to protect the separate identity of its brand?

8   Under what conditions would you recommend that a manufacturer brand a product which will be used as a part or material in the production of another article?

9   Give some examples of middlemen's brands other than those mentioned in this chapter. How do you account for the substantial increase in middlemen's brands over the past twenty-five years?

10   Why do some firms sell an identical product under more than one of their own brands?

11   Who do you forecast will be the winner of the "battle of the brands"?

12   What marketing strategy should a manufacturer adopt when his largest retail customer decides to buy a product from another source and put the store's brand on it? The retailer will continue to stock the first manufacturer's product, but heavy store promotional effort will be placed behind the store's brand.

13   "Middlemen's brands sell for lower prices than do manufacturers' brands." Prove or disprove this statement by a survey of at least fifteen products sold

in local drugstores or supermarkets. Be sure you are comparing packages of similar size in each case. How can you be certain that the two brands of a particular product on your list are of comparable quality?

14 Give examples of products that are excellently packaged. Give examples of some that are very poorly packaged.

15 Explain how packaging policies may be related to, or may implement, a firm's promotional program.

16 Name some products which you feel are well labeled and some which are poorly labeled.

17 "Self-service selling and television advertising have increased the importance of packaging and labeling." Explain.

18 If grade labeling is adopted, what factors should be used as bases for grading the following products?

a. Sheets and pillowcases   d. Canned peaches
b. Suntan lotion   e. Frozen orange juice
c. Blankets

19 Give examples of products in which the careful use of color has increased sales. Can you cite examples to show that poor use of color may hurt a company's marketing program?

20 Explain how the need to guarantee and service a product may influence the distribution system and the pricing structure for this product.

case 6. CLAREMONT CANDLE COMPANY

Addition of lower-priced product to manufacturer's line

After a long period of fairly constant annual sales volume, the sales curve of the Claremont Candle Company has been declining during the past few years. This trend has been bothering the president, Mr. Dale Fidino, because during the same period consumer income, especially consumer *discretionary* income, has increased steadily. Mr. Fidino is concerned that consumer motivation regarding the use of candles in the home may be changing; the primary demand for candles may have reached a peak and may even be declining. He feels strongly that the company must make some changes in its marketing program if the direction of this sales curve is ever again to turn upward.

The Claremont Candle Company has been in the wax and tallow business for over one hundred years, and today it is one of the largest producers of wax candles in the United States. Operations originated in England, where the candles were made by hand dipping them in a cauldron of molten tallow. Around 1900, the American plant and general offices were established in Kansas City, Missouri. This location was selected because of the close proximity of slaughterhouses—the source of raw materials of tallow and lard.

Claremont markets a complete line of high-quality candles in a wide variety of colors, shapes, and sizes. The bulk of the sales are made to the consumer market, primarily through large department stores and gift shops all over the country. The largest-volume item is a 15-inch smokeless, dripless, odorless beeswax candle, packaged six or twelve to a box and retailing for 50 to 60 cents per candle. Another significant market is the religious institutional market. Claremont has a sales force of twenty men selling to wholesalers who supply candles to churches and other religious institutions.

Periodic marketing research studies by the company have revealed that candles in general—and certainly Claremont's high-priced ones in particular—find a market primarily among people with above-average incomes, living in older, larger homes. These are the people whose homes have separate dining rooms and who generally live in a slower-paced, more gracious, elegant manner than is usually found in today's fast-paced society. This is the market where dining is an occasion and where candle-lit dinners or at least candle-decorated tables are the rule rather than the exception.

Mr. Fidino believes that this is a declining market. He wants to reach the large middle-income market living in housing developments in suburbia or in the new high-rise apartments he has seen springing up in so many cities. He thinks that the key to reaching this new market successfully is to introduce a lower-priced line of candles. He has in mind a retail price of 10 or 15 cents for a 15-inch candle. Mr. Fidino reasons that the lower-income and middle-income families will not pay 50 to 60 cents per unit just to have the gracious effect of candlelight in their homes. This market would, however, use candles in greater quantity if they could be purchased for about 15 cents each. At the same time, the company would continue to market its high-priced prestige line.

Investigation has shown that the addition of a lower-priced line would not present any major production problems. In fact, the quality of the new line would approximate that of the prestige products. The same wax and the same wick could be used for both product groups. The packaging and colors would be less expensive for the new line, and some new manufacturing equipment would be needed. The new products would be differentiated in style and design from the higher-priced candles.

Mr. Lawrence Scarlett, the vice-president of marketing, does not agree with the president's suggestion for adding the line of lower-priced candles. Mr. Scarlett has said that it is poor marketing strategy to trade down during a period of rising incomes, rising prices, and generally good business conditions. His proposal is to stick with the higher-priced products and do a more aggressive job of promoting them. He likens this to the promotional job which the California wine makers have done in increasing consumers' acceptance of wine with dinner and their understanding of the "proper" wine to use for each occasion.

Mr. Scarlett anticipates real problems in the distribution of the low-priced candles. He doubts that the present retailers would accept the new line. To seek new outlets such as drugstores, supermarkets, and variety stores would antagonize the existing retailers. Also, the present sales force has had no experience selling to the type of retail dealer that would probably be used for the new line. (Unanswered at this point is a question regarding the brand policy for the new line—would it be tied in any way to the brand of the higher-priced candles, or would the new products carry a totally unrelated name?)

A compromise solution for broadening the product base has come from the plant manager. He has proposed adding a line of holiday novelties for Christmas, Easter, Thanksgiving, Halloween, etc. As an illustration, for the Christmas season the company would produce such articles as wax Christmas trees, Santa Clauses, toy reindeers, sleighs, angels, and Christmas candles. These products would all be made from the same wax and tallow as the candles, and they would be fitted with wicks so as to burn as candles. To reduce production costs, the plant manager has developed a manufacturing process whereby the hot wax could be run through a soft-ice-cream machine to incorporate more air into the wax, thus reducing the total poundage of wax about 60 per cent per product. In this way, these products could be sold profitably at a competitive price in supermarkets and variety stores.

As a related marketing strategy, Mr. Fidino wants to change the packaging of the company's candles so they would be sold in pairs rather than only in dozens or half dozens. He contends that candles are not used by the dozen. If the products were available in a "twin-pack," consumers would have an opportunity to purchase a greater variety of colors and lengths; in the long run, these customers would use more candles.

Two of the top executives are fighting this packaging recommendation bitterly. They contend that as a result of twin packaging, the housewife would buy fewer candles than she would if they were packed in lots of six or twelve. These two men believe that if a consumer bought twelve candles at a time, she would be more apt to use them quickly and would soon be in the market for another dozen. If, on the other hand, she bought candles two at a time, she would have a tendency to use them only for decoration. That is, she would conserve them to prolong their life over several festive occasions.

QUESTIONS

1   Should the Claremont Company add the line of lower-priced candles?

2   Should the company add the line of holiday novelty items?

3   If the lower-priced candles and/or holiday novelties are added to the company's

product line, should these products be branded so as to associate them with the higher-priced candles?

4   Should the company package candles in pairs?

case 7. AURORA ELECTRONICS COMPANY (C)

Adding a new product to a manufacturer's line

The executives of the Aurora Electronics Company are trying to decide whether they should produce and market an FM auto radio. The company is a small manufacturer of electronic products including antenna systems, high-fidelity sets and speaker systems, radar and counter-radar devices, electronic instrumentation, radio communications, ultraviolet equipment, and other industrial products. Over 90 per cent of the company's sales volume is sold directly to agencies of the Federal government, primarily the Department of Defense and the Atomic Energy Commission. The quality of this company's products is very high, and the firm enjoys an excellent reputation. The company's dependence upon the whims of government contracts has caused management to seek to diversify its line by adding consumer and/or industrial products which could be sold to nongovernmental markets. Presently the company has only one such product, an electronic garage-door opener which is sold as a component part to a large manufacturer of garage doors. Mr. Stacy, the president of Aurora Electronics, handles the selling work himself. The company has no sales manager or salesmen.

The product which the engineering department is proposing for commercial development is an FM auto radio. It is a three-part unit—a tuner, an amplifier, and a junction box—which can be installed so that it plays through the speaker system of the AM set already in an automobile. The FM parts can be mounted under the seat, in the trunk, or under the hood of the car, and the tuning dial can be placed under the dashboard or in any other appropriate place. The product is very plain in external appearance, as are the products of competition. Executives in the company differ regarding the importance of the appearance of a product of this nature. The product requires technical improvement before it will be ready for a mass market. In fact, management now wants to determine what product characteristics should be added. For example, should the set be restyled so that it has a more attractive appearance? Should it carry push buttons or automatic signal-seeking devices?

FM auto radios have several product advantages over AM radios. FM programming is far superior to AM programming. FM radios have a fine tonal quality, and ordinarily they do not experience much interference from overhead wires, tall buildings, and passing automobiles. The Aurora Electronics model is superior to competitive models in its tonal quality and in its ease of installation. The company feels that there is a growing market for this product, and the studies which they have made indicate that the market potential is adequate to sustain the necessary output. The market is concentrated within metropolitan centers because FM reception is good only within a range of about 25 miles from the FM station. Several competitive models are on the market at the present time. Probably the two best ones are German imports. One of these is the Becker radio, a combination AM-FM set which sells for $160 to $600 installed. Becker radios are featured as original equipment on the Mercedes-Benz cars. Another German import, the Blau Punkt (Blue

Spot), is made by a firm which supplies about 85 per cent of the European car radios. Present users of the Blau Punkt have evidenced general satisfaction with the product, and newspaper reports have pointed out that in the Chicago area alone, there are some five thousand of these radios in use, with excellent prospects for sustained growth. In general, research has shown that an adequate market exists but that an outstanding marketing program is needed to tap it. The Blau Punkt retails for about $140 installed. There is a persistent rumor in the trade that Motorola has developed an FM car radio and will begin to market it commercially in the very near future.

The radio presents no production problems for Aurora Electronics. The company could use its present plant, equipment, manpower, and sources of supply. Entirely new channels of distribution would have to be developed, however. Management is thinking of going through radio wholesale houses and automotive supply houses and also hopes to reach automobile supply stores such as Western Auto Supply, Gambles, and the large mail-order houses. Automobile radio sales and repair shops are also considered excellent prospects for retail dealerships. The company plans to sell the product for about $75 at the factory. Total manufacturing and other direct costs would be $57, thus leaving the company with $18 per unit to cover overhead and the necessary promotional programs. Wholesalers in this industry customarily receive the margin of 15 per cent and retailers earn 40 per cent of selling price. Thus if the company sells through wholesalers to retailers, the retail price will be approximately $145. If they bypass wholesalers and sell directly to large retail outlets, however, the retail price will be about $125. Two competitive radios—the Gonset and the Hastings—are available in just the FM tuner alone. One model sells for $70, and the other for $109. Both of these models are also available with the entire set—the power supply, audio amplifier, and speaker. Gonset sells the entire package for $120, and Hastings sells its complete set for $190.

The company realizes that its lack of a marketing department would pose a problem, but its service manager is quite anxious to accept the challenge of selling the new product. He is an alert, intelligent, and very enthusiastic young man and has been with the company about four years. His formal educational background is in engineering, although currently he is taking courses in business administration. He has had considerable experience working with the company's existing product line, but no experience in selling.

QUESTIONS

1   Should the company add the FM auto radio to its lines? If not, why?
2   If so, what product features, such as design, appearance, push-button tuning, etc., should be added to the product? Keep in mind that each additional feature costs something and thus may increase the selling price.

case 8. McGREGOR COMPANY

Organization for new-product planning and development

In his long-range planning activities, Mr. Rodney Bruning, the president of the McGregor Company, forecasts the continuation of changing consumer buying patterns in the luggage industry over the next several years. He also recognizes that the prospects for growth in the industry are very favorable. At the same time, these changes in consumer behavior and the potential growth market will probably be accompanied by an increasing severity of competition. As a consequence of these and other factors, Mr. Bruning doubts whether the company's present program for planning and developing new products can meet the market challenges of the future. He is convinced of the importance of product planning and thinks possibly that his company needs to formalize, or at least to strengthen, the organization and management of this function. He is concerned particularly with two aspects of product planning and development. One is the procedure for generating new-product ideas, and the other is the organizational structure needed to implement the planning and development of new products.

Established around the turn of the century, the McGregor Company today markets three seemingly unrelated lines of merchandise. With general offices and production facilities in New England, it is one of the largest manufacturers of luggage in the world. Soon after World War II, McGregor acquired a furniture company in Dallas, producing mainly folding tables and chairs. Recently McGregor added a line of desk accessories—calendar pads, pen holders, leather and plastic desk blotters, etc. McGregor manufactures some of these accessories and purchases others, but all are marketed under the McGregor brand. The luggage line accounts for roughly 60 per cent of the company's annual sales volume, the furniture represents 35 per cent, and the accessories 5 per cent.

Historically, the luggage industry has been centralized in New England and the mid-Atlantic states, but today luggage manufacturers are found in many parts of the country. In fact, one of the largest in the world is located in Denver, Colorado, and another major producer is in Seattle, Washington. In recent years, a trend toward concentration has characterized this industry, thus lending support to Mr. Bruning's forecast of increasing competition. Ten years ago, there were about 470 luggage firms in the United States; today there are no more than 250. The largest company has possibly 25 per cent of the market, and the second largest around 10 per cent. Mr. Bruning estimates that 10 per cent of the factories account for 90 per cent of the world's production of luggage.

In luggage, McGregor manufactures and markets a complete line of men's and women's nonleather cases. Most of the products are vinyl-covered, over aluminum or magnesium frames, and are lined with a good quality of rayon cloth. The products are sold nationwide directly to retailers. In addition, the company is becoming increasingly involved in foreign marketing. Management has franchised companies in Western Europe, Canada, South America, and Japan to produce McGregor luggage. This involvement in international marketing is another factor which has stimulated Mr. Bruning's concern about product planning and development.

In the American market, Mr. Bruning sees changes in consumer behavior insofar as these people view luggage. It is no longer considered a once-in-a-lifetime type of purchase to be used until it is physically worn out. It is no longer just a utilitarian, heavy suitcase—a necessary burden for carrying clothes and other personal belongings. Mr. Bruning recognizes that today the element of fashion has been introduced in luggage. Manufacturers and consumers are increasingly concerned with the factors of style and design. The increase in leisure time plus the higher disposable income have resulted in more time spent in pleasure traveling. This means more of a market for luggage. While luggage is still a popular item for special gift-giving occasions such as graduation, retirement, weddings, and birthdays, sales are no longer so concentrated on these occasions. New items are being added to the traditional suitcase-type products. Attaché cases, for example, have enjoyed increasingly widespread market acceptance, whereas the traditional briefcase has declined in popularity.

At the present time, there is no formal system for generating ideas for new products at the McGregor Company, nor does the company have any systematized arrangement for processing new-product ideas from their inception through to the commercial marketing stage. McGregor utilizes a small, wholly owned subsidiary company for purposes of new-product research and for the styling and design of McGregor products. The subsidiary company's management is autonomous and independent—a state which Mr. Bruning insists must be maintained if the company is to fulfill usefully its unique function. Ideas are also filtered out of customer complaints as relayed to the company through its retail dealers. Any executive, of course, can make suggestions. The company has not adopted the commonly used "employee suggestion box" system—that is, a system of financial awards for worthwhile suggestions and ideas from employees. Sometimes new-product ideas come as a by-product of marketing research among consumers, as done by an independent marketing research firm.

As far as organizational or procedural arrangements are concerned, the style and design subsidiary company informally feeds information (new-product ideas or even models of new products) to one of the McGregor executives. Sometimes the executive vice-president or even the president gets involved in the initial stages of decision making as to the disposition—acceptance, test market, rejection, etc.—of the new-product idea or model.

To bring about more effective management of product planning and development, Mr. Bruning is considering establishing a new-product committee, consisting of himself, the president of the subsidiary company, the vice-president of manufacturing, the vice-president of sales and marketing, and the product manager (a staff executive) of the luggage division. This committee would have responsibility for evaluating all ideas and new-product models as presented by the subsidiary style and design company. If the pilot model received the tentative approval of the committee, a short production run would be authorized so that the product could be test-marketed by the research firm retained by McGregor. If the test-market results were satisfactory, the new-product committee would authorize full-scale production and marketing. By including all key executives on the committee, Mr. Bruning feels that a new product would be well received by manufacturing and marketing departments because the vice-president at the head of each of these departments would have already approved the product.

The vice-president of sales and marketing feels that the usual managerial drawbacks of committee action would render a new-product committee ineffective as an organizational and administrative unit for product planning and development. Instead, he recommends that the company establish a new product-development department. In this way, the product-planning function would be recognized for the full-time activity that it really is. Such a department would devote an appropriate amount of time and effort to product planning over the long run.

The product manager, who reports to the vice-president of sales and marketing, has suggested that his domain of activity be enlarged to include the planning and development of new products. He argues that such an assignment is a logical extension of his present responsibilities. He could take a new-product idea or model and carry it through all the development and testing stages. If the product were to be marketed on a commercial basis, it could be turned over to the appropriate department.

QUESTIONS

1 What organizational structure should the McGregor Company establish for the planning and development of new products?

2   What sources should the company use in order to generate ideas for new
       products?

case 9. CANADIAN-WESTERN PAINT COMPANY
Brand policy in company merger

Now that the Canadian-Western Paint Company has acquired 100 per cent control of the
Hawkins Paint Company, the executives of Canadian-Western must decide what brand and
labeling policies will be established for the existing product lines of the two firms. Currently,
there are varying degrees of duplication in the two companies' product lines, geographical
markets, and advertising media. By using one brand and one company name, Canadian-
Western could possibly effect economies in television and newspaper advertising, stationery,
packaging, labeling, and other operational areas of the marketing program.

The Canadian-Western Paint Company, established in 1910, has its main offices and
manufacturing plant in Vancouver, British Columbia. The firm produces a complete line of
paints, lacquers, and varnishes under its Lion Gate brand. A line of brushes and other
painting equipment and supplies is purchased from other manufacturers, but is marketed
by Canadian-Western under the Lion Gate brand. Annual sales volume is now approximately $15 million. The company's geographical market covers the three westernmost
Canadian provinces, from British Columbia eastward through Alberta into Saskatchewan.
Sales branches are maintained in Victoria, British Columbia; Calgary and Edmonton, Alberta;
and Saskatoon, Saskatchewan. Company salesmen sell to about 450 retail and wholesale
accounts including paint, lacquer, and varnish wholesalers and retail paint stores, hardware
stores, lumber and building materials dealers, and department stores. The Lion Gate brand
has a high degree of consumer recognition and acceptance. The company advertises
extensively, using television primarily, but also relying heavily on newspapers and outdoor
poster panels as promotional media.

When it was purchased by the Canadian-Western Paint Company, the Hawkins Paint
Company had been operating for over seventy years. The manufacturing plant and general
offices are located in Winnipeg, Manitoba, with a sales branch in Calgary. The company's
paint, lacquer, and varnish products are sold under the Hawkins brand, and these products
pretty well duplicate the Canadian-Western line. Hawkins's annual sales volume is approximately $4 million. Company salesmen have around two hundred retail and wholesale
accounts in Manitoba, Saskatchewan, and Alberta. Among these accounts, particularly
among the older ones and particularly in Manitoba, surveys have shown that there is a
strong dealer loyalty to the Hawkins brand. Furthermore, this brand is well accepted among
painting contractors and household consumers. This brand loyalty and acceptance decline,
however, the further west we get from Manitoba.

Until about ten years prior to the merger, the Hawkins Company had been extremely
successful. During the past decade, however, its profit performance has declined, even
though the sales volume has held steady. At the time of the merger, Hawkins was operating
at a loss, and the morale of its employees was low. Clarence Bullen, the vice-president of
marketing at Canadian-Western, feels that Hawkins's profit decline was caused by its poor
management. As an example, too often "deals" or "concessions" were made to existing

accounts in order to keep their business. Some customers who would normally be considered retailers were reclassified as distributors (wholesalers) and thus were granted larger discounts. Also, the company has become quite inactive lately in its advertising program, and there is concern that its image might be changing unfavorably.

The paint, lacquer, and varnish industry in western Canada is highly competitive. Already, competitors of Canadian-Western have contacted most of the Hawkins accounts, stating that Canadian-Western was absorbing Hawkins and that all dealer and distributor relations would be changed. Because of the internal turmoil that has existed in the Hawkins operations in recent years, Canadian-Western cannot counter this type of competition, as it normally could.

At this point, the Canadian-Western executives are debating what the brand policy of their company should be, in light of the recent acquisition of Hawkins. The advertising manager, Harry Foster, believes that the best course of action would be to carry on as before. That is, both the Lion Gate and the Hawkins brands would continue to be used, and the two separate company product lines would be marketed. Mr. Foster points out that it is important to keep in mind the geographical market coverage of the two firms. Between them, they cover the four western provinces in Canada. Canadian-Western markets in British Columbia, Alberta, and Saskatchewan; Hawkins sells in Alberta, Saskatchewan, and Manitoba. Thus, Hawkins does not market in British Columbia, and Canadian-Western is unknown in Manitoba, but there is a territorial overlap and conflict among existing accounts in Alberta and Saskatchewan.

Clarence Bullen has advocated a different alternative. He would drop the Hawkins brand now and concentrate all efforts on the Lion Gate label. In this way the company would be promoting only one name, and this would result in cost-saving efficiencies such as one set of television commercials, billboards, newspaper advertisements, labels, and packages.

He does realize that his recommendation poses some problems in that it might be difficult to convince the existing Hawkins dealers regarding the advantages of a one-brand program. Also, by dropping the Hawkins brand, the company would risk losing the dealer brand loyalty attached to the Hawkins name and the consumer recognition of, and preference for, that label. Furthermore, the Lion Gate label is unknown in Manitoba.

The president thinks that both the Foster and the Bullen recommendations leave much to be desired. Neither of them, for example, solves the problem of what to do about the conflicting accounts and duplication of effort in Alberta and Saskatchewan. The president is considering the possibility of either a totally new name or a name that would combine the two existing ones—a name such as Lion Gate–Hawkins, for instance. He also raises this question: Must our course of action involve an immediate major change, or could we possibly initiate a series of small moves which would constitute a major change over a period of two to four years?

QUESTION

1   What brand policy should the Canadian-Western Company adopt now that it has acquired the Hawkins Company?

PART FOUR

DISTRIBUTION STRUCTURE

11

DISTRIBUTION CHANNELS AND THE RETAIL MARKET

Our product is now ready for its market. The next general step in the marketing process is to determine what methods and routes will be used to bring the product to the market. This involves establishing distribution policies and strategies, including selecting channels of distribution and providing for physical handling and distribution. First, however, we should make certain that management understands something of the concepts and principles underlying the distribution system.

CHANNELS OF DISTRIBUTION

A *middleman* is an independent business concern standing between the producer and the ultimate household consumer or industrial user. A middleman performs activities and renders services in connection with the purchase and/or sale of products as they move from producer to consumer; either he takes title to the merchandise as it flows between producer and consumer or he actively negotiates the transfer of title.

The essence of a middleman's operation is his active and prominent role in negotiations involving the buying and selling of goods; his income arises directly from the proceeds of these transactions. It is his part in transfer of ownership which differentiates a middleman from other institutions, such as banks, insurance companies, and transportation firms, which help in the marketing process but do not take title and are not actively involved in purchase and sales negotiations. Whether or not a firm actually handles the products is not relevant to the definition of a middleman. Some middlemen warehouse and transport merchandise, while others do not physically handle it at all.

A common method of classifying middlemen is on the basis of whether they take title to the products involved. *Merchant* middlemen actually take ownership title to the goods they are helping to market. *Agent* middlemen do not take title, but they do actively assist in the transfer of title. Brokers, selling agents, and manufacturers' agents are examples of agent middlemen. The two major groups of merchant middlemen are wholesalers and retailers. It should be noted particularly that all retailers are merchant middlemen. When people urge the elimination of middlemen, they are usually speaking of wholesale middlemen alone. Ordinarily, they realize that they cannot get along without retailers.

A *channel of distribution* (sometimes called a trade channel) for a product is the route taken by the *title* to the goods as they move from the producer to the ultimate consumer or industrial user. A channel always includes both the producer and the final customer for the product, as well as all agent and merchant middlemen involved in the title transfer. The channel does *not* include firms such as railroads, banks, and other nonmiddleman institutions which render a marketing service but play no major role in negotiating purchases and sales. If a consumer buys apples from the grower at his roadside stand, or if a manufacturer sells a shirt by mail direct to a college student, the channel is from producer to consumer. If the shirt manufacturer sold to a department store which in turn sold to the college student, the channel would be producer—retailer—consumer.

The channel for a product extends to the last person who buys it without making any significant change in its form. When its form is altered and another product emerges, a new channel is started. When lumber is milled and made into furniture, there are separate channels for the lumber and the furniture. The channel for lumber may be lumber mill—broker—furniture manufacturer. The channel for the finished furniture might be furniture manufacturer—furniture wholesaler—retail furniture store—consumer.

Concept of channel structure

To understand a channel of distribution, one should first recognize that it is a structure. A structure is an organism that has dimensions of length, breadth, and depth; it has shape and is usually complex. A structure is organized and is evolved in order to do a job. As related to channels of distribution, a structure may be viewed in several ways.[1] A distribution structure may represent a choice among alternative channels of distribution, or it may involve a description of the different marketing situations faced by the various firms (retailers, wholesalers, producers) within the structure. It may be considered as a series of functions which must be performed in order to market products effectively. Any structure may be evaluated from a socioeconomic point of view.

The distribution structure is a highly complex organism, made up of a great variety of reasonably diverse institutions. Little systematic research has been done on it. Its constantly changing nature makes thoughtful analysis difficult and renders a description of it quickly out-of-date. Another factor obscuring a careful study of the distribution structure is the oversimplified treatment it receives in marketing literature and Bureau of the Census data. In the Census of Business, each separate establishment is placed in a traditional, single category depending upon which category represented over 50 per cent of the firm's annual sales volume. Thus if a company does 60 per cent of its business at retail and the rest at wholesale, it is classed as a retailer. This system of classification suggests a more orderly structure than actually exists. It effectively reduces the number of categories into which firms are sorted and avoids hybrid, nondescript classifications. However, hybridity is too common among marketing firms to be ignored.[2]

A channel as a total system

To maximize benefits to all groups concerned (producers, middlemen, and consumers), a channel of distribution should be treated as a unit—a total system of action. Within this systems concept, a channel would include the marketing organizational units of a manufacturer as well as the organizations of the middlemen used by this manufacturer. Consequently, there is a real need to coordinate the manufacturer's activities with those of the middlemen used in the distribution of the given product. A distribution system properly established and operated then becomes a significant competitive differential advantage for a company.

Unfortunately, a trade channel is all too often treated as a fragmented assortment of competing, independently operating organizations. A manufacturer may view his own retailers as his competition, or a middleman may be in conflict with his supplier, rather than recognizing that the real threat is other middlemen or the distribution systems of other manufacturers. That is, the real competition is between distribution systems of different producers, rather than between the organizational units within one producer's system.

[1] John A. Howard, *Marketing Management: Analysis and Decision*, Richard D. Irwin, Inc., Homewood, Ill., 1957, pp. 179–181.

[2] Phillip McVey, "Are Channels of Distribution What the Textbooks Say?" *Journal of Marketing*, January, 1960, p. 61.

It is true that power structures do exist in trade channels simply by virtue of the fact that a distribution system is comprised of separate, independent companies. Power struggles may also exist between groups *within* a company. Two marketing units—the advertising department and the field sales force, for instance—may look upon each other as competitors, quite contrary to the philosophy of total marketing underlying the market concept.

A channel as an investment

In addition to thinking of a channel of distribution as a structure and as a total system, management should also recognize that a channel represents a financial investment in the same sense that the plant, equipment, or any other asset is an investment. If profit maximization is a company goal, then the selection of a marketing channel should be based on the estimated rate of return to be earned on the capital investment in the channels. Thus "the process of channel selection should be considered as an investment decision by a manufacturing firm."[3]

Importance of middlemen

In any economy except a very primitive one, it is often not economically feasible or convenient for a producer to deal directly with an ultimate consumer. Think for a moment how inconvenient and complicated our daily existence would be if there were no retail middlemen—no drugstores, newspaper stands, supermarkets, or gasoline stations. If we live in a large city, we might think that we could buy things wholesale, but if there were *no* middlemen, there would be no wholesalers. Other bases for appraising the importance of marketing channels and middlemen are discussed in the following sections.

Concentration, equalization, dispersion   Frequently the quantity and assortment of goods produced by a firm are out of balance with the variety and amounts wanted by consumers or industrial users. A businessman needs paper, pencils, typewriters, and desks. A homeowner wants grass seed, topsoil, fertilizer, a rake, a rototiller, and a roller, and eventually he hopes to need a lawn mower. No single firm produces all of the items either of these users wants, and no producer may sell any of them in the small quantity the user desires. Obviously there is a need for someone to perform the function of balancing or equalizing what various producers turn out with what the final customers want. This is part of the task of marketing.

The job to be done involves (1) collecting or concentrating the output of various producers, (2) subdividing these quantities into amounts desired by

[3] Eugene W. Lambert, Jr., "Financial Considerations in Choosing a Marketing Channel," *Business Topics*, Winter, 1966, p. 25. This author suggests that channel choice is determined primarily by financial considerations rather than what are generally thought of as marketing factors.

the customers and gathering the various items together in the assortment or variety wanted, and (3) dispersing this assortment to consumers or industrial buyers.[4] In a few cases, the task of concentrating, equalizing, and dispersing is simple enough to be done by the producer and final customer working closely together. A copper miner may sell directly to the smelter firm; iron-ore producers may sell directly to the steel mill. In most cases, however, the producer and consumer are not able to work out the proper quantity and assortment. A specialist in concentration, equalization, and dispersion is needed, and this is the role of the middleman.

Creation of utility Middlemen aid in the creation of time, place, and possession utilities. In classical economic theory, production is defined as the creation of utility, and several types of utility are recognized. One is form utility, in which something is added in a chemical or physical manner to a product to make it more valuable. Lumber is made into furniture and flour into bread, thus creating form utility. Other utilities are equally valuable to the final user. Furniture located in Grand Rapids, Michigan, or High Point, North Carolina, in April is of little value to people in Austin, Texas, or Los Angeles, California, who want the furniture to give as Christmas presents. Transporting the furniture from Michigan to Texas increases its value: place utility is added. Storing it from April to December adds another value—time utility. The final value of possession utility is created when the Texas and California families buy the items.

Problems in management of distribution channels

To establish the channels of distribution for a firm, a marketing executive must undertake the following studies or tasks:

Understand the retail and wholesale markets and the types of middlemen available in both (Chapters 11 to 13). Because we are better acquainted with retailers than with wholesalers, we shall consider them in this order, thus reversing the normal positioning in a channel and going from the known to the unknown. Also, by beginning with the retailers, we focus attention first on consumers' problems.

Understand the various conflicts which continually exist between and within channels. These conflicts, as well as the possibility of bypassing or eliminating some of the traditional middlemen, are analyzed in Chapter 14.

Determine which channels to use, that is, the type or kind of middlemen (if any) to be used at each stage in the channel (Chapter 15).

---

[4] The concepts of concentration, equalization, and dispersion were first suggested to the author by Fred E. Clark in Fred E. Clark and Carrie P. Clark, *Principles of Marketing*, 3d ed., The Macmillan Company, New York, 1942. For an expanded, more up-to-date analysis of this aspect of distribution, and one which uses the terms "accumulation," "allocation," and "assorting," see Wroe Alderson, *Marketing Behavior and Executive Action*, Richard D. Irwin, Inc., Homewood, Ill., 1957, pp. 201–211.

Determine the intensity of distribution, that is, the number of outlets desired in each stage (Chapter 15).

Select the individual middlemen after evaluating them in terms of which services the manufacturer needs and which he can furnish himself (Chapter 15).

Determine the methods and procedures to be used in the physical distribution of the product (Chapter 16). This problem involves the strategic use of transportation and warehousing facilities and services in a firm's marketing program.

NATURE OF RETAIL MARKET

If a supermarket sells some floor wax to a gift shop operator who wants to polish the floor tiles in his store, is this a retail sale? Can a wholesaler or a manufacturer engage in retailing? When a gas station runs a big sale on tires and advertises that the products are being sold at the wholesale price, is this retailing? Are all the sales of a retail store considered retail sales? "Retailing," "retail store," "retail sales," and "retailers" are terms that should be defined not only to clarify their legal implications but also to avoid any possible misunderstanding in later discussions.

Retailing includes all activities directly related to the sale of goods or services to the ultimate consumer for personal, nonbusiness use. While most retailing is done through retail stores, it may be done by any institution. A manufacturer selling brushes or cosmetics door-to-door is engaging in retailing, as is a farmer selling strawberries at a roadside stand. Any firm—manufacturer, wholesaler, or retail store—which sells something to the ultimate consumer for his nonbusiness use, regardless of how it is sold (by person, telephone, mail, or vending machine) or where it is sold (in a store or at the consumer's home), is making a *retail sale*.

A *retailer* or a *retail store* is a business enterprise which sells *primarily* to ultimate consumers for nonbusiness use. A key word in the last definition is "primarily." A retailer may sell items infrequently to industrial users, but these are wholesale transactions, not retail sales. If over one-half of his dollar volume of business comes from sales to ultimate consumers, that is, sales at retail, he is classed as a retailer.

Ease of entry into retailing

It is easier to go into retailing than virtually any other trade, profession, or line of business. To practice medicine or law, one must pass state licensing examinations. To start a manufacturing or wholesaling firm, one must have a substantial sum of money to acquire a plant, equipment, and merchandise. To enter a laboring trade in many parts of the country, one must acquire union membership, and some unions have strict apprenticeship provisions. But to operate a retail store there are no examinations, and the necessary business licenses are easy to acquire. Some suppliers may even furnish merchandise and store fixtures on a consignment basis. Furthermore, many people entering retailing have the idea that no real training or special experience is needed.

There are important economic and social implications in the ease with which people may enter retailing. Often, underfinanced, poorly qualified people come into the field. Soon they fail, thus causing economic waste and inefficient use of human and economic resources. Mortality is higher among retail establishments than in any other classification of business and industry.

On the bright side, ease of entry results in fierce competition and added value for the consumer. Except perhaps in a small town, it is rather difficult to establish an unregulated, monopolistic position in retailing. Certainly, large-scale enterprises exist in retailing, and in some markets there is substantial concentration of business among a relatively small percentage of firms. Yet these giants usually compete with one another, and the consumer benefits.

Ease of entry has also contributed to volatility and change in the retail structure. Change is occurring constantly, but it is essentially evolutionary and not revolutionary. Actually there is inherent stability underlying retailing. Basically retail stores have not changed much in two thousand years; some of the types of stores which existed then still exist today. It is true that periodically a new type of institution emerges and threatens to extinguish existing outlets. The department store arose in the post-Civil War era; mail-order houses and chain stores developed in the 1920s; supermarkets and self-service retailing came to the fore in the 1930s and 1940s; discount houses developed in many large cities in the 1950s. Each of these newcomers forced a change in the operations of existing institutions, and at the same time the new ones eventually made adjustments and became a stable part of the retailing structure. These new types of stores did not crowd out competitors, as was threatened in practically every case. Instead, the newcomers rather quickly gravitated to a modest position in terms of their portion of total retail sales, leaving the basic structure unchanged.

table 11–1

Total retail trade in United States, selected years

Retail sales have more than doubled since 1948. Even after allowing for the increase in population and the rise in price levels, we find a huge increase in physical volume of merchandise sold. In contrast, note the remarkable stability in the number of retail establishments since 1948.

	1965	1963	1958	1954	1948
Number of stores (000)		1,708	1,795	1,722	1,770
Total sales ($000,000)	$284,300	$244,202	$200,365	$169,968	$130,521
Average sales per store		$141,200	$111,700	$ 98,700	$ 73,800

sources: U.S. Census of Business: 1963, Retail Trade, United States Summary; U.S. Census of Business: 1954; 1965 estimate from *Survey of Current Business*, February, 1966, back cover.

There are close to 1.7 million retail stores in the United States, and their total annual sales volume in 1965 was about $284 billion. In contrast, there are about 280,000 wholesaling establishments (excluding manufacturers' sales branches and offices) and about 300,000 manufacturers. The figures in Table 11–1 show that there is a remarkable stability in the total number of stores in the country. In spite of the population boom and rising consumer income over the past twenty to twenty-five years, there were about as many retail establishments in 1948 as in 1963. The increase in total sales volume, however, has been tremendous. In absolute amounts, total retail sales volume is about seven times as large today as before World War II and more than twice as great as during the years immediately following the war. Of course, the census figures in Table 11–1 do not take into consideration two factors influencing the rise in total dollar volume. One is the big rise in the price level during the period covered in the table, and the other is the increase in population. Nevertheless, even after allowing for these two factors, the retail sales per capita as measured in 1965 dollars were still considerably higher in 1965 than in 1948. That is, there has simply been a huge increase in the physical volume of merchandise sold at retail.

Costs and profits of retailers

Information regarding the costs of retailing is very meager. By gleaning data from several sources, however, we can make some rough generalizations. Certainly, careful studies would prove of great value, not only to manufacturers and wholesalers but also to economists, businessmen, legislators, and other groups who are trying to evaluate the efficiency of our marketing system.

Total costs and profits As nearly as can be estimated, the total average operating expense for all retailers combined is about 25 to 27 per cent of retail sales. This figure does not include the expenses of bars and restaurants, which do some processing. Wholesaling expenses are estimated at about 8 per cent of the *retail* dollar or about 10 to 11 per cent of *wholesaling* sales. Thus retailing expenses in total are about 2½ times the total of the costs of wholesaling when the expenses are stated as a percentage of sales of the middlemen in question.[5]

[5] See Harold Barger, *Distribution's Place in the American Economy since 1869,* Princeton University Press, Princeton, N.J., 1955, p. 60; and Paul D. Converse, "The Puzzle of Marketing Costs," *Journal of Marketing,* April, 1957, pp. 439–441. Barger found a rather narrow range of fluctuation in the total of wholesaling plus retailing costs in the United States since 1869.

A reader should be careful to note the base used for cost figures which are stated as percentages. The figures of 25 to 27 per cent for retailers and 10 to 11 per cent for wholesalers cannot be added together because they are computed on two different bases. The 25 to 27 per cent is based on the *retailers'* selling price, and the 10 to 11 per cent is based on the *wholesalers'* selling price. Before adding retailing and wholesaling costs together, they must be converted to a common base. Thus the operating

The proportionately higher retailing costs are generally related to the expense of dealing directly with the consumer. In comparison with wholesalers' customers, consumers demand more services. Also, the average retail sale is smaller, the rate of merchandise turnover is lower, buying is done in smaller lots, rent is higher, expenses for furniture and fixtures are greater, and salespeople cannot be used efficiently because the customers do not come in at a steady rate.

Costs and profits by kind of business   Studying the expenses of retailers in total is not nearly so meaningful as studying the expenses of one classification of retailers because the expense ratios vary from one type of store to another. Table 11–2 shows expenses as a percentage of sales when stores are classified by the nature and extent of product lines handled. Total operating expenses range from 14.2 per cent of net sales for farm equipment stores, through 14.4 per cent for grocery stores, 29.5 per cent for drugstores, and 37.9 per cent for medium-sized furniture stores, to 44.1 per cent, for florists. Table 11–2 also shows the average net operating profit *before* income taxes for selected kinds of businesses for selected years.

Costs and profits by method of operation   Within the kinds of businesses noted in Table 11–2, expenses vary according to the method of operation. Thus self-service supermarkets have operating expenses of 14 to 17 per cent, while grocery stores with salesmen and free delivery and credit approach 25 to 30 per cent of sales. Full-service department stores report expenses from 33 to 35 per cent, depending upon the sales volume of the store. General merchandise stores engaged in discount selling (discount houses) have operating expenses of 10 to 20 per cent.

ECONOMIC BASES OF RETAILING

It is very easy to get into retailing and just as simple to be forced out. Consequently, the social and economic justification for the retailer's existence must be based upon the services he offers. He exists only because he does a better job than his competitors in his primary responsibility—catering to the consumer —and in his secondary job—serving producers and wholesalers.[6]

Importance to consumers

The function of the retailer is to make the consumer's buying job as easy and convenient as possible. Essentially, the retailer acts as the consumer's purchas-

---

expenses of wholesalers total about 10 to 11 per cent of their sales, but this is only about 8 per cent of the final price paid by the consumer.

[6] For some thoughts on which activities a retailer himself should perform and which ones he should share, shift, or contract out, and for an identification of some factors which seem to influence the retailer's choice of alternatives, see Stanley C. Hollander, "Who Does the Work of Retailing?" *Journal of Marketing*, July, 1964, pp. 18–22.

table   11–2

Operating expenses and net operating profit margins as percentage of net sales of selected businesses, selected years*

Wide differences exist in the operating ratios of various types of retailers. Grocery stores' expenses are 14 per cent of net sales, while shoe stores have an expense ratio of 33 per cent. How do you account for these differences? Remember that net profit percentages are very low, even before income taxes are deducted.

Kind of business	Operating expense, per cent	Net operating profit, per cent†
Auto dealers[a]	14.0	0.5
Farm equipment dealers[b]	14.2	3.3
Farm supply stores	14.4	1.5
Grocery stores	14.4	1.5
Liquor stores (package)	17.1	2.6
Meat markets	19.3	1.4
Lumber dealers	21.1	3.4
Gasoline service stations	22.1	1.1
Sporting goods stores	26.6	2.0
Dry goods and general merchandise stores	27.6	1.9
Camera and photographic supply stores	28.5	2.4
Men's furnishings stores	29.3	3.5
Women's ready-to-wear stores	29.4	2.9
Paint and wallpaper stores	30.1	3.0
Hardware stores[c]	30.3	2.2
Drugstores[d]	30.5	5.3
Children's- and infants'-wear stores	30.8	1.7
Women's accessory and specialty stores	31.5	2.2
Auto accessory and parts stores	31.7	2.7
Office supply and equipment dealers[e]	31.9	2.4
Shoe stores (family)[f]	33.1	3.8
Music stores	33.3	2.5
Floor coverings stores	34.0	1.7
Candy, nut, and confectionery stores	35.4	0.4
Appliance-radio-television dealers[g]	36.8	0.2
Furniture stores[h] ($250,000–$500,000 sales)	37.9	0.3
Gift, novelty, and souvenir stores	38.1	1.9
Jewelry stores (cash and open credit)	40.7	3.7
Restaurants	44.0	3.3
Florists	44.1	3.3

* Years involved range from 1950 to 1960.

† *Before* income taxes, but *after* allowance for owners' salaries.

SOURCES: [a] National Automobile Dealers Association. [b] National Retail Farm Equipment Association. [c] National Retail Hardware Association. [d] *Lilly Digest,* Eli Lilly and Company. [e] National Stationery and Office Equipment Association. [f] *Men's Wear* magazine, July 24, 1959. [g] National Appliance and Radio-TV Dealers Association. [h] National Retail Furniture Association. All other data from *Operating Ratios for Forty-one Lines of Retail Trade,* Dun and Bradstreet, Inc., New York, 1959.

ing agent; this task involves anticipating his wants. Then the retailer has the responsibility of supplying the right kind of goods at a reasonable price. The retailer also performs the service of *bulk breaking*, that is, dividing large quantities into smaller units, such as individual cans, bottles, or boxes, appropriate for consumer use. The retailers offer a large variety and assortment of merchandise, including appropriate qualities, sizes, colors, styles, and seasonal items.

Retailers perform the function of transporting and storing the goods so that they will be readily available when and where the consumer wants them. Thus, time and place utilities are created. Furthermore, in many cases, a retailer will arrange for the product to be delivered from the store to the consumer's home. Retailers usually assume certain consumer risks in that they guarantee the goods they sell. Often retailers provide an installation and repair service.

Financing is another important function of retailers. They offer consumers open-book charge accounts payable once a month, revolving credit plans, and long-term installment programs. Retailers also add to the convenience and ease of consumer purchasing. They offer convenient shopping locations, considerable market information, personal salesmen, and other services, such as ample parking space, clothing alterations, and lessons on product use.

Importance to producers and wholesalers

For the producers and wholesalers, the retailer acts as a specialist in selling. He offers physical facilities and manpower so that the producers and wholesaling middlemen can have a point of contact with consumers near the consumers' homes. He also uses advertising, display, and personal selling to aid in moving the producers' products. In determining the needs and wants of the consumer, the retailer can act as an interpreter of consumer demand and relay vital information back through the channel of distribution.

By dividing large unit quantities into consumer-sized amounts, the retailer is performing a service to manufacturers as well as to consumers. It would be highly uneconomical for manufacturers to package and ship their goods in the quantities demanded by consumers. Retailers' storage activities also help both producers and consumers. By ordering and accepting delivery in advance of the season, the retailer removes some of the risk burden from the manufacturer.

CLASSIFICATION OF RETAILING MIDDLEMEN

To better understand the role that retailing middlemen play in the channel structure, we shall classify them on the following bases:

1. Size of store
2. Extent of product lines handled
3. Geographic location
4. Form of ownership
5. Method of operation

This list is not all-inclusive, nor are the bases mutually exclusive. A given store or group of stores may be classed in any one of the five ways mentioned. Also, cross-classification is possible. For instance, we may group all stores first by form of ownership (corporate chain, independent, manufacturer-owned); then, within each type of ownership we may subdivide the stores according to their product lines.

Size of store

Classifying retailing institutions according to their sales volume recognizes the fact that stores of different sizes present different management problems. Buying, promotion, financing, personnel relations, and expense control are influenced significantly by the volume size of the store. When we discuss retailing on the basis of store size, we find that a dichotomous situation exists. In fact, it is almost a dilemma. Retailing is at one and the same time both a small-scale and a large-scale operation.

Quantitative measurement   Most retailing establishments are very small. In 1963, about 71 per cent of the stores operating the full year had an annual sales volume of less than $100,000, but these stores accounted for only 17 per cent of all retail sales (see Table 11–3). Retailing is probably the best example of small business in the United States, particularly when we include retailers of services such as restaurants, barbershops, and garages.

table   11–3

Retail trade in United States, 1963: by annual sales volume

Although most retailers are small, there is a high degree of concentration in retailing. Seventy-one per cent of the stores had an annual sales volume under $100,000 in 1963, and only 2.4 per cent of the stores had annual sales over $1,000,000. However, these few stores accounted for 38 per cent of total retail sales.

Annual sales	*Establishments*			*Sales volume*		
	Number (000)	*Per cent*	*Cumulative, per cent*	*($000,000)*	*Per cent*	*Cumulative, per cent*
Total, all stores	1,708			244,202		
Establishments operated entire year, total	1,532.3	100.0		232,043	100.0	
Annual sales:						
$1,000,000 or more	36.1	2.4	2.4	89,096	38.4	38.4
500,000–999,000	43.4	2.8	5.2	30,062	13.0	51.4
300,000–499,000	57.6	3.8	9.0	21,935	9.5	60.9
100,000–299,000	306.1	20.0	29.0	50,683	21.8	82.7
20,000– 99,000	736.0	48.0	77.0	36,709	15.8	98.5
Under $20,000	353.1	23.0	100.0	3,558	1.5	100.0

SOURCE: U.S. Census of Business: 1963, Retail Trade, Sales Size.

Although most retailers are small, at the same time there is a high degree of concentration in retailing: a small number of establishments account for a substantial share of retail trade. In Table 11–3, we see that stores with an annual volume of over $1 million accounted for only 2.4 per cent of all establishments but for about 38 per cent of the total volume.

As impressive as the figures in Table 11–3 may seem, they still do not tell the full story of large-scale retailing, because they represent a tabulation of individual *store* sales and not individual *company* volume. A single company may own many establishments, as in the case of chain stores. When retail sales are analyzed by companies, the high degree of concentration becomes even more evident. Table 11–4 shows the sales of the twenty largest retailers in the country in 1965. (Their net profit as a percentage of sales is also shown. The small size of the average profit—2.4 per cent—among these giants may surprise people

table   11–4

Twenty largest retailers in United States, 1965: by sales volume

The $35 billion total sales of these giant retailers represented one-eighth of all retail sales in the United States, and yet their average profit was only 2.4 per cent of net sales. What are some of the marketing implications of this concentration for a maker of department store merchandise?

	Company	Sales ($000)*	Profit as per cent of sales
1	Sears, Roebuck	6,390,000	5.1
2	Great Atlantic & Pacific Tea	5,118,978	1.0
3	Safeway Stores	2,939,043	1.7
4	Kroger	2,555,109	1.2
5	J. C. Penney	2,289,209	3.4
6	Montgomery Ward	1,748,360	1.4
7	F. W. Woolworth	1,443,322	5.1
8	Federated Department Stores	1,330,737	5.3
9	Acme Markets	1,200,750	0.9
10	National Tea	1,161,948	1.0
11	Food Fair Stores	1,119,640	0.8
12	Allied Stores	961,353	2.3
13	Winn-Dixie Stores	915,339	2.5
14	Jewel Tea	873,229	1.7
15	May Department Stores	869,169	5.3
16	S. S. Kresge	862,441	2.7
17	W. T. Grant	839,715	3.7
18	Grand Union	779,683	1.4
19	E. J. Korvette	719,941	1.4
20	First National Stores	684,492	0.3

* Net sales, including all operating revenues. For companies not on a calendar year, the 1965 figures are for any fiscal year ending not later than Apr. 1, 1966. Sales of subsidiaries are included when they are consolidated.

SOURCE: *Fortune*, July 15, 1966, pp. 256–257.

who feel that retailing is highly profitable.) Sales of these twenty firms alone totaled $35 billion, or approximately one-eighth of the total value of retail trade.

Competitive positions of large and small retailers   The relative competitive positions of large-scale and small-scale retailers may be evaluated in the light of several factors.

DIVISION OF LABOR   The opportunity to enjoy the advantages of division of labor both at the executive level and in the manpower ranks is one of the strongest factors favoring large-scale retailers. Large retailers can afford to hire managerial specialists for each major function, such as buying promotion, and accounting. The small store usually cannot pay enough money or offer enough future opportunity to attract a high-caliber full-time person to perform these functions. The owner-manager may be a good executive, but he has to divide his time among too many activities to be effective in all of them.

FLEXIBILITY OF OPERATIONS   Small stores generally are more flexible in their management practices than are large units. Small retailers can stock merchandise to suit specific local needs, and they can adopt a flexible policy regarding services. In short, they do not have to check with headquarters or follow a company manual in every case.

BUYING POWER   Large-scale institutions have a buying-power advantage. They can buy in bigger quantities than small stores and secure higher discounts. They can achieve additional economies by purchasing from manufacturers. Sometimes this buying power is instrumental in acquiring other benefits, such as allowances for advertising, preferential treatment in case of shortages, and sole dealership rights in a given market.

USE OF ADVERTISING   Large stores can make effective use of advertising. It is not economically feasible for a corner grocery store to advertise in a metropolitan daily paper or on television. A large department store or a grocery chain with several stores blanketing a city can make good use of these media because the media match the market; there is little waste circulation.

RETAILER'S OWN BRAND   Large retail institutions are in a good position to develop and promote their own brands. For the small store, the potential sales volume from its own brand is more than offset by the funds required to promote the brand and guarantee its quality.

FINANCIAL STRENGTH   Underlying many of the points noted here is the fact that large retailers are usually in a better financial position. When they need money for expansion or for some other purpose, they can attract investors or borrow from banks and other lending institutions much more easily than small retailers can. A strong financial position enables a store to take advantage of all cash discounts offered, and these are extremely important in retailing because of the low net profit margins. A good financial position also enables a store to attract valuable franchises and attention from leading brand manufacturers. The financial strength of a retailer is a key point in a manufacturer's selection of individual middlemen.

INTEGRATION—HORIZONTALLY AND VERTICALLY   Large retailers handle a sufficient volume of merchandise to make it worth their while to take over wholesaling functions and sometimes even manufacturing operations. A large grocery chain may buy or set up a bakery just to supply its own stores. Many large retailers do their own warehousing and are thus vertically integrated into the wholesaling field.

COST OF OPERATIONS   There is a lack of precise information regarding the effect which size has on operating expenses. Generally, large stores have higher operating expense ratios than small stores. The expenses in large organizations also include the wholesaling activities conducted by these firms. Certainly, large stores have higher overhead expenses than do small ones. Part of the advantage of management and labor specialization is offset by the higher cost attendant upon the division of labor. Large stores also have a greater percentage of total employees in nonselling jobs.

EXPERIMENTATION, INNOVATION, AND MARKETING RESEARCH   With their specialized executive manpower and great financial strength, large retailers are in a good position to conduct all kinds of needed marketing research. They can experiment with new ideas. They can afford to risk more on innovative features, such as a daring new style of clothing or a new selling method (self-service in housewares or automatic vending of staple clothing items). A multistore organization can test something in one store before committing all units to the new practice.

LEGAL CONSIDERATIONS   Large-scale retailers have been a major target of legislators. Time and again, laws have been passed to equalize the economic position of large and small retailers. Fair-trade laws, which allow a producer to set the minimum price at which a retailer may sell his products, prevent a large store from substantially underselling a small one. Other legal measures have been aimed at the price which the retailer pays for his goods. The Robinson-Patman Act, for example, attempts to control the buying power of the large retailer. These laws are discussed in greater detail in Chapters 19 and 20.

Extent of product lines handled

Retail stores may be classified according to the extent of the product lines they carry. In this classification, stores are grouped as general merchandise stores, single-line stores, and specialty stores. Subdivisions within these three groups are recognized by names which consumers typically use in identifying retail stores. That is, we speak of department stores, variety stores, gas stations, and so on.

The relative importance of these various kinds of stores as measured by sales volume is shown in Table 11–5. In 1963, food stores accounted for almost one-quarter of the total retail trade, and the automotive group represented 18 per cent. Figures in the table also show the shift in the relative importance of each type of store from 1948 to 1963.

One note of caution should be observed when interpreting the figures in Table 11–5. As years go by, sales figures for stores classified as they are in this table are becoming less and less meaningful as true indicators of the relative volume of the different commodities. The reason is that there has been a pronounced trend toward scrambled merchandising, that is, the practice of adding new, unusual, unrelated lines to the lines customarily sold in a particular type of store.

General merchandise stores   Institutions which offer a large variety of lines, usually with some depth of assortment in each line, fall into the classification of general merchandise stores. The classification includes department stores, dry goods stores, variety stores, and general stores. As a group, these retailers account for 12 per cent of the total retail trade. Department stores—usually considered a major segment of the retailing structure—represent a little over 8 per cent of all retail sales, and variety stores contribute less than 2 per cent of the total.

table   11–5

Total retail sales and percentage of total sales: by kind of business, in billions of dollars

Food stores and automobile dealers together accounted for more than 40 per cent of total retail sales in 1963. When interpreting the data here, remember that a store often carries merchandise lines not formerly associated with that type of store. Consider the products stocked by a large "drugstore."

	1963 sales	Percentage of total sales			
Kind of business	*($000,000)*	*1963*	*1958*	*1954*	*1948*
Retail trade, total	$244,202	100.0	100.0	100.0	100.0
Lumber, building materials, hardware,					
farm equipment dealers	14,608	6.0	7.2	7.7	8.6
General merchandise group	30,002	12.4	10.9	10.5	12.3
Department stores	20,537	8.4	6.7	6.2	7.3
Variety stores	4,538	1.8	1.8	1.8	1.9
Food stores	57,079	23.4	24.5	23.4	22.7
Eating and drinking places	18,412	7.5	7.6	7.7	8.3
Automotive dealers	45,376	18.6	15.9	17.6	15.6
Gasoline service stations	17,760	7.3	7.1	6.3	5.0
Apparel and accessory stores	14,040	5.7	6.3	6.5	7.5
Furniture, home furnishings,					
equipment stores	10,926	4.4	5.0	5.1	5.4
Drugstores, proprietary stores	8,486	3.5	3.4	3.1	3.1
Other retailers	21,309	8.7	9.2	9.4	9.7
Nonstore retailers	6,204	2.5	2.7	2.7	1.8

SOURCES: U.S. Census of Business: 1963, 1954, Retail Trade, United States Summary.

DEPARTMENT STORES: IMPORTANCE AND RELATIVE MERITS   To be considered a department store for the Census of Business classification, an institution must employ at least twenty-five people, and in its variety of merchandise it must carry furniture, home furnishings, appliances, apparel for the family, and household linens and dry goods.

Department stores are highly organized business enterprises. Traditionally, the overall store management has been organized into four divisions: merchandising, sales promotion, store operation, and accounting control. Today many stores have recognized a fifth major division by elevating personnel relations to a position in the top-management structure. Merchandising or product planning, headed by a general merchandising manager, is usually the key to a store's success. Under the merchandising manager are the department buyers. In effect, each department is a business in itself, and the buyer has considerable autonomy. He determines what items will be bought, how much will be purchased, when it will be delivered, and how it will be displayed.[7]

Another department store feature of importance to producers is the common use of leased departments. The store leases a department to an outside firm which will establish and operate it. To all external appearances, a leased department is operated by the store itself. Beauty shops, restaurants, and departments handling hearing aids, optical goods, millinery, vacuum cleaners, and groceries are frequently leased.

Leased departments offer several advantages to a department store. They help to round out a store's line with no risk to the store. This is especially advantageous in fields where fashion risks are high. Leased departments may bring to the store a highly qualified specialist in a given product field and thus relieve the store's own managerial burden. Stores can also gain financially by leasing out a department whose establishment would require considerable capital outlay.[8]

The lessee is in a favorable position because his rent is often based on a percentage of his sales volume. In such cases, the rent is a variable expense, and the store assumes a significant part of the risk of poor sales. Also, the lessee enjoys the prestige of the store, and he can make use of other store services, such as delivery and credit.

In addition to the general merits of large-scale retail operation (specialized management, buying power, etc.), other advantages accrue to department stores in particular. Department stores offer a wider variety of products and services than any other type of retail institution where the customer comes to the store.

[7] For some suggestions on a new organizational structure to control the merchandising (product-planning) function in a department store chain, especially where sales by the branch stores are becoming larger than those in the main, downtown store, see Louis P. Bucklin, "Merchandising in Department Store Chains," *California Management Review*, Summer, 1964, pp. 41–46.

[8] For an analysis of (1) when a department store should lease a department, (2) how to evaluate a lessee, and (3) some managerial safeguards in leasing, see Robert D. Entenberg, "Leased Departments Can Be a Sound Investment," *Department Store Economist*, April, 1962, p. 34.

(A form of nonstore retailing—the mail-order house—may carry more lines than a department store.) The opportunity for one-stop shopping is almost unlimited. This in turn gives the store a chance to do suggestive selling and to lead the customer from one department to another.

Department stores have a prestige atmosphere or reputation which sets them apart as civic institutions. Window space is often used to promote a local attraction, such as an opera, a charity fund drive, or a football game. Visitors to a city go through the department stores, and local residents go downtown to see the store decorations at Christmastime; such tribute is rarely paid to a grocery store or appliance dealer.

Department stores suffer from several specific limitations as well as from those generally associated with large-scale activity. Operating costs are considerably higher than for most other kinds of retail business; they range from 33 to 35 per cent of sales, depending upon the sales volume of the store. One of the peculiar features of department stores—their many services—also contributes significantly to the high operating expense. Since department stores have a relatively slow rate of turnover and since some of their major product lines, such as apparel, go out of fashion rapidly, they may need to take markdowns on much of their merchandise in order to sell it.

A substantial problem confronting department stores has been their location—typically in the heart of the downtown shopping district. The population exodus to the suburbs and the traffic problems downtown have combined to force many department stores to open branches in the suburbs. The big downtown store, with its large investment, high tax location, and high cost operations, must be maintained, but it reaps a decreasing share of the total business in the area. Department stores are running into strong competition on other fronts as well. In the late 1940s and 1950s the high gross margin of department stores gave impetus to the development of discount selling.

Besides building branches in suburban shopping centers, department stores are making other concerted efforts to meet the new competition. Working with other downtown merchants, the stores are spearheading movements to revitalize downtown areas. Stores have been modernized and redecorated, and better municipal transit service and expanded parking facilities are being developed.[9] Competition from discount sellers is being met with alternative, retaliatory strategies.[10] One course of action—and perhaps one which is leading from weakness—is to convert to self-service, feature discount prices, and generally eliminate services. Another course is to trade up, drop the lines which compete with discount houses, emphasize fashion, and offer more services. This may be a good course of action for high-priced specialty shops, but it is a danger-

---

[9] For some case histories and examples of what various chain organizations (department stores, variety stores, and others) have done to revitalize the downtown areas, see S. O. Kaylin and Martin Ezra, "Recapturing the Downtown Marketplace," *Chain Store Age* (Executives Edition), September, 1964, p. 20.

[10] Stuart U. Rich and Bernard Portis, "Clues for Action from Shopper Preferences," *Harvard Business Review*, March–April, 1963, pp. 132–149.

ous path for department stores. Perhaps the best alternative for department stores—a compromise—is to upgrade merchandise lines and stress fashion, while at the same time offering on a limited basis some of the discounters' attractions and features.

VARIETY STORES   A limited-price variety store carries a large variety of lines of inexpensive convenience products usually sold from open displays on a self-service, cash-and-carry basis. A minimum number of services are provided. Although these stores are still called five-and-ten-cent stores, they have long since expanded their lines and traded up the quality and price levels of their merchandise. In addition to upgrading their stores and adding such nontraditional product lines as high-priced art, glassware, tires, and garden supplies, the large variety store companies have established separate chains of discount stores.[11] The great bulk of the variety store business is done by giant chain organizations, such as the F. W. Woolworth Company, the W. T. Grant Company, S. H. Kress, and S. S. Kresge. According to the Census of Business, 72 per cent of all variety store sales in 1963 were made by chains with more than 100 stores.

Single-line stores   This category of retailing institutions includes stores which carry a considerable assortment of a related line or group of products. Thus we find stores identified by the names of the individual line of products featured: grocery stores, appliance stores, furniture stores, building materials stores, hardware stores, and sporting goods stores. Usually, the larger the store, the more complete its assortment. In some cases, stores of this type carry two related lines, such as men's and women's clothing. Of course, the relative competitive merits of small- and large-sized stores apply to single-line stores as well as to other categories of retailers.

Specialty stores   Specialty stores constitute that class of retail institution which carries a limited variety of products. Typically they handle only one part of a single line of convenience or shopping goods. Examples of this type of store include dairy stores, tobacco shops, bakeries, meat markets, men's shoe stores, millinery shops, and furriers. Specialty stores should not be confused with specialty goods. Actually, specialty shops often do not carry specialty goods. The term "specialty" in relation to the store implies a limited line of merchandise, rather than the well-known, branded products which people are willing to expend considerable effort to purchase. Although there is some chain store activity in this field, the majority of the business is done by independent small-scale retailers.

Because specialty stores handle a limited line of merchandise, they usually have an excellent assortment. In the apparel field, they often feature the newest fashions. Frequently they are the exclusive dealers for certain brands in a given

[11] See Thomas J. Murray, "The Changing World of Woolworth," *Dun's Review and Modern Industry*, November, 1965, p. 46; and "Kresge's Triple-threat Retailing," *Business Week*, Jan. 29, 1966, p. 126.

market. Successful specialty stores usually have highly capable buyers who are expert judges of what will sell. Because they limit their merchandise to a narrow field, these stores can often buy in reasonably large quantities and thus secure favorable prices.

Two limitations facing a specialty store are its inability to diversify risks among many product lines and its inability to capitalize on the sale of related merchandise or impulse items.

Geographic location

Classifying retail stores according to their geographic location tells us something about consumer buying patterns. It also brings out the general conclusion that retail trade is concentrated in relation to population. Thus an analysis of the geographic location of retail trade can be used to evaluate regional market potentials for many products.

Regional distribution   Table 11–6 shows that there is a reasonably close relationship among the number of retail stores, their total sales, and population when these factors are classified by census regions. Where the share of population exceeds the share of retail sales (South Atlantic and East South Central regions) or where sales are relatively higher than population (Pacific and East North Central regions), these variations may be attributed to the differentials in per capita income among the regions.

table   11–6

Comparison of regional percentage distribution of population, retail sales, and number of stores, 1963

A reasonably close relationship exists between the geographical distributions of population, retail sales, and number of stores. Why do you suppose that sales are relatively higher per store in the Pacific and East North Central regions?

Region	Number of establishments, per cent	Retail sales, per cent	Population Dec. 31, 1963, per cent
United States, total	100.0	100.0	100.0
New England	6.0	6.2	5.8
Middle Atlantic	19.7	19.2	18.7
East North Central	19.5	20.7	20.1
West North Central	9.3	8.6	8.4
South Atlantic	14.1	13.3	14.6
East South Central	6.5	5.1	6.5
West South Central	9.5	8.6	9.4
Mountain	4.0	4.1	4.0
Pacific Coast	11.4	14.2	12.5

SOURCES: Retail sales—U.S. Census of Business: 1963, Retail Trade, United States Summary, from data on p. 11. Population—"Survey of Buying Power," *Sales Management,* June 10, 1964, p. 96.

Urban-rural distribution   As one might expect, the great bulk of the retail stores and retail sales is concentrated in the very small land mass made up of standard metropolitan areas. A *standard metropolitan area* is defined by the Federal government as a county or a group of contiguous counties with a total population of at least 100,000 and a central city with a minimum population of 50,000. The boundaries of metropolitan areas may cross state lines, but the counties must constitute a socially and economically integrated unit. Virtually all employment must be nonagricultural. The government has devised a list of about 220 standard metropolitan areas. In 1963 they accounted for 70 per cent of the retail sales and for 60 per cent of the stores. With the continuing decline in farm population as a percentage of total population, and the further development of interurbia, we can expect even more concentration of retail sales within metropolitan areas.

Distribution within urban parts of metropolitan areas   Within the central city and its adjacent cities and suburbs in a metropolitan area, there are several discernible types of shopping districts; together these constitute a retailing structure which should be recognized by marketing men. The hub of the retailing activity traditionally has been the central downtown shopping district—the location of the main units of department stores, major apparel specialty stores, departmentized specialty stores, and single-line jewelry and furniture stores. This district is the heart of shopping goods stores, although convenience goods also are readily available. The major arterial streets and boulevards and all forms of public transportation usually converge in this shopping district. The downtown area draws customers from a wide market, in some cases from over 100 miles.

In the older, larger cities in the East and Midwest, we often find a secondary shopping district.[12] This may be located in the main city about 5 to 8 miles from the downtown area; it may also be found in the "downtown" areas of older suburbs, such as Oak Park and Evanston, Illinois. These districts are not planned or controlled for marketing purposes and thus are differentiated from the modern, planned suburban shopping centers. Secondary districts often contain a branch of a downtown department store and branches of specialty or limited-line stores. Shopping goods are available, but not in so wide an assortment as in downtown areas. Also, secondary districts do not draw customers from so wide a radius as do downtown stores.

A third type of shopping district found in cities is a string-street development or a small cluster of neighborhood stores. Most of the retailers are small, and convenience goods stores predominate, although some small furniture or apparel stores also locate in these districts. In small districts of this type, the stores usually complement one another, although as the districts expand, com-

---

[12] With a few exceptions, such as Seattle or Los Angeles, Western cities do not have secondary shopping districts because most of these cities did not become large enough to support such a district until after World War II. By that time, major retailing developments were taking place in planned suburban shopping centers.

peting stores will be found. The trading area in a neighborhood district is quite small compared with that in a secondary or downtown district.

Since World War II, another significant type of shopping district has arisen in metropolitan areas—the planned, controlled suburban shopping center. Such a center differs from all other shopping districts in that it is carefully planned, developed, and controlled by one organization. The developer may be a major downtown department store or an individual promoter-investor-developer. The center consists of several stores built around a branch of one or two downtown department stores. Ideally there is at least one specialty or limited-line store to compete with each department in the department store, thus affording the consumer ample opportunity to shop and compare products. Many different kinds of convenience goods stores are found in these centers. Larger regional centers may have a bank, a theater, medical and dental offices, a travel bureau, and insurance agencies. Huge parking lots also are included. Large centers may have over one hundred stores, although a center may include only ten to fifteen stores and still be a planned, controlled shopping center.

The success of suburban shopping centers lies essentially in their appeal to, or conformity with, consumer buying patterns. A wide selection of merchandise is available; stores are open evenings; an informal atmosphere encourages mothers to dress informally and bring the children; plenty of free parking space is available. The success of these centers is enhanced by the group effort of the member stores. By coordinating their promotional efforts, all stores benefit; one builds traffic for another. Many stores in these centers are too small to do effective, economical advertising on their own, but they can make good use of major media by tying in with overall shopping center advertising and promotion. They also cash in on the general prestige and reputation of the center.

QUESTIONS AND PROBLEMS

1   "You can eliminate the middleman, but you cannot eliminate his functions." Discuss.

2   Which of the following institutions are middlemen? Explain.

a.	Food broker	g.	Chain supermarket
b.	Stockbroker	h.	Bank
c.	Real estate broker	i.	Grain elevator
d.	Department store	j.	Hardware wholesaler
e.	Railroad	k.	Fuller Brush salesman
f.	Advertising agency	l.	Radio station

3   What is a channel of distribution and how is it related to the physical distribution of the product?

4   "Middlemen are important in marketing, but the fewer of them we can use in the trade channel for a product, the lower the cost of marketing will be." Discuss.

5   Explain the concept of "utility" as it is used in economic theory. Explain how

time, place, and possession utility may be created in the marketing of the following products. What business institutions might be involved in creating these utilities?

a. Sewing machines
b. Fresh peaches
c. Nail files
d. Hydraulic grease racks used in garages and service stations

6   Define the terms "retailing," a "retail sale," and a "retailer." Explain the three concepts in light of the following situations:

a. Avon cosmetics saleslady selling door-to-door
b. Farmer selling his produce door-to-door
c. Farmer selling his produce at his roadside stand
d. Sporting goods store selling uniforms to a professional baseball team

7   How do you account for the wide differences in operating expenses among the various types of retail stores shown in Table 11–2?

8   Why is retailing more expensive than wholesaling? Why is retailing inherently less efficient than manufacturing?

9   What functions does a retailer provide for consumers? Do all stores perform the same functions? Explain.

10   The mortality rate among retail stores is one of the highest among all types of business institutions. How do you account for this?

11   "Retailing is typically small-scale business." "There is a high degree of concentration in retailing today; the giants control the field." Reconcile these two statements, using facts and figures where appropriate.

12   Referring to the ten criteria given in this chapter for evaluating competitive positions of large-scale and small-scale retailers, on which counts are small stores in a stronger competitive position than large-scale retailers? In light of your final score, how do you account for the numerical preponderance of small retailers?

13   What courses of action might a small retailer follow to improve his competitive position?

14   What can department stores do to offset their competitive disadvantages?

15   Distinguish between a specialty store and a limited-line store, giving some examples of each type in the city where your school is located.

16   "Single-line stores or specialty stores often have greater buying power than department stores." Explain.

17   What can single-line and specialty stores do to compete effectively with department stores?

18   What effect has the growth of suburban shopping centers had on department stores? On downtown specialty stores? On small retailers?

19   Identify the various types of shopping districts in a nearby city. Relate this structure to the one described in this chapter.

20   What factors would you consider and what requirements would you set if you were to establish and develop a planned suburban shopping center?

21   What is the relationship between the growth and successful development of planned suburban shopping centers and the material studied regarding the consumer in Chapters 4 to 6?

12

RETAILERS
AND METHODS
OF OPERATION

In the preceding chapter, retailing institutions were classified and analyzed on the basis of the size of the store as measured by sales volume, the extent of the product lines handled, and the geographic location. In this chapter, retailers are discussed in terms of form of ownership and method of operation.

RETAILERS CLASSIFIED BY FORM OF OWNERSHIP

Classified according to form of ownership, retail institutions fall into two major groups: independent stores and corporate chain stores. A third group, which we shall consider here, are voluntary associations of independents who band together in chain-like fashion in order to compete more effectively with the corporate chain store organization. Other less important ownership categories, such as leased departments, company stores, consumers' cooperatives, and government commissaries, account for a negligible percentage of total retail trade.

Corporate chain store

A *chain-store system* is an organization consisting of two or more stores centrally owned and managed and handling generally the same lines of products on the same level in the distribution structure. Technically, two or more units may constitute a chain, although today many merchants who consider themselves small-scale independents have two or three more units which they have opened up in shopping centers and newly populated areas. These retailers ordinarily do not think of themselves as a chain. Consequently, it might be more meaningful to consider a larger number of units as a reasonable minimum when categorizing a store as a chain. (The Census of Business uses multiunit classification categories starting with 2, 4, 6, 11, 26, 51, and 101 units.)

Central ownership is the key factor which differentiates corporate chains from voluntary associations of independent wholesalers or retailers. The third element in our definition of a chain-store system is central management. Individual units in a chain have very little autonomy. Buying is highly centralized with respect to both the physical purchasing and the determination of what will be bought. Centralized management also leads to considerable standardization in operating procedures and policies among the units in the chain.

Many chains are also vertically integrated, but this feature is not essential for definition or classification purposes. Safeway Stores, the large grocery chain, maintains large distribution centers where they buy from producers, do their own warehousing, and then distribute to their own stores in their own trucks. Some chain organizations, such as the A & P Company, actually own and operate manufacturing plants to supply some of their needs. Another form of vertical integration has resulted in manufacturer-owned retail chains. Some examples are shoe chains (Flagg Brothers), apparel chains (the Bond Clothing Company), and gasoline service stations (the Standard Oil Company of California).

Importance   In number of stores and total sales, independent single-unit stores constitute by far the largest segment of retail trade when institutions are classed by ownership. In fact, the 1963 Census of Business shows that about 87 per cent of all stores are single-unit stores and that they account for about 63 per cent of all retail sales. Of course, the other side of these statistics suggests the degree of concentration in retailing. Organizations with eleven or more stores did 26 per cent of total retail business with only 7 per cent of total stores. Chains with more than 100 units accounted for only 4 per cent of all stores, but they did 16 per cent of all retail business.

The importance of chains varies considerably from one type of commodity to another (see Table 12–1). Chains dominate the variety store business, where firms with eleven or more stores account for close to 80 per cent of all variety store sales. Chains of food stores, department stores, and shoe stores are also important. Since the end of World War II, there has been a significant increase in the amount of business done by multiunit organizations in the department store field. In 1963, 85 per cent of total department store sales came from companies with four or more units. This trend reflects the opening of branch stores in suburban markets as well as the expansion of chains.

Competitive advantages   Chain-store organizations are large-scale retailing institutions and, as such, enjoy the general competitive advantages of large-scale retailing discussed in Chapter 11. In addition, chain stores per se have some particular merits.

LOWER SELLING PRICES   Chain stores traditionally have been credited with selling at lower prices than independents. This is an image chains have projected to the public, but the claim of lower prices needs careful scrutiny because it can be misleading. It was probably more justified in the past than it is today. Many independents have improved and streamlined their operating methods and have thus reduced their costs. They have also pooled their buying power so that in many instances they can buy products at the same prices as the chains.

table   12–1

Percentage of sales made by various chains, 1963

Large chains dominate the variety store business. Does this indicate an absence of competition in the field? There are several giant chains among food stores, and yet in that retail field, companies with eleven or more units account for less than one-half of food store sales.

| | Percentage of sales | | |
Kind of business	*Four or more stores*	*Eleven or more stores*	*Over 100 stores*
Total retail sales	30.1	25.5	15.8
Limited-price variety stores	80.9	78.3	72.2
Department stores	85.6	70.5	33.0
Shoe stores	50.8	44.3	34.0
Food stores	48.9	44.2	32.1
Apparel and accessories stores			
(not including shoe stores)	32.8	24.6	11.0
Drugstores	26.1	22.5	11.0
Lumber, building materials, hardware,			
farm equipment dealers	12.3	8.1	2.1
Furniture, appliance, home furnishings			
stores	14.1	7.4	1.5
Gasoline service stations	11.5	9.6	6.4

SOURCE: U.S. Census of Business: 1963, Retail Trade, Single Units and Multiunits.

It is very difficult to compare prices of chains with those of independents. The merchandise is often not exactly comparable because many chains sell items under their own brands. It is difficult to compare the price of Del Monte peaches with A & P peaches. Also, it is not accurate to compare the price of a product sold in a cash-and-carry, no-customer-service store with the price of an identically branded product in a full-service store. The value of services should be included in the comparison.

When the chains do have a price advantage, it is traceable to one or more of three factors. First, chain-store operating costs may be lower than those of independents. Chains usually offer fewer "free" services. They reduce costs by careful buying and careful inventory controls which maximize their rate of turnover and minimize the number of slow-moving items in stock. Chains further reduce operating costs by doing their own wholesaling and, in some instances, their own manufacturing. This feature of vertical integration makes for economies of scale and a more effective operation.

The second factor holding prices down is that chains normally are satisfied with a lower percentage of net profit; they depend upon huge sales volume to maximize their dollar profit. Some of the large food chains, for example, show net profits of 1 to 2 per cent of net sales, and this is *before* income taxes.

The third factor is the buying ability of the chains. The quantities in which they buy—carloads and even trainloads—and their ability to contract often a year in advance for the entire output of a farm or factory enable them to secure a very favorable price. Chain-store buyers typically are specialists and are very skilled in their business. Because of the chain store's buying practices and buying ability, manufacturers and other producers are attracted to chains: these sellers realize that by making contact with one person or one buying group, they may get their products into hundreds of retail outlets.

OPPORTUNITY TO USE ADVERTISING AND SALES PROMOTION   Chain organizations are in a much better position to make effective use of advertising and sales promotion than even large independents. This competitive advantage is more a result of the multitude of chain outlets than of the total volume size of the corporation. That is, a grocery chain may have twenty-five medium-sized stores blanketing a city, and an independent competitor may have one huge supermarket doing three to four times the business of any single unit of the chain. Yet the chain can use the metropolitan daily newspaper as an advertising medium with much less waste circulation than can the independent. Many chains make effective use of national advertising media.

ABILITY TO SPREAD RISKS   Chain stores do not have all their eggs in one basket or in one store. Even large-scale independent department stores or supermarkets cannot match this advantage of the chain. A multiunit operation automatically has spread its risks among many members. If one store is located in a declining or disappearing market, that store can be closed and any loss absorbed by other, still healthy outlets.

FLEXIBILITY FOR EXPERIMENTATION   In many respects a chain is bogged down in red tape and administrative inflexibility solely because the multiunit operation requires standardization. This same multiunit operation, however, offers a number of opportunities for flexibility. As a case in point, one outlet's slow-moving merchandise can be moved to another outlet whose customers might view it more favorably. The company can experiment with layouts, different store fronts, or new types of merchandise by introducing any of these features into a few stores before committing itself to a full-scale introduction.

Competitive disadvantages   Chain stores suffer the limitations of all large-scale retailing institutions, as well as a few additional ones.

STANDARDIZATION AND INFLEXIBILITY   The feature of standardization, the hallmark of a chain store system and a major factor in its success, is not an unmixed blessing. Chains have not always been able to adjust rapidly to local competition or to take full advantage of local market opportunities because store managers could not act without first getting approval from a central office. The geographic decentralization of stores and their separation from the home office encourage administrative rigidity. Individual store managers frequently have no autonomy with respect to the merchandise they carry.

Chains are well aware of these limitations and have instituted several measures designed to give store managers greater freedom and to lessen the rigidities of merchandising policies. Chain-store executives, however, are also aware that in decreasing the amount of standardization, they run the risk of increasing their operating costs. Consequently, the single-unit store undoubtedly will continue to enjoy the advantage of flexibility in competition with a chain.

PERSONNEL PROBLEMS   Chain stores are particularly susceptible to the personnel problems associated with large-scale businesses. Store managers are shifted from one store to another, thus making it difficult for them to establish real rapport with other employees or with a particular community. In a single-unit department store, although it may be huge, the employees know that the top executives are close at hand in the same building. In a chain store, top management may be in another city, and employees may have little loyalty to, or real interest in, the firm.

POOR PUBLIC IMAGE   Up to the time of World War II, the chains were generally held in very low regard and high suspicion by a great many American consumers. Some of the common criticisms were: chains are run by absentee ownership; they drain money from a community; they do not pay their fair share of taxes; they have miserable personnel policies, such as long hours and low pay; they are monopolistic and engage in unfair competition; they employ "sharp" retailing practices, such as giving the customer short weight and adulterated products. Many of these charges were half-truths, and others were not true at all. Nevertheless, this poor image undoubtedly presented substantial obstacles to chain development. Changing social and economic considerations, along with more enlightened, socially responsible chain store management, have improved the situation, but chains will probably never enjoy the degree of public sympathy and support that local, independent merchants do.

ANTI-CHAIN-STORE LEGISLATION   In the 1930s, popular resentment against corporate chains led to the enactment of several major pieces of anti-chain-store legislation at both the state and Federal levels. Although these laws do not apply exclusively to chain retailers (some apply also to manufacturers and other middlemen), they restrict chain stores most, and usually were designed to do so. Today the Federal laws are enforced with great vigor because of judicial interpretations through the years, but many state laws have been tempered somewhat.

At the Federal level, the Robinson-Patman Act (1936), amending the Clayton Antitrust Act of 1914, is probably the most significant anti-chain-store law. This law affects the chains in three ways: it places restrictions on discounts allowed for quantity buying; it prohibits allowances to chains for performing brokers' services; and it limits the granting of allowances for advertising and other promotional activities. The Robinson-Patman Act is discussed in greater detail in Chapter 19.

Major state laws affecting chains are the resale-price-maintenance laws, unfair-sales-practices acts, and chain store tax laws. Resale-price-maintenance (fair-trade) laws prevent a retailer from selling a product below the price stipulated by the manufacturer. Thus chains are not able to undersell other stores on fair-trade items, regardless of the chains' lower operating costs, willingness to take lower profit margins, and offer of fewer services. Unfair-practices acts prohibit the sale of merchandise at a price lower than cost plus a small markup. Fair-trade and unfair-practices acts are discussed in Chapter 20. Chain-store tax laws were passed by twenty-nine states and still exist in twelve. These laws provide for graduated tax rates. The state tax per store usually depends upon the number of stores the chain has, either within the given state or in the entire nation.

Franchise systems involving small, independent retailers

One of the strongest competitive limitations facing corporate chains since the end of World War II has been the increased effectiveness of independent retailers and wholesalers who have copied chain-store marketing methods. Independents have adopted self-service methods in many types of stores; they have improved store appearance and layout; they have sought better locations, including suburban shopping centers; they have improved their merchandising practices by eliminating some slow-moving items and keeping fresh stock; and they have improved their accounting and inventory control systems.

Probably the most effective measure adopted by small independents, however, has been their practice of voluntarily associating with wholesalers, manufacturers, or other retailers in some form of contractual franchise system. In some instances these associations resemble a corporate chain so closely that about the only significant difference is that the retail stores are not centrally owned. These voluntary affiliations coupled with the limitations of large, corporate-chain forms of retailing and the changing nature of the consumer market are resulting in a revitalization of the small, independent retailer.[1]

Nature of franchise systems   The concept of franchising is blurred sometimes by the broad, loose usage of the term and by the many variations in the scope and content of franchise agreements. Historically in marketing, a franchise was defined narrowly as "a system under which a manufacturer granted to certain dealers the right to sell his product or service, in generally defined areas, in exchange for a promise to promote and merchandise the product in a specific manner."[2] Perhaps at this point it will be more useful if we broaden our interpretation of franchising to include any contractual arrangement between a franchiser (a supplier, who may be a manufacturer or a wholesaler) and a series of independent franchisees (either wholesalers or retailers). The franchiser grants the right to sell certain goods or services in generally defined markets; he usually provides equipment (where appropriate), the products or services for sale, and managerial services. In return the franchisee agrees to market the product or service in a manner established by the supplier.[3] Within the broader definition we find two main types of franchising systems—one is a voluntary association of retailers and/or wholesalers; the other is a retailer network initiated and sponsored by a manufacturer.[4]

ASSOCIATIONS OF INDEPENDENT RETAILERS   These associations may take any of several forms, but the two most important are wholesaler-sponsored groups and retailer-sponsored groups, also known, respectively, as voluntary chains and retailer cooperative chains. A *voluntary chain* is an association of independent retailers, initiated and sponsored by a wholesaler for the primary purpose of assuring the wholesaler of a series of profitable retail outlets for his products. The connecting link between the wholesaler and the retailer is a contract. In some instances, the wholesaler who sponsors a group of independent stores also belongs to a federation or association of similar group-sponsoring wholesalers. As an example of one of these federations in the food field, the Independent Grocers Alliance (IGA) grants a franchise to a wholesaler, who in turn licenses his member retailers as IGA stores.

The essence of the contract in a wholesaler-sponsored chain is that the wholesaler will furnish various services to the member retailers, who in turn

[1] See Alton F. Doody and William R. Davidson, "Growing Strength in Small Retailing," *Harvard Business Review*, July–August, 1964, pp. 69–79.

[2] Charles M. Hewitt, "The Furor over Dealer Franchises," *Business Horizons*, November, 1958, p. 81.

[3] See William P. Hall, "Franchising: New Scope for an Old Technique," *Harvard Business Review*, January–February, 1964, pp. 60–72.

[4] For the point of view that these two systems are sufficiently different that they should be identified as separate concepts and that the term "franchise selling" should be limited to the manufacturer-sponsored system, see Leonard J. Konopa, "What Is Meant by Franchise Selling?" *Journal of Marketing*, April, 1963, pp. 35–37.

will buy all or almost all their merchandise from this wholesaler. By virtue of the tremendous buying power of the combined retail units, the wholesalers are able to buy at prices competitive with corporate chain organizations. Wholesalers offer various marketing and management services, such as proposals for store layout, effective display methods, advertising aids, accounting and stock control systems, delivery of merchandise to the store, reasonable credit, and field supervisors. Sales volumes of voluntary chains, particularly the combined organizations such as IGA, are big enough to enable them to market under their own brand. This practice provides lower-cost buying opportunities, offers promotional advantages, and prevents consumers from making direct price comparisons with merchandise offered by corporate chains.

A *retailer cooperative chain* is an organization instituted and sponsored by a group of independent retailers who jointly buy and operate a wholesale warehouse. The formal tie is stock ownership in the cooperative warehouse. The retailer members usually maintain their separate identities, as in the Associated Grocers and the Certified Grocers—two of the larger retailer cooperative chains in the food field.[5]

Retailer-sponsored chains have the same basic purpose as wholesaler-sponsored chains—to enable independent wholesalers and retailers to meet more effectively the competition from corporate chain stores. These associations of independents differ from each other in the following respects: (1) sponsorship of the association—retailer or wholesaler; (2) ownership of the wholesale house—retailer or wholesaler; (3) the connecting link between wholesaler and retailer—contract or stock ownership; (4) the nature and amount of services provided by the wholesaler.

MANUFACTURER-SPONSORED SYSTEMS   This type of franchise system follows the narrow definition stated earlier. That is, a manufacturer sets up a network of retail outlets by contracting with new or established independent operators. The contract may cover (1) a single department in a store (Russell Stover candies or Mode O'Day clothes), (2) only one brand within a department (Magnavox or Maytag appliances), or (3) the entire retail outlet and all aspects of its operation (dealerships for autos, farm equipment, earth-moving equipment, or petroleum products; McDonalds or Dairy Queen drive-ins; Holiday Inns and Howard Johnson restaurants; Fred Astaire dance studios; Hertz or Avis auto rentals; Kelly Girl part-time help).[6]

Extent of franchising systems   Wholesaler-sponsored chains (IGA and Super Valu Stores, for example) are more prevalent in the grocery field than in any other line of retailing, although these chains do exist in fields of hard-

---

[5] Associated Grocers also sponsors in the West a chain of independently owned but look-alike stores—the Thriftway Stores.

[6] For a comprehensive analysis of manufacturer-sponsored franchising, see Edwin H. Lewis and Robert S. Hancock, *The Franchise System of Distribution*, The University of Minnesota Press, Minneapolis, 1963.

ware (Ace Hardware Co.), variety stores (Ben Franklin stores), auto supplies (Western Auto Supply Co.), and drugs (Walgreen Co.).[7] Retailer-sponsored chains are also quite significant in the grocery field, but otherwise they are not very important in the total retailing picture. Group affiliations of independent retailers have been growing rapidly in many fields since World War II. In fact, in grocery products these associations are growing at a faster rate than the corporate chains. From 1947 to 1963, according to *Progressive Grocer*, the share of grocery store sales transacted by corporate chains (eleven or more units) increased from 35 to 41 per cent. The market share accounted for by voluntary chains and retailer cooperatives rose from 31 to 49 per cent during the same period. Sales by unaffiliated independents declined sharply, from 34 to 10 per cent of the total market.[8]

Among manufacturer-sponsored systems, the concept of franchising an entire retail outlet (as contrasted with a single department or one brand within a department) is not new—oil companies and automobile manufacturers have done this for years. What is new, however, is its substantial growth since about 1950 and its spreading into many new fields. In addition to a huge volume in food and refreshment services, today manufacturer-sponsored franchise selling also embraces a variety of other products and services including auto mufflers, putting greens, paint, part-time office help, hearing aids, motels, and dance studios.[9]

Competitive advantages   Franchising has many economic and social factors encouraging its growth. In voluntary groups a manufacturer may reach hundreds of independents simply by contacting one wholesaler. A manufacturer-sponsored system offers a manufacturer an opportunity for greater control and supervision over the pricing, advertising, and selling of his product—a sharp contrast with the situation he faces when distributing through giant retailers. Franchising also provides a supplier with the means for rapid market expansion and a wide distribution system at a relatively low cost; the franchisee typically puts up some of the money. With his own money at stake, a fran-

[7] Walgreen's is an interesting example of a corporate chain. It has almost five hundred retail stores of its own, and through its wholesale division it has franchised almost two thousand "Walgreen Agency Drug Stores." These independent retailers provide additional outlets for Walgreen-branded products, while at the same time benefiting from Walgreen's advertising, product lines, protected territories, and managerial guidance.

[8] As quoted in Seymour Freedgood, "Uncle to 1,700 Grocers," *Fortune*, March, 1965, p. 130. This article describes the development and present-day activities of Super Valu stores, one of the country's largest voluntary food-chain sponsors. See also "A Supermarket Chain That Isn't a Chain," *Business Week*, Aug. 22, 1964, p. 81.

[9] See Richard Osk, "The Big Franchise Sell," *Sales Management*, Sept. 17, 1965, p. 25; see also "Franchising Finds It's an Industry," *Business Week*, June 19, 1965, p. 72.

chisee has more incentive and is apt to be a more dedicated entrepreneur than a store manager hired by the manufacturer.

In both types of franchise systems, retailers are identified as a group; thus a manufacturer can make effective use of cooperative advertising programs, display materials, and other promotional features. The group buying power enables the independent retailer members to obtain lower-cost merchandise and a better selection of the latest products. Furthermore, the retailers are able to do a better job of retail store management because of the administrative services and advice furnished by the wholesaler, particularly in voluntary chains. Finally, the opportunity to use group advertising enhances the competitive position of these retailers.

In a manufacturer-sponsored network particularly, franchising enables a person to realize a dream that many people have—the opportunity to own his own business. This goal now can be reached, and with the added security that the business has been tested. Also, the franchisee's investment is relatively small, and it is easier for him to borrow the necessary funds now that a big national firm is behind him. He may be an independent, small-scale retailer, and yet he is backed by the buying power, promotional programs, and management know-how of a big company.

Limitations   In the author's opinion, the biggest single competitive weakness of all independent retailers, whether affiliated or not, is their assumption that the sole advantage of the chain is its buying power. In fact, the Robinson-Patman Act was largely based on this premise. Through the years many retailers have come to the conclusion that this assumption is false, but too many still fail to realize that the real strength of a large-scale institution lies in its superior management personnel and specialized management practices.

Ignorance or disregard of this fact today places major limitations on voluntary associations of independents. Too often these retailers reject the management advice given by field supervisors. Many retailers still think of the association as a buying aid only and make little use of advertising, display, accounting, and other association services. In general, the problem is simply that these retailers are independent in every sense of the word. They want to be in business for themselves, and they do not take kindly to outside direction or supervision. Furthermore, there is always the problem of attracting new, desirable franchisees and of providing for management succession in established, successful outlets.

Future outlook   On balance, the future of franchise selling looks very encouraging. It will undoubtedly expand and be adopted in new industries. Already we have seen combined franchising operations in the case of a Ben Franklin variety store, a Western Auto store, and a supermarket grouped together under one roof as a small shopping center. The franchise system should grow because it is making significant contributions to the American economy.[10] Franchising has established high operating standards for retail and service businesses, and it has improved the efficiency of management. The system has broadened the range of goods and services offered to the public; it also increases the stability of retail outlets by reducing the risk of failure. Finally, it creates new business enterprises and broadens the economic base of the country by its encouragement of small business.

RETAILERS CLASSIFIED BY METHOD OF OPERATION

Manufacturers and wholesalers will find some value in analyzing retail middlemen according to their methods of operation. The two broad categories observed here are in-store retailing and nonstore, or outside-of-the-store, retailing. Major methods of in-store retailing which should be considered are full-service retailing, supermarket retailing, and discount retailing. Major forms of nonstore retailing are mail-order selling, automatic vending, and personal selling on a door-to-door basis.

Full-service retailing

This is the traditional form of in-store, across-the-counter retailing where the customer comes to the store, is waited on by a salesman, and may avail himself of other store services. It is no secret that this form of retail selling has declined considerably over the past thirty years or so. It is still prevalent, however, and probably will remain so in product lines where high-fashion goods are involved or where a salesman's demonstration, explanation, or fitting is needed.

Supermarket retailing

It is somewhat difficult to analyze supermarket retailing because there is no universally accepted definition of the term. To some people it is a *type* of retail institution found in the grocery business. To others, the term describes a *method* of retailing and may be used in connection with stores in any field.

In this discussion, a *supermarket* will be defined as a large-scale, departmentized retailing institution offering a wide variety of merchandise (including groceries, meats, produce, and dairy products), operating largely on a self-service basis with a minimum of customer services, and featuring a price

[10] Lewis and Hancock, *op. cit.*, pp. 85–92. See also Richard W. Hansen, "The Growth and Development of Cooperative Retail Chains and Their Marketing Significance," in L. George Smith (ed.), *Reflections on Progress in Marketing*, American Marketing Association, Chicago, 1965, pp. 110–118; in this study the author includes both retailer- and wholesaler-sponsored groups as "cooperative retail chains."

appeal and usually ample parking space. No minimum sales volume is established as a criterion in this definition. It is believed that in selecting a channel of distribution, a manufacturer or a wholesaler is more concerned with the marketing policies and methods of a type of retailing institution than with its precise volume.

The major marketing policies and strategies of a supermarket are stated or implied in the above definition. First, these stores operate largely or entirely on a self-service basis, and they characteristically offer very few services, such as credit or delivery. Second, the limited service feature, combined with the large buying power and willingness to take low percentage profit margins, means that supermarkets can sell at low prices. This low-price appeal has been one of the most important factors underlying the historical development and present-day importance of supermarkets. A third marketing characteristic of supermarkets is that they offer a wide variety of merchandise, and it looks as if the trend toward product diversification will continue.

Development of supermarkets   Supermarkets, as we know them today, had their start in the Depression days of the early 1930s. They were established in barnlike buildings, with wooden crates for shelves and with merchandise procured from sources faced with economic failure. They were owned and operated by *independents* attempting to compete with the chain stores. Those "pine board" operations were a far cry from the supermarket palaces of today. As large-scale retailers, supermarkets enjoy the general advantages attributable to scale, and they also may escape one of the serious problems of bigness, namely, the impersonal relations that exist between store and customer. Because most consumers who shop in supermarkets prefer to be left alone, the big store's lack of friendly, sociable salesclerks who know the customer by name may be no limitation.

Supermarkets are rapidly taking over food retailing. In one study, *Super Market Merchandising* estimated that 75 per cent of total grocery sales were done by supermarkets in 1965, as compared with only 31 per cent in 1948. Food chains have been particularly active in supermarket retailing. Chains with eleven or more stores accounted for about 60 per cent of all supermarket units and 70 per cent of all supermarket sales in 1965.[11]

These figures suggest that grocery supermarkets are reaching a saturation point and that their rate of expansion will soon level off. Today's food supermarkets are running out of small, full-service stores with which to compete; the large retailers are competing fiercely with one another. Further growth will probably come in response to population expansion and geographic shifts in population. There are other factors which have a retarding effect on grocery

[11] "The True Look of the Super Market Industry," *Super Market Merchandising*, April, 1966, pp. 38–55, especially pp. 42, 53. In this study, one criterion in the definition of a supermarket was a minimum annual sales volume of $500,000.

supermarket expansion. One is that the stores are growing so large that an enormous amount of capital is needed to establish a supermarket. Another is that choice locations become harder to find as the market becomes saturated.[12]

One way to attract new groups of consumers would be to offer additional services. This, of course, would be a reversal of the supermarket principle; it would increase operating costs and selling prices. It might be self-defeating, because it would drive away price-conscious consumers. Supermarket operating methods are being employed by retailers in many fields, and this will erect competitive hurdles in the path of product-line expansion by grocery supermarkets.

Another noteworthy development in recent years has been the spread of discount selling as a competitor of food supermarkets. Discount department stores started the movement by establishing discount-food departments in the stores. These departments operate with a lower gross margin and fewer services than conventional supermarkets. To meet this competitive, evolutionary development in food marketing, separate "free-standing" discount supermarkets are being established. In 1965, the combined sales volume of food departments in discount department stores and that of the free-standing discount supermarkets equaled 14 per cent of total conventional supermarket sales.[13]

Advent of supermarket methods in nonfood fields   Some of the features of supermarket operations have been employed with varying degrees of success in nonfood fields. The most frequently adopted measure has been self-service, with the accompanying open displays of merchandise. Many new or remodeled drugstores, variety stores, hardware stores, bookstores, and other types of retailers have made this shift. In some department stores, the departments selling greeting cards, housewares, notions, and men's furnishings have been placed on a self-service basis. These stores, especially the department stores, have made little attempt to adopt the other limited-service features of supermarket retailing.

Discount retailing and the discount house

One of the most significant parts of the "revolution in retailing" which occurred in the decade following World War II was the development of the modern

[12] For some research guidelines and a model for effective supermarket location, see Bernard J. LaLonde, "New Frontiers in Store Location," *Super Market Merchandising,* part 1, February, 1963, p. 107, and part 2, March, 1963, p. 70; see also Bernard J. LaLonde, *Differentials in Supermarket Drawing Power,* Michigan State University, Bureau of Business and Economic Research, Marketing and Transportation Paper no. 11, 1962.

[13] "The True Look of the Super Market Industry," p. 46; see also "How Discounters Undersell Supers," *Super Market Merchandising,* part 1, January, 1963, p. 45, and part 2, February, 1963, p. 66.

discount house. This institution or method of selling entered the retailing field as a brash innovator and forced a reexamination of traditional pricing structures and operating margins, costs, and methods.

What is a discount house? Is it a retailing *institution* which is separately discernible and which is capable of being defined so as to differentiate it, or are we really talking about a *method* of retail pricing and sales promotion which is applicable to almost any type of store? Actually there is nothing new about discount selling—the practice of selling below the list price or the regular advertised price. There is also nothing new about discount houses; they have existed in some form for many years. If this is the case, one may wonder why suddenly in the late 1940s and early 1950s there was so much excitement about them. The reason is that the discount houses of the pre-World War II era were of a different type. They reached a small percentage of the consumers and therefore had very little impact on other retailers. Many of these early discount houses were small establishments which displayed no merchandise; instead, they selected from manufacturers' catalogues and placed orders by model or style number. Generally, they were not widely advertised or publicized, and access to them was restricted in some fashion.

The discount houses which emerged after World War II, however, and which caused so much consternation in the ranks of traditional retailers, are different. They are large stores, freely open to the public, advertising widely, carrying a reasonably complete selection and variety of well-known brands of hard goods (appliances, home furnishings, sporting goods, jewelry), consistently selling below nationally advertised list prices, operating in heavily traveled but low-rent districts, having a minimum of expensive buildings and fixtures, and offering a minimum of customer services and usually plenty of free parking space. The quantitative importance of discount selling is somewhat difficult to assess because we lack commonly accepted definitions. However, the tremendous impact of discount selling on the retailing structure in the United States is generally recognized.

Growth of discount retailing   To understand the early success of the discount house, let us examine the reasons why some retailers were able to sell at low prices, and then analyze the market to see why consumers were so receptive to a low-price–no-service appeal. First, what factors led to the traditional retail markup on appliances and other products that are typically discounted? In the 1930s, electric appliances, such as refrigerators and mixers, were relatively new products and were generally classed as luxuries. Consequently, manufacturers had to offer retailers large markups—30 to 40 per cent —to encourage them to stock the products and perform the necessary services. Personal selling was required to demonstrate, explain, and truly *sell* these items. Retailers had to advertise the products and promote them in the local market. The products were not mechanically perfect, and the dealers had to service and repair them.

After World War II, product and market considerations had changed substantially. Products were presold to consumers through national advertising by the manufacturers. Many brands were well known and required little local promotion. The products were of better quality and needed fewer repairs, so the manufacturer's guarantee on parts was sufficient for the consumer.

After the war a new consumer market emerged—a vast middle-income market—composed in large part of people who had been in low-income groups. These people were price-conscious and were used to shopping where few services were provided. They were the people with whom supermarket methods of selling had been so successful. The supermarkets conditioned these consumers for discount selling—low prices and few services. Also, this market had a pent-up demand from the war years. With so many wants and limited income, people were forced to place importance on price when buying.

The situation was ripe for major changes in retailing. Most retailers, however, either failed to grasp the significance of the situation or paid no heed; instead, they maintained their traditional markup policies. On the other hand, the discount sellers saw the tremendous possibilities in a low-margin, high-turnover type of operation, with few services but big price reductions. Their operating methods enabled them to limit expenses to 12 to 18 per cent of sales, as compared with the 30 to 40 per cent found in department and limited-line stores.

Recent developments in discount retailing   Discount selling has led to a revision of traditional retailing margins. Manufacturers have altered their channels of distribution to include discounting retailers. Small-scale retailers have been forced to drop discounted products or else meet the discount-house price by offering fewer services and adopting more efficient methods. Large-scale retailers, such as department stores, have responded in several ways. In selling appliances, some stores have abandoned the one-price system and are bargaining with the customers. Others conduct almost a continual warehouse sale. Still others have realistically lowered their markups on discounted products.[14]

The discount houses themselves are changing. Some are upgrading their image to that of a "promotional department store," and some have opened stores in suburban shopping centers. In general, all discounters are trading up in products and services. In the early 1950s, discount sellers ordinarily did not carry food products or soft goods. Today many have added soft goods, including a line of wearing apparel. In fact, reasonably expensive, high-fashion women's ready-to-wear is carried in a number of large discount houses. We noted earlier that discount-food supermarkets have been established as separate stores or as departments in discount houses. Separate discount department stores are even being established by "conventional" retailers such as Woolworth (Woolco), Kresge (K-Mart), and Grand Union (Grand-Way).

[14] See Charles E. Silberman, "The Department Stores Are Waking Up," *Fortune*, July, 1962, p. 143.

The discount sellers' risks and operating costs are, of course, being increased as they add more expensive merchandise, broaden their assortments, move into fancier buildings and locations, and add more services. Vastly intensified competition is also causing real financial problems for many discounters, and there are signs of a slowdown in the dizzying rate of entry into the field.[15]

As discount houses and conventional retailers imitate one another and adopt each other's strong points, we can see discount sellers losing their identity as a distinctive form of retailing institution. Perhaps price will cease to be their principal appeal for consumer patronage. Instead, mature discount houses will have to rely more on the forms of nonprice competition (services, quality products, good location, believable promotion, ethical standards, etc.) used by older types of retailers.[16]

Nonstore personal selling

One of the oldest retailing methods in history is to have buyer and seller meet and transact their business at the buyer's home or at some other nonstore location. This is called door-to-door or house-to-house selling. Unfortunately, these titles are a poor way to describe nonstore personal selling. They suggest a cold canvass, wherein the salesman literally goes from door to door, without advance selection or qualification of prospects. Actually, relatively little selling is done in this haphazard way.

Nonstore sales may be made by either producers or retailers selling directly to consumers. Farmers sell fresh produce or eggs on a door-to-door basis. Bakery and dairy products are frequently distributed in this fashion. Many manufacturers also use this method, including makers of cosmetics (Avon), brushes (the Fuller Brush Company), costume jewelry (Sarah Coventry), housewares (Stanley Home Products), reference books (World Book Encyclopedia), vacuum cleaners (Electrolux), and plastic kitchenware (Tupperware). At the retailer level, automobile dealers do some door-to-door selling; rugs, draperies, appliances, home heating, and other departments in department stores often have their salesmen call directly on people at home.

The oldest and most common way for a "direct-to-home" salesman to

[15] See Kenneth Ford, "Discounting: Why It's Tougher Now," *Printers' Ink*, Mar. 22, 1963, p. 19; and "Is Success Spoiling Discount Stores?" *Business Week*, June 26, 1965, p. 97.

[16] William R. Davidson and Alton F. Doody, "The Future of Discounting," *Journal of Marketing*, January, 1963, pp. 36–39. For a research study on (1) what the discount store means to consumers, (2) what the discount store signifies in terms of competition with other retailers, and (3) who the discount stores see as their competition, see *Discount Stores: A Picture of Their Position Today in Metropolitan Chicago*, The Chicago Tribune Company, Chicago, 1964.

For another study indicating (1) who shops at discount stores, (2) why they shop there, and (3) what merchandise-price-convenience mix attracts them, see Stuart U. Rich and Bernard Portis, "Clues for Action from Shopper Preference," *Harvard Business Review*, March–April, 1963, pp. 132–149.

reach his prospects is simply a door-to-door canvass of a neighborhood. Another way is "party-plan" selling, in which one customer acts as the hostess of a party to which she invites several friends. The salesman, who is at the party and actually stages it, has a larger prospective market under more advantageous conditions than if he had approached each of the "guests" individually on a house-to-house basis. For her role in the affair, the hostess is given merchandise gifts or cash; the amount usually depends on how many attended the party or how much they purchased. Another house-to-house approach is to make the initial contact in a store, by telephone, or by having the prospect mail in a coupon. Then the salesman follows up by calling at the prospect's home.

According to the Census of Business in 1963, house-to-house selling accounted for about 1.0 per cent of all retail sales. Because of definitional limitations in the census, some forms of house-to-house activity are excluded from these figures, which therefore understate the full measure of this type of retailing. Even then, door-to-door selling is not a substantial part of the total retailing picture. At the same time, however, there are indications that an increasing number of companies are using this method to sell a widening variety of products.[17] Also, interestingly enough, a number of American firms feel that there is a big, profitable growth market overseas which can be reached by door-to-door selling.[18]

In-house selling is becoming increasingly attractive to consumers because it offers the ease and convenience of buying at home, plus personalized service. From the company's point of view, door-to-door selling provides an opportunity for the most aggressive forms of retail selling, plus the chance to demonstrate a product in the customer's home. A sales talk can be prepared in detail, with the assurance that this "canned" talk is more apt to reach prospective customers if it is given by a door-to-door salesman than if it is passed through wholesalers on to retailers' salesmen.

It is questionable whether the cost and profit factors of door-to-door selling are an advantage or a limitation. By eliminating the middleman, consumers may think they are saving money. Yet actually products sold door-to-door are probably higher-priced than those sold in stores, although price comparisons are difficult because the products are not identical. Sellers, in turn, are attracted by the seemingly high profit margins. Retail prices are easy to maintain at the producer's suggested level. The biggest single selling expense —salesmen's commissions and expenses—is a variable one because salesmen usually are paid a straight commission on sales and they pay their own expenses out of their commissions. Higher net profits are hardly possible, how-

[17] See "The Return of Door-to-door Selling," *The Wall Street Journal*, Jan. 8, 1964, p. 1.

[18] Thomas J. Murray, "The Overseas Boom in Door-to-door Selling," *Dun's Review and Modern Industry*, November, 1964, p. 35. To tap this market further, several American companies who use this selling method are building manufacturing facilities in foreign countries.

ever, unless the producer can perform all wholesaling and retailing functions at a lower total cost than if separate middlemen were used. On balance, the presence of higher profits is frequently a mirage.

The problems inherent in door-to-door selling explain why it will probably remain a minor form of modern retailing. First, while offering some conveniences to a consumer, it also runs counter to other buying habits, such as the desire to select from a wide assortment of merchandise or to shop and compare price and quality. This method of selling has acquired a poor reputation because many door-to-door salesmen have been nuisances or even unscrupulous, fraudulent operators. Many communities have passed laws regulating or even prohibiting this method of selling. Another limitation is that managing a door-to-door sales force poses tremendous problems. Good salesmen are extremely hard to find, and the turnover rate is high. Often they are poorly selected, inadequately trained, and insufficiently supervised. On top of everything else, door-to-door selling is the most expensive form of retailing. Salesmen's commissions alone run as high as 40 to 50 per cent of retail price. When we add to this the costs of managing the sales force, plus freight on the merchandise, we often get total margin requirements which are higher than a corresponding total of wholesalers' and in-store retailers' margins.

Nonstore, nonpersonal selling

Two other forms of nonstore retailing that involve no personal contact between buyer and seller are mail-order selling and automatic vending.

Mail-order selling   In mail-order selling, a consumer may (1) buy out of a catalogue, (2) mail in an order form appearing in an advertisement, or (3) use an order form received from the seller directly through the mail. Some of the mail-order houses (Sears, Montgomery Ward, Spiegel, Penney) are *general merchandise* houses offering an exceptionally wide variety of product lines with much depth of assortment in each line. Other institutions might be termed *specialty* houses in that they limit the number of lines they carry—books, records, garden supplies, or novelties, for example. Even some manufacturers or producers (apparel, cheese, fruits, etc.) sell directly by mail.

Traditional methods of contacting the consumer have been modified somewhat to meet changing competitive conditions. Today the large mail-order houses maintain catalogue order desks in their retail stores. They also have catalogue order offices in many communities, where a customer can come in person to place an order. Mail-order retailing accounts for only about 1 per cent of total retail sales, according to the Census of Business. This figure understates the total amount of mail-order retailing because it does not include mail-order business of department stores and producers. The percentage-of-sales figure also hides the fact that the mail-order business is highly concentrated in the two mail-order giants—Sears, Roebuck and Company and Montgomery Ward.

Mail-order retailing enjoys some competitive advantages. Operating costs are lower than for in-store retailing. Labor costs per dollar sales are low; mail-order houses are in low-rent locations, and they do not need elaborate store fixtures. Mail-order retailing also fits in with some consumer buying habits. A wide variety of merchandise is offered by the general merchandise houses. Also, the consumer can leisurely shop the catalogue and then place an order without the inconvenience of going to a store. Stated prices seem lower because they usually are quoted f.o.b. warehouse, that is, without the freight charges which the consumer must pay.

Mail-order retailing has some drawbacks both for the consumer and for the seller. Except where items are displayed at catalogue stores, customers must place their orders without actually seeing the merchandise they are buying. This limitation is counteracted to some extent by liberal return privileges and guarantees and by excellent and accurate catalogue presentations. Customers must plan their purchases well in advance in order to allow time for delivery. Mail-order houses have attempted to speed delivery by establishing branch warehouses and by transmitting orders by teletype. Mail-order houses have little flexibility. Catalogues are costly and must be prepared long in advance of the season. Price changes and new merchandise offerings can be announced only through the issuance of supplementary catalogues, and these are a weak selling tool.

Several of the factors which accounted for the early growth of mail-order retailing no longer exist. Automobiles and good rural roads have made city stores easily accessible to farmers, and rural retailing, in general, has improved. Far from being in a state of decline, however, catalogue buying by mail and telephone is resurging. The convenience of in-home, "one-stop" shopping appeals to a large group of consumers who are showing signs of revolting against standing in line, shopping from limited selections, getting no help from salesclerks, and fighting the traffic and parking problem.[19]

Automatic vending   Today an amazingly wide variety of products are sold through coin-operated machines which automatically vend merchandise (or services) without the aid or presence of a salesclerk. Usually the machines are owned by a vending machine operating company which rents the space needed for desirable locations. In 1965, according to the National Automatic Vending Association, the total volume of products sold through vending machines was $3.8 billion (approximately 1.5 per cent of total retail trade), with the bulk of this volume coming from cigarettes, soft drinks, candy, and hot beverages.[20] The remainder was spread over a wide field of such diverse

[19] See *Grey Matter* (retail edition), November, 1963.

[20] This volume does not include any business done through jukeboxes, pinball machines, slot machines, and similar amusement devices. In fact, the National Automatic Merchandising Association excludes from its membership anyone owning, operating, or otherwise connected with these amusement machines.

goods as hosiery, cosmetics, film, sandwiches, T-shirts, fishing worms, and such services as laundering and insurance policies.

Vending machines can expand a firm's market by reaching customers where and when it is not feasible for stores to do so. Products sold through vending machines typically have low unit values and low markups, so they are relatively expensive to sell through regular retail stores. Many stores use vending machines as a complementary form of retailing; some have placed a bank of machines outside the store to get nighttime business. Another major expanding market for automatic vending lies in the field of in-plant feeding, that is, the feeding of employees of factories, offices, and other places where large numbers of workers must be fed in a short period of time. The outlook for "robot retailing" is promising. Even department stores are experimenting with vending machines.

Automatic vending still faces major problems, however. In the first place, operating costs are high, and there is a continual need for machine maintenance and repair. New machines make former expensive models obsolete before they are depreciated. The prices of automatically vended products are frequently higher than store prices of the same products. A second significant problem is that products which can be sold successfully by machine must be well-known, presold brands with a high rate of turnover. They must be reasonably low in unit value, small and uniform in size and weight, and generally of a convenience goods nature. Only a limited amount of processing can be accomplished. A related set of problems concerns the extent to which automatic vending is compatible with consumer buying habits. Normally, consumers like to feel or see a product before buying; also the machine offers no opportunity to return unwanted merchandise.

TRENDS AND PROSPECTS

Producers and wholesalers of consumer goods and marketing men who work with them must understand the retail market before they can intelligently develop distribution policies and strategies. In this chapter we have noted many current developments and trends in particular retailing institutions.

The retailing structure is not a static structure; rather, it is a complex, dynamic organism, with stress particularly on the word "dynamic." Three major forces causing change are (1) the changing consumer markets served by retailers, (2) the retailers' own constant search for more effective and profitable methods, and (3) the manufacturers' realization that they need mass-marketing methods to keep up with the mass production of goods.

These forces have been responsible for the pronounced trend toward product diversification—scrambled merchandising. Retailers are constantly seeking higher-margin items to add to their lines. One type of store will add products which traditionally have been handled by other types of outlets. As a result, there is considerable similarity among various kinds of stores. The same forces have encouraged the development of suburban shopping centers and caused the relative decline of the downtown shopping district.

In retailing methods, these forces have been responsible for the growth of supermarket merchandising, discount selling, and automation. Advances in automated retailing—not just automatic vending—seem inevitable. Automatic wrapping, marking, materials handling, and record keeping will combine with vending machines to hasten the arrival of a completely automatic store. Automated retailing will have an increasingly significant impact on mail-order houses, supermarkets, department stores, and other retailers.[21] No doubt we shall experience continued increases in forms of in-home buying, especially shopping by catalogue and telephone.

There is a trend toward concentration of retail trade among a relatively small number of large-scale institutions. No matter how we classify retailers (by geographic area, depth and breadth of lines handled, ownership, or retailing methods), it is obvious that fewer stores are doing a steadily increasing share of the retail business. Concentration has developed through mergers of corporate chains, voluntary associations of independents, and the expansion of chains into new geographic markets. Many years ago it was pointed out—and it is still true today—that the decision to go it alone "is being made more and more only by the smaller, the weaker, the least competent distributors."[22]

An important by-product of concentration in retailing has been the increasing power of large retailers in the marketing system. No longer are these retailers at the mercy of manufacturers and wholesalers. Some retailers have integrated backward to take over wholesaling and manufacturing activities. Others have established their own brands in effective competition with manufacturers' brands. This does not mean, however, that the large retailer is always the dominant figure in the distribution scheme. One student of marketing has observed that a retailer cannot look only to other retailers for his competition. He must realize that the manufacturer and the consumer also are his competitors in that they are striving to make their own best bargain.[23]

The real issue is: Who can perform the marketing tasks most efficiently? Consumers have very little loyalty toward any retailer or other marketing institution. Also, other groups are providing what traditionally were considered retailing functions; manufacturers are supplying market information through advertising and other forms of communication. Consumers themselves are buying on a self-service, cash-and-carry basis, and are thus performing marketing activities once done by retailers.

[21] Charles R. Goeldner, "Automation: Evolution in Retailing," *Business Horizons,* Summer, 1962, pp. 89–98; see also "Unattended Store: How Close Is It?" *Printers' Ink,* Jan. 11, 1963, p. 11.

[22] Victor Lebow, "Our Changing Channels of Distribution," *Journal of Marketing,* July, 1948, p. 21.

[23] Malcolm P. McNair, "Significant Trends and Developments in the Postwar Period," in William Lazer and Eugene J. Kelley (eds.), *Managerial Marketing: Perspectives and Viewpoints,* rev. ed., Richard D. Irwin, Inc., Homewood, Ill., 1962, p. 497.

The other side of the concentration picture shows the ever-present fact that the great majority of retailers are small businessmen. Ease of entry into retailing contributes to this situation. In the major industry classification, few industries have a higher percentage of small businessmen than does retailing; only farming and fishing and, possibly, the service trades (although most businesses here are retailers) surpass retailing in the percentage of small businesses.

Inasmuch as the tendency to trade up in services over a period of years is found among all types of minimum-service retailers, including discount sellers, chain stores, supermarkets, and mail-order houses, the following generalization may be made: no type of retail institution will succeed over a long period of time if its *principal* method of operation involves a reduction of services to consumers. Price appeal through minimum service apparently has temporary advantages only. Sooner or later the consumer begins demanding services and is willing to sacrifice price advantages to get them.

Observing the changes in the retail scene during the past ten years, one might feel that there had been a great revolution. Actually, the changes are evolutionary; many follow similar patterns through the years. One such pattern is the cycle of retailing—the wheel of retailing. As Professor McNair has so succinctly explained it:[24]

The cycle frequently begins with the bold new concept, the innovation. The innovator has an idea for a new kind of distributive enterprise. At the outset he is ridiculed, condemned as "illegitimate." Bankers and investors are leery of him. But he attracts the public on the basis of a price appeal made possible by the low operating costs inherent in his innovation. As he goes along he trades up, improves the quality of his merchandise, improves the appearance and standing of his store, attains greater respectability. Then, if he is successful, comes the period of growth, the period when he is taking business away from the established distribution channels that have clung to the old methods. Repeatedly something like this has happened in American distribution. . . .

The maturity phase soon tends to be followed by top-heaviness, too great conservatism, a decline in the rate of return on investment, and eventual vulnerability. Vulnerability to what? Vulnerability to the next revolution of the wheel, to the next fellow who has the bright idea and who starts his business on a low-cost basis, slipping in under the umbrella that the old-line institutions have hoisted.

This familiar cycle can be observed in several instances in the past 100 years. First the department stores supplanted small retailers in the cities during

[24] Quoted in *Sales Management*, Nov. 21, 1958, p. 9. See also M. P. McNair, "Significant Trends and Developments in the Postwar Period," in A. B. Smith (ed.), *Competitive Distribution in a Free, High-level Economy and Its Implications for the University*, The University of Pittsburgh Press, Pittsburgh, Pa., 1958, pp. 17–18. For an excellent critical analysis and refinement of McNair's "wheel of retailing" hypothesis, see Stanley C. Hollander, "The Wheel of Retailing," *Journal of Marketing*, July, 1960, pp. 37–42. Professor Hollander concludes that the wheel hypothesis is not valid for all retailing but does seem to describe a fairly common pattern in industrialized, expanding economies.

the late 1800s and early 1900s. In the 1920s mail-order houses hit their peak. In that same decade the chain stores grew at the expense of independents, particularly in the grocery store field. In the 1930s the independents retaliated with supermarkets which proved so successful that the chain stores copied the method. In the 1950s the discount houses—young innovators—placed tremendous pressure on department stores, which had become staid, mature institutions. By the early years of the 1960s the discount houses had passed the youthful stage and soft-goods discounters were appearing. Now we wait to see what new institution or method will be the innovator in the 1970s. By the same token, manufacturers must keep abreast of the inevitable changes in the retailing institutional scene and be ready to appraise the potential of any retailing innovators.[25] Also, established retailers must be alert to meet the challenge with innovations of their own. Truly, a retailer must be ready, willing, and able to innovate, for the alternative is to die.

QUESTIONS AND PROBLEMS

1   "High-price, high-quality, high-fashion merchandise lines ordinarily do not lend themselves to chain store operation." Why?

2   Do chains sell at lower prices than independents? Why? Compare prices on several items carried by both chain stores and independents in your community.

3   What are chains doing to counteract their competitive operating disadvantages?

4   Following are some critical statements made about chain store organizations. Evaluate these charges.

   a.   Chains are absentee-owned; they drain money from a community.
   b.   Chains are monopolistic; they run independents out of business.
   c.   Chains do not pay their fair share of taxes.
   d.   Chains pay substandard wages.

5   Carefully distinguish between a retailer cooperative chain and a voluntary chain. Are there examples of either type in your community?

6   In what ways does a corporate chain (Safeway, A & P, or Sears, Roebuck) differ from a voluntary chain such as IGA or Red & White?

7   With all the advantages attributed to voluntary associations of independents, why do you suppose some retailers are still unaffiliated?

8   What factors should be considered by an independent retailer who is trying to decide whether to join a retailer cooperative or a wholesaler-sponsored chain?

9   "The only significant competitive advantage which chains have over independents is greater buying power. If buying power can be equalized through anti-chain legislation or by having the independents join some voluntary association, then independents can compete equally with the chains." Discuss.

10   "The supermarket, with its operating-expense ratio of 15 to 20 per cent, is the most efficient institution in retailing today." Do you agree? In what ways might supermarkets reduce their operating expenses?

[25] Gerald B. Tallman and Bruce Blomstrom, "Retail Innovations Challenge Manufacturers," *Harvard Business Review*, September–October, 1962, pp. 130–141.

11   "In an attempt to counterbalance the ever-increasing cost of personal salesmen in retail stores, all retailers within a few years will rely on either automatic vending machines or the self-service feature of supermarket retailing." Discuss.

12   Are there any limits to the types of products which may be sold profitably by supermarkets?

13   Name some discount houses in your community or in a large nearby city. Is there a distinction between "discount selling" and a "discount house"?

14   How have department stores and other affected retailers met the challenge of the discount house?

15   Many retailers consider discount houses unethical, illegitimate retailers engaged in unfair competition. Why is such a criticism made? Do you agree with it?

16   "House-to-house selling is the most efficient form of retail selling because it eliminates both the wholesalers and the retail stores." Discuss.

17   In view of the fact that door-to-door selling is generally the costliest of all retailing methods, from a social and economic point of view how can you justify its continued existence?

18   "The factors which accounted for the early growth of mail-order retailing no longer exist, so we may expect a substantial decline in this form of selling." Discuss.

19   Why would a retailer install vending machines to sell products that he already carries in his store?

20   What are the conditions which you think will limit the growth of in-home buying? Of automatic vending?

21   It is very easy for anyone to enter the field of retailing. This ease of entry undoubtedly contributes to the high mortality rate among retailers, with the resultant economic waste and inefficient use of resources. Should entry into retailing be restricted? If so, how could this be done?

22   What recommendations do you have for reducing the costs of retailing?

23   Looking to the future, what retailing institutions or methods will decline and which ones will increase in importance? Explain.

13

THE WHOLESALE MARKET AND WHOLESALING MIDDLEMEN

"Let's eliminate the middleman" and "The middleman makes all the profit" are cries which have been echoed by many consumers, businessmen, labor representatives, and legislators through the years. Typically these people are focusing their complaints on the wholesaling segment of the distribution structure. Historically, the wholesaler has been a truly powerful figure in American marketing. During the past twenty-five to fifty years, however, countless manufacturers and retailers have made successful attempts to eliminate the wholesaler from their trade channels. For 150 years or more, various writers have been forecasting the decline and disappearance of the wholesaler as a significant factor in marketing. Yet wholesaling middlemen continue to be an important force, and in many cases a dominant figure, in the distribution system.

NATURE AND IMPORTANCE OF WHOLESALING

For several marketing and legal reasons, the wholesaling concepts discussed here should be defined precisely and distinguished carefully from the corresponding retailing terms. For example, when manufacturers are establishing their pricing structures, they must often allow wholesalers and retailers different discounts because the two groups perform different services and thus have different operating costs to cover. State fair-trade laws, unfair-sales-practices acts, chain-store taxes, and the Federal Robinson-Patman Act usually apply to retailers and wholesalers in different ways.

Wholesaling broadly defined

Wholesaling or wholesale trade includes the sale, and all activities directly incident to the sale, of products or services to those who are buying for purposes of resale or for business use. Thus, broadly viewed, sales made by one manufacturer to another are wholesale transactions, and the selling manufacturer is engaged in wholesaling. A retail variety store is engaged in wholesaling if it sells pencils or envelopes to a restaurant or a grocery store. That is, wholesaling, broadly defined, includes sales of any firm to any customer except an ultimate consumer who is buying for personal, nonbusiness use. As in defining retailing, the key element and only real criterion in identifying wholesaling and wholesale sales is the status of the purchaser or his purpose for buying.

The narrower definition of wholesaling

While the above general definition of wholesaling is accurate, it is too broad to be of practical value for our purposes of understanding the role of wholesaling middlemen and establishing channels of distribution policies. For analytical convenience, the definition must be limited. Therefore we shall be concerned with companies and establishments which are engaged *primarily* in wholesaling. We shall exclude retailers who occasionally make a wholesale sale. We shall also exclude sales of manufacturers, farmers, and mineral producers because their major activity is not wholesaling; primarily, they are engaged in creating form utility rather than time, place, and possession utilities. If a manufacturer operates a physically separate establishment, such as a sales branch where the main function is wholesaling and not manufacturing, however, this establishment will be included as a wholesaling middleman. Thus ownership of the establishment does not determine its classification. It may be owned by a manufacturer (a sales branch), a retailer (a retailer cooperative warehouse), or a farmer (a cooperative grain elevator) and still be considered a wholesaling establishment.[1] Some wholesaling establishments occasionally make a

[1] One inconsistency here concerns chain-store warehouses. In recent years, the Census of Business has not classed chain-store warehouses as wholesaling establishments. It does, however, include retailer-owned cooperative warehouses in the whole-

retail sale; but again, for analytical convenience, a firm that does over 50 per cent of its business at wholesale is classified as a wholesaling institution by the Census of Business.[2]

Wholesalers and wholesaling middlemen

The term "wholesaler" applies only to a *merchant* middleman engaged in wholesaling activities; that is, he takes title to the goods he handles. "Wholesaling middlemen" is the all-inclusive term, covering wholesalers and other wholesaling middlemen, such as agents and brokers, who do not take title to the merchandise. Thus a food broker or a manufacturers' agent is not a wholesaler, but he is a wholesaling middleman. Sometimes one hears the terms "jobber" and "distributor"; although usage varies from trade to trade, in this book these terms are considered synonymous with wholesaler.

Development and economic justification of wholesaling

Up to the beginning of the nineteenth century, the major wholesaling firms in this country were export-import companies. They purchased raw materials and sent them to Europe for manufacturing and other processing. In return they imported finished goods and distributed them to trading posts, general stores, and small shops throughout the young country. Early in the nineteenth century, the processing of raw materials began in the United States. As finished goods industries sprang up and as the consumer markets expanded westward, domestic wholesalers developed and grew in importance, and the import-export houses declined.

Up to the end of World War I, the merchant wholesaler remained the kingpin in the channel structure. In general, manufacturers were small and poorly financed. They had no knowledge of the market, and it was not economically feasible for them to establish their own sales forces to go directly to the retailers or even to deal directly with other manufacturers. At the same time, the retailers were also small, geographically scattered, and financially weak.

Even though large-scale activity in manufacturing developed in the late 1800s and the early 1900s, manufacturers still had to rely largely on wholesalers to reach the retailers. After World War I, however, large-scale retailers, such as corporate chains, began to expand considerably. Thus the existence of large-scale businesses in manufacturing and in retailing set the scene for a shift in the balance of power. While the wholesaler has remained remarkably

saling section. Many marketing people believe that chain-store warehouses should be classed as wholesaling institutions and tabulated accordingly in the Census of Business.

[2] One writer refers to this as the "Procrustean bed" treatment by the census. See Phillip McVey, "Are Channels of Distribution What the Textbooks Say?" *Journal of Marketing*, January, 1960, pp. 61–65.

healthy and has continued to grow over the last thirty years, it is true, however, that he does not enjoy his old-time, almost monopolistic position in most channels of distribution.

Most manufacturing companies in the United States are still small and specialized. They have inadequate capital with which to maintain the sales force necessary to contact many scattered small retailers. Even among manufacturers who have sufficient capital, output is too small to justify the necessary sales force. Conversely, the typical retailer buys in small quantities and has a limited knowledge of the market and sources of supply. Wholesalers can pool the orders of many retailers and so furnish a market for a small manufacturer, and at the same time perform a buying service for retailers.

A wholesaler may be described as a marketing specialist. His usefulness in a channel of distribution is subject to the same considerations involved in the decision to utilize any other specialist. One writer has summed up three general economic reasons why a manufacturer should consider using a wholesaler.[3] First, normally a firm is seeking optimum utilization of its financial resources, and a wholesaler can perform the physical handling and shipping of products at an operating expense percentage lower than that at which most manufacturers can do the job. The wholesaler takes a net profit margin which is so low that manufacturers scorn it. Second, a manufacturer is concerned with the most effective use of his manpower resources, and in tight labor markets it makes some sense to use existing wholesaling distribution facilities rather than duplicate them. Finally, a wholesaler offers a manufacturer an opportunity to increase sales volume at a more rapid rate than that at which total expenses will rise.

Size of total wholesale market

In 1963 there were about 308,000 wholesaling establishments in the United States, and they had a total annual sales volume of $358 billion. Table 13–1 shows that in each Census of Business since 1939, the number of establishments increased substantially over the preceding census year. The 1963 total wholesale trade represented an increase of 25 per cent over 1958 and of 53 per cent over 1954.

Of course a substantial part of this increase is traceable to the rise in the price level. Even if each year's wholesale trade were expressed in 1963 dollars, however, one would still observe a major increase.

Classification of wholesaling middlemen

One widely used basis for classifying wholesaling middlemen is by ownership of the goods; wholesaling institutions are divided into two groups according to

[3] Howard T. Hovde, "The Impact of Wholesaling in a Changing Economy," *Report of the Twenty-eighth Annual Conference on Distribution*, Boston, 1956, pp. 91–93.

whether or not they take title to the merchandise they handle. Those who do take title are called *merchant middlemen* and are exemplified by wholesalers and sales branches of manufacturers. *Agent middlemen,* such as manufacturers' agents and brokers, do not take title; instead, they actively help in negotiating the transfer of title between a buyer and a seller.

Ownership of the wholesaling establishment is another basis for classification. Some wholesaling establishments, such as sales branches and sales offices, are owned by producers. Others are owned by retailers; retailer cooperative chain warehouses and warehouses of corporate chain stores are in this category. The great majority of wholesaling establishments, however, are owned by wholesaling middlemen themselves.

A third way to group the institutions is according to the service furnished to suppliers and customers. The two main categories are full-service, or full-function, wholesaling middlemen and limited-function middlemen.

Census classification of wholesaling middlemen   The Census of Business has developed a five-way classification which cuts across ownership of the establishment and ownership of the product and, to some extent, is based upon the method of operation. A marketing executive should understand the classification used in the census because it is a major source of quantitative data. The five groups are merchant wholesalers, manufacturers' sales offices and branches, agents and brokers, petroleum bulk stations and terminals, and assemblers of farm products. The number of establishments and the 1963 sales volume for each classification are shown in Table 13–2. The percentages of total wholesale sales accounted for by each group in 1963, 1958, 1954, and 1948 are also given. There has been stability among the five groups over the past twenty to twenty-five years. The only major change since before World War II seems to be that manufacturers' sales offices and branches have gained at the expense of agents and brokers. This may be due to the fact that as

table   13–1

Total wholesale trade in United States compared with total retail sales

Total wholesale sales in 1963 have increased 25 per cent over 1958 and 54 per cent over 1954. How do these figures compare with growth in retail sales?

Year	Number of wholesaling establishments	Wholesale sales (billions)	Retail sales (billions)
1963	308,000	$358.4	$244.2
1958	287,000	285.7	200.4
1954	250,000	234.0	170.0
1948	216,000	180.6	130.5
1939	190,000	53.8	42.0

SOURCES: U.S. Census of Business: 1963, Wholesale Trade, United States Summary, Retail Trade, United States Summary; and U.S. Census of Business: 1954, 1948.

market potentials have increased in various areas, many manufacturers have established branches in territories once served by agent middlemen.

MERCHANT WHOLESALERS   These wholesaling middlemen take title to the merchandise they handle; they are the largest single segment of wholesaling institutions when measured either by number of establishments or by sales. With sales of $157.4 billion done by approximately 209,700 establishments in 1963, merchant wholesalers accounted for 44 per cent of the total wholesale trade.

MANUFACTURERS' SALES BRANCHES AND SALES OFFICES   These establishments are owned and operated by manufacturers but are physically separated from the manufacturing plants. The distinction between a sales branch and a sales office is that a branch carries merchandise stock and an office does not.

table   13–2

Total wholesale trade and percentage of total sales: by type of operation

Merchant wholesalers have maintained the largest share of the market—a consistent 42 to 44 per cent. How do you account for the relative decline of agents and brokers?

Type of operation	Number of establishments, 1963 (to nearest 1,000)	1963 sales (billions)	Percentage of total sales			
			1963	1958	1954	1948
United States, total	308	$358,386	100.0	100.0	100.0	100.0
Merchant wholesalers	209	157,392	44.0	42.7	42.9	42.4
Service wholesalers	*	*	*	41.0	41.0	40.3
Limited-function wholesalers	*	*	*	1.7	1.9	2.1
Manufacturers' sales branches and offices	29	116,443	32.5	30.8	29.6	28.1
Merchandise agents and brokers	25	53,245	15.0	16.3	16.8	18.2
Selling agents	3	8,292	2.4	2.4	2.6	3.4
Manufacturers' agents	11	10,941	3.0	3.4	3.1	2.0
Brokers	5	13,855	3.9	3.5	4.6	5.1
Commission men	3	9,524	2.7	4.1	3.7	4.0
Others	3	10,633	3.0	2.9	2.8	3.7
Petroleum bulk plants and terminals	31	21,485	6.0	7.1	6.8	5.8
Assemblers of farm products	14	9,820	2.5	3.1	3.9	5.5

* Figures not available in 1963 census.

SOURCE: U.S. Census of Business: 1963, 1958, 1954, 1948; Wholesale Trade, United States Summary.

Sales branches and offices accounted for 33 per cent of the total wholesale trade in 1963, an increase from 28 per cent in 1948.

AGENTS AND BROKERS   These middlemen do not take title to the merchandise they handle, but they do actively negotiate the purchase or sale of products for their principals. The main types of agent middlemen are brokers, commission men (in the marketing of agricultural products), manufacturers' agents, and selling agents. Altogether in 1963, there were about twenty-five thousand firms of agents and brokers, doing a total volume of $53 billion. This represented 15 per cent of all wholesale trade, a decline from 18 per cent in 1948.

PETROLEUM BULK PLANTS AND TERMINALS   Basically these are merchant wholesalers or manufacturers' sales branches. That is, they are owned by independent wholesalers and perform all the usual wholesaling services, or they are owned and operated by petroleum refiners. They are separately noted in the Census of Business because of their special physical plant facilities and their somewhat different operations. These middlemen are engaged in the buying, storing, and wholesale selling of gasoline, oil, gases, and other bulk petroleum products. In 1963 there were 31,000 such establishments, with a total sales volume of $21.5 billion, which was 6 per cent of all wholesale trade.

ASSEMBLERS OF FARM PRODUCTS   The final major census classification includes various firms engaged in buying raw farm products from agricultural producers or fish and seafood products from fishermen. In contrast to the four other types of wholesaling middlemen tabulated in the census, assemblers buy in *small* quantities from *many* producers and sell in *large* quantities to *fewer* customers. After the products are concentrated in large economical quantities, they are sold to other wholesaling middlemen in central wholesale markets or to industrial users, such as food processors. Assemblers are tabulated separately because their methods of operation, their physical facilities, and the products they handle all pose a different set of problems. In terms of ownership of goods or ownership of establishment, however, assemblers are similar to some of the middlemen already mentioned. For instance, assemblers are merchant wholesalers in that they take title to the products and usually perform many marketing services, such as storage, delivery, and dissemination of market information. In 1963 there were 14,000 assemblers' establishments, with annual sales of almost $10 billion. This was 2.5 per cent of the total wholesale trade. Assemblers are considered in more detail in Chapter 25, which is devoted to the marketing of agricultural products.

Customers of wholesaling middlemen

One might expect that total retail sales would be considerably higher than total wholesale trade because retail prices on a given product are higher than the wholesale price and because many products sold at retail never pass through a wholesaler's establishment and so are excluded from total wholesale sales.

Total sales figures belie this line of reasoning (see Table 13–1). In each case, the volume of wholesale trade is about 40 per cent higher than total retail sales.

The explanation for this seemingly upside-down situation may be found in an analysis of the customers of wholesaling middlemen (Table 13–3). Only about 34 per cent of all wholesale sales are made to retailers for resale purposes. About 41 per cent are made to industrial users and would not be reflected in retail sales. These industrial markets include sales to manufacturers and also sales to retailers and wholesalers who use the products in their busi-

table   13–3

Sales of wholesale establishments, selected years: by class of customer

Only 33 per cent of wholesale sales are made to retailers for resale. A declining share (59 per cent, down to 41 per cent) of merchant wholesalers' sales are made to retailers. How do you account for this? Who are the main customers of agents and brokers?

Type of operation	Year	Retailers for resale	Industrial or business users	Other wholesale establishments for resale	House-hold con-sumers	Export market
				Percentage of sales made to:		
Merchant wholesalers	1963	40.8	37.6	14.5	1.2	5.9
	1958	45.9	31.7	15.3	1.6	5.5
	1954	45.2	32.0	15.1	2.8	4.9
	1948	46.9	31.8	13.7	1.6	6.0
	1939	58.9	23.6	11.1	1.9	4.5
Manufacturers' sales branches and offices	1963	32.4	44.1	19.2	0.4	3.9
Manufacturers' sales branches	1948	40.7	35.4	20.5	0.7	2.7
Manufacturers' sales offices	1948	19.6	51.6	26.2	0.1	2.5
Agents and brokers	1963	18.6	44.5	31.6	1.0	4.3
	1954	13.8	43.7	37.1	2.1	3.4
	1948	16.1	41.8	36.5	0.4	5.2
Assemblers of farm products	1963	13.2	49.3	27.8	7.6	2.0
	1954	6.8	45.1	34.6	10.9	2.5
	1948	9.4	32.6	51.8	5.3	0.9
Total, all types of establishments	1963*	33.5	41.3	19.2	1.1	4.8
	1948	38.4	35.3	21.1	1.1	4.1

* Petroleum bulk stations and terminals not included.

SOURCE: U.S. Census of Business for respective years.

nesses. About 19 per cent of all wholesale trade consists of sales made by one wholesaling middleman to another.

A substantially smaller percentage (from 59 per cent in 1939 down to 41 per cent in 1963) of merchant wholesalers' sales are made to retailers for resale today than before World War II. Large quantities of *industrial* products are now sold through merchant wholesalers, and larger quantities of *consumer* products are now sold directly by producers to retailers, thus bypassing the wholesaler. Furthermore, manufacturers' branches carrying stocks of merchandise do appreciably more of their business with retailers than the offices which have no inventories do. Apparently, retailers prefer to buy from a wholesaling middleman who performs the storage function. On the other hand the manufacturers' sales offices without stocks find industrial users a good market, possibly because the products bought by industrial users can be shipped directly from the factory. A final point concerns the customers of agents and brokers. Some people labor under the illusion that these middlemen sell only to wholesalers. Actually, industrial users are the main customer group (45 per cent) for agents and brokers.

Geographic distribution of wholesale trade

There is much geographic concentration of wholesale trade in the United States. Retail trade must follow the population, but the location of wholesaling

table 13–4

Regional distribution of wholesale trade, 1958 and 1963: by geographic regions

Wholesale businesses are concentrated in the Middle Atlantic and East North Central areas. How does this compare with the geographic distribution of retail sales?

| | Per cent of wholesale | | | |
| | Establishments | | Sales | |
Geographic region	1963	1958	1963	1958
United States, total	100.0	100.0	100.0	100.0
New England	5.4	4.8	4.4	4.8
Middle Atlantic	21.6	28.0	27.1	27.8
East North Central	19.0	20.8	20.5	20.8
West North Central	10.8	9.8	9.6	9.9
South Atlantic	11.9	10.0	10.6	10.0
East South Central	4.9	4.2	4.2	4.2
West South Central	9.7	7.8	7.8	7.8
Mountain	4.3	2.8	2.9	2.8
Pacific	12.4	11.8	12.9	11.9

SOURCE: U.S. Census of Business: 1963, Wholesale Trade, United States Summary.

establishments is influenced chiefly by transportation facilities, freight rate structures, and the products' physical characteristics.

Almost 50 per cent of the total wholesale trade (as measured by the location of the wholesalers' establishments rather than the customers' location) is concentrated in two census regions—the Middle Atlantic and East North Central (Table 13–4). By the same token, these two regions in 1963 accounted for about 40 per cent of the total retail sales and of the total population (Table 11–6). The New York City area alone is a very important wholesaling center; 19 per cent of total wholesale trade in 1963 came from the combined New York–Northeastern New Jersey metropolitan areas. In Table 13–4 we see a slight, but perhaps significant, trend away from this concentration. From 1958 to 1963 there was a *decrease* in the relative number of wholesale establishments located in the Middle Atlantic and East North Central regions and a small relative *increase* in every other region. The share of total wholesale sales increased slightly in the South and West at the expense of the East and Midwest.

Operating expenses and profits of wholesaling middlemen

The average total operating expenses for all wholesaling middlemen combined has been estimated at about 11 per cent of wholesale sales.[4] It has also been estimated that operating expenses of retailers average about 27 per cent of retail sales (omitting bars and restaurants, which do some processing of products). Therefore, on a broad average, the expenses of wholesaling middlemen take about 8 per cent of the consumer's dollar.

Expenses by type of operation   Table 13–5 shows operating expenses as a percentage of net sales for the major categories of wholesaling middlemen as classified in the Census of Business. Merchant wholesalers have the highest average operating expenses (13.5 per cent), and agents and brokers the lowest (3.6 per cent). Sales branches of manufacturers have higher expenses than sales offices—10.6 per cent compared with 4.2. This is because branches have the extra cost of handling merchandise stocks.

Care should be exercised when interpreting these figures. For instance, we should not conclude that agents and brokers are highly efficient and merchant wholesalers inefficient because of the disparity in operating expenses. The cost differentials are traceable to the differences in the amount and nature of services provided by these institutions. Also, a more careful analysis is necessary before we hand accolades to manufacturers' sales branches and offices which seem to have lower expenses than service wholesalers. Even when merchant wholesalers in given product lines (paper products, machinery) are compared with manufacturers' sales branches in the same line, the branch

---

[4] Harold Barger, *Distribution's Place in the American Economy since 1869*, Princeton University Press, Princeton, N.J., 1955, p. 60.

ordinarily shows a lower operating cost ratio. Careful analysis shows that the comparison is often "loaded" in favor of the manufacturers' branch operations. Branches and sales offices are located only in the markets offering the highest potential sales and profits. Thus the manufacturers' operations would get more sales per dollar of effort. Often, too, a branch is not allocated its full share of costs. Many indirect administrative expenses are charged in full to the home office, even though the branches share in the benefit. Finally, costs of manufacturers' sales branches and merchant wholesalers are not always comparable because of differences in services provided.

Expenses by kinds of goods handled Expense analyses based on broad categories of wholesaling establishments, as shown in Table 13–5, give a general picture of wholesaling costs. An executive in a given company, however, is probably interested in more detailed cost data. There are tremendous variations in the wholesaling costs of different products. Product considerations such as perishability, value in relation to bulk, rate of turnover, special storage and handling requirements, and technical selling needs influence the operating cost ratio. According to the 1963 Census of Business, for example, operating expenses of wholesalers of a general line of groceries were 6.7 per cent of sales, and tobacco distributors' costs were 5.6 per cent of sales. At the other extreme, distributors of office equipment and supplies had average expenses of 32 per cent of sales, and wholesalers of professional equipment and supplies, 24 per cent.

table 13–5

Operating expenses as percentage of net sales of wholesaling middlemen, 1963: by type of operation

Merchant wholesalers have the highest operating costs (13.5 per cent). Are they less efficient as a class than agents and brokers, whose expenses are only 3.6 per cent of sales? Why are manufacturers' sales branches a higher-cost operation than manufacturers' sales offices?

Type of operation	Operating expenses, percentage of net sales
Merchant wholesalers, total	13.5
Domestic service wholesalers	14.6
Manufacturers' sales branches (with stocks)	10.6
Manufacturers' sales offices (without stocks)	4.2
Agents and brokers	3.6
Brokers	2.8
Selling agents	3.9
Manufacturers' agents	6.0
Petroleum bulk plants, terminals	11.9 (1958)
Assemblers of farm products	9.0

SOURCE: U.S. Census of Business: 1963, Wholesale Trade, United States Summary.

Net profits   Net operating profits expressed as a percentage of net sales are extremely modest for wholesaling middlemen and are considerably lower than those for retailing middlemen. Table 13–6 shows the net profits for selected wholesalers as reported in a study made by Dun and Bradstreet. Out of twenty-nine product lines, chemical goods wholesalers were the only type for which the median net profit percentage was over 2.5 per cent. Medians range from 2.7 per cent for chemical products down to less than 0.40 per cent for distributors of tobacco products and poultry products.

table   13–6

Median net profits of selected wholesalers, 1963

The surprising feature is the low rate of net profit (as a percentage of net sales) earned by most wholesalers. The highest rate here is only 2.7 per cent (chemicals), while two other groups (poultry and tobacco products) each earned less than one-half of 1 per cent.

Kind of business and number of wholesalers	Net profit as percentage of net sales
Air-conditioning and refrigeration equipment (43)	1.60
Apparel and accessories (100)	0.76
Automobile parts and accessories (212)	1.88
Chemicals and allied products (51)	2.72
Cigars, cigarettes, and tobacco (84)	0.36
Commercial and industrial machinery and equipment (205)	1.71
Confectionery (36)	0.57
Dairy products (65)	1.04
Drugs and drug sundries (102)	0.98
Dry goods (128)	0.88
Electrical parts and supplies (143)	1.10
Electronic parts and equipment (51)	1.74
Farm machinery and equipment (48)	2.14
Fruits and produce, fresh (56)	1.12
Furniture and home furnishings (62)	1.54
Groceries (201)	0.63
Hardware (203)	1.29
Household appliances (102)	1.10
Lumber and building materials (156)	1.69
Meats and meat products (57)	0.79
Metals and minerals (57)	2.14
Paints and varnishes (47)	1.51
Paper (151)	1.01
Petroleum products (69)	1.95
Plumbing and heating supplies (184)	1.58
Poultry and poultry products (34)	0.35
Shoes (50)	0.81
Tires and tubes (39)	2.31
Wines and liquors (79)	0.96

SOURCE: "The Ratios of the Wholesalers," *Dun's Review and Modern Industry,* October, 1964, p. 62.

FULL-FUNCTION, OR SERVICE, WHOLESALERS

A *service wholesaler*—sometimes called a full-function wholesaler—is an independent merchant wholesaler who generally performs a full range of wholesaling functions. He may be called simply a wholesaler, or he may go under the name of distributor, mill supply house, industrial distributor, or jobber, depending upon the usage in his line of business. He may handle consumer and/or industrial products, and these goods may be manufactured or nonmanufactured and imported or exported. The Census of Business lists five groups of service wholesalers: wholesale merchants and distributors, terminal grain elevators, importers, exporters, and wagon distributors. The wholesale merchants and distributors represent about 93 per cent of the establishments and 87 per cent of the sales of the five groups. Consequently, the discussion here really revolves about the service wholesalers of manufactured goods in the domestic market.

Importance

The service wholesaler in the domestic marketing of manufactured products is the most important single type of wholesaling middleman if various quantitative measures are used as criteria. In 1963 these middlemen accounted for 63 per cent of all wholesaling establishments and 38 per cent of wholesale sales. Furthermore, the trend in the number of establishments and sales volume of these wholesalers shows significant increases since the end of World War II (see Table 13–7).

table 13–7

Number of establishments and sales volume of service wholesalers of manufactured products in domestic market, and total retail sales

Service wholesalers have certainly maintained their competitive position in the distribution structure, although some people had forecast a substantial decline in their importance. What are the most challenging competitive problems facing service wholesalers?

| | Service wholesalers | | | | Retail sales | |
Year	Number of establishments (to nearest 1,000)	Per cent increase over 1948	Sales volume (billions)	Per cent increase over 1948	(Billions)	Per cent increase over 1948
1963	194,000	61	$135.9	104	$244.2	87
1958	171,000	43	102.9	55	200.4	53
1954	151,000	26	86.1	30	170.0	30
1948	120,000		66.6		130.5	

SOURCE: U.S. Census of Business: 1963, 1954.

The most important conclusion to be drawn from Table 13–7 is that the service wholesaler has more than held his own in the competitive struggles within the distribution structure. In spite of the upsurge in their activity, service wholesalers cannot afford to become complacent. As noted in Table 13–3, service wholesalers face competition not only from other service wholesalers, and agents or brokers, but also from direct-selling manufacturers and their sales offices and sales branches and from direct-buying retailers.

Rack jobber   The rack jobber, called a "rack merchandiser" in the census, emerged after World War II as supermarkets added nonfood items. The rack jobber has expanded to serve drugstores, hardware stores, variety stores, and other stores which have instituted the self-service method of retailing. The general-line grocery wholesalers were in no position to add health and beauty aids, housewares, etc. Regular wholesalers in these nonfood lines could not easily sell to supermarkets for at least three reasons. First, the wholesalers' regular customers, such as drugstores or hardware stores, would complain loudly and probably withdraw their business. Second, too many different wholesalers would have to call on the supermarket to fill all the nonfood lines, and the retailer would object to so many wholesalers. Third, a single supermarket ordinarily would have too small an order in any one nonfood line to make it profitable for the wholesaler in that line.

One rack jobber (or a very few) can furnish all the nonfood items in a supermarket. The rack jobber furnishes the rack or shelves upon which to display the merchandise, and stocks only the fastest-moving brands on these racks; he is responsible for maintaining fully stocked racks, building attractive displays, and price-marking the merchandise. In essence, the retailer merely furnishes floor or shelf space and then collects the money as the customer goes through the check-out stand.

With the expansion of nonfood items in supermarkets, the position of rack jobbers should become stronger and more attractive. The only significant threat to his position is the possibility that the nonfood business in supermarkets will grow so large that retailers will want to deal directly with the manufacturers. Presently the rack jobber can perform the wholesaling services of buying, warehousing, and delivery at a lower cost than can most supermarkets—even supermarket chains. The rack jobber has high operating expenses, however— 18.3 per cent of sales in 1958.

Classification by line handled

Before manufacturers establish a channel structure or before retailing executives determine their sources of supply, they will want to analyze the depth and breadth of the product lines various service wholesalers carry.

General merchandise wholesalers   These wholesalers emerged over a century and a half ago to serve general stores, and to the extent that general stores still exist today, general merchandise wholesalers still serve them. They also serve hardware stores, electrical supply stores, auto accessory dealers, drugstores, and, in some cases, department stores. They carry merchandise in a wide variety of lines, but the trend is toward single-line concentration. Among the three classes of service wholesalers discussed in this section, general merchandise wholesalers are by far the least important in sales and in number of establishments.

General-line wholesalers   These wholesalers sell primarily to limited-line retail stores. They carry a complete assortment of merchandise within a broad product-line category, such as drugs, hardware, groceries, or sporting goods. A hardware wholesaler, for example, will carry electrical supplies, plumbing and heating products, housewares, paints, builders' hardware, tools, toys, and many other kinds of products typically found in a large retail hardware store. These institutions have the largest total sales of the three classes discussed here, and they continue to be important in the wholesaling picture of the large number of small retail stores.

Specialty wholesalers   These wholesalers carry only a part of a broad general line. In the dry goods apparel field, for example, there are wholesalers of shoes, of piece goods, of curtains and draperies, or of hosiery and lingerie. In machinery products there are industrial distributors of air-conditioning and commercial refrigeration equipment and wholesalers of farm and garden equipment.

These wholesalers offer to retail customers or industrial users the advantages of specialization. Within a narrow range of products, specialty wholesalers carry an exceptionally complete assortment. They bring considerable product information and technical know-how to their customers. Compared with the other groups of service wholesalers discussed in this section, they have a faster rate of stock turnover, lower capital needs for inventory, and fewer management problems. Their orders are usually smaller, however, and their operating costs are higher than those of general-line wholesalers. As one typical illustration, the operating expenses in 1963 for general-line drug wholesalers were 13.3 per cent of sales as compared with 17.5 per cent for specialty wholesalers.

Classification by geographic market

It is also useful to analyze service wholesalers according to the geographic markets they cover.

Local wholesalers   The market of local wholesalers is limited to one large city or to a trading area in which they have a competitive advantage. Over the nation as a whole, local wholesalers are far more numerous than regional or national wholesalers. In three major expense items—selling, transportation, and warehousing—local firms are generally able to maintain lower operating cost rates than firms with broader geographic markets. This gives local firms a significant competitive advantage. Because local wholesalers' salesmen can usually return home at night, traveling expenses are minimized. Transportation costs are lower because merchandise can be shipped in economical carload quantities for a greater percentage of the distance from manufacturer to retailer. Local wholesalers usually have ready access to market information regarding their customers and their merchandise needs. This tends to reduce credit losses and the expense incurred by overage or unwanted merchandise.

Regional and national wholesalers   National wholesalers cover all of the United States or at least several census regions. They are not very numerous, but they are very large in sales volume and are important within their product lines. Regional wholesalers cover several wholesaling areas and usually several states. In addition to New York and Chicago, the cities of Atlanta, Dallas, Denver, Minneapolis, San Francisco, and Seattle are frequently home office cities for regional wholesalers.

The big drawback to both regional and national wholesalers is their high operating costs. They may attempt to overcome this limitation in several ways. First, they may establish branch warehouses in cities outside the home office city. In fact, some big wholesalers, such as McKesson and Robbins in drugs, are essentially chain organizations. In these cases the regional or national wholesaler can ship in economical quantities to branch warehouse cities and thus compete with local wholesalers, at least on transportation costs. If sales offices are maintained in branch cities, then the salesmen's travel expenses also may be reduced. Another measure adopted by these wholesalers is to establish and promote their own brands. This makes price comparisons with manufacturers' brands more difficult and enables the wholesaler to establish a stronger hold on his market.

Services rendered to customers and suppliers

Growth among service wholesalers has occurred in the face of strong competition from other wholesaling middlemen and from large manufacturers and retailers who are attempting to bypass the wholesaler. In light of the fact that nobody is subsidizing the wholesaler, the presumption is that his existence is maintained and justified by the socioeconomic services which he renders. This will be clearer if we examine briefly the services that wholesalers render to their customers and to manufacturers.

Buying   Wholesalers act as purchasing agents for their customers whether they are small retailers or industrial users. The wholesaler determines in advance what his customers will want and then he has the merchandise on hand when the customers are ready for it. Wholesalers have a broad knowledge of sources of supply and are able to assemble in one place the products from hundreds of different sources. A good wholesaler has trained buyers constantly in touch with the appropriate markets, who seek out new and better products and acquire other types of market information. Through the use of wholesalers, the retailer can talk to a few salesmen—the wholesalers'—and thus have access to all these manufacturers. Essentially the same situation prevails among industrial users. These users often prefer to buy from industrial distributors rather than from manufacturers, especially when the product is not technical, has a small unit value, and is purchased infrequently and in small quantities.

In serving as the purchasing agent for retailers and industrial users, the wholesaler also indirectly but significantly aids manufacturers. By ordering enough of a given item to take care of the needs of several retailers, the wholesaler is able to submit a larger order than any of his individual customers could place. Many operating costs, such as order filling, billing, and shipping, are therefore lower per dollar of sales.

Selling   Just as the wholesaler is of inestimable value in the buying services he provides for his customers, so too is he of importance in the selling function he performs for manufacturers. As has been noted before, most manufacturers are small and have limited financial resources. They can build a good product, but they need someone to sell it. The wholesalers perform this service.

The key to an appreciation of the selling activity of wholesalers is a recognition of the nature of the retail market. Of the 1.7 million stores, about 87 per cent are independent, single-unit operations; most of these are small, and many are located in small towns. A wholesaler can afford to sell to these small scattered retailers because he represents many manufacturers and can carry many items. Consequently, he can usually get orders large enough to justify his widespread operations.

The cost of direct selling from manufacturer to retailer would be prohibitive, and even if a manufacturer attempted direct distribution, retailers would often reject it. In many cases the retailers know, respect, and trust the wholesaler as a result of past business dealings. The manufacturer is a stranger and would not be accorded the same welcome.

For industrial products, the industrial distributor offers a manufacturer essentially the same selling services as a wholesaler of consumer goods. The distributor provides a manufacturer who has no marketing facilities, or who is manufacturing a narrow line and cannot support a sales force, with an excellent means of reaching the market. He is frequently in a good position to know who influences a customer's buying decisions. The prestige which an established industrial distributor enjoys makes him an excellent middleman for introducing a new product.

A firm using a wholesaler to help distribute its products is faced with certain problems in the selling area. Since the wholesaler is not an employee of the firm, it has little control over his selling methods. The wholesaler represents many firms and can provide only part-time selling effort for the products of any of them. Furthermore, a wholesaler is in business to make a profit, and if it is to his advantage, he may at any time attempt to switch customers from the products of one manufacturer to those of another.

Dividing, or bulk breaking   One service provided by wholesalers—dividing, or bulk breaking—is probably of equal value to their customers and to manufacturers. The wholesaler buys in carload or truckload lots from a manufacturer and resells in case lots or less. Because of transportation costs alone, manufacturers find it economically unjustifiable to sell in small quantities directly to retailers. By shipping in carload or truckload quantities, the transportation costs are computed at the carload or truckload rate. If the manufacturer had to ship in smaller quantities to the retailer, the much higher less-than-carload or less-than-truckload rate would be charged. Furthermore, many manufacturers refuse to sell in the less-than-carload or less-than-truckload quantities, and many retailers will not buy in the larger quantities.

Transportation   In addition to buying in such quantities that the transportation costs are minimized for both manufacturer and customer, a wholesaler furnishes other transportation services to his customers. Since he usually provides quick and frequent delivery, retailers and industrial users need not carry large inventories. Consequently, their costs are reduced bcause their investments in inventory, insurance, and storage costs are lower. For the retailer, there is less risk that the merchandise will spoil or become obsolete and require markdowns.

Warehousing   Wholesalers create both place and time utility through their warehousing activities. The customer's opportunity to order frequently and in small quantities implies that the wholesaler has the desired merchandise on hand where and when the retailer wants it. Furthermore, wholesalers ordinarily have better storage facilities and can make more effective use of a given amount of space than their customers.

Manufacturers also benefit from this efficiency of storage, particularly manufacturers of seasonal items. Consider the warehousing problems of two manufacturers, one making skis and the other producing baseball equipment. A wholesaler can store these two alternate seasonal items in a single unit of space. As the space is emptied of skis during the fall and winter, it can be filled with baseballs and gloves.

Financing   In general, wholesalers aid their customers financially through open-book credit. They usually offer a cash discount if the customer pays his bill within a given period of time after the date of invoice or the receipt of goods. If the customer does not pay within that cash discount period, however, he still has several weeks or months, depending upon the practices in the trade, before the bill falls due. In many cases wholesalers have carried retailers for extended periods of time when the retailers were unable to collect on their customers' accounts.

The financing activities of a wholesaler tend to reduce a retailer's capital requirements. We have already mentioned the advantage of being able to maintain a low inventory. In addition, on seasonal merchandise, such as fishing tackle or Christmas items, wholesalers often deliver the merchandise in advance of the season but do not require payment until after the season is under way. Thus the retailer actually pays for his goods with the money he receives for selling them. This is very close to consignment selling or grubstaking.

In most cases, manufacturers either could not or would not offer comparable aid. They are too far removed from the retailers and industrial users to risk granting credit, and they are not nearly so able to get current, detailed, and accurate credit information as is the wholesaler. Furthermore, the bookkeeping involved in dealing on credit with small customers renders the activity economically unfeasible from a manufacturer's standpoint.

By granting credit to retailers, the wholesaler is indirectly providing financial help to manufacturers. In addition, wholesalers often supply a more direct form of financial aid to producers. Wholesalers will buy in advance of a season or will accept and store several shipments, paying for them well in advance of the time they will be resold to retailers. Wholesalers also help by generally paying their bills promptly, thus further reducing a manufacturer's capital requirements.

Risk bearing Several of the points already mentioned suggest ways in which wholesalers bear or reduce risks for their customers and for manufacturers. In addition, wholesalers usually guarantee the merchandise they sell, and the retailer can thus get immediate satisfaction on claims involving faulty or defective merchandise.

Simply by taking title to the merchandise, a wholesaler reduces a manufacturer's risk. If the product deteriorates, goes out of fashion, or for some other reason does not sell, the wholesaler usually bears the burden. To the extent that the wholesaler performs the storage function, he also performs the risk-bearing function. Finally, a manufacturer's credit loss is reduced by dealing with wholesalers; the wholesaler is absorbing the higher risk venture of granting credit to retailers.

Management services and advice By furnishing managerial services and advice, especially to retailer customers, wholesalers have significantly solidified and strengthened their own position in the market. The existence of a full-function wholesaler is dependent upon the economic health and well-being of small retailers. Therefore, by helping the retailer the wholesaler really helps himself. Some of the managerial services provided by wholesalers today include training of retail salesclerks; advising on, and helping with, store displays and store layout; and establishing better systems for inventory control and accounting. Wholesalers can supply information regarding new products, competitors' prices, special sales by manufacturers, and other data regarding market conditions.

LIMITED-FUNCTION WHOLESALERS

A small group of merchant wholesalers who have received much attention in marketing literature through the years, possibly more attention than their numerical importance merits, are the limited-function wholesalers. These are merchant middlemen who do not perform all the usual wholesaling functions. In 1958, after declining in importance since the end of World War II, they represented only 3 per cent of all wholesaling establishments and less than 2 per cent of wholesale trade. The decline has continued, so that except for truck distributors, they were no longer identified separately in the 1963 Census of Business. The activities of most of these wholesalers are concentrated in a few product lines. In general, operating costs are lower for limited-function wholesalers than for service wholesalers, but this is to be expected because of the differential in services performed. The major types of limited-function wholesalers are truck jobbers, drop shippers, cash-and-carry wholesalers, and retailer cooperative warehouses. The retailer cooperative warehouse was discussed in the preceding chapter; the others are briefly examined at this point.

A *truck distributor* or jobber (sometimes still called a "wagon jobber" in memory of the days when he used a horse and wagon) is a specialty wholesaler, chiefly in the food field. He carries nationally advertised, fast-moving, and perishable or semiperishable specialty goods, such as candies, dairy products, potato chips, and tobacco products. The truck jobber establishes a route of retail store customers. The unique feature of his method of operation is that he sells and delivers merchandise during his call. His competitive advantage lies in his ability to furnish fresh products so frequently that the retailer can buy perishable goods in small amounts and have a minimum risk of loss. The major limitation of a truck jobber is his high operating-cost ratio—13 per cent in 1963—which is caused primarily by the small size of his orders and the inefficient use of delivery equipment. A truck is an expensive warehouse.

The *drop shipper*, sometimes called a "desk jobber," gets his name from the fact that the merchandise he sells is delivered directly from the manufacturer to the customer and is called a "drop shipment." Drop shippers take title to the products, but they do not physically handle the goods. They operate almost entirely in coal and coke and in lumber and building materials. These products are typically sold in carload quantities, and freight is high in comparison with unit value. Thus it is desirable to minimize the physical handling of the product.

Cash-and-carry wholesalers do not grant credit or deliver merchandise to their retailer or industrial user customers. These wholesalers handle a limited line of staple merchandise which has a rapid rate of turnover. They are especially active in the wholesaling of grocery and tobacco products, calling on small establishments which cannot be served profitably by full-function wholesalers. Some regular wholesalers have established cash-and-carry departments to handle small, financially risky accounts and to compete with cash-and-carry wholesalers.

AGENT WHOLESALING MIDDLEMEN

Another important group of wholesaling middlemen consists of agents and brokers. These middlemen are distinguished from merchant wholesalers in two important respects: agent middlemen do *not* take title to the merchandise, and they typically perform fewer services for their clients and principals. For these reasons, the average operating expenses for agents and brokers in 1963 were only 3.6 per cent, as compared with 14.6 per cent for service wholesalers (see Table 13–5). There were 25,300 establishments of agents and brokers in 1963, and they had a total sales volume of $53.2 billion. They constituted 8 per cent of all wholesaling middlemen and transacted 5 per cent of the total volume of wholesale trade (Table 13–2). Based on sales volume, the major types of agent middlemen are manufacturers' agents, selling agents, brokers, and commission men. The first three of these are discussed in this chapter, while commission merchants are described in Chapter 25, where we discuss agricultural marketing. Auction companies, import agents, and export agents are less important types of agent middlemen.

All agent middlemen have some reasonably common characteristics which help to explain the role they play. One such similarity concerns their customers. A restudy of Table 13–3 may correct a general misconception regarding the role of agent middlemen in channels of distribution. It is erroneously believed that these middlemen almost always act between a manufacturer and a wholesaler. Actually less than one-third of the agent middlemen's sales are to wholesalers. Industrial users are the major customers, accounting for 45 per cent of the agents' sales.

A second common characteristic of agent middlemen is that they are usually compensated by a percentage commission based on the volume of sales or purchases they negotiate. The third point is that agent middlemen generally either act as a substitute for a manufacturer's sales force or serve as an addition to the sales force, thus enabling a manufacturer to sell in markets located beyond the limits of his own salesmen. A final common characteristic, and one which sometimes creates a problem, is that although most agent middlemen ostensibly are working for a seller (they are paid by a seller), they often act in the best interest of the buyer. Apparently their idea is that they can always get another supplier, but customers are hard to find and hold.

Manufacturers' agents

A manufacturers' agent (frequently called a "manufacturers' representative") is an agent commissioned by a manufacturer to sell part or all of the producer's products in a restricted territory. In some respects, the manufacturers' agent resembles one of the manufacturer's salesmen, and in some respects he is similar to a manufacturer's sales office or branch. The agent, however, is independent and is in no way an employee of the manufacturer. He has little or no control over the price and terms of a sale; these are established by the manufacturer. Because a manufacturers' agent sells in a restricted territory, a producer may use several agents if his market is national or if it covers more than one geographic region. The size of an agent's territory usually depends upon the density of its potential. One territory may be limited to the Chicago metropolitan area; another may cover Washington, Oregon, Idaho, western Montana, and Alaska. Unlike a broker, a manufacturers' agent has a continuing, year-round relationship with his principal. He usually represents several noncompeting manufacturers of related products and can pool into one profitable sale the small orders which otherwise would go to several individual manufacturers. For this reason, he can operate in markets that none of his principals could individually afford to enter. Besides, buyers may prefer to deal with one representative rather than with direct salesmen from several manufacturers.

Manufacturers' agents are used extensively in the distribution of many types of consumer products and industrial products, such as machinery and equipment, electrical products, sporting goods, dry goods, apparel, some food items, furniture, metals, and automotive supplies. The main service offered to manufacturers by this agent middleman is selling. He seeks out and serves markets which the manufacturer himself cannot profitably reach. Furthermore, because a manufacturers' agent does not carry nearly so many lines as a regular wholesaler, the agent can offer a higher-caliber, more aggressive form of selling service. Some manufacturers' agents carry merchandise inventories and thus perform a warehousing function. Operating expenses depend upon the product sold and whether the merchandise is stocked. Some representatives operate on a commission as low as 2 per cent, while others charge as much as 20 per cent. These commissions cover operating expenses and net profit. On an overall basis, the operating expense ratio is about 6 per cent for agents.

There are some limitations which a manufacturer may face if he decides to use manufacturers' agents. If the agent does not carry merchandise stocks, the manufacturer may be at a competitive disadvantage because he cannot fill orders quickly. Most agents cannot furnish customers adequate technical advice and repair service, nor are they equipped to install major products. While the agent's commission may be reasonably low, the additional cost of services that the manufacturer must perform himself may result in a total marketing cost which is higher than it would be if another type of middleman were used. Finally, because the agent normally has no authority to set the price or to alter the price established by the manufacturer, a seller may lose out in competitive bidding situations where on-the-spot authority to change prices is required.

Manufacturers' agents may be used in three characteristic situations:

1. In a small firm, usually a new one, with a limited number of products and no salesmen, manufacturers' agents may do all the selling.

2. In a firm which wants to add a new and possibly unrelated line of products to the existing product mix, where the present salesmen either are not experienced in a new line or cannot reach the new market, the new line may be given to manufacturers' agents. Thus a company may have both salesmen and agents covering the same geographic market.

3. In a firm wishing to enter a new geographic market which is not yet sufficiently developed to warrant sending salesmen, manufacturers' agents familiar with that market may be used. If a company has been selling from the Atlantic Coast to the Rocky Mountains and now wishes to extend into the Pacific Coast states, it can employ agents who know potential customers and may already be calling on them with other products.[5]

Selling agents

A selling agent is an independent middleman who is used essentially in place of a manufacturer's entire marketing department. This agent typically performs more marketing services than any other type of agent middleman, and he also has more control and authority with respect to the marketing program of his client-principal. A manufacturer will employ one selling agent to market the full output of the firm over its entire market. Selling agents are used most in the marketing of textiles and coal, although they are also found to some extent in the distribution of apparel and of food, lumber, and metal products. Their operating expenses average about 4 per cent of sales.

In addition to acting as the manufacturer's sales force, a selling agent in textiles typically offers information and advice regarding the styling of the merchandise, an important function where fashion merchandise is involved. Agents usually have considerable authority in establishing prices and terms of sale, and they frequently supply financial aid to manufacturers. Because of their critical position in a manufacturer's operations, selling agents sometimes really run their clients' companies—a sort of "tail wagging the dog" situation in which manufacturers are pretty much at the agents' mercy.

Despite the apparent similarity between a selling agent and a manufacturers' agent, there are some fundamental differences between the two. First, a manufacturer uses only one selling agent, whereas he would use several manufacturers' representatives if he took this alternative. Manufacturers' agents have restricted territories; selling agents do not. Second, if a selling

[5] For a comprehensive study of manufacturers' agents, see Thomas A. Staudt, *The Manufacturers' Agent as a Marketing Institution*, U.S. Department of Commerce, Bureau of the Census, Washington, D.C., 1952. An interesting story of the day-to-day operations of a manufacturers' agent is told in R. A. Smith, "Ninety-nine Lives of Charlie Soames," *Fortune*, January, 1953, p. 100.

agent is used, a manufacturer will have no salesmen; if manufacturers' representatives are used, a seller will often have a sales force of his own. Third, selling agents have far more control over prices and terms of sale. Fourth, selling agents always sell the entire output of a firm; manufacturers' agents usually sell only part of the product line in all the market, or all the product line in part of the market.

Brokers

Brokers are agent middlemen whose prime responsibility is to bring buyers and sellers together. They furnish considerable market information regarding prices, products, and general market conditions. Brokers do not physically handle the goods; also, they do not work on a continuing basis with their principals. Most brokers work for sellers, although about 10 per cent represent buyers. A broker has no authority to set prices; he simply negotiates a sale and leaves it up to the seller to accept or reject the buyer's offer. Because of the limited services provided, brokers operate on a very low cost ratio—about 3 per cent of net sales.

Brokers are most prevalent in the food field. Their operation is typified by a seafood broker handling the pack from a salmon cannery. For possibly three months out of the year, the cannery is in operation. The canner employs a broker (the same one each year if relationships are mutually satisfactory) to find buyers for the salmon pack. The broker provides information regarding market prices and conditions, and the canner then informs him of the price he desires. The broker seeks potential buyers among chain stores, wholesalers, and others. When a transaction is completed, the broker receives his commission—usually 2 per cent of the total sale. When the entire pack is sold, the agent-principal relationship is discontinued until possibly the following year.

An evolutionary development in the food brokerage field should be noted. Through the years many brokers have established permanent relationships with some principals and are offering services or performing activities which more accurately would classify these middlemen as manufacturers' agents. They still call themselves food brokers, however, and they are classed as brokers in the Census of Business.

WHOLESALING SERVICES PROVIDED BY NONMIDDLEMEN

There are several types of firms which are not middlemen but which do provide important services for manufacturers and middlemen alike.

Fairs, trade shows, and exhibitions

Many industries periodically hold trade shows, fairs, or exhibitions of products. Some hold these affairs annually in one city, while others have three or four shows a year, each in a different city. For example, there are annual furniture shows in Chicago, Grand Rapids, Dallas, and High Point, North Carolina. These are not permanent exhibitions; they last for a few days or a week. They offer an opportunity for a manufacturer to display his wares and make contacts with wholesalers and retailers. Middlemen in turn contact suppliers and customers. Furthermore, manufacturers can see what competitors are offering, and the middlemen can see what competitors are buying.

Merchandise marts

Several cities have central market facilities where manufacturers or wholesaling middlemen rent space and exhibit their products on a reasonably permanent basis. The Merchandise Mart and the Furniture Mart in Chicago are good examples of such facilities. Show rooms are not usually open to consumers, but the exhibits offer retailers and wholesalers an opportunity to see what is available and to place orders.

Public warehouses

Bonded public warehouses are independently owned and operated storage facilities which provide warehousing and other wholesaling functions. Many specialized types are available, such as cold-storage warehouses and grain elevators. These institutions may be used by manufacturers or wholesaling middlemen in lieu of maintaining their own storage facilities. A manufacturer may rent space in several public warehouses located throughout his market, thus maintaining stocks of merchandise at strategic locations near his wholesalers or other customers. Upon notice from the manufacturer, the warehouseman will fill an order and make arrangements for shipping it. Public warehouses are discussed in more detail in Chapter 16, where we consider the management of physical distribution.

Freight forwarders and transportation companies

Railroads, truckers, and other common carriers, as well as freight forwarders, which typically provide some wholesaling services, are discussed in Chapter 16.

Our survey of the major types of wholesaling middlemen and of the services they render, their costs, and typical situations in which they might best be used gives some insight into the way a firm establishes a channel structure for its products. Wholesaling middlemen are specialists in marketing. A producer must decide which wholesaling services he needs and then select the right institutional specialist to perform these services. When a manufacturer criticizes the high cost of a given wholesaler, he may be using the wrong type of wholesaler; or, he may be paying for services which he does not need or is not using.

QUESTIONS AND PROBLEMS

1   A large furniture warehouse is located in a major Midwestern city. The following conditions exist with respect to this firm:

    a.   All merchandise is purchased directly from manufacturers.

    b.   The warehouse is located in the low-rent, wholesaling district.

    c.   Merchandise remains in original crates; customers use catalogues and swatch books to see what the articles look like and what fabrics are used.

    d.   About 90 per cent of the customers are ultimate consumers, and they account for 85 per cent of the sales volume.

    e.   The firm does quite a bit of advertising, pointing out that consumers are buying at wholesale prices.

    f.   Crates are not price-marked. Salesmen bargain with customers.

    g.   Some 10 per cent of sales volume comes from sales to small retail furniture stores.

    Is this firm a wholesaler? Why or why not?

2   Which of the following are wholesaling transactions?

    a.   A farmer sells fresh produce to a restaurant.

    b.   A chemical manufacturer sells chemicals to a fertilizer manufacturer.

    c.   A drug wholesaler sells drugs to a hospital; to a drug retailer.

    d.   A retail lumberyard sells plywood to a building contractor; to a homeowner for his "do-it-yourself" project.

3   Carefully distinguish among the following: wholesaler, wholesaling, jobber, wholesaling middleman, distributor.

4   Historically, what have been the economic justifications for the existence of wholesaling middlemen? Which of these still exist?

5   What conditions account for the fact that manufacturers' sales offices and branches have maintained a steadily increasing share of total wholesale trade, while the agents' and brokers' share has declined in each census year since 1948? See Table 13–2.

6   What trends are pointed up in a study of the customers of wholesaling middlemen? What has caused these developments?

7   How do you account for the substantial variation in operating expenses among the major types of wholesalers shown in Table 13–5?

8   In comparing the operating-expense ratio for retailers and for wholesalers in Tables 11–2 and 13–5, we see that wholesalers typically have lower operating expenses. How do you account for this?

9   What competitive advantages do general-line wholesalers have over specialty wholesalers or general merchandise wholesalers?

10   What competitive advantages do local wholesalers enjoy over regional ones? Name some wholesalers' brands carried by stores in your area. Why are regional wholesalers in a better position than local firms to sponsor their own brands?

11   What activities could regular wholesalers discontinue in an effort to reduce operating costs?

12   Why does the regular wholesaler have to engage in financing activities when we have banks? In transportation activities when we have trucks, trains, etc.?

13   What services does a full-function wholesaler provide for a manufacturer?

14   What types of retailers, other than supermarkets, offer reasonable fields for entry by the rack jobber? Explain.

15   Explain the conditions under which a manufacturers' agent is likely to be used.

16   Carefully distinguish between a selling agent and a manufacturers' agent.

17   What is the economic justification for the existence of the broker, especially in light of the few functions he performs?

18   Which type of agent middleman, if any, is most likely to be used in each of the following situations? Explain your choice in each instance.

     a.   A small manufacturer of a liquid glass cleaner to be sold through supermarkets

     b.   A small manufacturer of knives used for hunting, fishing, and camping

     c.   A salmon canner in Alaska packing a high-quality, unbranded product

     d.   A small-tools manufacturer who has his own sales force selling to the industrial market and who wishes to add backyard barbecue equipment to his line

     e.   A North Carolina textile mill producing unbranded towels, sheets, pillowcases, and blankets

19   Looking into the future, which types of wholesaling middlemen do you think will increase in importance and which ones will decline? Explain.

14

COMPETITIVE CONFLICTS AND COOPERATION IN DISTRIBUTION CHANNELS

In Chapter 11 we established the concept that a company's trade channel should be regarded as a total system of distribution, rather than as a fragmented assortment of independent institutions operating in an uncoordinated fashion. Manufacturers and middlemen alike should understand that the middlemen used by a manufacturer are only a logical extension and component of a systematic organization which starts with the manufacturer and is designed to maximize marketing effectiveness in the sale to the final customer. The systems concept of distribution suggests then a need for, and the value of, cooperation and coordination among channel members. Yet power structures do exist in trade channels, and a struggle does continually go on among channel members.

At the root of this struggle is institutional change, several examples of which were observed in our study of retailing and wholesaling institutions. This change, in turn, is caused first by the shifting nature of market demand and second by the economic growth and competitive activity among the institutions. It is axiomatic that change begets conflict and that conflict very often results in change.

While pressures for institutional change have mounted over the years, we should recognize at the same time that strong psychological and socio-logical barriers stand in the path of this change. These barriers often persist in the face of economic analyses showing that the change may result in channels which will offer economic advantages and that resistance to change may extend the life of uneconomic channels.

Several of these noneconomic barriers may be identified.[1] One is the presence of group solidarity and collective action among resellers of common backgrounds—retail druggists, for example. Sometimes entrepreneurial values—particularly those of small retailers—place higher ratings on stability than on growth, and this of course tends to restrict innovation. Even in larger organiza-tions, change may be resisted because it "violates group norms, creates un-certainty, and results in loss of status." Finally, a firm's position in the channel may be correlated to its acceptance or resistance to change. That is, the "insiders" in the dominant channel, the "strivers" who want to become part of that system, and the "complementors" who assist the first two groups are all emotionally and economically committed to the dominant channel. They endeavor to maintain the *status quo* against the minor intrusions of "transients" and the major threats from "outside innovators" who would realign the exist-ing structure.

NATURE OF THE CONFLICTS

Three separate forms of competitive conflicts within channels of distribution may be identified. Two of these occur on the horizontal level of distribution: the first is competition between middlemen of the same type—hardware store versus hardware store, or industrial distributor versus industrial distributor; the second is competition between different types of middlemen, but still on the same level—hardware store versus paint store, or industrial distributor versus manufacturers' agent. The third type of competitive conflict is vertical in nature, involving institutions on different levels of distribution—manufac-turer versus wholesaler, for example.

Competition on the same level of distribution

On the same level of distribution, perhaps the main form of conflict has been the competition engendered by "scrambled merchandising"—that is, the prac-

---

[1] Bert C. McCammon, Jr., "Alternative Explanations of Institutional Change and Channel Evolution," in Stephen A. Greyser (ed.), *Toward Scientific Marketing*, American Marketing Association, Chicago, 1964, pp. 477–490; see also Joseph C. Palamountain, *The Politics of Distribution*, Harvard University Press, Cambridge, Mass., 1955.

tice of a middleman of diversifying his product assortment by adding merchandise lines not traditionally carried by that type of institution. This practice, which started before World War II, has spread pretty well throughout the fields of retailing and wholesaling. Today it continues to show signs of increasing, rather than decreasing, in intensity.

We have seen grocery supermarkets, as an illustration, add toiletries, drugs, clothing, magazines, small appliances, records, alcoholic beverages, lawn and garden supplies, and other nonfood lines. The retailers who traditionally sold these lines become irritated both at the grocery stores for diversifying and also at the manufacturers for using these "unorthodox" channels. The stimulus for product proliferation among middlemen and the crossing of traditional channel lines may come from any of three general sources—the market, the middleman, or the manufacturer.

Market-inspired   Preference for one-stop shopping and the trend to self-service selling are two changes in consumer buying behavior which have encouraged the development of scrambled merchandising. To an increasing extent, consumers want convenience in their shopping. They prefer to go to one store and buy food, toothpaste, and a couple of inexpensive cooking pans, for example, rather than having to visit three different retailers. Also, the consumer acceptance of—even preference for—self-selection of merchandise has acted as an incentive for many stores to add new product lines which lend themselves to self-service selling.

Middleman-inspired   The middleman's constant search for more effective and profitable marketing methods has furnished an impetus to the growth of scrambled merchandising. A retailer, such as a food supermarket, operating on a gross margin of 16 to 18 per cent is bound to be attracted to items such as drug sundries or housewares, where the margin may be about 30 per cent.

Some retailers seek to increase their store traffic by adding new merchandise lines. Furniture stores have added small appliances, and jewelry stores have added records and miscellaneous gift items for this purpose. In other situations, any really new product is usually very attractive to all types of retailers who consider the item even remotely marketable in their store. Consequently, product innovation will continue as a big factor in the further scrambling of traditional product assortments.

A substantial segment of a middleman's total costs are fixed, and furthermore they are common to all products sold. That is, they cannot be identified directly with any given product, nor do they vary directly with sales volume in the short run. This cost factor is a real incentive for a retailer or wholesaler to add new product lines to broaden the base over which he can spread his fixed costs. This proliferation, of course, contributes to scrambled product lines and intensifies the degree of channel conflict.

Manufacturer-inspired   Sometimes the stimulus for scrambled merchandising comes from the manufacturer. As a case in point, consider the manufacturers who have taken over the responsibility for repair service on their products. Appliance manufacturers used to be limited in the type and number of retailers they could use because it was essential that the dealer be prepared to service and repair the appliances. Once the manufacturer assumes that responsibility, he can sell through many new types of retailers who formerly were not qualified.

In another situation, a manufacturer may add new products to his line and want new types of outlets so as not to antagonize his existing middlemen. Thus he keeps harmony in his present channels, but creates conflict in the new, nontraditional outlets. Finally, improvements in production technology may change the shape and location of a manufacturer's cost curve. His break-even point may be higher, or he may be in a position to decrease his unit costs considerably by increasing his output. In any event, a burden is placed on the marketing department to find new markets (and thus possibly new types of middlemen) for the potential increase in output.

Conflict between different levels of competition

Perhaps the most severe competitive conflicts in distribution systems today are of a vertical nature—that is, between retailer and wholesaler, between manufacturer and retailer, or between manufacturer and wholesaler. Retailers may make some sales to institutions and other industrial users, thus competing with wholesaling middlemen, as when stationery stores sell office supplies to other retail stores, for example. Producers compete with retailers by selling house-to-house, by selling through the manufacturers' own retail stores, or by selling at the point of production—at the factory or farm. Conflicts frequently develop between manufacturers and agent middlemen when manufacturers place their own sales forces in territories well developed and heretofore covered by the agents. The remainder of this chapter is devoted to the vertical types of conflict.

WHO CONTROLS THE CHANNELS?

In marketing literature, authors have generally taken a manufacturer-oriented approach to channels of distribution. The implication is that the manufacturer is the one who makes the decisions regarding type of outlet, number of outlets, and even the selection of individual outlets. This is a one-sided point of view. Actually, the middleman has considerable freedom and power to make his own choices in establishing channels for products. "The selection of a multi-stage channel is not the prerogative of a manufacturer unless his franchise is coveted by the middlemen he seeks, as being more valuable to them than their franchise would be to him."[2] Certainly the name and reputation of Macy's, Safeway, or Sears, Roebuck and Company, and of other strong retailers mean more to the consumers than most of the brands sold in these stores. Large retailers

[2] Phillip McVey, "Are Channels of Distribution What the Textbooks Say?" *Journal of Marketing*, January, 1960, pp. 61–65.

today are challenging manufacturers for channel control, just as the manufacturers challenged the wholesaler fifty years ago. Even a small retailer may be influential in a local market, and his prestige may become greater than that of his suppliers. McVey observed: "In some instances his local strength is so great that a manufacturer is virtually unable to tap that market, except through him. In such a case the manufacturer can have no channel policy with respect to that market."

Actually, the questions of who *is* the channel leader and who *should be* remain largely unsettled.[3] The position supporting leadership by the manufacturer is production-oriented; he creates the new products, and he needs the increasing sales volume to derive the benefits and economies of large-scale operations. A large retailer may use the same arguments, especially if he provides new-product ideas or specifications. Also, one can argue that the retailer is the natural leader under the marketing concept—standing closest to the consumer, knowing his wants, and being his purchasing agent. Perhaps the best answer to the channel-control questions is a compromise—a balance of power should exist rather than a general or prolonged domination by any one level in the distribution channels.

MANUFACTURER VERSUS WHOLESALER

A significant channel conflict during the past half-century has been between the manufacturer and the wholesaler, as manufacturers have tried to bypass wholesalers and deal directly with retailers. Ordinarily, the battle is between the producers and wholesalers of manufactured *consumer* products. As a rule, it does not involve wholesaling middlemen for industrial products. There is a tradition of direct sale in the industrial field, and where middlemen are used, the need for their services has long been recognized. Nor does this conflict involve agent middlemen for consumer goods to any great extent. The relationships between a manufacturer and his agent middlemen are relatively peaceful for two reasons. First, these relationships are established on a temporary basis. Brokers work with a manufacturer only part of the year; manufacturers' agents know in advance that they may lose their franchises as soon as the territory can support the manufacturer's sales force. Second, agent middlemen offer fewer services than wholesalers. This means that there are fewer areas of possible conflict with manufacturers.

Historical background of the conflict

The clash of interests between wholesalers and manufacturers in the marketing of manufactured consumer products can be best understood by reviewing the

[3] This paragraph is adapted from Bruce Mallen, "Conflict and Cooperation in Marketing Channels," in L. George Smith (ed.), *Reflections on Progress in Marketing*, American Marketing Association, Chicago, 1965, pp. 74–77; see also Bruce Mallen, "A Theory of Retailer-Supplier Conflict, Control, and Cooperation," *Journal of Retailing*, Summer, 1963, pp. 24–32ff.

position of the wholesaler before 1920, the changing position of the manufacturer over the years, the changing position of the retailer since 1920, and,
finally, the net effect these changes have had on the wholesalers and manufacturers.

Historically, the wholesaler has occupied a position of major importance
in distribution systems. Before 1920, he was dominant because both manufacturers and retailers were small and poorly financed. In addition, retailers
were widely dispersed over the entire country. In effect, the wholesaler served
as the sales force of the manufacturer and as the purchasing agent for the
retailer. In so doing, he granted credit to the retailers, an especially important
service in the days when our economy was largely agricultural and cash was
available only at harvesttime. Poor transportation and communications systems
forced the wholesaler to perform the storage function—carrying large inventories to be able to satisfy his retail customers. He carried a wide assortment
of products, even from competing manufacturers. Essentially he was an order
taker; he did no aggressive selling, nor did he consider this his function.

As a result of the risks he took and the broad scale of his services, the
wholesaler had high operating costs. To cover these costs he needed a wide
margin of profit. Through the nineteenth and the early part of the twentieth
centuries, wholesaler institutions suffered increasingly from inertia, a low caliber
of management, and a lack of flexibility in management. The firms did not
adjust to changing economic and social conditions. Thus we see the familiar
picture of an organization which reaches a stage of maturity and faces little
competition.

During the last half of the nineteenth century and the first part of the
twentieth, the position of the manufacturer changed substantially. Manufacturing was becoming more efficient, production management was of a higher
caliber, and the net effect was a reduction in manufacturing costs. Furthermore, manufacturers were beginning to realize that it was better to make a
small profit on the sale of many units than a wide margin on the sale of a
few units. Manufacturers were quick to learn that the best means of achieving
increased volume was through a change in marketing methods. Aggressive
selling effort, lower prices, product identification through branding, and advertising and sales promotion were recognized as keys to mass markets. Once
the manufacturer embarked upon these programs, he disliked giving wholesalers the customary wide margin on sales which his policies were stimulating.
In fact, manufacturers urged wholesalers to take lower percentage margins
in the interest of achieving higher total dollar volume and dollar profits.

After World War I, the position of the retailer changed considerably.
Large-scale retailing institutions developed in great numbers, and retail markets
became concentrated in geographic areas in and around metropolitan centers.
New organization forms, particularly the corporate chains, were developing.
Large-scale operations entailed large buying power, well-financed retailers,
better-managed firms, and so on. Large-scale retailers also were economically

able to assume many wholesaling functions. All these factors encouraged retailers to go directly to the manufacturers to purchase their merchandise.

The growing influence of the manufacturer and the retailer had a significant effect upon wholesaling middlemen. Wholesalers were caught between large-scale, integrated retailers on the one hand and large-scale, direct-selling, integrated manufacturers on the other. As the wholesaler saw his prestige reduced, he fought back. He realized that he could not afford to promote aggressively the products of any one manufacturer, and he resented any cut in his discount margin. By refusing to cooperate to any extent in the manufacturer's efforts to promote products to retailers and by installing his own brands of merchandise, the wholesaler further increased the conflict between himself and the manufacturer. The net effect of the wholesaler's reaction was to push the manufacturer further in the direction of the large-scale retailer.

Manufacturers' side of the conflict

From the point of view of the manufacturer, it seems that there are good reasons to try to bypass the wholesalers. In this section we shall see what those reasons are and then evaluate the alternative channels open to manufacturers.

Reasons for bypassing wholesalers   Basically, either because they are dissatisfied with the wholesalers' services or because of market conditions, manufacturers favor direct sale from manufacturer to retailer or to consumer.

WHOLESALERS' FAILURE TO PROMOTE PRODUCTS AGGRESSIVELY   A complaint voiced frequently by manufacturers is that the wholesalers ordinarily will not aggressively promote the products of individual producers—that wholesalers essentially are order takers, not salesmen. To really sell a product, manufacturers say, wholesalers demand special incentives, such as larger discounts or exclusive territorial franchises.[4]

Wholesalers agree that these charges leveled by the manufacturers are largely true. Generally speaking, all products are the same to the wholesaler, and he does not feel that it is his responsibility to promote those of one manufacturer over those of another. With the thousands of items typically carried by wholesalers, it is not possible for their salesmen even to mention each item to prospective customers, much less try to sell each one.

WHOLESALERS' FAILURE TO PERFORM STORAGE FUNCTION   In some cases, manufacturers have eliminated wholesalers because they failed to provide the traditional storage services that the producers were used to. Manufacturers have been forced to carry larger stocks and to bear a greater share of the

---

[4] For a report on how manufacturers can use their pricing policies to stimulate wholesalers to promote products more aggressively, see Martin R. Warshaw, "Pricing to Gain Wholesalers' Selling Support," *Journal of Marketing*, July, 1962, pp. 50–54.

market risk. Several factors have encouraged wholesalers to reduce their storage services and to buy on a hand-to-mouth basis. Improved transportation and communication services, for example, make it possible for wholesalers to get necessary merchandise much more quickly today than in years gone by.

DEVELOPMENT OF WHOLESALERS' OWN BRANDS   Also adding to the manufacturers' desire to bypass the wholesaler is the fact that many middlemen have developed and are aggressively promoting their own brands in direct competition with manufacturers' brands.

MANUFACTURERS' DESIRE FOR CLOSER MARKET CONTACT   Manufacturers sometimes bypass wholesalers in an attempt to control their products over a greater proportion of the distance from producer to ultimate consumer or industrial user. This interest on the part of the manufacturer is particularly evident where installing, servicing, and repairing the product play a significant role in the product's sales success. Furthermore, by eliminating the wholesaler, the manufacturer can better learn how his product is moving in the market and what the consumer's reaction to it is.

NEED FOR RAPID PHYSICAL DISTRIBUTION   If products are subject to physical perishability or fashion obsolescence, it may be essential to reduce the channels to the shortest length possible. Where fashion obsolescence is concerned, it is far too slow and risky to distribute through wholesalers. For products such as women's ready-to-wear or millinery, orders are frequently placed by telephone and shipped by airplane.

COST OF WHOLESALERS' SERVICES   One of the biggest pitfalls in the marketing process is the assumption that manufacturers can perform the traditional wholesaling functions at a lower cost. Many producers have learned the hard way that bypassing the wholesaler may actually increase the cost of marketing or result in poor market coverage or an otherwise inferior marketing program. Eliminating the wholesaler results in economy only if the manufacturer and/or the retailer can perform the wholesaler's functions more effectively. Even when his research shows that costs will be lowered by eliminating wholesalers, the producer should still investigate further to determine whether the wholesaling services will be performed adequately and whether his long-range market and profit position will be improved.

PREFERENCE OF RETAILERS FOR BUYING DIRECTLY   Many retailers believe that they can get lower prices on merchandise, more advertising allowances, and better service and merchandise selection if they deal directly with manufacturers. Usually the retailers who prefer to buy directly are large-scale enterprises. Consequently, manufacturers seek their business and try to meet their needs.

Courses of action open to manufacturers   If a manufacturer wishes to bypass wholesalers, he has three major alternative channels: he may sell directly to the retailer, he may establish sales offices or branches and sell directly through them to the retailer, or he may bypass the retailer as well as the wholesaler and sell directly to the ultimate consumer. If a manufacturer prefers to use a wholesaler but needs more aggressive selling, he may employ a group of missionary salesmen.

Whatever alternative channel of distribution is used in lieu of wholesalers, direct selling inevitably places a greater financial burden on the manufacturer and adds immeasurably to his management problems. He must operate a sales force, handle the physical distribution of the product, and operate a credit system. Direct selling does not normally result in as intensive a market coverage as wholesalers can provide. Manufacturers are also faced with small-order problems. Finally, once a manufacturer embarks upon a program of direct selling, he must be ready to face competition from his former wholesalers who are now pushing competitive products.

SELL DIRECTLY TO RETAILERS   A decision to sell directly to retailers without the use of sales offices or branches should be based on the situation surrounding five factors. The first is the *market*. An ideal retail market for direct selling is one made up of large-scale retailers who are geographically concentrated, who buy in large quantities, and who maintain central buying offices. Thus we find such retail organizations as corporate chains, mail-order houses, and voluntary chains buying directly from manufacturers. In addition, a manufacturer may establish profitable direct-sale arrangements with specialty stores. While the volume of a specialty store may not be so great as that of a department store or supermarket, the specialty store nevertheless presents an attractive volume outlet in its limited product line. Frequently a shoe store, a clothing store, or a retailer of photographic equipment and supplies will have a sales volume greater than that of a corresponding department in a department store.

The *product* considerations which make direct sale possible or in some cases even necessary are (1) physical or fashion perishability, (2) high unit value or high gross margin, (3) demand for custom-made or specially constructed products, (4) importance of mechanical servicing or installation, (5) manufacturer's output consisting of a full line of related products, and (6) large total order.

Adequately qualified marketing executives are usually a prerequisite for a successful direct-selling program. When circumventing a wholesaler, a manufacturer creates countless managerial problems with respect to organizing and operating a sales force.

In direct selling, preferably both the manufacturer and the retailer should have *financial strength*. If the manufacturer employs a field selling force, the financial requirements will be especially heavy. Also, someone must take over the credit risks and responsibilities previously assumed by the wholesalers.

Sometimes a manufacturer can eliminate a wholesaler only if there are excellent *physical distribution facilities* for the product. The existence of public warehouses, for instance, may enable a manufacturer to perform the storage function normally handled by wholesalers.

OPEN SALES OFFICES OR BRANCHES   Salesmen working out of sales offices or branches under decentralized management may be desirable when the following conditions exist:

1.   There is a concentrated market for the product.

2.   The manufacturer has a large sales force and needs to supervise it closely.

3.   The company places greater emphasis on personal selling than on advertising in its promotional programs.

4.   There is a need to install, service, and repair the product.

5.   Customers demand rapid, economic delivery, and the company does not want to use public warehouses.

Executives in a manufacturing establishment should recognize that branch organizational structures raise substantial financial and operating problems. Not only are operating costs higher because of duplication of manpower and effort, but there is also the fixed cost attendant upon the investment in the branch, plant, and equipment. Operating decisions must be made regarding which functions will be decentralized and which will be handled in the home office. For instance, who is to have the authority and responsibility for hiring, training, promoting, and firing salesmen? Who is to have the authority to grant credit and change prices?

On balance, the statement made by Professor Tosdal many years ago still seems pertinent. He said, "If there is any general rule to be applied to the establishment of branch organizations, it is to the effect that the burden of proof is upon those who advocate establishment of branches rather than upon those who oppose such extensions."[5]

SELL DIRECTLY TO CONSUMER   Various distribution methods may be used to make this short channel effective (see Chapter 12). The producer may employ personal, nonstore selling (house-to-house) or mail-order selling. He may establish retail stores, or he may sell directly to the consumer at the point of production, either the factory, farm, boat dock, or some other location.

USE MISSIONARY SALESMAN   When a manufacturer wants to use a wholesaler but also wants to have the advantages of aggressive selling, he may employ missionary salesmen. Also known as promotional salesmen, detail men, or factory representatives, they perform a number of services and may be used under several different conditions. Typically, missionary salesmen call upon a retailer and aggressively promote the product of the manufacturer. If the salesman secures any orders, he passes them on to the jobber, and the jobber receives his normal commission. Missionary salesmen may be used to install point-of-purchase displays in retail stores or to introduce new items to retailers. Sometimes these salesmen are called in to close difficult sales which whole-

[5] Harry R. Tosdal, *Introduction to Sales Management*, 4th ed., McGraw-Hill Book Company, New York, 1957, p. 513. As one indication of current trends, see "Branch Distribution Trend Gains," *Business Week*, Sept. 10, 1960, p. 65.

salers have not been able to handle themselves. These factory representatives may train retail salesmen, particularly when technical product information is necessary. They may also seek new accounts and stand ready to handle complaints. Because using this sales force is a step short of establishing a sales office or branch, it is less expensive and presents fewer management problems.

Wholesalers' side of the conflict

The wholesaler in his turn is often dissatisfied with the actions of the manufacturer. Marketing administrators should understand and evaluate the wholesaler's complaints. Then these executives should analyze the alternative courses of action open to wholesalers who want to meet the competitive threat of being bypassed.

Reasons for wholesalers' dissatisfaction   Some of the reasons wholesalers are unhappy with manufacturers are implicit in our earlier discussion. The grievances stated here are not all-inclusive, but should establish the tenor of the wholesalers' objections.

MANUFACTURERS FAIL TO UNDERSTAND TRUE ROLE OF WHOLESALERS From the wholesaler's point of view, probably the main irritant is the manufacturer's failure to understand or accept the fact that the primary obligation of the wholesaler is to serve his customers. The wholesaler's responsibility as a service agent for the manufacturer is only secondary.

MANUFACTURERS EXPECT TOO MUCH   Wholesalers often feel that manufacturers' expectations with regard to storage, warehousing, and other services are excessive and are far greater than the wholesaler's discounts justify. As explained earlier, the wholesaler is in no position to promote individual products aggressively, nor can he actively push point-of-purchase displays and other promotional material.

MANUFACTURERS SKIM CREAM OFF MARKET   Wholesalers note that often they are used only in the early stages of territorial development. Then, when the market is intensively cultivated, the manufacturers bypass them and deal directly. Wholesalers also note that manufacturers often use middlemen only in the least profitable segments of the market. In the concentrated, fertile segments, producers sell directly to retailers or industrial users. While this observation is accurate, the wholesaler should understand that his real worth lies in being able to reach markets which the manufacturer himself cannot penetrate profitably.

MANUFACTURERS SELL TO RETAILERS WHO USE THEIR OWN BRANDS Manufacturers often sell products to retailers who place their private brands on the product; wholesalers object to this practice because these products compete with the manufacturers' own brands carried by the wholesaler. Here perhaps the wholesalers are tilting at windmills. Retailers who sell under their own brand names are large-scale organizations; if one manufacturer refuses to sell to them, they will get the merchandise from another. And in any event, their brands will still be in the market competing with those carried by the wholesaler.

Courses of action open to wholesalers   Wholesalers have taken several measures to improve their competitive position in channels of distribution and to meet the threat of being eliminated. All these measures attempt (1) to improve efficiency to such an extent that neither suppliers nor customers can find more desirable means of accomplishing marketing tasks and (2) to tie retailers to the wholesaler in one way or another.

IMPROVE INTERNAL MANAGEMENT   Many wholesalers have taken significant steps to modernize their establishments and to upgrade the caliber of their management. These have been refreshing changes. New, functional single-story warehouses have been built outside the congested downtown areas, and mechanized physical-handling equipment has been installed. In the office, electronic computers and machine accounting systems have streamlined the inventory and accounting controls and have thus reduced losses from obsolete, slow-moving items.

Many wholesalers have added limited-function departments and have otherwise increased the flexibility of their operations.

Another cost-cutting, efficiency-inducing factor has been the adoption of selective selling. That is, the frequency with which a wholesaler will call on his accounts is based on some system of priority: less profitable accounts will be visited less frequently, and really low-profit accounts may be solicited only by mail or telephone.

These and other innovations have generally had the effect of lowering operating costs or of giving the retailer far better service for the same money. Much remains to be done, of course. Activities related to managing the sales force, for instance, have not kept pace with improvements in clerical operations and in the physical handling of products.

PROVIDE MANAGEMENT ASSISTANCE FOR RETAILERS   In growing numbers, wholesalers are coming to realize that their success is totally dependent upon the success of their small, independent retail customers. Therefore, anything the wholesalers do to improve the retailers' operations is really in their own self-interest. Management guidance for retailers may take several forms. Using their own salesmen or other field employees as management advisers, wholesalers can help retailers choose store locations, improve their store layouts, and install better accounting and inventory processes; they can help retail store operators do a better job of selecting, displaying, and promoting their merchandise.

FORM VOLUNTARY CHAINS   Voluntary chains of retailers formed by wholesalers have proved to be an effective device for meeting the competitive challenges that exist today in channels of distribution. This structure was discussed in Chapter 12. In a voluntary chain, a wholesaler enters into a contract with several retailers, agreeing to furnish them with various management services and large-volume buying advantages. In turn, the retailers agree to do all or almost all their buying from the wholesaler.

DEVELOP AND PROMOTE OWN BRANDS   Many large wholesalers have successfully established and developed their own brands. If a wholesaler is connected with a voluntary chain of retailers, the chain provides the wholesaler's brand a built-in market. Private brands help the retailers, too, because consumers cannot easily compare private-brand prices with those of manufacturers' brands carried in other stores.

SEEK LEGISLATIVE AID   A final method used by wholesalers to meet the competition of other institutions is to seek legislative aid at the state or Federal level. While the author does not recommend this method as the long-run salvation of the wholesaler, it seems to be a favorite and first choice of many wholesalers. Wholesaler organizations were instrumental in getting the Robinson-Patman Act passed, and they also fought vigorously for the passage of state fair-trade and unfair-practices laws. (These laws are discussed in Chapters 19 and 20.) One intent of these laws was to neutralize the large-scale buying power of giant retailers, such as corporate chains and large, independent department stores. As noted in the discussion of retailing institutions, a fundamental error made by many middlemen—wholesalers and retailers alike—is to believe that the only advantage corporate chains have over small independents is large buying power. Even if all stores bought merchandise at the same price, the other advantages of large-scale enterprises would clearly enable them to out-compete the smaller merchants.

In the author's opinion, legislative aid can help the wholesaler only temporarily. It obscures his basic problems and therefore postpones their effective long-range solution. The wholesaler's real salvation and opportunity for growth lie in his ability to improve the internal management of his establishment and to help the small-scale, independent retailer become a more effective institution.

Future of the wholesaler

In the 1920s and 1930s, it was frequently forecast that the full-function merchant wholesaler was a dying institution. Statistics given in Chapter 13, however, show that since World War II the wholesaler has actually improved his position.[6]

There are two broad but basic reasons for the comeback of the merchant wholesaler. One is a fuller realization of the true economic worth of his services. The other is the general improvement and modernization of his management methods and operations. The bandwagon to eliminate the whole-

[6] For a good summary analysis of the revitalization of the wholesaler, see Edwin H. Lewis, "Comeback of the Wholesaler," *Harvard Business Review*, November–December, 1955, pp. 115–125. For an example of how the world of wholesaling is continuing to change dramatically in one traditional wholesaling stronghold—the grocery field—see William Applebaum, "Management Responsibilities Facing the Wholesale Grocer," *Journal of Marketing*, July, 1964, pp. 68–73.

saler proved to be a blessing in disguise. Innumerable firms tried to bypass the wholesaler and came to realize that the net result was unsatisfactory. They could not perform some of the wholesaling functions at all, or they found the cost prohibitive. In many cases, it became evident that the wholesaler was able to provide the manufacturers and retailers more and better services, and to provide them more efficiently and at a lower cost, than these firms themselves could.

Wholesalers are still the controlling force in the channels used by many firms. These producers are totally dependent upon the service wholesaler or some other type of wholesaling middleman. We must not conclude, however, that only low-cost wholesalers can survive in the competitive market. Even seemingly high-cost wholesalers are thriving. A high operating-cost ratio is not necessarily a result of inefficiency. Instead, it is usually a result of more and better service. Many wholesalers' costs are high only because they offer an established distribution system (granted, it may be nonaggressive) and many other services which ease the producers' marketing and financial burdens.

On balance, the service wholesaler's position seems reasonably secure. His elimination is justified only when the alternative channel structure is more effective and less costly. As long as there are many small-scale producers located in widely scattered, sparsely populated markets, there will be a real need for wholesalers. Because these market conditions will undoubtedly exist for some time to come. it looks as if the service wholesaler is truly here to stay.

MANUFACTURER VERSUS RETAILER

Today, perhaps even more significant than the conflict between manufacturers and wholesalers is the struggle for channel control which goes on between manufacturers and retailers. A very basic reason for the conflict is this: *"The people who manufacture the goods and the people who move the goods into the hands of the ultimate consumer do not share the same business philosophy and do not talk essentially the same language."*[7] In manufacturing corporations, management's point of view is typically characterized as a psychology of *growth*. His goals are essentially dynamic and evolving; he is forever climbing to the top and is not content to rest on past accomplishments. In sharp contrast, the psychology of the small- and medium-sized retailer is essentially *static* in nature. His goals are easily and well defined and are far more circumscribed than those of the manufacturing corporation executive; at some point the retailer levels off into a continuously satisfying plateau.

Domination versus cooperation

In the struggle between manufacturer and retailer, each group has a series of weapons it can use in its efforts to dominate.[8] A manufacturer can use his

[7] Warren J. Wittreich, "Misunderstanding the Retailer," *Harvard Business Review*, May–June, 1962, p. 147. The balance of the paragraph is drawn from this article.

[8] See Mallen, "Conflict and Cooperation in Marketing Channels," pp. 77–83.

promotional program to build a strong consumer preference for his product. Legal weapons are available to him in the form of franchise contracts, consignment selling, or outright ownership of the retail store. As a negative method of dominating, the manufacturer may refuse to sell to uncooperative retailers. Suggestive devices such as premarking the price on products or advertising the resale price are weaker control methods.

Retailers are not necessarily unarmed in this situation. By effective advertising programs or by establishing their own brands, they can develop consumer preferences for their stores. A retailer can either concentrate his purchases with one supplier or spread his buying among many sources, depending upon the number of manufacturers involved and which strategy is most effective for him.

On the other side of the coin, fortunately, channel members seem to realize that their common interests and reasons for cooperating with one another do outweigh any reasons for conflict. Perhaps manufacturers and retailers alike understand that it is in their own best interests to treat a distribution channel as a total system—to consider a channel as an extension (forward or backward, as the case may be) of their own internal organizations.[9] To implement this concept, a manufacturer should do the sort of thing for a retailer that he does for his own marketing organization. That is, the manufacturer can provide advertising aids, training for dealer salesmen, managerial assistance, etc. Retailers can reciprocate by carrying adequate inventories, promoting the product, and building consumer goodwill. (These methods of mutual, day-to-day cooperation are elaborated on in Chapter 15.)

Manufacturer involvement in retailing

To an increasing extent, manufacturers are becoming involved in retailing. The pressures stimulating this trend are identifiable.[10] More and more large retailers are integrating backward into manufacturing, and they are also expanding the number of products being sold under their own private brands. As retailers limit their product assortments to only the fastest-moving brands, and as the battle for shelf space becomes more intense, many manufacturers are apt to be crowded out of stores or relegated to inferior positions.

If a manufacturer does intend to get involved in retailing, probably the best course of action for him is to develop some sort of coordinated distribution system, rather than relying on the traditional, fragmented marketing

[9] For additional insight on this point, see Valentine F. Ridgeway, "Administration of Manufacturer-Dealer Systems," *Administrative Science Quarterly*, March, 1957, pp. 464–483; and Peter Drucker, "The Economy's Dark Continent," *Fortune*, April, 1962, p. 103. For some suggestions on how manufacturers can coordinate their activities with the giant retailers, see Eugene Whitmore, "A Long, Long Way from Mom & Pop," *Sales Management*, June 4, 1965, p. 21.

[10] See *Grey Matter*, "Gravity Exerting Stronger Pull on Marketing," in J. Howard Westing and Gerald Albaum (eds.), *Modern Marketing Thought*, The Macmillan Company, New York, 1964, pp. 42–44.

channels. Either of two routes may be used to reach this goal. The first is a vertically integrated system in which the manufacturer owns the retail outlets —a system used by Hart, Schaffner & Marx and the Sherwin-Williams Company, for instance. The other alternative is a contractual arrangement—a franchise agreement—between the manufacturer and independent retailers. Franchising, which was discussed in Chapter 12, provides a system of countervailing powers by which manufacturers can battle large retailers for markets and by which small, independent retailers can compete with renewed vigor. Since World War II, there has been a significant growth in both types of centrally coordinated systems, but the most rapid rate of expansion has been in the contractually integrated networks.[11]

Dual distribution   The increased use of one form of dual distribution is another real source of conflict between manufacturers and retailers. Broadly defined, *dual distribution* is the practice whereby a supplier uses more than one type of channel or marketing organization to distribute his product. We are concerned here with the type of dual distribution in which a manufacturer sells the same brand, or two brands of basically the same product, to the same market through *competing* channel networks. A paint manufacturer, for instance, may distribute through a series of retail stores which he owns, at the same time using conventional channels of independent paint wholesalers and retailers—all aiming at the same market. The general practice is not new; for years it has been carried on by oil companies, tire manufacturers, and paint companies. But what is new is the surge in its growth and its adoption in industries heretofore generally untouched.[12]

The impetus for this growth is coming from several sources. In many industries, increasing competition has spurred manufacturers to open their own stores in markets where no satisfactory outlet is available. Some manufacturers establish their own stores as testing grounds for new products and marketing techniques. In suburban markets, small retailers often do not have the financial resources to open a store in shopping centers. Consequently, many large manufacturers must open their own stores in these centers if they want suitable outlets.

To conclude, in this chapter we have taken a macro point of view as we studied the never-ending, constantly evolving, dynamic competitive conflict and cooperation occurring in distribution systems. In the next chapter we shall

[11] Bert C. McCammon, Jr., "The Emergence and Growth of Contractually Integrated Channels in the American Economy," in Peter D. Bennett (ed.), *Marketing and Economic Development*, American Marketing Association, Chicago, 1965, pp. 496–515.

[12] Thomas J. Murray, "Dual Distribution vs. the Small Retailer," *Dun's Review and Modern Industry*, August, 1964, p. 28; see also Lee E. Preston and Arthur E. Schramm, Jr., "Dual Distribution and Its Impact on Marketing Organization," *California Management Review*, Winter, 1965, pp. 59–70.

return to our microanalysis and examine the process in which marketing executives select a channel of distribution and establish working relationships with individual middlemen.

QUESTIONS AND PROBLEMS

1   We are seeing an increase in "scrambled merchandising" on the retail level of distribution. What effect do you think this trend will have on wholesaling middlemen?

2   What factors determine who controls the channel of distribution for a given brand?

3   "Large manufacturers always control the channels used to reach local markets." Do you agree? In your college community, are there examples of strong manufacturers who are unable to tap the local market except through local independent retailers?

4   Explain the role played by each of the following factors in the conflict between manufacturers and wholesalers, particularly in the marketing of consumer products:
   a.   Traditional position of the wholesaler before 1920
   b.   Changing position of the manufacturer since the late 1800s
   c.   Changing position of the retailer since 1920

5   Why is there considerably less friction between manufacturers and wholesalers in the industrial goods field than in the consumer goods field?

6   Explain the reasons why the manufacturer is dissatisfied with the performance of the wholesaler. Do you agree with the manufacturer's point of view?

7   What can a manufacturer do to stimulate wholesalers into performing a more aggressive, effective job of promoting the manufacturer's products?

8   Use examples to explain how bypassing a wholesaler will sometimes *increase* the cost of marketing.

9   If a large department store must still rely on wholesalers in some instances, how do you account for the fact that specialty stores, which are much smaller, buy directly from manufacturers?

10   Why are regular wholesalers relatively unimportant in the marketing of women's high-fashion wearing apparel, furniture, and large electrical equipment?

11   Many manufacturers have established sales branches or offices in markets where various types of wholesalers are already in existence. Why is this done?

12   "The use of missionary salesmen is a fine compromise between the use of a wholesaler and the complete elimination of the wholesaler." Discuss this idea, showing how missionary salesmen may offset manufacturers' objections to wholesalers.

13   In the channel conflict, what are the wholesaler's reasons for being dissatisfied with the manufacturer? Assuming you are the manufacturer, what would be your rebuttal to these points?

14   In one region of the country, a general merchandise wholesaler had been supplying small, independent variety stores for years. Recently, two of the national limited-price variety chains entered the area and are giving the independents some stiff competition. Should this general merchandise wholesaler establish his own voluntary chain, signing up as members his present independent retail accounts? Would your recommendation be the same if the field were hardware stores? Drugstores? Stores selling low-priced shoes for the entire family?

15   "The future of the wholesaler depends upon his ability to increase his own efficiency and to furnish managerial aids to his retailers." Discuss, pointing out the alternatives if the wholesaler fails to meet this challenge.

16   What marketing conditions might encourage a manufacturer to adopt a policy of dual distribution at the retail level?

17   For many years, a manufacturer of vacuum cleaners has sold to consumers through leased departments in department stores. Sales have been disappointing in many cities in recent years, so the firm is considering a change in its channels of distribution. Presently the company hires, trains and compensates the salesmen who work in the leased departments. The department stores exercise only nominal supervision over these salesmen to ensure that they follow store policies regarding credit, returns, repair, etc. The alternative channel being seriously considered is to sell direct to the consumer on a door-to-door or party-plan basis. The salesmen presently in the leased departments would serve as the nucleus of the new sales force. Should the manufacturer discontinue using leased departments and sell directly to the consumer?

15

ESTABLISHING CHANNELS OF DISTRIBUTION

The preceding chapters have described the types of middlemen available on both the retailing and wholesaling levels. The real capacity of a marketing executive can be measured by his ability to use this background to establish and manage the channels of distribution which will maximize his company's profit position over the long run. Marketing executives frequently find that establishing channels for their products and solving the problems connected with channel management are among their most difficult tasks. In part this difficulty is traceable to the dynamic nature of the distribution structure and its propensity for change. Competitive conflicts constantly call for attention and sometimes force channel adjustments. Long channels compound a producer's problem because he is far from his ultimate consumers or users. Also, frequently he has little or no control over his middlemen and cannot get from them necessary current market information regarding his markets and products.

Three steps are involved in this decision-making phase of the marketing process. First, a manufacturer must select the general channel to be used, keeping in mind the goals of the company's marketing program and the job to be done by means of the distribution system. Second, assuming he is going to use middlemen, he must make a decision regarding the *number* of middlemen or the intensity of distribution to be used at each level and in each market. Finally, again assuming he will use middlemen, he must select the specific firms which will handle his product, and then establish and manage the day-to-day working relationships with them.

Only infrequently—as when a new company is started or when an established firm introduces a new product or enters a new market—will a marketing manager establish a distribution system from the ground up. The more usual task of channel management involves a continuing evaluation, and possibly a modification or reorganization, of the existing structure. Far more marketing executives are involved with the day-to-day working operations of the distribution system than with any other step in channel selection.

The reader may have noted that the task of establishing channels is approached from the manufacturer's or producer's point of view. Middlemen also face channel problems essentially similar to those of a producer. Furthermore, the control of the channels used by manufacturers and the freedom of choice regarding these channels may actually rest with wholesaling and/or retailing middlemen. Simply as a framework for analysis in this chapter, however, channel policies and strategies will be studied from the vantage point of the producer.

MAJOR CHANNELS OF DISTRIBUTION

Actually there are several alternative channels, and in most industries each alternative is used by at least a few firms. Even to describe the major channels used for consumer products and for industrial goods is risky because it may suggest an orthodoxy which does not exist. Nevertheless, that risk is taken in the following section, which outlines the most frequently used channels for the two major classes of products. These channels are illustrated in Fig. 15–1.

Distribution of consumer goods

Five channels are widely used in the marketing of consumer products. In each, the manufacturer has the additional alternative of using sales branches or sales offices. Some students will justifiably conclude that consideration of these institutions triples the number of alternatives. Furthermore, whenever wholesalers are used, goods may be distributed from one large wholesaler to several sub-jobbers and then to retailers, thus placing two wholesaling links in the chain. It

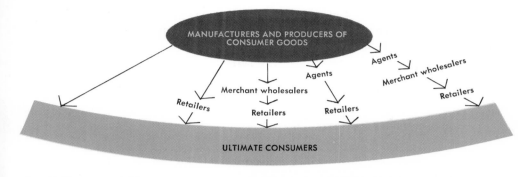

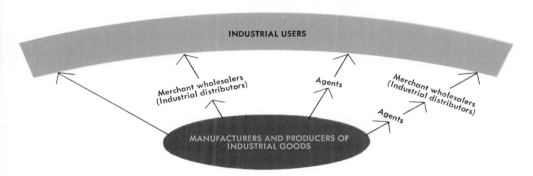

MAJOR MARKETING CHANNELS AVAILABLE TO MANUFACTURERS AND PRODUCERS

fig. 15–1

In each channel, a manufacturer or producer may use his own sales branches or personnel to reach the next institution. The channel leading directly from the producer to the consumer at the upper left of the diagram represents door-to-door selling and direct mail. In any channel, two levels of merchant wholesalers may be involved—one wholesaler sells the product to another wholesaler.

is evident, therefore, that our suggestion that there are only five major channels is an oversimplification, but one which seems necessary if we are going to discuss this unwieldy subject in a few paragraphs.

Producer—consumer   The shortest, simplest channel of distribution for consumer products is from the producer to the consumer, with no middlemen involved. The producer may sell from house to house, as many dairies and some agricultural producers do, or he may sell by mail.

Producer—retailer—consumer   Many large retailers buy directly from manufacturers and agricultural producers. Also, some manufacturers—the

Sherwin-Williams Paint Company, the Bond Clothing Company, and the Florsheim division of the International Shoe Company, for example—have established their own retail stores, although this is not a common practice.

Producer—wholesaler—retailer—consumer   If there is a "traditional" channel for consumer goods, this is it. As was noted in preceding chapters, small retailers and small manufacturers by the thousands find this channel the only economically feasible choice.

Producer—agent—retailer—consumer   Instead of using wholesalers, many producers prefer to use a manufacturers' agent, selling agent, broker, or another agent middleman to reach the retail market, especially *large-scale* retailers. A manufacturer of a glass cleaner selected a food broker to reach the grocery store market, including the large chains. A manufacturer of a line of fishing lures used manufacturers' agents to reach sporting goods stores, hardware stores, and other retailing institutions.

Producer—agent—wholesaler—retailer—consumer   When trying to reach *small* retailers, the producers mentioned in the preceding paragraph often use agent middlemen, who in turn go to wholesalers who sell to small stores.

Distribution of industrial products

Four general types of channels are widely used in reaching industrial users. Again, a manufacturer may use a sales branch or a sales office to reach the next institution in the channel, or two levels of wholesalers may be used in some cases (see Fig. 15–1).

Producer—industrial user   This direct channel accounts for a greater *dollar* volume of industrial products than any other distribution structure. Manufacturers of large installations, such as locomotives, generators, and heating plants, usually sell directly to the users.

Producer—industrial distributor—user   Producers of operating supplies and small accessory equipment frequently use industrial distributors to reach their markets. Manufacturers of building materials, construction equipment, and air-conditioning equipment are only a few examples of firms which make heavy use of the industrial distributor.

Producer—agent—user   Firms without their own marketing departments find this a desirable channel. Also, a company which wants to introduce a new product or enter a new market may prefer to use agents rather than its own sales force.

Producer—agent—industrial distributor—user   This channel is similar to the preceding one, except that for some reason it is not feasible to go through agents directly to the industrial user. Probably the unit sale is too small to sell directly, or perhaps decentralized inventories are needed to supply the users rapidly. In such cases, the storage services of the industrial distributor are required.

SOME GENERALIZATIONS ABOUT DISTRIBUTION CHANNELS

A few broad generalizations may serve as a guide to management in its task of developing channels of distribution. First, channel analysis should begin with the final customer and work backward to the producer because, essentially, channels of distribution are determined by consumer buying habits. This point, of course, is in complete alignment with the philosophy of the marketing concept. Thus if a significant percentage of the potential customers wish to buy on credit or prefer to shop in the evenings, the manufacturer should see to it that the retail section of the channels includes the appropriate outlets.

A second generalization is that the channels finally established must be totally appropriate to the basic objectives of the firm's marketing program. If the company's goal is to render the best possible servicing for its complex industrial product, then a short channel should be used. If management sees as its goal the widest possible distribution of its product line, then obviously an exclusive franchise policy at the retail level is *not* appropriate.

Third, the channels should provide a firm with access to a predetermined share of the market, including a definite level of intensity of market penetration. A manufacturer of golfing equipment seeking as broad a market as possible made a mistake in establishing channels which included only department stores and sporting goods stores at the retail level. The executives should also have considered channels which would reach discount houses and the professional shops at country clubs, as well as the major trading-stamp companies that included the products in their premium catalogues.

Fourth, the channels must be adequately flexible so that the use of one channel will not permanently close off another. A manufacturer of small appliances (irons, toasters, etc.) distributed only through appliance wholesalers and then to appliance retailers. The company had an offer from a drug chain to buy the products directly from the manufacturer. The appliance retailers threatened to discontinue the line if the manufacturer placed it in drugstores, and the producer decided to turn down the drug chain's offer. Subsequently, a competitive manufacturer accepted a similar offer and profited considerably.

A fifth point to keep in mind is that there is a high degree of interdependence among all firms in the channel for any given product. There can be no weak link in the chain if it is to be successful. In effect, each firm in the channel becomes his brother's keeper. Manufacturers using wholesalers are only as good as the wholesalers; wholesalers in turn are successful only if their retailers do well.

A sixth observation is that constant evolutionary and sometimes almost revolutionary changes are occurring. Channels of distribution and middlemen are always on trial. Sometimes in the course of categorizing institutional middlemen a person may succumb to the notion that markets are segmented or otherwise protected so that the different channels or the several types of middlemen do not compete with one another. Actually, there is considerable competition, and this is one of the economic forces making for constant change. The dynamic factor of change should remind us of the earlier observations that continuing evaluation (rather than sporadic, one-shot studies) is needed in channel management and that day-to-day administration is a more usual task than selection of the basic channel or determination of the intensity of distribution.

Two other generalizations are corollaries of the preceding one. Middlemen survive only when their existence is economically sound and socially desirable. Nobody subsidizes or otherwise keeps a middleman in existence if he does not serve well. Furthermore, new middlemen and channels arise to do new jobs or to do those that are not being done well.

FACTORS AFFECTING CHOICE OF CHANNELS OF DISTRIBUTION

In the course of making decisions with respect to its channels of distribution, management should carefully analyze its market, its products, its middlemen, and the company itself.

Market considerations

Referring to the generalization that channels of distribution should be determined by customer buying patterns, we note that the nature of the market is the most important factor influencing the choice of channels of distribution.

Consumer or industrial market   The most obvious point to consider is whether the product is intended for the consumer or the industrial market. If it is going to the industrial market, retailers will not be included in the channel. If it is going to both markets, the company will want to use more than one channel.

Number of potential customers   A large potential market is likely to necessitate the use of middlemen. If the market is relatively small, the company may be able to use its own sales force to sell direct. A related consideration is the number of different industries to which the company sells. A firm selling drilling equipment and supplies only to the oil industry used its own sales force and sold directly to the users; one reason for this channel choice was the relative narrowness of the market. (Incidentally, this company also maintained a few sales branches in order to have the centralized stocks of parts and supplies readily available for its customers.) For a paper products manufacturer, this aspect of the market led to an opposite decision. The company's products ultimately were sold to many different industries and to many firms in each industry. Consequently, the manufacturer made extensive use of industrial distributors.

Geographic concentration of market   Firms selling to the textile or the garment industry will find that a large proportion of the buyers are concentrated in a few geographic areas. Direct sale is more feasible than if the market were spread over the entire nation. Even when a market is truly national, some segments have a higher density rate than others. There are more potential customers for office machines in Chicago or Los Angeles than in Albuquerque or Chattanooga. In densely populated markets, a seller may establish sales offices or branches, but he will decide to use middlemen in markets where the numbers of potential customers are less heavily concentrated. A company selling hard-rock mining equipment has a geographically concentrated market, and direct sale is feasible. On the other hand, the same company may sell drills, compressors, and other construction equipment to contractors all over the country. Here the lack of a geographically concentrated market, or of market segments with high density rates, forces the company to use industrial distributors.

Order size   The volume of sales which may be made to individual firms will influence the channels used to reach these companies. A food products manufacturer will sell directly to large grocery chains because the total volume of business makes this channel economically desirable. The same manufacturer cannot sell to small grocery stores in sufficient quantities to warrant direct sale, so wholesalers will be used because they afford a larger volume potential. One reason industrial operating supplies are typically sold through industrial distributors is that the volume purchased by most industrial users is too small to justify direct sales.

Customer buying habits   The buying habits of ultimate consumers and industrial users, the amount of effort the consumer is willing to expend, the desire for credit, the preference for one-stop shopping, and the desire for the services of a personal salesman significantly affect channel policies.

Product considerations

The unit value of a product, its physical characteristics, and other product considerations have a strong influence on the choice of distribution channels. Special governmental regulations and the channels used for competitive products also play a part.

Unit value   The unit value of a product influences the amount of funds available for distribution. Usually, the lower the unit value of a product, the longer the channels of distribution. In contrast, if the product is of high unit value, more funds are derived from each unit sold, and the company is more apt to use shorter, more costly channels. This is one reason why industrial installation type of products are sold direct, while small accessory equipment items usually go through industrial distributors or agents. However, when products of low unit value are sold in large quantities or are combined with other goods so that the total unit *sale* is large, shorter channels may be feasible.

Bulk and weight   Management must consider the cost of freight and handling in relation to the total value of the product. A producer of a heavy, bulky item, where freight is a significant part of the total value, will seek to minimize the physical handling of the product and will prefer to ship in carload or truckload quantities. This is one reason drop shippers are used in the marketing of coal and building materials. Although the title may go through middlemen, the physical product is shipped directly to the industrial user or retailer.

Perishability   Products subject to physical or fashion perishability must be speeded through their channels. Typically the channels are short. If middlemen are used for physically perishable products, they may be selected because of their special storage facilities. Manufacturers of nonperishables have wider choices in channel selection. They can offer better guarantees to middlemen and normally will find more middlemen willing to carry their goods.

Technical nature of a product and servicing required   An industrial product which is highly technical often will be distributed directly to the industrial user. The manufacturer must have salesmen and servicemen who can explain the product to potential customers and who can provide considerable presale and postsale service. Wholesalers normally cannot do this. Consumer products of a technical nature provide a real distribution challenge for the manufacturer. Ordinarily he cannot sell the goods directly to the consumer. As much as possible, he will try to sell directly to retailers, and even then the servicing of the product may pose problems.

Custom-made versus standardized products   This factor is somewhat related to the preceding one. If a product is custom-made, it will probably be distributed directly from producer to ultimate consumer or industrial user. One important exception is found in tailor-made consumer products, such as home furnishings, where retailers are widely used. In these instances, the retailers do not carry merchandise stock. They have samples, illustrations, and catalogues from which consumers may order.

Extent of product line   A manufacturer's channel choice is influenced appreciably by the extent of his product line. In the field of home appliances, for example, a firm is almost required to produce a full line of products if it wishes to secure desirable wholesalers and retailers. In other instances, the broader the line, the shorter may be the channel. The manufacturer with only one item may have to use wholesaling middlemen, whereas he could go directly to retailers if he had several products which could be combined in one large sale. Again using the appliance field as an example, a retailer ordinarily cannot buy a carload of washing machines alone, but he might buy a carload of mixed appliances.

Company considerations

The one factor which tells most about a company and has the greatest influence on channel policies is probably its size. Although size in and of itself means little, the company that has been successful enough to become large is almost certain to have the financial strength, the capable management, the ability to provide services for middlemen, and the desire to control the channel for its product. Given comparable market and product considerations, a large firm is more apt to have shorter channels than is a small enterprise.[1]

Reputation Well-known companies with good reputations are in a better position to acquire channels and middlemen of their choice than are unknown businesses.

Financial resources A financially strong company needs middlemen less than one which is financially weak. A business with adequate finances can establish its own sales force and even branch organizations; it can also grant credit or warehouse its own products, whereas a weak firm would have to use middlemen to obtain these services.

A financially weak firm may deal directly with retailers or industrial users if they can take the entire output of the plant. Some large chains have such working agreements with manufacturers. Usually the product is sold under the retailer's brand. The obvious disadvantage of this arrangement is that the producer is completely at the mercy of its one large customer.

Experience and ability of management Channel decisions are affected by the marketing experience and ability of the management. Many companies lacking marketing know-how prefer to turn the job over to middlemen. New companies, built upon the engineering and production abilities of management, often rely heavily on middlemen to do the marketing job. An established company planning to sell a new product or enter a new market is likely to use middlemen until it acquires experience in the new field.

Desire for control of channel A manufacturer may establish as short a channel as possible simply because he wants to control the distribution of his

---

[1] For evidence of the strong relationship between the size of a firm, the channels it uses, and the method of organizing the marketing function, see Robert E. Weigand, "The Marketing Organization, Channels, and Firm Size," *Journal of Business*, April, 1963, pp. 228–236.

product, even though the cost of the more direct channel is higher. The producer may feel that he can give his product more aggressive promotion by controlling the channel. Also, he can better control such factors as freshness of merchandise stocks and the retail prices of the goods.

Services provided by seller   Often a producer's channel decision is influenced by the quantity and quality of marketing services he can provide in relation to those demanded by the middlemen. Frequently manufacturers can sell their products to retail chains only if the goods are presold through heavy advertising. Other middlemen may demand that the manufacturer build in-store displays or send missionary salesmen to call on retailers and industrial users.

Middlemen considerations

The final set of factors to be analyzed by a manufacturer deals with the middlemen. These are particularly important because so often middlemen control the channel for a given producer's product.

Services provided by middlemen   A producer should select middlemen who will provide the marketing services he himself either is unable to provide or cannot economically perform. If a product needs aggressive promotion to enter a new market, a manufacturers' agent can usually provide the service better than a full-function wholesaler. If a product requires special storage facilities, a wholesaler may provide these facilities best. In these examples we can see the relationships between the nature of the product and the services provided by middlemen.

Availability of desired middlemen   An administrator should recognize that the middlemen he desires may not be available. They may be carrying competitive products and may not wish to add another line. In any event, the manufacturer may have to alter his entire channel. One producer of industrial machinery who could not secure desirable distributors in a metropolitan market opened a sales office in that city. It proved so successful that eventually he opened branches or offices in several other markets and discontinued his use of industrial distributors in those cities.

Attitude of middlemen toward manufacturer's policies   Sometimes a manufacturer's choice of channels is limited because his marketing policies are not acceptable to certain types of middlemen. The producer's unwillingness to guarantee the product against a price decline will eliminate many middlemen from consideration. Some types of retailers and wholesaling middlemen are interested in carrying a line only if they can get an exclusive franchise in a territory.

Sales volume possibilities   A point calling for very careful study is the determination of which channel offers opportunities for maximum sales volume.

All other factors being equal, a producer will select a channel offering the greatest potential volume over the long run. There are two problems inherent in that statement, however. The first is the difficulty of forecasting which channel will offer the largest potential volume. The second is that realistically all other things are not equal. A high-volume channel may also be a high-cost channel, or a firm may secure maximum volume but lose all control over its distribution.

Cost requirements   The final point to analyze is the cost of selling through alternative channels. Expenses should be equated with functions performed by the middlemen. As noted in preceding chapters, a high-cost middleman is not to be excluded automatically from consideration. His cost may be high only because he provides so many services. When analyzing these costs, a firm should study the *total* channel expense rather than the expense of *separate* types of middlemen.

Analysis of cost by channels of distribution is a difficult task. (See Chapter 29 for a discussion of this topic.) If such an analysis is not made, however, management has no sound foundation for judging channel expenses. Furthermore, even after a cost analysis shows which is the lowest-cost channel, then the products, the market, or other considerations may indicate that this channel is not the best choice.

SELECTION OF CHANNELS FOR NEW PRODUCTS OR NEW COMPANIES

Special channel problems are faced by an established company adding a new, unrelated product to its line or by a new company starting out either with a new type of product or with an established product. Three important considerations will influence the decision making in these situations. The first concerns the newness of the product and the extent to which the consumers realize they want it. A manufacturer of men's suits who adds shirts to his line faces different channel problems from those of an appliance manufacturer who adds electronic clothes washers which require no water. In the latter case a primary demand must be created, and provisions must be made in the channel to educate the consumers regarding the new product and to instruct them in its use.

Second, for any new product or new company the promotion requirements are particularly high. Aggressive selling is needed. We have seen that wholesalers do not perform this service; yet they may be needed to reach retailers or industrial users. The manufacturer, faced with the need to spend huge sums on advertising and to establish a missionary sales force, has several alternatives. Instead of using wholesalers, he may develop his own sales force to call directly on retailers or industrial users; or he may compromise by employing a manufacturers' agent and giving him a large enough commission to encourage him to sell the product intensively and aggressively.

The third point is that the company may find it difficult to establish the channels it wants simply because the middlemen are not eager to take on an unknown company or an unknown product. In this case the manufacturer may have to use any channel which will accept the product and hope that in time he can change to more appropriate channels.

USE OF MULTIPLE CHANNELS OF DISTRIBUTION

A manufacturer may use multiple channels either to reach different markets or to sell to the same market.

A firm selling the same products to both consumer and industrial markets would usually establish separate channel structures. In like manner, differences in the size of the buyers or the market densities often result in the use of more than one channel. A manufacturer of food products will sell directly to large grocery chains, but to reach smaller stores he will use another channel which includes grocery wholesalers. A producer may establish sales branches in a concentrated market and from these branches send out a sales force to reach wholesalers or to go directly to retailers. In more sparsely populated markets, the same producer will use manufacturers' agents instead of sales branches or his own sales force.

Sometimes a producer is reaching different markets, and thus is using multiple channels, because he is selling an assortment of unrelated products. Firms producing oleomargarine and paint, or rubber products and plastics, illustrate the point. These firms may also have organized their sales forces into separate divisions according to the various customer groups or product lines.

As we noted in the preceding chapter, a particularly significant development in dual distribution (and a source of channel conflict) has been the increased use of *competing* channel systems by manufacturers to sell the same brand to the same market.

DETERMINING INTENSITY OF DISTRIBUTION

After a manufacturer has decided upon the general channels he will use, he should next determine the number of middlemen—the intensity of distribution—to be employed at the wholesaling and retailing levels in the channels. In this respect, a manufacturer has three major alternative courses of action. These are not neatly compartmentalized alternatives. Instead, the degrees of intensity of distribution form a continuum, or phases in a scale. At one end is *intensive* distribution, in which the manufacturer tries to get maximum exposure for his product by having it sold in every outlet where final customers might possibly look for it. The second alternative is *selective* distribution, in which the producer selects a limited number of wholesalers and/or retailers in a given geographic area. The third possibility is *exclusive* distribution, which involves the use of only one wholesaling middleman or retailer in a specified geographic market.

Intensive distribution

Ordinarily the policy of intensive distribution is adopted by the manufacturers of consumer convenience goods. Consumers demand immediate satisfaction for this class of product and will not defer a purchase in order to get a particular brand. In the field of industrial products, intensive distribution is usually limited to operating supplies or other highly standardized items, such as janitorial supplies, small tools, and some lubricants. Retailers often control the extent to which the policy of intensive distribution can be implemented. For example, a new manufacturer of toothpaste may want distribution in all supermarkets, but these retailers may limit their assortment to the four fastest-selling brands. Intensive distribution also places most of the burden of advertising and promotion on the shoulders of the manufacturer. Wholesalers and retailers are not going to help advertise a product that all competitors are selling.

Selective distribution

Selective distribution covers a wide range of market exposure or distribution intensity. A business which adopts this policy may have only a few outlets in a particular market, or it may have a large number but still have something short of intensive distribution. The policy of selective distribution lends itself especially well to manufacturers of consumer shopping or specialty goods and industrial accessory equipment, for which most customers have a brand preference. Even makers of convenience goods often limit the number of their outlets to some extent because it simply is not profitable to sell to every existing outlet.

When a firm adopts a selective distribution policy at the retail level, there will normally be a reduction in the number of wholesalers used. Conversely, a firm may limit the number of retail outlets by the simple expedient of first limiting the number of wholesalers to whom it sells. Adopting a selective distribution policy at the retail level may make it possible for the manufacturer to eliminate or bypass wholesalers completely.

Many companies have switched to selective distribution in order to achieve higher profit levels. Although they forecast a decline in sales volume, many of them actually increased their volume substantially because they were able to do a more thorough selling job with the smaller number of accounts.

A company may decide to adopt a selective distribution policy after some experience with intensive distribution. The reasons for the change usually hinge upon the high cost of intensive distribution or the unsatisfactory performance of middlemen. Some customers perennially order in small, unprofitable amounts. Others may be poor credit risks. Still others may be chronic complainers, frequently returning goods they ordered or demanding extraordinary services. Finally, some retailers may be eliminated because they are not providing adequate repair and maintenance facilities to service the products.

Once the executives in a firm decide to follow a selective distribution policy, special requirements ordinarily fall upon the chosen outlets. The fewer the number of outlets, the heavier the requirements. For example, the limited number of middlemen are expected to display the products more prominently and to promote them more aggressively than if distribution were unlimited.

Exclusive distribution

Under an exclusive distribution policy the supplier enters into an agreement with a particular wholesaling middleman or retailer whereby the supplier will sell only to that wholesaler or retailer in the given market. Under these exclusive distributorships (with a wholesaler) or exclusive dealerships (with retailers) the middlemen are sometimes prohibited from handling a directly competitive line of products.[2]

When used   A new firm having difficulty establishing a distribution system and securing desirable middlemen or an established firm trying to market a new product may attract outlets by offering exclusive franchises. Some risk is involved in using exclusive selling agreements to secure initial distribution because if the manufacturer later wants to terminate the exclusive arrangement, considerable ill will may be engendered. Exclusive dealerships are frequently used in the marketing of consumer specialty products. Expensive men's suits, sold under heavily advertised brands, fall into this category. When department stores or very large specialty stores are granted these franchises, a manufacturer often gets a bonus in the form of several outlets in the one market because the retailers open branch stores in suburban shopping centers.

Management often adopts an exclusive distribution policy when it is essential that the retailer carry a large inventory in order to ensure customers an adequate choice. This form of distribution is also desirable when the dealer or distributor must furnish installation and repair service. Manufacturers of farm machinery, large construction equipment, and commercial heating and air-conditioning equipment frequently use exclusive distributorships for this reason.

Evaluation from manufacturer's standpoint   From a supplier's point of view, several marketing advantages stem from an exclusive distribution policy. In the first place, this policy helps the manufacturer control the retail segment

---

[2] In technical language, a contract wherein the middleman agrees not to handle competitive products is known as an "exclusive dealing" agreement. On the other hand, the terms "exclusive selling," "exclusive dealerships," "exclusive distributorships," and "exclusive distribution" refer only to arrangements whereby the seller agrees not to sell to other retailers or wholesalers in the particular market; they say nothing about other products.

Frequently the term "exclusive agency" is used to describe exclusive dealerships, and the retailer is referred to as the "exclusive agent" for the product. No agency relationship exists in a legal sense. The retailer buys the product outright and legally performs in his own interest. He is not the legal agent of a manufacturer-principal. Because he is an independent retailer, the term "exclusive franchise" would more appropriately describe his relationship with the manufacturer.

of his channel. He is better able to determine what the retail price of his product will be, and he is in a position to approve advertisements featuring his products. A dealer is more likely to be cooperative and to promote the product aggressively because he realizes that his future is tied to the success of the manufacturer. With fewer accounts, the manufacturer is able to reduce credit losses and marketing costs. His billing, shipping, and order-filling functions are simplified. The dealer will probably carry a complete stock and be more willing to service the products than he would be if there were broader distribution.

On the other hand, there are a few serious competitive limitations to this distribution policy. Probably the most significant is that the manufacturer substantially limits the number of his sales outlets. He may lose the business of some customers who would normally buy the manufacturer's brand if it were more conveniently located. Also, the manufacturer will suffer if his exclusive dealer incurs customer ill will. Essentially, the manufacturer has all his eggs in one basket, and he is pretty much dependent upon the retailer. Another problem facing the manufacturer is the difficulty of getting good dealers. Often the best ones in a market are already taken by competitors. Finally, a manufacturer who does a considerable amount of national advertising will have a great deal of waste circulation if his advertisements reach many people who do not live in the vicinity of his dealers.

Evaluation from retailer's standpoint   A significant advantage of an exclusive dealer is that he reaps all the benefits of the manufacturer's marketing and advertising activities in the particular market and gets all repeat sales. He finds it easier to maintain the margin on the product because he is protected from price-cutting competitors. Finally, if he does not carry competitive lines, he may increase his rate of stock turnover in the exclusive product line and also reduce his investment in inventory. Because he is important to the manufacturer, the lone retailer probably gets better treatment from him.

For a retailer, the main drawback to an exclusive dealership is that he becomes wedded to the manufacturer. If the manufacturer does a good job with the product, the dealer prospers. But if the manufacturer fails, the dealer is powerless to do anything but sink with him.

Dealership agreements often require the retailer to invest a considerable sum of money in equipment and facilities. If the agreement is then canceled, he stands to lose a major investment; having cut himself off from other suppliers, he may have virtually no opportunity to acquire a product line of another firm. Another hazard from the retailer's standpoint is that once the volume is built up in a market, the manufacturer may add other dealers. The retailer is often at the mercy of the manufacturer; it is a one-sided arrangement in this respect, particularly if the brand is strong and the franchise is valuable. High quotas and other demands and activities of the manufacturer may put a heavy strain on the retailer. To keep the valuable franchise, the middleman may have to give up his independence and operate almost as a sales branch.

Legal considerations   Although exclusive distribution is not illegal, Federal laws and judicial interpretations have imposed some restrictions on three major aspects of its use. One aspect is *exclusive dealing contracts*, the arrangement whereby the franchise holder is prohibited from carrying similar product lines from competing manufacturers. A second involves *tying contracts*, under which the exclusive dealer or distributor is required to carry a manufacturer's full line if this supplier so desires. The third arrangement is the *closed sales territory*, wherein the manufacturer limits each franchise holder to selling only to buyers located within the assigned exclusive territory.

None of the three arrangements is automatically illegal. Section 3 of the Clayton Antitrust Act of 1914 specifically states, however, that exclusive sales or lease contracts are unlawful if their effect "may be to substantially lessen competition or tend to create a monopoly in any line of commerce." It is under this provision that unreasonably restrictive exclusive dealing contracts and tying contracts have typically been ruled illegal. Questions on the legality of closed sales territories usually involve Section 5 of the Federal Trade Commission Act of 1914, which prohibits unfair competition which may be in restraint of trade.

Exclusive dealing contracts have been declared unlawful rather consistently if the manufacturer's sales volume is a substantial part of the total volume in a market or if the volume done by the exclusive dealers is a significant percentage of the total business in an area. That is, the law is violated when the competitors of a manufacturer are essentially shut out from a substantial part of the market because of this manufacturer's exclusive dealing contract.

In recent years, probably the key case affirming this position was the one involving the Standard Oil Company of California. The Supreme Court ruled that Standard's exclusive dealing contracts (covering gasoline and other products) with its independently owned Chevron stations were unlawful because they were a substantial threat to competition.[3] About six thousand dealers in seven Western states were involved. Together they represented 16 per cent of the service stations and only 6.7 per cent of the total sales volume of all these products in the seven-state area.

By inference in some judicial decisions and by outright statement in others, it has been made clear that exclusive dealing is not illegal in all situations. In fact, where the seller is just getting started in a market or where his share of the total market is so small as to be negligible, his negotiation of exclusive dealing agreements may not only improve his competitive position but also strengthen competition in general.

Ordinarily there is no question of legality when a manufacturer agrees to sell to only one retailer or wholesaler in a given territory, provided there are no limitations on competitive products. Also, a manufacturer can sell to

[3] *Standard Oil Company of California* v. *United States*, 337 U.S. 293 (1949).

dealers who do not carry competitors' products, just so this is a voluntary decision on the part of the franchise holder.

With regard to tying contracts, apparently a dealer can be required to carry a manufacturer's full line as long as the dealer is not prohibited from carrying competitive products. The arrangement is questionable, however, if a supplier forces a dealer or a distributor to take slow-moving, less attractive items in order to acquire the really desirable products.

Closed sales territories may be illegal because they restrict the franchise holders. They may also tend to create a monopoly for a product in a given territory in that buyers cannot play exclusive dealers in different territories against one another. Perhaps the safest policy is to assign each reseller a geographical area of primary responsibility rather than a closed sales territory.[4]

SELECTING AND WORKING WITH INDIVIDUAL MIDDLEMEN

When all is said and done, middlemen can often make or break a manufacturer. They are the ones who personally contact the final customer, whether he is an ultimate consumer or an industrial user. Consequently, a manufacturer's entire channel effort fundamentally is designed to reach one goal— that of maximizing the marketing effectiveness at the point of final sale. This generalization supports the systems concept of a channel of distribution, as set forth early in Chapter 11 and developed further in Chapter 14. That is, to maximize the effectiveness of a distribution channel, it must be treated as a complete system and not as a series of independent, competing, self-oriented links. Thus, the success of a manufacturer's distribution effort depends ultimately upon how well he selects his individual middlemen and then administers the action system involving these distributors and dealers.

This final step in establishing channels is particularly important at the *wholesaling* level because a manufacturer uses fewer wholesalers than retailers. Furthermore, the choice of wholesaling middlemen preempts to a considerable extent the manufacturer's choice of retailers. At the *retail* level, the choice of individual middlemen is particularly important when the producer has decided upon a policy of selective or exclusive distribution. A manufacturer may create considerable ill will for himself when he terminates an exclusive franchise or drops some of his selected accounts. Not only are feathers ruffled among the retailers who are dropped, but also dealers in other markets may begin to lose their regard for this supplier.[5]

[4] For some managerial guidelines in formulating sales policies in view of pertinent exclusive dealing legislation and its interpretation, see Leonard J. Konopa, "Exclusive Dealing Arrangements in Marketing," *Business Topics*, Summer, 1964, pp. 63–72.

[5] For a comprehensive report of some two hundred United States and Canadian manufacturers, describing the criteria they employ in selecting and evaluating their distributors and dealers, how these standards are used, and the methods of finding and investigating potential middlemen, see Roger M. Pegram, *Selecting and Evaluat-*

Factors affecting choice of middlemen

Several factors may contribute to a successful business operation by a middleman. Some, such as business conditions and competition, are external to the firm's operation and generally are not controllable by the wholesaler or retailer. Other points which are internal and controllable by the middlemen include the caliber of their executives, their ability to advertise, and the soundness of their merchandising or product planning.

The manufacturer should establish qualifying criteria or standards for each factor so he will know what he is looking for. Then he must find the available middlemen who meet these predetermined standards. Here we may again observe that channel research is one of the most difficult types of marketing research. To get the desired information regarding potential middlemen will undoubtedly involve some kind of field research. When the manufacturer has a prospective retailer in mind for a selective or exclusive dealership, the producer probably should talk with the retailer's suppliers and competitors. If possible, the manufacturer should find out what the retailer's customers are like and what they think of the store. It is important to make certain that all information is currently accurate. A store that was doing an outstanding job in promotion last year may have lost the key executive who was the guiding force behind this success. In another case, a middleman may have recently assumed financial commitments which will deplete his working capital and make him a slow-paying account for the next full year.

Access to desired market   In the selection of an individual wholesaler or retailer, by far the most important factor to consider is: Does he sell to the market I want to reach? This really is the *sine qua non* of middleman selection. If he does not now reach the manufacturer's desired market, it is doubtful that the manufacturer's products will induce him to change substantially his customer list.

Location   A good location is particularly important at the retail level, but it must also be considered in selecting wholesaling middlemen because a firm's location is often closely related to its ability to reach a desired market.

A retailer's location must be considered with respect to shopping centers, competitive outlets, and trading areas. A manufacturer who wants to select a specialty store in a shopping center will first want to determine whether the shopping center is the most desirable one in the market. In one case, a shopping center had no leading department store, and therefore a specialty store was not selected in this center. Even the location of the retail store within the shopping center may be an important consideration.

---

ing *Distributors*, National Industrial Conference Board, Studies in Business Policy, no. 116, New York, 1965. This report includes case studies, executives' comments, and excerpts from company policy and procedure manuals.

Manufacturers of shopping goods will try to select retailers who are located close to competitors and are in an area where there is heavy customer traffic. One producer preferred retailers who had a downtown location as well as branches in the suburbs. In this way he acquired several stores in a market but still had exclusive franchises.

Product-planning policies A manufacturer should carefully consider the product policies of prospective wholesalers or retailers. To illustrate, a manufacturer ordinarily seeks stores where his line will complement rather than compete with the store's other products. If he refuses to sell to middlemen who carry a competing line, then he must seek outlets which have no such line or which are willing to drop their present lines. A garment manufacturer had such a policy, and his products were so attractive to retailers that many stores discontinued their previously handled brands in order to get his line.

Depth or assortment typically carried by a dealer within a product line may influence a manufacturer's or wholesaler's choice of outlet. A manufacturer of health and beauty aids produced a wide line of products in several sizes, types of packaging, and colors. Department stores and large drugstores would carry the full assortment, but supermarkets wanted only one or two sizes of a few fast-moving items. This manufacturer could not rely only on supermarkets for his retail distribution. He had to use other stores which were willing to carry a larger proportion of his complete assortment.

A manufacturer must consider the comparative quality and price of other lines in a store. Even if the retailer were willing, a manufacturer should not be interested in selling his line of dresses which start at $59.95 to stores whose highest-priced lines of other dresses are $29.95.

Buying practices of middlemen often influence a manufacturer's decision. Irregular, hand-to-mouth buying is not so desirable as fewer but larger orders placed on a planned basis. A wholesaler of office supplies and equipment dropped several retail accounts, and one reason was that these retailers bought sporadically and in small quantities.

Most manufacturers are interested in finding out whether the retailer prefers to handle and aggressively promote products carrying his own private brand. Finally, the pricing policies and practices followed by middlemen should influence a manufacturer. As an illustration, a producer who is opposed to resale price maintenance should normally avoid dealers who demand it. By the same token, if the manufacturer wants to maintain a suggested retail price, he must avoid dealers who are well-known price-cutters or who might use the brand as a price football.

Promotion policies If a manufacturer must rely on middlemen to do the bulk of the promotion, he will select them differently from the way he would if he himself planned to advertise and otherwise promote the product heavily. Some manufacturers have been forced to shun large retailers, who otherwise were desirable, because these dealers demanded promotional allowances, displays, or product demonstrators. The manufacturers either could not afford these promotional devices or preferred to use other methods.

For producers of many types of goods, the nature of the middleman's personal selling activities is important. A manufacturer of earth-moving equipment and other construction machinery made it a point to ascertain the technical abilities of salesmen of industrial distributors before granting a franchise in a territory. If a product does not lend itself to the self-service method of retail selling, then obviously the many stores employing this method are eliminated from further consideration.

Services available to customers   The consumer's acceptance of discount selling, with its limited services but low prices, has changed managerial thinking with regard to the necessity of services. However, this does not mean that manufacturers and middlemen can consider customer service a thing of the past. Where service is important, a manufacturer should judge the potential middlemen on the basis of the services they normally offer to their customers. Manufacturers and wholesalers of big-ticket consumer products, such as furniture and appliances, usually prefer retailers who supply credit and delivery services for their customers. Middlemen for many industrial products must be able to provide their customers with good mechanical service and rapid delivery of parts and supplies.

Physical plant and equipment   A middleman's plant layout, operating facilities, and transportation or warehouse facilities may be important considerations for a manufacturer. Storage facilities with temperature and moisture controls are indispensable for some products.

Financial ability   A manufacturer should investigate a middleman's financial condition and the financing services he provides for his customers and suppliers. Naturally a manufacturer will prefer middlemen who pay their bills regularly and promptly. In some cases a manufacturer will select an individual retailer who is small and financially insecure because he holds great promise for the future.

Quality of management   An overall factor for a manufacturer to consider is the caliber of executives in a middleman's business. Their capacity to manage—that is, their ability to perform all aspects of the management process, such as planning, organizing, and staffing—is crucial to the success of the firm. The quality of management is reflected in all aspects of the middleman's business.

The working relationship

In the administration of a channel system (as we saw in the preceding chapter), some institutions assume the role of *primary* (controlling) organizations, while others occupy secondary roles.[6] Regardless of whether the manufacturer or the middlemen hold the controlling position, a real interdependence exists between the two groups. Unless the manufacturer is successful, the welfare of the dealer is in jeopardy, and conversely the manufacturer has a vital interest in his dealers' success. The greater the share of his total business that a dealer derives from the sale of a given manufacturer's product, the greater is his dependence on that supplier.

There is also a community of interest in what each organization—manufacturer and middleman—expects from the other in support of an effective total marketing program. A series of rewards and penalties may be invoked by either party to encourage the other to perform as expected in line with the needs of the distribution system. The major reward for either party is in the form of increased profits. A manufacturer can also use programs of recognition or financial incentives to further reward a dealer. Probably the most powerful penalty which a manufacturer can assess is to terminate his sales agreement with a dealer. A middleman, in turn, can penalize a manufacturer by not promoting his products adequately, by pushing a competitor's products, or ultimately by dropping the manufacturer's line entirely.

A middleman has a right to expect the manufacturer to provide well-designed, properly priced, salable products for which consumer demand has been built by a good advertising program. A manufacturer may also grant territorial protection in the form of an exclusive franchise.

On a day-to-day basis, a manufacturer can furnish promotional and managerial assistance in many forms. Preparing sales manuals for middlemen and conducting sales training programs for dealer or distributor salesmen are only two examples. A manufacturer's in-store promotional aids may be useful, and his missionary salesmen are often welcomed because they can check stock, build displays, and work with salesclerks. Middlemen should be notified about price changes and stock conditions, and they should be completely informed about new products. Manufacturers can offer managerial assistance in accounting systems, buying activities, and advertising. Managerial advice should be available for a middleman when he selects a location for a new store, arranges a store layout, modernizes an existing store, or switches to a self-service operation.[7]

Day-to-day working relationships between the manufacturers and their middlemen determine the ultimate success of the arrangement. Friction can develop easily if there is not a real spirit of cooperation. An open, clear channel

[6] Ideas in this and the following paragraph are adapted from Valentine F. Ridgeway, "Administration of Manufacturer-Dealer Systems," *Administrative Science Quarterly*, March, 1957, pp. 464–483.

[7] As examples of what two manufacturers have done to improve the quality of management among their dealers, see "New Growth Rings for U.S. Plywood," *Business Week*, July 24, 1965, p. 72; and "Weyerhaeuser & Dealers Form Marketing Partnership," *Industrial Marketing*, December, 1964, p. 123; see also *Building a Strong Distributor Organization*, National Industrial Conference Board, Experiences in Marketing Management, no. 6, New York, 1964.

of communication between the two is an absolute requirement. As we noted in the preceding chapter, however, unfortunately this communication system is weakened because manufacturers and middlemen often have conflicting business philosophies and speak different languages.

In return for the products and services which he supplies, the manufacturer has a right to expect certain assistance and cooperation from middlemen in day-to-day relationships. Some of these points have been developed at greater length in the preceding chapters on the distribution system. A retailer or wholesaler may be expected to carry adequate stocks of merchandise, undertake some advertising and sales promotion, grant credit to customers, and possibly service the product. The amount of help to be provided in each of these activities depends upon the product itself and the nature of the middleman's franchise. More is expected from holders of exclusive franchises than from middlemen used in intensive distribution.

ANALYSIS AND EVALUATION OF CHANNELS OF DISTRIBUTION

In the face of changing conditions in the market and among middlemen, constant appraisal of channel activity is mandatory. Yet a surprisingly large number of companies assume that the channel job is completed once their channels are established. Executives who regularly sponsor product innovation and who insist on a new advertising campaign twice a year often seem perfectly content with an archaic distribution structure. Failure to keep one's channel abreast of the market can seriously hurt a firm's profit position.

Several types of quantitative and qualitative marketing research may be undertaken to aid a business in appraising its channels. In a quantitative sense, a company may analyze the sales volume performance of each of its middlemen to determine whether they are getting an adequate volume from each territory, product line, and customer group. The need for a cost analysis by channels of distribution has already been mentioned. These kinds of quantitative analyses are discussed in more detail in Chapters 28 and 29.

To do a proper job of evaluating a middleman's performance, a manufacturer must establish standards and then develop methods for measuring the middlemen's performance against these predetermined criteria. A commonly used standard of performance is a sales quota. The manufacturer sets the number of units or the dollar volume of each of his products which a middleman must sell in a given time period. Other bases for appraising performance include the total amount of advertising he devoted to the manufacturer's products, the middleman's treatment of competitive lines which he handles, his promptness in paying bills, or the number of complaints which the manufacturer receives from his customers. External factors, such as new competitors and general business conditions in a market, should often be taken into consideration when measuring performance.

Another type of valuable research involves determining the attitudes and reactions of middlemen and even final customers toward the manufacturer, his products, and his marketing policies. Essentially, the manufacturer is trying to get some "feedback" from his middlemen and final customers. Middlemen's attitudes may be uncovered by a formal questionnaire survey conducted either by the manufacturer himself or by an outside research agency. A few years ago, a major home appliance manufacturer employed a research firm to determine what the appliance dealers' attitudes were toward the manufacturer's salesmen, distribution system, and advertising programs.[8] The main findings were that dealers wanted the products to be presold through advertising and to be of high quality, and they wanted the manufacturer's service facilities close by. Additional findings regarding what the dealers expected from the manufacturer's salesmen were incorporated into the latter's sales training program.

Many companies try to determine middlemen's attitudes simply by informal observations and investigations made by salesmen or by a company executive who has contact with the middlemen. Usually middlemen are quite willing to express their opinions to the manufacturer.

QUESTIONS AND PROBLEMS

1   Which of the channels illustrated in Fig. 15–1 is most apt to be used for each of the following products? Defend your choice in each case.
   a.   Life insurance   f.   Iron ore
   b.   Single-family residence   g.   Toothpaste
   c.   Farm tractor   h.   Women's shoes
   d.   Newspaper printing press   i.   Men's shoes
   e.   Office furniture   j.   Refrigerators

2   "The great majority of industrial sales are made directly from the producer to the industrial user." Explain the reason for this in terms of the nature of the market. In terms of the nature of the product.

3   The text suggests that products subject to physical perishability must be speeded through the channels and that typically the channels are short. Yet in the marketing of agricultural perishables, very long channels with several types of middlemen are used. How do you reconcile these statements?

4   A small manufacturer of fishing lures was faced with the problem of selecting his channel of distribution. What reasonable alternatives does he have? In your analysis, consider particularly the nature of his product and the nature of his market.

5   What special channel problems are involved with new products and new companies? What recommendations do you have for overcoming each of the problems?

6   What is the usual relationship between the intensity of a company's distribution and the length of its channels of distribution?

7   Is a policy of intensive distribution consistent with the buying habits for convenience goods? For shopping goods? Is intensive distribution normally used in the marketing of any type of industrial goods? Explain.

   [8] "What Dealers Can Tell about Sales," *Printers' Ink*, Mar. 29, 1963, p. 66.

8 Why would a manufacturer ever want to abandon intensive distribution in favor of selective distribution?

9 Assume that a manufacturer of builders' hardware wanted to move to a selective distribution system. How would he go about determining which accounts to keep and which to eliminate?

10 Carefully distinguish between "exclusive dealing" and an "exclusive dealership."

11 From the manufacturer's viewpoint, what are the competitive advantages of exclusive distribution?

12 What are the drawbacks to exclusive selling from the retailer's point of view? To what extent are these alleviated if the retailer controls the channel for the particular brand?

13 What is a tying contract? Is it illegal under the Clayton Antitrust Act?

14 Identify a few retailers near your school who have exclusive franchises for particular products. Study these retailers and determine to what extent they comply with the factors discussed in this chapter in connection with selecting individual middlemen.

15 How can a manufacturer determine whether an individual retailer or wholesaler sells to the market the manufacturer wants to reach?

16 A manufacturer of a well-known brand of men's clothing has been selling directly to one dealer in a Western city for many years. For some time, the market has been large enough to support two retailers very profitably, and yet the present holder of the franchise objects strongly when the manufacturer suggests adding another outlet. What alternative does the manufacturer have in this situation? What course of action do you recommend that he take?

17 Interview local retailers to determine which manufacturers are making an effort to get some "feedback" from their dealers. Specifically, what techniques have these manufacturers adopted?

18 "A manufacturer should always strive to select the lowest-cost channel of distribution." Do you agree? Should he always try to use the middlemen with the lowest operating costs? Explain.

16

MANAGEMENT OF PHYSICAL DISTRIBUTION

After the channels of distribution have been established and the individual middlemen selected, a firm can turn its attention to the physical distribution of its product through these channels. Physical distribution is concerned with the movement of the right amount of the right products to the right place at the right time.

TOTAL SYSTEM CONCEPT OF PHYSICAL DISTRIBUTION

Physical distribution in marketing is essentially a problem in logistics. Logistics is normally considered a military term; it is concerned with the details of transporting, quartering, and supplying troops. Supplying the troops, in turn, is concerned with transporting and handling equipment and materials. An army cannot afford to have one of its units in a position where it has guns but no ammunition, or trucks but no gasoline. By the same token, a private business is in a weak position when it has orders but no merchandise to ship, or when it has a good supply of machinery in Atlanta but an urgent customer in New Orleans. These situations indicate the importance of *location* in marketing, whether it is the location of a store, warehouse, or stock of merchandise. The appropriate assortment of products must be in the right place at the right time in order to maximize the opportunity for profitable sales volume. *Physical distribution*, then, is the management of the physical flow of products and the establishment and operation of efficient flow systems.[1] In its full scope, the management of physical distribution for a manufacturer would involve not only the movement of *finished goods* from the end of the production line to the final customer but also the flow of *raw materials* from their source of supply to the beginning of the production line. Similarly, a middleman would manage the flow of goods *onto* his shelves as well as *from* his shelves to the customer's home or store.

The task of physical distribution may be divided into the five parts listed below. What is done in one area, however, very definitely affects decision making in others. A decision on the location of a warehouse may influence the selection of the transportation carrier. The decision on the carrier influences the optimum size of the shipment.

1. Determine the inventory locations and establish a warehousing system.
2. Establish a materials-handling system.
3. Maintain an inventory control system.
4. Establish procedures to process the orders.
5. Select a method of transportation.

From time to time in this book, it has been pointed out that marketing is a total, integrated system of business action and not a fragmented series of operations. Nowhere is this idea seen more clearly than in the matter of physical distribution. But it has not always been this way. Traditionally— and unfortunately this is still true in too many firms—the activities involved in physical distribution have been fragmented, and managerial responsibility for them has been compartmentalized into units which often have conflicting, and even diametrically opposite, goals. The production department, for instance, sets the production schedule and is interested in long production runs so as to minimize the unit manufacturing costs, even though the result may be abnormally high inventory costs. The traffic department looks at the freight rates rather than at the total cost of physical distribution. Thus carriers with low ton-mile charges are often selected, even though this may mean undue time spent in transit and require larger inventories to fill the

[1] The flow concept is captured in the term "rhochrematics," which was coined from the Greek words *rhoe*, meaning "a flow," as a river; *chrema*, meaning "products," "materials," or "things"; and *-ics*, the abstract ending for any of the sciences. See Stanley H. Brewer, *Rhochrematics: A Scientific Approach to the Management of Material Flow*, University of Washington, Bureau of Business Research, Management Series, no. 2, Seattle, Wash., 1960.

long pipelines. The finance department wants to minimize funds tied up in inventories, while the sales department wants to have a wide assortment of products available at locations near the customers. Under managerial conditions such as these, it is not possible to optimize the flow of products.

At this point, we are interested in studying physical distribution from the viewpoint of the *user* of the services (transportation, warehousing, etc.) rather than through the eyes of the *seller* of the services. At times, however, it will be necessary to examine in some detail what the seller of these services has to offer because only then can the user decide what is his best course of action. Nevertheless, it will be helpful to keep in mind that our viewpoint is that of the user who is concerned with integrating physical distribution into his marketing program.

By viewing physical distribution as a system of business action, management is dealing with a large number of related variables. Problems in such a situation may be solved by means of various statistical and mathematical techniques. Some of these techniques were developed and used in World War II in connection with problems of military logistics. For instance, operations research—a technique involving the use of statistical probability theory, mathematical models, and other concepts—has been particularly helpful in such problems as determining the number and location of warehouses, the optimum size of inventories, and transportation routes and methods. Improvements in computers and other electronic data-processing equipment have made it possible to handle and process rapidly the large quantities of data needed in these quantitative analyses. In our survey treatment in this chapter, however, we shall be concerned with the fundamentals and the conceptual aspects of physical distribution management rather than with the details and methods of quantitative analysis used in solving problems in this field.[2]

The total cost approach

As part of the systems concept, executives should understand and apply the *total cost approach* to the management of physical distribution in a company's marketing program. A firm has several alternative methods of physically handling and distributing its products. The administrators should try to optimize the cost-profit relationship of these various choices after analyzing the

---

[2] For a more complete textual treatment of physical distribution as an integrated systems concept, see J. L. Heskett, Robert M. Ivie, and Nicholas A. Glaskowsky, Jr., *Business Logistics*, The Ronald Press Company, New York, 1964; James A. Constantin, *Principles of Logistics Management*, Appleton-Century-Crofts, Inc., New York, 1966; Edward W. Smykay, Donald J. Bowersox, and Frank H. Mossman, *Physical Distribution Management*, The Macmillan Company, New York, 1961; or Frank H. Mossman and Newton Morton, *Logistics of Distribution Systems*, Allyn and Bacon, Inc., Englewood Cliffs, N.J., 1965.

total cost of physical distribution, rather than considering separately the costs of shipping, storage, handling, or some other fragmented activity in physical distribution.

Too often an executive looks at the cost of only one aspect of physical distribution—transportation, for example—and tries to minimize the cost of this single activity. Possibly he frowns on the apparent high cost of shipment by air freight or shipments in small units. He does not see that efforts to reduce transportation expenses may result in increases in warehousing expenses, which more than offset the saving in freight costs.

The airlines particularly have been conscious of the total cost concept because unit freight rates are appreciably higher for air transportation than for land or sea shipment. The Armour Pharmaceutical Company (a division of the Armour Company) found that the higher costs of air freight were more than offset by the savings in lower inventory costs, less insurance and interest expense, lower crating costs, and fewer lost sales due to depletion of stock. The company eliminated all except one warehouse, cut inventories by 50 per cent, boosted the rate of stock turnover, and found it could supply markets which had previously been inadequately served.[3]

The point being made here is not that air freight is the best method of transportation. (In fact, Armour later substantially reduced its business with airlines in some parts of the country.) Rather, the idea is that physical distribution should be viewed as a total process and its costs analyzed accordingly. Then management can expect to get a better picture of its operations, better communications with its field activities, and consequently greater control over its distribution system.

Implicit in the total cost concept is the thought that management should strive for an optimum balance between total cost and customer utility. That is, rather than seeking *only* to minimize the total costs of physical distribution, executives should also consider customer want satisfaction in connection with this segment of the firm's marketing program. It may be necessary to incur something above the lowest possible total costs of physical distribution in order to achieve something nearer an optimum level of customer utility.

INCREASING ATTENTION TO PHYSICAL DISTRIBUTION MANAGEMENT

Fortunately, in recent years we have witnessed a significant increase in the emphasis which American business management is placing on physical dis-

---

[3] George M. Shutes, "Airfreight from a Marketing Viewpoint," *Journal of Marketing*, October, 1960, pp. 39–43. Additional case histories showing the application of the total cost concept in physical distribution are related in "Air Cargo Closes a Warehouse," *Sales Management*, Mar. 20, 1964, p. 131; "Why Raytheon Takes to the Air," *Sales Management*, Oct. 2, 1964, p. 47; and "Reorganizing Distribution for Higher Profits," *Industrial Marketing,* February, 1963, p. 77.

tribution; happily, there are no signs at all that this trend is abating. A major reason for the increased attention is the fact that physical distribution expenses are a substantial cost factor in many industries. To cite just one study, these costs ranged from about 10 per cent of sales in the machinery industry to 30 per cent in the food industry.[4] For many products, the largest single operating expenses are those involved in physical distribution. For other products, costs equal to as much as one-half of the wholesale price are incurred in performing transportation and warehousing activities. Not only do these costs already loom large, but they are increasing. The Sterling Drug Company, for instance, reported that it could ship 500 pounds of drugs by truck from New York to Chicago for $16.50 in 1960. Five years later, that cost had risen to $18.90, an increase of about 15 per cent.[5] Increases in the variety of products and in the number of sizes, colors, models, etc., sold by a firm also add to the complexities and costs of its physical distribution system. These expenses are a prime factor in establishing geographic limits for a firm's markets.

Through the years, management has made substantial progress toward optimizing the costs of manufacturing and other production activities. Cost reductions have also been effected in many areas of marketing. This leaves physical distribution as a prime target; it is the new (and perhaps the last) major frontier for cost cutting. By treating this activity as a total system, rather than as a set of fragmented parts, business can take a significant stride toward greater efficiency.[6]

In addition to cost considerations, other factors are also accounting for the increased attention being devoted to physical distribution management.[7] Improvements in inventory control and advances in computer capabilities have resulted in a trend toward more frequent ordering of small quantities. Sellers catering to these customers are finding that their existing methods of distributing products do not give the required levels of service. Another factor forcing a review of distribution systems is the dramatic break in recent years from traditional institutional patterns. (These changes were observed earlier in Chapters 11 to 14.) Governmental enforcement of price legislation is encouraging companies to base their discounts and other price differentials on cost differences, so these firms are forced to study their distribution systems carefully to determine their actual costs. Finally, where competitive marketing strategies were at one time centered largely around

[4] Richard E. Snyder, "Physical Distribution Costs," *Distribution Age*, December, 1963, pp. 35–42.

[5] H. Jay Bullen, "New Competitive Selling Weapon: Physical Distribution Management," *Sales Management*, May 7, 1965, p. 41.

[6] See Donald D. Parker, "Improved Efficiency and Reduced Cost in Marketing," *Journal of Marketing*, April, 1962, pp. 15–21. See also "The Next Place for Paring Costs," *Business Week*, May 1, 1965, p. 132.

[7] Wendell M. Stewart, "Physical Distribution: Key to Improved Volume and Profits," *Journal of Marketing*, January, 1965, pp. 65–70.

price and product features, now we are recognizing that effective and reliable physical distribution services can constitute a significant competitive differential.

A FIRM'S STRATEGIC USE OF PHYSICAL DISTRIBUTION

The strategic use of business logistics may enable a company to strengthen its market position by providing more customer satisfaction and by reducing total operating costs. The management of this activity can also affect a firm's marketing mix—particularly its product-planning, pricing, and channels of distribution policies.[8]

Reduce distribution costs

Many avenues to cost reductions may be opened by the effective management of a company's physical distribution activities.[9] Effectively systematizing these activities may result in a simplification, such as the elimination of warehouses, which will cut costs. Inventories—and their attendant carrying costs and capital investment—may be reduced by consolidating stocks at fewer locations and by shortening the replenishment cycle in warehouses. Sometimes a redesigned package permits more efficient transportation and warehousing. Savings may be effected by the selection and use of efficient procedures and technological innovations available for materials handling, order processing, communications, transportation, etc.

Generate additional sales volume

A properly designed logistics system can also help in several ways to generate additional sales volume.[10] Such a system will minimize out-of-stock conditions, the result being an increase in both sales and customer satisfaction. A responsive system can shorten the customer's order cycle and thus reduce his inventory requirements. Cost savings can be passed on to customers in the form of larger discounts. Increased efficiencies in physical distribution often enable a seller to expand his geographical market coverage. All in all, an effective logistics system tends to solidify supplier-customer relationships, and it may even free marketing personnel so that they can concentrate more on promotion and other marketing activities.

[8] For a report on ways to achieve needed improvement in the physical distribution system, see John F. Magee, "The Logistics of Distribution," *Harvard Business Review*, July–August, 1960, pp. 89–101. This article points out that the distribution system in a firm can significantly affect product design, plant investment, and organization.

[9] Stewart, *op. cit.*, pp. 68–69.

[10] *Ibid.*, p. 68.

Adjust to rate, time, and place differences in production and consumption: creation of time and place utilities

There are several conditions under which management can make profitable use of both transportation and warehousing facilities in adjusting its rate, time, and place of production to meet the market demand for the firm's product. To illustrate, there may be a market situation of year-round consumption but only seasonal production or availability, as in the case of agricultural products. Proper use of warehousing facilities will enable a producer to store the seasonal surplus so that it can be marketed long after the production season or harvest has ended.

In other cases warehousing helps to adjust conditions of seasonal consumption but year-round production, as in the case of snow skis. A manufacturer likes to produce on a year-round basis in order to operate his plant efficiently. Consequently, enough surplus stocks are warehoused during the off-season so that the peak-season demand may be met without the need for overtime operation or additional plant capacity.

In a slightly different market situation we often find that seasonal demand and seasonal production do not occur simultaneously. In our industrial economy, the bulk of manufactured products are made in anticipation of demand, not in response to firm orders. Hence a manufacturer will produce Christmas tree ornaments or toys during the spring and summer so that they may be sold to wholesalers and moved to retailers in time for shelf display in November. Before November, there is ample opportunity for the strategic use of warehousing facilities in connection with the amount and location of inventory stocks.

In effect, and in an economic sense, the main function of the transportation subsystem in physical distribution is to add value to products through the creation of *place utility*. A fine suit hanging on a garment manufacturer's rack in New York City has less value to a retailer or consumer in Baltimore than a similar suit displayed in the retailer's store. Transporting the suit from New York to the retailer in Baltimore creates place utility and adds value to the product. Also, speed in transportation may save valuable production time, prevent loss of orders, and create place utility more rapidly.

The economic value of storage (as a key part of warehousing) is the fact that it creates *time utility*. A product may be properly located with respect to its market, but the timing may be such that there is no present market demand. Precious value is added to this item simply by holding and properly preserving it in storage until the demand rises. Time utility is created and value added when bananas are picked green and allowed to ripen in storage or when meat is aged and tobacco cured in storage. Storage is essential when there is an imbalance in the timing of production and consumption.

In this discussion a careful distinction is made between warehousing and storage. *Storage* is the marketing activity which involves holding and properly preserving products from the time of their production until their final sale. *Warehousing* embraces storage plus a broad range of action-oriented functions, such as assembling, dividing (bulk breaking), and preparing products for reshipping. In many respects, warehousing is related both to transportation and to storage.

Stabilize prices

Careful management of warehousing and transportation facilities can help to stabilize prices for an individual firm or for an entire industry. If a market is temporarily glutted with a certain product, sellers can warehouse the product until supply and demand conditions are more favorable. This managerial use of warehousing facilities is commonly found in the marketing programs for agricultural products and other seasonally produced goods. The judicious movement of products from one market to another may relieve gluts in one area, enable a seller to avoid a market with depressed prices, or allow a seller to take advantage of a market which has a shorter supply and higher prices.

Determine choice of channels and location of middlemen

Administrative decisions regarding the management of inventory—its location, handling, transporting, and control—have an important bearing on a manufacturer's selection of his trade channels and the location of his middlemen. Logistics considerations may become paramount, for example, when a company has decided to decentralize its inventory, and now must determine how many sites to establish and whether to use wholesalers, its own branch warehouses, or public warehouses. One manufacturer may select merchant wholesalers who perform storage and other warehousing services, while another may prefer to use a combination of manufacturers' agents and public warehouses. The agents can solicit orders, provide aggressive selling, and do the necessary promotional work, while the orders can be physically distributed through and from the public warehouses.

Logistics facilities may influence a manufacturer's decision on where to locate his branches or in what cities he will seek wholesalers. Sometimes a company wants to locate a branch in a small town or a suburban community, but finds that the additional freight and handling costs from the nearest transportation center are prohibitive. Physical distribution facilities thus force the company to establish its branch in the central city.

A note of caution should be sounded at this point. Rarely are channels selected primarily on the basis of physical distribution considerations. Instead, logistics is only one factor to consider in this case. We can recall from the preceding chapter that the nature of the market and other factors heavily influence channel decisions. In fact, when making channel decisions, the logistics system should usually be considered only insofar as it relates to the nature of the market or the product.

There are many ways in which effective traffic management can aid a company's total marketing program and improve its overall profit picture. First, a good traffic manager will see to it that his company is enjoying the fastest, lowest-cost routes and the lowest possible rates on whatever method of transportation the administrator has decided upon. The pricing of transportation services is one of the most complex and complicated parts of the American business scene. To read a rate or tariff schedule properly (this is the carrier's "price list") is a real art and requires considerable practice.

Another service which a traffic manager can render his company is the auditing of freight bills. This job is necessary because carriers sometimes charge a higher rate than the one which should apply. They are not intentionally trying to defraud the shippers; they are simply misinterpreting the complex rate schedule. A careful audit can save a company thousands of dollars annually in the form of refunds for overcharges. Some transportation consultants make a living performing this auditing and claim service for their clients.

A good traffic manager can also negotiate with carriers in order to get his products reclassified or to get a special rate. A company may offer to ship larger quantities on a given carrier if lower rates are granted. The traffic manager should investigate the possibility of having his company operate its own private carriers, especially its own trucking system. If this possibility seems reasonable for a shipper, it can be an effective bargaining tool in getting reduced rates from common carriers.

DETERMINE INVENTORY LOCATIONS (ESTABLISH WAREHOUSING SYSTEM)

The name of the game in logistics is inventory management in the fullest sense of the term. Executive judgment must be exercised regarding the size, location, handling, and transporting of the inventories. Decision making in these four areas is interrelated. Decisions on the number and locations of inventory sites, for example, will influence decisions on inventory size and transportation methods. These interrelationships are often quite complex; they rarely occur in simple, consecutive, straight-line order. The problem of what should be decided first or where management should start in the logistics planning process resembles the "chicken or the egg" proposition.

One place where planning can begin is with a determination of the number and location of inventory sites. Final judgments will depend greatly on the nature of the market (its size, density, and location), the nature of the product, and the seller's financial position. (These considerations were discussed in the preceding two chapters in connection with the selection of channels and the company-branch-versus-the-wholesaler controversy.)

Perhaps basic to the inventory location problem is the company's intended strategy regarding inventory deployment—is it to be heavily concentrated or dispersed throughout the market? Each strategy has its merits and limitations. Centralizing the inventory means that it can be reduced in total size, can be better controlled, and is more responsive to unusual requests. Efficiency in warehousing and materials handling should be increased. On the other hand, centralizing the stocks of products will probably mean higher total transportation charges and slower delivery service to some segments of the market. Dispersing the inventory presents the other side of the coin on any of the points just noted.

To make a decision on the number and location of inventory centers requires consideration of many variables—transportation methods, freight rates, transit times, warehousing costs, customer buying patterns, and production costs and schedules, to mention just a few of the factors involved. Fortunately, the problem lends itself nicely to quantitative analysis and computer programming. With the aid of operations research techniques, a company can simulate the operations and predict the results of several plans of action.

The distribution-center concept

Perhaps the answer, and an effective compromise, in the concentration-dispersion inventory deployment controversy is for a company to establish one or more *distribution centers*. Planned around markets rather than transportation facilities, the basic thought behind the distribution-center concept is to develop under one roof a speedy, efficient, fully integrated system for the flow of products—taking, filling, and delivering orders to customers. The distribution center is a "new look" in warehousing, having achieved prominence only since the 1950s, but the concept is rapidly being adopted by many well-known firms.[11] The Borden Company, for instance, planned to cut from 136 warehouses down to 16 to 18 distribution centers. After a three-year study, Libby, McNeill & Libby eliminated 214 warehouses and in their place established 5 distribution centers. Similar patterns have been followed by the Raytheon Co. (electronics), the Whirlpool Corp. (appliances), the Bigelow-Sanford Co. (carpeting), and many other firms.

Aided by the use of the latest techniques in data processing, materials handling, record keeping, and inventory control, firms are able to process orders efficiently and rapidly. This new distribution system has lowered distribution costs by reducing the number of warehouses, cutting excessive inventories, curtailing inconsistent deliveries, and eliminating out-of-stock conditions. Storage time and delivery time have been cut to a minimum, thus putting in practice the adage that manufacturers and middlemen are in business to sell goods, not

[11] "The New Nerve Centers of Distribution," *Dun's Review and Modern Industry*, June, 1963, p. S-104. See also Joel F. Olesky, "Distribution Comes of Age," *Dun's Review and Modern Industry*, January, 1965, p. 36; and Donald J. Bowersox, *Food Distribution Center Location: Technique and Procedure*, Michigan State University, Marketing and Transportation Paper no. 12, East Lansing, Mich., 1962.

to store them. Products can be assembled in the distribution center and redistributed quickly with a minimum of handling.

Ownership and types of warehouses

A firm (manufacturer, wholesaler, or retailer) has the option of operating its own private warehouse or of using the services of a public warehouse. A private warehouse is more likely to be used if a company moves a large volume of products through it and there is very little, if any, seasonal fluctuation in this materials flow. A competitive limitation to private warehousing is that it represents a relatively fixed or inflexible expense item. Also, it requires an expenditure of managerial time and talent.

Public warehouses offer storage and handling services and facilities to any interested individual or company. The users pay only for the cubic space occupied by their goods, and they pay only for the time during which this space is occupied. Several types of public warehouses are in wide use today. Probably the most common is the *general merchandise* warehouse, which stores practically any kind of manufactured or nonmanufactured product needing protection from the weather but having no special temperature, humidity, or handling requirements. Various types of *special commodity* warehouses are used for particular agricultural products, such as grains, wool, cotton, and tobacco. Ordinarily each of these warehouses handles one kind of product and offers special services particularly required for that product. Another widely used type of public warehousing facility is the *cold-storage* warehouse.

A particular type of general merchandise warehouse or special commodity warehouse is the *bonded* warehouse. This is used to store products on which a Federal tax must be paid before they can be sold. Some imported goods, alcoholic beverages, and tobacco products are typically stored in these facilities. The warehouse is bonded by the U.S. Department of the Treasury. An advantage of bonded warehouses is that the import duty or excise tax need not be paid until the merchandise is sold.

Services offered by public warehouses

The best-known and most widely used service offered by public warehouses is storage. Products can be stockpiled in appropriate physical condition and in strategic locations until the seller wishes to distribute them to customers. In addition to storage, public warehouses offer other services.

Dividing bulk shipments and reshipping   Public warehouses receive large quantity shipments, such as carload units, and bulk break, or divide, them into smaller units and then reship the smaller quantities to predetermined customers. In this way a seller can combine several less-than-carload orders into one carload shipment and consign the car to a warehouse located near the several buyers. The shipper enjoys the lower carload rate from his shipping points to the warehouse location. Actually, the warehouseman may be acting as a freight forwarder, since products are not actually stored but simply handled and reassembled for final delivery. Some public warehouses accept products shipped in bulk and then package the goods according to the seller's specifications.

Specialized management and labor   Because they are specialists in the activities which they perform, public warehouses can offer the advantages and services of specialization in management, labor, and facilities. They can provide management advice with respect to physical distribution. Also, they have the latest machinery and equipment required for efficient loading, storing, and handling of products.

Financing   Public warehouses can aid the owner of goods financially by issuing a warehouse receipt and providing a field or custodian warehousing service. A warehouse receipt may be used as collateral to secure a loan from a bank. When the goods are sold, the loan may be paid off and the ownership receipt redeemed so that the merchandise may be released from the warehouse and delivered.

Field warehousing (also called custodian warehousing) works in the following manner. Assume that some products are stored in the owner's private warehousing facilities and that he wants to get a bank loan on the merchandise without having the expense of moving it to a public warehouse. The owner calls in a public warehouseman and leases to him a section of the warehouse which contains the merchandise in question. A field warehouse is not limited to a portion of a regular private warehouse. It may be an office cabinet, locked desk drawer, office safe, open yard, storage tank, grain elevator, or some other storage facility. The products may even be shipped from a manufacturer to his wholesaler's warehouse and then placed under a field warehousing plan. The warehouseman issues a receipt for the goods, and this receipt again serves as collateral for a bank loan. The leased area, in effect, becomes a public warehouse, and the goods cannot be removed until the receipt is redeemed.

Substitute for company branch warehouse or wholesalers   A very significant advantage of public warehouses is that they may be substituted both for a company branch warehouse system and for wholesalers. In addition to the bulk-breaking and reshipping services mentioned above, public warehouses will provide office and display space for sellers. These storage firms will also accept and fill orders for vendors. A manufacturer can ship in carload quantities to a public warehouse, just as he can ship to his own branches or wholesalers. Public warehouses enable him to maintain decentralized stocks of merchandise so that he can satisfy hand-to-mouth buyers and fill orders rapidly. Public storage and warehousing costs are variable expenses requiring no capital investment. A firm does not pay for unused capacity, as it often must with a branch warehouse. Furthermore, public warehouses afford greater flexibility in the location of merchandise stocks. If a seller wishes to change or add inventory locations, he can easily change public warehouses.

Protection and security through government regulations   Legislative action at both the Federal and state levels has afforded considerable protection and security to firms using the services of public warehouses. These laws are the guarantee which makes warehouse receipts acceptable as bank collateral, and they also curtail abuses and unethical practices by warehouse operators.

ESTABLISH A MATERIALS-HANDLING SYSTEM

The selection of the proper equipment to handle products is an important aspect of the management of physical distribution. Too often insufficient administrative attention is devoted to this activity. This careless attitude is surprising in light of the fact that the cost of handling products is a substantial part of the total cost of physical distribution.

In this discussion of materials-handling equipment, we include the warehouse building itself. Historically, warehouses have been multistory buildings located in congested, run-down parts of town. Their operation has been characterized by elevators, chutes, and other highly expensive vertical methods of moving products. Modern warehouses are huge, sprawling, one-story affairs located in outlying parts of town where land is less expensive and loading platforms are easily accessible to motor trucks as well as railroad spurs. Ramps have replaced stairs, and forklift trucks, conveyor belts, motor scooters, and other mechanized equipment are used to move merchandise. In some warehouses the order fillers are even equipped with roller skates. As a result, handling costs are often appreciably lower than in the old style of multistory warehouse.[12]

With respect to materials-handling equipment, an executive should first be acquainted with what equipment is available, and then he should select that which is best fitted for his particular warehouse operation. Many firms have found that "palletization" (the use of pallets to aid in mechanical handling of merchandise) makes physical handling more economical. On the other hand, products which are oddly shaped or are handled in small quantities may not lend themselves to the use of pallets.

"Containerization" is a fledgling cargo-handling system which is gaining increasing acceptance in the physical distribution system. The system involves enclosing a shipment of products in containers of metal, wood, or some other material, and then transporting them by rail, truck, and/or ship unopened from the time they leave the shipper until they reach their destination. The bright

[12] See Martin Ezra, "Warehouse Mechanization Moves Ahead," *Chain Store Age*, June, 1963, p. 13; "Marriage of Computer and Conveyor Systems Produces Automated Warehouse," *Chain Store Age*, February, 1964, p. 13; and "A Computer Ships the Shoes," *Business Week*, July 11, 1964, p. 96.

future of containerization is not without its roadblocks, however; shippers and carriers are seeking to solve the problems of lack of standardization of containers, labor's unenthusiastic reaction to the system, and the need for revisions in transportation rate schedules.[13]

MAINTAIN INVENTORY CONTROL SYSTEM

A key activity in a firm's physical distribution system is the maintenance of effective control over the size and composition of the inventories. Inventory represents a sizable investment in many companies. Also, from a macro point of view in the economy as a whole, inventories are often analyzed as a factor influencing general economic conditions. The goal of inventory control is to minimize the investment and fluctuations in inventories, while at the same time providing prompt order-filling services for customers.

Perhaps the greatest boon to inventory control in recent years has been the improvements in computer technology. This factor has enabled management to shorten the order-delivery cycle and to reduce substantially the level (size) of inventories. Through use of the computer, a greater variety of more detailed, accurate information is more speedily available than was heretofore considered possible.

Inventory size may be determined by balancing the market needs and cost factors. Market demands on inventory can be anticipated by analyzing the sales forecast. Thus, the more accurate the forecast, the greater is the probability of optimizing inventory size. The cost factors to consider are (1) acquisition costs, i.e., the costs of making or buying the products to put in inventory, and (2) carrying or holding costs—warehousing expenses, interest on investment, losses due to spoilage and pilferage, inventory taxes, etc.

The inventory's upper limit will also be influenced considerably by the desired level of customer satisfaction, that is, what percentage of orders the company should be able to fill promptly from inventory on hand. Out-of-stock conditions result in lost sales, loss of goodwill, and maybe even a loss of customers. Yet to be able to fill 100 per cent of the orders promptly may require an excessively costly inventory. One authority estimates that about 80 per cent *more* inventory is required to fill 95 per cent of the orders than to fill only 80 per cent.[14]

Related to the size question is the need to establish the optimum quantity to reorder (make or buy) when it is time to replenish inventory stocks. The determination of this "economic order quantity" (EOQ) for a manufacturer moves us back into the production-scheduling process. Once again we see the

[13] In *Dun's Review and Modern Industry*, see "Containers: The Boom Begins," May, 1966, p. 113; John L. Eyre, "Containerization: The Unhappy Marriage," June, 1965, p. 134; and Lassor Blumenthal, "Containerization: The Route to Integrated Transportation," June, 1964, p. 110.

[14] Magee, *op. cit.*, p. 92.

total system aspect of physical distribution; no single segment can be decided in isolation. Decisions on the size of the EOQ will be made by balancing acquisition costs, carrying costs, and the desired level of satisfaction in filling customers' orders. Here again, the capabilities of operations research techniques, plus the use of the computer, can provide management with the analytical tools that help in decision making.

Closely related to the inventory control system and every bit as valuable to management are merchandise planning systems. Two commonly used systems are basic stock lists and model stock plans. Both planning systems are based essentially on an analysis of past sales.

The *basic stock list* is widely used in the distribution of staple goods where identical or closely related items are carried year after year. Under this system, reasonably detailed information is maintained for every item the company keeps in stock. That is, separate records are maintained for each size, color, material, or other significant feature of a given product. The information includes sales of the item, minimum limits when reordering is necessary, and the quantity to be reordered.

For fashion merchandise the most widely used merchandise planning system is called a *model stock plan*. The same items are not carried year in and year out in product lines subject to fashion changes, so a basic stock list is not feasible. A certain style of women's dress, suit, or shoes may be carried for only one fashion season, but there are other factors in the area of fashion merchandise which do remain reasonably constant and thus lend themselves to planning. For example, a dress manufacturer or the dress department in a department store will find that the percentage of total unit dress sales in each size remains about the same over a period of years. Perhaps size 12 dresses account for 16 per cent of total sales, size 14 dresses represent 24 per cent, etc. Also, the manufacturer or retailer may find that each price line accounts for about the same share of unit sales each year. Consequently, a firm can plan what it considers an ideal, or model, stock on the basis of size, price line, or any other product characteristic which remains reasonably constant for several seasons.

ESTABLISH PROCEDURES TO PROCESS ORDERS

As another step in a physical distribution system, management needs to establish a procedure for handling and filling orders; this should also include provision for credit-granting decisions, invoice preparation, and collections on past-due accounts. A considerable amount of consumer ill will can be generated if a company makes mistakes or is slow in filling orders. From the company's standpoint, the activities connected with handling and filling orders offer opportunities for a substantial reduction in marketing expenses.

Processing orders includes activities in two areas—the pertinent office work and the physical task of assembling and shipping. The goal here is to do these jobs quickly, accurately, and as economically as possible, commensurate with good service. This function of order processing lends itself nicely to automation or mechanized operation.

SELECT METHOD OF TRANSPORTATION

A major decision involving the logistics system of a company is that of determining which agencies will be used to ship the products from the manufacturer to the middlemen or final customers or from one middleman to another. (At this point, we are concerned primarily with *intercity* shipments.) The transportation routes and the freight rate structure are important determinants of the geographic limits of a company's market, the outline of its sales territories, and the location of its inventory stocks. When the decision is made regarding the method of transportation to be used, the company may establish its own facilities, such as its own truck, rail, or barge line, or it may employ common carriers.[15]

Before making the decision, however, management should understand the relative merits, costs, special features, and services of each of the five major forms of transportation: railroads (freight, express, and parcel post), trucks, water, pipelines, and airplanes. The relative importance of each, along with some trends in its use, is shown in Table 16–1. Note that the figures reflect *intercity freight* traffic only. Ocean coastal traffic between United States ports is not included. Virtually all farm-to-farm and intracity freight movements are made by motor truck. Consequently, the figures for water and truck carriers really understate the importance of these methods of transportation by a considerable margin. Nevertheless, Table 16–1 is illuminating. It shows that railroads are still by far the major intercity freight carrier. Although their relative position has declined steadily since 1930, the actual ton-miles of freight carried by railroad has increased about 75 per cent since that time. Even excluding intracity freight traffic, the use of motor trucks has expanded phenomenally over the past thirty years.[16]

Railroads

Railroads are particularly well adapted for long hauls of carload quantities of bulk products which are low in value in relation to their weight and the freight

[15] Transportation carriers are often divided into three types: common, contract, and private. A *common* carrier is one which is granted operating rights by a government regulatory agency, such as the Interstate Commerce Commission. The carrier operates on announced schedules and rates and is expected to handle merchandise from any shipper. *Contract* carriers operate in a less restricted and less regulated manner. They enter into contracts with individual shippers and agree to move specified shipments for specified periods of time. *Private* carriers are owned and operated by individual firms for the shipment of their own goods only.

[16] For an excellent annual series of articles on current developments in transportation, see "The Special Report on Transportation," a special supplement published as part of the May or June issue of *Dun's Review and Modern Industry*.

charges. Thus these carriers are low-cost agencies for the shipment of items such as coal, sand, gravel, minerals, and agricultural and forest products. On the other hand, railroads are limited by their inflexibility—they can go only where the track is laid. Railroads have been hurt and trucks have been helped by the growth of markets, including suburban markets, not located on rail lines.

In spite of the many services that railroads have instituted, the nature of the market is such that air, highway, water, and pipeline carriers will probably make further inroads on the railroads. Marketing executives, however, should be aware of the various services offered by railroads because for many products and in many marketing situations, railroads are still the lowest-cost, most efficient method of transportation.

Carload versus less-than-carload freight rates   Railroads offer substantial savings to firms which can ship in carload (c.l.) quantities as compared with less-than-carload (l.c.l.) shipments. For many items the c.l. freight rate is as much as 50 per cent less than the l.c.l. rate. This is a tremendous incentive to shippers of large quantities of products, especially to shippers of minerals, agricultural products, and similar goods where freight expenses are a significant percentage of total value.

Combined shipments   Long ago the railroads realized that they were vulnerable to competition from other types of carriers when it came to handling l.c.l. shipments. Consequently, the railroads have developed several measures

table   16–1

Estimated distribution of intercity freight traffic in United States: in millions of ton-miles

Railroads are still the major carrier for intercity freight. While the physical volume of rail freight has increased substantially, the railroads' share of the market has declined considerably since 1930. Freight shipped by truck or pipeline has increased from 9 per cent of the total in 1930 to 40 per cent in 1965. If we consider intracity freight, which carrier is most important?

Carrier	Ton-miles, 1965	Per cent of total			
		1965	1950	1940	1930
Railroads	705,000	43.5	56.2	61.3	74.3
Great Lakes	108,000	6.7	10.5	15.5	14.8
Rivers and canals	151,000	9.3	4.9	3.6	1.7
Motor trucks	375,000	23.1	16.3	10.0	3.9
Oil pipeline	280,000	17.3	12.1	9.6	5.3
Air carriers	1,800	0.1			
Total	1,620,800	100.0	100.0	100.0	100.0

SOURCE: *Yearbook of Railroad Facts*, Association of American Railroads, Washington, D.C., 1966, p. 39.

designed to reduce the cost of l.c.l. shipments, to speed them up, and generally to make the railroads a more attractive carrier for firms wishing to ship in smaller quantities. These measures provide for combining into a c.l. quantity the freight from one or more companies who are shipping products to customers located in one area. The pooled freight can go at carload (c.l.) rates and can be delivered much more rapidly than if its component parts were sent separately in l.c.l. units. Sometimes the initiative in pooled shipments is taken by a group of retailers who arrange to buy a carload of some item, have it loaded at the shipping point, and then provide for the distribution of the individual orders when the car reaches its destination.

Railway express   The Railway Express Agency is a separate company owned by the major railroads. Air express is just one branch of the Railway Express Agency. Railway express offers pick-up and delivery service; it will ship orders with freight collected on delivery, and its shipments move on passenger trains or at passenger-train speeds. The rates are higher than for carload freight shipments, but the service is admirably suited for small shipments of perishables and other products where the freight cost is low in relation to the item's value.

In-transit privileges   Two in-transit privileges offered by railroads are (1) diversion in transit and (2) the opportunity to process some products en route. *Diversion in transit* allows a seller to start a shipment moving in one general direction and to establish or change destination while the car is en route, just so long as the new destination involves a forward movement of the car and no backtracking. The charges are computed on the basis of the through rate or long-haul rate from the point of origin to the ultimate destination, plus a small charge for diversion. This is a valuable service to shippers of perishable products which are subject to frequent price fluctuations and to variations in price from one city to another on any given day. To illustrate, a Washington cooperative may want to ship Red Delicious apples to Eastern markets. Several carloads will be shipped from Wenatchee, Washington, to Chicago, or they may just be shipped eastward with the specific destination to be determined sometime after the shipment leaves Wenatchee. Before the shipment reaches Chicago, the shipper may receive word that prices in the Chicago market are temporarily depressed because of a heavy supply in relation to the demand but that there is a good market in Memphis. Consequently, at the appropriate "diversion point" (probably Chicago in this case) the cars will be rerouted to Memphis. The freight charges will be based on the through rate from Wenatchee to Memphis. A shipment may be diverted several times before reaching its final destination.

Under the privilege of *processing in transit*, a shipper may have his product unloaded, graded, manufactured, or otherwise processed in some manner while en route, and then have it shipped on to its final destination. As an example, livestock may be shipped from a Western state to Chicago. En route the animals may be unloaded, watered, and fattened in feedlots, but the through rate to Chicago will apply. Wheat may be shipped from Spokane to Minneapolis, where it may be made into flour and the flour shipped to Detroit. Again, the shipper has the privilege of processing in transit. The through rate is usually substantially less than the combined rates from origin to processing point and from processing point to destination.

Piggyback and fishyback services   In recent years the railroads have attempted to meet competition from trucks by offering a "piggyback" service to shippers. Under this arrangement loaded truck trailers are carried on railroad flatcars. The product can be loaded on trucks at the seller's shipping dock and need not be handled again until they are unloaded at the buyer's receiving station. This combination of truck and rail transportation offers more flexibility than railroads alone can offer. Also, eliminating much of the handling of the goods tends to decrease damage and pilferage.

"Fishyback" service involves transporting loaded truck trailers on barges or ships. The trailers may be carried piggyback fashion by railroad to the ship's dock, and then at the other end they can be loaded back onto the trains for the completion of the rail haul. In an alternative use of the fishyback service, railroads are not used at all. Merchandise is trucked directly to ports, where the trailer vans are loaded on barges. At the end of the water journey the vans are trucked to the receiving station.

Freight rate structure   A few comments on the railroad rate structure may give some indication of the enormous complexity of transportation rates. Railroads are used as examples because they frequently set standards for rates on other types of carriers. Also, railroad rates are often used as a basis for comparison when analyzing shipping costs on trucks, airlines, or barges. Most products shipped by railroad go under a class rate or a commodity rate, although bargaining and competition from other carriers have led to the establishment of special rates for particular products in certain parts of the country.

Class rates have been established in an attempt to simplify the problem of determining shipping rates for thousands of items shipped between countless points of origin and destination. Many classes have been set up, and each has its own rate per 100 pounds shipped over a given distance. Products which are reasonably similar in size, value, perishability, or some other distinguishing feature are grouped into one class. Several thousand manufactured products are classed in this manner, and their shipping costs are figured accordingly. Within each class, the rates may vary according to distance, but the ton-mile charges are less as the length of the haul increases. Also, there are regional differences in class rates for the same distance. Further complications enter the picture in at least three ways. First, thousands of new rates are filed each year with the Interstate Commerce Commission. Second, attempts are always being made to have products changed to a lower class. Third, a slight change in the description of what is being shipped may move a product from one class to another.

Commodity rates have been established for the shipment of bulky, low-value products, such as sand, gravel, iron ore, lumber, coal, grains, and other agricultural products. A separate rate is set for each product going between two specific points. Thus there is one commodity rate for lumber shipped from Seattle to Boise, Idaho. About 85 per cent of railroad freight moves under commodity rates, about 5 per cent under class rates, and 10 per cent under some type of special or exception rate.

Commodity rates per ton-mile generally are lower than class rates because of the lower value of products shipped. It is the shipment of the class rate type of products, however, which is being taken over to such a great extent by the highway and air carriers. The shifting of this higher-revenue traffic away from railroads is one factor contributing to their economic decline.

Trucks

The tremendously increased use of highway transportation which was noted in the discussion of Table 16–1 is traceable largely to three factors: an improved system of highways, new developments in equipment for trucking and materials handling, and the competitive advantages of this method of transportation. Trucks have proved to be a very effective transportation medium for short hauls of high-value merchandise. Highway carriers have the advantages of speed and flexibility of movement. Once the merchandise is loaded at the shipper's dock, it can be sent directly to the buyer without any loading or unloading between. Truck shipments require less handling and therefore less careful and expensive packaging than rail shipments; usually there is less damage in transit.

Another factor favoring highway transportation is its lower total freight cost for many products. This is not because of lower freight rates for trucks. Actually rail and truck freight rates are similar for shipping many products in many parts of the United States. The difference is due largely to the fact that trucks go from the seller's loading dock to the buyer's receiving platform. Railroads go from terminal to terminal, and there are added costs in moving products to and from the terminals.

Waterways

A considerable amount of freight is transported by ships and barges on inland and coastal waterways. These waterways are especially good for shipping bulky, low-value, nonperishable products, such as petroleum, sand, gravel, coal, grain, and metallic ores. Water transportation is the cheapest and also the slowest of all major methods of shipping. Its use is sometimes limited by climatic conditions.

Pipelines

Pipelines are a rather special method of transportation in that they are largely limited to carrying petroleum products, especially crude oil and natural gas. While pipelines are technically common carriers open to use by any shipper, most of them are used to ship the products of the companies who own the lines. They are obviously limited in use because of their inflexibility. Pipeline shipping of crude oil costs less than rail transportation but more than water transportation.

Airlines

Although the newest of the major methods of transporting products, the airlines have undoubtedly done more than any other type of carrier to spearhead the systems approach and total cost concept in physical distribution. Obviously unable to compete on the basis of rates or ton-mile costs alone, the airlines had to demonstrate that the use of air freight would result in savings in other distribution elements (smaller inventory, faster delivery, fewer warehouses, less expensive packaging, etc.), which would tend to offset the higher air transportation costs.[17] Even though air freight rates have been reduced considerably over the years, they still average around 20 cents per ton-mile (for piston-engine planes), compared with 5 to 8 cents for trucks and 3 to 6 cents for railroads. Some newer jet cargo airplanes, however, can operate profitably at 10 cents per ton-mile.

Air express (door-to-door shipment) and air freight (terminal-to-terminal shipment) together account for only a small part of 1 per cent of total intercity freight shipments, although the tonnage has increased steadily and appreciably over the past several years. These total figures, however, conceal the wide use of air freight, and the important role it plays, in certain marketing situations. To an increasing extent, the use of air freight as a transportation method is being dictated by management's customer-oriented sales thinking, and not only by its orientation toward total cost savings.

The strongest selling point for air freight is its speed. This factor has enabled many industries and firms to expand their market limits and to open new markets. Products subject to physical deterioration (fresh-cut flowers, biologicals, fresh seafood, radioisotopes) can be delivered to many more markets by air than by any other carrier. Sears, Roebuck and Company, for example, has taken advantage of the speed of air freight to compete with firms which

[17] For a landmark study on this topic, see Howard T. Lewis and James W. Culliton, *The Role of Air Freight in Physical Distribution,* Harvard University, Graduate School of Business Administration, Cambridge, Mass., 1956. The Stanford Research Institute later conducted an extensive study, analyzing 261 case histories, to determine how and why industry is using air freight. See "Sky Shipping: New Horizons for Marketers," *Sales Management,* Nov. 15, 1963, p. 44; and Ellis D. Slater, "The Effect of Air Freight on Company Policies," *Michigan Business Review,* March, 1964, pp. 25–27.

have merchandise stocks much nearer to the market. Montgomery Ward has a warehouse in Denver, and yet one way in which Sears competes effectively in that market is by using daily air freight shipments from its Kansas City warehouse, about 600 miles away.

Speedy delivery can have beneficial effects on inventory control. Both the inventory size and the number of warehouse locations may be reduced; this means a cut in the inventory costs and a reduction in the risks from physical deterioration or obsolescence. By using air freight, stores which feature fashion apparel merchandise do not have to maintain such a large inventory, with its concurrent risk of fashion obsolescence.

Costly shutdowns in manufacturing operations can often be avoided by the air shipment of repair or replacement parts. Packaging costs can be reduced when products are shipped by air because less transit time is involved and there is less physical abuse than with other transportation methods.

Freight forwarders

The freight forwarder is a specialized marketing institution which has developed through the years to serve firms who ship in l.c.l. quantities. Freight forwarders do not own their own transportation equipment, but they do provide a valuable service in physical distribution. Their main function is to consolidate l.c.l. shipments or less-than-truckload shipments from several shippers into carload and truckload quantities. Their operating margin generally is the spread between c.l. and l.c.l. rates. That is, the shipper pays l.c.l. rates, and the freight forwarder transports the products at c.l. rates. The freight forwarder also picks up the merchandise at the shipper's place of business and arranges for delivery at the buyer's door. In addition to this pick-up and delivery service, an l.c.l. shipper enjoys all the advantages of speed and minimum handling associated with c.l. shipments, even though he pays l.c.l. rates. Also, freight forwarders provide the small shipper with traffic management services; they select the best transportation methods and routes. In recent years freight forwarders have become quite active in connection with air transportation.[18]

ORGANIZATIONAL RESPONSIBILITY FOR PHYSICAL DISTRIBUTION

A significant question which may be asked of American business is: Who is in charge of physical distribution? All too frequently in the past, the answer has been "no one." We observed earlier that activities within the system are often not integrated or coordinated and that managerial responsibility is consequently compartmentalized into units which may even have conflicting goals. It is encouraging to note, however, that there is a marked trend toward the establishment of a formal department responsible for the management of all

[18] See "Air Freight Forwarder Finds Ceiling Unlimited," *Business Week*, Oct. 16, 1965, p. 87.

physical distribution activities.[19] One study suggested that a prospective physical distribution department passes through four stages: (1) shipping—total organizational fragmentation; (2) traffic—a managerial specialist in transportation is used; (3) movement—the dawn of a systems viewpoint; and (4) physical distribution—the activities are planned and operated as a system in the full sense of the word.[20]

Assuming that a company has a physical distribution department, the next organizational question is: To whom should the head of this department report? At the risk of charges of "empire building by the marketing people," current enlightened managerial thinking suggests that physical distribution should be the responsibility of either the chief marketing executive or a separate department whose head reports directly to the president of the company. In any event, logistics management should be viewed by top management as one of its prime responsibilities.[21]

QUESTIONS AND PROBLEMS

1   In some companies, activities such as processing and shipping orders, maintaining an inventory control system, and locating warehouse stocks throughout the market are treated as separate, fragmented activities. What are some of the administrative and operational problems which are likely to occur in this type of arrangement?

2   "The goal of a modern physical distribution system in a firm should be to operate at the lowest possible *total* costs." Do you agree? Discuss.

3   Name some products for which the costs of physical distribution constitute at least one-half of the total price of the goods at the wholesale level. Can you suggest ways of decreasing the physical distribution costs of these products?

4   "Storage adds value to products in that it creates time utility. At the same time, the value of a product may be totally destroyed by storing it too long." Explain.

5   Explain how a marketing manager can use transportation and warehousing facilities to stabilize the prices of his products.

6   How is a middleman's management of his inventories related to the physical distribution system of a manufacturer who supplies this middleman?

[19] See Joel F. Olesky, "Distribution Comes of Age," *Dun's Review and Modern Industry*, January, 1965, p. 79; and H. Jay Bullen, "New Competitive Selling Weapon: Physical Distribution Management," *Sales Management*, May 7, 1965, p. 48. A 1963 study by *Transportation and Distribution Management* magazine, covering medium- and large-sized companies, indicated that 44 per cent had some type of distribution department and estimated that eventually some 60 per cent of American manufacturing concerns will have such a department.

[20] J. L. Heskett, "Ferment in Marketing's Oldest Area," *Journal of Marketing*, October, 1962, pp. 40–45; see also Robert E. Weigand, "The Management of Physical Distribution: A Dilemma," *Business Topics*, Summer, 1962, pp. 67–72.

[21] See, for example, Anthony E. Cascino, "Top Management Looks at Physical Distribution," in Peter D. Bennett (ed.), *Marketing and Economic Development*, American Marketing Association, Chicago, 1965, pp. 727–739.

7   "Inventory size will be smaller but transportation expenses will be larger if a manufacturer follows an inventory-location strategy of concentration rather than dispersion." Do you agree? Explain.

8   "The use of public warehouse facilities makes it possible for a manufacturer to bypass wholesalers in his channels of distribution." Explain.

9   If a public warehouse can provide so many wholesaling services, why have these warehouses not largely eliminated full-function wholesalers and manufacturers' sales branches?

10   What is the relationship between inventory management and the "economic order quantity" in production scheduling?

11   Referring to Table 16–1, how do you account for the substantial increases in share of intercity freight shipped by trucks, at the apparent expense of the railroads?

12   How are transportation decisions related to packaging policies?

13   Why are l.c.l. shipments so much slower and more costly than c.l. shipments?

14   What alternatives does a manufacturer have if he must ship in l.c.l. quantities, but the competitive price structure for his product is such that he cannot afford to pay the high l.c.l. freight rates?

15   Visit a local railroad freight office and find out what products in the region are shipped under some form of in-transit privilege.

16   As traffic manager of a large department store in the big city nearest your campus, you are asked to determine the best transportation method and route for the shipment of each of the following items to your store. In each case your store is to pay all freight charges. Unless specifically noted, there is no time urgency involved.
   a.   Fresh salmon from Seattle, Washington. Total shipment weighs 200 pounds.
   b.   An assortment of various types of large appliances from Evansville, Indiana. Total weight is 20,000 pounds.
   c.   A refill order of 200 dresses from New York City. This is a "hot" fashion item, so speed is of the essence.
   d.   Sheets, pillowcases, and towels from a mill in Alabama. Total weight is 100 pounds.
   e.   Ten sets of dining-room furniture from Grand Rapids, Michigan.

17   Under what conditions is a company apt to select air freight as its main method of transporting its finished goods?

18   "The head of the physical distribution department should report directly to the chief marketing executive." Do you agree? Discuss.

case 10. CROCKETT ELECTRIC COMPANY
Selection of channels of distribution

The vice-president in charge of production and engineering at the Crockett Electric Company saw an automatic garage-door opener at a home show and has become interested in the possibilities of adding a similar article to his company's line. He has approached the marketing department executives with the product idea, and they were interested enough to do some preliminary marketing research. Studies have shown that a large market potential exists and that only a minute part of this potential has been tapped. Many competitive models exist, but none has had any degree of market acceptance or success. In brief, here is a product with a terrific potential, but as yet no firm has been able to capitalize on these opportunities.

Crockett's engineers have now developed a patentable electronic door opener. The product is fairly simple. It consists of two units, one of which is to be installed inside the garage. The other is a portable unit which can be mounted in some convenient location within the car or placed in the glove compartment. The user simply pushes a button on the portable unit in the car to open or close the garage door. Once the car is in the garage, the door can also be closed by turning off the garage light. Additional automobile units can be purchased for families with more than one car. The entire product is transistorized. Crockett's model would retail for about $225, which is well within the range of competitive prices. The product can be installed easily and inexpensively by the homeowner, according to simple and clear instructions.

So far, one important product weakness has been discovered. The unit in one person's car sometimes opens garage doors in other homes having a similar product. This weakness would become increasingly critical as more units of the product were sold. The executives have horrible visions of what might happen in a row of suburban houses with all the garages equipped with Crockett door openers: one person driving down the street and pushing the button in his car unit might open all the garage doors in the block, one by one. The engineers are hard at work on this problem, and have just about perfected a mechanism which would make it possible to set different electronic signals for each door opener produced.

The Crockett Electric Company is a large Midwestern manufacturer of a wide line of industrial and consumer electrical products, including industrial switching and timing equipment, motors, radio and television components, and a line of small appliances sold under middlemen's brands. Annual sales are approximately $150 million. The company has its own sales force operating out of five regional offices (Chicago, New York, Atlanta, Dallas, and Los Angeles). Salesmen sell directly to large industrial users, to government agencies, and also to several types of industrial distributors.

Currently, the executives are trying to determine what channels to use for the door opener. Part of their indecision stems from the fact that they do not know whether they are dealing with an industrial or a consumer market. Mr. Shannon, the marketing vice-president, feels that the door opener is a consumer product. He is not, however, certain whether it should be sold through wholesalers and retailers of building materials, whether it should go through channels for home appliances, or whether it should be treated like power lawn mowers and other patio and garden equipment. Mr. Moyer, the sales manager, definitely feels that the door opener is an industrial product. He thinks that once a house is built and sold, the resident consumer will not add the door opener and that Crockett should reach the people who are building the homes. Consequently, he thinks that the product should be sold directly to architects and to building contractors engaged in large suburban housing developments. Mr. Moyer also feels that there is a substantial market among all sorts of industrial users, such as manufacturing plants, retail stores, gasoline service stations, automobile repair garages, parking garages, warehouses, and any other type of company with large overhead doors for loading docks.

A related question facing these executives is whether to use the company's present sales force and, if so, to what extent. The product itself presents no problems in this respect. The salesmen are ably qualified to sell it. None of the proposed channels, however, involves middlemen on whom the sales force is presently calling. Thus an entirely new customer list must be developed. Also, the salesmen would have only one product to sell to these newly added middlemen. It is questionable whether it would be profitable for Crockett's present salesmen to sell the door opener. The executives are considering the feasibility of using manufacturers' agents to reach the appropriate parties.

QUESTIONS

1   Do better market opportunities lie in treating the door opener as a consumer or an industrial product?
2   Which channels should be used to reach your recommended market?
3   Should the company use its present sales force to sell the door opener, should it establish a separate sales force, or should manufacturers' agents be used? Is there still another reasonable alternative here?
4   Should Crockett select one distributor in each geographic market and offer him an exclusive franchise?

case 11. FASHION-LINE LUGGAGE COMPANY

Adding new trade channels and increasing intensity of distribution

The Fashion-Line Luggage Company, with its home office and factory in a large Eastern city, is one of the nation's biggest manufacturers of a full line of men's and women's non-leather luggage products. In the past, the company used plastic or bass plywood for most of its luggage frames. Currently, the company is producing one line made from fiber glass and one made from magnesium. Frames for these lines are covered with plastic and lined with a high quality of rayon satin. The hardware is either brass or stainless steel.

The company uses national advertising extensively to promote its luggage as a high-quality fashion item. Illustrations in advertisements feature the company's products in settings such as resorts, airline terminals, and business offices. In the ads, the product is used by smart, well-dressed women and obviously successful business executives. The advantages of the slim-line design and the light weight are stressed. New models are brought out periodically but not annually.

Fashion-Line's products are distributed by the company's sixty-man sales force directly to leading department stores and luggage stores. While the company does not follow an exclusive distribution policy, its distribution is highly selective. For example, in a city with a population of 500,000, the company may sell to only five or six, or even fewer, retailers. The retailers are required to carry a rather extensive inventory of Fashion-Line's products and to maintain a good-sized display on the selling floor. The various articles in the product line carry retail prices ranging from $14.95 to $69.95. The retailer is allowed a 40 per cent margin on this price.

In the past, the company was a strong supporter of fair-trade pricing. This is a price policy whereby a manufacturer signs a contract with his retailers. The retailer agrees to sell at, or not below, the price stipulated by the manufacturer. The management still endorses the principle of fair-trade pricing but realizes that in many states the laws have been declared unconstitutional or rendered valueless by court decisions. Consequently, the firm now places a suggested retail price on a tag attached to each unit produced. Because the product is a good seller, is in great demand, and generally offers a valuable franchise, the manufacturer has been able to maintain its suggested prices at the retail level.

A few retailers who sought to cut the prices soon lost their franchises on the grounds that they did not properly handle, display, or sell the product. A few years ago, Fashion-Line broadened its distribution base by selling to two large trading-stamp firms who now offer the luggage as a premium in their stamp redemption catalogues. Samples of the products are prominently displayed in the stamp redemption centers maintained by the two companies.

At the present time, the executives are considering possibilities for substantially increasing the sales volume. Mr. Thompson, the president, feels that the company should sell through discount houses in large metropolitan markets. For years, several of these retailing distributors have wanted to carry Fashion-Line's products but have not been able to acquire a regular source of supply from which to purchase in large quantities. Products from two of Fashion-Line's major competitors have appeared to a growing extent in discount houses throughout the country. Of course, if Fashion-Line markets through discount houses, the company will not be able to maintain suggested retail prices on its products. Mr. Thompson is also concerned about the impact of discount-house sales on his present retailers.

Mr. Koll, the vice-president in charge of sales, believes it is a mistake to use discount houses as retail outlets. He fears that Fashion-Line will lose control over the retail distribution of its products. He also thinks that selling to discount houses will destroy, or at least run counter to, the high-quality and high-fashion image established through the years by the company's distribution and promotional programs. Instead, he recommends that Fashion-Line strive to increase the numbers of outlets of the type presently used. Instead of selling through only three to six retailers in a city of 500,000, for example, he thinks the company can handle as many as ten or twelve and still maintain control over price, display, inventory, and other conditions at the retail level. The company has few outlets in towns with populations under 25,000 or 30,000, and Mr. Koll suggests that hundreds of these communities offer real possibilities for at least one dealership.

QUESTIONS

1   Should the Fashion-Line Company sell to discount houses?

2   Should Mr. Koll's recommendation for additional selective retail outlets be adopted?

3   What other changes in the company's distribution system do you recommend in order to increase its sales volume substantially?

case 12. MIDWEST ENGINEERING CORPORATION

Changing channels of distribution for industrial products

In order that his company might continue to grow and to meet the competitive challenges in today's marketplace, Mr. Everett McGovney, the general sales manager of the Midwest Engineering Corporation, thinks that it might be necessary to change the channels of distribution which the company has been using for several years. The Midwest Engineering Corporation, located in Milwaukee, Wisconsin, manufactures and markets a line of soft drink dispensers for top-of-the-counter or under-the-counter installation. These dispensers are the type which mix concentrated syrup with precooled carbonated water, and are designed for operation by a personal attendant.

The basic product unit consists of a tank for the carbon dioxide (CO_2) gas cylinder and the dry refrigeration unit, a three- or four-flavor dispensing valve and head, and the necessary tubing, regulators, and fittings. A syrup tank is an optional but usually purchased accessory. The product line consists of seven models, each in a different size and design and each with different features intended for specific markets. For example, six different types of valve-dispenser heads are offered so that a customer can select the valve which best fits his locational needs. Attachments are available for making hot drinks or ice or for dispensing soda water or ice water (as well as the standard orange, cola, root-beer, and lemon-lime flavors). Most of the basic models are priced at $600 for a three-flavor unit and $675 for a four-flavor dispenser. Syrup tanks are an additional $22 to $28, depending upon their size.

For four of its models, the company markets the identical dispenser under two brands —the Cummings brand and the Mix-A-Soda name. The other three models are sold only under the Mix-A-Soda label. The Cummings-branded dispensers are sold exclusively to soft drink bottlers (Pepsi-Cola, 7-Up, Coca-Cola, etc.), and these products carry the trademark decorations and colors of the bottler's franchise. Mix-A-Soda dispensers are sold to independent soft drink equipment dealers and distributors, and the dispensers do not carry any franchise identification.

The company's products enjoy a very wide potential market. The soft drink bottlers themselves sell to a diversified list of users. In addition, the Mix-A-Soda models are ideal for drugstores, soda fountains, restaurants, bars, and any other place where soft drinks are dispensed over the counter by a personal attendant. The Midwest Engineering Corporation has one large model designed for volume locations such as stadiums, large drive-in restaurants, schools, and theaters.

To reach its market, the Midwest Engineering Corporation has a sales organization headed up by Mr. McGovney, the general sales manager. Reporting to him are four division managers whose territories blanket the United States, a product training manager, a national accounts manager, and the fourteen manufacturers' agents now used by the company. It is the division manager's responsibility to work with these manufacturers' agents and to direct their activities. These agents are used by the Midwest Engineering Corporation only to sell the Cummings dispensers directly and exclusively to soft drink bottlers. The agents, of course, also carry other companies' product lines marketed to the bottling industry. The Cummings line receives about 40 per cent of the agents' time. The agents are paid a commission of 6 per cent on the sales of all Cummings dispensers in their territories. They receive no allowance for expenses, guarantees, or advances of commissions from Midwest Engineering.

The division managers are also responsible for selling the Mix-A-Soda line directly to independent soft drink equipment dealers and distributors. Agents are not used in marketing the Mix-A-Soda brand, nor does the company have any salesmen, other than the four division managers. These managers are paid a salary plus all expenses, and they also receive a year-end bonus. Salaries plus bonus average about $10,500, and annual expenses average about $7,000 per manager.

The Midwest Engineering Corporation has enjoyed a satisfactory and constant rate of growth during the past six years. However, competition is increasing appreciably, and the high rate of annual sales increases which was experienced initially has now leveled off. Sales last year totaled $3.64 million, $2.24 million of which came from Cummings sales made by the manufacturers' agents, and $1.4 million from sales of the Mix-A-Soda brand. Selling expenses were 10.6 per cent of net sales volume. Annual net profit has been satisfactory.

At the present time, Mr. McGovney is considering the alternative of establishing a group of company salesmen and discontinuing the use of manufacturers' agents. He envisions a staff of ten men, plus a field sales manager. To initiate this program, three of the present division managers would become members of the field sales force, and the fourth division manager would be promoted to the position of field sales manager. Possibly some of the present manufacturers' representatives would be interested in working directly as company salesmen, but it is highly unlikely that more than one or two would be both interested in, and qualified for, the job. The remaining five or six salesmen who are required would be recruited from among men known in the bottling industry. If qualified men are not available, a company training program would be instituted to provide the required manpower.

From the increased sales volume which a company sales force is expected to produce, a more rewarding compensation plan could be instituted in order to induce present division managers and manufacturers' representatives to become field salesmen. For these experienced men, a compensation plan based on salary plus commission plus all expenses would provide a net income of $12,000 a year, plus all company fringe benefits such as insurance and pension plan. Inexperienced men could expect to net about $8,000 a year plus fringe benefits at the start.

Mr. McGovney realizes that sales returns in some territories may be sparse for awhile. He is so confident the plan will work, however, that he anticipates having smaller territories and a sales force of fifteen men (a 50 per cent increase) in four years. He points out that ten company salesmen spending 100 per cent of their time on Midwest products would be considerably more effective than fourteen representatives spending only 40 per cent of their time. Furthermore, a direct sales force would be more effective because its training, supervision, and motivation could be directed by company management. Also, comments from customers indicate that they prefer to do business directly with company salesmen rather than with manufacturers' agents. The majority of the Midwest Engineering Corporation's competitors are currently operating their own sales forces. Mr. McGovney would like to implement the change in the distribution structure immediately, before knowledge of the move can leak to the manufacturers' representatives and to the rest of the industry at large.

The advertising agency account executive, Mr. George Coolidge, who manages the Midwest Engineering Corporation's advertising program, thinks Mr. McGovney's plan is premature. Possibly in the future he would endorse it, but at the present time he believes the company is not big enough or strong enough to make the channel changes successfully. He urges that the company continue to use agents but work with them more effectively. He argues that Mr. McGovney is grossly underestimating the cost and difficulty of establishing and operating a company sales force, as well as the time required for such an undertaking. Furthermore, the manufacturers' representatives will no longer be active and strong supporters of Midwest's products; instead, they will turn into fierce and effective competitors.

Seeking a compromise alternative, Mr. Lee Allen, the production manager, proposes that the company phase into a direct sales-force distribution structure. This would be started by placing company salesmen in territories which had sufficient volume to support them. Manufacturers' agents would continue to be used in the remaining territories which now have less market potential. He argues that it would be difficult to change the company's distribution structure and marketing philosophy all at once. However, he is convinced that, with adequate planning and preparation, the changes could be accomplished successfully over a period of time.

QUESTIONS

1   Should the Midwest Engineering Corporation change its channels of distribution structure?

2   If so, should the company adopt Mr. McGovney's proposal for a company sales force?

case 13. RED FEATHER OIL COMPANY

Manufacturer-retailer relationships

Over a period of almost ten years, the market position of the Red Feather Oil Company has been deteriorating in its Omaha, Nebraska, sales district. The top marketing executives of Red Feather believe that a major factor accounting for this decline has been the ineffectiveness of the men who have been the district sales managers in Omaha. Three different men have held the position over the past eight years. None of the three has seemed able to stimulate Red Feather's service station managers effectively, to establish good working relationships with those dealers, or to stem the declining sales and profit position of the service stations in the district. Recently, Mr. Charles Rucker was appointed as the new district sales manager in Omaha, having been transferred from a similar position in Cincinnati. His assignment is to uncover the reasons for the poor performance of the Red

Feather stations in the Omaha district and to establish a program for improving dealer performance and manufacturer-dealer relationships.

The Red Feather Oil Company is one of the world's largest producers of crude oil and manufacturers of petrochemical products. Many of the company's chemicals and synthetic rubber products are marketed all over the United States as well as in several foreign countries. The domestic market for refined petroleum products covers thirty-five states, from the Atlantic Ocean to the Rocky Mountains. Gasoline is retailed through thousands of service stations, over half of which are owned and operated by independent managers.

Red Feather maintains forty service stations in the Omaha metropolitan area. These stations constitute only 1 per cent of the total Omaha market and, of course, are faced with severe competition. All forty are owned by the firm; that is, Red Feather purchased the property and financed the buildings and the major equipment. The company's investment varies with each individual station, but in general it is substantial. The firm's policy is to lease these individual outlets to dealers, who run them as their own business in accordance with very general standards and responsibilities as dictated by Red Feather. Each dealer is responsible for minor equipment and accessories that he needs to run the station. This constitutes an average investment of $6,000 to $10,000 for each service station manager. The Omaha office employs three salesmen to serve the stations in the district. These men make weekly calls and record fuel requirements; fuel is sold to the dealers on a consignment basis. The salesmen are also responsible for informing the dealers of local advertising efforts and for supplying them with promotional supplies and suggestions from headquarters. These salesmen serve as the communications link between the Omaha district office and the dealers.

Shortly after his appointment to his new position, Mr. Rucker began to study the Omaha situation by checking company records, by discussing district problems and past efforts with employees, and by visiting all the stations and dealers. He found that the situation was indeed serious, since ten of the forty service stations were lying idle, having been closed at some time during the past ten years. Since Red Feather owns these outlets, their closure constitutes a big expense. The industry-wide figure for obsolescence of service stations due to changing population and highways is about 5 per cent. Mr. Rucker discovered that none of these stations had become obsolete because of shifts in traffic patterns or population. Instead, their closure was traceable to other factors, ranging from general unprofitability and dealer incapability to serious financial problems.

The following list of five unsatisfactory conditions summarizes reasonably well the situation in the Omaha district:

1. Many of the stations are shabby-looking and run down, in comparison with those of competitors.

2. Dealers in many cases are offering poor service and following inadequate marketing policies, where such policies exist at all.

3. Dealers are often unable to meet existing debts on time and are generally in poor financial shape.

4. Dealers feel that they are fighting the company; there exists an unsatisfactory relationship between them and Red Feather.

5. Red Feather's well-equipped dealer school, located in the Omaha office, is not being used.

Mr. Rucker has concluded that he should concentrate his attention on three main problem areas. The first involves the methods being used to select managers to run the service stations. In the past, just about anyone who had the necessary capital and some experience was given a dealership. Rucker knows that it is difficult to find good dealers, especially men who have both the capability and the capital, but he believes that an effort could be made to improve their quality. Red Feather recruits most of its dealers through leads from salesmen and present dealers. This, incidentally, is a general industry practice.

Second, Mr. Rucker feels that he must find a way to improve the overall financial status of the dealers. While choosing better-qualified men for dealerships would undoubtedly help the situation, this alone would not completely solve the problem. He also contends that the physical condition of the stations will improve when dealers' financial problems are solved. The third problem is the general lack of communication between the dealers and the Omaha district office. Mr. Rucker believes that somehow the dealers should be made to feel that they are a part of the company, and that the relationship between them and the company must and could be improved.

QUESTIONS

1. What policies or procedures should the company adopt in order to attract highly qualified station managers?

2. How can the district sales office help the dealers with their financial and general management problems?

3. What should Mr. Rucker do in order to develop a better relationship between the Red Feather Oil Company and its dealers in the Omaha district?

PART FIVE

17

PRICE
AND
PRICING
OBJECTIVES

"How much do you think we ought to sell it for?" This is a question frequently asked by executives who have the responsibility for pricing the products or services they are marketing. The question would be more accurately worded if they asked, "How much do you think we can get for this item?" or "How much should we ask for it?" The question would then be in accord with the generalization that *prices are always on trial*. No price should ever be considered permanent. In fact, far from being final, a price is simply an offer, a suggestion, or an experiment to test the pulse of the market. If the customers accept the offer, that is fine. If they reject it, the price usually will be changed as quickly as possible, or the product may even be withdrawn from the market. The volatility of a company's pricing structure calls for the utmost in executive capability in most firms. Before being concerned with actual price determination, however, an executive should understand the meaning and importance of pricing, and he should determine what his pricing goals are.

IMPORTANCE OF PRICE

Pricing is considered by many the key activity within the capitalistic system of free enterprise. Price becomes a hub around which the system revolves; it is the balance wheel which keeps the system operating on an even keel. Imperfections in pricing are an indication of imperfections in the system.

The market price of a product influences wages, rent, interest, and profits. That is, the price of a product influences the income earned by, or the price paid for, the factors of production—labor, land, capital, and entrepreneurship. In this way, price becomes a basic regulator of the entire economic system because it influences the allocation of these resources. High wages attract labor, high interest rates attract capital, and so on. Conversely, low wages, low rent, or low profits reduce the availability of labor, land, and risk takers.

Criticism of the American system of reasonably free enterprise and the public's demand for further restraints on the system are often triggered by, or based on, a reaction to price or pricing policy.

Certainly a company's pricing structure, more than any other segment of the marketing program, is influenced by state and Federal legislation. We have restraining laws affecting product policies (packaging, labeling), distribution policies, and promotional activities, but the key legislative regulations in marketing apply to pricing. Because of these legal considerations, executives are hesitant to disclose information about their companies' pricing structures, policies, and practices. This hesitancy adds to the difficulty of acquiring the empirical data so badly needed if businessmen are to learn more about pricing and price determination.

The price of a product or service is a major determinant of the market demand for the item. Price will affect the firm's competitive position and its share of the market. As a result, price has a considerable bearing on the company's revenue and net profit. The revenue is equal to unit price times the volume of units sold. The volume itself, that is, the *quantitative* measure of demand, is affected by the price. The profit is equal to revenue minus costs. To some extent, costs are a function of volume, and costs themselves are measured by their price. Price affects the market segment that will be reached by a firm. Because a person's income so often determines his other socio-economic characteristics, the price may influence the *qualitative* nature of the company's market as well as its quantitative limits.

The price of a product also affects the firm's marketing program. In product planning, for example, if management wants to improve the quality of its product or add differentiating features, this decision can be implemented only if the market will accept a price high enough to cover the costs of these changes. In the channels of distribution, a properly priced product not only helps to attract the general types of middlemen needed, but it can also attract desirable individual wholesalers and retailers. The pricing structure will determine whether the manufacturer or his retailers will be expected to finance the bulk of the promotional program. Unless a price can be set high enough to pay for the advertising or personal selling, these efforts will have to be curtailed or omitted.

At the same time, there are usually countervailing forces limiting the importance of pricing in a company's marketing program. Differentiated product features, a persuasive advertising campaign, or a strong brand preference may be more important to a consumer than price. Thus, these forces may engender rigidities or a "stickiness" in the pricing mechanism, so that it does not respond so quickly and precisely to changes in demand or supply. Thus, the traditional, theoretical role of price as an allocator of scarce resources is modified somewhat in today's economic system.

To put the role of pricing in a company's marketing program in its proper perspective, then, let us say this—price is important, but not all-important, in explaining marketing strategy and marketing success. One study among manufacturing companies, for example, identified product-related activities and sales effort as the most important factors contributing to marketing success in a firm; one-half of the respondents did not even list price as one of the top five factors.[1] Three situations may account for this relatively low ranking of pricing: (1) Because supply generally exceeds demand, most sellers must be highly competitive (or collusive) in their pricing; (2) today's relatively affluent consumer is interested in more than just price; and (3) a seller may achieve some pricing freedom through successful product differentiation.

MEANING OF PRICE

Undoubtedly many of the difficulties associated with price determination and price policies start with the rather simple fact that often we do not really know what we are talking about. That is, we do not know the meaning of the word "price," even though it is true that the concept is quite easy to define in familiar terms.

In economic theory, we learn that price, value, and utility are related concepts. Utility is the attribute of an item that makes it capable of want satisfaction. Value is the quantitative expression of the power a product has to attract other products in exchange. We may say the value of a certain hat is three baseball bats, a box of fancy red Delicious apples, or 30 gallons of gasoline. Because our economy is not geared to a slow, ponderous barter system, we use money as a common denominator of value and use the term "price" to describe the money value of an item. Price is value expressed in

[1] Jon G. Udell, "How Important Is Pricing in Competitive Strategy?" *Journal of Marketing,* January, 1944, pp. 44–48. In another study, the presidents of some four hundred large corporations reported that personal selling was the most important factor in a company's marketing mix; see "Top Executives Rank Salesmanship Tops, Study Shows," *Sales Management,* Mar. 18, 1966, p. 120.

terms of dollars and cents, or whatever the monetary medium may be in the country where the exchange occurs.

Practical problems connected with a definition of price arise, however, when we try to state simply what the price of a pint of fresh strawberries or an office desk is. Harry paid 30 cents for a pint of strawberries, while Bill paid only 10 cents and was also allowed to eat all the strawberries he wanted at the seller's location; the 10-cent price was what he paid for the strawberries he took home with him. The price quoted to Harry for an office desk was $325, while Bill paid only $175.

At first glance it looks as if Bill got the better deal in each of these examples. Yet when we get all the facts we may change our opinion. Harry bought his strawberries at the local supermarket. Bill responded to a strawberry grower's advertisement which stated that if one came out to the farm and picked the berries himself, they would cost 10 cents a box. The grower furnished the pint-sized boxes and allowed Bill to eat all he wanted while he was berry picking. Harry's desk was delivered to his office, he had a year to pay for it, and it was all beautifully finished. Bill bought a partially assembled job with no finish on it. (He was a do-it-yourself fan.) He had to assemble the drawers and legs and then painstakingly stain, varnish, and hand-rub the entire desk. He arranged for the delivery himself, and he paid cash in full at time of purchase. Now let us ask the question of who paid the higher price in each case. The answer is not so easy as it seemed at first glance.

These examples illustrate how difficult it is to define price in an everyday business situation. Many variables are involved. The definition hinges around the problem of determining exactly what it is that a person is buying. This relates to the problem posed in Chapter 8, that of trying to define a product. In pricing we must consider more than the physical product alone. A seller usually is pricing a combination of the physical product plus several other services and want-satisfying benefits. Sometimes it is difficult even to define the price of the physical product alone. On one model of automobile a stated price may include radio, heater, power steering, and power brakes. For another model of the same make of car these four items may be priced separately. In another situation the price may be defined as that which the buyer pays or the seller nets, with the difference being the freight charges. Some sellers quote a price that includes various services (alterations, installation, credit, delivery), while others price these individual services separately. Where a trade-in is involved, price will be stated in terms of money plus a product.

In the above examples it was implicitly assumed that the transaction involved an ultimate consumer or industrial user. The same types of problems exist, however, when we attempt to define price in transactions between producers and middlemen.

In summary, price is the amount of money (plus possibly some goods) which is needed to acquire in exchange some combined assortment of a product and its accompanying services. Obviously there is a large number of possible combinations of a finished or partially complete product and the various services which may accompany it.

PRICING OBJECTIVES

We have observed that before a company can do a marketing job properly, management needs a goal. Pricing is no exception. Management should decide upon the objectives of pricing before determining the price itself. Very few firms, however, consciously establish pricing objectives or clearly state their specific price policies; very, very few have written statements of their pricing goals.

We can theorize on pricing objectives within a company, and we can draw conclusions from personal observation, but empirical data are hard to come by. One landmark study of pricing has been made. In the 1950s The Brookings Institution completed a study to determine the price policies and the methods of price determination used by a representative group of twenty large firms. Part of the study was devoted to pricing goals. Dr. A. D. H. Kaplan had the major responsibility for the study and the final published report.[2] As an outgrowth of the Brookings Institution study, Prof. Robert F. Lanzillotti published a helpful article devoted entirely to the pricing objectives of the twenty firms.[3] While the scope of the study was limited to large companies, many of the findings are applicable to smaller firms. Much of the material in this chapter is drawn from the original study and the subsequent article.

Even when pricing goals are stated by a company, it should be recognized that they may be only a rationalization or a pious hope. The key point of interest is the extent to which the company actually can implement the objectives. Obviously they are more easily realized in a large, dominant firm than in a small one.

Executives hesitate to talk or write about pricing, not only because they fear government action under pricing laws, but also because the information will benefit competitors. Consequently, they state their goals in terms which are socially acceptable. In the Brookings Institution study, in almost no instance did a firm state that its goal was to maximize profits by charging all that traffic would bear over the long run. Many firms had both principal and collateral goals. Table 17–1 summarizes the pricing goals of the twenty companies along with data on rate of return on investment and average share of market.

The main goals in pricing may be classified as follows:

1. Achieve target return on investment or on net sales.
2. Stabilize prices.
3. Maintain or improve a target share of the market.

[2] A. D. H. Kaplan, Joel B. Dirlam, and Robert F. Lanzillotti, *Pricing in Big Business*, The Brookings Institution, Washington, D.C., 1958.

[3] Robert F. Lanzillotti, "Pricing Objectives in Large Companies," *American Economic Review*, December, 1958, pp. 921–940.

4. Meet, follow, or prevent competition.

5. Maximize profits.

The first four goals were cited most often by the companies included in the Brookings Institution study. Any of the five may be applicable to small firms, but the third, fourth, and fifth are easiest for a small business to aim for.

Achieve target return on investment or net sales

Many firms seek to achieve a certain percentage return on investment or on net sales. The return on investment was the goal most frequently mentioned by the subjects of the Brookings Institution study. Target-return pricing may be defined as building a price structure designed to provide enough return on capital used for specific products, groups of products, or divisions so that the sales revenue will yield a predetermined average return for the entire company. Target return may be a short-run (one year) or a long-run goal; it is mostly the latter. If an estimate is made of standard volume expected over the long run, fluctuations will occur in short-run volume, but they will average out.

Many retailers and wholesalers use target return on net sales as a pricing objective for short-run periods. They set a percentage markup on sales which is large enough to cover anticipated operating costs plus a desired profit for the year. In such cases the *percentage* of profit may remain constant, but the *dollar* profit will vary according to the number of units sold.

According to the Brookings Institution study, target return on investment was typically selected as a goal only when one or both of two conditions were present. First, ordinarily the firms were leaders in their industry, or they sold in protected markets. For example, target return on investment was a stated goal of General Motors, International Harvester, Aluminum Corporation of America, the DuPont Company, Standard Oil Company of New Jersey, Johns-Manville Corporation, and Union Carbide Corporation. Second, this goal was typical in connection with new and unique products and for low-unit-price, high-volume, standardized items. The length of time over which the target is to be reached varies among companies but tends to be shorter for new products than for established products. This is because management wishes to recoup research and development costs as soon as possible. Variations exist in the rigidity with which companies adhere to the goal of target return. In industries characterized by widely fluctuating prices, target return often serves only as a bench mark.

Table 17–1 shows specific target return percentages stated by some firms; other companies considered target return a general goal but gave no specific percentages. This table also shows the average and range of return on investment actually earned after taxes over the nine-year period from 1947 to 1955. In several cases—General Motors, General Electric, and United States Steel—the actual returns exceed the goal. There are at least three explanations for this discrepancy. First, the targets may have been minimum ones. Second, the period from 1947 to 1955 was an unusually prosperous one. Finally, pricing on a historical cost basis does not provide adequate profit to expand or replace present capital.

Some of the reasons most frequently stated by companies for selecting a particular level of return were as follows:

1. It is a fair or reasonable rate. The concept of "fair and reasonable" is important to these companies because most of them are very much in the public eye. Their pricing structure is of great interest to the Antitrust Division of the Justice Department, the labor unions, and the public in general. To avoid charges of monopoly or restraint of trade, they must set "fair and reasonable" prices.

2. It is traditional in the industry.

3. Management wants to reach or improve a corporation's average return over a recent period.

4. It was what the company felt it could get in the long run.

The Brookings Institution study discovered a trend toward the adoption of some form of target return as a pricing objective either for particular products or for the entire company. Some of the major reasons for this trend are:

1. An increasing awareness of the interrelationship of profit, capital, and investment, and the importance of planning and budgeting for this triumvirate.

2. The desire for a common basis for evaluating performance of products and divisions in the company.

3. The fact that cost-plus government contracts focus attention on rate of return.

4. The tendency to copy successful large firms which have been using target return as a pricing goal for some time.

Stabilize prices

Another major pricing objective of some enterprises is to stabilize prices. In some degree this goal is a corollary to that of a target return on investment. That is, price stability is one approach to a target return.

The goal of stabilizing prices is often found in industries that have a leader. Usually the goal of the price leader is to stabilize prices. In industries where demand can fluctuate frequently and sometimes violently, large companies, especially, will try to maintain stability and steadiness in their pricing. In the Brookings Institution study, United States Steel and the Kennecott Copper Corporation were pointed out as two firms which apparently sought this goal, but often with considerably less than total success. The American Can Company, The Aluminum Corporation of America, and some of the chemical companies seemed to have achieved a greater degree of price

table 17-1

Pricing goals of twenty large industrial corporations

Company	Principal pricing goal	Collateral pricing goals	Rate of return on investment (after taxes) 1947–1955[a]		Average market share[b]
			Ave.	Range	
Alcoa	20% on investment (before taxes); higher on new products (about 10% effective rate after taxes)	1. "Promotive" policy on new products 2. Price stabilization	13.8	7.8–18.7	Pig and ingot, 37%; sheet, 46%; other fabrications, 62%[c]
American Can	Maintaining market share	1. "Meeting competition" (using cost of substitute product to determine price) 2. Price stabilization	11.6	9.6–14.7	Approx. 55% of all types of cans[d]
A & P	Increasing market share	"General promotive" (low-margin policy)	13.0	9.7–18.8	n.a.
Du Pont	Target return on investment—no specific figure given	1. Charging what traffic will bear over long run 2. Maximum return for new products — "life cycle" pricing	25.9	19.6–34.1	n.a.
Esso (Standard Oil of N.J.)	"Fair-return" target—no specific figure given	1. Maintaining market share 2. Price stabilization	16.0	12.0–18.9	n.a.
General Electric	20% on investment (after taxes); 7% on sales (after taxes)	1. Promotive policy on new products 2. Price stabilization on nationally advertised products	21.4	18.4–26.6	[e]

Company	Principal pricing goal	Collateral pricing goals			Market-share goal or other
General Foods	33⅓% gross margin: ("⅓ to make, ⅓ to sell, and ⅓ for profit"); expectation of realizing target only on new products	1. Full line of food products and novelties 2. Maintaining market share	12.2	8.9–15.7	n.a.
General Motors	20% on investment (after taxes)	Maintaining market share	26.0	19.9–37.0	50% of passenger automobiles[f]
Goodyear	"Meeting competitors"	1. Maintaining "position" 2. Price stabilization	13.3	9.2–16.1	n.a.
Gulf	Following price of most important marketer in each area	1. Maintaining market share 2. Price stabilization	12.6	10.7–16.7	n.a.
International Harvester	10% on investment (after taxes)	Market share: ceiling of "less than a dominant share of any market"	8.9	4.9–11.9	Farm tractors, 28–30%; combines, cornpickers, tractor plows, cultivators, mowers, 20–30%; cotton pickers, 65%; light and light-heavy trucks, 5–18%; medium-heavy to heavy-heavy, 12–30%
Johns-Manville	Return on investment greater than last 15-year average (about 15% after taxes); higher target for new products	1. Market share not greater than 20% 2. Stabilization of prices	14.9	10.7–19.6	n.a.
Kennecott	Stabilization of prices		16.0	9.3–20.9	n.a.
Kroger	Maintaining market share	Target return of 20% on investment before taxes[g]	12.1	9.7–16.1	n.a.
National Steel	Matching the market— price follower	Increasing market share	12.1	7.0–17.4	5%

table 17-1—Continued

Company	Principal pricing goal	Collateral pricing goals	Rate of return on investment (after taxes) 1947–1955[a]		Average market share[b]
			Ave.	Range	
Sears, Roebuck	Increasing market share (8–10% regarded as satisfactory share)	1. Realization of traditional return on investment of 10–15% (after taxes) 2. General promotive (low-margin) policy	5.4	1.6–10.7	5–10% average (twice as large a share in hard goods as in soft goods)
Standard Oil (Indiana)	Maintaining market share	1. Stabilizing prices 2. Target return on investment (non specified)	10.4	7.9–14.4	n.a.
Swift	Maintaining market share in livestock buying and meat-packing		6.9	3.9–11.1	Approximately 10% nationally[h]
Union Carbide	Target return on investment[i]	Promotive policy on new products; "life cycle" pricing on chemicals generally	19.2	13.5–24.3	[j]
U.S. Steel	8% on investment (after taxes)	1. Target market share of 30% 2. Stable price 3. Stable margin	10.3	7.6–14.8	Ingots and steel, 30%; blast furnaces, 34%; finished hot-rolled products, 35%; other steel mill products, 37%[k]

NOTE: n.a.—not available.

ᵃ Federal Trade Commission, *Rates of Return (after Taxes) for Identical Companies in Selected Manufacturing Industries, 1940, 1947–1955*, Washington (1957), pp. 28–30, except for the following companies, whose rates were computed by the methods outlined in the Commission Report: A & P; General Foods; Gulf; International Harvester; Kroger; National Steel; Sears, Roebuck; and Swift.

ᵇ As of 1955, unless otherwise indicated. Source of data is company mentioned unless noted otherwise.

ᶜ *U.S. v. Alcoa et al.*, "Stipulation Concerning Extension of Tables III–X," dated May 31, 1956, U.S. District Court for the Southern District of New York.

ᵈ As of 1939, U.S. Department of Justice, *Western Steel Plants and the Tin Plate Industry*, 79th Cong., 1st Sess., Doc. No. 95, p. 1.

ᵉ The company states that on the average it aims at not more than 22 to 25 per cent of any given market. Percentages for individual markets or products were not made available, but it is estimated that in some markets, e.g., electrical turbines, General Electric has 60 per cent of the total market. Cf. Standard and Poor's, *Industry Surveys*, "Electrical-Electronic—Basic Analysis," Aug. 9, 1956, p. E 21.

ᶠ Federal Trade Commission, *Industrial Concentration and Product Diversification in the 1,000 Largest Manufacturing Companies: 1950*, Washington, January, 1957, p. 113.

ᵍ Target return on investment evidently characterizes company policy as much as target market share. In making investment decisions, the company is quoted as follows: "The Kroger Company normally expected a return on investment of at least 20% before taxes." See McNair, Burnham, and Hersum, *Cases in Retail Management*, McGraw-Hill Book Company, Inc., New York, 1957, pp. 205ff.

ʰ This represents the average share of total industry shipments of the four largest firms in 1954. Cf. *Concentration in American Industry*, Report of Subcommittee on the Judiciary, U.S. Senate, 85th Cong., 1st Sess., Washington, 1957, p. 315.

ⁱ In discussions with management officials, various profit-return figures were mentioned, with considerable variation among divisions of the company. No official profit target percentage was given, but the author estimates the *average* profit objective for the corporation to be approximately 35 per cent before taxes, or an effective rate after taxes of about 18 per cent.

ʲ Chemicals account for 30 per cent of Carbide's sales, most of which are petrochemicals, a field that the company opened thirty years ago and still dominates; plastics account for 18 per cent—the company sells 40 per cent of the two most important plastics (vinyl and polyethylene); alloys and metals account for 26 per cent of sales—top United States supplier of ferroalloys (e.g., chrome, silicon, manganese), and the biggest United States titanium producer; gases account for 14 per cent of sales—estimated to sell 50 per cent of oxygen in the United States; carbon, electrodes, and batteries account for 12 per cent of sales—leading United States producer of electrodes, refractory carbon, and flashlights and batteries; and miscellaneous—leading operator of atomic energy plants, a leading producer of uranium, the largest United States producer of tungsten, and a major supplier of vanadium. Cf. "Union Carbide Enriches the Formula" *Fortune*, February, 1957, pp. 123ff.; Standard and Poor's *Industry Surveys*, "Chemicals—Basic Analysis," December 20, 1956, p. C 44; and "Annual Report for 1955 of the Union Carbide and Carbon Corporation."

ᵏ The range of the corporation's capacity as a percentage of total industry capacity varies from 15 to 54 per cent, as of January, 1957. For more detail see *Administered Prices: Hearings Before the Subcommittee on Antitrust and Monopoly of the Senate Committee on the Judiciary*, 85th Cong., 1st Sess., pt. 2, *Steel*, Washington, 1958, pp. 335–336.

SOURCE: Robert F. Lanzillotti, "Pricing Objectives in Large Companies," *American Economic Review*, December, 1958, pp. 924–927.

stability. Price leadership within an industry may shift; for example, in the aluminum industry it is apparent that since the end of World War II, Alcoa's strength as a price leader has declined as Reynolds and Kaiser aluminum companies have grown in size.

Price leadership does not necessarily mean that the goal of stability is reached by having all firms in the industry charge the same price as that set by the leader. Price leadership means only that some regular relationship exists between the leader's prices and those charged by other firms. Some companies may regularly sell at a level above or below that set by the leader. In a given geographic market, "minor" oil companies frequently price their gasoline at 1 or 2 cents a gallon under the level charged by the "majors."

Companies seeking stability in their pricing are very anxious to avert price wars, even when demand is declining. Furthermore, if small firms cut prices or deviate too much from the established relationship with the price leader, the leader may step in with a temporary but sharp price cut in order to get the recalcitrants back in line. Price leaders increasingly are taking a long-run point of view in achieving stability. Their goal, in a sense, is a case of "live and let live." The companies are willing to forgo maximizing profits in times of prosperity or short supply if they have the opportunity to earn a reasonable profit during less prosperous periods.

Many retailers and manufacturers of consumer products have attempted to stabilize prices throughout a market by resorting to suggested resale prices or to out-and-out resale price maintenance supported by law.

Maintain or improve target share of market

In some companies, both large and small, the major pricing objective is to maintain or increase the share of the market held by the firm. One factor that makes market share a desirable or workable goal is that a company can usually determine what share of the market it enjoys. In some respects, market share is a better indicator of corporate health than target return on investment, especially in times of prosperity and increasing markets. A firm might be earning what management considers a reasonable return, but what is "reasonable" may be based on a market of some years ago. Unless management keeps fully abreast of conditions in an expanding market, this "reasonable" profit may be too small; the company may be getting a decreasing share of the market. By making market share a pricing objective, and thus focusing attention on it, the company is less apt unknowingly to lose its former market position.

In the Brookings Institution study of goals, market share seemed to be almost as important as a target return on investment. A & P, for example, constantly seeks to increase its share of the market through continuous low pricing. Sears, Roebuck and Company states that its objective is to realize its traditional return on investment of 10 to 15 per cent after taxes, but the company consciously seeks to achieve a satisfactory share of the market for its various product lines. Although Sears states no fixed percentage of market as a goal, management feels it is doing a successful job when its market share reaches 8 to 10 per cent. In the study, it was not usually possible to compare target share of the market with the actual share realized by the companies. Either data were lacking or management hesitated to disclose its target share percentages.

Large firms may try to limit their share of the market for one reason or another. In some cases they fear government intervention or restraint if they get too large. General Motors, with approximately 50 per cent of the automobile market, has been in this situation for years. Certainly some adjustments are needed either in a company or in an economic system when companies must consciously hesitate to do the most complete, aggressive, and consumer-satisfying marketing job of which they are capable. Some companies —General Electric and Johns-Manville, for example—prefer to have a *relatively* small market share, say, 20 per cent rather than 50 per cent, because they would rather work to expand a smaller share than to defend a larger share.

Meet or prevent competition

Countless firms, regardless of size, consciously price their products to meet, follow, or sometimes even prevent competition. When a company seeks simply through trial and error to find a price at which its output can be sold, we can almost say that it has no pricing objective. At least it has no control over the goal and the means used to reach it.

Large rubber companies, such as Goodyear Tire and Rubber Company, generally feel that they can exercise very little influence over the market-determined price. In an industry where there is a price leader and where the product is highly standardized, most firms have a "follow-the-leader" policy. National Steel Corporation and the Kroger Company pursue this policy as a rule. Gasoline companies profess that they simply set their prices to meet competition, particularly during a price war. The major firms usually wait until they have proof that the price in a market has broken. Then they cut their prices in order to meet the competition.

Some firms consciously price to prevent competition. Normally this goal or practice is not publicly admitted, but it has been brought to light in court cases involving manufacturers and retailers in the food field. When introducing a new product, a company will frequently set a low price in order to discourage competition. Usually this policy is unsuccessful. If the new item is popular enough, other producers will be attracted into the field regardless of the pricing policy of the innovator.

Maximize profits

The pricing objective of making as much money as possible is probably followed by a larger total number of companies than any other policy yet mentioned. Even businesses which price to meet competition often do so because that is the best way to maximize profits.

The trouble with this goal is that the term "profit maximization" has an ugly connotation. It is connected in the public mind with profiteering, high prices, and monopoly. In economic theory or business practice, however, there is nothing wrong with profit maximization. Theoretically, if profits become unduly high because supply is short in relation to demand, new capital will be attracted into a field to better balance demand and supply. In the marketplace, it is difficult to find many situations where a monopolistic situation has existed over an extended period of time. Substitute products are available, purchases are postponable, or competition increases, and prices are thus kept at a reasonable level. Where prices may be unduly high and entry into the field is severely limited, public outrage soon balances the scales. If market conditions and public opinion do not do the job directly, government restraints which represent the feeling of the public will soon bring about moderation.

A profit maximization policy is apt to be far more beneficial to a company and to the public if practiced over the long run rather than when a short-run point of view is taken. Pricing by companies who cannot see beyond the end of their next month's profit and loss statement often results in repercussions which may be extremely detrimental to the firms. Practiced over the long run, profit maximization should result in a socially desirable allocation of resources. Efficient firms are rewarded and inefficient firms disappear. Profits attract new capital into a field. Prices are kept at a reasonable level, and supply is sufficient to satisfy market demands.

To maximize profits over the long run, firms may have to accept short-run losses. A firm entering a new geographic market or introducing a new product frequently finds it advantageous to use relatively low prices in order to build a large clientele. Such companies often do not expect to show a profit for the first few years, but they are laying a solid foundation for adequate profits over the long run.

If profit maximization is selected as the pricing goal, it should be viewed with respect to the company's entire marketing program. The goal should be to maximize profits on total output rather than on each single item. A manufacturer may maximize total profits by practically giving away some articles which will attract the buyer's attention or will stimulate sales of other goods. Through its sponsored broadcasts and telecasts of athletic events, the Gillette Company frequently promotes razors at very low, profitless prices. Management hopes that once a customer acquires a Gillette razor, he will become a long-term profitable customer for Gillette blades. In this way the company maximizes its profits in total but not on each product in its line. A retailer often finds the best way to maximize profits over his entire store is to offer well-known items as "leaders." They are sold at a very small profit or even at a loss, but they attract so many customers to the store—customers who stay to buy other items—that the overall profit picture of the store is enhanced considerably.

The first step in establishing a price system is consciously to formulate an objective and state it clearly in writing. Once the pricing objective is agreed upon, the executives can move to the heart of price management—the actual determination of the base price.

QUESTIONS AND PROBLEMS

1   Why would management in a labor union be interested in the prices on products sold by a firm which employs the union's members?

2   Two students paid 69 cents for identical tubes of toothpaste at a leading department store. Yet one student complained that he paid a much higher price than the other. What might be the basis for this complaint?

3   Explain how two nonresident students may each pay $1,100 a year for out-of-state tuition and fees at a large Western university, and yet someone can claim that the two students in no way paid the same price for a college education.

4   "Watching television commercials is too high a *price* to pay to see a baseball game." "Having to put up with Mr. ——— (a news analyst with a syndicated column in many newspapers) is part of the high *price* we pay for freedom of the press." Are these correct interpretations of the concept of price?

5   Which of the five general pricing objectives discussed in this chapter is socially the most desirable?

6   Are the top executives in the finance, marketing, and production departments all likely to vote for the same pricing objective in a firm? In what respects might these three executives prefer different objectives?

7   In Table 17–1, which companies stated target return as their principal pricing goal? Which of these firms exceeded the target? How do you account for the excess? Are these monopolistic companies?

8   Explain how the chosen pricing objective may influence a firm's promotional program. Which goal will involve the largest, most aggressive promotional campaign?

9   "The goal of price stabilization is marked by nonaggressive marketing strategies and is usually found only in mature companies." Discuss.

10   Are the principal and collateral pricing goals compatible in each of the following companies? (Refer to Table 17–1.)
     a.   The American Can Company
     b.   The Gulf Oil Company
     c.   The National Steel Company

11   What conditions seem to be characteristic of the large companies listed in Table 17–1 which stated that price stabilization was a pricing goal?

12   Evaluate target return on investment or net sales as a pricing goal for a manufacturer. Consider the merits and limitations from both a business-competitive and a social point of view.

13   What marketing conditions might logically lead a company to set "meeting competition" as a pricing objective?

14   Is profit maximization compatible with each of the other major pricing goals?

15   "Profit maximization is an antisocial pricing goal." Discuss.

18

PRICE
DETERMINATION
IN PRACTICE

It is now time to suggest a procedure which will result in the establishment of a specific price in a practical business situation. No single procedure is used by all firms. One critical reason for the lack of exact pricing models or formulas is the lack of sufficiently detailed information on costs at various volumes and on demand at various prices.

PROCEDURE FOR PRICE DETERMINATION

The price determination procedure used here can be divided into six steps:[1]

[1] Another approach suggested by a careful student of pricing was built on the philosophy that price determination is best accomplished by developing a long-run, policy-oriented approach to price. He suggested a sequential, multiple-stage, six-step approach: (1) selecting market target, (2) choosing a brand image, (3) composing a marketing mix, (4) selecting a pricing policy, (5) determining a pricing strategy, and (6) arriving at a specific price. In this approach it is important that the se-

1. Estimate the demand for the product.
2. Anticipate the competitive reaction.
3. Establish the expected share of market.
4. Select the price strategy to be used to reach the market target.
5. Consider company policies regarding products, channels, and promotion.
6. Select the specific price.

At this point we are concerned with determining only the basic or list price of the product or service. Later we shall deal with specific policies regarding discounts, freight allowances, price lines, and other factors which may somewhat alter this basic price. Ordinarily the original price setter is a producer, although sometimes a large middleman sets or strongly influences the original price.

The same general steps are followed in pricing a product, whether it is a new article or an established one. Pricing an established product often offers very little challenge because the exact price or a very narrow range of prices may be dictated by the market. At the same time, some stages in the pricing procedure are particularly important and difficult for a new article. Consequently, any special conditions involved in pricing new products will be woven into the discussion where appropriate.[2]

Estimate demand for product

The first step in pricing a product is to estimate the total demand for the item. This is easier to do for an established product than for a new one. The seller is not certain that a new product will have any demand at all. Two practical steps in demand estimation are, first, to determine if there is a price which the market expects, and second, to estimate the sales volume at different prices.

The "expected" price   The expected price for a product is the price at which customers consciously or unconsciously value the product; it is what they think the product is worth. Often, rather than being one specific dollar

---

quence be followed because each stage simplifies decision making in the following one, narrows the range of price, and reduces the likelihood of error. Reasonable alternatives are reduced in number as management progresses through the stages. See Alfred R. Oxenfeldt, "Multi-stage Approach to Pricing," *Harvard Business Review*, July–August, 1960, pp. 125–133. For another procedure, see Stephen J. Walsh, "A Planned Approach to New Product Pricing," in *Pricing: The Critical Decision*, American Management Association, Management Report no. 66, New York, 1961, pp. 45–57.

[2] For one study (covering 146 companies) indicating the factors which influenced the pricing of new products, the location of responsibility for new-product pricing, and the prevalence of pretesting new-product pricing decisions, see "Pricing New Products," *Conference Board Recorder*, January, 1964, pp. 7–14.

amount, the expected price can be determined within a range; it might be "between $250 and $300" or "not over $10."

It is surprising sometimes how shrewd customers can be in evaluating a product. In the case of a new product, however, direct competition and price comparison are often slight in the early life of the product, so the manufacturer has considerably more latitude in setting his price than is the case with older products. If customers have no predetermined idea of the value of a product, there is a broader possible range of prices which the market might expect. The seller may set a higher initial price on the product than would be possible if it were an established item subject to comparison. Then, after the market has developed an image of a high-priced article, the seller can lower the price and the market may think it is getting a bargain.

A producer must also think of the middlemen's reaction to the price. Middlemen are more likely to give an article favorable treatment in their stores if they approve of its price. Because of their extensive experience and wide knowledge of competitive and substitute products, retail or wholesale buyers can frequently examine an item and make an accurate estimate of the selling price that the market will accept.

A manufacturer should not feel that it is impossible to change the expected price, particularly on a new product. This may be done by:[3]

1. adding product features which increase the apparent value of the article by more than the actual cost of the added features,
2. selecting distribution channels which reach customers who will see the article in comparison with more expensive items, or
3. using an advertising program to increase the value of the product in the customer's eye.

Research may uncover the fact that the expected price is below the level at which the firm can make or buy the product. Unless adjustments can be made in production costs, the relatively low expected price may preclude the production or purchase of the item.

It is possible to set a price too low. If the price is much lower than that which the market expects, often sales will be lost. For example, it would probably be a mistake for a well-known cosmetics manufacturer to put a 19-cent price tag on lipstick or to price its imported perfume at $1.29 an ounce. Either customers will be suspicious of the quality of the product, or their self-concepts will not let them use such low-priced merchandise. Furthermore, the firm may hurt or even lose its reputation for high-quality, prestige products. More than one seller has raised the price of his product and experienced a considerable increase in sales. In terms of market-demand curves,

[3] Alfred R. Oxenfeldt, "Pricing New Products," *Establishing a New-product Program*, American Management Association, Management Report no. 8, New York, 1950, p. 25.

this situation is referred to as inverse demand—the higher the price, the greater the unit sales.

How does a seller determine the expected price? He may submit the article to an experienced retailer or wholesaler for appraisal. Manufacturers of industrial products sometimes approach engineers and other technical men working for prospective customers. By showing models or blueprints, the manufacturer can solicit informed judgments on what the price "ought to be." Another possibility is to observe prices of comparable competitive products. A third alternative is to survey the potential consumers. They may be shown the article and asked what they would pay for it. This approach can bring misleading answers because there is often a considerable difference between what a person *says* the product is worth and what he will actually pay for it. A much more effective approach is to market the product in a few limited test areas. By trying different prices under controlled research conditions, the seller can determine at least a reasonable range of prices. When it is not practical to produce a sufficient quantity to test the market, the seller may have to rely on some form of depth interviewing of potential customers.

Estimates of sales at various prices   It is extremely helpful in price determination to estimate what the sales volume will be at several different prices. These estimates involve a consideration of the demand elasticity of the product. A product with an elastic market demand should usually be priced lower than an item with an inelastic demand. By estimating the demand for its product at different prices, management, in effect, is determining the demand curve for the item. These volume estimates at different prices are important also in relation to determining break-even points, which are discussed later in this chapter.

Anticipate competitive reaction

Present and potential competition is an important influence on price determination. Even a new product is not totally free from competition. Any possible distinctiveness is limited in that it is ordinarily only a matter of time until some form of competition will be felt strongly. The threat of *potential* competition is greatest when the field is easy and inexpensive to enter and the profit prospects are encouraging.

Competition can come from three *existing* sources. First, from directly similar products: the manufacturer of Wheaties must consider the price set on Kellogg's cornflakes or General Foods' Post Toasties. Second, from available substitutes: for many years United States Steel considered only such competitors as Bethlehem Steel Corporation (directly similar). Now the steel producers must be alert to prices on aluminum and plastics because for many end products steel is no longer the only reasonable alternative material. Third, competition may come from unrelated items seeking the same consumer dollar.

The next step in price determination, and one which tends to narrow still further the range of the probable pricing decisions, is to determine what share of the market the company expects to capture. An aggressive firm seeking a larger share of the market ordinarily will price differently from a company which is content with its present share. Sometimes the drive for a certain market share is characterized by heavy advertising and other forms of nonprice competition rather than by price appeals.

The expected share of the market will be influenced by present production capacity, costs of plant expansion, and ease of competitive entry. It would be a mistake for a firm to aim for a larger share of the market than its plant capacity can sustain. If a new product is priced low in an attempt to gain a broad market, and if the market response is extremely favorable, the company may not be able to fill its orders.

If management is not interested in expanding its plant because ease of competitive entry and potential competition undoubtedly will drive down future profits, the initial price will be set relatively high. The company will seek only that share of the market which can be handled with existing capacity.

Any one of several pricing strategies might be employed by management to achieve the predetermined share of the market. By focusing attention on two alternatives which are polar extremes, we can highlight many of the pertinent issues. These alternatives are popularly referred to as "skim-the-cream" pricing and "penetration" pricing. They are most appropriate to the pricing of new products.[4]

Skim-the-cream pricing   The cream-skimming strategy involves setting a price which is high in the range of expected prices. The seller may continue with this strategy for an indefinite period, or he may later lower the price in order to tap other segments of the market. Cream skimming is probably most effective with a highly distinctive article which is aggressively promoted in the early stages of its life cycle.

There are at least five reasons why skim-the-cream pricing may be particularly suitable for new products. First, demand is likely to be less elastic in the early stages of a product's life cycle. In the early stages, price is less

[4] These opposite strategies are discussed in Joel Dean, *How to Price a New Product*, Small Business Administration, Management Aids for Small Manufacturers, no. 62, Washington, D.C., April, 1955; see also Joel Dean, "Pricing Policies for New Products," *Harvard Business Review*, November, 1950, pp. 45–53. Much of the discussion in this section is adapted from these two sources.

important, competition is at a minimum, and the product's distinctiveness lends itself to real salesmanship. Second, this strategy can effectively segment the market on an income or buying-power basis. The first appeal is to that segment of the demand curve which responds to distinctiveness and exclusiveness in a product and is relatively insensitive to price. Later on, the seller can lower his price and appeal to segments of the market which are highly sensitive to price.

A third advantage of cream skimming is that it acts as a strong hedge against a possible mistake in setting the price. If the original price is too high and the market does not respond, management can easily lower it, but it is very difficult to raise a price which proves to be too low to cover costs or lower than the product's popularity warrants. Fourth, high initial prices can often generate more revenues and profits than can low prices in the early stages of market development. Thus funds can be earmarked for market expansion. Finally, high initial prices can be used to keep demand within the limits of a company's productive capacity. A low initial price which brings more business than a firm can handle may result in the permanent loss of the goodwill of many customers.

Penetration pricing   In this strategy, a low initial price is set in order to reach the mass market immediately. This strategy can also be employed at a later stage in the product's life cycle. Many a firm has saved its product from a premature death or at least from premature old age simply by switching to penetration pricing from cream skimming.

Compared with cream skimming, penetration pricing is a more aggressive competitive strategy and is likely to be more satisfactory when the following conditions exist: First, the quantity sold is highly sensitive to price; that is, the product has a highly elastic demand; second, substantial reductions in unit production and marketing costs can be achieved through large-scale operations; third, the product faces very strong competition soon after it is introduced to the market; fourth, there is an inadequate high-income market to sustain a skim-the-cream price.

The nature of potential competition will critically influence management's choice between the two pricing strategies. If competitors can enter a market easily and quickly and if the market potential for the product is very promising, management probably should adopt a policy of penetration pricing. Low initial pricing may do two things. First, it may discourage other firms from entering the field because the investment needed in production and marketing facilities will be too great in light of the anticipated low profit margin. Second, low prices may give the innovator such a strong hold on his share of the market that future competitors cannot cut into it. On the other hand, cream skimming may be more feasible where market potential is not large enough to attract the big competitors. While percentage margins per unit of sale may be attractive, the total dollar profits will be too small to attract large firms.

Another major step in the pricing procedure is to consider a company's marketing policies with respect to the product itself, the distribution system, and the promotional program.

Product policies   We have already observed that the price of a product is influenced substantially by whether it is a new item or an older, established one. Other aspects of the product and product policies must be considered by management in setting a price. For example, product perishability influences a firm's pricing policy. The importance of a product in its end use also must be considered. To illustrate, price competition is largely absent and a stable price structure exists among manufacturers of packaging materials, industrial gases, and aluminum fabrications. These products are only an incidental part and cost of the final product.

Whether the article will be sold under a middleman's brand or under the manufacturer's own brand will affect the price established by the manufacturer. The interdependence of the product mix is another consideration. Where products are related, the manufacturer's price set on any one item affects all others in the line. Thus General Motors cannot establish the price for a Chevrolet without considering the prices of other General Motors cars. On the other hand, in a firm such as General Mills, which sells Wheaties and airplane controls, or in Union Carbide, which sells Prestone and industrial oxygen, there is greater flexibility in pricing. A manufacturer or middleman who offers free mechanical service and installation probably will charge a higher price than one who does not.

Channels of distribution   The channels selected, the types of middlemen used, and the gross margin requirements of these middlemen in light of the services they perform will influence a manufacturer's price. A firm selling through wholesalers and also directly to retailers often sets a different factory price for each of these two classes of customers.

Promotional methods   The promotional methods used and the extent to which the job is done by the manufacturer or the middlemen is still another factor to consider in pricing. If the bulk of the promotional responsibility is placed upon retailers, they ordinarily will require a larger margin than if the product is heavily advertised by the manufacturer. Even when a manufacturer promotes heavily, he may want his middlemen to use local advertising, store display, and other types of promotion to tie in with his national advertising. Such a decision must be reflected in the dealer's margin and, consequently, in the manufacturer's price.

While there is no mechanical or magic formula, it is possible to suggest some models which management can follow. This stage in pricing procedure warrants detailed discussion.

BASIC METHODS OF SETTING PRICE

In the pricing procedure just outlined, the final step is to narrow the range of expected prices to the point where a specific selling price is established. Over the years many different methods have been used by individual companies to accomplish this task. Most of these approaches to price setting, however, fall under one of the following major methods:

1.   Prices may be based on total cost plus a desired profit.

2.   Prices may be based on a balance between estimates of market demand and costs of production and marketing.

3.   Prices may be set by competitive market conditions.

Prices based on costs

In its simplest form, the cost-plus approach means that the selling price for a unit of a product is equal to the unit's total cost plus an amount to cover the anticipated profit on the unit. As an example, a contractor figures that the labor and materials required to build and sell ten houses will cost $150,000, and his other expenses (office rent, depreciation on equipment, wages of management, etc.) will equal $50,000. On this total cost of $200,000, he anticipates a profit of 10 per cent of cost. Cost plus profit amounts to $220,000. Therefore each of the ten houses will sell for $22,000.

While this is a very simple, easily understood, and easily applied pricing method, it has one serious limitation. It disregards the fact that there are different types of costs and that they all do not act alike as output increases or decreases. Referring to our housing example, if the contractor sold only eight houses, his total sales would be $176,000. His labor and materials chargeable to eight houses would total $120,000 ($15,000 per house). He would still incur the full $50,000 overhead expenses, however, so his total cost would be $170,000, leaving a profit of only $6,000, or about $750 per house instead of the anticipated $2,000.

Different cost concepts   A more sophisticated approach to cost-plus pricing takes into consideration the several types of costs and their different reactions to changes in level of output. That is, the total unit cost of a product will change as output expands or contracts. The following classification of cost concepts is important for our purposes:

1. Total fixed costs
2. Total variable costs
3. Total cost
4. Average fixed costs
5. Average variable costs
6. Average total costs
7. Marginal costs

Three of these concepts may require some elaboration. *Total fixed costs* are elements, such as rent, executives' salaries, and property taxes, which remain constant regardless of level of output. Even if production ceases entirely, these costs continue. We shall, however, implicitly assume here that we are dealing with a fixed plant capacity and a short-run period of time. Over the long run, *all* costs tend to be variable.

With respect to *average variable costs,* we shall, under a simplified assump-

fig. 18–1

This graph shows the relationships among total fixed costs, total variable costs, and total cost so that their significance in pricing can be seen. The effect of total variable costs in this simplified example is to make total cost a slowly ascending curved line.

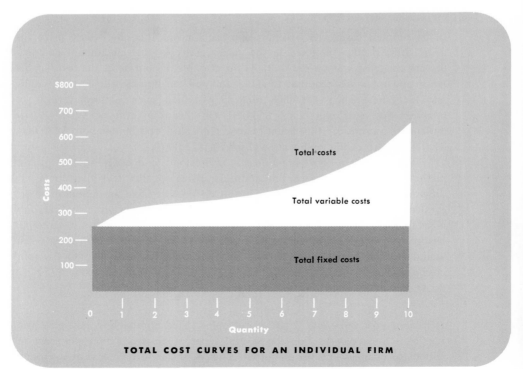

TOTAL COST CURVES FOR AN INDIVIDUAL FIRM

table 18-1

Costs for individual firm

Total fixed costs never change, despite increases in quantity. These costs are incurred for land rent, executives' salaries, and other items which remain constant no matter what quantity is being produced. Variable costs represent increasing costs for input of materials, labor, power, etc., as production quantity rises. Total cost is the sum of all fixed and variable costs. The other measures in the table are simply methods of looking at costs per unit and always involve dividing costs by number of units produced according to the formulas at the tops of the columns.

Quantity output, Q	Total fixed costs, TFC	Total variable costs, TVC	Total costs, TC = TFC + TVC	Marginal costs per unit, MC	Average fixed costs, AFC = TFC ÷ Q	Average variable costs, AVC = TVC ÷ Q	Average costs per unit, ATC = TC ÷ Q
0	$256	$ 0	$256		Infinity	$ 0	Infinity
1	256	64	320	$64	$256.00	64	$320.00
2	256	84	340	20	128.00	42	170.00
3	256	99	355	15	85.33	33	118.33
4	256	112	368	13	64.00	28	92.00
5	256	125	381	13	51.20	25	76.20
6	256	144	400	19	42.67	24	66.67
7	256	175	431	31	36.57	25	61.57
8	256	224	480	49	32.00	28	60.00
9	256	297	553	73	28.44	33	61.44
10	256	400	656	103	25.60	40	65.60

SOURCE: Adapted from Paul Samuelson, *Economics*, McGraw-Hill Book Company, New York, 1961.

tion, keep these constant. In such a case the *total* variable cost will increase with each additional unit of output. The direct labor and material costs *per unit*, however, will remain the same. In a more typical production operation, unit variable costs are relatively high for the first few units of output. Then, as total output increases, the average variable costs come down because of quantity discounts on material, more efficient use of manpower, etc. Beyond some optimum point, average variable costs will increase as expanded output results in overtime pay, overuse and crowding of plant facilities, and generally less efficient use of labor and materials resources.

Marginal cost is the cost of producing and selling one more unit, that is, the cost of the most recent or last unit. If it costs $500 to produce sixty units and $527 to produce sixty-one units, the marginal cost is $27.

These seven cost concepts and their interrelationships may be studied in Table 18–1 and in Figs. 18–1 and 18–2, which are based on the table. Figure 18–1 shows the relationship among the curves representing the *totals* of (1) all costs, (2) fixed costs, and (3) variable costs, respectively. Here we can see that total fixed costs are represented by a straight line because they are constant within a short-run period. As output increases, total costs increase by the amount of variable cost incurred by each unit. Thus the total cost curve is a line which rises to the right. In Fig. 18–1, however, variable costs are not constant per unit; therefore, the total cost line is curved. If variable costs were constant, the total cost line would be straight.

Fig. 18–2 graphically displays the interrelationships among the various *average unit* costs. The average variable cost curve (AVC) would be horizontal if the average variable costs were constant. In our example, it curves downward until the eighth unit is passed; then diminishing returns set in. The average total cost curve (ATC) will slope downward as long as marginal costs are less than average unit costs. Even though the marginal costs are up after the fifth unit, the average cost curve continues to slope downward until after the eighth unit. This is because marginal costs, even though going up, are still less than average costs. The marginal cost (MC) and the average total cost curves intersect at the lowest point of the average total cost curve. Beyond that point (the eighth unit in the example) the cost of producing and selling the last unit is higher than the average of all units. Therefore, from then on the average total cost will rise. The reason for this is that the average variable costs are increasing faster than the average fixed costs are decreasing. Producing the ninth unit reduced average fixed costs from $32 to $28.44, but average variable costs rose $5. The average total cost curve will slope downward as long as average variable costs increase less than the average fixed costs decrease.

The marginal cost, as shown by the marginal cost curve in Fig. 18–2 and in column (5) of Table 18–1, is a critical figure to keep in mind. This represents the cost of producing and selling the last unit. Later in the analysis we shall see that to maximize profits a firm theoretically will continue producing

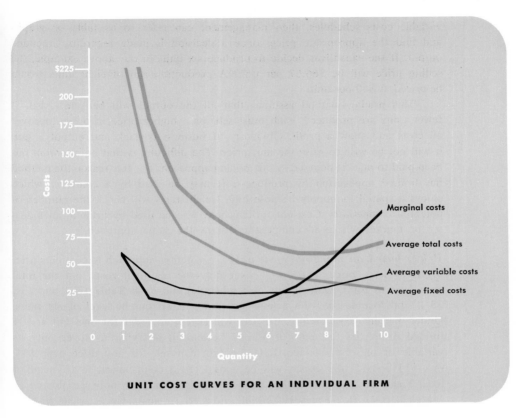

UNIT COST CURVES FOR AN INDIVIDUAL FIRM

fig. 18–2

Here we see how unit costs change as quantity increases. The average total cost per unit is generally U-shaped. It starts quite high because total fixed cost is spread over so few units. As quantity increases, average fixed cost declines, thus pulling down the average total cost line. But the total cost per unit will start to slope upward when the quantity produced begins to put a strain on the productive capacity of the plant, which shows in increasing average variable costs. The increase in costs is also reflected by the acute U shape of the marginal cost line. The cost of producing one more unit goes up as workers are crowded, machines are overburdened, and other troubles are encountered. What is the most logical solution to this problem for a manufacturer who has a profitable product but encounters rising unit costs as a result of high quantity produced?

and selling as long as the sales revenue from this last unit (called marginal revenue) exceeds the cost of the unit.

Refinements in cost-plus pricing Once management understands that all costs do not behave the same as output increases or decreases, then refinements are possible in price setting based on the cost-plus approach. If we assume that the desired profit is included either in the fixed costs or in the variable costs schedules, then management can refer to its table or graphs and find the appropriate price, once a decision is made regarding intended output. If the executives decide to produce six units in our above example, the selling price will be $66.67 per unit. A production run of eight units would be priced at $60 per unit.

This pricing method assumes that all the output will be sold. Also, if fewer units are produced, each must sell for a higher price in order to cover all costs and show a profit. Obviously, if business is slack and output is cut, it will not be wise to raise the unit price. The difficulty is that no attention has been paid to market demand in this pricing approach. For this reason the method has limited application by producers. It may be used by a company which enjoys a spatial monopoly because high freight rates will check the number of potential competitors. Cost-plus pricing may also be used by firms in an industry or market where all competitors follow the same approach.

Prices based on marginal costs only   Another approach to cost-plus pricing is to set a price which will cover only the marginal costs, not the total costs. Let us refer again to the cost schedules shown in Table 18–1 and Fig. 18–2 and assume that the firm is operating at an output level of six units. Under marginal cost pricing, the firm will accept an order for one unit at $31 instead of at the full cost of $66.67 because it is trying to cover only its variable or out-of-pocket costs. If the firm can sell for any price over $31, say, $33 or $35, the excess will be considered a contribution to payment of fixed costs. Obviously all orders cannot be priced to cover only variable costs. Marginal cost pricing may be feasible, however, if management wants to keep its labor force employed during a slack season or if the executives wish to keep the plant running rather than face costly shutdowns and startups. Marginal cost pricing may also be used in an introductory campaign for a new product or when one product is expected to attract business for another. As an example of the last point, a department store may price meals in its tearoom at a level which covers only the marginal costs, reasoning that this facility will bring shoppers to the store, where they will buy other merchandise.

Cost-plus pricing by middlemen   Cost-plus pricing is widely used by retailing and wholesaling middlemen. At least it seems this way upon first glance. A retailer, for example, pays a given amount to buy a product and have it delivered to his store. Then he will add to the acquisition cost an amount (his markup) which he estimates is necessary to cover his expenses and still leave a reasonable profit. To simplify his pricing and accounting, he may add the same percentage markup to all his products. This is an average markup which he has determined through experience will be large enough to cover the costs and profit for his entire business. If a clothing store buys a garment for $30, including freight, the item will be priced to sell at 66⅔ per cent over cost, or $50. (Store policy will probably result in this price being set at $49.95; pricing at odd amounts is discussed in Chapter 20.) The price of $50 will give the retailer a markup of 40 per cent of his selling price or 66⅔ per cent based on his merchandise cost. Different types of retailers will require different percentage markups because of the nature of the products handled, services offered, etc. A self-service supermarket has lower costs and thus a lower average markup than a full-service delicatessen. Furniture and jewelry stores have higher markups than do drugstores. The topic of markups is discussed in more detail in the Appendix.

To what extent is cost-plus pricing truly used by middlemen? At least three significant indications suggest that what seems to be cost-plus pricing is really market-inspired pricing. In the first place, most retail prices which are set by applying average percentage markups are really only price *offers*. If the merchandise does not sell at the original price, that figure will be lowered until it reaches a level at which the merchandise will sell. The second indication of market influences is the fact that many retailers do not use the same markup on all the products they carry. A supermarket will have a markup of 6 to 8 per cent on sugar and soap products, 15 to 18 per cent on canned fruits and vegetables, and 25 to 30 per cent on fresh meats and produce. These different markups for different products definitely reflect competitive considerations and other aspects of the market demand. Some items are slower moving than others, and some face stiffer competition; in other cases store location will influence the initial markup. Middlemen find, perhaps through trial and error, what percentage markup will bring in the greatest dollar volume and profit margin from the market. Then this market-reflecting markup is expressed as if it were a cost-plus approach.

The third consideration here is that the middleman usually does not set the basic price. The manufacturer's price is set so as to allow each middleman to add his customary markup and still sell at a retail price circumscribed by the competitive market. That is, the *key* price is set by the manufacturer with an eye on the market.

Evaluation of cost-plus pricing   This book has emphasized that a firm must be market-oriented and must cater to consumers' wants. Why, then, are we now considering cost-plus pricing? Actually, it provides a good point of departure in the discussion of price determination. Also, it is spoken of so widely in business that we must understand it. Adherents of cost-plus pricing point to its simplicity and its ease of determination. They say costs are a known quantity, whereas attempts to estimate demand are fraught with guesswork.

This opinion is questionable on two counts. First, it is doubtful whether adequate, accurate cost data are available. We know a fair amount about cost-volume relationships with respect to production costs, but what we know is still insufficient. Furthermore, our information regarding marketing costs is woefully inadequate. Certainly there is a dearth of information about costs of new products, because sales volume is still an unknown quantity. Really, when we consider costs in relation to pricing, we are, at best, usually dealing with approximations. The second point concerns the inexactitude of demand estimations. The difficulty of constructing a demand schedule estimating sales volume at various prices is great. Nevertheless, sales forecasting and other research tools can do a surprisingly helpful job in this area. Certainly crude, inexact estimates are better than none at all, and estimates are essential if a firm is to do a reasonably proper job of pricing.

Critics of cost-plus pricing do not say costs should be disregarded in pricing. Costs should be a determining influence, but not the only one. They are a floor under a firm's prices; if prices stay under this floor for a long period of time, the firm will be forced out of business. Ordinarily a company will not sell its products below cost, but it may sell particular items at or below cost if they are needed to round out the line or to generate market acceptance and customer traffic for other profitable items. At the other end of the scale, costs plus a reasonable profit should not act as a ceiling price. The market should set the upper level of prices.

Some students of pricing claim that the cost-plus method is used today to set the price of over one-half of all our products. This conclusion exaggerates the incidence of cost-plus pricing. Many firms say they use cost-plus as the method of setting their basic prices, but really they are using some form of market-inspired pricing.

Costs furnish a good point from which to start computing price. Management can determine a tentative price on a cost-plus basis but then make adjustments in the cost-plus price when it is able to measure demand factors. When used by itself, cost-plus is a weak and unrealistic method of pricing because it completely ignores the influences of competition and market demand.

Break-even analysis

One way to use market demand as a basis for price determination and still consider costs is to approach pricing through a break-even analysis. A break-even analysis involves developing tables and/or charts which will help a company determine at what level of output the revenues will equal the costs, assuming a certain selling price. Sales at levels above the break-even point will result in a profit on each unit, and the farther above the break-even point a firm goes, the higher will be the total and unit profit. Output at any stage below the break-even point will result in a loss to the seller. Break-even analysis also is a valuable pricing tool if the company's pricing objective is to maximize profits.

Determination of break-even point   The method of determining the break-even point is illustrated in Table 18–2 and Figs. 18–3 and 18–4. In our hypothetical situation, the company's fixed costs are $250 and its variable costs are constant at $30 a unit. Thus the total cost of one unit is $280; for five units the total costs are $400 ($30 multiplied by 5, plus $250). In

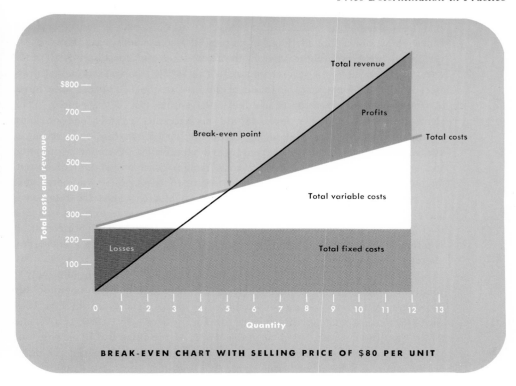

BREAK-EVEN CHART WITH SELLING PRICE OF $80 PER UNIT

fig. 18–3

Here the break-even point is reached when the company sells five units. Fixed costs, regardless of quantity produced and sold, are $250. The variable cost per unit is $30. If this company sells five units, total cost is five times $30, or $150, plus $250, or $400. At a selling price of $80, the sale of five units will yield $400 revenue, and costs and revenue will equal each other. At the same price, the sale of each unit above five yields profit.

Fig. 18–3 the selling price is set at $80 a unit. Consequently, every time a unit is sold, $50 is contributed to overhead. That is, the variable costs or the out-of-pocket costs are $30 per unit, and these expenses are incurred in producing each unit. But any revenue over $30 can be used to help cover the fixed costs. At a selling price of $80 the company will break even if five units are sold. Stated another way, the variable costs for five units are $150 and the fixed costs are $250, for a total cost of $400. This is equal to the revenue from five units sold at $80 each. Stated as a formula:

$$\text{Break-even point in units} = \frac{\text{Total fixed costs}}{\text{Unit contribution to overhead}}$$

It is important to note the assumptions and limitations underlying the computations in the preceding paragraph and in Fig. 18–3. First, we assume that total fixed costs are constant. This is true only over a short period of time and within a limited range of output. It is reasonably easy, however, to develop a break-even chart wherein the fixed costs, and consequently the total costs, are stepped up at several intervals. This is what happens in actual practice; a good example may be found in the case of the size of the sales force. A static level of fixed costs assumes a given number of salesmen. When demand reaches a higher level, it will be necessary to add one or more salesmen. This involves a sudden increase in fixed marketing costs to cover the additional men's salaries, expenses, and supervision. A second assumption in our example is that the variable costs remain constant per unit of output. In the earlier discussion of the cost structure of the firm, it was noted that the average variable costs in a firm usually fluctuated. Thus the total costs were shown as a curved line in Fig. 18–1, and the average variable cost line in Fig. 18–2 was curved and sloped rather than straight and horizontal. It is also possible to develop a break-even chart for a company with a fluctuating average variable cost.

Another limitation of Fig. 18–3 is that it shows a break-even point only if the unit price is $80. It is possible and highly desirable to compute the break-even points for several different selling prices. Therefore, in Fig. 18–4 the break-even point is determined for four prices—$60, $80, $100, and $150. Fig. 18–4 is also based on Table 18–2. If the price is $60, it will take sales of approximately 8.3 units to break even; at $150, only about 2.1 units. Every different selling price will result in a different break-even point.

Break-even analysis related to market demand   Up to this point in our discussion of break-even analysis, we have found that its major limitation as a realistic pricing tool is that it ignores the market demand at the

table   18–2

Computation of break-even point

At each of several prices, we wish to find out how many units must be sold to cover all variable costs plus total fixed cost. At a unit price of $100, the sale of each unit contributes $70 to cover the overhead expenses. We must sell about 3.6 units to cover the $250 fixed cost. See Figs. 18–3 and 18–4 for a visual portrayal of data in this table.

(1)	*(2)*	*(3)*	*(4)*	*(5)*
	Unit variable	*Contribution*	*Overhead*	*Break-even*
Unit	*costs,*	*to overhead,*	*(total fixed*	*point**
price	*AVC*	*(1) − (2)*	*costs)*	*(4) ÷ (3)*
$ 60	$30	$ 30	$250	8.3 units
80	30	50	250	5.0 units
100	30	70	250	3.6 units
150	30	120	250	2.1 units

* To nearest decimal point.

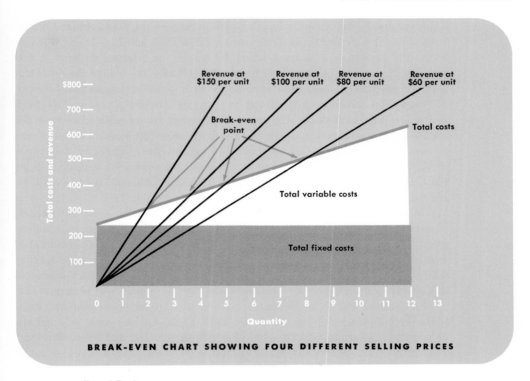

BREAK-EVEN CHART SHOWING FOUR DIFFERENT SELLING PRICES

fig. 18–4

Here the company is experimenting with several different prices in order to determine which is the most appropriate. There are four different prices and four break-even points. At a price of $60, the company will start making a profit after it has sold 8.3 units. At the opposite extreme, the break-even point for a price of $150 is about 2.1 units.

various prices. It is still essentially a tool for cost-plus pricing. The revenue curves in Figs. 18–3 and 18–4 show only what the revenue will be at the various prices *if* (and it is a big if) an unlimited amount can be sold at these prices. The curve *presumes* that the company can sell any output at the given price. Actually this presumption smacks considerably of a perfectly competitive market, an unrealistic situation in practice. So far, our break-even charts show only the amount which must be sold at the stated price in order to break even. The chart does not tell us whether we *can* actually sell this amount. The amount which the market will buy at a given price may be below the break-even point. For instance, at an $80 unit selling price, the break-even point is five units. If the market will buy only three or four units, the firm will not break even; it will show a loss.

This deficiency in break-even analysis can be remedied by estimating the total demand which actually exists at several different selling prices.[5]

[5] This approach to pricing first came to the author's attention in Edward R. Hawkins, "Price Policies and Theory," *Journal of Marketing*, January, 1954, p. 234.

Then this market information can be superimposed on the predetermined break-even data. This procedure is illustrated in Table 18–3 and Fig. 18–5. Management first constructs a demand schedule, that is, its estimate of what it can sell at various prices. Columns (1) and (2) of Table 18–3 show this information. From these figures, total revenue at each price is determined—column (3)—and this information is plotted on a graph. The *DD* curve in Fig. 18–5 is the resulting total demand curve. Students may be more familiar with the traditional demand curves which slope downward to the right. The difference is that the usual demand curve shows *average* revenues, while the *DD* curve in Fig. 18–5 represents *total* revenues. Basically the curves are developed from the same demand schedule. In fact, a traditional demand curve could be plotted from the figures in columns (1) and (2) of Table 18–3.

After the total *DD* curve is drawn, it is placed on the break-even chart, which already shows several revenue lines representing different unit selling prices. To maximize profits, management finds the point on the demand curve which is the greatest vertical distance above the total cost curve. The specific selling price selected is the one represented by the revenue line which intersects this point on the *DD* curve. The optimum level of output also is determined by this intersection. In our example, $100 is the selling price, and five units is the output which will maximize profits at $100. An $80 price will sell six units and bring profits of $50. The other two prices, $60 and $150, however, will result in losses of $40 and $10, respectively, because demand at these prices is less than the output needed to break even.

table   18–3

Relations among break-even analysis, total revenue from market demand, and profits

By comparing market demand and break-even point at each unit price, we find which price will maximize profits. Note that at a $60 price the break-even point is 8.3 units; yet the market will buy only seven units at the price, so a loss would result. Explain why there is a $50 profit at the $80 price. This is shown graphically in Fig. 18–5.

(1)	(2)	(3)	(4)	(5)	(6)
					Total profits (spread between TR and TC at number of units sold)
Unit price	Market demand at the price, in units	Total revenue TR = (1) × (2)	Break-even point	Total cost (TC) of units sold*	(3) − (5)
$ 60	7	$420	8.3	$460	$ −40
80	6	480	5.0	430	50
100	5	500	3.6	400	100
150	2	300	2.1	310	−10

* Computed from cost data in Table 18–2. (Unit variable costs are $30, and total fixed costs are $250.)

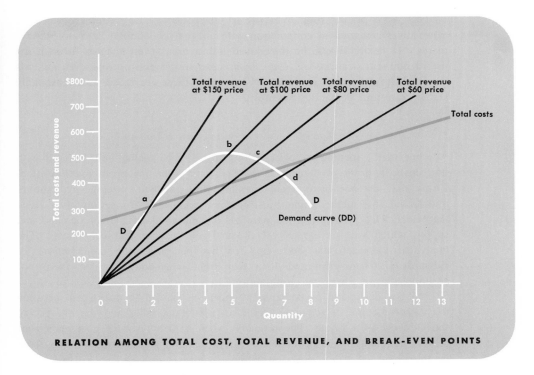

RELATION AMONG TOTAL COST, TOTAL REVENUE, AND BREAK-EVEN POINTS

fig. 18–5

Superimposing the total demand curve on the break-even chart graphically shows which price will maximize profits. We seek the point at which the demand curve is the greatest vertical distance above the total cost line (point b in this case). Then we determine which price is represented by the total revenue line intersecting the demand curve at this point; $100 is our price. Note that the lower price of $60 would result in a loss of $40 (point d is below the total cost line).

Evaluation of break-even analysis   Certainly no one should claim that break-even analysis is the perfect pricing tool.[6] Some of its limitations have already been touched upon. That is, many of the underlying assumptions are unrealistic in a practical business operation. It assumes that costs are static, and it requires an empirical determination of the company's cost curve. Break-even analysis has a very limited value as a pricing tool in firms whose costs fluctuate frequently and widely and whose product mixes vary considerably. On the revenue side, break-even analysis often oversimplifies or assumes as static a revenue activity which really is highly volatile. It also assumes that one can accurately estimate demand at different prices.

These limitations should not lead management to dismiss break-even

[6] This subject is treated in Joel Dean, *Managerial Economics*, Prentice-Hall, Inc., Englewood Cliffs, N.J., 1951, pp. 326–341. Much of the discussion here stems from this source.

analysis as a pricing tool. While it is not perfect, it is extremely valuable, especially when used in conjunction with an analysis of total demand. Refinements and flexibility can be introduced into a break-even analysis through the use of mathematical models. Even in its most simple form, break-even analysis is very helpful because in the short run many firms are faced with reasonably stable costs and demand structures.

Prices based on balance between supply and demand

Another major method of price setting involves balancing unit demand with unit costs in order to determine the best unit price for profit maximization. Firms that do not have profit maximization as their pricing goal should understand this method, and possibly they can use it for setting their basic list prices. This pricing method parallels the marginal analysis of demand and supply which was developed by classical and neoclassical economists. The analytical approach has been updated by the pioneering contributions of Edward H. Chamberlin and Joan Robinson, who developed the theory of monopolistic, or imperfect, competition.[7]

In our discussion of demand, we must be careful to distinguish between the demand curve or schedule facing an individual seller and the one facing the industry as a whole. Theoretically, when a firm operates in a market of perfect competition, its demand curve is horizontal at the market price. That is, the single seller has no control over the price, and he can sell his entire output at the market price. Even in a perfectly competitive market, however, the industry has a downward-sloping curve. That is, for the industry as a whole, more units can be sold at lower prices than at higher prices.

The market situation facing most firms in the United States today is one of monopolistic, or imperfect, competition, characterized by product differentiation and nonprice competition. By differentiating his products, an individual seller has some control over his prices. In effect, each seller becomes a separate "industry"; his product is to some extent unlike any other. An individual seller in monopolistic competition has a downward-sloping demand curve. That is, he will attract some buyers at a high price, but to broaden his market and to sell to more people, he must lower the price.

If the price is to be set by a balancing of demand and supply, the price setter must understand the concepts of average and marginal revenue in addition to average and marginal cost. Marginal revenue is the income derived from the sale of the last unit—the marginal unit. Average revenue is the unit price at a given level of unit sales; it is total revenue divided by the number of units sold. Referring to the hypothetical demand schedule in Table 18–4, we see that the company received an additional $70 (marginal revenue) from

[7] Edward H. Chamberlin, *Theory of Monopolistic Competition*, 8th ed., Harvard University Press, Cambridge, Mass., 1957; and Joan Robinson, *Economics of Imperfect Competition*, The Macmillan Company, New York, 1933.

the sale of two units instead of one; the fifth unit brought a marginal revenue of $53. After the sixth unit, however, the total revenue declined each time an additional unit was sold. Hence there was a negative marginal revenue.

The downward-sloping demand curve which faces most firms is an average revenue curve. It shows how many units will be sold at various unit (average) prices. To make an average revenue curve slope downward, the marginal revenue must always be less than the average revenue. That is, as unit sales increase, the revenue from the last unit becomes progressively smaller (see the revenue curves in Fig. 18–6). The firm's average unit cost curve (average fixed costs plus average variable costs) and its marginal cost curve have been placed in Fig. 18–6, along with the revenue curves, in order to depict graphically the price-setting process.

The firm will continue to sell as long as the revenue it gets from the last unit sold exceeds the cost of producing this last unit. That is, output continues as long as marginal revenue exceeds marginal costs. At the point where they meet, output theoretically should cease. Certainly management will not want to sell a unit at a price less than the costs of production. Thus the point of production is where marginal costs equal marginal revenue. This is quantity *OE* in Fig. 18–6. The price is determined by locating the point on the average revenue curve which represents *OE* output. Remember that average revenue represents the unit price. Thus the unit price at *OE* output is *EC*; this is the same as *OB* on the main vertical axis. At price *EC* the average unit cost is *DE*. Thus the company enjoys a unit profit of *DC*. Total profit is *OE* times *DC* (quantity times unit profit). This is the area bounded by *ABCD*.

table   18–4

Demand schedule for individual firm

At each market price, a definite quantity of the product will be demanded at any given time. Thus changing the unit price upward or downward will result in a differing number of units sold and a differing amount of total revenue. Marginal revenue is simply the amount of additional money gained by selling one more unit. In this example, the company no longer gains marginal revenue after it has sold the sixth unit at a price of $60.

Units sold	Unit price (average revenue)	Total revenue	Marginal revenue
1	$80	$ 80	
2	75	150	$70
3	72	216	66
4	68	272	56
5	65	325	53
6	60	360	35
7	50	350	−10
8	40	320	−30

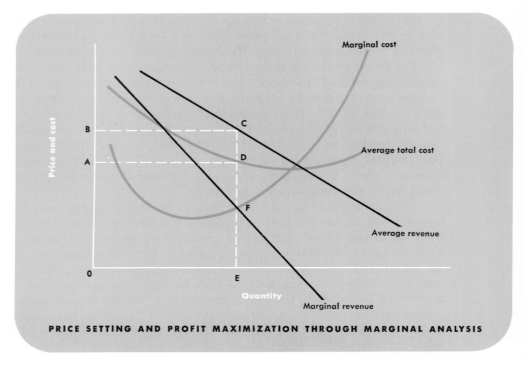

PRICE SETTING AND PROFIT MAXIMIZATION THROUGH MARGINAL ANALYSIS

fig. 18–6

Maximum profit occurs at the point where the marginal revenue curve intersects the marginal cost curve. In most situations, the company will not produce one more unit if the revenue derived from selling that unit would be less than the cost of producing and selling it.

Supply and demand analysis as a basis for price setting has enjoyed only limited use. Businessmen usually claim that the analysis does not take into consideration important variables that exist in the dynamic, real-life market situation. They feel that more and better data are needed for plotting the curves exactly. Demand and supply analysis can be used, they feel, to study past price movements, but it cannot serve as a practical basis for setting prices.

Those who are skeptical of the practical values of supply and demand analysis at the present time should take heart: management's knowledge of costs and demand is improving. Better methods of forecasting have been a boon in this area. Data-processing equipment is bringing more complete and detailed information to management's attention all the time. Earlier in the chapter it was pointed out that management usually can estimate demand within broad limits, and this is helpful. Also, experienced management in many firms can do a surprisingly accurate job of estimating marginal and average costs and revenue.

Cost-plus pricing is one extreme among pricing methods; at the other end of the scale is a method whereby an individual firm's prices are set in relation *only* to the competitive market price. Cost in no way determines the price. In fact, usually it is the other way around—price determines the firm's costs. Pricing on the basis of market alone is the strategy most closely related to the pricing objectives of meeting or preventing competition. This price-setting method can also be used when a company sets profit maximization or a target return on investment as a goal. The seller's price may be set right at the market price level in order to meet competition, or it may be set either above or below the competitive market level, and still be related to this level.

Pricing to meet competition   Management may decide to price a product right at the competitive level when any one of several situations exists. A firm is most likely to use this pricing method when the market is highly competitive and the product is not differentiated significantly from competitive models. Ordinarily, new products are sufficiently differentiated for the seller to have some control over price. To some extent, this method of pricing reflects market conditions which parallel those found under perfect competition. That is, effective product differentiation is absent, buyers and sellers are well informed about the market price and market conditions, and the seller has no discernible control over the selling price. Most producers of agricultural products must set their prices to meet competitive market levels. Even when farmers act as a group, as in an agricultural cooperative, they have very little, if any, real influence over the selling price, at least not in the short run. Manufacturers of gray goods in the textile industry, most manufacturers of automobile tires, and small firms producing well-known, standardized products— all ordinarily use the market-based method of pricing.

The market-based method of pricing is also used when a traditional or "customary" price level exists. Candy bars, soft drinks, and chewing gum, for example, are traditionally priced at a nickel or a dime. In the face of rising costs, most sellers, rather than trying to change the price of a candy bar from 5 cents to 6 or 7 cents, will accept the nickel price and then tailor their costs to the market price by reducing the quantity or quality of the bar. The sharp drop in revenue which occurs when the price is raised above the customary level gives an indication that the individual seller faces a kinked demand (see Fig. 18–7). The customary price is at *P*, the location of the kink in the curve. If the seller tries to go above that level (*OA*), the demand for his product drops sharply, as indicated by the flat average revenue curve above point *P*. At any price above *OA*, the demand is highly elastic. Below price *OA*, the demand is highly inelastic, as represented by the steeply sloping average revenue curve and the negative marginal revenue curve. That is, the total revenue decreases each time the price is reduced to a level below *P*. The customary price is so strong that a reduction in price by one firm will not increase the firm's unit sales very much, certainly not enough to offset the loss in unit or average revenue.

Sometimes a manufacturer faces a customary price line used by his retailers. This is typical of the apparel and clothing accessories industries. A shoe manufacturer, for example, may have to set a factory price on his shoes so that his retailers can sell them in the $14.95 or the $19.95 line and still get their normal or usual markup.

Up to this point in our discussion of pricing to meet competition, we have observed market situations which involved many sellers. Oddly enough, the same pricing method is often used when the market is dominated by only a few sellers. This type of market is called an oligopoly. The products of all

fig. 18–7

The kink occurs at the point of the customary price (OA). Above OA, demand declines rapidly. A price set below OA will result in very little increase in volume, and consequently the marginal revenue is negative. Which part of average revenue reflects an elastic demand and which segment shows inelastic demand?

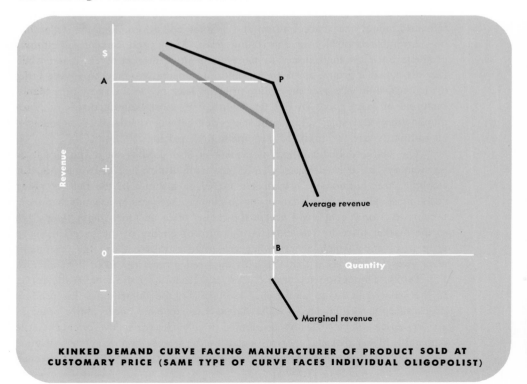

KINKED DEMAND CURVE FACING MANUFACTURER OF PRODUCT SOLD AT
CUSTOMARY PRICE (SAME TYPE OF CURVE FACES INDIVIDUAL OLIGOPOLIST)

manufacturers are reasonably similar, and the demand is usually inelastic. The demand curve facing an individual seller in an oligopoly is a kinked one, as in Fig. 18–7. An oligopolist must price at the market level in order to maximize profits. Selling above the market price will result in a drastic reduction in total revenue because the average revenue curve is so elastic above point *P*. If an oligopolist cuts below the market price, all other members of the oligopoly must respond immediately; otherwise the price-cutter will enjoy a substantial increase in business. Therefore, the competitors retaliate with comparable price cuts, and the net result is that a new market price is established at a lower level. Each member of the oligopoly gets about the same share of the market that he had before, but his unit revenue is reduced by the amount of the price cut. Theoretically, an oligopolist gains no advantage by cutting his price. For his own good, he will simply set his price at a competitive level and let it stay there. In reality, price wars are often touched off in an oligopoly because it is not possible to fully control all sellers of the product. Assuming the absence of collusion, every so often some firm will enter the market with a price reduction, and all others usually must follow in order to maintain their respective shares of the market.

Pricing to meet competition is also found in industries where there is a price leader. In the steel industry, for example, the United States Steel Corporation is the acknowledged leader. The Brookings Institution study brought out that the National Steel Corporation simply followed the prices set by United States Steel, regardless of its own cost of production.[8]

The market-equated method of pricing is rather simple to apply. A firm ascertains what the going price is, and after allowing for customary markups for middlemen, it arrives at its own selling price. Next it must determine whether it can make and sell the item at that price. To illustrate, a manufacturer of men's dress shoes is aware that his retailers want to sell the shoes for $19.95 a pair. He sells directly to the retailers, and they want an average markup of 40 per cent of their selling price. Consequently, after allowing $7.98 for the retailers' markup, the manufacturer's top price is about $12. He then decides whether $12 is enough to cover his production and marketing expenses and still leave him a reasonable profit. Sometimes he faces a real squeeze in this matter, particularly when his costs are rising but the market price is holding firm.

Pricing below competitive level   A variation of market-based pricing is to set a price at some point below that which is considered the competitive level. This method of pricing is usually found at the retail level of distribution, although it is not unknown among manufacturers. Since the end of World War II, the most talked-about example of this kind of pricing has been

---

[8] A. D. H. Kaplan, Joel B. Dirlam, and Robert F. Lanzillotti, *Pricing in Big Business*, The Brookings Institution, Washington, D.C., 1958, pp. 13–24, 204–205.

discount-house pricing. Discount houses typically price well-known, nationally advertised brands 10 to 30 per cent below the suggested retail list price or the price actually being charged by most other retailers. They operate on the principle of low markup and high volume. The manufacturer's reputation for quality merchandise usually offsets customer concern about the reputation of the retailer.

Often firms prefer to operate on the basis of fewer services but lower prices. For years, Macy's New York store advertised that its prices were at least 6 per cent below those charged by stores which granted credit. Pricing below competition is also a good way for a company to penetrate a new market. It is a method particularly adaptable to products with an elastic demand; that is, in general, the type of product upon which the discount houses built such huge volume. At the manufacturing level, pricing below market is a strategy employed by small fringe firms attempting to compete with much larger organizations.

Pricing above competitive level   Manufacturers or retailers sometimes set their prices above the market level. This may be done by a producer who follows a temporary or even a permanent strategy of cream skimming. Usually above-market pricing can be done only when the product is unique or distinctive or when the seller has acquired prestige in his field. An outstanding women's specialty clothing store is able to price an article above the market level just because the article carries the store's label. At the national level, this is probably possible for such organizations as I. Magnin, Saks Fifth Avenue, Neiman-Marcus, or Marshall Field and Company. Most cities have a prestige clothing, jewelry, furniture, or even food store where price tags are noticeably above the competitive level set by other stores which handle similar types of products.

QUESTIONS AND PROBLEMS

1   What marketing conditions have served to reduce the importance of the price-setting function in many companies today?

2   What is the expected price for each of the following articles? How did you arrive at your estimate in each instance?
   a.   New type of carbonated cola beverage which holds its original carbonation long after it has been opened; packaged in 8-ounce and 32-ounce bottles
   b.   Men's dress shoes made entirely of long-wearing, high-quality plastic which simulates leather
   c.   Nuclear-powered, 21-inch, table-model television set guaranteed to run ten years without replacing the original power-generating component; requires no battery or electric wires
   d.   Automatic garage-door opener for residential housing

3   Name some products for which you think an inverse demand exists. Within which price range does this demand exist for each product on your list?

4 Who in a manufacturing firm should have the responsibility for setting the basic price on a product? In a department store, who has this job? Under what circumstances is it customary for the salesmen to set the price?

5 Give some examples of products which have an elastic demand. An inelastic demand.

6 For each of the following products, do you recommend that the seller adopt a cream-skimming or a penetration pricing strategy? Support your decision in each instance.
   a. Original models of women's dresses styled and manufactured by Dior
   b. A new wonder drug
   c. An exterior house paint which wears twice as long as any competitive brand
   d. A cigarette really totally free of tars and nicotine
   e. Instant beer
   f. Atomic-powered motor boat, family-sized

7 Discuss the following propositions:
   a. Skim-the-cream pricing is feasible only when the seller employs an exclusive or a highly selective distribution policy.
   b. Penetration pricing is practical only when a firm engages in intensive distribution.

8 Referring to Fig. 18–2, at what point does the marginal cost curve (MC) intersect the average total cost curve (ATC)? Explain why the ATC curve is declining up to the intersection point and rising beyond it. Explain how the MC curve can be rising while the ATC curve is still declining.

9 In Table 18–1, what is the marginal cost of the seventh unit produced?

10 "Without exception, the marginal cost is always equal to the variable cost of the marginal unit." Do you agree?

11 What are the merits and limitations of the cost-plus method of setting a basic price?

12 In a break-even chart, is the total *fixed* cost line always horizontal? Is the total *variable* cost line always straight? Explain.

13 Referring to Table 18–2 and Fig. 18–4, what are the break-even points at prices of $50 and $90 if the variable costs are $40 a unit and the fixed costs remain at $250?

14 Referring to Table 18–2 and Fig. 18–4, find the break-even point for selling prices of $60 and $100 if the fixed cost totals $400.

15 "Beyond the break-even point, all revenue from sales is pure profit. Consequently, once the break-even point is achieved, it behooves the seller to increase his advertising and personal selling efforts in order to get more of these profitable, above-break-even-point sales." Discuss.

16 Does supply and demand analysis in relation to pricing have any practical value for the businessman?

17 Referring to Fig. 18–6, why would the firm normally stop producing at quantity *OE*? Why is the price set at *EC* (same as *OB*) and not at *EF* or *ED*?

18 Are there any stores in your community which generally price above the competitive level? How are they able to do this?

19   A soft drink manufacturer has been pricing his 10-ounce bottled drink to sell for 10 cents at retail. The product has strong market acceptance in its regional market, competing favorably with Coca-Cola, Pepsi-Cola, 7-Up, and other well-known brands. For some time, production and marketing costs have been increasing, and management must now take some action. Which of the following courses of action should the company follow? Can you propose a better alternative?

a.   Raise the price to 13 cents or two bottles for 25 cents
b.   Reduce the quality of the beverage
c.   Reduce the quantity to 8 ounces
d.   Curtail the advertising

19

PRICE POLICIES AND STRATEGIES

After management has set the basic or list price for its product, it must turn its attention to the many facets of the price system that require the formulation of specific policies. What kind of quantity discount schedule shall we adopt? Should we fair-trade our products? Shall we insist upon f.o.b. pricing, or shall we occasionally absorb freight?

In this chapter and the next, we shall discuss ten problem areas in pricing, listed below, which call for executive policy making. We shall also consider the more important legal aspects of some of the price policies.

1. Discounts and allowances
2. Geographic price policies
3. One price versus variable price
4. Pricing multiple products
5. Price lining
6. Resale price maintenance
7. "Leader" pricing

8. Guarantee against price decline
9. Psychological pricing
10. Price competition versus nonprice competition

Many of the price policies discussed here are closely related to, and can be explained by, some of the general economic theory noted in the preceding chapter. That is, many "pricing policies are special cases of the general theory of monopolistic competition."[1]

DISCOUNTS AND ALLOWANCES

Discounts and allowances result in a deduction from the list price. The deduction may be in the form of cash or some other concession, such as a free case of merchandise. The philosophy underlying discounts and allowances is that the customer will in return perform some marketing activities whose value to the seller will be equivalent to the amount of the discount or allowance. Commonly used forms include quantity, trade, cash, and seasonal discounts; and promotional, brokerage, and freight allowances. Allowances for freight are discussed later in this chapter; the others are considered at this point.

Quantity discounts

Quantity discounts are deductions offered from list prices by a seller in order to encourage a customer to buy in larger amounts or to concentrate his purchases with this seller. The discounts may be based on dollar or unit purchases.

Cumulative and noncumulative quantity discounts   A *noncumulative* discount is based upon an individual order of one or more products. Thus a retailer may sell golf balls at $1 each or at three for $2.50. A manufacturer or a wholesaler may set up a quantity discount schedule such as the following, which was used by a manufacturer of industrial adhesives. Noncumulative

Boxes purchased on single order	Percentage discount from list price
1–5	
6–12	2.0
13–25	3.5
Over 25	5.0

quantity discounts are expected to encourage large orders. Many expenses, such as billing, order filling, shipping, and salesmen's salaries, are about the same whether the seller receives an order totaling $10 or $500. Consequently, selling expense as a percentage of sales decreases as the order becomes larger.

A cumulative discount is based on the total volume (dollars or units)

[1] Edward R. Hawkins, "Price Policies and Theory," *Journal of Marketing*, January, 1954, p. 233. This article contains a good discussion of the relations between price policies and the estimate of the demand curve facing an individual seller.

purchased over a period of time. These discounts are an advantage to a seller because they tie customers more closely to him. They are really patronage discounts in that the more total business a buyer gives a seller, the greater is the discount. They are especially applicable to the sale of perishable products. The seller wants to encourage a customer to buy fresh supplies frequently so that the merchandise will not grow stale. Thus the discount is based on total purchases over a month, rather than on each separate order.

Either type of quantity discount can be used nicely by a company producing several related or even nonrelated products which are apt to be purchased by a single buyer. Often the sales of a slow-moving item can be stimulated if it is offered in an attractive discount package with more popular items. Finally, quantity discounts can help a manufacturer effect real economies and efficiencies in the production end of the business as well as in selling. Large orders can result in more efficient, lower-cost production runs. A cumulative discount based on total orders from all units in a retail chain may enable a producer to make much more effective use of his production capacity, even though orders are shipped in small amounts with no savings in marketing costs.

Discount schedules can create ill will between buyers and sellers. The buyer whose purchases are just below the next bracket often pressures the seller to give him the higher discount. A salesman may be tempted to overload his customers by urging them to buy larger quantities than they need in order to get higher discounts. Management faces a real problem in the task of constructing the discount schedule. Cost studies and analyses of customer buying habits are usually necessary in order to set up the proper discount percentages and quantity brackets. A drawback to cumulative discounts is that they are in no way related to the size of individual orders; hence there is no premium attached to buying in large, economical units.

Trade discounts

Trade discounts, sometimes called "functional" discounts, are a reduction from list price offered to middlemen or other types of buyers in payment for marketing functions which they will presumably perform. A manufacturer may quote a retail list price of $400 with trade discounts of 40 per cent and 10 per cent. The retailer pays $240 ($400 less 40 per cent), and the wholesaler pays the manufacturer $216 ($240 less 10 per cent). The wholesaler is given the 40 and 10 per cent. He is expected to keep the 10 per cent to cover the costs of his wholesaling functions, and pass on the 40 per cent to the retailers. It should be noted that the 40 and 10 do not constitute a total discount of 50 per cent off list price. Each discount percentage in the "chain" is computed on the amount remaining after the preceding percentage has been deducted. Trade discounts vary considerably from one industry to another because of differences in the normal markups required by various types of middlemen and differences in the traditional channels used.

In addition to allowing a middleman his usual markup in payment for functions he performs, trade discounts serve other purposes. They are usually high enough to cover high-cost middlemen, who otherwise would not be interested in handling the product. A large discount, however, may offer retailers an opportunity to sell below list. They can show the list price to the customer and make him feel he is getting a bargain. In another situation, many companies publish annual or seasonal catalogues with list prices. The net price can be varied simply by changing the amount of the trade discount. Therefore, if prices change, the seller does not have to print a new catalogue; he just changes the trade discount on the particular item.

When only list prices are published, it is difficult for buyers to compare competitive offerings unless they have the seller's current trade discount schedule and are also able to calculate the net price.

Trade discounts originated in the traditional channel and trade relationships which existed within each industry. A wholesaler was a wholesaler, and his functions were easy to distinguish from those of a retailer. Today, however, channel structures are far more complex, and price differentials occasioned by trade discounts are much more difficult to justify on a cost basis. Unless management makes a detailed marketing cost analysis by classes of customers, it can hardly prove that the discounts are equivalent, or even related, to the cost differentials incurred in dealing with these different classes of customers.

Cash discounts

A cash discount is a deduction from price granted to the buyer for paying his bill within a specified period of time. The discount is computed on the net amount due after first deducting trade and quantity discounts from the initial price. If a buyer owes $360 after the other discounts have been granted, and he is offered terms of, say, 2/10, n/30 on an invoice dated November 8, he may deduct a discount of 2 per cent ($7.20) if he pays his bill within ten days after the date of invoice (by November 18); otherwise he must pay the entire bill of $360 in thirty days (December 8). In a cash discount, two elements are present—the percentage reduction itself and the time period within which the bill must be paid. There are many different terms of sale because practically every industry has its own combination of these two elements. For example, one may see 2/10, n/30; 1/10, n/60; 2/10 e.o.m. (2 per cent discount if paid within ten days after the end of the month); 3/10, n/60 r.o.g. (the ten-day discount period starts upon receipt of the goods).

Most buyers are extremely eager to have their accounting departments pay the bills in time to earn the cash discounts. The discount in a 2/10, n/30 situation may not seem like very much. But management must realize that this 2 per cent is earned just for paying twenty days in advance of when the entire bill is due. If a buyer fails to take the cash discount in a 2/10, n/30 situation, he is, in effect, borrowing money at a rate of interest which, if computed on an annual basis, would be 36 per cent. (Figuring a 360-day year, there are eighteen periods of twenty days each in the year. Eighteen periods at 2 per cent each equals 36 per cent.)

Seasonal discounts and forward dating

If a firm is producing an article, such as air conditioners or lawn mowers, which is purchased on a seasonal basis, management may want to consider the strategy of granting a seasonal discount. This is a discount of, say, 5, 10, or 20 per cent which is given to a customer who places an order during the slack season. Off-season orders enable the manufacturer to level out his production schedule and make better use of his facilities.

Forward dating is a variation of both a seasonal discount and a cash discount. A manufacturer of fishing tackle will seek orders from wholesalers and retailers during the winter months. The bill will be dated, say, April 1, and terms of 2/10, n/30 may be offered as of that date. Thus the seller can get orders in December and January which help him to level out his production. The wholesale or retail buyers do not have to pay their bills, however, until after the season starts.

Promotional allowances

Promotional allowances are price deductions granted by sellers to buyers in payment for promotional services performed by the buyer. These allowances may also be in the form of promotional aids and materials supplied by the seller. To illustrate, a manufacturer of builders' hardware gives a certain quantity of "free goods" to dealers who prominently display his line. A clothing manufacturer pays one-half the space charge of an advertisement placed by a retailer and featuring the manufacturer's product. A luggage manufacturer provides advertising display materials for all his retailers. The use of promotional allowances as a promotional strategy rather than a price strategy is discussed in Chapter 21.

Brokerage allowances

When the services of a broker as a wholesaling middleman are employed in the producer's channel of distribution, the broker is paid a certain percentage of the sales volume he generates. This payment is called a "brokerage fee" or a "brokerage allowance" and is really just another form of trade discount. Because of the legal implications in certain types of brokerage arrangements, these allowances are noted separately instead of being included with trade discounts. Many times in the past, the commission which the seller normally paid a broker was *instead* paid to large-scale buyers who performed the services usually ascribed to brokers. Today, however, the Robinson-Patman Act prohibits a seller from paying a brokerage fee to the buyer or any firm owned or controlled by the buyer.

The Robinson-Patman Act and price discrimination

The discounts and allowances discussed in this section may result in different prices for different customers. Whenever price differentials exist, there is price discrimination; the terms are synonymous. In certain situations, price discrimination is prohibited under the Robinson-Patman Act. This is one of the most important Federal laws affecting a company's marketing program. Federal laws apply only to interstate commerce, but the interpretation of what is "interstate" is quite broad.

Background of the act   In 1890, after many years of public discontent with the monopolistic and collusive practices in restraint of trade by large manufacturers, Congress passed the Sherman Antitrust Act. The intent of the law was to declare illegal, monopolies and combinations in restraint of trade in interstate commerce. Less than satisfactory success with the enforcement of this law led Congress to seek other methods of regulating the trade practices of large companies. Consequently, in 1914 Congress passed two laws—the Clayton Antitrust Act, which generally outlawed price discrimination, and the Federal Trade Commission Act, which prohibited unfair competition. It was felt that monopolies were nurtured by price discrimination and unfair competition. Therefore, by declaring these two business practices illegal, Congress presumably had removed the conditions necessary to develop monopolies and other combinations in restraint of trade.

The years following World War I, however, saw the development of large-scale retailing among mail-order houses and chain stores and the subsequent decline in the competitive position of the small store. The Depression of the early 1930s focused attention still further on the plight of the small-scale merchant. Three questionable trade practices involving price discrimination were pinpointed as particular sources of the large retailers' competitive advantage. They included unearned quantity discounts, dummy brokerage allowances, and pseudo promotional allowances, and were labeled a "triumvirate of evil" by an oratorical legislator. The Clayton Antitrust Act proved inadequate to cope with these practices because, in the course of administering and enforcing the price-discrimination sections of this law, the government found too many weaknesses and loopholes. Consequently, in 1936, during an era of anti-chain-store feeling, the Robinson-Patman Act was passed to amend Section 2—the price-discrimination section—of the Clayton Antitrust Act.

Main provisions of the act   The Robinson-Patman Act was intended to curb the practices of large-scale retailers only, but it was written in such general terms that through the years it also has become applicable to manufacturers.

PRICE DISCRIMINATION   Price discrimination is prohibited between different purchasers of products of like grade and quality if the effect of this discrimination may be substantially to lessen or injure competition with the person who either grants or knowingly receives the benefits of such discrimination or with customers of either of them.[2]

INJURY TO COMPETITION   Not all price differentials are illegal under this law. One exception involves the impact on competition. Price differentials are considered unlawfully discriminatory only when their effect *may be* substantially to lessen competition. This provision is broad but not unlimited. To establish a prima facie case of price discrimination, the government has to prove only that a *reasonable probability* of injury to competition exists; *actual* injury does not have to be proved by the government.[3] The injury-to-competition section also applies to three levels of trade. It is unlawful for a seller to discriminate in price if this may lead to a substantial lessening of competition (1) with other sellers, (2) among firms buying from the discriminating seller, or (3) among the customers of these buyers. Thus manufacturer A cannot discriminate if this may unduly hurt other manufacturers, Mr. A's wholesalers, or any retail customers of these wholesalers.

OTHER EXCEPTIONS AND DEFENSES   Price differentials are allowable in response to changing conditions which affect the market for, or the marketability of, goods. For example, differentials are allowed in response to seasonal obsolescence, physical deterioration of products, distress sales, or going-out-of-business sales.

---

[2] For an analysis of the "like-grade-and-quality" proviso and the inconsistencies and implications in its interpretations, see Jacky Knopp, Jr., "Branding and the Robinson-Patman Act," *Journal of Business*, January, 1966, pp. 24–34; and Jacky Knopp, Jr., "What Are 'Commodities of Like Grade and Quality'?" *Journal of Marketing*, July, 1963, pp. 63–66. Most frequently, the interpretation problems center around "private" branding; that is, price differentials are established by a manufacturer who sells a product under his own brand or label and also sells a physically and chemically identical product under a middleman's brand.

[3] *Corn Products Refining Company v. Federal Trade Commission*, 324 U.S. 726 (1945). In this same decision (p. 742) the Supreme Court apparently contradicted itself or was not careful in its choice of words, for it said that there need be only a reasonable *possibility* that the discriminations *may* have harmed competition. This unfortunate choice of words became part of the basis for the Supreme Court's decision against the Morton Salt Company. See *Federal Trade Commission v. Morton Salt Company*, 68 S. Ct. 822 (1948). The Morton Salt case probably marked the peak of the period of strict interpretation of the "injury-to-competition" clause. Later decisions reverted to the idea that a reasonable probability of injury must exist. Also, there must be proof of substantial and continuing injury, not trivial or sporadic injury, before a prima facie case can be established. See *Minneapolis-Honeywell Regulator Company v. Federal Trade Commission*, 191 F. 2d 786 (1951); certiorari dismissed, 344 U.S. 206 (1952).

Price differentials may be granted if they do not exceed differences in the cost of manufacture, sale, or delivery resulting from differences in the quantity sold or from different methods of sale or delivery of the product. These differentials are allowable even though there is a reasonable probability of injury to competition. This "cost proviso" is a main defense available to firms engaging in differential pricing.

The hitch is that the burden of proof rests with the seller and not with the Federal Trade Commission or other plaintiffs in a case. Almost of necessity, a firm must show a detailed marketing cost analysis if it hopes to use the cost defense in Robinson-Patman cases. Furthermore, the history of enforcement of the act suggests that the differential prices should be established *as a result of* a marketing cost analysis. Too often, firms have discriminated in price and then, when called to task by the Federal Trade Commission, have tried to justify their price differentials by after-the-fact cost studies. Usually these companies have lost their cases. "Anyone who has not considered costs when creating price differences should expect a long, difficult, and expensive experience in preparing and attempting to sustain a cost defense."[4]

Another major defense available under the act is the "meeting-competition" defense. A firm may rebut a prima facie case of price discrimination by showing that its lower price was set "in good faith to meet an equally low price of a competitor." Also, a seller may furnish services and facilities to a buyer if this is done in good faith to meet the services or facilities furnished by a competitor. Through the years, this defense has proved to be something less than satisfactory to most defendants. Usually the decision has been that good faith was lacking when this defense was used in support of price differentials. Also, the Federal Trade Commission has maintained that this defense is only procedural, shifting the burden of proof back to the Commission; the Commission does not consider this a substantive defense which absolves or frees the defendant from the charges brought under the law. In spite of the Federal Trade Commission's opinion on this matter, however, the courts in recent years seem to have established that meeting the equally low price of individual competitors is a complete or substantive defense against charges of price discrimination.[5]

---

[4] Donald J. Fennelly, "On the Judging of Mince Pies," *Harvard Business Review*, November–December, 1964, p. 79. This article presents an accountant's view of the cost defense, and it offers six proposals for introducing greater clarity and equity into the enforcement and observance of the Robinson-Patman Act.

For a report on the court's treatment of the cost defense in the 1960s and an examination of the analytical methods used by the Supreme Court and the Federal Trade Commission as they evaluate cost defenses presented to them, see Robert A. Lynn, "Is the Cost Defense Workable?" *Journal of Marketing*, January, 1965, pp. 37–42.

[5] *Federal Trade Commission v. Standard Oil Company (Indiana)*, 355 U.S. 396 (1958). See also *Standard Oil Company (Indiana) v. Federal Trade Commission*, 340 U.S. 231 (1951).

BUYER'S LIABILITY   The Robinson-Patman Act includes an innovation in trade regulations in that the buyer is as guilty as the seller if he (the buyer) knowingly induces or receives an unlawful price discrimination. This provision is intended to restrain large-scale buyers from demanding discriminatory prices. Prior to the Robinson-Patman Act, a seller who succumbed and granted the differential could be found guilty, and the pressuring buyer would go scot-free.

In general, the interpretations of this provision have shown that it is largely ineffectual in restraining buyers. From a practical standpoint, it has been difficult to prove that the buyer "knowingly" received an unlawful price differential. The courts have ruled that it is not the buyer's responsibility to prove that the price differentials were equal to the seller's cost savings. The buyer cannot be expected to acquire access to the seller's accounting records. Rather, it is up to the Federal Trade Commission to prove that sufficient cost savings did not exist. Also, in the Automatic Canteen Company case, the Supreme Court ruled that the Federal Trade Commission must show that (1) the buyer knew he was getting a lower price and (2) the buyer knew this price could not be justified under the act.[6]

In the same decision, however, the Supreme Court suggested that a buyer's knowledge of prevailing trade practices in his industry might be ample evidence that this buyer knew whether or not he was receiving discriminatory price advantages. In subsequent years, decisions in Circuit Courts of Appeals based on the Supreme Court's inferences in the Automatic Canteen case have supported and strengthened the Federal Trade Commission in its administration of the buyer's-liability section of the Robinson-Patman Act.[7]

BROKERAGE PAYMENTS   The Robinson-Patman Act tackles the problem of unearned brokerage payments by declaring that it is unlawful to pay or receive brokerage allowances except for services rendered. Essentially it is illegal for a seller to pay brokerage fees directly to a buyer or to anyone owned or controlled by the buyer.

While interpretations by the Federal Trade Commission and the courts make the meaning of this section clear, its soundness from a marketing viewpoint is highly questionable. For example, the buyer for a chain of grocery stores may approach a food canner and offer to buy a quantity of canned

[6] *Automatic Canteen Company of America v. Federal Trade Commission*, 346 U.S. 61 (1953). See also Edward W. Barrett, Harper W. Boyd, Jr., Dascomb R. Forbush, and Ralph Westfall, "The Automatic Canteen Company Case and Buyer's Liability under the Robinson-Patman Act," *Journal of Marketing*, January, 1954, p. 246.

[7] See *American Motor Specialties Co., Inc. v. Federal Trade Commission*, Commerce Clearing House, Trade Regulation Reporter, ¶ 69,712, as reported in "Legal Developments in Marketing," *Journal of Marketing*, October, 1960, pp. 72–73; see also *Mid-South Distributors et al. and Cotton States Inc. et al. v. Federal Trade Commission*, Commerce Clearing House, Trade Regulation Reporter, ¶ 69,939, as reported in "Legal Developments in Marketing," *Journal of Marketing*, July, 1961, p. 83.

fruits and vegetables, or the chain may purchase through a firm acting as its agent. In either case the chain or its agent is performing all the services normally provided by a broker working for the seller. Prior to the passage of the Robinson-Patman Act, it was common practice for a large buyer to seek, and for a seller to grant freely and openly, the usual brokerage commission. The seller was granting a form of discount to his customers in return for their performance of functions which the seller would otherwise have to provide. In outlawing such practices under the Robinson-Patman Act, the courts have said that buyer and seller are at arm's length in a transaction and that it is not possible for a buyer or anyone working for him to render services to a seller. Any services performed by the buyer are for his own benefit and not that of the seller. Consequently, the "except-for-services-rendered" clause is virtually interpreted out of the act when a buyer seeks a rebate or allowance in lieu of the usual brokerage fee.

To strengthen even more the prohibition against a buyer's getting a brokerage allowance from a seller, the courts have ruled in several cases that the brokerage section stands alone in the act; it is not connected with any other section. Thus the cost defense is not permissible under this section, nor is the defense of meeting competition in good faith. Truly the food brokers—the originally intended beneficiaries of this section—have a protective umbrella held over them.

PROMOTIONAL ALLOWANCES   Various types of promotional services and facilities, or payments to buyers in lieu of these services or facilities, are lawful under the Robinson-Patman Act only if they are offered to all competing customers on proportionally equal terms. The Supreme Court has ruled that injury to competition does not need to be proved in order to show a violation of these sections. Furthermore, the cost defense is not admissible, but a firm may use the defense that it discriminated in order to meet competition in good faith.[8] In the interpretation of the sections on promotional allowances, the real problem is to determine what is meant by "proportionally equal terms." This concept and its practical application are examined in Chapter 23, in connection with a firm's promotional program.

History of interpretation of the act   The Robinson-Patman Act is probably one of the most ambiguous, controversial laws ever written for the purpose of regulating trade. It is extremely difficult to set forth many helpful generalizations for use by marketing executives. Some sections, such as those covering brokerage payments and buyer's liability, are reasonably clear. In others, as one writer has said, "twenty-three years of enforcement have produced crystal-clear confusion."[9] One respected legal authority who has been involved in

[8] See *Exquisite Form Brassiere, Inc. vs. Federal Trade Commission*, 301 F. 2d, 499 (1961); certiorari denied, 82 S. Ct. 1162 (1962).

[9] W. David Robbins, "A Marketing Appraisal of the Robinson-Patman Act," *Journal of Marketing*, July, 1959, p. 15.

Robinson-Patman litigations sums up his opinion regarding the regulatory impact of the act: [10]

On balance, a quarter century of Robinson-Patman administration has probably restrained more competition than it has preserved. The Act's chartless enforcement became a "numbers game" which largely missed the "big buyer" —the Congressional target—and often boomeranged on the smaller competitor, the Act's intended beneficiary. Overall, although the Act's prohibitions are porous, it has fostered a regulatory climate which inhibits competition and breeds restraint.

Anticipating no congressional revision of the act and doubting any administrative reorientation toward it, Rowe sees the judicial process as the best hope for adapting "this relic of the Great Depression to the economic setting of a more dynamic age."

Legality of quantity discounts   Because quantity discounts result in different prices to different customers, these differential or discriminatory prices are potentially illegal under the Robinson-Patman Act if the necessary injury to competition can be shown. To justify its price differentials stemming from its quantity discounts schedule, management must rely on the cost defense provided in the act. In a nutshell, quantity discounts are legal if the resultant price differentials do not exceed the differentials in the cost of manufacturing, selling, or delivering various quantities of the product. The price differentials may be less than the cost savings, but they must not exceed the differences in cost.

A study of the quantity discount cases brought under the Robinson-Patman Act will show that cumulative discounts have virtually no chance of being defended, because it is not possible to show that the discounts make due allowance for differences in cost only.

Noncumulative discounts can be based upon corresponding cost differentials, but defendants have used the cost defense successfully in very few cases over the past twenty-five years. There are two main reasons for this poor record. In the first place, very few companies have sufficiently detailed marketing cost information upon which to build a cost defense. Even today, most firms have not awakened to the need for detailed information on marketing expenses, even though they may have been keeping detailed records on production costs for years. The second reason for the lack of success with the cost defense was suggested earlier. Too often a company has made a cost study *after* the discount schedule was set up and *after* the Federal Trade Commission has issued a complaint. Thus it was obvious that the company did not

[10] Frederick M. Rowe, *Price Discrimination under the Robinson-Patman Act*, Little, Brown and Company, Boston, 1962, p. 551.

base the schedule on cost differentials, for the company really did not know what the differentials were until the case came up.

Legality of trade discounts   There is no specific statement about functional discounts in either the Clayton Act or the Robinson-Patman Act. Consequently, the legal status of trade discounts is still a little fuzzy. Three landmark cases brought under the Clayton Act established the point that separate discounts could be given to separate classes of buyers.[11] That is, one discount could be given to wholesalers and another to retailers, so long as all buyers within a given group were offered the same discount. Whether a firm was classified as a retailer or as a wholesaler depended entirely upon the status and motives of the customers and not upon the nature of the buying operation or the quantity of the purchases. Therefore, a large chain selling to ultimate consumers would be classed as a retailer, even though it purchased in larger quantities than many wholesalers and even though it performed wholesaling functions in its buying.

Presumably, functional or trade discounts are legal under the Robinson-Patman Act if they are genuinely offered to different classes of customers in return for services rendered. It might also be presumed that the legality of a manufacturer's trade discount schedule would be helped if the differentials in the schedule were reasonably related to cost savings resulting from the use of the various classes of middlemen.

Because of lack of specific coverage in the act, and because changes in distribution patterns have upset traditional channel structures, it seems reasonable to assume that functional discounts will be increasingly scrutinized and challenged by the Federal Trade Commission in the years to come.

GEOGRAPHIC PRICE POLICIES

When establishing a price structure, a seller must consider the factor of freight costs involved in shipping the product to the buyer. This consideration grows in importance as freight becomes a larger part of total variable costs. Pricing policies may be established whereby the buyer pays all the freight, the seller bears the entire cost, or the two parties share the expense. The decision can have an important bearing on the geographic limits of a firm's market, the location of its production facilities and sales branches, the source of its raw materials, and its competitive strength in various market areas.

F.O.B. point-of-production pricing

In one widely used geographic pricing system, the seller quotes the selling price at the factory, mill, or other point of production and has the buyer

---

[11] *Mennen Company v. Federal Trade Commission*, 288 Fed. 774 (1923); certiorari denied, 262 U.S. 759 (1923); *Great Atlantic and Pacific Tea Company v. Cream of Wheat Company*, 277 Fed. 46 (1915); *National Biscuit Company v. Federal Trade Commission*, 299 Fed. 733 (1924), certiorari denied, 266 U.S. 613 (1924).

pay the entire cost of transportation. This is usually referred to as f.o.b. mill or factory pricing. Of the five systems discussed in this section, this is the only one in which the seller does not pay any of the freight costs. The seller pays the costs of loading the shipment aboard the carrier—hence the term "f.o.b.," or "free on board." The title to the merchandise passes to the buyer at that point, and he assumes all costs and responsibilities for shipping. Even though this policy is usually thought of as a manufacturer's pricing policy and therefore is labeled f.o.b. factory or some other point of production, it is used by many middlemen. Cash-and-carry wholesalers price their merchandise f.o.b. warehouse. Many discount houses and other retailers sell on an f.o.b. store basis, and the consumer pays the delivery costs.

Under the f.o.b. factory price policy, the seller nets the same amount on each sale of similar quantities. The delivered price to the buyers varies according to the freight charges. Although the Federal Trade Commission has, in general, considered an f.o.b. mill pricing system nondiscriminatory, this pricing policy has serious economic and marketing implications. In effect, f.o.b. pricing tends to establish a geographic monopoly for a given seller. Freight rates prevent distant competitors from entering his market. He in turn is increasingly priced out of markets that are far from his factory. At the same time, buyers located some distance from the seller pay heavy freight bills. If freight is a significant part of the total cost of the seller's product, it can have considerable influence on the size of his market. Many manufacturers have had to locate their plants close to the source of high-freight materials which were priced f.o.b. factory.

Uniform delivered pricing

Under a uniform delivered pricing system, the same delivered price is quoted to all buyers, regardless of their locations. This policy is sometimes referred to as "postage stamp pricing" because of the similarities of the pricing of mail service. Actually, the seller is pricing f.o.b. at the buyer's location. The seller receives varying factory net prices on each sale depending upon the amount of his shipping costs.

A uniform delivered price is typically used where transportation costs are a minor item in the seller's total cost structure. The policy is also used by many retailers who feel that "free" delivery is an additional service which will strengthen their market position.

It has been generally established by the Supreme Court that a uniform delivered price is legal when it is truly maintained over the seller's entire geographic market.[12] A uniform delivered price does mean, however, that the seller is absorbing freight on shipments to distant customers and overcharging on freight (called "phantom" freight) in sales to buyers located near the shipping point.

[12] *Federal Trade Commission v. A. E. Staley Manufacturing Company*, 324 U.S. 746 (1945); see particularly p. 757.

Under a uniform delivered price system, buyers located near the seller's factory are paying for some of the costs of shipping to more distant locations. The counterargument is that an f.o.b. factory system gives an undue advantage to buyers located near the factory. Critics of f.o.b. factory price usually are in favor of a uniform delivered price. They feel that the freight expense should not be isolated and charged to individual customers any more than any other single marketing or production expense. From a marketing standpoint, a uniform delivered price is a convenient method of quoting price. It also lends itself to national advertising.

Zone delivered pricing

Under a zone price policy, a seller's market is divided into a limited number of broad geographic zones, and a uniform delivered price is set within each zone. Zone delivered pricing is quite similar to the system used in pricing parcel post services and long-distance telephone service. A firm which quotes a price and then says "slightly higher west of the Rockies" is using a two-zone pricing system.

Whether the company uses a single-zone pricing system (uniform delivered price) or a multizone system, the freight charge built into the delivered price is approximately an average of the charges at all points within a zone area. Therefore a seller either absorbs some of the freight costs or includes phantom freight in sales to all points, with one exception. This exception is sales made to buyers who are located at the point in the zone where the actual freight costs are equal to the arbitrary freight figure included in the selling price.

When a zone delivered price system is employed, the seller must walk a neat tightrope to avoid charges of illegal price discrimination among buyers or among customers of the buyers. This means that the zone lines must be drawn so that all competing buyers are in the same zone. This condition is almost impossible to meet in the dense market areas of the East and the Midwest.

Freight absorption pricing

A freight absorption price policy may be adopted to offset some of the competitive disadvantages of f.o.b. factory pricing. With an f.o.b. factory price, a firm is at a price disadvantage when it tries to sell to buyers located in markets nearer to competitors' plants. In order to penetrate more deeply into these markets, a seller may be willing to absorb some of the freight costs. As a policy, freight absorption usually means that seller A will quote to the customer a delivered price which is equal to A's factory price plus the freight costs which would be charged by the competitive seller located nearest the customer.

Our seller can continue to expand the geographic limits of his market as long as his mill net after freight absorption is larger than the marginal costs on the units sold. Freight absorption is particularly adaptable to a firm whose total fixed costs are heavy or whose fixed costs per unit of product are high and whose variable costs are low. In these cases, management must constantly seek ways to cover fixed costs, and freight absorption is one answer.

The legality of freight absorption is reasonably clear. The policy is legal if it is done independently and not in collusion with other firms. Also it must be done only to meet competition. In fact, if practiced properly, freight absorption can have the effect of strengthening competition because it can break down spatial monopolies and barriers around protected markets. Predatory freight absorption with the intent of destroying competition obviously would be unlawful.

Basing-point pricing

Even though it is not so widely used as it once was, and even though its legality is questioned, the basing-point system is extremely important. Under this system the delivered price of a product is equal to (1) the price at the point of production plus (2) published freight charges between the basing point nearest the buyer and the buyer's location. The actual shipping point has no bearing on the computation of the delivered price. A basing point itself is simply an arbitrary location from which delivered prices are computed by all competing sellers in an industry. Usually all basing points used by an industry are also important production points for the commodity, but not all production locations are basing points. Thus there are fewer basing points than production centers, and, as we shall see later, this factor has considerable influence on the legality of basing-point pricing.

To illustrate basing-point pricing, let us assume that a buyer is located in Kansas City and that Chicago is the nearest basing point. The established freight rates between Chicago and Kansas City for the product in question are $15 a unit. Manufacturers are located in Detroit, Chicago, and Kansas City. Freight charges between Detroit and Kansas City are $25 a unit. Let us assume also that all three manufacturers can produce and sell the product for $100 a unit at their factories. The delivered price in this example is $115—the price at point of production plus freight from the basing point closest to the buyer, regardless of the actual shipping point. The Chicago seller would have a mill net of $100; he just breaks even in this transaction. The Detroit manufacturer would have to absorb $10 of freight and would net only $90 at his factory. The Kansas City manufacturer would have a mill net of $115 because he would receive $15 in nonincurred, or phantom, freight.

Sellers may use either a single or a multiple basing-point system (a two-city basing-point system is shown in Fig. 19–1). Probably the best-known single basing-point system was the Pittsburgh-plus system used for years in the steel industry. The delivered price quoted for any steel product was equal to the mill price plus freight from Pittsburgh, regardless of where the sellers were located. This system generally aroused no objections so long as the steel producers were all located in or near Pittsburgh. As the industry expanded into Birmingham, Chicago, Cleveland, and other cities, however, trouble developed. Buyers located in Chicago, for example, objected to paying phantom freight from Pitts-

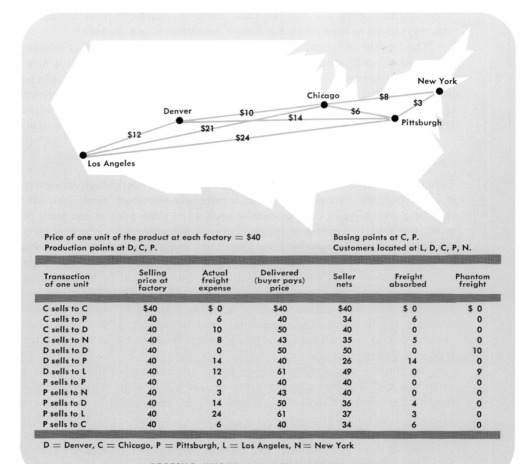

Price of one unit of the product at each factory = $40
Production points at D, C, P.

Basing points at C, P.
Customers located at L, D, C, P, N.

Transaction of one unit	Selling price at factory	Actual freight expense	Delivered (buyer pays) price	Seller nets	Freight absorbed	Phantom freight
C sells to C	$40	$ 0	$40	$40	$ 0	$ 0
C sells to P	40	6	40	34	6	0
C sells to D	40	10	50	40	0	0
C sells to N	40	8	43	35	5	0
D sells to D	40	0	50	50	0	10
D sells to P	40	14	40	26	14	0
D sells to L	40	12	61	49	0	9
P sells to P	40	0	40	40	0	0
P sells to N	40	3	43	40	0	0
P sells to D	40	14	50	36	4	0
P sells to L	40	24	61	37	3	0
P sells to C	40	6	40	34	6	0

D = Denver, C = Chicago, P = Pittsburgh, L = Los Angeles, N = New York

PRICING UNDER A BASING-POINT SYSTEM

fig. 19–1

Dollar amounts shown between various locations represent freight rates for shipping one unit of the product between the two given cities. The figures in the table show prices in this system, which has two basing points.

burgh when they purchased from Chicago mills. Although mills in or near Chicago might enjoy receiving phantom freight, they also might object to the single basing-point system. Under it, sellers located long distances from the basing point could not take advantage of their locations by offering lower prices to nearby customers.

Eventually a multiple basing-point system developed in the steel industry, and several other cities were designated as official basing points for various classes of steel products. As long as some sellers' locations are not designated as basing points, however, and as long as these sellers are closer to some buyers than is the nearest basing point, phantom freight is inescapable.

Characteristics of industries using basing-point system   In addition to the steel industry, such industries as cement, sugar, gypsum products, plate glass, heavy chemicals, lumber products, and corn products have used the basing-point system. These industries have several common characteristics which are conducive to the use of basing-point pricing. In the first place, the product in each is a standard, nondifferentiated item. Sugar is sugar, and window glass is window glass; price is all important, and brands are not significant. Another point is that freight constitutes a substantial cost element. Furthermore, fixed expenses constitute a large part of total costs, and excess capacity typically exists in basing-point industries. Thus, there is a constant threat of price-cutting by firms willing to accept orders at any price above variable costs. Even though total costs are not covered, any return over variable costs is a contribution to overhead. Finally, there are relatively few firms in the industry, and it is rather easy to get agreement on the use of the system and to enforce the agreement.

Evaluation of basing-point system   Several rather strong objections are typically raised against the basing-point pricing system. One is that it is not possible to justify the phantom freight. This is an unearned element, and it results in price discrimination. Another incriminating objection is that collusion is required to make the basing-point system work. The use of a freight rate book, published by the industry's trade association and rigidly followed when quoting prices, is considered evidence of collusion by many people.

Another criticism of basing-point pricing is that it eliminates price competition and makes for rigidity in the pricing structure. All sellers quote the same delivered price at any one location. Usually any attempt to cut below the "proper" price is met with swift and strong retaliation from competitive sellers. One seller cannot effectively take advantage of the fact that he is located nearer to buyers than other sellers are. Without a basing-point system, new plant development might be encouraged in markets where present demand exceeds supply and where there are good growth prospects. These new sellers could use their locational advantage to serve as the basis of a price advantage. Finally, there is a considerable amount of transportation crosshauling, which results in duplicate use of transportation facilities and resources. Because the delivered price is the same regardless of shipping point, a Birmingham firm, for example, may buy from a Pittsburgh seller, and a Pittsburgh firm may buy from a Birmingham seller. The result is two shipments between Birmingham and Pittsburgh where there would have been none if the buyers had purchased from the nearest sellers.

A number of advantages are stated in support of basing-point pricing, but they have some fundamental weaknesses. A frequently mentioned merit is that basing-point systems prevent the growth of spatial, or geographic, monopolies. Without this system, buyers would be at the mercy of the nearest seller. Consequently, many buyers are said to prefer basing-point pricing. This argument is weak on at least three points. First, if a seller were really prospering in his geographic area because outsiders could not overcome the freight barriers, other sellers would soon build competitive plants in the area. Second, distant sellers could still enter the market by absorbing freight on an independent basis. Finally, the buyers who are located near the sellers and who are paying phantom freight are certainly not in favor of basing-point pricing.

Another stated advantage of the system is that it prevents predatory price-cutting and chaotic conditions in an industry. Eliminating the system would force locational readjustment, and some sellers would be forced out of business. Individual firms which would suffer from these locational and other changes would no doubt prefer the *status quo*. In our system of free enterprise, however, an underlying thesis is that the system operates freely enough to allow entry, exit, and other changes by individual firms and that the net result is a more efficient system which better benefits society as a whole. While some individual firms may suffer, the entire economy is better off.

Legality of basing-point pricing   There is no law against the basing-point system per se. In various cases since about 1920, however, the Federal Trade Commission has sought to have the system outlawed, whether it was practiced by one company independently or by members of an entire industry working together. In the 1940s the Commission met with considerable success. Cases were brought separately against two large manufacturers of glucose, a corn syrup used in candy manufacturing. These firms employed a single basing-point system, using Chicago as the basing point, even though some of their plants were located elsewhere. There was no charge of collusion between the two sellers. Nevertheless, the Federal Trade Commission and the Supreme Court ruled in each case that the single basing-point system used by these firms involved phantom freight, was discriminatory, and thus was illegal under the Robinson-Patman Act.[13] A later and possibly even more important case involved the Federal Trade Commission's proceedings against the Cement Institute (a trade association) and its members, who were using a multiple basing-point system.[14] In this case the system was ruled illegal on two major counts. First, it was ruled to be unfair competition, and thus a violation of Section 5 of the Federal Trade Commission Act, because it was proved that collusion and combination in restraint of trade existed in the employment of the pricing system. Second, the multiple basing-point system was ruled unlawfully discriminatory and thus a violation of the Robinson-Patman Act.

In spite of these decisions, the legality of basing-point pricing is still not entirely clear. The Cement Institute case was decided in part by the fact that combination and conspiracy in restraint of trade were shown. The status of

[13] *Corn Products Refining Company v. Federal Trade Commission*, 324 U.S. 726 (1945); and *Federal Trade Commission v. A. E. Staley Manufacturing Company*, 324 U.S. 746 (1945).

[14] *Federal Trade Commission v. Cement Institute et al.*, 68 S. Ct. 793 (1948).

basing-point pricing where there is no proof of collusion is not entirely clear. Nevertheless, in the Cement Institute decision the Supreme Court referred to the glucose cases where there was no hint of collusion. From this reference, we can infer that a basing-point system is inherently discriminatory (because of phantom freight) and thus unlawful under the Robinson-Patman Act, whether or not collusion is present.

QUESTIONS AND PROBLEMS

1. Carefully distinguish between cumulative and noncumulative quantity discounts. Which of these two types of quantity discounts has the greater economic and social justification? Explain your position, disregarding the legal considerations for the time being.

2. A manufacturer of appliances quotes a list price of $500 a unit for a certain model of refrigerator. He then grants trade discounts of 35, 20, and 5 per cent. What is his selling price? Who might get these various discounts?

3. A building materials manufacturer sold a quantity of his product to a wholesaler for $350, and the wholesaler in turn sold to a lumberyard. The wholesaler's normal markup was 15 per cent, and the retailer usually priced the item to include a 30 per cent markup. What is the selling price to the consumer?

4. Interview a few different types of local retailers (restaurant, clothing store, sporting goods store, furniture store, etc.) and determine what terms of sale are customarily applied to their purchases. What accounts for the variations among the different types of retailers?

5. Two families living in the same apartment house each purchased a set of dining-room furniture from the same retailer. One family was charged $25 more than the other family. Is this a violation of the Robinson-Patman Act? Explain.

6. The Robinson-Patman Act prohibits price discrimination, yet manufacturers and wholesalers often charge different prices to different customers. Is this illegal?

7. Company A sells to all its customers at the same published price. A sales executive finds that company B is offering to sell to one of A's customers at a lower price. Company A then cuts its price to this one customer, but maintains the original price to all other customers. Is this a violation of the Robinson-Patman Act?

8. Using examples, explain the provisions of the section of the Robinson-Patman Act which deals with brokerage allowances.

9. What recent court cases have involved the Robinson-Patman Act? Briefly explain the situation in each case. The Commerce Clearing House's loose-leaf service on trade regulations is one source of information. The "legal-developments" section in the *Journal of Marketing* is another likely source.

10. Carefully explain the cost-defense provision in the Robinson-Patman Act.

11. Name some products which logically might be sold under a uniform delivered price system.

12. "An f.o.b. point-of-production price system is the only geographic price system which is fair to all buyers." Discuss.

13   Distinguish between a uniform delivered pricing system and a zone delivered system.

14   Explain how the basing-point system of pricing enables a seller to expand his market.

15   "The pricing system based on freight absorption has all the desirable features but none of the undesirable features of the basing-point system." Discuss.

16   If an Eastern manufacturer wants to compete in Western markets, where he is at a significant disadvantage with respect to freight costs, what pricing alternatives are open to this firm to help it overcome the freight differential?

17   "Adopting a multiple basing-point system eliminates the inherent undesirable features of basing-point pricing." Discuss.

20

PRICE POLICIES AND STRATEGIES (cont.)

The preceding chapter covered geographic price policies and several aspects of discounts and allowances. In this chapter we shall continue the discussion of price policies and strategies by considering eight additional problem areas.

ONE-PRICE VERSUS VARIABLE-PRICE POLICY

Rather early in its pricing consideration, management should decide whether the company will follow a one-price policy or a variable-price policy. While adopting one will not necessarily preclude the use of the other, normally it is not strategic to waver back and forth.

Under a *one-price* policy the company charges the same price to all similar types of customers who purchase similar quantities of the product under essentially the same terms of sale. Discounts and allowances may be granted under this policy if they are offered on equal terms to all comparable customers.

When a *variable-price* policy is used, the company will sell similar quantities to similar buyers at different prices. Sometimes variable prices are offered when the buyer and seller are friends; in other cases, sellers want the business of certain customers and will offer them favorable differential prices. Usually, however, under this policy the price is set as a result of bargaining.

In the United States, the one-price policy has been used more than variable pricing, particularly at the retail level. This is in contrast to many foreign countries where the final price is customarily determined by bargaining and haggling. A one-price policy is by no means the rule in the United States, however. In the marketing of any product where a trade-in is involved, variable pricing abounds. Thus a one-price policy is virtually unknown in automobile retailing, even though posted factory list prices may suggest that the same price is offered to all.

A one-price policy builds customer confidence in a seller, whether at the manufacturing, wholesaling, or retailing level; weak bargainers need not feel they are at a competitive disadvantage. The policy is also a great time-saver; it makes for a more orderly transaction process. Finally, this policy can be adopted whether personal salesmen are used or not. It lends itself nicely to self-service retailing, mail-order selling, and automatic vending.

A variable-price policy also has some advantages. It offers the seller flexibility in his dealings with different customers. The seller may wish to make price concessions to woo a buyer away from a competitor, or the seller may want to give a buyer a better deal because the customer shows promise of becoming a large-scale buyer in the future. Some sales representatives may have to use price concessions as the means of closing a sale.

On balance, however, variable-price policy is generally less desirable than a one-price policy. In sales to business firms, not to consumers, variable pricing is likely to be in violation of the Robinson-Patman Act. Variable pricing generates considerable ill will when the word gets around that some buyers acquired the product at lower prices. Price competition, while effective at the time, often offers only a short-run gain. Variable pricing can trigger a price war and bring strong retaliation in some industries. In most retail stores, variable pricing would result in chaotic selling conditions and a virtual absence of managerial control.

PRICING MULTIPLE PRODUCTS

Most firms market several lines of products or offer a breadth of products within one line. As the number of products increases, the pricing problems become more complex and difficult. When setting the basic list price for multiple products, management uses the same general methods it would if only one product were being marketed.

No article produced or carried by a company is an island unto itself, however. It is related to the company's other products through market demand, through cost, or through both. Management must consider these interrelationships when pricing the company's full complement of products.

On the *cost* side of the pricing equation, it can be seen that some products present joint cost situations. In the product lines of a meat-packer, for example, many products are derived from one beef carcass. In pricing related products, management may decide that each article must recoup its full cost plus a profit or that each must cover only variable costs, with any return above that level considered a contribution to overhead.

On the *demand* side, the products may differ but be related in quality, design, uses, or sizes. These interrelationships reduce management's flexibility in pricing because the executives always must consider the effect the original price or any price change will have on the prices of other products. A manufacturer of outboard motors sells a line of products in which one of the relative differences is the size of each model as measured by its horsepower. Thus when pricing a 15-horsepower motor, the executive must consider this price in relation to the ones set for motors of 7.5, 10, and 25 horsepower.

A key consideration in the pricing of multiple products is the degree to which the market for each size, quality level, brand, etc., can be isolated from the market for other sizes, brands, and quality levels. In the above example, if various sizes of outboard motors were sold to separate markets, isolated from one another, then each size could be priced without reference to the others. These markets usually are not isolated, however; they overlap and actually represent a continuum.

Another key consideration in pricing multiple products is that the firm should be trying to achieve a pricing goal on its total output or for a related group of products but not necessarily for each individual item. This point was mentioned in Chapter 17 in connection with the goal of profit maximization. If a company can increase its total profits by pricing certain articles below total costs or even below variable costs, then this is sound marketing strategy. In order to make possible a larger over-all profit, a firm may have to carry losing products just to round out its line.

PRICE LINING

Price lining is found more commonly among retailers than among wholesalers or producers. It consists in selecting a limited number of prices at which the store will sell its merchandise. A shoe store may sell several styles of shoes at $14.95 a pair, another group at $19.95, and a third assortment at $24.95. Price lining is used extensively in the retailing of all types of apparel. Many years ago, Woolworth's and other variety stores got the nickname "five-and-ten-cent stores" because of their policies of price lining everything at one of these two levels.

For the consumer, the main benefit of price lining is that it simplifies buying decisions; the choice of price is limited. From the retailer's point of view, the policy is advantageous because it helps the store owner to plan his purchases. A dress buyer, for example, can go into a market looking for dresses which may be retailed for $19.95, $29.95, or $39.95.

On the surface, price lining may seem to ease management's pricing decisions because the retail price is already set. Initially, however, the company had to decide how many lines to have and at what level each price line should be. Furthermore, every time the retailer wants to make a purchase, he has fundamentally the same pricing decisions to make that an executive in any other non-price-lining company has. The only difference is that in a price-lining company, the cost must fit into the price. The retailer still has the alternative of equating marginal cost and marginal revenue or of using cost-plus pricing in the form of his usual markup. The decision is made with respect to the price paid for the merchandise rather than the price at which it will be sold.[1]

Two big problems in price lining center around the task of setting the initial price lines and the difficulties encountered when the costs are increasing. In determining the price lines, management does not want too many or too few, and care must be taken that they are not too close together or too far apart. If they are too close together, the consumer may not be able to see why one item is x dollars higher than another. If they are too far apart, sales may be lost because some consumers want an article at the price in between the two levels.

Rising costs can put a real squeeze on price lines; a company hesitates to change its price line every time costs go up. But if costs increase and prices remain stationary, profit margins are compressed, and the retailer may be forced to seek products with lower costs. Where longtime relationships exist between manufacturers and retailers, or where price lines are traditional, as in 5- and 10-cent candy bars, manufacturers may reduce the product's size or quality (and thereby its costs) and enable retailers to hold prices at existing levels.

RESALE PRICE MAINTENANCE

Some manufacturers want to set or control the prices at which retailers will resell their products. They can do this by means of suggested resale prices or by means of a resale-price-maintenance policy supported by law.[2]

For some producers who follow a policy of suggested list prices, the price is just a guide for retailers; it is a list price on which discounts may be computed. For others, the suggested price is so rigidly enforced that a retailer's franchise

[1] For a discussion of the application of economic theory to the policy of price lining, see Edward R. Hawkins, "Price Policies and Theory," *Journal of Marketing*, January, 1954, pp. 237–238.

[2] For a description and analysis of methods used to encourage retail price stability by manufacturers of consumer goods, see Louis W. Stern, "Approaches to Achieving Retail Stability," *Business Horizons*, Fall, 1964, pp. 75–86. This investigation showed that the most effective and legally justifiable methods were those involving restricted distribution, market segmentation, and reductions in discounts and allowances. Methods which seemed inadequate included fair trade, granting promotional allowances, and moral suasion.

will be canceled if he does not adhere to the manufacturer's list. Normally, strict enforcement of the suggested list price is possible only when a manufacturer uses a selective or exclusive distribution pattern and when the brand is a desirable one from the retailer's point of view.[3]

One of the most controversial of all price policies is that of resale price maintenance established under state and Federal laws. The policy is employed by manufacturers, and it governs prices at the retail level. Resale-price-maintenance laws have come to be known as "fair-trade" laws. This is truly a strategic choice of titles: who can argue against fair trade? Opponents use the term "resale price-fixing."

Legal aspects of resale price maintenance

The Depression days of the 1930s spawned the state fair-trade laws. The intent of the laws was to protect small-scale retailers from the onslaught of large retailers, especially the chain stores. At the peak of their popularity, these laws existed in all states except Vermont, Missouri, and Texas. There also was no such legislation in the District of Columbia.

State legislation   In general, the state laws follow one of two model acts. In one model the manufacturer sets the *exact* price at which the product will be sold at retail. Under the other, the producer sets the *minimum* resale price. These laws are voluntary; the manufacturer does not have to fair-trade his products. They apply only to branded, copyrighted, or otherwise identifiable products sold in free and open competition. Usually under the laws a retailer may cut below the fair-trade price if he is holding a distress sale or discontinuing the product. In such cases, however, several of the laws first give the manufacturer the opportunity to buy back the stock at invoice price.

The key provision of the state fair-trade laws is known as the "nonsigners" clause. It states that when a manufacturer signs a fair-trade contract with one retailer in a state, every other retailer in the state is bound by this contract after due notice of the price has been given.

No state agencies have been set up to enforce these contracts. Enforcement is left up to the individual companies or groups of companies. It is a tremendous task and constitutes one of the greatest weaknesses in the laws.

Federal legislation   There was some concern, however, that resale price maintenance in interstate commerce was price-fixing in violation of the Federal antitrust laws, so, in 1937, the Miller-Tydings Act was passed as a piece of enabling legislation. It is an amendment to the Sherman Antitrust Act. It is not a Federal fair-trade law; it simply enables a firm in one state to fair-trade its products in any other state *which has a fair-trade law* without being in violation of the antitrust laws.

[3] See Louis W. Stern, "Economic Factors Influencing Manufacturers' Decisions concerning Price Maintenance," *Journal of Retailing*, Spring, 1965, pp. 30–37ff.

The Miller-Tydings Act and the state fair-trade laws withstood legal attack from many sources until 1951, when the nonsigners clause was held to be invalid in interstate competition.[4] In 1952 this loophole and others were plugged by the passage of the McGuire Act as an amendment to the Federal Trade Commission Act. The right to use the nonsigners clause in interstate commerce was specifically approved, and thus the teeth were restored to the state laws.

Current status of fair-trade legislation   The fair-trade laws are effective in fewer than thirty states. In the others, either the laws have been ruled unconstitutional or the nonsigners clause has been ruled invalid.

Realizing that fair-trade legislation on the state level is proving to be largely ineffective, the proponents of legalized resale price maintenance are exerting tremendous pressure to have a Federal fair-trade law passed. In recent sessions of Congress, a bill has been introduced which would allow a manufacturer of an identifiable product to fix its resale price. Notification to middlemen would be accomplished by advertising the resale price or by attaching a notice to the product. This bill was drafted originally by an agency of the National Association of Retail Druggists. It is, interestingly enough, strongly opposed by the Federal Trade Commission, the Antitrust Division of the Department of Justice, the Department of Agriculture, the Department of Commerce, and countless business interests.[5]

Prevalence of resale price maintenance   It is estimated that not more than 5 to 10 per cent of retail sales have ever been covered by fair-trade contracts. Resale price maintenance was especially prevalent in the drug trade— in toiletries, drug sundries, patent medicines, etc. This pricing practice also has been used by manufacturers of leather goods, photographic equipment, sporting goods, liquor, and small appliances.

Fair trade has virtually never been used on grocery items—a major segment of total retail trade. One reason for this is that grocery prices fluctuate too frequently; the task of notifying all grocery outlets would be unfeasible. Fair trade in food lines is also risky because most of the large grocery retailers have their own highly accepted brands. These middlemen's brands can easily be substituted for fair-traded manufacturers' brands. Fair trade is not at all practical where trade-ins are customary, as in large appliances, automobiles, and similar products. If refrigerators were fair-traded, for example, a discount seller could cut below fair trade by offering a large trade-in allowance on an old ice cube tray.

---

[4] *Schwegmann Bros. v. Calvert Distillers Corporation,* 341 U.S. 384 (1951).

[5] For a presentation of opposing sides of the "quality stabilization" controversy, see Stanley C. Hollander and James L. Fri, "A Debate: The Quality Stabilization Bill," *Business Horizons,* Spring, 1964, pp. 5–20.

Evaluation of resale price maintenance

Before a firm makes a decision on resale price maintenance, management should study the policy from the viewpoints of the manufacturer, the retailer, and the consumer.

Manufacturer's viewpoint   A manufacturer may want to fair-trade his product in order to advertise its price or to prevent its being used as a loss leader. He may fear that price cuts will damage his product's prestige. If price reductions are prolonged or permanent, as they would be in the hands of some large retailers, consumers may feel that the regular list price is an inflated indication of the product's value. Also, if the product becomes a price football, dealers who sell at the regular list price may discontinue the product or push substitute brands.

Another factor is that a manufacturer may want to protect his small dealers from the price competition of large-scale retailers because he feels that he needs small dealers. A price-cutting retailer may not be able or willing to give the selling effort and in-store promotion desired.

On the other hand, the competitive limitations of fair trade far outweigh any advantages which this policy may seem to have for manufacturers. It is doubtful that the absence of a fair-trade policy really can hurt the prestige of a product. Consumers are used to paying different prices at different outlets. If the product is a good one and is properly promoted by the manufacturer, many retailers will continue to carry it because of consumer demand.

Also, the factor of substitution is a two-edged sword. Some manufacturers fear that retailers will bury a product which is not fair-traded. At the same time, a product which is fair-traded may not be promoted and may not even be carried by many of the large-volume, low-cost retailers. The key words here are "low cost." For example, Sears, Roebuck and Company did not handle Sunbeam appliances while they were fair-traded. After the Sunbeam Corporation discontinued its fair-trade policy, however, some of their appliances were carried in the Sears catalogues and stores. Most large-volume, *high-cost* retailers, such as department stores, did carry Sunbeam and other fair-traded appliances. Manufacturers should also remember that a major reason why some middlemen have instituted their own brands and why these have been so successful is that they have had a price advantage over the higher fixed price of fair-traded manufacturers' brands.

Finally, it may be virtually impossible to enforce fair-trade contracts if any distribution policy except exclusive distribution is followed. Because of enforcement problems, a fair-trade policy has been discontinued by many formerly staunch advocates.

Retailer's viewpoint   Small retailers and high-cost, large retailers have traditionally favored fair trade. Small retailers are unable to match the price cuts offered by large stores; smaller operators do not have enough sales volume on other items or on the price-cut items to offset the loss from price reduction. Sometimes the large stores can *sell* to consumers at a lower price than small dealers can *buy* from their wholesalers.

One may wonder how retailers can afford to cut below list price. Some retailers do it to attract customers to the store; this is called "leader pricing" and is discussed in the next section. Price cuts may also be possible because the retailer buys in such large quantities that he gets substantial discounts or because he offers a minimum of service.

Fair trade has drawbacks for retailers as well as for manufacturers. The economic, social, and moral effects of the nonsigners clause are important. These points have been argued in the courts for over twenty-five years, and opinion is still substantially divided. This author's opinion is that the clause is undesirable. It seems that one retailer should not be bound by the interests of another. Also, if a retailer buys a product and assumes all risks of ownership, this should be a sufficient basis for letting him determine the price at which he will sell it.

Another disadvantage of fair trade is that it eliminates price competition at the retail level. Fair trade protects the high-cost, inefficient operator who wishes to maintain high unit margins even though he sells only a relatively small number of units. On the other hand, fair trade penalizes the retailer who prefers to earn a small profit per unit of sale and depend upon huge volume to reach his total profit goal. Retail price maintenance also penalizes the low-cost retailer who is not able to use his competitive advantage by passing on to consumers the lower prices resulting from the efficiency of his operation. Particularly does fair trade work to the advantage *of* the full-service retailer and *against* the retailer whose costs are low because he offers few services or none at all.

It is difficult to show that fair trade has helped the small merchants. In fact, in some respects it has hurt the retail drug industry; drug products, with their high gross margin protected by resale-price-maintenance laws, have been extremely attractive to other stores, especially supermarkets. As a result, today a substantial volume of drug items is sold through grocery stores. Furthermore, it is difficult to show that independent druggists have been better off through the years than independent retailers in grocery, apparel, or other non-fair-trade fields.

Consumer's viewpoint   From the point of view of the consumer, it is difficult to build a case in support of fair trade. Some people claim that fair-trade laws tend to keep prices on all products at a reasonable level. Without fair trade it is claimed that prices would be cut on a few items but raised on articles whose prices are not so well known to consumers. Proponents of fair trade state that the policy ensures wide, fair distribution of products and makes it possible for consumers to buy items at conveniently located small stores.

On balance, these arguments seem rather weak. Convenience of location is not measured in the same way today as it was in the 1930s. The biggest objection to fair trade from the consumer's viewpoint is that, as various studies have shown, prices are higher on an item when it is fair-traded than when it is not.[6] Also, if consumers are willing to forego services and instead enjoy lower prices, this alternative is not open to them if the product is fair-traded.

LEADER PRICING AND UNFAIR-PRACTICES ACTS

Many firms, primarily retailers, cut prices temporarily on a few items in order to attract customers. This price and promotional strategy, involving the use of loss leaders, is called "leader pricing." Leader items are, or should be, well-known, heavily advertised articles which are purchased frequently. Actually the term "loss leaders" is a misnomer; "profit leaders" would be more descriptive of the goal of the policy. The idea is that customers will come to the store to buy the advertised leader items and then stay to buy other regular-priced merchandise. Hopefully, the net result will be an increase in total volume and total profits.

Today about twenty-five states have unfair-sales acts, unfair-practices acts, or unfair-sales-practices acts to regulate leader pricing. Originally passed in some thirty states in the 1930s, these laws were part of a general drive against chain stores and other large-scale retailers. The intent was to prohibit predatory price-cutting, leader pricing, and other sales below cost. In contrast to the voluntary fair-trade laws, the unfair-practices acts are mandatory. They apply to all middlemen and to sales of all products, whether or not they are branded or specifically identifiable.

The states have followed one of two model laws. Under one model, a reseller is prohibited from selling an item below invoice cost, including freight, plus a stated markup which is usually 2 per cent at wholesale and 6 per cent at retail. Under the other model law, the minimum price is set at invoice cost, including freight, plus the retailer's or wholesaler's cost of doing business.

The general intent of these laws is commendable. They eliminate much of the predatory type of price-cutting; however, they permit firms to use loss leaders as a price and promotional strategy. That is, a retailer can offer an article below full cost but still sell above cost plus 6 per cent markup. Furthermore, under the unfair-practices acts, low-cost, efficient businessmen are not penalized, nor are high-cost operators protected. Differentials in retailers' purchase prices can be reflected in their selling prices, and savings resulting from the absence of services can be passed on to the customers.

On the other hand, the unfair-sales-practices acts have some glaring weaknesses. In the first place, the states do not establish provisions or agencies for

---

[6] For one study of the impact of a national fair-trade law on consumer prices, see Jerome C. Darnell, "The Impact of Quality Stabilization," *Journal of Marketing Research*, August, 1965, pp. 274–282. According to this study, a Federal fair-trade law would increase the consumer price index by one to ten points, depending upon the extent to which fair trade currently prevails.

enforcement. It is the responsibility and burden of the injured party to seek satisfaction from the offender in a civil suit. Another limitation is that it is difficult or even impossible to determine the cost of doing business for each individual product. It is on this point that some states have declared their laws unconstitutional. The third weakness is that the laws seem to disregard the fundamental idea that the purpose of a business is to make a profit on the total operation and not necessarily on each sale of each product.

GUARANTEE AGAINST PRICE DECLINE

A producer must decide whether or not he will make a refund or rebate to his middlemen in case he reduces his price within a stated period of time after filling their orders. Some sellers guarantee the price until orders are delivered or received; others protect the price well into the season when the merchandise is being sold by the middlemen. If a manufacturer must reduce his price, he simply credits each middleman's account with an amount equal to the unit price cut times the number of units the middleman has on hand.

Wisely used, a price-guarantee policy is especially worthwhile for firms producing goods subject to seasonal fluctuations in demand. This policy should encourage middlemen to place large orders well in advance of the season. Then the manufacturer can keep his plant operating in what would otherwise be a slack season. During periods of falling prices a middleman can order in large amounts and have no fear of taking a loss if prices decline still further.[7]

This policy has some limitations from the standpoint of the manufacturer. If he has sold huge quantities of merchandise and the price drops, he may be faced with a heavy financial loss. The cost of policing the policy is an important factor, especially if the manufacturer guarantees the price until the merchandise is resold. Middlemen might inflate their inventory figures, and bad customer relations might be created, if the manufacturer used his salesmen to check the middlemen's stocks. Another drawback is the fact that price guarantees encourage inventory speculation by middlemen. They have no risk at all. If prices go up, they gain; if prices drop, the guarantee protects them. Speculative buying will be limited if the manufacturer guarantees his price only until the shipment is received by the middleman. The final limitation is that price guarantees may lead to price rigidity. Even when market conditions call for a price cut, manufacturers may hesitate to reduce their prices because they dislike having to give a rebate.

PSYCHOLOGICAL PRICING—ODD PRICING

Several price policies can be grouped under the general heading of psychological price policies. Already we have touched upon three of these: price lining,

---

[7] For a report on a guaranteed annual price, an innovative pricing policy offered to large buyers by the leading lumber producers, see "Lumber Tries 'Annual Price,'" *Business Week*, July 25, 1964, p. 98.

prestige pricing above competitive market levels, and the use of customary prices at the market level. We also pointed out that if a price is set below the expected level, sales will suffer. Actually, volume can be increased by raising the price.

At the retail level, another psychological pricing policy is commonly used. Prices are set at odd amounts, such as 19 cents, 49 cents, $19.95, etc. Automobiles are priced at $2,995 rather than $3,000, and houses sell for $16,950 instead of $17,000. The practice originally developed as a control measure over theft by retail salesclerks. Odd pricing usually forces a clerk to make change, and this in turn forces him to ring up the sale on the cash register.

In general, retailers believe that pricing items at odd amounts will result in larger sales. Thus 49 cents or 98 cents will bring greater revenue than 50 cents or $1. Furthermore, retailers believe that buying psychology is such that odd prices will bring more sales volume than the next *lower* even-numbered price. That is, at 49 cents or 98 cents a firm will sell more units than at 48 cents

fig. 20–1

Some segments of the curve slope negatively; that is, as the price declines, volume also decreases. The zigzag shape reflects the idea that a familiar odd price will bring more sales volume than the prices immediately below these figures. Thus by pricing an article at 49 cents or 98 cents, the company will sell more units than at 48 cents or 96 cents. Do you agree? What types of stores use odd pricing? What products lend themselves to odd pricing?

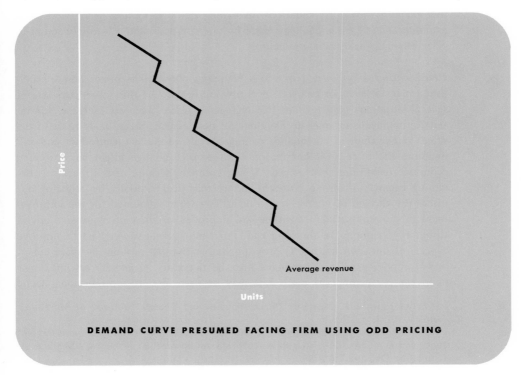

Price

Average revenue

Units

DEMAND CURVE PRESUMED FACING FIRM USING ODD PRICING

or 96 cents. In this situation the seller's average revenue curve would have a zigzag shape, as shown in Fig. 20–1.[8]

There is little concrete evidence to support the retailers' belief in the value of odd prices. Various studies have reported inconclusive results.[9] Odd pricing is often avoided in prestige stores or on higher-priced items. Thus expensive men's suits are priced at $150, not $149.95.

PRICE COMPETITION VERSUS NONPRICE COMPETITION

In the course of developing its marketing program, management has a choice of emphasizing price competition or nonprice competition. Rarely is one of these strategies employed to the exclusion of the other, but one can be intentionally stressed and depended upon more than the other.

Price competition

With monopolistic competition, product differentiation, and advertising so prevalent in the economy today, we may overlook the fact that there is still a considerable amount of price competition. Management may decide to engage in price competition by regularly offering prices which are as low as possible. Often when this is done the seller also offers a minimum of services. In their early years, discount houses, chain stores, and mail-order houses competed in this manner. Two other situations involving price competition which we should examine are (1) price changes made by our company and (2) our reaction to price changes made by a competitor.

Price changes by our firm   A company may cut its prices below established market levels or below a level previously used by this seller. Any one of several situations may prompt this change in price. As costs increase, for instance, management may decide that the best course of action is to raise the price, rather than to cut quality or aggressively promote the product and still maintain the price. Another reason for the price change might be worsening economic conditions in a market. If our company's share of the market is declining because of strong competition, we may react initially by reducing our price. We should, of course, try to determine what accounted for the improvement in our competitor's position—an improved product or aggressive advertising, for example. In the long run, our best alternative may be to improve aspects of our own marketing program, rather than to rely on the price cut.

Temporary price adjustments may be necessary to correct an imbalance in inventory. Temporary price cuts may be used also as a promotional tactic

[8] From Edward R. Hawkins, "Price Policies and Theory," *Journal of Marketing*, January, 1954, p. 235.

[9] For example, see Eli Ginsberg, "Customary Prices," *American Economic Review*, June, 1936, p. 36. See also studies reported in Edward R. Hawkins, "Methods of Estimating Demand," *Journal of Marketing*, April, 1957, p. 433.

when introducing a new product or in an effort to stimulate sales of an existing product. One study of temporary price reductions on three consumer items (regular coffee, cleansing tissue, and frozen dinners) established some useful guidelines for management. Professor Hinkle concluded:[10]

1. Off-season reductions are more profitable than equal or even greater reductions during high-volume seasons.

2. Frequent price cuts on the same brand bring successively smaller gains in market share.

3. Temporary price reductions seldom prevent new brands from gaining a foothold in the market.

4. Price cuts on new brands are more effective than price cuts on established products.

5. Price reductions seem to have little power to reverse a declining sales trend.

Before changing a price, management should consider several factors. Price-cutting may be advisable, for example, only when the seller is faced with an elastic demand curve. By reducing its price, management hopes that the volume will be increased sufficiently to increase total revenue. If demand is inelastic, a price cut will serve only to reduce total revenue.[11]

A seller should also determine what percentage sales increases will be necessary to offset any given percentage cut in unit price. For example, if unit prices are cut 20 per cent, sales must increase 25 per cent just to give the same dollar sales volume as before the cut. The formula is $X = \dfrac{C}{1 \text{ minus } C}$, where C is the percentage price cut, and X is the percentage by which sales must increase to give the same dollar sales volume as before the cut.

Management should also determine what affect a given price cut will have on gross margin and net profit, and what sales increase will be needed to offset this reduction. The formula regarding gross margin is $X = \dfrac{M \ (1 \text{ minus } C)}{M \text{ minus } C}$ minus 1, where C is the percentage price reduction, M is the gross margin percentage, and X is the percentage sales increase needed to earn as many gross margin dollars as before the cut. This formula assumes that unit production costs remain constant. Thus if a firm has a 30 per cent gross margin and cuts prices 10 per cent, it needs a 35 per cent increase in sales volume.

From the seller's standpoint the big threat and weakness in price-cutting

[10] *Marketing Science Institute*, July, 1965, p. 1; see also Charles L. Hinkle, "The Strategy of Price Deals," *Harvard Business Review*, July–August, 1965, pp. 75–85.

[11] For a new concept of price sensitivity—one which suggests that the pricing decision should rest on a better rationale than elasticity because often there are identifiable desensitizing factors (such as eccentricities in consumer behavior, unequal ability of salesmen, and difficulty in comparing different products)—see Richard T. Sampson, "Sense and Sensitivity in Pricing," *Harvard Business Review*, November–December, 1964, pp. 99–105.

is that competitors will retaliate, especially in oligopolistic market situations. The net result can be a price war, and the price may even settle permanently at a lower level. Price-cutting is most likely to be found in markets where there are several sellers and the products or services are reasonably similar. In this situation, a cut below market price will probably bring a large increase in volume.

It should be noted that an oligopoly is not necessarily found only among large firms. A group of small neighborhood merchants can constitute an oligopoly. Thus the druggist or the barbers in a community may try to avoid price competition because if one reduces his price, all must follow. The term "oligopoly" means "a few sellers." In a resort town where all of the grocery business is done by three small grocers, an oligopoly exists.

Reaction to competitors' price changes   We can assume that our competitors will change their prices. We may not know when the change will occur, what its magnitude will be, or whether it will be an increase or a decrease. But change they will. Consequently, we should at least be ready with some policy guidelines or, better yet, have a plan of reaction established. Advance planning is particularly necessary in the case of a competitive price reduction because time will then be of the essence. If a competitor boosts his prices, a reasonable delay in reacting will probably not be perilous; in fact, it may turn out to be the wise thing to do if his increase was a mistake. Our decision on what to do in the face of a price cut by a competitor will depend upon answers to such questions as: (1) Why did he cut his prices—is it a temporary move, or do we gauge it to be a long-run strategy? (2) *Can* we meet the price cut— that is, do we forecast that our cost-price-volume relationships permit a cut, or should we try to counter in nonprice fashion? (3) *Must* we meet the reduction—how important is this product or market to us, and how sensitive is the market to price competition?

Nonprice competition

In nonprice competition, a seller maintains a stable, constant price and attempts to improve his market position by emphasizing his product, distribution system, promotional program, or services. Of course, management still has the task of setting the price, and competitive prices still must be taken into consideration. Furthermore, the price may change over a period of time. Nevertheless, in a nonprice competitive situation the emphasis in the marketing program definitely is on something other than price.

By using terms familiar in economic theory, we can differentiate nonprice competition from price competition. In price competition a seller attempts to move up or down his demand curve by changing the price. In nonprice competition a seller attempts to *shift* his demand curve to the right by means of product differentiation, promotional activities, or some other device. This point

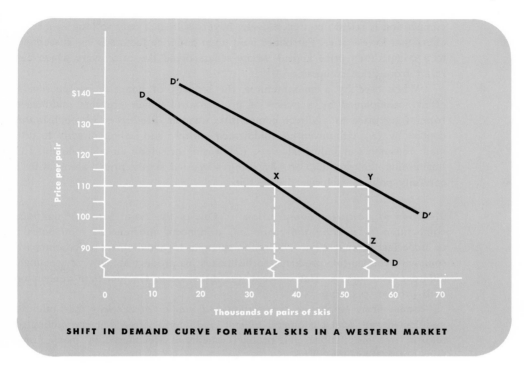

SHIFT IN DEMAND CURVE FOR METAL SKIS IN A WESTERN MARKET

fig. 20–2

Use of nonprice competition can shift the demand curve for a product. A company selling metal skis in a Western market used a promotional program to sell more skis at the same price, thus shifting DD to D'D'. Volume increased from 35,000 to 55,000 units at $110 (point X to point Y). Besides advertising, what other devices might this firm use to shift its demand curve? If price competition were used, at what price could the company sell 55,000 pairs?

is illustrated in Fig. 20–2. At $110 the producer of a given model of metal snow skis can sell 35,000 pairs a year in the western region of his market. On the basis of price competition alone, he can increase his sales to 55,000 if he is willing to reduce his price to $90. The demand curve facing him is still *DD*. However, he is interested in boosting his sales without any decrease in selling price. Consequently, he embarks upon a promotional program—a form of non-price competition—and he is able to inform and persuade enough new custom-ers to buy at the original $110 price so that his unit sales increase to 55,000 pairs a year. In effect, his entire demand curve has shifted to position *D'D'*.

There is an increasing use of nonprice competition in marketing. Com-panies want, at least to some extent, to be the masters of their own destiny. In nonprice competition, a seller's entire advantage is not removed when a competitor undersells him. Furthermore, customer loyalty is fleeting when price competition is relied upon exclusively; buyers will stick only so long as a seller offers that lowest price. Patronage built upon nonprice factors is less susceptible to a competitor's price appeal. Many sellers dread the price wars which can result from price competition.[12]

When used by a manufacturer, the strategy of nonprice competition is often accompanied by a policy of price control which prevents middlemen from using price as a direct competitive weapon. Producers accomplish this control by (1) circumventing middlemen entirely and selling directly to ultimate consumers or industrial users, (2) leasing or selling on consignment, (3) fair-trading the product, or (4) using suggested resale prices along with a carefully policed exclusive distribution.

Methods of nonprice competition   One of the major forms of nonprice competition is *product differentiation*, a concept inherent in monopolistic, or imperfect, competition. The seller attempts to avoid direct price comparisons with competitive products, so he makes his product actually or seemingly different from others. This concept was discussed in Chapter 9 in connection with product planning.

Some firms emphasize the *variety and quality of services* they offer to middlemen and final customers. Liberal credit terms, free delivery, unlimited returns, free installations, and product warranties are offered by many firms. Sometimes *convenience of location* can be used as the basis for nonprice competition. Suburban shopping centers stress this factor when competing with downtown shopping districts. At the manufacturing level, a firm may open sales offices or branches in order to serve its market better. Location can also be an important factor in direct price competition. A firm selling f.o.b. factory will stress the advantages of low freight costs when selling to nearby customers.

Although *trading stamps* have been used for many years as a method of nonprice competition, it was not until the 1950s that they became really popular. For several years, surveys have reported that more than four out of five families are stamp savers. In 1964, the value of stamps sold to retailers was estimated at $715 million, as contrasted with only $38 million in 1951.[13] (Interestingly enough, the same phenomenon is occurring overseas—in Japan, where trading stamps have increased rapidly in importance.[14])

Food stores are the largest single class of users of trading stamps, although gasoline service stations and drugstores also use them quite heavily as competitive devices. The stamp companies themselves constitute a big market. In 1964, consumers redeemed their stamps for $76 million worth of

[12] For a comprehensive study of abnormal competitive behavior in pricing, see Ralph Cassady, Jr., *Price Warfare in Business Competition*, Michigan State University, Bureau of Business and Economic Research, Occasional Paper no. 11, 1963.

[13] See "Trading Stamps: 1965," *Premium Practice*, March, 1965, p. 27.

[14] See A. J. Alton and George O. Totten, "Trading Stamps in Japan: Boom in the Making?" *Journal of Marketing*, April, 1965, pp. 12–17.

furniture (at retail), $87 million worth of housewares, and $117 million worth of soft goods, to name just a few types of merchandise whose manufacturers count stamp companies as major customers.

After a number of years of substantial growth, there is some indication, however, that the use of trading stamps in product marketing is reaching a saturation point and is leveling off. At the same time, perhaps, we can look for the increasing use of stamps as a nonprice promotional device in the marketing of services—banking, travel, etc.[15] A number of major retailers have discontinued the use of trading stamps, turning to other promotional devices. Several good studies have been made of the use and effects of trading stamps.[16] The net effect of stamps on retail prices, however, is still not entirely clear. As with many marketing problems, the answer is, "It depends." In some cases, prices seem to have increased in stamp-giving stores, but in other instances there were no price increases. The net effect is also influenced by whether a customer religiously saves and redeems all his stamps. Stamps cost the retailer 2 to 3 per cent of sales. (He pays $2 to $3 for a thousand stamps and then gives one stamp for every 10 cents' worth of purchases.) He can absorb this cost if he can cut some other promotional expense or if he can increase his volume so that the unit fixed costs are reduced enough to offset the 2 or 3 per cent increase in unit variable costs.

The early users in a market stand to profit most from trading stamps. But when many retailers begin to use them, as is the case today, this advantage decreases or disappears. The only way to avoid a drop in profits is to reduce other expenses or to raise prices. In most markets, competition seems to have prevented any significant rise in prices traceable to the use of trading stamps.

Retailers and customers alike have strong feelings about trading stamps. When a bill relating to stamps appears before a legislature, there are usually highly emotional reactions on both sides of the issue. Many retailers would probably discontinue giving stamps if they did not fear a loss of business. Apparently some consumers feel that they are getting something for nothing or that they are getting merchandise for which they otherwise would not save. If a customer accepts a 2 per cent cash discount in place of stamps, he will not usually save the pennies to buy the merchandise; if he accepts the trading stamps, however, he probably will accumulate enough to exchange them for the item.

[15] See Milton Alexander, "The Trading Stamp Hassle," *Sales/Marketing Today*, August–September, 1965, pp. 4–6; and "Are Trading Stamps Losing Their Punch?" *Business Week*, Sept. 4, 1965, p. 66.

[16] For example, see Harvey L. Vredenburg, *Trading Stamps,* Indiana University, Bureau of Business Research, Business Report no. 21, Bloomington, Ind., 1956; Albert Haring and Wallace O. Yoder, *Trading Stamp Practice and Pricing Policy*, Indiana University, Bureau of Business Research, Business Report no. 27, Bloomington, Ind., 1958; *Trading Stamps and Their Impact on Food Prices*, U.S. Department of Agriculture, Marketing Research Report no. 295, Washington, D.C.

Possibly the most important method of nonprice competition is *promotion*. In fact, nonprice competition is often considered a mixture of pricing and promotion. Certainly, along with product differentiation, promotion is a hallmark of nonprice competition and monopolistic competition. The topic of promotion is treated in the next three chapters.

QUESTIONS AND PROBLEMS

1   Under what marketing conditions is a company likely to use a variable-price policy? Can you name some firms which employ this policy, other than when a trade-in is involved?

2   Are retailers ever faced with the problem of pricing multiple products? Explain.

3   Name some products which you feel are priced out of line with other items sold by a company.

4   Should Congress pass a Federal resale-price-maintenance law?

5   Explain how the nonsigners clause works with respect to fair-trade laws.

6   Why is it that, historically, manufacturers frequently fair-traded their small traffic appliances (toasters, electric razors, etc.) but not their large appliances (refrigerators, washing machines, etc.)?

7   "Most of the real support for resale price maintenance has come from small, independent retailers who have demanded this form of protection against price-cutting chains and large independents. When manufacturers claimed that they were not interested in fair-trade pricing except to keep small retailers happy, they were distorting the truth." Do you agree?

8   Traditionally, resale price maintenance has been widespread in the retail drug field and virtually nonexistent in the grocery store field. Small, independent grocers, however, have done a pretty good job of competing with the chains through the years, while small independent drugstores have experienced a high mortality rate. How do you account for this situation? Is this strong evidence that resale price maintenance is not what is needed to help the small retailer in his competitive battle against the chains?

9   "The real battle over fair trade is between high-cost and low-cost retailers, not between small-scale and large-scale firms." Do you agree? Do you know of any chains or other large-scale, but high-cost, retailers who are in favor of fair trade? Do you know of any small firms opposed to it?

10   Is it unethical for a retailer to sell one or more items below his delivered cost?

11   What are the significant differences between fair-trade laws and unfair-sales-practices acts?

12   Distinguish between leader pricing and predatory price-cutting.

13   Explain the reasoning underlying the zigzag shape of the demand curve in Fig. 20–1. Does this demand phenomenon actually exist in real life?

14   "The use of periodic, temporary price cuts to stimulate consumer demand is not a wise marketing strategy." Do you agree? Discuss.

15   How should a manufacturer of prefinished plywood interior wall paneling react if a competitor cuts his price?

16   What factors account for the increased use of nonprice competition?

17   Why is the price of a product so seldom mentioned in national magazine advertising done by manufacturers?

18   Should trading stamps be abolished?

case 14. HILLCREST PRODUCTS, INC. (A)
Pricing a new product

The executives of Hillcrest Products, Inc., are trying to decide what the retail price should be for their new product—a glass cleaner—which is ready for marketing on a full-scale basis. Hillcrest Products, Inc., is a new company, and the glass cleaner is its first product to be marketed commercially, although it has developed and market-tested several other cleaning products. Plans call for the introduction of the other products as soon as they can be given adequate attention by management. Since the company is small, the executives wisely do not wish to spread their efforts over too many products at one time.

The new glass cleaner is liquid in form and golden in color. It will be competitive with such brands as Windex, Bon-Ami, Glass Wax, and Easy-Off. Windex is far and away the leading brand in sales. For example, the *Denver Post* survey of consumer brand preferences has shown that Windex is the brand purchased in about 70 per cent of the households using commercial glass cleaners. No other brand reaches over 10 per cent of this market.

Management in the Hillcrest company feels that its product is demonstrably superior to anything on the market. Market tests have shown that once consumers try this product, they strongly favor it over anything they have used previously. The product's main differential advantage is that it does not leave a film. The Hillcrest people feel that all other brands, regardless of their advertising claims, leave a film. Also, the Hillcrest product is nontoxic, a distinct advantage in households where there are small children.

The product comes in two attractively labeled packages—a Duo-Pak and a 16-ounce glass refill bottle. The Duo-Pak consists of a 16-ounce bottle plus an 8-ounce clear plastic bottle with a plunger-type spray dispenser top. The intent is that the consumer will fill the plastic bottle and use it, rather than the glass bottle, for actual cleaning work. The fact that the plastic is unbreakable is another favorable differentiating product feature. Both the Duo-Paks and the refills are packed twelve to a case.

Currently, Hillcrest markets through supermarket chains at the retail level, and the company uses a separate food broker to reach the chains in each brokerage area, such as Denver, Kansas City, Omaha, Oklahoma City, and Wichita. For example, chain buying offices in the Denver brokerage area represent stores in Colorado, Wyoming, northern New Mexico, and parts of Oklahoma, Kansas, Nebraska, and South Dakota.

Hillcrest has no desire to sell its product under resale-price-maintenance (fair-trade) contracts. In setting its own selling price, however, the company has to have some intended retail price in mind in order to allow for the necessary broker's fee and retailer's margin. The company plans to allow retailers a margin of 25 per cent of their selling price, and the brokers a fee of 10 per cent of Hillcrest's selling price.

The unit variable costs for Hillcrest's product packed in case lots are 33 cents for the Duo-Pak and 14 cents for the refill. These costs include the glass and plastic packages, the cardboard holder for the Duo-Pak, the liquid cleaner itself, the shipping carton, freight, and direct labor for filling the packages and preparing the cartons for shipment. Actually, the largest single direct costs are the glass and plastic packages. If the company could order these packages in lots of 50,000 or more, the unit cost could be reduced 2 cents.

The company conservatively expects to sell 1 million 16-ounce bottles during the first year in a 1:2 ratio of Duo-Paks to refills. It is difficult to estimate overhead very accurately at this stage. Administrative and office salaries will be about $35,000. Other overhead costs, including travel expense but excluding advertising, are figured at $16,000. Of course, the largest single indirect expense is advertising. The company expects to plow all available funds into advertising and display. If necessary, the company will operate at a loss for a few years rather than skimp on advertising. The advertising budget for the first year is set at $50,000.

The usual retail selling prices of competitive products in supermarkets are as follows:

Brand	Product	Price, in cents
Windex	20-oz bottle	40–45
Windex	14-oz aerosol can	59
Windex	8-oz bottle	14
Windex	Plunger-type spray dispenser	15
Easy-Off	15-oz aerosol can	49
Bon-Ami	15-oz aerosol can	65
Glass Wax	16-oz bottle	59

QUESTIONS

1 What unit retail prices do you recommend for the Duo-Pak and for the refill?
2 What should be Hillcrest's selling prices per case for Duo-Paks and for refills?
3 What is the break-even point in sales volume and in units, assuming that Duo-Paks and refills sell in a 1:2 ratio?

case 15. WHEATLAND COMPANY

Price policy for a repair service

The owner of the Wheatland Company is considering a change in the method he uses for setting prices on the repair service jobs performed by his firm. The Wheatland Company, located in a small town in western Kansas, is a wholesale repair service working on watches, clocks, and jewelry products. Mr. Cecil Claridge, the owner, was in the retail repair trade for about ten years before he started his own wholesale service company in 1950.

The Wheatland Company provides its services for retail jewelry stores and drugstores. Proprietors of jewelry stores are a market for this service because they need a place to send their excess repair work when their own repair departments become overloaded. Wheatland offers drugstore managers a place to send watch, clock, and jewelry items which these stores sold and which now need some form of repair service. Drugstores normally do not operate their own repair departments. Wheatland also offers a drugstore executive an opportunity to add a profit-making activity to his business by way of providing a watch and jewelry repair service which he may sell to his customers. Because of the sparse population in Wheatland's geographic market, there are many small towns which have no jewelry store but which do have a drugstore. These druggists are in a favorable position to handle much of the watch and jewelry repair business in their community by sending the products to Wheatland or to a competing company for the actual service work.

The wholesale repairing of watch and jewelry is a service industry which developed largely after World War II and which today has captured a large share of this type of repair work done in the United States. These central repair depots flourish because they free a jewelry retailer from repair work, thus enabling him to devote his energies and attention to the selling end of his business. Also, many jewelers find it more economical to send their repair work to a wholesale firm such as Wheatland, rather than to maintain their own retail repair departments in their stores. While the number of watches sold has greatly increased in recent years, the number of wholesale service centers has remained fairly constant. This situation may be attributed to improvements in timepieces, market acceptance of throw-away watches, and better oils and materials, all of which have reduced the amount of repair work needed per watch.

Currently the Wheatland Company is handling about nine hundred repair jobs a month from approximately one hundred accounts located in Kansas, Nebraska, Oklahoma, and eastern Colorado. Drugstores and jewelry stores each account for about one-half of Wheatland's business. At this volume, the company employs three full-time watch repairmen, one full-time jewelry repairman, one full-time man who divides his efforts between watch and jewelry repair jobs, and two girls (one part-time) who do the bookkeeping and other office work. Mr. Claridge does some repair work during peak load periods. He also spends quite a bit of time traveling the territory seeking new business and maintaining good relations with existing accounts.

In the repair market, price is probably the most important factor to the jewelry stores, while speed of service is more important to the drugstores. In all cases, of course, honesty and competent service are essential. The Wheatland Company is in a rather good competitive situation. There is just one other wholesale repair service in the area, and that is only a one-man operation. Of course, there are repair services of this type in the larger cities such as Kansas City, Topeka, Wichita, Oklahoma City, and Omaha, but these companies cannot match Wheatland for speed of service to customers.

Presently, the Wheatland Company uses a pricing system whereby each repair job is separately and individually priced on a cost basis. That is, each job is charged with the direct labor and materials used on that job, plus an amount added to cover overhead expenses and profit. Thus, in the case of a watch repair job, for instance, one price may be charged for a "clean, oil, and adjust" job, while another specific price would be assessed for a crystal repair or for a general cleaning and overhaul.

Mr. Claridge recognizes that there is something to be said for this method of determining a price. It is probably the fairest method in that each job is priced on the basis of actual cost. Also, because it is the traditional pricing system used in the jewelry repair business, the jewelry stores would probably prefer it out of habit, if for no other reason. Jewelry stores tend to send Wheatland only the more difficult repair jobs—the ones which may also take a considerable amount of time. The easier ones are done in the stores' own repair departments.

The present system does have some undesirable features. It is sometimes complicated in that it is difficult to allocate costs equitably. It is a waste of a skilled repairman's time to require him to write up a repair ticket with a summary of the work he performed and the price of the materials he used. Time is also wasted in the process of giving a price estimate to the retail store's customer. When a customer brings in a watch for repair, the jeweler may have to send it to Wheatland for an estimate; Wheatland then quotes a price to the store, who in turn contacts the customer. If the price is right, the store must notify Wheatland to go ahead with the work.

Mr. Claridge believes that the present pricing system for watch repairs is oriented too much toward the jewelry trade. Consequently, he is considering another system which he feels will appeal more to druggists. His proposal is for a single-price system. That is, every job would be priced at the same figure, no matter what the job is or how much labor and materials are used. The single price would probably be set at a figure which is an average price for a complete cleaning and overhaul—the most common type of watch repair job. This new system would apply only to watch repair jobs, which constitute the major segment of the business. Clock and jewelry repair jobs would continue to be priced on an individual job basis.

The proposed pricing method would enable a store to "preretail" a watch repair job. Mr. Claridge thinks his company can capture a greater segment of the repair business if the druggist can tell the customer, with no time delays for estimates, that the repair job will cost, say, $8 and that this will include all work, no matter how extensive.

Under a single-price system, Wheatland would save time and money because fewer records would have to be maintained. The repairmen would no longer devote as large a share of their time to nonrepair activities such as preparing cost statements on each job. The druggists would probably like the system because to them, quality and speed of service are more important than price.

A big question mark in the new system is the amount of work needed to sell the jewelry stores on the method. They might object to a change from the system which they have been accustomed to using. Another real problem is the fact that not all watch repair jobs are the "clean and overhaul" type. A customer would probably object to paying the flat rate for something like a crystal replacement or some other minor type of repair. Wheatland may have to establish more than one category of repair job, with a flat rate for each category, or else risk losing a profitable segment of the watch repair market.

QUESTION

1   What method should the Wheatland Company use for setting prices on watch repair jobs?

case 16.   DILLON ELECTRIC COMPANY*

Change in discount schedule

The demise of the fair-trade laws has come as a severe blow to the Dillon Electric Company of Chicago, Illinois. This company, which has an annual sales volume of over $30 million, manufactures a widely accepted full line of small household appliances. It has consistently been a major proponent of fair trade and has assiduously avoided dealing with

* Case written by Prof. John M. Hess, University of Colorado.

discount houses. It has been one of the most consistent prosecutors of price-cutters in the appliance business.

Dillon has established a strong dealer loyalty through its antidiscount activities and through its policy of "a fair margin for honest dealers." Discounters, of course, also favor the Dillon line because its prices are promoted and maintained so well that Dillon products make perfect discount merchandise. Dealer margins for the line have generally been broader than the margins for lines of competing small appliance manufacturers. The established prices on the line permit a 33 to 37 per cent margin for retailers and an 18 to 22 per cent margin for wholesalers. The range depends on the quantity purchased, the particular item, and the source of supply.

Excessive discounting of the line has begun to alienate dealers and to weaken the firm's distribution system. To combat this problem, Carl Gross, the vice-president of marketing, has proposed a reduction in dealer margins. He believes that narrow margins will solve the discount-house problem and will actually permit a better average maintained markup for legitimate retailers and wholesalers. His proposal calls for a reduction in margins for all lines. Under the new schedule, as shown in the table below, wholesalers will average a 12 to 14 per cent markup on their selling prices, and retailers will average 22 to 27 per cent on retail prices. Retail prices will be reduced, but the net to the company will vary only slightly.

Sample price schedule for Dillon Electric Company

Product	Former retail price	New retail price	Former wholesale price	New wholesale price	Former gross to manufacturer	New gross to manufacturer
Toasters	$22.95	$16.95	$14.90	$12.80	$11.90	$11.00
Standard mixers	56.95	44.95	38.00	34.00	31.00	30.00
Hand mixers	24.95	19.95	16.25	14.50	13.00	12.50
Blenders	42.50	33.95	27.30	24.40	21.80	21.00

QUESTIONS

1   How can retailers and wholesalers be persuaded to accept the innovation proposed by Mr. Gross?

2   Will this approach solve the discounting problem? What side effects may there be?

3   Are there other ways to control the discounting on this line? Should the company attempt to control it?

4   What action should the Dillon Electric Company take?

case 17. WARD-KNIGHT FURNITURE COMPANY
Use of trading stamps

The Ward-Knight Furniture Company is a retail furniture chain with a store located in each of five small towns within a radius of 30 to 150 miles from a large city with a population close to 500,000. Mr. Ralph Partlow, president of the company, is considering the use of trading stamps in one of the stores in the chain. This particular store is located about 30 miles from the metropolitan center. The town has a population of 20,000 and serves a trading area of 75,000 people, including a summer resort area. A four-lane freeway connects the small town with the downtown center of the large city. The economic base of the small town rests on farming and small industry. According to *Sales Management's* "Survey of Buying Power," this community offers an above-average market potential. In 1960, its Quality of Market Index was 117, and its Index of Sales Activity was 161. (The Quality of Market Index is a measure of purchasing power as compared with the national average of 100. The Index of Sales Activity shows the relation between a community's retail sales and population. It is computed by dividing the community's percentage of national retail sales by the community's percentage of national population.)

Ward-Knight has been located in this town for over fifty years. It is the leading furniture store in the community and has a sales volume of about $600,000 a year. It carries a complete line of furniture and carpeting and also a line of large and small appliances. It holds the franchise for many of the leading names in the field, such as Bigelow carpeting, Hoover vacuum cleaners, and Drexel, Heritage, Simmons, and Heywood-Wakefield furniture. Its competition comes from three other furniture stores, one of which is a specialty store selling only knotty-pine furniture. In addition, there are a Montgomery Ward store and four appliance stores. Over the years, the store has established a large and loyal local clientele. Times are changing, however, and the discount houses in the metropolitan center are beginning to make inroads into Ward-Knight's market.

Within a month or so Ward-Knight will open a brand-new store about one block off the main shopping street. There will be plenty of parking space, and the store will be located next to a large bank and across the street from a large supermarket. The floor space will almost triple that of the present store. Because of the opening of the new store, plus the fact that competition is growing, Mr. Partlow is seeking new methods of stimulating sales volume; hence his consideration of trading stamps. Trading stamps are prevalent in the area, but their use has been limited largely to food stores and gasoline stations. Mr. Partlow is intrigued by the idea of trading stamps as a promotional device in furniture stores; the cost would be $2 for 1,000 stamps. He would give ten stamps with each dollar's worth of purchases, which means that he would use one book for every $100 in sales. Thus his cost would be 2 per cent of sales. None of his competitors, either in his own town or in the metropolitan center, use trading stamps. This is an additional factor encouraging Mr. Partlow to adopt them in his store. His study of the use of trading stamps has led to the conclusion that they are an effective sales stimulant for a store whose competitors do not use stamps.

QUESTIONS

1 Should the company institute the practice of giving trading stamps with customers' purchases?

2 If you recommend against the use of trading stamps in this case, what other promotional or pricing strategies do you recommend to stimulate sales volume in the Ward-Knight Company?

PART SIX

PROMOTIONAL ACTIVITIES

21

THE PROMOTIONAL PROGRAM

Having completed an examination of the product planning, distribution structure, and price system in a firm, we must now examine the final operational area in a company's marketing program—the promotional activities. Chapters 21, 22, and 23 are devoted to the determination and management of the *promotional* mix, that is, the most strategic combination of advertising, personal selling, sales promotion, and other promotional tools that can be devised to reach the goals of the sales program.

When a home handicraft economy exists and a man makes a good product, his neighbors probably know about it. The "better mousetrap" theory is not realistic, however, in our modern economy. The present situation is far more accurately described in the statement "nothing happens until somebody sells something." This statement expresses rather succinctly the place of promotional activities in today's business scene. Promotional activities are probably the most criticized part of the entire marketing program. For this reason, the reader must keep an open mind and remember one thing: not to confuse a tool with its user. Without question, many advertisements are misleading, and many salesmen act in poor taste. This is no fault of the tool of advertising, but simply indicates that it has been used poorly. Yet it is human nature to blame the tool itself: a person will hammer a nail crooked and blame the poor quality of the nail; he will hit his finger and blame the hammer.

NATURE AND IMPORTANCE OF PROMOTION

Many people consider that "selling" and "marketing" are synonymous terms but actually selling is only one of the many components of marketing. Selling is defined by the American Marketing Association as "the personal or impersonal process of assisting and/or persuading a prospective customer to buy a commodity or a service or to act favorably upon an idea that has commercial significance to the seller."[1]

In this book, "selling" and "promotion" are used synonymously, although "promotion" is the preferred term. This preference is based on the belief that, in the minds of some people, selling suggests only the transfer of title or the use of personal salesmen but does not include advertising or other methods of stimulating demand. We are saying that promotion includes advertising, personal selling, sales promotion, and other selling tools. While the choice of words may be unfortunately similar, it should be noted particularly that "promotion" and "sales promotion" are different. "Promotion" is the all-inclusive term representing the broad field under discussion here, and "sales promotion" is only one part of it.

Basically, promotion is an exercise in information, persuasion, and influence. These three are related in that to inform is to persuade, and, conversely, if a person is being persuaded, he is probably also being informed. Many years ago, Prof. Neil Borden, of Harvard University, recognized the necessary place and pervasive nature of persuasion and influence in our socioeconomic system; he said that "The use of influence in commercial relations is one of the attributes of a free society, just as persuasion and counterpersuasion are exercised freely in many walks of life in our free society—in the home, in the press, in the classroom, in the pulpit, in the courts, in the political forum, in legislative halls, and in government agencies for information."[2]

Promotional methods

The two most widely used methods of promotion are personal selling and advertising. These activities are treated in Chapters 22 and 23, respectively.

---

[1] Committee on Definitions, Ralph S. Alexander, Chairman, *Marketing Definitions: A Glossary of Marketing Terms*, American Marketing Association, Chicago, 1960, p. 21.

[2] Neil H. Borden, *The Economic Effects of Advertising*, Richard D. Irwin, Inc., Homewood, Ill., 1942, p. 802.

Sales promotion, which is designed to supplement and coordinate personal selling and advertising efforts and which includes such activities as store displays, trade shows and exhibitions, and the use of samples or premiums, is discussed in this chapter. Another group of less widely used promotional methods includes mail-order advertising and selling, automatic vending, and auctions.

In addition, there is a group of marketing strategies which are in part promotional: such strategies as product differentiation, market segmentation, trading up, trading down, the use of trading stamps, and branding belong in this group. They have been discussed in earlier chapters in connection with market analysis, product planning, or pricing.

Importance of promotion in modern marketing

In the realistic marketplace, perfect competition does not exist. Under conditions of imperfect, or monopolistic, competition, with product differentiation, nonrational behavior, and less-than-complete market information, promotional activities are essential. Promotion is an adjunct or a function of imperfect competition. Several factors point up the need for, and importance of, promotion today. In the first place, as the physical distance between producers and consumers increases, and as the number of potential customers grows, the problem of market communication becomes a significant one. Furthermore, improvements in physical distribution facilities are expanding the geographic limits of markets.

Another factor contributing to the importance of promotional activities has been the development of channels of distribution which involve the use of wholesaling and/or retailing middlemen. Once middlemen are introduced into a marketing pattern, it is not enough for a producer to communicate only with the ultimate consumers or industrial users. It becomes essential that middlemen be informed about products. Wholesalers, in turn, must promote the products to retailers, and retailers must communicate with consumers.

The intensification of competition among different industries, as well as among individual firms within given industries, has placed tremendous pressures on the promotional programs of individual sellers. In the development of our economy of abundance, want satisfaction has replaced, to a great extent, the mere necessity of fulfilling basic physiological requirements. As consumers engage more and more in the satisfaction of wants rather than needs, they become more selective in their choices of alternative expenditures. To attract customers, a firm must have a good promotional program. Customer demand is largely dormant; it must be awakened and stimulated.

Promotional effort looms important in the overall operations of a business. It is usually the largest part of the total marketing expenses. All promotional expenses together often constitute the largest single cost in a firm—even larger than its total production costs.

Recession or an economic decline quickly points up the importance of selling. During such a period, there are no major problems in product planning —channels remain essentially the same, and the pricing structure is basically unchanged. The key problem is selling. Finally, promotion is needed to maintain the high material standard of living and the high level of employment which we enjoy in this country.

THE COMMUNICATIONS PROCESS

In any society, the nature of interpersonal relations depends in large measure upon the effectiveness of the interpersonal communications. Certainly in business in general, and in marketing in particular, the effectiveness of the system is related to the effectiveness of the communications. To go one step further, within the marketing system the promotional activity is basically an exercise in communications. If an executive understands something of the theory of communications, he should be able to better establish and manage a promotional program in his firm.

The word "communication" is derived from the Latin word *communis*, meaning "common." Thus, when you communicate, you are trying to establish a "commonness" with someone. Through the use of verbal or nonverbal symbols, you as the source send a message through a channel to a receiver in an effort to share an idea, attitude, or some other kind of information.[3] Fundamentally, a communications process requires only three elements—a *message*, a *source* of this message, and a *receiver*. However, to refine the process into a workable form—one which recognizes environmental practicalities—additional elements come into play. The information which the sending source wants to share must first be *encoded* into transmittable form and then later *decoded* by the receiver at the destination. Another element to be reckoned with is *noise* which may interfere at any stage with the transmission or reception of the message. The final element in the process—feedback—tells the sender whether the message was received and how it was perceived by the destination target. The feedback element is also the basis for planning ahead; the sender learns how he might improve his communications by using different channels, encoding, or messages.

These elements constituting a general communications system may be conceptualized in a model as diagramed in Fig. 21–1.[4] This same model, as adapted to the promotional activities in a company's marketing program, is illustrated in Fig. 21–2. The information source may be a person with an idea

[3] See Wilbur L. Schramm, "How Communication Works," in Wilbur Schramm (ed.), *The Process and Effects of Mass Communication*, The University of Illinois Press, Urbana, Ill., 1954, pp. 3–26.

[4] Adapted from David K. Berlo, *The Process of Communication*, Holt, Rinehart and Winston, Inc., New York, 1960, pp. 30–32. See also the model in Claude E. Shannon and Warren Weaver, *The Mathematical Theory of Communication*, The University of Illinois Press, Urbana, Ill., 1949, p. 5.

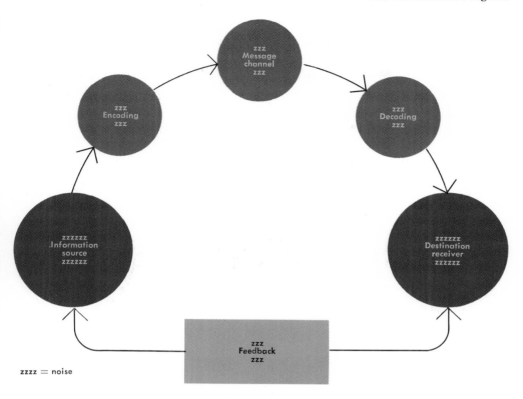

zzzz = noise

A GENERALIZED COMMUNICATIONS SYSTEM

fig. 21–1

to communicate. He will encode it into a transmittable form by putting it into written or spoken words, or perhaps even into a gesture of some sort (wave his arms, dim his bright lights). The coded message is then carried by print media, sound waves, or light waves to the destination—an individual, a church audience, or a university class, for example. Each receiver decodes (interprets) the message in light of his individual experiences or frames of reference. The closer the decoded message is to its encoded form (assuming it was encoded fully and accurately), the more effective is the communication. By the receiver's words or actions (feedback), the sender can judge the extent to which his message got through.

Let us illustrate the process with a marketing example. An executive wants to communicate a selling message to a consumer. The message is encoded into a radio commercial and carried to the consumer via a radio program and a receiving set. Hopefully, the consumer hears the commercial and interprets it. How effectively the message came through and how much it moved the con-

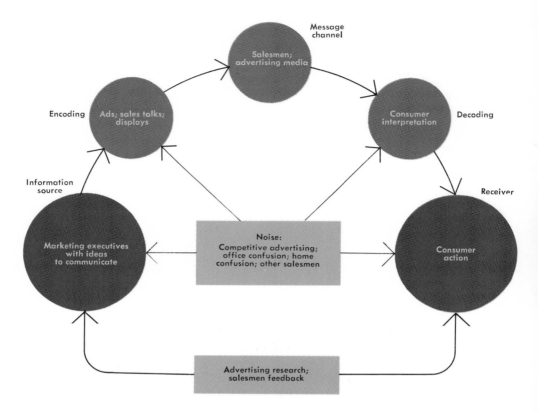

Message
channel

Salesmen;
advertising media

Encoding — Ads; sales talks;
displays

Consumer
interpretation — Decoding

Information
source

Marketing executives
with ideas
to communicate

Noise:
Competitive advertising;
office confusion; home
confusion; other salesmen

Receiver

Consumer
action

Advertising research;
salesmen feedback

A MARKETING COMMUNICATIONS SYSTEM
ILLUSTRATING ACTIVITIES IN PROMOTIONAL PROGRAM

fig. 21–2

sumer to action, the sender will try to determine through marketing research feedback. At any point in the process, interfering noise may reduce the effectiveness of the system. While the radio commercial is on, the children may be making noise in the house, or someone may ring the doorbell. Competitive advertisements, salesmen, or displays are also forms of noise. The consumer may counteract the house noise by turning up the radio volume. The sender can counteract the noise by preparing an especially good commercial or by running it at a time when doorbells and children are apt to be quiet.

In effect, the marketing executive uses his previous analysis of consumer characteristics and behavior to provide him with encoded symbols which can be used to communicate the merits of his product and the reasons for buying it. An analysis of the market for carbonated beverages, for instance, might show that one major market is the people who serve soft drinks at parties.

The seller can then encode his message in an advertisement which pictures the use of his product in an entertainment setting.

THE CAMPAIGN CONCEPT

When planning the total promotional program in a firm, management must ordinarily make use of the campaign concept. A *campaign* is a planned, co-ordinated, integrated series of promotional efforts built around a single theme or idea and designed to reach a predetermined goal. Although the term "campaign" is probably thought of most often in connection with advertising, it seems more appropriate to apply the concept of a campaign first to the entire promotional program. Then the total promotional campaign can be subdivided into its advertising, personal selling, and sales-promotion components, and the subcampaigns can be planned in more detail.

Many types of promotional campaigns may be conducted by a company, and several may be run concurrently. Geographically, a firm may have a local, regional, or national campaign, depending upon the available funds, objectives, and market scope. One campaign may be aimed at consumers and another at wholesalers and retailers. The stage of a product's life cycle may determine whether a pioneering or competitive campaign will be conducted. Sometimes a firm is most concerned with building an image or promoting its services through an institutional campaign. A campaign may run for a week, a month, a year, or even longer. Three to six months is quite common.

Perhaps the first step in developing a promotional campaign should be to establish the campaign goals and determine the campaign strategy. One writer has suggested some areas which should be considered in the course of setting this strategy:[5]

1. What is the relative emphasis to be placed on primary versus secondary demand stimulation?

2. What balance is desired between the immediacy of the action-response and the duration of the response?

3. Do we wish to influence everyone a little bit or a few people intensively?

4. At what point are we targeting our emphasis on the spectrum between brand awareness and brand insistence?

5. What issues or product features (both ours and our competitors') will we stress?

Early in the course of planning the campaign, management should decide what selling appeals will be stressed. This decision will be based to a large extent upon the specific objectives of the campaign and the research findings concerning the buying motives and habits of the customers. If the goal of a

[5] Dodds I. Buchanan, "A New Look at 'Old' Advertising Strategy," *Business Horizons*, Winter, 1965, pp. 85–96.

promotional campaign put on by an airline is to introduce its new jet service, the appeals might be to the customers' desire for speed, a quiet and restful trip, or fine food and courteous services. If the same airline wanted to increase its plane loadings of air freight, however, the ads and the personal selling presentation might stress low total cost of air freight, reduction in losses due to spoilage and handling, advantages of savings in packaging, or convenient schedules.

A campaign revolves around a central idea or focal point. This "theme" permeates all promotional efforts and tends to unify the campaign. A theme is simply the appeals dressed up in a distinctive, attention-getting form. As such, it is related to the campaign's objectives and the customers' behavior; it expresses the product's benefits. Frequently the theme takes the form of a slogan, such as Hallmark Card Company's "when you care enough to send the very best" or DeBeers' "a diamond is forever." Cigarette manufacturers use such themes as "the thinking man's filter, the smoking man's taste," "remember how good cigarettes used to taste?" and "it's what's up front that counts." Some companies use the same theme for several campaigns; others develop a different theme for each new campaign.

The key to success in a campaign depends largely on management's ability to activate and coordinate the efforts of its entire promotional task force and the physical distribution of the product. Unfortunately, this is not always the case; too often the effectiveness of the advertising part of the promotional campaign is reduced considerably because of a failure to coordinate advertising with the personal selling and sales-promotional efforts. Divided organizational responsibilities are frequently at the root of this problem.

In a successfully operated campaign, the efforts of all groups concerned will be meshed effectively. The *advertising program* will consist of a series of related, well-timed, carefully placed ads. The *personal selling effort* can be tied in by having the salesmen explain and demonstrate the product benefits stressed in the ads. In the case of seasonal campaigns, salesmen's calls will be timed so as to follow shortly after the campaign is opened. Also, the salesmen will be fully informed about the advertising part of the campaign—the theme, media used, schedule of appearance of ads, appeals used, etc. The salesmen, in turn, should carry this information to wholesalers and retailers so that they can become effective participants in the campaign. *Sales-promotional devices* such as point-of-purchase display materials need to be coordinated with the other aspects of the campaign. For each campaign, new display materials must be prepared, reflecting the ads and appeals used in the current campaign, in order to maximize the campaign's impact at the point of sale. Personnel responsible for the *physical distribution activities* must ensure that adequate stocks of the product are available in all outlets prior to the start of the campaign.[6]

[6] For an example of the use of the campaign concept in marketing strategy by one highly successful company, see "Gillette's Supersharp Strategy," *Sales Management*, Oct. 5, 1962, p. 39.

DETERMINATION OF PROMOTIONAL MIX

Determining the most effective promotional *mix* is another of the difficult tasks in marketing management. Several different promotional tools or combinations thereof may be used. The underlying difficulty is that management does not know the exact extent to which advertising, personal selling, or any other promotional tool will help achieve the goals of the sales program. The executives do not know how much should be spent on each promotional activity, nor do they know what to expect from the expenditure.

Guideposts to aid management in its decision regarding the promotional mix will be examined in the following section. First, we shall analyze the factors which influence the promotional mix. Second, we shall pose and analyze several questions of basic promotional strategy in order to illustrate the effect of the influencing factors. Finally, we shall examine the quantitative data from a research study to show the practical applications of the analytical material.

Factors influencing promotional mix

Four factors which should influence management's decision making with respect to promotional mix are (1) the amount of money available for promotion, (2) the nature of the market, (3) the nature of the product, and (4) the stage of the product's life cycle.

Funds available Regardless of what may be the most desirable promotional mix, the amount of money available for promotion is the real determinant of the mix. Businesses with ample funds can make greater and more effective use of advertising than enterprises with limited financial resources. Small or financially weak companies are likely to rely on personal selling, dealer displays, or joint manufacturer-retailer advertising. The use of personal salesmen may be inefficient compared with advertising in magazines or newspapers. Either of these advertising media can carry at least part of the promotional message to far more people at a much lower cost per person than can personal salesmen. To do an effective promotional job in advertising, however, may take a considerable sum of money. Therefore, a company that is financially weak must choose some alternative in the mix.

Nature of the market As is true in most problem areas in marketing, management's decision on the promotional mix will be influenced to a great extent by the nature of the company's market. This influence is felt in at least three ways.

GEOGRAPHIC SCOPE OF THE MARKET Businesses selling in local markets only will often use promotional ingredients quite different from those used by firms which have national markets. Personal selling may be adequate in a small local market, but as the market broadens geographically, greater reliance must frequently be placed on advertising.

CONCENTRATION OF THE MARKET   Market concentration influences a firm's promotional strategy in three basic ways. First, the total number of prospective customers is a consideration. The fewer the number of potential buyers, the more apt a seller is to stress personal selling rather than advertising.

The second consideration is the number of different types of potential customers. A market that is concentrated in one type of customer or industry will call for a different promotional mix from that required when a firm sells to many different customer groups. A firm selling large power saws and other cutting equipment used only by lumber manufacturers may be able to use personal selling effectively, and there will be very little advertising in its mix. Another company selling hand tools used by thousands of consumers and virtually all types of industrial users probably will include liberal portions of advertising in its mix, because personal selling would be prohibitively expensive in reaching the final customers.

Finally, even though a firm sells nationally, it may find its market concentrated in relatively few spots. In this type of market concentration, emphasis on personal selling may be feasible, whereas it would be unrealistic if the potential customers were widely distributed all over the country.

TYPE OF CUSTOMERS   The promotional strategy is influenced by whether the business is aiming its sales campaign at industrial users, household consumers, or middlemen. To some extent, this final point overlaps and summarizes the market considerations discussed above. To illustrate, a promotional campaign aimed at retailers or wholesalers will probably contain a greater percentage of personal selling than will a program designed to attract household consumers. In many situations the middlemen may strongly influence the promotional strategy used by a manufacturer. Often a retail store will not even stock a product unless the manufacturer agrees to do a certain amount of advertising.

Nature of the product   Consumer products and industrial goods frequently require different strategies. Within the category of consumer goods, a promotional mix is influenced by whether the product is generally considered a convenience, shopping, or specialty item. In industrial goods, installations are not promoted in the same way as operating supplies or raw materials.

A few examples will show how the general nature of a product influences its promotional requirements. Firms marketing convenience goods will normally rely heavily on manufacturers' advertising plus emphasis on dealer displays. Personal selling plays a relatively minor role. This mix is best because a convenience product is widely distributed, needs no special demonstration or explanation, and is competing with many brands that have reasonably equal acceptance. Furthermore, buying decisions are often made at the point of purchase.

In the field of industrial goods, the promotional strategy behind installations usually features heavy emphasis on personal selling. The market for such products is more easily pinpointed than the market for other types of industrial products. Also, the unit sales are typically large, products are often made to specification, and considerable presale and postsale personal service is necessary. Raw-materials sellers also rely on personal selling, often to the total exclusion of advertising. Many raw materials are unbranded, and the products of any one of several firms will fill a buyer's need. Personal services and persuasion from salesmen may be the only differentiating features offered by one seller over another.

Stage of the product's life cycle   In Chapter 8, we observed that products go through a life cycle, usually starting with the introductory period; then progressing through the stages of growth, maturity, and saturation; and finally ending in decline and possible abandonment. Strategy decisions for promoting a product should be influenced considerably by the stage of demand for the item—that is, the phase of its life cycle which it is in at a given time.

In the pioneering, or introductory, stage a seller must stimulate *primary* demand—the demand for a type of product—as contrasted with *selective* demand—the demand for a particular brand. Thus manufacturers first had to sell the consumers on the value of electronic kitchen ovens in general before it was feasible to promote Tappan, General Electric, or some other brand.

When a product is in the pioneering stage (so far as a prospective customer is concerned), the customer does not recognize that he wants the commodity. He does not immediately understand how it will benefit him. Therefore, the promotional strategy is to inform and educate the potential customer or industrial user. He must be told that the product exists, how it may be used, and what want-satisfying benefits it provides.

Normally, heavy emphasis must be placed on personal selling when a firm is promoting a new product or is pioneering in a new market. Trade shows, exhibitions, and fairs also may play a major role in the promotional mix, particularly in the case of industrial goods which go directly from producer to customer. Rather than call on each customer or each industrial plant individually, the company can promote its new product at a home show, automobile show, or some other type of trade show where the prospective customers will come to the seller's exhibit. Manufacturers rely heavily on personal selling in attracting middlemen to handle a new product. During the introductory stages of the product, the middlemen in turn often use more personal selling in their promotional mix than they will after the item gains broader market acceptance.

During the middle stages of a product's life, the promotional mix calls for increased emphasis upon advertising. Customers are aware of the want-satisfying benefits of the product, so advertising can perform whatever informational and educational tasks remain to be done. As a product moves through the middle stages and attracts stiff competition, more and more attention is devoted to advertising as a tool of persuasion rather than of information only.

Intense competition forces sellers to devote larger sums to advertising and thus contributes to the declining profits experienced in the maturity and saturation stages.

For most products, the promotional emphasis during the middle stages is on advertising, but this is not universally true. Some products are of such a technical nature that even after acceptance, they must be heavily promoted by personal selling.

Most products eventually reach the final stages of their life cycle—decline and possible abandonment. New and better products are taking their place. Manufacturers are discontinuing the production of the older goods, the profit rates are declining, and even promotional effort is substantially cut back. Wise marketing administrators usually feel that it is not sound to promote heavily a product which has a declining primary demand.

Questions of basic promotional strategy

The following analysis of seven important questions should put management in a better position to determine its promotional mix. This analysis is closely related to the four basic influencing factors discussed above.[7]

When should personal selling be main ingredient? Personal selling will ordinarily carry the bulk of the promotional load (1) when the company is small or has insufficient funds with which to carry on an adequate advertising program, (2) when the market is concentrated, or (3) when the personality of the salesman is needed to establish rapport or create confidence. Personal selling will also be emphasized when the product (4) has a higher unit value, (5) requires demonstration, (6) must be fitted to the individual customer's needs, as in the case of securities or insurance, (7) is purchased infrequently, or (8) involves a trade-in.

When should advertising be main ingredient? If the market for the product is widespread, as in the case of a national consumer market, advertising should receive heavy emphasis. Advertising works best when the seller wishes to inform many people quickly, as in an announcement of new store hours, a special sale, or a new credit policy.

Certainly not every product lends itself to advertising. Many years ago Prof. Neil H. Borden identified five criteria which may serve as guides for management in deciding whether the company should use advertising to increase the demand for its product.[8] If all five of these criteria are met, normally there is an excellent opportunity to advertise. However, this ideal condition rarely exists. Ordinarily a firm has a product which meets some, but not all,

---

[7] Several of these questions are discussed in greater detail in James D. Scott, *Advertising Principles and Problems*, Prentice-Hall, Inc., Englewood Cliffs, N.J., 1953, chap. 7.

[8] Neil H. Borden, *The Economic Effects of Advertising*, Richard D. Irwin, Inc., Homewood, Ill., 1942, pp. 424–428.

of these conditions. Then the decision on whether or not to advertise becomes more difficult.

The five criteria are as follows:

1.   The primary demand trend for the product should be favorable. Advertising works best when the market demand for a product is on the upswing. In spite of the layman's opinion, advertising cannot successfully sell a product that people do not want, nor can advertising reverse a declining primary demand trend.

2.   There should be considerable opportunity to differentiate the product. When this condition exists, it is easier to advertise because the company has something to say. For this reason, appliances, automobiles, and cosmetics are easier to advertise than salt and sugar. Products which are not easy to differentiate by brand may still be advertised by a trade association. Products advertised by the American Dairy Association, the Wool Growers' Association, or the Association of Natural Rubber Producers are cases in point. A retailer who cannot easily differentiate his product lines from those of his competitors may try to differentiate his services, such as credit or location, which are an adjunct to the sale of the product.

3.   The product should have hidden qualities. This condition affords the seller grounds for informing or educating the market through advertising. On this point, a sofa or a mechanical device is easier to advertise than are greeting cards. Where hidden qualities are important, consumers learn to rely on the dependability of a certain brand. Thus brand preference can be developed.

4.   Powerful emotional buying motives should exist for the product; then buying action can be stimulated by appeal to these motives. It is easier to build an effective advertising campaign for Metrecal or some other balanced diet for weight reduction than for an article such as clotheslines, hammers, or sheets. Prestige products or stores have achieved their status largely through advertising which appeals to existing emotional motives.

5.   The company must have sufficient funds to support an advertising program adequately.

When should promotional efforts by retailer be stressed?   If the product has important qualities which can be judged at the point of purchase, or if it is a highly standardized item, it lends itself to dealer display. So do products which are purchased on impulse. A product with a limited market, which makes advertising unreasonable, may also be promoted through the dealers. Dealer promotion is particularly important when the retailer is better known in the market than the manufacturer.

When should manufacturer-retailer cooperative advertising be used? There are really three questions involved here. First, when should a manufacturer list his dealers' names and addresses in his advertisements? Second, under what conditions should the manufacturer pay the retailer to mention the manufacturer's product in the retailer's advertisement? Finally, when should a retailer emphasize the manufacturer's product in the store's advertising and display?

In answer to the first of these questions, the retailers' names should be mentioned particularly when the manufacturer employs selective or exclusive distribution policies. It then becomes important to tell the market where the product may be obtained. Concerning the second question, the manufacturer may have to pay the retailer to promote the product in order to get the retailer even to carry the commodity. Also, the retailer may be in a position to demand payment when his name has better selling power than the manufacturer's. In answer to the third question, a retailer should emphasize the manufacturer's products in the store advertising and display when the manufacturer's name is very important. That is, the dealer wants his customers to know that he carries the line of the well-known manufacturer.

Is retailer promotion needed when manufacturer emphasizes advertising or personal selling? The answer to this question is "yes." Personal selling, advertising, and merchandise display work done by the retailer can be quite effective. No matter how much advertising the manufacturer does, he can always benefit from high-caliber selling at the retail level. Dealer advertising can be used to supplement the manufacturer's advertising. Promotional effort by a well-known, respected store can be the final impetus needed to penetrate a local market and to stimulate consumer buying action. This type of effort at the dealer level is particularly effective when the manufacturer's advertising is of the reminder or indirect-action type. When a retail store operates on a self-service basis, dealer display is almost imperative to move the product, regardless of how good a job the manufacturer has done in his national advertising. Displays serve as an excellent reminder to the customer, reinforcing what he has seen in the national advertising. They also serve as a reminder when products are purchased infrequently or when consumers do not use shopping lists.

If a retailer emphasizes personal selling, does he need to advertise? Under certain conditions the answer to this question is "yes." In the first place, advertising will help to attract the customer to the store. Regardless of the quality of personal selling, it is largely wasted if the retailer cannot first attract an adequate number of potential customers. Furthermore, the advertising can support the efforts of the personal salesmen. If the product is particularly high-priced or is purchased infrequently, again some promotional device is needed to attract the customers to the store; discretionary purchases are very easy to put off indefinitely.

Should promotional activity be continued when demand is heavy or exceeds capacity? The answer is a definite "yes." It is important that the manufacturer keep his name before the public. Boom conditions may pass, or the seller may acquire new plant capacity. A market is a dynamic institution, and customer loyalty is a "sometime thing"; old customers leave and new customers must be won. If conditions of high demand persist, they are certain to attract competitors. If they are temporary, the seller's heavy advertising may discourage competitors from coming in. In any event, the nature of the advertising message may change. When demand is heavy in relation to supply, the company will probably switch to institutional or indirect-action advertising.

Examples of promotional mix

The business applications of some of the points developed in this section are reflected in Tables 21–1 and 21–2. These tables summarize some of the findings made in a study of marketing expenditures in relation to the sales of ninety-three companies. With the exception of a few firms which sell services, the companies represented in the two tables are manufacturers. In some fields, such as soft goods, it is likely that retailers carry the bulk of the promotional burden. Seventy-four of the firms sell consumer goods (Table 21–1), and forty-three, industrial products (Table 21–2); some of the ninety-three firms market both types of commodities. The amount spent for three promotional activities—advertising, sales promotion, and personal selling—is shown as a percentage of net sales. It should be noted particularly that the "—" symbol indicates that data were not reported, not that there were no expenditures for the activity. In this study, sales promotion was defined as those marketing efforts which are neither advertising nor personal selling but which coordinate advertising and personal selling and make them more effective. Expenditures for catalogues, price lists, display materials, and promotional booklets are examples of sales promotion costs.

One main point which can be studied from the tables is the amount of the total promotional appropriation in relation to sales. Among consumer goods firms, the toiletries and cosmetics manufacturers devote as much as 35 to 45 per cent of net sales to promotion. At the other extreme, firms producing steel or aluminum spend almost nothing (as a percentage of sales) to promote their consumer products. In general, the proportion of sales revenue expended on the promotion of industrial goods is much smaller than that spent on promotion of consumer goods.

From the tables it is obvious that several of the firms did not clearly delineate expenditures for the many separate marketing activities. Instead, costs of two or more functions, such as advertising and sales promotion or sales promotion and marketing research, are lumped together. Nevertheless, the study does show the differences in the promotional mixes used by the various companies. In the consumer goods fields (Table 21–1), most of the cosmetics and toiletries manufacturers relied much more on advertising than on sales promotion or personal selling. These firms need to develop brand acceptance

table   21–1

Promotional costs as percentage of sales of consumer goods: by individual companies

> Note the wide variations in the promotional mixes used by different firms. Compare the cosmetics firm (no. 3) and the insurance company (no. 62). Also note the variations in total promotional appropriations. A paint company (no. 12) devoted 27 per cent of sales to promotion, while the promotion budget of an appliance company (no. 43) was only 8 per cent of sales. How do you account for these differences?

Number	Type of product	Advertising budget[a]	Advertising	Sales promotion	Sales force
1.	Toiletries and proprietaries	A	30.0	4.0	10.0
2.	Package goods	AA	25.0	8.0	8.0
3.	Cosmetics	C	24.0	5.0	7.0
4.	Cosmetics	AAA	22.0	2.0	10.0
5.	Housewares	B	20.0[b]	—[b]	3.5
6.	Perfumes and cosmetics	B	16.0	3.0	21.0
7.	Drug sundries	A	14.0	3.0	5.0
8.	Drugs	A	12.0	8.0	7.0
9.	Books	A	11.0	6.0	5.0
10.	Food	AAA	11.0	6.0	—
11.	Mail order	AAA	10.5	0.2	0.3
12.	Paints	B	10.0	2.0	15.0
13.	Housewares	B	10.0	2.0	6.0
14.	Beer	AA	9.5	6.4[e]	—
15.	Food and feed	AAA	8.1	3.2	6.1
16.	Food	AAA	7.0	5.0	3.0
17.	Food	AAA	7.0	4.5[e]	—[e]
18.	Small housewares	B	6.0	1.3	12.5
19.	Appliances	AAA	5.0	1.0	—
20.	Soft drinks	B	5.0	3.0	1.0
21.	Soft goods	C	5.0	6.0	12.0
22.	Nonferrous metals	AA	5.0[c]	—[c]	—
23.	Salt	C	5.0[c]	—[c]	—
24.	Packaged grocery products	AAA	4.8	0.7	1.2
25.	Beverages	A	4.6	1.4	—
26.	Tool manufacturing	C	4.0[c]	—[c]	10.0
27.	Paper converting	C	4.0	4.0	—
28.	Soft goods, textiles	A	4.0	1.0[f]	17.0
29.	Tires, foam rubber	A	4.0	4.0	—
30.	Pianos	C	4.0	0.3	5.0
31.	Chemicals	D	3.5	1.0	—
32.	Automotive parts	C	3.5	—	10.3
33.	Photographic equipment	C	3.3[c]	—	3.0
34.	Food	A	3.5	1.7	6.0
35.	Appliances	A	3.0	3.0	—
36.	Textiles	B	3.0	0.7	3.6

table   21–1—Continued

Number	Type of product	Advertising budget[a]	Advertising	Sales promotion	Sales force
37.	Shoe manufacturing	A	3.0	0.3[f]	4.5
38.	Marketing cooperative—fresh produce	C	3.0[c]	—[c]	10.0
39.	Baby foods	A	2.7	2.6	6.0
40.	Hand tools	B	2.5	0.9	7.1
41.	Home furnishings	B	2.5	2.0	6.0
42.	Power tools	C	2.5	—	—
43.	Appliances	A	2.5	1.5	4.0
44.	Airline	AA	2.2	0.7	—
45.	Building materials	A	2.2	1.9	4.8
46.	Liquors	A	2.0	—	—
47.	Basic metals	A	2.0	1.0	—
48.	Heating and air conditioning	A	2.0	0.5	4.5
49.	Soft goods	C	2.0	2.5	4.5
50.	Floor coverings	A	2.0[c]	—	—
51.	Plumbing and heating	A	2.0[c]	—	—
52.	Shoe manufacturing	D	2.0[c]	—	5.3
53.	Steel equipment	C	2.0[c]	—	16.0
54.	Transportation	AA	1.8	0.2	6.0
55.	Building materials	AA	1.5	0.7	8.0
56.	Automotive	D	1.5	—	3.0
57.	Rubber	C	1.5	1.5	4.5
58.	Rubber products	C	1.3	1.0	—
59.	Water pumps	D	1.3	1.3[f]	5.0
60.	Photographic equipment	B	1.3	0.7	3.0
61.	Food	A	1.0	0.3	—
62.	Insurance	A	1.0	0.5	17.5
63.	Textiles	B	1.0	1.0	0.5
64.	Petroleum	C	1.0	—	—
65.	Retail food chain	AAA	1.0[c]	—[c]	—
66.	Oil	A	0.7	0.3	—
67.	Petroleum	A	0.6	0.3	—
68.	Domestic pumps and water systems	C	0.6	1.0	—
69.	Over thirty industries	A	0.5	1.5	—
70.	Glass manufacturing	A	0.5	0.2	—
71.	Steel manufacturing	D	0.2	0.5	0.5
72.	Iron and steel	D	0.1	—	—
73.	Aluminum	B	0.1	0.1	—
74.	Building industry	A	0.1[d]	—[d]	—[d]

NOTE: Dash (—) indicates data not given.

[a] AAA—$10,000,000 and over; AA—$5,000,000–9,999,999; A—$1,000,000–4,999,999; B—$500,000–999,999; C—$100,000–499,999; D—under $100,000.

[b] Advertising, sales promotion, and marketing research combined.

[c] Advertising and sales promotion combined.

[d] Advertising, sales promotion, marketing research, and sales force combined.

[e] Sales promotion, marketing research, and sales force combined.

[f] Sales promotion and marketing research combined.

SOURCE: Dale Houghton, "Marketing Costs: What Ratio to Sales?" *Printers' Ink*, Feb. 1, 1957, pp. 54–55.

table 21–2

Promotional costs as percentage of sales of industrial goods: by individual companies

Sales-force expenditures are typically much higher than advertising appropriations. In the promotional mix, marketers of industrial goods usually emphasize personal selling to a much greater degree than firms selling consumer products. Why? Compare this table and Table 21–1; note that the total promotional budget for industrial products is typically a smaller percentage of sales than is true for consumer goods.

Number	Type of product	Advertising budget[a]	Advertising	Sales promotion	Sales force
1.	Paint	D	10.0	—	—
2.	Road construction and agricultural equipment	D	4.0[b]	—[b]	7.0
3.	Industrial fasteners, steel shelving and shop equipment	B	2.8	—	—
4.	Office equipment	C	2.5[c]	—[c]	—
5.	Instrument	C	2.0	0.9	9.0
6.	Tool manufacturing	C	2.0[c]	—[c]	10.0
7.	Paper converting	C	2.0	2.0	—
8.	Instruments and controls	C	2.0[b]	—[b]	15.0
9.	Electrical control	C	1.8	3.8	—
10.	Metalworking machinery	C	1.8	0.2	—
11.	Graphic arts	C	1.5	0.5	16.0
12.	Metalworking	C	1.5[c]	—[c]	5.0
13.	Metal cutting tools	C	1.2	—	5.6
14.	Industrial machinery	D	1.0	2.0	7.0
15.	Package grocery products	B	1.0	0.9	4.8
16.	Metal product—foundry and machining	C	1.0	0.8	5.5
17.	Automotive parts	C	1.0	0.5	4.5
18.	Building materials	B	1.0	0.3[d]	4.0
19.	Nonferrous metals	A	1.0[c]	—[c]	—
20.	Die cutting	D	1.0	—	10.0
21.	Basic metals	AA	1.0	—	—
22.	Aluminum	A	0.8	0.4	—
23.	Petroleum	B	0.8	0.3	3.0
24.	Chemicals and plastics	A	0.8	—	—
25.	Chemical and food processing, steel mill, and construction equipment	A	0.7	0.2	6.0
26.	Iron and steel	A	0.6	—	—
27.	Hand tools	C	0.5	0.2	2.4
28.	Materials handling	B	0.5	0.5	—
29.	Soft goods—textile	C	0.5	—	12.0
30.	Automotive	D	0.5	—	0.5
31.	Plate steel fabrication	D	0.4	0.5	0.5

table   21–2—Continued

Number	Type of product	Advertising budget[a]	Advertising	Sales promotion	Sales force
32.	Foundry	C	0.3	—	—
33.	Iron and steel	C	0.3	—	—
34.	Rubber products	D	0.3	—	—
35.	Photographic equipment manufacturing	D	0.2	—	—
36.	Food and feed	C	0.1	0.3	2.5
37.	Chemicals	B	0.1	—	—
38.	Glass manufacturing	D	0.1	—	—
39.	Oil	C	0.1	—	—
40.	Aircraft	C	0.1	—	—
41.	Heavy manufacturing and aircraft accessories	C	0.1	—	9.3
42.	Manufacturing conveyors and pneumatic tube systems	C	—	—	—
43.	Building industry	C	—	—	—

NOTE: Dash (—) indicates data not given.

[a] AAA—$10,000,000 and over; AA—$5,000,000–9,999,999; A—$1,000,000–4,999,999; B—$500,000–999,999; C—$100,000–499,999; D—under $100,000.

[b] Advertising, sales promotion, and marketing research combined.

[c] Advertising and sales promotion combined.

[d] Sales promotion and marketing research combined.

SOURCE: Dale Houghton, "Marketing Costs: What Ratio to Sales?" *Printers' Ink*, Feb. 1, 1957, p. 24.

in a highly competitive national market. The cost of personal selling in these industries probably stems mainly from the heavy use of manufacturer-financed demonstrator salesmen in retail stores. As might be expected, in a mail-order firm (no. 11) the ratio of advertising to all other promotional activities is about 20:1. On the other hand, a firm selling soft goods (no. 21) emphasizes personal selling. A tool manufacturer (no. 26), an automotive parts firm (no. 32), and a steel equipment company (no. 53) also emphasize personal selling. In these firms, the product requires more explanation, the market is more concentrated as a rule, and manufacturers' brands are not usually important.

The firms must depend upon personal selling to get middlemen to handle the product. A life insurance firm (no. 62) had about a 17:1 ratio of personal selling to advertising. Life insurance requires a promotional program carefully tailored to each individual customer. This obviously calls for heavy personal selling rather than mass advertising.

Among firms selling industrial products (Table 21–2), more reliance was placed on a sales force than on an advertising program. Some of the firms reported a very high ratio of personal selling to advertising. For example, a textile manufacturer (no. 29) stated a 24:1 ratio, and a die-cutting firm (no. 20) had a 10:1 ratio.

DETERMINATION OF TOTAL PROMOTIONAL APPROPRIATION

In determining how much money should be appropriated for the entire promotional program, management should consider promotional costs in light of the influence the program will have on production costs. Here is another instance where it is better to employ the total-cost approach instead of basing decisions on a fragmented cost analysis of individual activities. To illustrate, assume that a firm is operating in the declining stage of its cost curve. That is, as output increases, the unit costs of production decrease. By increasing its promotional appropriation, the company may be able to increase its total sales to the point where the reduction in unit production costs more than offsets the increased promotional expenditures.

It is extremely difficult to establish promotional appropriations. Management lacks reliable standards for determining how much to spend on advertising or personal selling in total or how much to spend on specific activities within each area. An even more serious problem is that management normally cannot assess the results of its promotional expenditures. A firm may add ten salesmen or increase its trade-show budget by $20,000 a year, but no one can determine what increase in sales or profits is to be expected, nor can anyone measure the relative values of the two expenditures. The growing number of companies using a scientific approach to advertising budgets may be presaging a breakthrough in this problem area. Such aids as electronic computers, mathematical models, operations research methods, and long-range budgeting are being used. It was noted in one study that, in general, advertising executives are indifferent to, or actively opposed to, these innovations but that top management is encouraging experimentation.[9]

Even though much trial and error and executive judgment are involved in decisions on the promotional budget, a few generalizations can be made. Usually a small company will spend a greater percentage of sales on promotion than will a large business. Apparently there is a point at which diminishing returns set in. Of course, the larger company will spend more in dollars and thus probably reap better returns. New products require proportionately larger expenditures than established products. By the same token, a new company will devote a larger percentage of sales to promotional activities than an established company.[10]

---

[9] See "Ad Budgets: A Growing Science," *Printers' Ink*, Dec. 16, 1960, pp. 16–22; see also James F. Engel and Martin R. Warshaw, "Allocating Advertising Dollars by Linear Programming," *Journal of Advertising Research*, September, 1964, pp. 42–48.

[10] For a summary of the essential factors to consider, the methods to use, and a recommended procedure for establishing an *industrial* advertising budget, see H. Jay Bullen, "What to Consider when Planning Your Ad Budget," *Industrial Marketing*, August, 1964, pp. 70–74.

Methods of determining appropriation

There are four basic methods of determining the budget allocation for promotion. They are frequently discussed in connection with the advertising appropriation alone, but they may also be applied to the total promotional appropriation.

Relation to income   The promotional appropriation may be related in some way to company income. First, the expenditures may be set as a percentage of past or anticipated *sales*. Second, the appropriation may be based on a percentage of net or gross *profit*. Third, some businesses prefer to budget a fixed amount of money per *unit* of past or expected future sales. Manufacturers of products which have a high unit value and a low rate of turnover (automobiles or appliances, for example) frequently use this last method. Fruit growers' cooperative associations assess member growers a certain amount per case of fruit sold through the cooperative.

The percentage-of-sales method is probably the most widely used of all those discussed here. It has achieved broad acceptance because it is simple and easy to calculate. It also sets the cost in relation to sales income and thus tends to act as a variable expense rather than as a noncontrollable fixed expenditure. Actually the method is unsound and logically inconsistent. By setting promotional expenditures for one year on the basis of sales in the preceding year, management is saying that promotion is a *result* of sales, when, in fact, it is a *cause* of sales. Even when promotion is set as a percentage of future sales, this method is logically indefensible. By forecasting future sales and then setting the promotional appropriation, management is still considering advertising and personal selling to be a result of sales. If sales depend upon promotion, as is truly the case, then they cannot be forecast until the promotional appropriation is determined. Another undesirable result of this method is that promotional expenditures will be reduced just when sales are declining. If the reasons for a sales decline are not clear, management can compound its difficulties by withdrawing promotional support at that time. Experience shows that a better course of action is to maintain the level of promotional activity, even if profits drop temporarily, until the basic causes of the sales decline can be determined and corrected.[11]

Task or objective   A much sounder basis for determining the promotional budget is to decide first what tasks the promotional program is intended to accomplish and then determine what the cost of promotion must be. Various

[11] For some research findings illustrating this point, see A. C. Neilsen, Jr., "Many Measurements Available to Increase Advertising Effectiveness," *Media/scope*, September, 1965, p. 72.

forms of this method are widely used today.[12] The task method forces manage-ment to define clearly, realistically, and in detail the goals of its promotional program. This method also involves management in long-run, rather than year-to-year, planning. Sometimes this approach is called the "buildup method" because of the way it operates. For example, a company may set as one goal the entry into a new geographic market or the full-market introduction of a new product. The executives decide that this venture will require ten additional salesmen. Compensation and expenses of these salesmen will cost a total of $170,000 per year. Salary for an additional sales supervisor and expenses for extra office and administrative needs will cost $20,000. Thus in the personal selling part of the promotional mix, an extra $190,000 must be appropriated. Similar estimates may be made for the anticipated cost of advertising, sales promotion, and other promotional tools to be used in connection with the goal of entering a new territory or introducing a new product.

Use of all funds available   A new company frequently plows all possible available funds into its promotional program. Management may expect to have to wait one to five years before it will earn a profit and be able to budget for its sales program in a different manner.

Follow competition   A weak method of determining the promotional appropriation, but one which is used enough to be noted here, is to match the promotional expenditures of competitors. Sometimes only one competitor is followed. In other cases management will have access to industry averages through its trade association, and these will become company bench marks. The system is weak on two counts at least. First, a firm's competitors may be just as much in the dark as the firm itself, and second, the firm's needs and goals may be quite different from those of its competition.

SALES PROMOTION

In Chapter 8, "merchandising" and "sales promotion" were called the two most loosely used terms in the marketing vocabulary. In fact, the sales promo-tion manager of a major oil company has referred to sales promotion as "muddled, misused, and misunderstood."[13] Many businessmen use the terms

[12] In the study referred to in the preceding footnote, most of the respondents stated that "the job to be done" was the single most important determinant of their adver-tising budgets. Yet in practice most of the firms began building their budgets with a set figure—usually either a percentage increase over last year's budget or a percentage of next year's sales forecast. Few companies actually first determined their advertising objectives, then planned the program to reach these goals, and finally calculated the cost of this program.

[13] See William R. Kelly, "Muddled . . . Misused . . . Misunderstood . . . That's Sales Promotion!" *Sales Management*, Jan. 15, 1954, p. 36.

synonymously with advertising or promotion in total. Today in the field of marketing we are beginning to get substantial agreement that sales promotion is a separately distinguishable field. In one survey, 90 per cent of the executives who were contacted reported that there was a clear, and in most companies, a formal, distinction between sales promotion and advertising.[14]

What then is sales promotion? The American Marketing Association says its preferred definition is, "those marketing activities, other than personal selling, advertising, and publicity, that stimulate consumer purchasing and dealer effectiveness, such as displays, shows and expositions, demonstrations, and various non-recurrent selling efforts not in the ordinary routine."[15]

In what ways are the sales promotion and advertising different? First, except for direct mail, advertising deals with media owned and controlled by others, while sales promotion tries to inform and persuade groups through tools and methods controlled by the company itself. Sales promotion deals with nonrecurring and nonroutine matters, in contrast to advertising or personal selling. Finally, while most companies could not exist profitably without advertising or personal selling, they could do without sales promotion. Frey called sales promotion the "plus" ingredient in the marketing mix.

In effect, a major function of sales promotion is to serve as a bridge between advertising and personal selling—to supplement and coordinate efforts in these two areas. Not only are we seeing an increase in the growth and stature of sales promotion, but also the trend is to integrate it as a part of the total marketing strategy. Often, for example, it is being introduced at the inception of a campaign, and not tacked on afterward.[16]

Importance of sales promotion

There is a saying in retailing that "it is the final three feet which count." This refers specifically to the distance from the retail salesclerk to the consumer, but the meaning can be broadened to suggest the importance of all activities at the point of purchase, whether it is a purchase by an ultimate consumer, middleman, or industrial user. Firms "have spent millions on determining the most effective techniques and appeals for luring the prospect into the dealer's place

[14] Albert W. Frey, *The Role of Sales Promotion*, Dartmouth College, Amos Tuck School of Business Administration, Hanover, N.H., 1957, p. 2.

[15] Committee on Definitions, Ralph S. Alexander, Chairman, *Marketing Definitions: A Glossary of Marketing Terms*, American Marketing Association, Chicago, 1960, p. 20. In this set of definitions, however, the American Marketing Association also observes that in retailing, sales promotion is interpreted to cover "all methods of stimulating customer purchasing, including personal selling, advertising, and publicity." Thus in retailing, "sales promotion" is used in a broad sense and is virtually synonymous with "promotion," as the term is used in this book and also by most manufacturers.

[16] Joel Harnett, "Sales Promotion: Marketing's Tiger by the Tail," *Printers' Ink*, Feb. 26, 1965, p. 47.

of business . . . but they have failed to follow through by studying how to get him to buy—and to buy *their* products—once he is inside the store."[17]

Today much consumer dissatisfaction with respect to retail selling could be alleviated by a good sales-promotional program. The growing use of self-service, automatic vending, and other sales methods where salesmen are not used also points up the need for sales promotion.[18] Accentuating this point is the high incidence of impulse buying and the tendency of retailers to diversify their product mix. Furthermore, sales-promotional devices are often the only promotional materials available at the point of purchase. Advertising media reach potential consumers at their homes, at their places of business, or in their travels. When the time for buying arrives, the impact of the advertisements may have worn off (or the prospect may not have even seen the advertisement), but sales-promotional devices at the point of purchase inform, remind, or otherwise stimulate the buyer. People who see the promotional devices are excellent prospects! They are usually in a buying frame of mind or they would not be there.

Services rendered by sales promotion

The sales promotion department of a manufacturer may work with many different groups—consumers, dealers and distributors, or other sections of the marketing department. Similarly, retailers engage in sales-promotional activities aimed at consumers. A manufacturer's sales-promotional program which is directed toward the consumer may be divided into two groups—activities intended to *educate or inform* the consumer and those intended to *stimulate* him. To inform the consumers, companies will prepare booklets and manuals, give demonstrations, and offer free consulting services. To stimulate consumers, many firms give away samples and premiums. Others conduct contests, offering prizes for the best statement which tells in twenty-five words or less why the consumer likes the given product. These various activities are intended to get the consumer to use the product or (as in a contest) to get him to think of all the possible reasons why he likes it.

Services rendered to dealers and distributors include such things as conducting training programs for the middlemen's salesmen, giving managerial advice, and installing displays. In summary, a manufacturer tries to increase the dealers' interest in the product and to enhance their effectiveness as merchants.

[17] Robert N. McMurry, "How to Win or Lose Sales at the Point of Purchase," *Journal of Marketing*, July, 1959, p. 41.

[18] For a report on the extent of use, the retailers' attitudes, the manufacturers' strategies, and the minimization of waste in connection with one major type of sales promotion—point-of-purchase displays—see Bert C. McCammon, Jr., "The Role of Point of Purchase Display in the Manufacturer's Marketing Mix," in Taylor W. Meloan and Charles M. Whitlo (eds.), *Competition in Marketing*, University of Southern California Press, Los Angeles, 1964, pp. 75–92.

Within the manufacturer's marketing department, the sales promotion division can perform services for the personal selling, advertising, and marketing research groups. Sales promotion people can prepare portfolios, sales manuals, demonstration kits, and other selling aids used by the salesmen. Also, in the field, the sales force can concentrate on product selling while the sales promotion men do all the missionary work with dealers and consumers. The marketing research department can get help in field survey work. The sales promotion department can aid the advertising people by preparing displays and other point-of-purchase advertising materials.

In conclusion, a marketing manager should well consider the role which sales promotion can play in a marketing mix. This activity should not be submerged in departments which are concerned primarily with advertising or the personal sales force. Once marketing executives become aware of the value of sales promotion work, they will undoubtedly use this tool more effectively to supplement the work of the marketing division. At the present time, unfortunately, much remains to be done systematically and empirically to determine the most effective use of sales promotion in a company's marketing program and to measure the results of using these promotional tools.[19]

When the key decisions have been made with respect to the total promotional program, management can concern itself with the administration of the personal selling and advertising programs, usually the two major components of the total promotional effort in a firm. These two areas are the respective subjects of the next two chapters.

QUESTIONS AND PROBLEMS

1   What is the difference between selling and marketing?

2   What is the relationship between the industrialization of an economy and the importance of promotion?

3   Are promotional methods and tools used in any type of economic systems other than capitalism?

4   What relationships and differences are found among the following items? Explain carefully.

     a. Promotion   c. Sales promotion
     b. Advertising   d. Personal selling

5   To what extent can a fine promotional program offset significant weaknesses in the product? In the distribution system? In the price structure?

6   Identify the central idea—the theme—in some current promotional campaigns.

[19] For conflicting points of view regarding whether we can quantitatively measure the effect which sales promotion has on sales, see John H. Weber, "Can Results of Sales Promotion Be Predicted?" *Journal of Marketing*, January, 1963, pp. 15–19; Milton J. Margolis, "How to Evaluate Field Sales Promotion," *Journal of Marketing*, July, 1963, pp. 42–46; and Lee Adler, "Sales Promotion Effectiveness *Can* Be Measured," *Journal of Marketing*, October, 1963, pp. 69–70.

7 Explain how the *nature of the market* would affect the promotional mix for the following products:
 a. Oil-well drilling equipment
 b. Plywood
 c. Golf clubs
 d. Precision instruments used by missile manufacturers
 e. Cigarettes

8 Discuss how the promotional mix and the promotional program for portable electric typewriters are apt to change as this product goes through its life cycle.

9 Using Borden's criteria, evaluate the advertisability of each of the following products. Assume sufficient funds are available in each case.
 a. Car batteries   c. Wall mirrors
 b. Mattresses   d. Small power tools

10 Can you name any products which are advertised heavily but which do *not* meet the criterion of having hidden qualities?

11 What influence do a manufacturer's channels of distribution have on his promotional program?

12 Referring to Tables 21–1 and 21–2, the manufacturers of industrial goods seem generally to spend a relatively larger share of their total promotional effort on personal selling than consumer goods firms. Consumer goods manufacturers, on the other hand, show larger advertising percentages than the industrial firms. How do you account for this?

13 If a manufacturer of a consumer product does a good job of advertising and personal selling, is promotion by the retailer needed? Why or why not?

14 Why is the percentage-of-sales method so widely used to determine the promotional appropriation when, in fact, most authorities recognize the task or objective method as the most desirable one?

15 Visit a supermarket, clothing store, and hardware store, and then make a list of all the sales-promotional tools or devices which you observed in each store. Which of these devices do you feel are particularly effective?

16 Is sales promotion effective for selling expensive consumer products such as houses, automobiles, or backyard swimming pools? Is your answer the same for expensive industrial products?

17 Explain how sales promotion can be used to offset weaknesses in retail salesmanship.

22

MANAGEMENT OF PERSONAL SELLING

The salesman has long been featured in song and story; he has been alternately praised and ridiculed. Truly, he is the backbone of marketing. Selling is essential to the health and well-being of our economic system, and it probably offers more job opportunities than any other single vocation today. Yet personal selling is frequently criticized, and it is very hard to attract qualified young people into selling jobs.

NATURE AND IMPORTANCE OF PERSONAL SELLING

The goal of all marketing efforts is to increase profitable sales by offering want satisfaction to the market over the long run. Personal selling is by far the major *promotional* method used to reach this goal. The number of people employed in advertising is in the thousands; in personal selling, the number is in the millions. In many companies personal selling is the largest single operating expense, often equaling 8 to 15 per cent of net sales. Advertising costs average 1 to 3 per cent of sales. Expenditures for salesmen's salaries, commissions, and travel expenses; the costs of operating sales branches; and the expenses of managing these salesmen all add up to a tidy sum.

Personal selling is the most important element in the entire marketing mix, according to a survey of 400 presidents of large corporations selected at random from a Dun & Bradstreet directory. This survey also underlined the fact that personal selling is becoming a popular route to the top in a company. "Selling is the quickest way for young people to grow into any business and to be rewarded handsomely."[1] Salesmen's jobs have increased in number and importance since 1960, and half the presidents anticipated that personal selling will take a still larger chunk of a company's total budget by 1970.

Relative merits

Personal selling consists in individual, personal communication, in contrast to the mass, relatively impersonal communication of advertising, sales promotion, and the other promotional tools. Consequently, compared with these other tools, personal selling has the advantage of being more flexible in operation. Salesmen can tailor their sales presentations to fit the needs, motives, and behavior of individual customers. Also, salesmen can see the customer's reaction to a particular sales approach and then make the necessary adjustments right on the spot. Objections and questions can be uncovered and answered immediately. A second merit of personal selling is the chance to minimize wasted effort. In advertising, much of the cost is devoted to sending the message to people who are in no way real prospects. In personal selling, a company has an opportunity to pinpoint its market target far more effectively than can be done with any other promotional device.

A third advantage of personal selling is that in most situations this tool can be used to make the actual sale. Advertisements can attract attention and arouse desire, but usually they do not get buying action and complete the transfer of title. Finally, salesmen can perform for management many other services which are not strictly selling jobs. They can collect credit information, reflect customer attitudes, and relay complaints to management. Some firms use their sales representatives to handle adjustments, perform major repair services, and act as fieldmen for marketing research projects. Of course it is questionable whether a company should use good salesmen for these nonselling tasks.

If personal selling has a major limitation, it is its high cost. Even though the use of salesmen enables a business to reach its market with a minimum of wasted effort, the cost of developing and operating a sales force is high. Another disadvantage is that personal selling is often limited by the company's

[1] "Top Executives Rank Salesmanship Tops, Study Shows," *Sales Management*, Mar. 18, 1966, p. 120.

inability to get the caliber of men needed to do the job. At the retail level many firms have abandoned their sales forces and shifted to self-service for this very reason.

Personal selling is not always the best promotional tool to use. In the preceding chapter we noted the product and market conditions under which a company should emphasize personal selling in its promotional mix.

Types of personal selling jobs

It is misleading to talk about *the* selling job, as if we could describe a typical salesman or meaningfully generalize about his job. Working in a retail store is not the same as selling electronic computers or executive airplanes; a missionary salesman who sets up window displays has a job quite unlike that of a creative insurance salesman. It should be worthwhile here to classify selling jobs according to the salesman's employer and then by his prospects and customers.

Selling for manufacturers The various types of selling jobs performed by manufacturers' sales forces include selling directly to other manufacturers and industrial users, selling to wholesalers and retailers, selling directly to consumers on a door-to-door basis, and doing sales-promotional work with middlemen.

SELLING TO INDUSTRIAL USERS One type of manufacturers' sales job involves selling industrial products to firms which will not resell the goods in their present form. The products sold will range from large, expensive installations to small industrial operating supplies. The job calls for able, high-caliber salesmen. Compensation is often quite high, and the men are given unlimited expense accounts. In jobs of this kind, we frequently find creative, professional salesmen, particularly when items of high unit value are being sold to top executives. *Creative selling* may be defined as the task of entering into the buyer's decision-making process before an order is formulated and obtaining cooperation through an offer to provide substantial services and information.

Creative salesmen must be well informed about the prospective buyer's problems and the product's benefits because the buyers themselves are well informed. These salesmen must display some aggressiveness because industrial purchases are often postponable. Also, they must be able to mix with top-level executives. That is, they must be able to discuss costs, manufacturing procedures, taxes, and personnel problems understandingly with these executives.

Another important facet of the industrial salesman's job is that of locating the persons within a plant who have authority in decisions to purchase. Frequently this is not the purchasing agent, who may be no more than a functionary who signs purchase orders and selects vendors on the basis of price, delivery date, and credit terms. Our salesman must locate and deal with the operating, maintenance, and design people who actually participate in internal decisions to purchase. And he must see them before the specifications of the purchases have been finalized.

SELLING TO WHOLESALERS   Another type of manufacturers' selling job involves selling to wholesaling middlemen. This job calls for creative selling as well as the ability to perform services for the wholesaler and his employees. As part of getting the order, the manufacturer's salesman may have to train the wholesaler's salesmen, help the wholesaler promote the product, adjust complaints, and, in general, service the account.

A reasonably high-caliber salesman is needed in this job. Usually he is paid by a combination plan which includes a salary plus some form of incentive. The manufacturer pays all the travel and other expenses. Most of the salesman's work is done in large cities, and since his territory may include several metropolitan centers, traveling is usually involved.

SELLING TO RETAILERS   Some manufacturers' salesmen sell directly to retailers. This job is quite similar to that of selling to wholesalers.

The initial task is to get the retailer to stock the product by showing him that there is a demand for it, that it will be a profitable item, and that the manufacturer will make the necessary guarantees. Because many retailers feel they can judge a product's merits and potential profitability, the salesman's job may be to negotiate prices and terms of sale or to explain his company's programs for advertising and sales promotion.

After the initial contact is made and an order obtained, the main activities center around keeping the retailer informed on new products and other developments and helping him to promote and resell the product, train his salesmen, and handle adjustments. Calls are made regularly over a reasonably set route.

SALES-PROMOTIONAL WORK WITH RETAILERS   Some manufacturers' selling jobs do not require creative product selling at all. They involve calling on retailers in order to build goodwill and coordinate the work of the wholesalers' or manufacturers' product salesmen with the company's advertising program. The salesmen are usually called missionary salesmen, promotional salesmen, or detail men; their job was described in Chapter 14. This type of job is pretty routine and does not require a particularly high-caliber salesman. Turnover is often high, compensation is relatively low, and supervision of the men is a real job.

SELLING DIRECTLY TO THE CONSUMER   This is the traditional door-to-door sales job. Sometimes it involves a literal door-to-door cold canvass, as in the case of Fuller Brush salesmen. More often, however, the salesmen make calls on a selective basis. This is probably the most difficult selling job of all; it requires both physical and mental stamina. It calls for the utmost in persistent, creative selling. Almost always the men are paid on a straight-commission basis.

The door-to-door sales job is very important for two reasons. First, it is an excellent training and proving ground for salesmen who want to move into other types of selling activity. If a fellow can be a success at door-to-door selling, he has a fine chance of succeeding in many other selling tasks. Second, this type of job attracts people who cannot or do not want to work full time.

Selling for wholesalers   The salesmen for a wholesaler are frequently labeled "order takers." These salesmen typically have so many products to sell that they cannot do much aggressive, creative selling. Salesmen for wholesalers of groceries, drugs, hardware, building materials, or industrial operating supplies may have thousands of different items listed in their catalogues. Their job is to call regularly on retail or industrial accounts in order to fill the customers' needs. If a salesman has been calling on a retailer for some period of time and has earned the retailer's trust and confidence, the store buyer usually will let the wholesaler's representative check the stock, take inventory, and write up the order himself.

Today many wholesalers are trying to remove the "order taker" stigma from their salesmen by training them to perform various promotional and managerial services for retailers. The retailers are encouraged to prepare their own orders from catalogues. The wholesaler's salesmen then devote their time to working with the dealer's salesmen, helping with advertising programs, building displays, and performing other similar tasks.

Normally this type of job does not require a highly qualified salesman. It is routine and calls for much detail work. Little traveling is involved except in sparsely populated parts of the country. The men are usually paid a salary plus a small incentive, and they have a limited expense account.

Selling for retailers   Selling jobs in retail stores are, in general, on a very low level; they offer a low salary and consequently do not usually attract properly qualified and motivated employees. The prospective customer has identified his want and has a reasonably clear idea of how to satisfy it. The retail salesclerk's job is to show the customer the merchandise, explain relative merits of competing products, make the sale, and arrange for necessary services, such as packaging, delivery, or credit. Because of management's dissatisfaction with salespeople, many stores have installed self-service methods of selling.

There are some exceptions to the retail selling job just described. Retailers of "big-ticket" items, such as automobiles, large appliances, and home heating plants, often have their salesmen call on the prospect at his home. Here there is more opportunity for creative selling, and sometimes these representatives are really good salesmen. Incidentally, the greater ability of these salesmen is reflected in a considerably higher level of compensation than is found among typical retail salesclerks.

DEVELOPMENT AND OPERATION OF A SALES FORCE

In a marketing program many executives may be involved in activities related to the management of a sales force. It is not within the scope of this book to cover these activities in detail, but we shall summarize the tasks involved in developing and operating a sales force.

Selecting salesmen

Importance of good selection program   As explained in Chapter 2, it is
the author's contention that staffing is the most important of all managerial
activities. In a promotional program the value of good selection is seen in several ways. First, since it is very difficult to find good salesmen, it is essential
that the selection program maximize the opportunity of getting the type of man
needed. Second, a sales manager is no better than his salesmen. No matter how
well managed a sales force may be, if it is distinctly inferior in quality to that
of a competitor, the competitor will win out. Third, if a sales force is well
selected, many other tasks in sales management such as training and supervision
are made easier. Also, selling costs will be reduced because turnover rates will
be lower. In addition to its many other advantages, a well-selected sales force
should be more productive and should build better customer relations than a
poorly chosen group.

Scope of selection task   The three major steps in sales force selection are
as follows:

1.   Determine the number and type of men wanted. This step includes an
analysis of the job and the preparation of a written job description. Management also must determine specifically what qualifications are needed to fill the
job as it is described.
2.   Recruit an adequate number of applicants.
3.   Select the qualified men from among the applicants.

The key to success in the first step is to establish the proper hiring specifications, just as if the company were purchasing equipment or supplies instead
of manpower. To establish these specifications, management must first know what
the particular sales job entails. This calls for a detailed job analysis and a written
description. It should include specific statements regarding the title of the job,
organizational relationships, job duties, and applicant qualifications. This written
description will later be invaluable in training, compensation, and supervision.

Determining the qualifications needed to fill the job is the most difficult
part of the selection function. We still really do not know all the characteristics
that make a good salesman. We do not know to what quantitative degree each
should be possessed, nor to what extent an abundance of one can offset the lack
of another. As an approach to the problem, some companies have analyzed the
personal histories of their past salesmen to determine traits common to the successful or unsuccessful performers. Sometimes it helps to interview people
when they leave the company to see if meaningful patterns can be uncovered.

A planned system for recruiting a sufficient number of applicants is the
next step in selection. A recruiting system has these characteristics:

1.   It is operating continually, not just when there are vacancies on the sales
force.

2.   It is systematic, reaching and exploiting all appropriate sources of applicants.
3.   It provides a continual flow of qualified applicants in greater numbers than the company can use.
4.   It is phased so that mechanical, initial steps can be delegated and will not require a high-level executive's time.

The third step involves two tasks. First, management must establish a system of measuring applicants against predetermined standards. Then it must activate the system so as to select the necessary number of men who have the proper qualifications. Sales managers should use all available selection tools in their effort to determine which applicants possess the desired qualifications. These tools include application blanks, interviews, references, credit reports, psychological tests, and physical examinations. Probably all companies use application blanks. They serve as records of personal histories and may be used to implement interviewing. Some companies assign scores to various answers on a blank and total the applicant's score. If this score is below a predetermined level, the applicant will usually be eliminated at that point.

The interview is the other most widely used selection device. Virtually no salesman is hired without one personal interview, and it is desirable to have several. Ideally these should be conducted in different physical settings and by different people. This should help to reduce the effect of one person's possible bias, to get other people's opinions, and to see how the recruit acts under different conditions. Usually an interview can help an employer to determine how badly the applicant wants the job, whether the company can assure him the success he wants, and whether he will work to his fullest capacity. Patterned or preplanned interviews are usually considered most desirable because they overcome many weaknesses found in the typical interviewing process. Interviews vary according to when they are given and who is interviewed (applicant, wife, family).

Assimilating new salesmen into the organization

When a salesman is hired, management should pay close attention to the task of integrating him into the company family. Often this step is overlooked entirely. The person is carefully selected and wined and dined to recruit him into the firm. Then as soon as he is hired, the honeymoon is over, and he is left to shift for himself. In such cases the man often becomes discouraged and may even quit. A wise sales manager will recognize that the new man knows very little about the details of his job, his fellow workers, or his status in the firm. A vital need exists to maintain clear and open two-way channels of communication between the new man and management.

Training salesmen

Another major phase of operating a sales force includes developing and conducting a training program. All salesmen, even experienced ones, need some training periodically. Training involves the following problem areas; in each instance, decisions will be based to a considerable extent upon the kind of training program involved—whether it is an indoctrination program, a refresher course, or some other type.

1. What are the goals of the program? In general, the aim of the program is to increase productivity and stimulate the men. In addition, executives must determine what specific ends they wish to accomplish. For instance, the goal may be to increase sales of high-margin items, to improve prospecting methods to develop new accounts, or to introduce the new season's line of products.

2. Who should do the training? The training program may be conducted by the line sales executives, by a company staff training department, or by outside training specialists.

3. What should be the content of the program? A well-rounded sales training program should cover three general topics: product knowledge, information about company policies and practices, and selling techniques. Salesmen must know everything possible about their own products and about competitive goods. Usually these subjects are covered in initial training programs, and information regarding new products is included in refresher courses and continuous training programs. The job description will provide an excellent guide to the content of the program.

Salesmen should also know the company history, the executives, and the policies concerning pricing, discounts, returns, delivery, guarantees, minimum orders, etc. Finally, new salesmen especially need to be instructed in whatever selling techniques are required for the particular product.

4. When and where should training be done? Some companies believe in fully training a man before he goes into the field. Others let a man prove he has some desire and ability to sell and then bring him back into the office or plant for intensive training. Both points of view have merit.

Firms may employ either centralized or decentralized training programs. A centralized program may involve a periodic meeting or convention which all salesmen attend, or the company may employ an organized school conducted on a continuing or periodic basis. A decentralized program may be held in branch offices, in traveling sales clinics, or during on-the-job training. Decentralized programs generally cost less than centralized programs. They do not take the man away from his work for long and do not disrupt home office routine. The trainee can learn right in the environment where he works and where his problems occur. The big problem with decentralized programs is that the quality of instruction is often inferior.

5. What instructional methods should be used? The lecture method can be employed to inform trainees about company history, policies, and practices. Demonstrations may be used to impart product knowledge or selling techniques. Round-table or panel discussions are often employed to analyze problems encountered by the salesman in his work. Role playing is an excellent device for

training a man in proper selling techniques. On-the-job training can be used in almost any phase of the program.

Compensating salesmen

To compensate their men, companies may offer both financial and nonfinancial rewards. The nonfinancial rewards involve giving a man an opportunity for advancement, satisfying his need for recognition of his efforts, and giving him a feeling of prestige, self-respect, and belonging. Financial rewards may take the form of direct monetary payment or of indirect monetary payment (paid vacations, pensions, and insurance plans).

Before designing a specific plan, management should understand the broad goals of a sound pay arrangement. It should enable a company to attract, keep, and develop desirable men. It should correlate a man's rewards with his efforts and results, particularly his results. A sound plan should enable management to control the activities of the sales force. It should ensure proper treatment of customers. To reach these general goals, the specific plan should (1) provide for a steady income as well as an incentive income, (2) be flexible, yet uncomplicated, and easy to understand, (3) be economical to administer, and (4) be competitive and still be fair to management and to the salesmen. In designing a compensation plan, management should, by referring to the job description, relate the pay plan to the salesman's job. As much as possible—and this is difficult—the plan should be based upon job elements which are controllable by the salesman and are also quantitatively measurable.

Establishing a compensation system really involves making decisions on two general problems—the *level* of compensation and the *method* of compensation. The level refers to the total dollar income which a salesman earns over a period of time. The method of compensation refers to the system or plan by which the salesman will reach the intended level. The level is influenced by the type of man required for the job and the competitive rate of pay for similar positions.

There are three widely used methods of compensating a sales force: straight salary, straight commission, and a combination plan. Today, probably well over one-half of the firms in the country use some kind of combination plan.

The straight-salary plan offers a maximum of security and stability of earnings for a salesman. Management is in a better position to control and direct the activities of the men because they are paid the same amount each month regardless of what tasks they perform. Turnover is usually minimized. Under this arrangement salesmen can consider the customers' best interests. A commonly stated drawback of the plan is that it does not offer adequate incentive for the men. Also, it is a fixed cost, unrelated to sales revenue. Determining the proper salary level is often a problem. Also, unless management provides a high quality of supervision and control, the company wastes the advantage of being able to direct the men under this plan. Straight-salary systems are typically used for compensating new salesmen and missionary salesmen, when opening new territories, or when the sale involves a technical product and a lengthy period of negotiations.

A straight commission tends to have just the opposite merits and limitations. It provides tremendous incentive for the salesmen, and the commission costs can be related directly to sales or gross margin. The sales representative has more freedom in his work, and his level of income is largely determined by his own efforts. On the other hand, it is difficult to control the men and to get them to do a fully balanced sales job; it is particularly difficult to get them to perform tasks for which no commission is paid. There is always the danger that they will oversell a customer, high-pressure him, or otherwise incur his ill will. Straight-commission plans may work well if:

1.   Great incentive is needed to get the sales.

2.   Very little nonselling missionary work is required.

3.   The company is financially weak and must relate its compensation expenses directly to sales or gross profits.

4.   The salesmen prefer the plan, or it is quite common in the industry.

5.   The company is unable to supervise the men.

The ideal way to develop a combination plan is to balance the best features of both the straight-salary and straight-commission plans with as few of their drawbacks as possible.

An important element in a salesman's financial affairs is the reimbursement for business expenses which he incurs in traveling or selling. The importance of salesmen's expense control is difficult to overrate. With shrinking profit margins and higher break-even points in a company's operations, many administrators are justly concerned over the travel and other expense items incurred by the sales force. It is essential that sales executives develop a plan to control these costs and reimburse the salesmen for them. In principle, a salesman should not make or lose money because of his expense account, nor should he forego any beneficial sales activities because he will not be adequately reimbursed for the attendant expenses. Most firms pay salesmen for these expenses under an expense account arrangement. Ordinarily arrangements for reimbursing salesmen for these expenses should be separated from the compensation plan. A substantial number of companies, however, let the salesmen pay all their own expenses from their total salaries or commissions.

Supervising salesmen

Another management responsibility involved in operating a sales force is to provide adequate supervision of the men. This activity can serve both as a method of continuation training and as a device to ensure that company policies and practices are being carried out. One of the values of supervision is that it affords a vertical two-way channel of communication between management and the sales force. Executives must determine how much supervision is needed to avoid either over- or undersupervising. There is probably little doubt that personal supervision is most effective. This may be done by field supervisors, branch managers, or the home office sales manager or his assistants. Other methods of supervision include the use of correspondence reports and sales meetings.

Motivating salesmen

Already we have noted that proper training programs, compensation plans, expense controls, and supervisory systems help to motivate a salesman. In addition, a company may employ such techniques as contests or conventions. In general, management is concerned with keeping morale at a high level and ensuring that the salesmen will produce to their full capacity. Poor morale can result in increased turnover, unsatisfactory sales performance, increased expenses, and development of outside interests. A good sales manager will recognize the common business and personal factors causing low morale, and he will establish a means of determining the state of morale among his sales force.

EVALUATION OF SALESMEN'S PERFORMANCE

Part of the task of managing a field selling force should include the job of establishing and operating an orderly procedure for evaluating the efforts of the salesmen.

Benefits

When the success of the entire marketing program rests to a great extent on the effectiveness of the sales force, anything which can be done to increase a salesman's productivity is highly desirable. Until an executive knows what his men are doing, he is in no position to make constructive proposals for improvement. By studying salesmen's activities and by establishing standards for what constitutes good performance, management should be able to upgrade salesmen's efforts in general.

Performance evaluation can help management to determine what factors are responsible for success in selling. By analyzing and comparing the characteristic activities of good and poor salesmen, management may be able to isolate and identify the factors that lead to sales success. Management may find, for example, that the top ten salesmen average 20 per cent more calls per week than the poorest ten men; it may find that the successful men spend more time giving managerial advice to retailers and training retail clerks.

Performance analysis can help the salesmen appraise and improve their own efforts. A salesman with a poor sales record may have known for a long time that he was doing something wrong but was unable to determine what it was because he had no objective standards by which to measure his performance.

In the management of a sales force, performance evaluation can be of help in several areas. It is an aid in determining what should be included in a training program, and it can help in sales supervision. If a supervisor knows some of the specific strengths and weaknesses of each salesman, then he can do a better job of guiding, directing, and training the men under him. Performance evaluation can also help management determine salary increases and promotion for the men.

An overall benefit of an appraisal of salesmen's performance is that it will normally have a favorable effect on the morale of the sales force. Evaluation means that the men are getting recognition. They ordinarily feel better when they realize that objective standards are being used to measure their efforts.

Bases for evaluation

A sales representative may be evaluated on the bases of (1) personal characteristics; (2) knowledge of company policies, products, competition, and customers; (3) sales activities (building goodwill, training customers' salesmen) *not* subject to quantitative measurement; and (4) sales activities which can be measured quantitatively. The last category warrants further discussion. It is best to use as many quantitative criteria as possible in conjunction with one another. By using the number of calls as the sole criterion, for example, management may rate salesman A at the top; when evaluating men on the basis of the number of orders per call or the average size of order, however, management may find that this man is at the bottom. Some widely used criteria are as follows:

1.   Sales volume in relation to quota. Probably the most frequently used criterion is a person's sales volume alone or his volume in relation to an assigned quota. Information should also be available regarding the man's sales of each product and his sales to each customer. Even then, volume analysis alone does not tell management whether the sales representative obtains profitable business, nor does it indicate in any way what kind of goodwill and customer relations a man is building.

2.   Gross margin.

3.   Number of calls per day (call rate). Obviously, a salesman cannot make sales unless he calls on customers personally, by mail, or by telephone. In general, the more calls a man makes, the more sales he makes. Consequently, a valid criterion in evaluating a man's performance is his call rate—that is, the number of calls he makes in some period of time.

4.   Number of orders.

5.   Size of orders.

6.   Orders per call (batting average). In this measure, the call rate and number of orders are correlated. The batting average is determined by dividing the number of orders (hits) by the number of calls (times at bat). A man with a high

call rate who has not been getting many orders will have a low batting average. By computing a man's batting average for each class of customer, management may find that some salesmen are much better at handling some customer groups than others.

7. Salesmen's expenses and expense ratios. This includes determining cost per call, cost per order, and the ratio between a man's direct selling expenses and his net sales.

8. New accounts.

In a properly managed marketing program, there will be a continuing program for the analysis and evaluation of salesmen's performance. Management should then be able to ascertain more precisely the extent to which the salesmen's efforts are misdirected, and steps may be taken to remedy the situation.

EFFECTIVE PERSONAL SELLING

A marketing executive should understand the fundamentals of effective salesmanship and be able to set forth a procedure for selling. We shall summarize briefly one procedure which can be used in personal selling.

Presale preparation

In the chain of events which will eventually or hopefully lead to a sale, the first step is to make certain that the salesman is prepared. This means that he must be well acquainted with his product, his market, and the techniques of selling. Before the salesman makes his first call, he should know as much as possible about the motivation and behavior of the market segment to which he will sell. He should be informed on the nature of the competition, the business conditions prevailing in his territory, etc.

Locating or prospecting for potential buyers

The salesman is now ready to locate customers. This second step toward a sale involves drawing up a profile of the ideal prospect. The salesman can examine records of past and present customers in his effort to determine the characteristics of such a prospect. From this profile he may develop a list of people or companies who are logical potential buyers of the product.

There are other ways a salesman can acquire a list of prospects. His sales manager usually will prepare a list for him; present customers can suggest new leads; present users may want later or different models of the product. The salesman might build a list of users of competitors' products. A little thought will often suggest logical prospects. For instance, salesmen of home furnishings, insurance, light fixtures, or telephone equipment find prospects in the regularly published lists of building permits issued. Salesmen of many products find leads among birth or engagement announcements in newspapers.

Preapproach to individual prospects

Before calling on prospects, the salesman should try to learn all he can about the person or company to whom he hopes to sell. He might want to know what products or brands the prospect is now using and what the reaction to them is. The salesman should try to find out the personal habits, likes, dislikes, etc., of the prospect. In general, the salesman should try to get all the information he can, so that he will be able to tailor his presentation to the individual buyer.

Sales presentation

The actual presentation of the salesman will start with an attempt to attract the prospect's attention. Next, he will try to hold the customer's interest while building a desire for the product. Then the salesman will try to close the sale. All through his presentation, he must be ready and able to meet any hidden or expressed objections which the prospect may have.

Attract attention—the approach   Several approaches are frequently used to attract the prospect's attention and start the presentation. In the simplest approach, the salesman merely greets the prospect, introduces himself, and states what he is selling or why he is calling. While this is direct, in many selling situations it is not so effective as other approaches. If the salesman was referred to the prospect by a customer, he might start out with a reference to this common acquaintance. Sometimes this is called the "Joe sent me" approach. The salesman might suggest the product benefits by making some startling statement. One sales training consultant often greets a prospect with the question, "If I can cut your selling costs in half, and at the same time double your sales volume, are you interested?" This approach parallels the strong, attention-getting headlines often used in advertisements. A fourth approach, which can be effective if the salesman has a new or unusual product, is simply to walk in and hand the product to the prospect. While the prospect looks it over, the salesman can start his sales presentation.

Hold interest and arouse desire   When the salesman has attracted the prospect's attention, he can hold his interest and stimulate his desire for the product by means of the sales talk itself. There is no common pattern here. Usually, however, a product demonstration is invaluable. Also, if it has not been possible to determine a prospect's specific needs during the preapproach, certainly this must be done in the course of the presentation. Whatever pattern is followed in the talk, the salesman must always show the prospect how the product will benefit *him*.

Many companies insist that their salesmen use a "canned" sales talk; that is, all representatives must give identical presentations verbatim or with very minor changes. Although many people may feel that this is a poor practice, it has been proved time and again that a canned sales talk can be effective. Salesmen can still project their own individual personalities, even though they all say essentially the same thing. These presentations ensure that all points are covered, they employ tested techniques, and they facilitate the sales training job considerably.

Meet objections and close the sale　　After he has explained the product and its benefits, the salesman should try to close the sale and write up an order. As part of the presentation, he may periodically venture a trial close in order to sense the prospect's attitude or willingness to buy. By posing some "either-or" questions, a salesman can start to bring the presentation to a head. That is, he may pose such questions as "Do you prefer the gray or the green model?" "How soon would you want this delivered?" or "Would you plan to charge this or pay cash?"

The trial close is important because it gives the salesman an indication of how near the prospect is to a decision. A salesman may lose a sale by talking too much. The prospect may be ready to buy at the beginning and then change his mind if the salesman insists on a full presentation. Sometimes sales are lost simply because the representative fails to ask for the order.

The trial close also tends to bring out the buyer's objections. Salesmen should encourage a buyer to state his objections; then the salesmen have an opportunity to answer and counteract them and to bring out additional product benefits or reemphasize previously stated points.

The toughest objections to answer are those which are hidden or unspoken. A salesman must uncover the real objections before he can hope to make a sale. Another difficult situation occurs when the prospect says he wants to "think it over." A generalization on this point is that the salesman must close the sale then and there, or the chances are that he will lose it.

Textbooks on salesmanship discuss different types of final closing techniques. The assumptive close is probably used as much as any other, and it can be used in a wide variety of selling situations. In this closing technique, the salesman assumes that the customer is going to buy, so it is just a case of settling the details. He will ask such questions as "When do you want this delivered?" "Is this a charge sale?" "Do you want this gift-wrapped?" or "What color have you decided upon?"

Postsale activities

An effective selling job does not end when the order is written up. Normally, sales success depends upon repeat business. Also, a satisfied customer will furnish leads to other prospects. Consequently, a representative must perform postsale activities and services as part of the selling process. Immediately after the sale, he should reassure the customer by summarizing the product's benefits and pointing out how satisfied he will be with its performance. If mechanical installation is necessary, the representative should make certain the job is done properly. He should ascertain that all points in the sales contract and the guarantee are clearly understood. It may be necessary to instruct the new owner in the use of the product. In the case of large industrial products, the salesman will often spend weeks or months in the customer's establishment, training operators and checking to be sure that the product is working smoothly within the buyer's system. In general, all these postsale activities have the objective of building customer goodwill and laying the groundwork for many years of profitable business relations.

REASONS FOR SHORTAGE OF QUALIFIED SALESMEN

In spite of the many job opportunities and the high levels of compensation in selling, there is an acute shortage of qualified people entering this field. Management is often forced to accept submarginal people. For several reasons, a talented prospect will consider a selling career only when he cannot qualify for any other job. Selling usually involves considerable traveling, and this often is a deterrent to family men. The career lacks social prestige and status. Also, many people have a poor image of the salesman owing to the abundance of traveling-salesman jokes and the fact that the only sales activities most people ever see are retail clerking and door-to-door selling. Most sales jobs in no way resemble these two activities. The majority of people are totally unaware of the many really good sales jobs which involve selling to manufacturers, retailers, or wholesalers.

One writer, in analyzing the problem, points out that selling is considered a white-collar job, salesmen receive a relatively high income, and the job offers freedom of action—all three factors being characteristic of high-prestige occupations. At the same time, selling's prestige is lowered because (1) no formalized education and training are required and (2) power and authority are lacking both in the job and in dealing with customers.[2]

Possibly a fundamental reason why people stay away from selling jobs is that these folks are just not talented enough to become salesmen. Consciously or unconsciously, people may recognize that sales work is one kind of activity that requires grasping the naked sword and coming to grips with reality in a situation stripped of all possibilities for excuse making. It is a virile activity that puts a man's mettle to the test every day. In a sense, sales work reduces the relationship between two people to a very simple test of power: Can I get you to buy? Most other jobs modify this relationship, allowing the worker to operate in a protected environment where he may affect sales indirectly and impersonally, without exposing himself to the possibility of failure and a recognition of his personal inadequacy.

[2] John L. Mason, "The Low Prestige of Personal Selling," *Journal of Marketing*, October, 1965, pp. 7–10; see also John L. Mason, "The Salesman's Prestige: A Reexamination," *Business Topics*, Autumn, 1962, pp. 73–77.

QUESTIONS AND PROBLEMS

1   Is it possible for a firm to sell a product successfully without the use of personal salesmen? If so, give some examples.

2   "At the retail level, all firms should adopt the self-service method of selling, and advertising should be used instead of personal salesmen. Advertising is a less expensive, faster, easier way to reach a mass market." Discuss the implications of these statements.

3   For which of the following products should the major promotional effort be placed on personal selling rather than advertising when dealing with the final customer? Support your decision in each case.
    a.   Mobile homes
    b.   Electronic computers
    c.   Television sets
    d.   Office furniture

4   How does the salesman's job vary in the following situations?
    a.   Fuller Brush man selling door-to-door
    b.   Salesman selling small, company airplanes to manufacturer of packaging materials
    c.   Manufacturer's salesman selling office machines to wholesaler of office supplies and equipment
    d.   Wholesaler's salesman selling office machines for use in retail stores; in offices of manufacturers

5   Present an orderly procedure for developing a job description for salesmen.

6   Prepare a job description for a manufacturer's salesman of sporting goods who sells directly to retail stores.

7   "Salesmen are born, not made." Do you agree? If so, why does a firm need a good training program? If not—that is, if you believe that salesmen are made, not born—why does a firm need a good selection program?

8   "A good selection program is desirable but not essential. Improper selection of salesmen can be counterbalanced by a good training program, by a good compensation system, or by fine supervision." Discuss.

9   What sources should be used for recruiting sales applicants in each of the following firms? Explain your reasoning in each instance.
    a.   A company selling executive airplanes to a manufacturer of paper products
    b.   A firm selling cosmetics door-to-door
    c.   A dress manufacturer selling high-fashion dresses to department stores and exclusive specialty shops
    d.   A grocery products wholesaler selling to retailers and institutions in the Pacific Northwest

10   "It is best to hire experienced salesmen because they do not require any training." Discuss.

11   "The best method of training salesmen is to put them out in the field and let them learn from experience." This has been called the "sink-or-swim" method. How would you answer this point of view?

12   What factors should be considered when determining the *level* of salesmen's compensation?

13   Compare the merits of a straight-salary plan and a straight-commission plan of salesmen's compensation. Name some companies or types of sales jobs in which each plan might be desirable.

14   What measure might be used to determine whether a salesman is using high-pressure selling tactics or other techniques which may injure customer relations?

15   In this chapter, many of the bases for evaluating salesmen's performance seemed to apply more to "outside" salesmen—those who go to the customers. What bases might be used to evaluate the performance of in-store retail salesmen?

16   How can a sales manager evaluate the ability of his salesmen to get new business?

17   What are some of the sources you might use to acquire a list of prospects for the following products?
a.   Automobiles   c.   Life insurance
b.   Baby furniture

18   What can a salesman do when customers object that the price of his product is too high?

19   What can be done to make selling more attractive as a career?

23

MANAGEMENT
OF ADVERTISING

A hunter ordinarily does not use a rifle to hunt ducks. If he did, the mass flight of ducks would pass over him and be gone before he had an opportunity to aim at more than a very limited number. He needs a device which will enable him to hit more ducks with the same amount of effort expended in using a rifle. Thus he will use a shotgun. By the same token, mass communication is needed to reach mass markets at a reasonable cost. Advertising and sales promotion are just the tools for this job. It is too costly and time-consuming to try to do the job with salesmen alone.

NATURE AND IMPORTANCE OF ADVERTISING

Advertising consists of all the activities involved in presenting to a group a nonpersonal, oral or visual, openly sponsored message regarding a product, service, or idea; this message, called an *advertisement,* is disseminated through one or more media and is paid for by the identified sponsor.

Some important considerations should be noted in connection with this definition. First, there is a significant distinction between advertising and an advertisement. The advertisement is simply the message itself. Advertising is a process—it is a program or a series of activities necessary to plan and prepare the message and get it to the intended market. Another point is that the public knows who is behind the advertising because the sponsor is openly identified in the advertisement itself. Also, payment is made by the sponsor to the media which carry the message. These last two considerations differentiate advertising from propaganda and publicity.

Types of advertising

An understanding of the different bases for classifying the types of advertising should be useful to an executive before he gets involved in the advertising program in his firm.

Product and institutional   All advertising may be classed as product or institutional. In product advertising, the advertiser is informing or stimulating the market about his products or services. Product advertising is often further subdivided into direct-action and indirect-action advertising. With *direct-action* advertising, the seller is seeking a quick response to his advertisement. An advertisement with a coupon may urge the reader to send in immediately for a free sample. Thursday-night and Friday-morning advertisements run by supermarkets list products featured in weekend sales. *Indirect-action* advertising is designed to stimulate demand over a longer period of time. Advertisements are intended to inform the customers that the product exists and to point out its benefits so that when they are in the market for the product, they will look favorably upon the seller's brand. Product advertising may also be subclassed as *primary-demand* and *selective-demand* advertising to correspond with the stages of the product's demand or life cycle. (This topic was discussed in Chapter 21.)

Institutional advertising is designed to create a proper attitude toward the seller and to build goodwill, rather than to sell a specific product or service. Institutional advertising may be further subdivided into three areas: patronage, public relations, and public service institutional advertising. In *patronage institutional* advertising, a seller is trying to attract customers by appealing to patronage-buying motives rather than product-buying motives. To illustrate, a retailer may inform his market about new store hours or a change in his delivery policy; a manufacturer may stress new credit and returned-goods policies when advertising in trade journals to attract wholesalers. *Public relations* institutional advertising is used to create a favorable image of the firm among employees, stockholders, or the general public. A manufacturer, for example, may run some ads telling what he is doing to reduce air or stream pollution caused by his plant's operations. *Public service* institutional advertising is illustrated by ads urging the public to support a Red Cross drive, to give to the United Fund, to vote, or to drive carefully. The New York Life Insurance Company has run a series of ads to help guide young people in their choice of a career.

National and local   National (general) advertising is that sponsored by manufacturers, wholesalers, or other producers. Local (retail) advertising is just that—advertising placed by retailers. Although the terms "national" and "local" are used synonymously with "general" and "retail" in the advertising business, this is an unfortunate and inexact comparison. It is true that most manufacturers and wholesalers sell in more than one local market, and it is also true that a retailer's market is usually confined to one locality. As currently used in the trade, however, the term "national" advertising refers only to the level of the advertiser and has no relation at all to geographic coverage. If a manufacturer or other producer places a single ad in only one city, this is still referred to as national advertising.

Another purposeful distinction may be drawn between a manufacturer's and a retailer's advertising. A manufacturer's advertising is designed to build a demand for his product. He does not care where the item is purchased, as long as the customer buys his brand. In retailer's advertising, the stress is on the store. A retailer does not care what product or brand you buy, as long as you buy it at his establishment. Therefore his advertisements often feature appeals to patronage motives, showing you what services he offers and why it is to your advantage to buy at his store.

Nature of market   Several classifications of advertising are based upon subdivisions of the market. Advertising differs depending upon whether the market target is the consumer, middleman, industrial user, or professional man. Consumer advertising is aimed at ultimate consumers who purchase for non-business, personal use. In trade advertising, the target may be retailers or other middlemen where the appeal is, "Buy this product to resell in your store at a profit." In industrial advertising, an industrial user is urged, "Buy this product to use in your business." The professional market is approached with advertising which says, "Recommend or specify this product for use by your patients or clients."

Another way to classify the market for advertising is on a mass-class basis. Advertising of widely used consumer goods is ordinarily aimed at a broad, heterogeneous mass market. Other advertising may carry a special appeal to fishermen, hot-rod lovers, teen-age girls, dude ranchers, etc.

Importance of advertising

Advertising in one form or another is used by virtually all manufacturers and retailers in the country. Examples of the goals which may be reached through advertising are discussed in the next section of this chapter. The importance of advertising may also be expressed by various quantitative measures.

Advertising expenditures in total and by media   One quantitative indication of the importance of advertising is the total amount spent on the activity in the United States. In 1965, total advertising expenditures exceeded $15 billion—an increase of 64 per cent in ten years. Table 23–1 shows the relative importance of the major advertising media. For years, newspapers have been the most widely used medium, based upon total advertising dollars invested. About 80 per cent of the expenditures for newspaper advertising goes for local rather than nationa! advertising. In recent years, the fastest-growing medium—television—took over second place, a spot held for many years by direct mail.

Advertising expenditures as percentage of company sales   When gauging the importance of advertising, it is often more meaningful to measure expenditures against a bench mark rather than simply to look at the total in an isolated position. Frequently, advertising expenses are expressed as a percentage of a company's sales.

One representative study showed that manufacturers of consumer products spend about 3 per cent of sales for advertising purposes, while manufacturers

table   23–1

Volume of advertising expenditures in United States: in millions of dollars

Annual volume of advertising expenditures passed the $15-billion mark in 1965, and newspapers maintained their first-place position. Note the rise of television. Do you think that radio and magazines will eventually cease to be important advertising media?

	1965		1960		1955	
Medium	*Amount*	*Per cent*	*Amount*	*Per cent*	*Amount*	*Per cent*
Newspapers	$ 4,435.0	29.4	$ 3,702.8	31.1	$3,087.8	33.6
Television	2,497.0	16.5	1,590.1	13.3	1,025.3	11.1
Direct mail	2,271.4	15.0	1,830.2	15.3	1,298.9	14.1
Magazines, including national farm publications	1,197.7	7.9	940.8	7.8	729.4	7.9
Radio	889.3	5.9	692.4	5.8	544.9	5.9
Business papers	678.5	4.5	609.3	5.1	446.2	4.9
Outdoor	180.0	1.2	203.3	1.7	192.4	2.1
Miscellaneous*	2,971.1	19.6	2,362.8	19.9	1,869.5	20.4
Total	$15,120.0	100.0	$11,931.7	100.0	$9,194.4	100.0

* Includes cost of advertising departments, transportation advertising, weekly newspaper advertising, regional farm publications, point-of-purchase material not included in direct-mail expenditures, and all other legitimate advertising expenditures not already covered.

SOURCE: "Advertisers' Guide to Marketing for 1963," *Printers' Ink,* Aug. 31, 1962, pp. 384–385, for 1955 and 1960 expenditures. Preliminary estimate for 1965 from *Printers' Ink,* Feb. 11, 1966, p. 12.

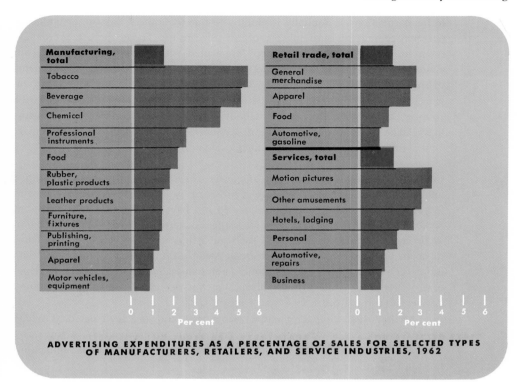

ADVERTISING EXPENDITURES AS A PERCENTAGE OF SALES FOR SELECTED TYPES OF MANUFACTURERS, RETAILERS, AND SERVICE INDUSTRIES, 1962

fig. 23–1

Advertising budgets in most industries are surprisingly low in relation to total sales. Even though a firm—an automobile manufacturer or a department store, for instance—may spend millions on advertising, this is usually a small percentage of the company's sales volume.

SOURCE: *A Graphic Guide to Consumer Markets: 1966,* National Industrial Conference Board, Inc., New York, pp. 80-81. Based on data from U.S. Treasury Department.

of industrial goods spend less than 1 per cent (see Tables 21–1 and 21–2). In a summary report based on other sources, the National Industrial Conference Board showed advertising as a percentage of sales for various types of manufacturers, retailers, and service industries (Fig. 23–1). In the majority of these industries, advertising was less than 2 per cent of sales.

Sometimes it may seem as if the public is bombarded on all sides by advertising; however, the total amount spent is usually small in relation to sales volume. For example, large department stores spend quite a bit on advertising, yet it amounts to only about 2 to 4 per cent of sales. Automobile manufacturers spend millions on advertising, and yet the total is about 1 per cent of their volume.

Number of people employed   Because of the glamour and publicity frequently connected with the advertising industry, one might think it is large in terms of manpower. Actually it employs modest numbers; job opportunities in personal selling far outnumber those in advertising. Today there are probably no more than 400,000 jobs directly connected with advertising. This total includes all people working in advertising agencies and advertising departments of manufacturers and middlemen, and all those working in an advertising capacity for all media. There are some four thousand advertising agencies in the country, and in total they employ about sixty thousand people.[1] Most advertising agencies and the advertising departments in most firms are very small, employing on the average less than ten people.

Cost of advertising versus cost of personal selling   Another quantitative indication of the use of advertising is provided by a comparison of its cost with the cost of personal selling. While we do not have accurate totals for costs of personal selling, we do know they far surpass advertising expenditures. In manufacturing, only a few industries, such as drugs, toiletries, cleaning products, tobacco, and beverages, have advertising expenditures which are higher than those for personal selling. In countless companies, advertising runs 1 to 3 per cent of net sales, while in many firms the expenses of managing and operating a sales force run from 8 to 15 per cent of sales.

At the wholesaling level, advertising costs are very low; personal selling costs may run ten to fifteen times as high. Even among retailers in total, and this includes those with self-service operations, the cost of personal selling runs substantially higher than for advertising.

Objectives of advertising

Fundamentally the only purpose of advertising is to sell something—a product, a service, or an idea. The intent may be to generate a sale immediately or at some time in the future. Nevertheless, the basic objective is to sell. Stated another way, the real goal of advertising is effective communication; that is, the ultimate effect of advertising should be to modify the attitudes and/or behavior of the receiver of the message.[2] Sometimes the public, and even an advertising businessman, overlooks this fact. The businessman is not interested in awarding a prize to his best-dressed salesman or to the one who is best liked by everybody. Instead, he wants to reward the salesman who has the best sales record.

[1] Frederic R. Gamble, *What Advertising Agencies Are: What They Do and How They Do It*, 2d ed., American Association of Advertising Agencies, New York, 1960, p. 25.

[2] See Charles E. Lee and Jarvis Woolverton Mason, "Advertising Objectives, Control, and the Measurement Controversy," *Business Topics*, Autumn, 1964, pp. 37–42. Another writer has characterized the function of advertising in a different way, although the ultimate goal is the same. In a sociological and psychological orientation, "the function of advertising is to help organize and modify the basic *perceptual processes* of the consumer, so that he is guided toward seeing and feeling a product in a given predictable way." See Irving S. White, "The Functions of Advertising in Our Culture," *Journal of Marketing*, July, 1959, pp. 8–14.

At the same time, forgetting that his real aim is to build an ad that will sell the most merchandise, he may be trying to earn awards for having the best copy, layout, or use of color in his advertisements. To a businessman such as this one, the advertisement is considered an end in itself, when really it is only a means to an end.

Specific objectives   The general goal of advertising is to increase profitable sales, but this goal is too broad to be implemented effectively in an advertising program. It is necessary to establish more specific objectives which can be worked into the program. A few examples of these more limited aims are listed below:

1.   Support personal selling program. Advertising may be used to open customers' doors for salesmen and to acquaint the prospect with the seller's company. Advertising can also reduce selling costs by doing some of the sales prospecting. It permits the salesmen to make fewer calls and enables the company to maintain contact with the customers between salesmen's calls.

2.   Reach people inaccessible to salesmen. A salesman may be unable to reach top business executives and professional men, or he may not be certain who makes the buying decisions in a company. In either case, there is a good chance that all these executives and decision makers will read a journal which carries the ads.

3.   Improve dealer relations. The goal of an advertising campaign may be to attract new dealers by showing them how profitable it is to carry the manufacturer's line. The purpose of other advertisements may be to give the names and addresses of retailers who carry the product.

4.   Enter a new geographic market or attract a new group of customers.

5.   Introduce a new product or a new price schedule.

6.   Increase sales of product. An advertising campaign may be designed to lengthen the season for the product (as has been done in the case of soft drinks), increase the frequency of replacement (as is done in campaigns for sparkplugs and light bulbs), increase the variety of product uses, or increase the units of purchase.

7.   Expand the industry's sales.

8.   Counteract prejudice or substitution.

9.   Build goodwill for the company and improve its reputation by rendering a public service through advertising or by telling of the organization behind the product.

DEVELOPMENT OF AN ADVERTISING CAMPAIGN

Up to this point in the analysis of advertising in the economy and in the firm, it has been tacitly assumed that the firm is going to advertise. Actually the first decision management must make in this area is whether or not it should advertise its products. Some guideposts to use in answering this question of basic promotional strategy have already been analyzed.

Once the decision is made to advertise, management can get on with the job of developing an advertising program or campaign. In Chapter 21, a campaign was defined as a planned, coordinated series of promotional efforts built around a central theme and designed to reach a specific goal. The series of ads used in the campaign must be integrated with the sales-promotional efforts and with the activities of the sales force.

Initial planning

In the course of planning the total promotional campaign, presumably management has already established its desired specific goals. It has decided what the central theme will be and what appeals will be stressed in light of consumer buying motives and habits. The total promotional appropriation has been determined and has been allocated among the various promotional tools, including advertising. Management can now concern itself with the selection of the advertising media and the creation and production of individual advertisements.

Selecting the media

Three levels of decision making are required in the selection of advertising media. First, management must determine what general types of media to use. Will newspapers, television, or magazines be used? If magazines are to be used, will they be shelter magazines such as *Better Homes and Gardens,* business magazines such as *Business Week,* or some other subtype? If television is selected, will it be local, national network, or spot telecasting? Finally, the specific medium must be chosen. The company which decides first on radio and then on local stations now must decide whether to use station WABC or KXYZ in city A.

Several factors should be considered in making media decisions. Some of these factors affect all three levels of media decision making, whereas others relate more specifically to only one or two levels.

Objective of the advertisement   Media choices are influenced both by the purpose of a specific advertisement and by the goal of an entire campaign. For example, if the goal of the advertising is to make appointments for salesmen who are going to call on industrial users, then the advertising company will probably use direct mail. If an advertiser wants to make last-minute changes in an advertisement, or if he wishes to place an ad inducing action within a day or two, he may use newspapers or radio. Magazines are not so good for this purpose because the ad must be placed weeks before the date of publication.

Media circulation   Media circulation must match the distribution patterns of the product. Consequently, the *geographic* scope of the market will influence the choice of media considerably. Furthermore, media should be selected which will reach the desired *type* of market with a minimum of waste circulation. A firm manufacturing shotguns, for example, will advertise in a magazine which appeals primarily to hunters. Media used to reach a teenage market will be different from those used to reach mothers with young children.

Requirements of the message   Management should consider the media which are most suitable for the presentation of the message to the market. Meat products, floor coverings, and apparel are ordinarily best presented in pictorial form; thus radio is not a good medium for these lines. If a product, such as insurance, calls for a lengthy message, outdoor advertising is poor. If the advertiser can use a very brief message, however, as in the case of salt, beer, or sugar, then billboards may be the best choice. Television can be used to show pictures, but not detailed ones.

Time and location of buying decision   The advertiser should select the medium which will reach the prospective customer at or near the time and place that he makes his buying decision. For this reason, outdoor advertising is often good for gasoline products. Grocery store ads are placed in newspapers on Thursday nights or Friday mornings in anticipation of heavy weekend buying.

Cost of media   The cost of the advertising media should be considered in relation to (1) the amount of funds available and (2) the circulation of the media. In the first instance, the amount of funds available may rule out television as a choice, or possibly the advertiser can afford local television but not national network. On the second count, the advertiser should try to develop some relationships between the cost of the medium and its circulation.

Cooperation and promotional aids offered by media   A manufacturer may want to tie in his advertising with that of his dealers. Consequently, he will look favorably upon media such as magazines which offer reprints for use in counter or window displays. Another firm may want some research done on local markets. Management may select the individual medium which can provide this service.

Characteristics of major types of media   In the process of selecting the media to use in a campaign, a marketing executive must consider the advertising characteristics of newspapers, magazines, and the other main classes of media. The term "characteristics" is carefully chosen instead of "advantages and disadvantages." To illustrate, one characteristic of radio as an advertising medium is that it makes its impression through the ear. For many products this feature is an advantage; for those which benefit from a colored photograph, this characteristic of radio is a drawback. For a third group of commodities, the ear-impression feature may be a neutral factor in media choice—neither an advantage nor a limitation.

NEWSPAPERS   As an advertising medium, newspapers are flexible and timely. They can be used to cover one city or several urban centers. Ads can be canceled on a few days' notice or inserted on one day's notice. Newspapers also give an advertiser an intense coverage of a local market because almost everybody reads newspapers. The local feature also helps in that the ads may be adapted to local social and economic conditions. Many newspapers offer promotional assistance, and they are an excellent source of market information. These media offer an opportunity to use a fair quality of color, and circulation costs per prospect are low. Newspapers are also helpful if the advertiser wishes to present his message to the market frequently. On the other hand, the life of a newspaper advertisement is very short.

MAGAZINES   Magazines are an excellent medium when a high quality of printing and color is desired in an advertisement. Magazines can be used to reach a national market at a relatively low cost per prospect. Through the use of class magazines, an advertiser is able to reach a selective audience with a minimum of waste circulation. Magazines are usually read in a leisurely fashion, in contrast to the haste with which other media are read. This is a particularly valuable point for the advertiser who must present his message at some length. Some of the less favorable characteristics of magazines are their inflexibility and the infrequency with which they reach the market, as compared with other media.

DIRECT MAIL   Direct mail is probably the most personal and selective of all the media. Because it reaches only the market which the advertiser wishes to contact, there is a minimum of waste circulation. The personal feature and the aspect of selectivity also mean that the copy itself can be extremely flexible. Direct mail is not accompanied by articles or other editorial matter, however, unless the advertiser provides it. As a result, the direct-mail advertisement itself creates its own circulation and attracts its own readership. Direct mail is quite costly in terms of prospects reached when compared with other media, but other media reach many people who are not real prospects. A severe limitation is posed by the difficulty of getting and maintaining good mailing lists.

TELEVISION   Television, the newest and fastest growing of all major media, is also probably the most versatile. It makes its appeal through both the eye and the ear; products can be demonstrated as well as explained. It offers considerable flexibility in terms of the geographic market covered and in terms of the time the message is presented. By making its impression through the ear, it can take advantage of the personal, dramatic impact of the spoken word. On the other hand, television is an extremely expensive medium. The message is not permanently recorded; thus if the prospect is not reached the first time, he is lost forever as far as that particular message is concerned. Television does not lend itself to long advertising copy, nor does it present pictures so clearly as magazines do. As in direct mail and radio, television advertisers must create their own audiences.

OUTDOOR   Outdoor advertising is a highly flexible, low-cost medium. Because it reaches virtually the entire population, it lends itself nicely to widely used consumer products which require only a brief selling statement. It is excellent for the reminder type of advertising, and it carries the impact of large size and color. There is complete flexibility in geographic coverage and in the intensity of market coverage within a given area. These advantageous features, however, carry with them some inherent drawbacks. Unless the product is a widely used consumer good, considerable waste circulation will occur. While the cost is low in terms of reaching an individual prospect, the total cost of a national campaign is quite high. There is no opportunity to present lengthy copy, and it is not possible to show much detail in the pictures.

Creation of advertisements

It may be said that the advertisements are the heart of the entire advertising program. All the other steps in the campaign are designed to aid in delivering the sales message to the market target in the most effective manner. Obviously the message itself is of considerable importance, so its creation constitutes a major phase in a campaign.

Before creating the advertisement, the people concerned should remember that the main purpose of advertising is to sell something and that the ad itself is a sales talk. The ad may be a high-pressure sales talk, as in a hard-hitting, direct-action ad; or it may be a very long-range, low-pressure message, as in an institutional ad. In any case it is trying to sell something. Consequently, it involves the same kind of selling procedure as a sales talk delivered by personal salesmen. That is, the ad must first attract attention and then hold interest long enough to stimulate a desire for the product, service, or idea. Finally, the ad must move the prospect to some kind of action. The desired action may lie anywhere within a virtually unlimited scope of possibilities, ranging from an immediate change in overt behavior to a slowly changing attitude or thought process.

Creating an advertisement involves the tasks of writing the copy—including the headline—selecting illustrations which may be used, preparing the layout, and arranging to have the advertisement reproduced for the selected media.

The *copy* in an advertisement is defined as all the written or spoken material in it, including the headline, coupons, and advertiser's name and address, as well as the main body of the message. The *illustration*—whether it is a photograph, drawing, reproduction of a painting, cartoon, or something else—is a powerful feature in an advertisement. Probably the main general points to consider with respect to illustrations are (1) whether they are the best alternative use of the space and (2) whether they are appropriate in all respects to the ad itself. The *layout* is the physical arrangement of all the elements in an advertisement. Within the given amount of space or time, the layout man must place the headline, copy, and illustrations. Decisions are made regarding the relative amount of white space and the kinds of type to be used. A good layout can be an interest-holding device as well as an attention getter. It should lead the reader in an orderly fashion throughout the entire advertisement.

EVALUATION OF ADVERTISING PROGRAM

At several stages in the course of the advertising program, management should carefully evaluate the effectiveness of what has been done or what is planned for the future. Executives may wish to evaluate an entire advertising campaign, a single advertisement, or some part of an individual advertisement. They may wish to appraise various aspects of the advertising media.

Importance

Advertising typically is one of the most highly criticized segments of our marketing system. While great strides may have been made to improve advertising through the years, much still remains to be done. We need to increase the effectiveness of advertising, and we also must find better ways to evaluate this effectiveness.

Management needs to test advertising in order to know not only *which* ads or campaigns are better than others, but also *why* they are better. This information will help management to get the most effective and economical combination of advertising ingredients, including the media.

Shrinking profit margins and increasing competition, both foreign and domestic, are forcing management to appraise all of its expenditures carefully. Top executives want more proof than they now have that advertising really does pay. They want to know whether dollars spent on advertising are resulting in proportionately as many sales as dollars spent on other activities.

Difficulty

Many problems and limitations confront a company in its efforts to measure the effectiveness of its advertising. This is one of the least-developed areas of marketing research. One problem is our inability to isolate or identify the precise effectiveness of any given advertisement or even an entire campaign. Except in the area of direct-mail advertising, we cannot attribute a given unit of sales to any specific advertisement or campaign. By the very nature of the marketing mix, all elements—including advertising—are so intertwined, and there are so many variables, that measurement of any one by itself is impossible. Many factors besides advertising influence sales success.

Even in evaluating a particular advertisement, management is likely to run into difficulty because one part of an ad may be more easily appraised, and thus given more emphasis, than another.[3] Essentially there are only two parts

[3] Clarence E. Eldridge, "Advertising Effectiveness: How Can It Be Measured?" *Journal of Marketing,* January, 1958, pp. 242–243.

of an advertisement—*what* is said and *how* it is said. One part deals with product attributes to be explained, and the other comprises the headlines, illustrations, and layouts. Over the years, a great deal has been done to improve the manner of presentation (the "how") because research has been able to establish and use criteria to measure its effectiveness. Most of the widely used measurement devices have emphasized the use of attention-getting devices in advertisements and the number of people who note, read, and remember the advertisements and the claims in them. Little has been done to aid management in its evaluation of the "what" part of an ad, and at the present time, the effectiveness of this part is quite difficult to judge.

Many individual advertisements, and even entire campaigns, do not aim primarily at immediate sales results; consequently, it is difficult to measure their effectiveness. Some advertisements simply announce new store hours, new service policies, or a new product. Probably the most difficult type of advertising to evaluate is that which is intended to build goodwill, increase prestige, create a company image, or influence attitudes. Institutional advertising falls in this category.

Presently used evaluative methods simply tell us which ad is the best among those being appraised. There are no standards for determining what must be included in an ad to ensure success. Furthermore, even though we test several advertisements in advance in order to select the one that is best, we still have no guarantee that sales results will be successful.[4]

Methods used to measure effectiveness

When confronted with the need to evaluate the effectiveness of its advertising, a company should not rely solely on the opinions of advertising experts or professional advertising men. They have been proved time and again to be poor judges of which ads will elicit favorable consumer response to a product, service, or idea. Often they are too concerned with the manner in which the message is presented—the "how" part of advertising. If possible, management should plan to use some testing technique which will sample customer reaction.

The effectiveness of an advertisement may be tested before the advertisement is presented to the public, while it is being presented, or after it has completed its run. The "sales results test" attempts to measure the sales volume stemming directly from the advertisement or series of advertisements being tested.

Most other types of tests are indirect measurements of advertising's effectiveness. One group, called "readership," "recognition," or "recall" tests, involves showing respondents part or all of the previously run advertisement to

[4] For encouraging reports from some of the companies which are making advances in measuring the effectiveness of their advertising, see Gail Smith, "How GM Measures Ad Effectiveness," *Printers' Ink,* May 14, 1965, p. 19; "Who Says Ad Impact Can't Be Measured?" (Du Pont's story), *Sales Management,* Apr. 19, 1963, p. 37; and "In the Land of the Blind . . . ," *Sales Management,* Feb. 19, 1965, p. 65.

determine whether it was read, what parts in it were remembered, and whether the respondent knows who sponsored it. The theory underlying these tests is that the greater the number of people who see, read, and remember an advertisement, the greater will be the number who do as the advertisement urges them. Another type of test involves measuring the number of coupons or other forms of inquiries which were received from certain advertisements.[5]

Sometimes marketing men use a consumer panel or consumer jury to appraise a group of advertisements and select the best one. With respect to radio and television advertising, several techniques are used to measure the quantity and quality of program audiences. The theory is that the number of people who will buy the sponsor's products varies proportionately with the number who watch or hear the program. As noted in Chapter 5, in connection with consumer motivation, marketing researchers in recent years have made increasing use of measuring techniques in the fields of psychology and sociology. These techniques have been used in part to measure consumer response to advertising.

Many of these various measurement devices have enjoyed some degree of success. In general, however, there is still a long way to go before really effective evaluation tools and techniques will be developed for advertising. Possibly our hope for the future lies in the more effective use of psychological and sociological testing methods and in the use of mathematical models and operations research.[6]

We should remember, however, that the basic goal of advertising is to sell something—to modify consumer attitudes or behavior. Therefore, when we deal with the evaluation of advertising's effectiveness, we should be more concerned with measuring advertising's ability to influence these attitudes and behavior, rather than with measuring the extent to which consumers recall or recognize given advertisements.

ORGANIZING FOR ADVERTISING

There are four widely used organizational arrangements employed to facilitate the work done in an advertising program. Within a company, the job may be done by a separate advertising department, or it may be handled by another department, possibly a general sales department, as only one part of its departmental responsibility. A third arrangement involves turning the entire advertising task over to an advertising agency, and the fourth combines the use of an advertising agency and the company's own department.

[5] For a series of research findings which refute the idea that a recall of advertised facts about a given product is a significant measure of the effectiveness of these ads, see Jack B. Haskins, "Factual Recall as a Measure of Advertising Effectiveness," *Journal of Advertising Research*, March, 1964, pp. 2–7.

[6] For some of the problems encountered in the use of standard econometric models, see Richard E. Quandt, "Estimating the Effectiveness of Advertising: Some Pitfalls in Econometric Models," *Journal of Marketing Research*, May, 1964, pp. 51–60.

Advertising management within the company

Advertising activities are sometimes administered by the department which operates the sales force. This arrangement is most common when advertising is a relatively unimportant part of the promotional mix or when the firm is small.

In larger businesses or in those where advertising is a substantial part of the promotional mix, advertising activities are usually administered by a separate department. Under these circumstances the head of the department should report to the marketing manager if the company is to adopt and implement the marketing concept. In some companies the advertising manager still reports directly to the president. It is considered a better arrangement, however, if all marketing activities are coordinated at an executive level below the president.

Large retailers often have their own advertising departments and do not use an advertising agency. The advertising department performs all the tasks involved in planning and executing the campaign. Many manufacturers have their own departments but also use an advertising agency. The question then arises of why a department is needed if the company has a good agency. In the first place, the department acts as a liaison between the agency and the company. The department approves the agency's plans and advertisements and has the responsibility of preparing and administering the advertising budget. Finally, direct-mail advertisements, dealer displays, and other activities ordinarily not performed by the agency are handled by the company department.

Advertising agency

An advertising agency is an independent company set up to render specialized services in advertising in particular and in marketing in general. Today the term "agency" is a legal misnomer. These firms are not agents in the legal sense but instead are independent companies. Advertising agencies started as space brokers for handling advertisements placed in newspapers. Through the years, however, the function of the agencies has changed. Their main job today is not to aid media but to serve advertisers.

Services rendered   Many agencies offer a broad range of marketing and advertising services. In the field of advertising alone, they plan and execute entire advertising campaigns. In radio and television, they are responsible for producing the entertainment as well as the commercials. There is a definite trend toward broadening still further the scope of their services. Many of these firms are becoming *marketing* agencies, offering many services which heretofore were performed either by another type of outside specialist or by the advertiser himself. A company's decision to involve its advertising agency in performing marketing (but nonadvertising) services for the firm will depend upon the extent to which company management perceives that (1) its competitive environment is rapidly changing (as contrasted with a stable environment), (2) the agency is knowledgeable about the products and the industry, and (3) the costs of agency services are lower than the costs of those provided by alternative sources.[7]

Reasons for using when a company has own department   Even when a company has a good advertising department, there are several reasons why it may be interested in using an agency. In the first place, the company normally does not have as many types of specialists as a medium- or large-sized advertising agency. Because an agency can spread the costs of its staff over many accounts, it can do more for the same amount of money.

The company can also get an objective, outside viewpoint from an agency, assuming that the agency representatives are not acting as "yes-men" in order to keep the advertiser's account. A related point is that the company can benefit from the agency's experiences with its many other products and clients. Another advantage not often fully recognized is the fact that an agency feels a greater pressure than the company's own department to produce effective results. Relations between an agency and a client are very easy to terminate, but it is difficult to get rid of an ineffective advertising department. Finally, because of the manner in which agencies are compensated, the use of an agency may not cost the advertiser a single penny.[8]

Agency compensations   There are two major methods of compensating advertising agencies: the commission method and the fee method. Under the typical commission system, an agency receives an amount equal to 15 per cent of the cost of the media time or space. The commission is paid by the media, who bill the agencies for the stated rate, less 15 per cent. Then the advertiser pays the full rate to the agency. Thus if an agency prepares and places an advertisement in magazine space worth $40,000, the media will bill the agency for $34,000 ($40,000 less 15 per cent); the agency in turn bills the client for the full $40,000. It is with this income of $6,000 that the agency performs its services. When agencies contract with outside specialists to do work for an advertiser, the agencies usually collect a commission on charges for this work. Most retailers and other local advertisers deal directly with the local media and pay lower rates. No agency commission is paid on these rates; if a local advertiser uses an agency, he usually pays a fee.

In the preceding section it was stated that agency services may not cost the advertiser a cent. In the above example, the company could have used its own department to prepare and place the advertisement, but the space would

---

[7] Derek A. Newton, "Advertising Agency Services: Make or Buy?" *Harvard Business Review*, July–August, 1965, pp. 111–118.

[8] For a guide on how to select and work with an advertising agency, see *Industrial Marketing,* April, 1966, sec. 2, Special Agency Guide; see also "How to Judge an Agency," *Dun's Review and Modern Industry,* October, 1958, p. 64.

still have cost the company $40,000. In addition, the company would have had the expense of preparing the advertisement.

For many years there has been considerable dissatisfaction with the straight-commission system. Profits of the agencies declined because they were forced by competition to perform more and more services without additional compensation. Large advertisers who bought much media time and space felt they were paying too much. Agencies received the same compensation whether they placed the same advertisement in ten different magazines or whether they had the extra expense of creating ten different ads. Furthermore, only accredited agencies were eligible to receive the commission.

The general rigidity of the system bothered many people, including, finally, the government. In the 1950s the Department of Justice sued the American Association of Advertising Agencies and several leading trade associations of publishers. The complaint was that these groups were fixing commission rates and allowing only favored or accredited agencies to receive the commissions, all this in restraint of trade. In 1956 these associations signed a consent decree in which they agreed not to establish fixed commission rates.

Today there is a definite trend toward the use of the fee method or a combination of commission and fee, although the straight-commission method is still probably the most widely used.[9]

REGULATION OF PROMOTIONAL ACTIVITIES

Because the primary objective of promotion is to sell something by means of informing, persuading, or otherwise communicating with a market, promotional activities attract attention. Consequently, abuses of the activities by individual firms are easily and quickly noted by the public. This situation in turn soon leads to public demand for correction of the abuses, assurances they will not be repeated, and general restraints on promotional activities. To answer this demand, regulations and other safeguards have been established by the Federal government and most state governments. In addition, many private business organizations, both profit and nonprofit in nature, have attempted to establish voluntary controls and guideposts for the direction of promotional activities.

For the most part, these regulatory measures have been applied far more to advertising than to personal selling or any other promotional tool. The probable reason for this unbalanced emphasis is that advertising is more centralized and is easier to control. There are far fewer media through which advertising messages may be carried than there are personal salesmen. Also, advertising messages are recorded, whereas usually there is no certain evidence of what a salesman said.

[9] See "Ad Agency Compensation and Services," *Conference Board Record*, February, 1964, pp. 17–23; and "A New Way of Life for Madison Ave?" *Business Week*, May 1, 1965, p. 76.

Federal regulation

Regulation of promotional activities is authorized in two major pieces of Federal legislation: the Federal Trade Commission Act and its Wheeler-Lea amendment, and the Robinson-Patman Act.

Federal Trade Commission Act and Wheeler-Lea amendment   The governmental measure which probably has the broadest influence on regulating the content of promotional messages in interstate commerce is the Federal Trade Commission Act and the Wheeler-Lea amendment. The main provision of this law bearing on promotional activities is Section 5. This section prohibits unfair methods of competition which have the effect of injuring a competitor. Wisely, no specific examples of unfair competition are spelled out in the law. Instead, it is up to the Federal Trade Commission to determine on a case-by-case basis whether a given act constitutes an unfair competitive act and thus is a violation of the law. Through the years the Commission has developed quite an extended list of what it has determined to be unfair or deceptive methods of competition. Included in this list are various forms of false, misleading, or deceptive advertising and personal selling.

Loopholes in the Federal Trade Commission Act led to the enactment of the Wheeler-Lea amendment in 1938. With respect to promotion, the amendment considerably strengthened the original act in at least three ways. First, it is a violation of the law if the unfair competitive act injures the public, regardless of the effect this competitive practice may have on a competitor. Under the original Federal Trade Commission Act, false or misleading advertising had to injure a competitor before a violation could be charged.

A second improvement specifically prohibits false, misleading, or deceptive *advertising* of food, drugs, cosmetics, and therapeutic devices.[10] This provision strengthened the Commission's position by specifying four types of products where advertising abuses exist and where the public's health is directly involved. Temporary injunctions may be granted which force the seller to cease the disputed advertising until a decision can be reached. Prohibition of false, misleading, or deceptive advertising under the law is not limited to these four types of products. False advertising of any product may be judged unfair competition and thus be a violation of the Federal Trade Commission Act.

The third significant change concerns enforcement of cease and desist orders issued by the Commission. Such orders automatically become effective in sixty days unless the defendant appeals to the Federal courts. Previously, a cease and desist order could be issued, but if there were no compliance, the Commission had the burden of seeking enforcement.

[10] The *labeling* of these four groups of products is not included within the scope of the Wheeler-Lea amendment. Labeling is regulated under the Food, Drug, and Cosmetic Act of 1938, a law which is administered by the Food and Drug Administration. This law was discussed in Chap. 10, along with a consideration of several other laws pertaining to labeling.

Robinson-Patman Act   The Robinson-Patman Act, which was discussed in connection with price policies, has two sections relating to promotional allowances. One refers to situations where the seller makes payments for promotional services and facilities provided by his customers, and the other pertains to situations where the seller himself provides promotional services and facilities instead of paying the customers for doing the job. The law states that the seller must offer the services, or payments for them, on a proportionally equal basis to all competing customers.

Prior to the Robinson-Patman Act, there were many abuses in the handling of promotional allowances. Large-scale retailers were often favored by manufacturers at the expense of small buyers. Many firms would furnish retail demonstrators to one leading department store in a city, even though many other stores in that city also purchased the firms' products. Many times, cash allowances were granted to large buyers when no services at all were performed in return.

Today if a manufacturer wants to furnish demonstrators, floor or window displays, cooperative advertising programs, extra commissions for salesmen to push his product, or any other type of promotional assistance, this promotional device or a comparable one must be made available on a proportionally equal basis to all firms competing in the resale of the product. "Proportionally equal basis" has sometimes been hard to define. Generally the courts have accepted the amount purchased as a basis for allocation. Thus if store A buys $150,000 worth of merchandise a year from a manufacturer, and store B purchases $50,000 worth, then store A may be offered promotional allowances valued at three times those offered to B.

A seller must offer only similar promotional allowances, not necessarily identical ones.[11] Not all buyers can make equal use of a given promotional aid, and, furthermore, identical allowances are often not economically sound. If a department store buying $100,000 worth of products a year is granted a demonstrator for forty hours a week, it probably makes little sense to furnish one for four hours a week to the store whose purchases total only $10,000. The small store might prefer additional window displays or extra commissions for its salesclerks. This requirement of similarity means that a seller cannot avoid his legal responsibility by saying that some small customers do not take advantage of the same offer he makes to large buyers.[12]

[11] This policy was set forth in *Trade Practices Rules for Cosmetics and Toilet Preparations Industry*, Federal Trade Commission, Washington, D.C., 1951. For a broader and more recent statement regarding promotional allowances, see Federal Trade Commission, *Guides for Advertising Allowances and Other Merchandising Payments and Services; Compliance with Sections 2 (d) and 2 (e) of the Clayton Act, as Amended by the Robinson-Patman Act*, U.S. Government Printing Office, 1960.

[12] For the marketing implications in a recent case involving cooperative advertising and indirect price discrimination in connection with Sections 2(d) and 2(e) of the Robinson-Patman Act, see Lawrence X. Tarpey, Sr., "The *Woman's Day* Case and Cooperative Advertising," *Journal of Marketing*, July, 1965, pp. 35–39.

State and local regulation

At the state and local levels we can note two types of legislation which regulate promotional activities. The first of these is patterned after the *Printers' Ink* model statute first developed by *Printers' Ink* magazine in 1911 to establish "truth in advertising" in intrastate commerce. Today almost all states have a *Printers' Ink* statute or one which is quite similar to it. Several states have established a separate state agency to handle various "consumer defense" activities.

A general type of local legislation which affects personal selling goes under the title "Green River" ordinance. This type of legislation is named after the town of Green River, Wyoming, one of the first places to enact such a law. Green River ordinances restrict the activities of salesmen who represent firms located outside the affected city and who sell door-to-door or call on business establishments. Ostensibly these laws were passed to protect local citizens from fraudulent operators. Actually the measures also serve to insulate local businesses from outside competition.

Regulation by private organizations

Several kinds of private organizations also exert considerable control over promotional practices of businesses. Many magazines, newspapers, and radio and television stations regularly refuse to accept advertisements which they feel are false, misleading, or generally in bad taste. Some trade associations have established a "code of ethics" which includes points pertaining to sales force and advertising activities. Some trade associations regularly censor advertising appearing in their trade or professional journals. Better Business Bureaus located in major cities all over the country are working to control some very difficult situations.

QUESTIONS AND PROBLEMS

1 Bring to class an example of each of the following types of advertising:
   a. Institutional (retail or manufacturer)   c. Primary demand
   b. Direct-action product

2 How do you account for the variations in advertising expenditures as a percentage of sales among the different types of companies shown in Table 23–2?

3 Several specific objectives of advertising were outlined early in this chapter. Bring to class some advertisements which illustrate at least six of these goals, or be prepared to describe a current radio or television advertisement which is attempting to achieve these objectives.

4 In what respects does the advertising of an automobile manufacturer differ from that of a large department store? Consider the objectives, nature, and scope of advertising as well as the nature of the products and markets of these two firms.

5   Which advertising medium is best for advertising the following products?

    a.   Life insurance   d.   Suntan lotion

    b.   Plastic clothespins   e.   Women's hosiery

    c.   Auto seat covers   f.   Industrial valves and gauges

6   Many grocery products manufacturers and candy producers earmark a good portion of their advertising appropriations for use in magazines. Is this a wise choice of media for these firms?

7   Why do department stores use newspapers so much more than local radio as an advertising medium?

8   Select two ads, one having effective copy and the other having poor copy. Do the same for headlines, use of illustrations, and layout. Explain your reasoning in each instance.

9   Why is it worthwhile to pretest advertisements before they appear in the media? Suggest a procedure for pretesting a magazine ad.

10   If there is so much merit in evaluating the effectiveness of advertising, why are some executives opposed to spending any money for this purpose?

11   What procedures can a firm use to determine how many sales dollars resulted from a given ad or from an entire campaign?

12   Many advertisers on television use program ratings to determine whether to continue the sponsorship of a program. These ratings reflect the number of families who watch the program. Are program ratings a good criterion for evaluating the effectiveness of advertising? Does a high rating indicate that sales volume will also be high? Should the Federal Communications Commission prohibit the use of TV program ratings? Discuss.

13   If a manufacturer has a good advertising agency, should he discontinue using his own advertising department?

14   Many manufacturers use an advertising agency to help with the company's advertising program, while most retailers do not use an agency. How do you account for this difference?

15   Explain how an advertiser may actually save money by using an agency. In your analysis, consider the factor of agency compensation.

16   Evaluate the commission and the fee methods of compensating advertising agencies.

17   How did the Wheeler-Lea amendment strengthen the Federal Trade Commission Act?

18   Explain the interpretation of "proportionally equal basis" in connection with manufacturers' granting advertising allowances. Consider especially the situations when retailers vary in size.

19   Do you think we need additional legislation to regulate advertising? Personal selling? If so, explain what you would recommend.

case 18. HILLCREST PRODUCTS, INC. (B)
Promotional methods to introduce new product

The executives of Hillcrest Products, Inc., are undecided about what promotional tactics to employ in the introduction of the company's new glass cleaner. This product, which cleans by means of emulsification and thus leaves no film, is to be sold in supermarkets in competition with such brands as Windex, Bon Ami, Glass Wax, and Easy-Off. Hillcrest's product is put up in a Duo-Pak—a combination of a 16-ounce glass bottle of the cleaner plus an 8-ounce plastic bottle with a plunger-type spray dispenser top. Sixteen-ounce refill bottles are also sold separately. Hillcrest is a new Western firm, capitalized at $500,000 to manufacture and market a line of cleaning products.

A large advertising program has been established for the first year, during which the company plans to enter several regional markets, including those centered in Denver, Kansas City, Omaha, Albuquerque–El Paso, Oklahoma City, Wichita, and Salt Lake City. Local newspapers and local radio and television stations are the principal media to be used. In-store displays will be used periodically in very large stores if the store managers are willing to allocate the necessary space. Now management wants to select an effective promotional tool to help move the product in its introductory stage in each community. One possibility is to offer the Duo-Pak at 10 cents off the regular price. All cases in the initial shipment to each store would be appropriately marked with this introductory offer. Then, after the initial shipment was sold, any reorders would be intended for sale at the regular price. One of the executives has suggested that a premium—a cellulose sponge—be attached to the product. The sponge is about 1½ inches thick and measures 4 by 6 inches. It would cost Hillcrest 7 cents. Preliminary market tests have shown that women shoppers feel that the sponge has a retail value of 39 to 49 cents. One recognized problem is that the combination of the sponge and the Duo-Pak would be a bulky item to display in supermarkets, where shelf space is at a premium. Another possibility is to "sample" a city. This would involve mailing or delivering on a door-to-door basis a 4-ounce sample bottle of the glass cleaner. Procter & Gamble and Lever Brothers have used this promotional device effectively to introduce new products. A variation of sampling the actual product would be to mail every household a coupon worth 10 cents on the purchase of the Duo-Pak. The company estimates it would cost 4 cents for each complete mailing piece, including production costs plus the necessary postage. To get this rate, the company would have to order in lots of 100,000 from the printer. A mailing service could be used to handle the process of assembling the coupon in an envelope and mailing it.

Hillcrest's advertising agency has suggested placing the 10-cent coupon in each newspaper advertisement for an introductory period of a few weeks. This would cut the cost of a coupon-mailing campaign. In fact, this method is the least expensive of all five suggested, since not every buyer would use his coupon. On the other hand, the effort required to cut out the newspaper coupon and bring it to the store would reduce its incentive and promotional value.

1 Which of these promotional devices should the company employ as an introductory offer?

2 What other devices should the company consider for this purpose?

case 19. OHIO TIRE AND RUBBER COMPANY

Advertising program among franchised retailers

What is known today as the Ohio Tire and Rubber Company was founded in 1934 in a small town in Ohio, when Mr. Atkins developed a piece of equipment which he called a "rubber welder." This machine was able to join two pieces of rubber together in such a way that they would remain attached even while being used under extreme environmental conditions. With the help of a few employees, Mr. Atkins manufactured the machine in his garage. He also served as the sales force, traveling throughout the area and calling upon service stations, tire repair shops, and garages. The rubber welder found an eagerly waiting market among tire repair shops and garages in Ohio and Indiana. In fact, many of the customers called upon by Mr. Atkins were so favorably impressed with the capabilities and potentialities of the rubber welder that these repairmen wanted to have exclusive rights to the use of the machine in their markets. It was from these requests that Mr. Atkins developed the franchising arrangements used by the Ohio Tire and Rubber Company today.

Later in the 1930s, Mr. Atkins, using the same basic rubber-welding principles, designed and manufactured a machine which would put a complete new tread on a tire casing. This retreading machine was also well accepted by the garages and tire repair shops. When new tires were not available during World War II, the tire retreading business boomed, and the Ohio Tire and Rubber Company expanded its operations considerably. After the war, as new tires once more became plentiful, the market for tire retreading machines slumped. To offset the decline in his business, Mr. Atkins signed an agreement with the B. F. Goodrich Company. Under the agreement, Ohio's franchised retail dealers were provided with Goodrich's well-known national brand of tires and tubes to sell along with their other products and services.

Today the Ohio Tire and Rubber Company remains as it has always been—a manufacturer and supplier; it is not a retailer. The company does, however, serve as the "parent" company for approximately one hundred retailers from coast to coast who operate as Ohio-franchised dealers. Virtually all these franchised holders are either tire repair and retread shops or auto repair garages specializing in tire maintenance and front-end service. Under the terms of the franchise agreement, Ohio grants each dealer the right to sell Ohio products and services and to use the Ohio name in a territory protected from encroachment by any other Ohio franchise holder. The retailer owns his own building and equipment and handles his own advertising.

The Ohio Tire and Rubber Company manufactures the tire retreading and repairing equipment used by its franchised dealers. In addition to manufacturing the tread rubber and the various tread matrices which are used in the retreading machines, the Ohio Company also produces wheel alignment equipment, wheel balancing equipment, and automotive truing machines for servicing the front-end mechanisms in automobiles. All these pieces of equipment are sold directly to the franchised retailers.

A few years ago, the Ohio Company discontinued carrying the Goodrich brand of tires and tubes and started selling under the Ohio name a line of tires and tubes purchased from another large manufacturer. Also under its own brand, Ohio supplies to its franchise holders a line of batteries, shock absorbers, brake linings, and front-end repair parts. Annual sales of the Ohio Company have reached $10 million, and the largest part of this volume is from the sale of new tires.

At the present time, the Ohio Company itself does no advertising. The only advertising of Ohio products and services is done at the local level by the franchised retailers. The parent company provides the dealers with point-of-purchase advertising materials and grants them an advertising allowance of 1½ per cent of their purchases from the Ohio Company. From time to time, several dealers will group together and advertise jointly in their immediate market area. For example, some years ago, three stores in the Portland, Oregon, market started a joint advertising program by sharing the cost of a $50-a-month advertising program in local newspapers. This has grown, until today eighteen stores in the western Oregon area cooperate in a $40,000-a-year local advertising effort.

Mr. Atkins has become increasingly concerned that his company's promotional efforts are inadequate to meet the stiffening competition his company is facing in its bid for tire and parts replacement business. All his major competitors—Sears, Montgomery Ward, the major tire companies, the major petroleum companies, discount houses, and department stores—are advertising heavily. In view of this competitive promotion, Mr. Atkins is considering the use of national advertising by his company to support the local promotional efforts of the franchised dealers. Also, strong requests have been received from many dealers, urging the Ohio Company to do some advertising on television and in national magazines.

Mr. Atkins envisions an annual appropriation of about $500,000 for this advertising. He wants to use spot commercials on black-and-white television and periodic advertisements in magazines such as *Sports Illustrated* and the *Saturday Evening Post*. He would use both product and institutional advertising and would contract with an advertising agency to do the work.

By embarking upon a national advertising campaign, Mr. Atkins believes the company would increase its prestige and upgrade its image among consumers. This type of promotion would help to attract new franchise holders. It would also pave the way for expansion of product lines. For some time, Mr. Atkins has hoped that the Ohio Tire and Rubber stores could be patterned after the retail outlets of the Firestone and the Goodyear companies, where a wide variety of merchandise is carried.

The vice-president of sales, Mr. R. K. Llewellyn, is not in favor of the national advertising idea. Instead, he believes the Ohio Tire and Rubber Company should increase its support of the dealers in their local promotional programs. He fears that the cost of national advertising would be prohibitive. He would prefer to do no advertising rather than waste money on an inadequate program. In his view, the money could be better spent by increasing the dealers' advertising allowance to 5 per cent of purchases and by furnishing more and better point-of-purchase advertising materials. To stimulate the dealers to do more newspaper advertising, Mr. Llewellyn would have the Ohio Company provide, at no cost to these dealers, all the necessary matrices (mats) for the ads. The only cost to the dealer would be the space charges.

Regardless of the direction taken in their promotional programs, both Mr. Atkins and Mr. Llewellyn are wondering what the main appeal should be in these programs. On one hand, the company could emphasize the quality of its products. The idea would be to build brand recognition for the Ohio name and to stress product benefits of the tires, tubes, and other items sold to consumers. On the other hand, both executives realize that "quality of service" is a very effective advertising appeal. For example, a few years ago, the two largest Ohio Company dealers handled the B. F. Goodrich tire. They have since switched to the new Ohio private-branded tire, and these firms are still the two top dealers, and their volume on new tires has increased. This would seem to indicate that consumers are more interested in the dealer and his services than in the brand name of the products he sells. Furthermore, by using the "service-center concept" as an appeal, the company might better attract new retailers and increase the market for its retreading equipment and front-end alignment equipment.

QUESTIONS

1 Should the Ohio Company engage in national advertising, or should it only give more support to retailer advertising at the local level?

2 Should the company's main promotional appeal stress "quality of service" or "quality of product"?

...MPANY

...ion-type product by small company

Si ... arted thirteen years ago, the promotional efforts of
th ... of the mailing of a pamphlet in answer to inquiries,
pl ... inder and president, George Van Loonen, has made
ar ... s. Because sales have fallen off recently, Mr. Van
L ... er the company should establish some sort of an
o ... Van Loonen Company, located in Newark, New
Je ... ural steel products used in the construction industry.
Sa ... l from $1.6 million to $2.0 million annually, varying
w ... iction industry.
... e assortment of equipment used by structural con-
tr ... a-long booms, stiff legs, loose-neck booms, buckets,
fo ... s, counterweight boxes, and center hitches. Most of
th ... h unit value and are custom-designed and built to
fi ... stomers; the company produces very few stock items.
... ny designed an extra-long boom (300 to 360 feet)
... over competitive products. These are tubular booms
built in 40-foot sections out of a high-tensile-strength steel (called "T-1"). Because each boom is custom-made, the company does not maintain an inventory of sections of the boom. The Van Loonen product is lighter, and yet more durable, than the booms designed and

built by the many crane manufacturers. Also, it can be installed on older machines. This feature is attractive to, and strengthens the competitive position of, contractors who cannot afford a new machine.

In addition to its manufacturing operation, the Van Loonen Company also does quite a bit of repair and redesign work in the New York area. The repair work involves mainly straightening bent parts and rebuilding worn parts. The company will redesign a piece of equipment so that it is adaptable for a wider range of jobs or so that it can be used on another machine.

Most of the company's business comes from east of the Mississippi River, with the biggest concentration in New York City and northern New Jersey. Presently, this market consists mostly of customers with whom the company has been dealing for years and who know Mr. Van Loonen personally. However, a potential world-wide market exists for Van Loonen products. The extra-long T-1 boom, for example, has been sold on a limited basis to heavy contracting companies in Europe, Australia, and South America. Again, the limited promotional efforts have kept the Van Loonen Company largely an unknown quantity.

A rather unusual market situation exists for the extra-long T-1 type of boom manu-factured by the Van Loonen Company. Only three other firms compete with Van Loonen in the sale of long booms, and each of these competitors makes a boom designed for use on only his own machines. Thus, if a contractor wants to buy a long T-1 type of boom for his machine and this machine is not made by one of the three competitors, this contractor is a logical prospective customer for the Van Loonen Company. That is, the Van Loonen Company has a large untapped market and one which cannot be reached by the three competitors. Yet most contractors do not realize they can increase the use and value of their present machines by adding the long boom because they erroneously believe that the use of the long boom requires a newer, heavier machine.

The president and the chief engineer are the main executive officers in the company. Actually, this is about as close to a one-man operation as a company this size can get. The president is the heart and force behind the company. He does all the policy making, includ-ing that relating to pricing, distribution, product planning, and promotion. In pricing, for instance, the large extent of custom-made products makes it difficult to establish any pricing standards. The president sets the price on each order, depending upon the product's intended use. He seldom grants discounts; when given, they are based on the size of the order and the length of time the customer has been doing business with the company.

The chief engineer is important in the organization, not so much because of his training but because the law requires that all structures built or used in New York City be certified by a licensed engineer. Since he holds a license from New York City, this engineer has the right to certify blueprints.

At the present time, the company is doing no promotion other than mailing an infor-mational pamphlet in answer to inquiries received in the office. There is no personal selling and no direct mail or other kind of advertising of any type. The most effective promotion has been the word-of-mouth advertising done by the long-standing customers located in the greater New York area. This limited promotion, plus the personal contacts made by Mr. Van Loonen, brought in all the business the company could handle for the first ten years of its life. Since the T-1 boom was developed three years ago, the company has had suffi-cient orders for it. Even during the past year, when orders began to decline, the president and chief engineer continued to think that the company's limited promotional efforts were sufficient.

Now, however, it is becoming increasingly apparent to Mr. Van Loonen that these limited efforts are not at all adequate. He realizes that he has about saturated the market which exists for the long booms in New York. He must expand into other parts of the United States and even into foreign countries. His funds are quite limited, although he does estimate that the company could devote about $20,000 for some initial promotion.

The chief engineer has suggested that the company institute a program of direct-mail advertising. The mailing list would include contractors who build large structures of the type where the long boom is needed. These structures include apartment houses, office buildings, dams, bridges, and government installations such as missile bases and facilities built by the National Aeronautics and Space Administration (NASA) for its aerospace research activities. Such a campaign would make the Van Loonen product known to these builders and explain to them the many uses of the T-1 boom. The engineer points out that direct-mail advertising would be less expensive than magazine or trade-journal advertising, and also less expensive than using personal salesmen.

In spite of the increased cost, Mr. Van Loonen would prefer to hire one salesman to call on the type of contractor the engineer would reach by direct mail. The president believes that a salesman would be far more effective in that he could evaluate a contractor's machines and the needs of the construction job. Then he could explain how the Van Loonen custom-made boom would help this contractor meet his own special requirements.

QUESTION

1   What type of promotional program should the Van Loonen Company develop to reach the market outside the greater New York area?

case 21. SUNSET PHOTOGRAPHIC STUDIOS, INC.

Promotional efforts to enter a new market

In light of growing pressures in many communities to adopt new, or to strengthen already existing, Green River ordinances restricting activities of traveling salesmen, the executives of the Sunset Photographic Studios are reappraising the promotional methods used to support their mobile retail units. This company takes portrait photographs. It does its own developing, retouching, finishing, and oil-coloring work. The home offices are in Nashville, Tennessee, and finishing plants are located in Birmingham, Nashville, Cincinnati, and Dallas.

The company operates a chain of retail outlets located in almost all states east of the Mississippi River, as well as in Louisiana, Arkansas, Texas, Oklahoma, and Colorado. About seventy-five of the retail outlets are permanent studios in medium- and large-sized cities. In addition, the company maintains a large number of traveling or mobile units which visit communities for a period of a few days to a few weeks, depending upon the market potential in the town. Some communities are visited only once a year, and others three or four times a year. For these units the company usually rents office and studio space in a local hotel or motel. The traveling unit is fully staffed and equipped. The staff includes personnel to do promotional work in advance of the unit's visit, one or more photographers, and the clerical help needed to arrange the photographic sittings, show proofs to the customers, take orders, and do the record keeping. The finished portraits are mailed to the customers either prepaid or on a c.o.d. basis.

The quality of the work done by the Sunset company is excellent, and the firm enjoys a reputation for dependability and responsibility. Operating as it does on a traveling basis, the company is particularly concerned about its reputation in the various towns. Management knows that success depends upon repeat visits and favorable word-of-mouth advertising from past customers. The company's prices are reasonable; in fact, Sunset's photographs are frequently priced below those of local competitors. From its inception some thirty years ago, the firm has followed the pricing strategy of low unit profit margins, depending upon a large sales volume to return satisfactory total profits. This pricing policy is one of the factors which irritate local photographers in many cities.

Before arriving in a town, the company sends ahead a group of door-to-door salesmen and saleswomen who sell introductory offers—a $2 coupon entitling a customer to one 8-by-10 black-and-white photograph which regularly sells for $7.50. The salesmen are paid on a straight-commission basis. They also set up appointments for taking the photographs. Of course, when the subject arrives for his sitting or after he sees the proofs, the company hopes to increase the original order. Actually, the company loses money if the customer does not buy more than the original $2 order.

The practice of selling coupons on a door-to-door basis has been used successfully for years by the company, and it is still bringing in satisfactory sales volume. Several factors, however, are making the executives wonder whether the method has about outlived its usefulness. Except in small towns, it is difficult to reach enough prospects in a short period of time by this method. As the company has grown in size and prestige, the executives have thought that possibly door-to-door selling is damaging the firm's image. One man has stated that this type of selling was all right in the early days, when the firm was starting, but now more socially acceptable methods should be used. In some communities, Green River ordinances are increasingly hindering the operation of the advance men.

The company is considering other promotional methods for entering new markets. Mr. Huff, the sales manager, has suggested party-plan selling. He has been impressed with the apparent success enjoyed by firms selling jewelry, home products, and cosmetics in this manner. The lady giving the home party could be rewarded by portrait photographs of members of her family, or she could select from other prizes. This method would enable one salesman to reach more prospects in a shorter period of time than he could by approaching them on a door-to-door basis. Local service clubs, garden clubs, church groups, sports clubs, and similar organizations are considered good prospects for party-plan selling. Also, on college and university campuses, the dormitories and the fraternity and sorority houses are considered excellent prospects and a substantial market potential.

The manager of the Cincinnati plant, who came up through the company ranks as a salesman and photographer, is more inclined toward extensive use of local newspaper advertising. The advertisements could include the $2 coupon. The use of a newspaper might also earn the newspaper's support if legislative attempts were made to prohibit firms such as Sunset Photographic Studios from selling in the town. Of course, the other side of the coin is that the local merchants might put pressure on a newspaper publisher so that he would not accept advertising from an outside company such as Sunset.

QUESTIONS

1   Which of the three methods should the company emphasize?

2   Should promotional methods used in towns visited several times a year be different from those used in communities visited only once a year?

3   Should the promotional program for new markets be different from that employed in communities that the company has previously visited?

PART SEVEN

MARKETING IN
SPECIAL FIELDS

24

MARKETING OF SERVICES

As we developed a marketing program for an individual company in Parts 3 to 6, our thoughts were focused largely on the domestic marketing of manufactured goods. The marketing programs in three additional fields will be considered separately, although briefly, in this chapter and the two that follow. The areas to be discussed are the marketing of services, the marketing of agricultural products, and the marketing of American products in foreign countries. In each case, we are again concerned with building a marketing program around the constituent parts of the marketing mix—the product, the distribution system, the price structure, and the promotional program. Marketing research should be used as much as possible, and the program should be based upon findings from a careful market analysis.

In the first chapter of this book, we defined marketing as a system designed to plan, price, promote, and distribute goods and *services* to markets. Then we promptly devoted the intervening twenty-two chapters largely to the marketing of *products*, dealing with such things as credit, delivery, and management advice only when they were associated with, and incidental to, the sale of goods. Now we shall rectify that imbalance a bit. In bare-bone outline, it is true, the marketing of services is the same as the marketing of products in that marketing research is used to build a marketing program to reach preanalyzed markets. Although the skeletons may be similar in the marketing of goods and services, the flesh put on the bare bones often results in finished figures that are significantly different in appearance.

NATURE AND IMPORTANCE

Out of every dollar that we as consumers spend, about 41 cents goes for services, and the forecast is that this figure will increase, rather than decrease. Yet relatively little has been written in the way of a conceptual, integrated, all-encompassing study to guide marketing executives in service concerns.[1]

Definition and scope of field

Perhaps one reason for this paucity of literature is that no common definition and boundaries have been established to delimit the field of services. The American Marketing Association defines services as "Activities, benefits, or satisfactions which are offered for sale, or are provided in connection with the sale of goods."[2] Under this interpretation, we would include (1) intangible benefits or satisfactions offered for sale independently of other goods or services (insurance, investments, some medical service); (2) intangible activities which require the use of tangible goods (amusement, house rentals, transportation service); and (3) intangible activities purchased jointly with products or other intangible activities (credit, training dealer salesmen). For our purpose, this definition is too broad and lacks the preciseness needed for useful marketing analysis. Particularly, we should separate out those services which exist only in connection with the sale of a product or another service. Thus, when we talk about the marketing of services, using the above three-way classification, we are talking only about those activities listed in parts (1) and (2).

Consequently, in this chapter we shall define "services" as separately identifiable, intangible activities which provide want satisfaction when marketed to consumers and/or industrial users and which are not necessarily tied to the sale of a product or another service. Therefore, we include such services as

---

[1] For two noteworthy exceptions to this statement, see Donald D. Parker, *The Marketing of Consumer Services*, University of Washington, Business Study Series, no. 1, Seattle, Wash., 1960; and Eugene M. Johnson, *An Introduction to the Problems of Service Marketing Management*, University of Delaware, Bureau of Economic and Business Research, Newark, Del., 1964.

[2] Committee on Definitions, *Marketing Definitions: A Glossary of Marketing Terms,* American Marketing Association, Chicago, 1960, p. 21.

medical care, insurance, repair service (but not the repair parts purchased), and entertainment; we exclude credit, delivery, and packaging services which exist only when there is a sale of an article or another service.[3]

We are concerned primarily with the services sold by some business or professional firm with profit-making motives—commercial services—in contrast to those sold by nonbusiness organizations such as churches, public schools, and the government. One useful classification of commercial services is given below. No attempt is made to separate these services according to whether they are sold to household consumers or industrial users. In fact, most are purchased by both market groups. Only a few—advertising agency service and management consulting service, for example—are purchased solely by industrial users.

1. Housing (includes rentals of hotels, motels, apartments, houses, and farms).

2. Household operations (includes utilities, house repairs, repairs of equipment in the house, landscaping, and household cleaning).

3. Recreation (includes rental and repairs of equipment used in participating in recreation, amusement, and entertainment activities; also admission to all entertainment, recreation, and amusement events).

4. Personal care (includes laundry, dry cleaning, beauty care).

5. Medical and other health care (includes all medical service—dental, nursing, hospitalization, optometry, and other health care).

6. Private education.

7. Business and other professional services (includes legal, accounting, management consulting, and marketing consulting services).

8. Insurance and financial (includes personal and property insurance, bank services, credit and loan service, investment counseling, and tax service).

9. Transportation and communications (includes freight and passenger service on common carriers, automobile repairs, and automobile rentals).

Extent of growth of services

Even assuming some definitional and measurement problems, nevertheless the statistics on expenditures for consumer services alone tell quite a growth story. Almost every year since 1947, expenditures for these services have increased both in total dollars and as a percentage of total personal consumption expenditures. (See Table 24–1.) From 1950 to 1965, expenditures for these services about tripled ($62 billion to $175 billion), while personal expenditures for durable and nondurable goods only doubled ($128 billion to $254 billion). As a

---

[3] For another definition, identifying marketed services as a "market transaction by an enterprise or entrepreneur where the object of the market transaction is *other than* the transfer of ownership (and title, if any) of a tangible commodity," see Robert C. Judd, "The Case for Redefining Services," *Journal of Marketing*, January, 1964, pp. 58–59.

percentage of gross national product, service expenditures rose from 22 to 26 per cent in the twenty-year period following World War II (1946 to 1965). Services accounted for 41 cents of the personal consumption dollar in 1965, as against only 31 cents in the late 1940s. In Fig. 24–1, we see graphically that expenditures for services have increased relatively more than expenditures for durable and nondurable goods since World War II.

To say that 41 cents out of every dollar we spend goes for services is really a gross understatement of their economic importance. These figures represent service expenditures for personal consumption only; they do not include the

table   24–1

Expenditures for personal services as a percentage of the gross national product and total personal consumption expenditures, for selected years, 1946–1965

The share of consumer dollars spent on services has increased rather steadily since World War II (41 per cent in 1965, as against 31 per cent in 1947). How do you account for this increase? Is there likely to be a continued increase in the expenditure percentage devoted to services?

				Service expenditures as percentage of:	
				---	---
Year	*Services*	*Personal consumption expenditures*	*Gross national product*	*Personal consumption expenditures*	*Gross national product*
		In billions of current dollars			
1940	26.0	70.8	99.7	36.7	26.1
1946	45.3	143.4	208.5	31.6	21.7
1947	49.8	160.7	231.3	31.0	21.5
1948	54.7	173.6	257.6	31.5	21.2
1949	57.6	176.8	256.5	32.6	22.5
1950	62.4	191.0	284.8	32.7	21.9
1951	67.9	206.3	328.4	32.9	20.8
1952	73.4	216.7	345.5	33.9	21.2
1953	79.9	230.0	364.6	34.7	21.9
1954	85.4	236.5	364.8	36.1	23.4
1955	91.4	254.4	398.0	35.9	22.9
1956	98.5	266.7	419.2	36.9	23.5
1957	105.0	281.4	441.1	37.3	23.8
1958	112.0	290.1	447.3	38.6	25.0
1959	120.3	311.2	483.6	38.6	24.9
1960	128.7	325.2	503.8	39.6	25.5
1961	135.1	335.2	520.1	41.5	26.0
1962	143.0	355.1	560.3	40.3	25.5
1963	152.3	373.8	589.2	40.7	25.8
1964	162.6	398.9	628.7	40.8	25.9
1965	174.7	428.7	676.3	40.8	25.8

SOURCE: Data for 1946–1964 from Business Statistics: 1965 (a biennial supplement to *Survey of Current Business*), p. 1; 1965 data from *Survey of Current Business*, February, 1966, back cover.

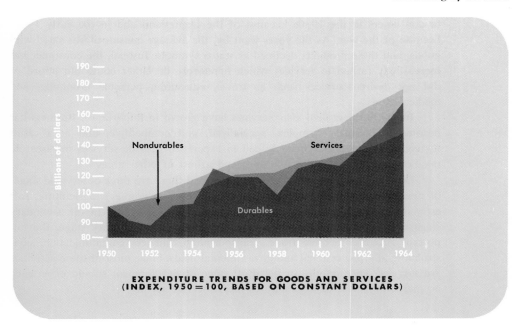

EXPENDITURE TRENDS FOR GOODS AND SERVICES
(INDEX, 1950 = 100, BASED ON CONSTANT DOLLARS)

fig. 24-1

Since 1950, expenditures for services have increased about 80 per cent, as contrasted with the 50 per cent increase in spending for nondurable goods. (These are constant-dollar figures; increases in price levels are eliminated.) How do you account for the erratic shape of the line representing expenditures for durable goods?

SOURCE: *A Graphic Guide to Consumer Markets: 1966,* National Industrial Conference Board, Inc., New York, p. 46.

vast amounts spent by industrial users who purchase services. The truth of the matter is that we do not have accurate measurements reflecting total sales of services. This lack of complete statistical data is traceable, in part at least, to the definitional problems just discussed. In its published data on selected services, for instance, the Bureau of the Census includes complete information on personal services, repair services, business services, and amusement, to name a few, but excludes such items as medical care, legal service, and private education. Another type of quantitative-measurement problem arises in product-associated services. When autos are repaired, how much should be added to the service statistics, and how much included in retail sales of products (the repair parts)? Nonetheless, it seems quite clear that there has been a significant growth in the market for services over the past two decades.

To understand the reasons for this boom in services, we must understand what has been happening in our economy since World War II. The long period of prosperity has meant higher incomes, increased leisure time, and generally a rise in living standards. In the early stages of a period such as this, people first expend their rising incomes on goods. This was particularly true after World War II, when there was a huge backlog of demand for products denied to consumers in the 1930s because of the Depression and in the early 1940s because of the war. As the years went by, the average consumer was sated with goods, and these products declined as status symbols. Instead, the consumer has increasingly turned to services which heretofore he either could not afford or did not desire—services such as travel, education, personal grooming, and medical care.

In the business field also, services have grown in importance. Business has become increasingly complex, specialized, and competitive, and as a result management has been forced to call in experts to provide services in research, taxation, advertising, labor relations, and a host of other areas.[4]

One theory of economic growth holds that there are three observable stages of development.[5] In the primary stage (low-level economies), agriculture, forestry, hunting, and fishing occupy the population's attention. In the secondary stage, the major emphasis is on manufacturing. In the tertiary stage, the important activities involve trade, transportation, finance, communication, construction, and professional and governmental fields. Since most of these activities are services, an economy in the third stage of development should experience an increasing share of expenditures in the service sector.

CHARACTERISTICS OF SERVICES

Services possess several distinctive characteristics which have significant marketing implications. These differentiating features create marketing problems and result in marketing programs which are often substantially different from those found in connection with the marketing of products.

Intangibility

Services are intangible. The impossibility of a customer's tasting, feeling, seeing, hearing, or smelling a service before he buys it places some strain on the marketing organization. This burden falls mainly on a company's promotional program, where the salesmen and the advertising department must concentrate on the benefits to be derived from the service, rather than emphasizing the service itself. An insurance company will promote service benefits such as guaranteed payment of the children's college expenses, protection against losing one's life's savings in a damage suit resulting from an auto accident, or a retirement income of so many dollars a month. The telephone companies tell us in their advertising that long-distance telephoning brings us the pleasure of talking to friends and relatives in distant cities; another series of telephone advertisements

---

[4] Johnson, *op. cit.*, p. 12.

[5] Colin Clark, *The Conditions of Economic Progress*, 3d ed., Macmillan & Co., Ltd., London, 1957, p. 491, as cited in William J. Regan, "The Service Revolution," *Journal of Marketing*, July, 1963, pp. 57–62; see also William J. Regan, "Economic Growth and Services," *Journal of Business*, April, 1963, pp. 200–209.

shows how companies can cut selling and inventory costs, and often save a sale, by using long-distance calls.

On the other hand, the factor of intangibility offers some competitive advantages to a firm. Problems of physical distribution are eliminated. There is nothing to store or handle; there is no inventory to control; and a company will never be faced with losses from a decline in inventory values.

Inseparability

Services often cannot be separated from the person of the seller. A corollary to this point is that given services are often created and marketed simultaneously. For example, a beauty operator is creating the service of a haircut and dispensing the service at the same time. Of course, preparation and training may be done in advance.

From a marketing standpoint, inseparability means that frequently direct sale is the only possible channel of distribution, and one seller's services cannot be sold in very many markets. This characteristic also limits the scale of operation in a firm. One man can repair only so many autos in a day or treat only so many medical patients. Also, because each man—that is, each "service institution"—is a specialist, the service company often cannot add a variety of other services to its line the way a department store or supermarket can.

As a modification of the inseparability feature, there may be a tangible representation of the service by someone other than the creator-seller. A travel agent, insurance broker, or rental agent, for instance, may represent and help promote the service which will be sold by the institution producing the service.

Heterogeneity

It is impossible to standardize output among several sellers of presumably the same service. As a matter of fact, it is not possible to standardize completely even the output of one seller. A railroad does not give the same quality of service on each trip; all repair jobs a mechanic does on automobiles are not of equal quality. Complicating this characteristic is the fact that often it is difficult to judge the quality of a service. (Of course, we can say the same for some products.) It is particularly difficult to forecast the quality in advance of buying a service. A person pays to see a ball game without knowing whether it will turn out to be an exciting one, well worth the price of admission, or a low-quality, dull performance.

In light of these problems of standardization and quality evaluation, the service company should pay particular attention to the "product-planning" stage of its marketing program. Management must do all it can to ensure consistent and high-quality performance. In this way, the company can build the customer confidence and good reputation that are so vital to repeat business and to favorable word-of-mouth advertising.

Perishability and fluctuating demand

Services are highly perishable, and they cannot be stored. Unused electrical power, empty seats in a stadium, and idle repairmen in a garage all represent business which is lost forever. Furthermore, the market for services fluctuates considerably by seasons, by days of the week, and by hours of the day. Many ski lifts lie idle all summer, and golf courses in some areas go unused in the winter. College football stadia are used mainly in the fall, and then only one day a week. Use of city buses fluctuates within a day.

The combination of perishability and fluctuating demand offers product-planning, pricing, and promotion challenges to executives in a service company. They might look for new uses for idle plant capacity in off-seasons. Through advertising, they can show consumers the advantages of using city transportation facilities during nonpeak hours. In an attempt to level demand, telephone companies price at lower rates on nights and weekends. When a service is offered only once, as in any given baseball game, the seller should price in order to fill all seats.

THE MARKETING CONCEPT AND SERVICE MARKETING

The growth in services has generally been attributed to the maturation of our economy and the rising standards of living in our affluent society. "It is significant that very little credit for this growth has been given to marketing developments in the service industries."[6] Traditionally, executives in service companies have not been marketing-oriented. They have lagged behind sellers of products both in accepting the market concept and in implementing it in their company management. Service organizations have also generally been slow in adopting or making efficient use of promotional methods, "product" strategies, and other marketing techniques. With a few notable exceptions, such as the insurance industry and, more recently, the telephone companies, marketing management in service firms has not been especially creative; innovation has typically come from product-associated companies.

To illustrate, the major impetus for the increased use of electrical power has come from appliance manufacturers, not electric utilities. For years, commercial banks made a customer feel as if they were doing him a big favor by holding his money for him; loans were granted grudgingly, and it never occurred to the banker that he was the buyer—that really a borrower was "selling" his need for a loan. The laundry and dry-cleaning industry stood still, despite increased competition from home laundry equipment and coin-operated dry-cleaning establishments and despite the development of wash-and-wear and permanently pressed fabrics. The repair industry has left a trail of dissatisfied and even irate customers for years.

[6] Eugene M. Johnson, "Marketing Is Key to Success in Service Business," *Sales/Marketing Today*, November, 1964, p. 8.

Perhaps we can identify the reasons for this lack of a marketing orientation. No doubt the intangibility of services poses more difficult marketing problems than those which product sellers face. In many service industries —particularly professional services—the sellers think of themselves as producers or creators, and not as marketers, of the service. They are proud of their ability to repair a car, diagnose an illness, fly a plane, sing a concert, or give a good haircut. They do not think of themselves as businessmen; it is not "ethical," for example, for a doctor or a lawyer to advertise. Failure of management to recognize that competition existed may account for lack of interest in marketing in some industries—banking, railroads, and public utilities, for instance.

The all-encompassing reason, however, seems to be that top management has yet to recognize how important marketing is to the success of a firm. This failure is reflected in three areas of weakness.[7] First, these executives have a limited view of the marketing function and of the business they are in. They equate marketing with selling and fail to consider other parts of the system. Movie producers thought of themselves as being in the business of making movies; instead, they were really marketing entertainment. Railroad executives saw their task as running a railroad, instead of marketing a transportation system or a total materials-handling system. The second point—a consequence of the first—is that management fails to recognize that many of its problems are marketing problems; and once this fact is recognized, management may still not act quickly. Finally, there has been insufficient coordination of all marketing activities in service firms. Many service firms lack an executive whose sole responsibility is marketing—a counterpart of the vice-president of marketing in a goods-producing company.

Fortunately, this total situation seems to have improved markedly over the past decade.[8] While there may still be a long way to go in some service fields (perhaps in repair services, personal grooming, and others where small businesses predominate), the overall future prospects look good for the recognition and acceptance of the marketing concept in service industries.

A PROGRAM FOR MARKETING OF SERVICES

Because we are dealing with intangibles, the task of determining the marketing-mix ingredients for a total marketing program in a service industry is perhaps more difficult and therefore requires more skill and sophistication than is true in product-marketing firms.

[7] *Ibid.*, pp. 8–11.

[8] For some examples, see "United Charts a New Flight Plan," *Business Week*, Aug. 14, 1965, p. 128; "How to Make a Last Place Product (the New York Mets baseball team) a Banner Success," *Sales Management*, Apr. 16, 1965, p. 34; " 'A Hell of a Way to Run a Railroad,' " *Sales Management*, Mar. 4, 1966, p. 28; Johnson, *An Introduction to the Problems of Service Marketing Management*, pp. 36–44 (transportation, communication, banking, and insurance services).

Market analysis and market planning

Procedural considerations involved in market analysis and planning are essentially the same whether a firm is selling a product or a service. A marketer of services should understand the components of population and income as they affect the market for his services. In addition, he must carefully analyze his customers' motivation for buying his services—that is, *why* do they want his services, and does each segment of his market have the same or different motives? Also, the seller must determine the buying patterns for his services— when, where, and how do they buy, who does the buying, and who makes the buying decisions?

Some of the trends pointed up in Chapters 4 to 7 are particularly worth watching because they carry considerable influence in the marketing of services. As an example, increases in disposable income and discretionary buying power mean that consumers can buy more than basic personal and household necessities. Consequently, they become a growing market for more and better medical care, insurance, or transportation service. The increasing number of working women means greater markets for many services. Women will now pay for services such as laundry or household repairs which formerly they performed themselves. Shorter working hours have resulted in increases in leisure time. More leisure time plus greater income mean increased markets for recreation and entertainment services. Another concomitant of increases in buying power has been the increased demand for convenience. Several types of services may be purchased as a result of this factor.

A service industry may be able to segment its market on some basis and then use an appropriate marketing strategy to reach each segment more effectively. The airlines, for instance, identified the youth market (ages twelve to twenty-one) as a separate unit and then established a youth fare (half price with a membership card or on a space-available basis) to reach that market segment.

To determine people's attitudes toward, and motives for buying, its service, a company may use motivation research. The diaper service industry did just that. Faced with a negative attitude toward its service, the industry employed a research firm to find out what people thought of diaper service, why they thought it, and what might be done to reverse the poor image. Based on these findings, a promotional campaign was initiated which was successful in creating a more favorable image.[9]

Planning and developing the service

Product planning and development should have its counterpart in the marketing program of a service industry. Management should use an organized, sys-

[9] Martha W. Lear, "Diaper Service," *McCall's*, January, 1964, p. 84.

tematic procedure to determine (1) what services will be offered, (2) what the company's policies will be with respect to the length and breadth of the service line offered, and (3) what, if anything, needs to be done in the way of service attributes such as branding or providing guarantees.

Unfortunately, planning and developing the service has been a neglected activity in most service firms until very recent years, and it is still ignored in too many cases. The basic reason for this neglect goes back to the lack of a marketing orientation in service industries and their narrow view of what business they are in. A motion-picture firm which thinks its job is to "make movies" (instead of marketing entertainment) is not apt to get involved in creating and marketing a filmed comedy series for television. A bank which considers itself a savings depository (instead of a marketer of financial services) is not apt to provide drive-up windows, charge account plans, bill-paying service through checking accounts, or evening-hours banking service. By taking the broad view of the range of its service offerings, a company may stay in business long after narrower firms have disappeared. An electric utility which thinks of its business as marketing energy (instead of producing electricity) will not be dismayed when solar radiation or atomic energy is used as a source of power.

New services are just as important to a service company as new products are to a product-marketing firm, even though service companies may not face the problem of obsolescence to as great an extent. Similarly, improving existing services is every bit as important as improving existing products. Certainly much of the procedure for developing new products and many of the criteria for selecting new products (as discussed in Chapter 8) are equally applicable in a service firm.

A service industry can expand or contract its "product line," alter existing services, and trade up or down—in the same way that a product-marketing organization does. Dry cleaners, for instance, have expanded into laundry services, mothproofing, storage, dyeing, and clothing alterations and repairs. Auto insurance firms have added life and fire insurance. The reasons for these line expansions are familiar—the company wants to increase its total volume, reduce seasonal fluctuations in volume, cater to changing buying patterns such as the desire for one-stop shopping, etc. Some railroads have simplified their line by dropping passenger service or by abolishing freight stations at some small, unprofitable locations. Some service firms have effectively expanded their line by working jointly with companies selling related services.[10] Automobile rental firms have working arrangements with airlines, railroads, and hotels, so that when a customer flies or goes by train to his destination, a car will be ready for his use at that point, and he will have a hotel room reserved. Travel agencies combine many transportation and recreation services in one package.

In some respects, policy making is easier for services than for products.

---

[10] See Parker, *op. cit.*, p. 117.

Tasks related to packaging, color, labeling, and style are virtually nonexistent in marketing services. However, in other areas—branding and standardization of quality, for instance—the job in service industries poses greater problems. Branding is difficult because consistency of quality is hard to maintain and because the brand cannot be physically attached to a service. In fact, branding is not used very widely in the marketing of services.

Standardization of quality in a service is an extremely important goal to strive for. In some fields such as beauty care, medical care, and some of the recreation industries, no attempt is made to mass-produce a service; instead, the sellers often offer custom-tailored service for each customer. Even in these cases, however, the customer wants consistency of quality, and this consistency is very difficult to achieve because the service is produced and sold in individual units—one haircut, one appendectomy, or one dance lesson.

Channels of distribution for services

When developing a distribution system for his services, a seller is concerned only with the transfer of ownership. No problems of physical distribution such as bulk breaking, transportation, or warehousing are involved. Channels of distribution for services are generally very simple when compared with channels for products. Most services are sold directly from producer to consumer or industrial user. No middlemen are used because the service cannot be separated from the person of the seller, nor is it feasible to use a tangible representative of the service. Public utilities, medical care, repair service, and others are typically sold without middlemen. The only other channel frequently used involves one agent middleman. We see this channel used in the sale of securities, transportation, housing rentals, labor, and entertainment. Sometimes dealers are trained in the production of the service and then are franchised to sell it, as is the case with the Sanitone dry-cleaning process, Fred Astaire dance studios, Kelly Girl part-time office help, and Holiday Inn motels.

Whether the seller markets directly or uses an agent to reach his customers, the seller's or agent's *location* with respect to the potential market is all important. Services cannot be delivered to a customer, so the seller should select a convenient, accessible location where there is maximum customer traffic. Many motels and restaurants have either moved or gone out of business because a new highway drew away traffic when it bypassed their formerly good locations. Banks have increased their business by moving the tellers' windows to a location accessible to autos on a drive-in basis.

The inability to use middlemen to any great extent limits the geographical market that a service seller can reach. On the other hand, it gives this seller a chance to serve his customers better. It also provides the seller with a golden opportunity to get customer feedback quickly and in sufficient detail so that he can improve his marketing program.

Pricing of services

Perhaps nowhere in the marketing of services is there greater opportunity for managerial creativity, skill, and imagination than in the area of pricing.[11] Price determination is critically important here because of the discretionary nature of customer buying. In the case of most services, personal or business, the customer may postpone his purchase or even perform the service himself. Only rarely does a buyer face the situation where he needs a service immediately and the number of sellers is quite limited. Another factor to consider is that markdowns are not possible in many cases. If there are empty seats at a given concert or athletic contest, it is not possible to hold them over and offer them at a lower price later.

These considerations suggest that the elasticity of demand for a service should influence the price set by the seller. Interestingly enough, sellers often recognize an inelastic demand; then they charge higher prices. But they fail to act in opposite fashion when faced with an elastic demand, even though a lower price would increase unit sales, total revenue, utilization of facilities, and probably net profit.

The basic methods of price determination for services are generally the same as for products. Cost-plus pricing is used for various kinds of repair service where the main ingredient is direct labor and the customer is charged on an hourly basis. The price equals the repairman's wages plus an amount to cover overhead and profit. For other services (rentals, entertainment, legal counseling, management consulting), the prices are determined primarily by market demand and competition; it is pretty much a case of what the traffic will bear.

Certainly perfect competition does not exist to any extent, if at all, in the pricing of services. Because of the inability to standardize quality, services are highly differentiated, and it is virtually impossible to have complete market information. Also, in any given market, such as a neighborhood, there are geographical limits within which a buyer will seek a service, and consequently there is not a large number of sellers. The heavy capital investment required to produce many services (transportation, communications, medical care) limits the freedom of entry and exit considerably.

In some service industries, the private seller will establish a price, but it must be approved by a regulatory agency of the state or Federal government. State public utility commissions regulate the prices on gas, electrical, and telephone services. Freight and passenger railroad rates are regulated by the Interstate Commerce Commission; auto and fire insurance rates must ordinarily be approved by state insurance commissioners. This public regulation of prices, however, need not stifle the opportunity for imaginative, skillful pric-

---

[11] For a good discussion of pricing of services, see Parker, *op. cit.*, pp. 38–43.

ing designed to stimulate sales.[12] Lower rates for long-distance telephoning on nights and Sundays and different prices which benefit large-volume users of electricity are examples of creative pricing to increase market penetration.

Sometimes a trade or professional association is a price setter within an industry. Barber unions set the price on haircuts, and a laundry and dry-cleaning association sets the price on cleaning a suit of clothes. Fees charged by doctors, architects, accountants, and advertising agencies are frequently influenced strongly by professional associations.

Many of the areas of pricing policies discussed in Chapters 19 and 20 must also be considered by executives in a service firm. Thus we see quantity discounts in the pricing of electrical power; cash discounts are offered if you pay your auto insurance premium once a year instead of quarterly or semi-annually. Doctors and management consultants use a variable-price policy, whereas a movie theater has a one-price policy at any given time of day. A motel or apartment owner offers multiple services (one-bedroom, two-bedroom, suites), and he must price one service in relation to another in his line. Geographical pricing policies may be involved, although the variable here is time, not freight charges. A repairman will charge more if he must go out of town some distance, and a doctor will charge more for house calls than office calls.

Promoting the service

Management's task is especially difficult when the company must build a promotional program around intangible service benefits; it is so much easier to sell something which can be seen, felt, and demonstrated. In the marketing of services, we find that personal selling, advertising, and indirect forms of promotion are all used extensively.

Personal selling is important because of the close relationship between the buyer and the seller. Brands are used very little, so brand preferences and loyalties cannot be depended upon. Also, self-service or automatic vending cannot be used very much. Whether selling consumer or industrial services, the salesman can often build or destroy customer goodwill toward the firm. Consequently, it is imperative that management do a careful, effective job in selecting, training, supervising and otherwise managing the sales force. In most service industries where personal selling is the main promotional tool used, high-caliber salesmen are usually required.

Not much more needs to be said here about advertising because the principles and procedures are generally the same as those developed in Chapter 23. Small firms can often make effective use of local advertising. Also, a group of small local firms can participate in joint advertising ventures. National trade

---

[12] Martin W. Warshaw, "Effective Marketing: Key to Public Utility Growth," *Michigan Business Review,* November, 1962, p. 20.

associations (laundry, dry cleaning, and others) have done considerable national advertising to stimulate primary demand for their services. Even though a service is intangible, store displays that show the benefits or results of using the service can be effective.

Many service firms, especially in the recreation-amusement-entertainment field, benefit considerably from free publicity. Sports coverage by newspapers, radio, and television media help in this matter, as do newspaper reviews of movies, plays, and concerts. Travel sections in newspapers have helped sell transportation, housing, and other services related to the travel industry.

As an indirect means of promotion, doctors, lawyers, and insurance men may participate actively in community affairs as a means of getting their names before the public. Other service firms (banks, utilities, railroads) may advertise to attract new industry or more population, knowing that anything which helps the community grow will automatically mean an expanded market for them.

A promotional program in a service company should have two major goals. One is to portray the service benefits in as appealing a manner as possible. The other is to build a good reputation. Because the firm is marketing intangibles, a good reputation is perhaps even more important in a service company than in a product-marketing business. Excellent performance in any area of a company's marketing program, of course, will enhance the image of the firm, but the promotional effort can play an especially helpful role. Advertising campaigns can stress dependability of the service—its consistent, high quality. Ads can also emphasize the courteous, friendly, efficient service.

A service firm's promotional effort can be even more effective if the seller can tie in with something tangible—a distinctive color, as used by Howard Johnson or Holiday Inn, or a personal symbol like Smokey the Bear, Reddy Kilowatt, or Wolley Segap (to promote use of yellow pages in telephone books).

FUTURE OUTLOOK IN SERVICE MARKETING

There is every reason to believe that services will continue to take an increasing share of the consumer dollar, just as they have done generally over the past twenty years. This forecast seems reasonable even if we should experience periods of economic decline, for history shows that the demand for services is less elastic than the demand for products. The market for services did not slump as much as expenditures for goods during the Depression of the early 1930s and the recessions of 1948–1949, 1954, and 1960.

Our enthusiasm may be dampened a bit when we realize that, with all the growth in service marketing since World War II, consumer expenditure patterns have returned only to what they were in 1929. In that year, services accounted for about 40 per cent of total personal consumption expenditures; in 1932, services expenditures reached a high of 46 per cent of the total. Also,

some of the growth during the past twenty years is attributable to price inflation. The price level for services has increased more rapidly than the prices
of goods since World War II.

Nevertheless, there has been real and significant growth, and it should
continue. Much of the growth does not show in government statistics; it is
hidden. The market for business services is on the upswing. Also, today an
increasing part of the total price and cost of a product stems from the service
sector of the business—credit, delivery, sales training, etc.

Undoubtedly, in the total picture there will be some changes in the service
mix. Not all types will grow at the same rate. The shift in the total mix plus
the forecasted growth pose some real marketing challenges for executives in
service industries. They will have to adopt a marketing orientation in their
firms or run the risk of losing out in the competitive race.

One student of service marketing has posed the following series of five
propositions supporting the forecasts for growth:[13]

1.   We have exhausted much of the growth potential in domestic markets for
goods, so manufacturers are turning to markets which are more difficult to
serve but which have higher rates of return. These are markets where com-
modity-associated services provide utilitarian satisfactions to business and functional satisfactions to household consumers. Also, higher incomes and higher
consumption levels will provide bigger markets for service industries such as
medicine, education, travel, and research.

2.   Mass-production techniques long used in manufacturing products are now
being applied in the development of service technologies. Production systems
are being developed which will routinize services so they can be provided
faster, more conveniently, and at lower unit costs for the mass markets. In
this respect, we have seen how data-processing systems have been developed
successfully for communications and information services. Language laboratories, teaching machines, and programmed learning systems are mechanizing
the field of education services.

3.   As a wider market is reached by means of technologies in service systems,
we can expect a growing impersonalization of these services.

4.   The impersonalized attention and substitution of manufactured equipment
will encourage a reduction in the extrinsic values of a service, even though
the intrinsic values may be the same or higher. In the medical field, for instance, technology may improve the accuracy of the diagnosis and the quality
of the remedy (intrinsic essentials); the delivery of these services to more and
more people will probably result in a decrease in the extrinsic elements such
as abundant personal attention and loving care from the family doctor.

5.   In the long run, however, we can expect a proliferation of services which
are adaptable to a wide variety of tastes, just as the mass production of com-

[13] Regan, "The Service Revolution," pp. 60–62.

modities has led to a diversity in product choice today. The qualitative standards of tomorrow's services will probably be different from those of today or yesterday. Intrinsically, the service may be the same or better, but extrinsically, it will probably be poorer until we find an acceptable substitute for personalization. Even if we could dramatically increase the supply of teachers, doctors, and other research specialists, however, it is doubtful that society would support the traditional high unit cost system.

QUESTIONS AND PROBLEMS

1 When defining services, from a marketing standpoint why is it useful to exclude the group of services (credit, delivery, training dealer salesmen, etc.) which exist only in connection with the sale of a product or another service?

2 How do you account for the substantial increase in expenditures for services relative to expenditures for products since the end of World War II?

3 Even with the surge in expenditures for services since the 1940s, they still do not command as large a share of total consumer expenditures as they did during the Depression of the early 1930s. How do you account for this situation?

4 What are some of the marketing implications in the fact that services possess the characteristic of intangibility?

5 Why are middlemen rarely used in the marketing programs of service firms?

6 Services are highly perishable and are often subject to fluctuations in demand. In marketing its services, what can a company do to deal with or offset these factors?

7 Cite some examples of service marketers who seem to be customer-oriented and describe what these firms have done in this vein.

8 "Traditionally, marketers of services have *not* been marketing-oriented." Do you agree? If so, how do you account for this deficiency?

9 Present a brief analysis of the market for each of the following services. Make use of the components of a market as discussed in Chapters 4 to 7.
   a. Laundry and dry-cleaning firm located in shopping center adjoining your campus
   b. Four-bedroom house for rent at a major seashore resort
   c. Bowling alley
   d. Nursing home

10 What are some of the ways in which each of the following service firms might expand its line?
   a. Advertising agency   c. Automobile repair garage
   b. Telephone company

11 Explain why the concept of demand elasticity is so important in the pricing of services.

12 "Personal selling should be the main ingredient in the promotional mix for a marketer of services." Do you agree? Discuss.

13 What steps can a service-marketing firm take to improve its brand image or to increase customer brand loyalty?

14   When athletic contests are televised, the area within 50 or 75 miles of the event is often "blacked out." When there is a sellout on seats for the event, should the blackout restriction be removed?

15   In what ways does the marketing of services differ from the marketing of products?

25

MARKETING AGRICULTURAL PRODUCTS

The decline of the small farmer as an economic institution is changing the face of agricultural marketing as we have known it for decades. Instead, the growth of large-scale production in agriculture is focusing attention on the marketing problems in *agribusiness*. To an increasing extent, these producers are looking on themselves as businessmen, not as farmers. Also emerging, albeit slowly, among these growers is a consumer orientation—as witness, for example, the year-round marketing of turkey, the development of lean pork, and the packaging of frozen chicken by separate parts (all legs or thighs or breasts, etc.).

The marketing of agricultural products is fundamentally the same as the marketing of manufactured goods, although significant differences often exist with respect to the marketing methods and institutions used. In the marketing mix for agricultural products, for instance, methods of distribution and policies regarding channels and middlemen are very important because direct sale is usually not easy. On the other hand, aspects of product planning and promotion usually draw little attention from individual producers. Agricultural marketing is different also in that individual agricultural producers ordinarily have no significant control over the marketing of their output. In this discussion, we are concerned with agricultural products only so long as they remain in their natural state. Once they are subjected to any significant amount of processing or change in form, they are classed as manufactured products.

MARKETING IMPLICATIONS OF AGRICULTURAL PRODUCTION

Several aspects of agricultural production have a great influence on the marketing of the products. In the first place, the scale of operation in agriculture is often small and specialized, and the producing units are usually located great distances from the major markets. Furthermore, a major segment of the market is made up of small but numerous units—household consumers. As a result, in the marketing of agricultural consumer goods there is a definite need for middlemen who can assemble or concentrate the output of small producers and later disperse it to consumers and industrial users.

Another pertinent aspect of agricultural production is that supply reacts very slowly to price changes or to changes in demand. In the short run, if prices rise, it is not possible to increase appreciably the output of crops or livestock. By the same token, when prices decline, farmers or growers can rarely withhold supply from the market in an attempt to stabilize prices. The actions of a single farmer are negligible in affecting price. Even where farmers act as a group, as in a producers' cooperative, either their inability to store products more than a few months or their financial needs force them to send their output to market. Consequently, prices of most agricultural products fluctuate frequently, freely, and considerably. The resultant risks to the grower are serious.

A third consideration is the difficulty of controlling the quality of a product. The quality of animals or crops varies not only among units produced on a given farm, but also from farm to farm and from region to region. This factor increases the importance of grading agricultural products according to predetermined standards. Effective standardization and proper grading are imperative when industrial users (canners, textile mills, tobacco manufacturers, etc.) demand uniformity among the units of raw materials they use.

With respect to transportation and warehousing, first, it is difficult to control the quantity of goods produced; second, production is seasonal, although the demand for most agricultural commodities is fairly steady throughout the year; and finally, most agricultural goods are bulky, perishable, and of low unit value.

Within given grades, most units of a commodity are homogeneous. This characteristic, coupled with the factor of small producing units, makes it very difficult for a single grower to use advertising, personal selling, or other forms of promotion.

PRODUCT PLANNING

Classification of products

The twofold classification of consumer goods and industrial goods applies to agricultural products as well as to manufactured goods. Consumer farm products are those which ultimately will be sold to household consumers in essentially the same form in which they were produced. That is, they will not undergo any significant processing which changes their form, but they will be cleaned, trimmed, purified, graded, and packed. In this category, the main examples are fresh fruits and vegetables, eggs, and fluid milk. It is estimated that consumer farm products account for about 20 per cent of the dollar value of all agricultural commodities sold.

Industrial farm products, which represent the other 80 per cent, are those which are used as industrial raw materials. In this category we find all grains, fiber crops, tobacco, and most of the livestock and poultry. Also, large quantities of fruits and vegetables are canned, dried, pickled, or otherwise processed and are classed as industrial goods.

Some commodities may fall in either category, depending upon whether they are processed or not. Although consumer farm products are generally marketed differently from industrial commodities, various stages in the marketing systems for both classes may be similar. For example, in the early stages of the channels of distribution for fruits or vegetables, the same types of middlemen and the same marketing methods are often used, regardless of the final destination of the commodities.

Product policies

Product-line policies are not a major consideration for producers of agricultural goods. What a farmer grows is ordinarily determined to a great extent by soil, climate, and other factors beyond his control. If he wishes to add to his product line or expand his product mix, his alternatives are limited. He lacks the authoritarian privilege of policy making. Within the broad constraints of soil and climate, however, over a period of years groups of producers have changed their product mix in response to market demand. Improved strains of cotton and corn are available for industrial users; livestock producers are responding to overweight Americans' demand for leaner meats.

In the marketing of agricultural products, the use and importance of packaging are increasing, especially with respect to consumer products. The trend toward self-service in retailing and the consumers' desire for convenience and sanitation are contributing to this development, but packaging is usually done by the middlemen, not by the producers.

Generally there is very little branding or differentiating of products among growers. Within given grades of wheat, for example, farmer Brown's wheat is not distinguishable from farmer Green's. In a number of cases, however, growers' cooperatives have succeeded in differentiating their products through branding and advertising. This aspect of agricultural marketing is discussed later in this chapter under Promotional Program.[1] While standardization and grading play a major role in product planning, other product considerations such as color, style, design, and labeling are normally not important for agricultural goods.

DISTRIBUTION SYSTEM

Individual producer versus industry as a whole

When considering the channels of distribution system in agricultural marketing, we may distinguish between problems faced by an individual grower and those encountered by the entire industry. For an individual farmer, the distribution problems are fairly simple because he has very few alternatives. Most growers must sell in nearby local markets where there are limited numbers of buyers. Rarely is it feasible to sell in a central market or to shop around among several local markets. Growers of some products, such as fruits and vegetables, may sell some of their output directly to consumers or to retailers, but again this is not a common practice. Generally an individual grower does not control the distribution of his product after it leaves his hands.

For the industry as a whole, the channels of distribution and the management of physical distribution are probably the most complex aspects of the entire marketing process. Transportation and warehousing are extremely important. In general, the agricultural industry must depend upon several levels of distribution and several types of middlemen.

As suggested earlier, the key factor underlying the complexity of the distribution system and the need for many middlemen is the nature of the producers and ultimate buyers. In large central markets, supply must be adjusted to demand. Then the assembled supply must be divided and dispersed

---

[1] For a study on the influence of brands on consumer preferences for one relatively homogenous agricultural commodity (frozen turkeys) which indicated that a carefully planned and executed brand promotion program can be a powerful tool in overcoming marketing anonymity, see James C. Makens, "The Pluses and Minuses of Branding Agricultural Products," *Journal of Marketing*, October, 1964, pp. 10–16; for the success which United Fruit Company has had with its Chiquita brand on bananas, see "Branding a Well-known Product," *Sales Management*, Nov. 10, 1964, p. 160.

through many middlemen until it reaches the final buyers in the small quantities they desire.

Traditional market structure

Historically, agricultural goods have moved through a distribution structure which included a series of wholesaling markets—local assembling markets, central markets, and secondary wholesaling markets designed to disperse the goods. In the case of consumer products, a retailing market would be added. This wholesaling structure developed in the decades prior to World War I. It reflected three factors: the concentrated population centers in the East and the Midwest, the distant producing centers in the South and the West, and the importance of railroad transportation in hauling bulky, low-value products over the long distances separating the production areas from the market centers. Among the many different commodity groups (cotton, grains, livestock, fruits and vegetables, tobacco, etc.) the market structure varies insofar as names of middlemen and types of facilities are concerned. Nevertheless, underlying these superficial differences, one can observe a common structure.

Local assembling markets Ordinarily it is too costly, inefficient, and inconvenient for individual growers to try to deal directly with the middlemen. Therefore, in the first stage of the distribution system, agricultural products are assembled in local markets. Thousands of these markets are found throughout the agricultural producing areas. They are located in small towns and at other convenient places where farmers and ranchers can bring their crops and animals and find prospective buyers. Livestock pens, cold-storage warehouses, grain elevators, or just the buyers' offices may serve as the market location.

The primary function of the local markets is to assemble or concentrate the commodities so that they may be shipped in economical units such as carloads or truckloads. Another important function of the local markets is to provide an immediate cash outlet for the farmer's crop or livestock. Many local markets have facilities for grading, packing, and storage. Communication services are usually available also.

Central markets The next step in the traditional distribution process for agricultural goods has been to move them from the local markets to a few large central or terminal markets. Terminal markets for fresh consumer-bound produce are found in large population centers, such as Chicago, New York, Philadelphia, Baltimore, Los Angeles, Atlanta, and Seattle. Frequently certain cities become identified as central markets for given commodities, particularly those used as industrial raw materials. For example, Chicago, Minneapolis, and Kansas City are markets for grain; Boston for wool; Memphis, New Orleans, Savannah, Dallas, and Houston for cotton; Chicago, Kansas City, Omaha, Sioux City, and Denver for livestock.

The location of the central markets in certain cities may be attributed to several factors. Usually these terminals enjoy good transportation service and facilities and a favorable freight rate structure. Often they are processing or exporting centers for a particular product. Many are favorably situated in the midst of a great consuming market, or they are located between the consuming areas and the producing areas.

All the necessary marketing functions are performed in the terminal markets. They are the last step in the assembly or concentration process and the first step in the dispersion process. Excellent, highly specialized facilities are provided for such activities as transportation, physical handling, storage, grading, and packing. Communication and market information services are highly developed. Financial services are available from banks or other institutions which specialize in the financing of the particular commodities being distributed through a given central market. Perhaps the most valuable feature of these markets is their abundance of highly specialized and highly skilled manpower.

Historically, terminal markets have been the location of price-making activities. Many buyers and sellers gravitate to these markets, representing regional, national, or even international demand and supply. Consequently, their negotiating activities are really price-making forces. The resulting central market prices often serve as the basis for price quotations in local assembling markets and in the various dispersion markets. To determine the price in a local market for wheat, we would start with central market quotations and then deduct the shipping and handling charges and the middlemen's commissions involved in the exchange of title and physical movement of the product from the local to the central market. Often sales are made in these markets, but the physical product usually need not enter them. Samples of wheat may form the basis of a transaction in the Chicago market, while the carload of wheat will be shipped from a North Dakota grain elevator to a miller's factory in Minneapolis.

The heart of many terminal markets is an organized commodity exchange —a center of transactions and price-making activities. Examples include the Chicago Board of Trade, the Kansas City Board of Trade, the New Orleans Cotton Exchange, and the New York and Chicago Mercantile Exchanges. The commodity exchange is an independent organization composed of members (agent and merchant middlemen and representatives from processing and manufacturing firms) who trade in the given commodities. The exchange itself does no buying or selling. It simply provides a place where these activities may be carried out under supervision and prearranged rules determined by the member buyers and sellers. The commodity exchange furnishes a considerable amount of market information and also supplies facilities for settling disputes among member traders.

Secondary dispersion markets   In central markets, agricultural raw materials are sold in carload quantities to manufacturers and processors. Agricultural consumer goods are dispersed in carload and truckload quantities to large retail chain organizations. Middlemen operating in central markets normally prefer to deal in carload quantities. Since retailers cannot ordinarily buy in these large units, they must seek some other source of supply. Consequently, a separate wholesaling market structure, which we shall call a "secondary dispersion market," has developed in between the large terminal wholesaling market and the retail markets. The retail market itself may be considered a secondary dispersion market. The retail market for agricultural consumer goods, however, is not significantly different from the retailing structure discussed in Chapters 11 and 12.

Secondary wholesaling markets may be found in virtually every medium- and large-sized city in the country, including cities where large terminal markets are located. In central market cities, secondary wholesalers buy from middlemen in the central markets and sell to small retailers. In other cities, the secondary wholesalers may be supplied by central market sources, or they may buy directly in local markets, thus bypassing the central markets. In some cases, secondary wholesalers buy directly from growers, thus bypassing both the local and the terminal markets. Wholesalers in secondary dispersion markets may also sell agricultural raw materials to small local manufacturers and processors.

Changes in traditional market structure

Over the past three to four decades, significant changes have occurred in the distribution patterns and market structures for agricultural products. A decentralization of markets, owing to the growth of regional markets, has reduced the dependence upon large central markets. Another significant change is that traditional markets are now being bypassed.

Several factors account for these shifting tides. Improved communication services make complete, up-to-the-minute market information available to farmers and middlemen throughout the country. Farmers can get price quotations from central markets and thus are in a better bargaining position locally. An improved, expanded highway network and the growth of a trucking industry offer farmers access to more distant and larger markets. Also, large-scale retailers often go directly to growers or to local or regional markets. Improvements in storage, grading, and handling facilities in local and regional markets have brought about many changes in market patterns. Another factor is the expansion of population into the South, the Southwest, and the West. As population centers grew in new areas, a new group of regional markets arose to meet the demand. Finally, the decentralization of manufacturing and processing industries using agricultural raw materials has lessened the dependence on the traditional terminal markets for many commodities.[2]

[2] For an analysis of some of the reasons for the transition from the old terminal market system to a highly decentralized one, see R. L. Kohls, "The Terminal Market Decline," in J. Howard Westing and Gerald Albaum (eds.), *Modern Marketing Thought*, The Macmillan Company, New York, 1964, pp. 384–387.

Middlemen in agricultural wholesaling

In the various wholesaling markets for agricultural goods there are many different types of buyers. Some are buyers for retail chains or institutions such as hotels; others are employed by processors or manufacturers. In addition, there is a wide variety of middlemen in these markets. These middlemen may be distinguished by the functions they perform, whether they take title to the goods they handle, the types of commodities in which they specialize, or their organizational structures.

Assemblers   In local and regional markets the dominant type of middlemen may be grouped under the title "assemblers." These firms are merchant wholesalers. Often they are local resident buyers who operate in only one local market. They also include representatives from middlemen in central markets, independent wholesalers who travel from one local market to another, and farmer-owned cooperative marketing associations. As their name implies, their chief function is to concentrate output from several farmers into a large economical shipping unit. This is in sharp contrast to the typical wholesaler of manufactured products, one of whose chief functions is to buy in large quantities from manufacturers and then bulk break or disperse merchandise in smaller quantities to retailers or industrial users. Assemblers usually can offer a farmer cash for his crop, basing the price on central market quotations. In general, local assemblers have established relationships with middlemen in central markets, so the local wholesalers have a ready market for the output. For many types of products, assemblers also provide grading, packing, and storage services.

Commission men and merchant wholesalers   In the marketing of many agricultural products such as fresh fruits and vegetables, grains, and livestock, a very important and widely used middleman in the large central markets is a commission merchant, also called a commission man or a commission house. The term "commission merchant" is actually a misnomer; this handler is really an agent middleman. In many transactions today, he does not take title to the commodities he handles.

The commission method of operation in central markets may be described briefly as follows. An assembler in a local market (possibly a local resident produce buyer or a grain elevator) consigns a shipment to a commission merchant in a central market. These firms usually have established working relationships over a period of years. The commission man meets a train or truck and takes charge of the shipment. It is his responsibility to handle and sell the goods. He arranges for any necessary storage, grading, and other services prior to the sale. He finds a buyer at the best possible price, makes the sale, and arranges for transfer of shipment. He deducts his commission, freight charges, and other marketing expenses and remits the balance as soon as possible to the local market shipper. In some cases, commission men extend credit to local shippers or make advance payments on carloads consigned to them.

Commission dealing was quite common in the past, particularly in the marketing of fresh fruits and vegetables. In years gone by, transportation facilities were poor, storage facilities were inadequate, grading standards meant little, and communication services were slow and insufficient. Consequently, commission men hesitated to accept the great risks of ownership, or if they did offer to buy carloads outright, their offering price was too low for the shippers. They preferred to accept the risks of commission selling.

During the past twenty to thirty years, however, commission dealings in fresh produce have declined. To an increasing extent, commission men are taking outright title to the goods they handle. Today it is not at all uncommon to find wholesale carlot receivers who act as commission men (agent middlemen) in some transactions and as merchant wholesalers in others. Three reasons underlie the decline in commission selling of fresh fruits and vegetables. First, many shippers lost faith in the system: some commission men abused their trust and shortchanged the shippers, taking advantage of the fact that shippers were far away and knew little about market conditions. Second, facilities for physical handling, storing, and shipping have improved so that losses from perishability are reduced. Finally, improved dissemination of market information means better data on prices and demand and supply in a given market.

Commission selling is still widespread in such commodities as grain and livestock; these products are not so perishable, and there is always a market for them. The key to the continued success of a commission merchant is his ability to sell at prices satisfactory to the shipper, to move the commodities quickly with minimum losses due to perishability, and to manage the commodities properly and in good faith. The organized systems of trading on commodity exchanges and the improved dissemination of information have reduced the likelihood of abuses.

Brokers   At all levels in agricultural marketing, brokers function much as they do in the marketing of manufactured goods. They bring buyer and seller together, acting as the agent for either party, but not *both*. Compared with commission men, brokers have less power and perform fewer services. In fact, one reason a buyer or seller uses brokers *is* that he wants to retain more control over the transaction.

Auctions   Auctions are used extensively in the distribution of fresh fruits, tobacco, and livestock. Auctioning is really a method of selling rather than a middleman operation. Fresh fruit auctions are usually held in central market locations; tobacco and livestock auctions are held in local or regional marketing centers. An auction company is a private firm. It provides facilities for storing and exhibiting commodities to be auctioned, it provides the auctioneer, and it arranges for a place to hold the auction. Ordinarily the auctioneer prepares a catalogue or some other listing of the quantities and grades of commodities to be sold.

In fresh fruit auctions, the sellers are usually independent assemblers in local markets or farmer-owned cooperative associations. The buyers are typically wholesalers in secondary dispersion markets or representatives from retail chains. In some cases, bidding will be done by brokers representing other buyers. In livestock and tobacco auctions, the sellers are usually independent farmers or farmer-owned cooperative associations, and the buyers are representatives from meat-packers or manufacturers of tobacco products.

Auctions offer the advantage of moving a large quantity of products in a short period of time. This feature is particularly attractive to sellers of highly perishable fruits. The bidding is open, so sources of supply and demand operate in free and open competition to set market prices. On the other hand, auction selling is expensive. Even though the actual sales commission may be only 2 per cent, the costs of receiving, storing, and exhibiting the products, plus the time spent by buyers and sellers in attending the auction, raise total expenses to a fairly high level. Open-market bidding can lead to extreme price fluctuations. Also, the sellers whose output is sold near the end of the auction probably get a lower price than those whose goods are sold in the early bidding.

Direct sale by producers

The great bulk of agricultural products still moves through wholesaling middlemen in local and central markets. At the same time, some farmers sell directly to industrial users and to retailers or consumers. Highly perishable fruits and vegetables frequently are sold by the growers directly to canners and other processors. In fact, to assure himself of a supply, a processor may contract for the entire output of several growers in an area. Producers of highly perishable items like this arrangement because they are assured of a ready market.

Growers of consumer products sometimes sell a share of their output directly to consumers on a door-to-door basis, in public markets, or at roadside stands. While the farmer gets a higher price, direct marketing is an extremely costly, risky, and inefficient method. A small share of consumer farm products is also sold directly to retailers in nearby communities.

PRICE DETERMINATION

Generally speaking, the individual producer of agricultural products has no control or influence over the price he receives for his output. For this reason, most of the pricing policies discussed in Chapters 19 and 20 are not pertinent to agricultural marketing.

In many respects the pricing of agricultural products reflects more closely the classical theoretical concept of perfect competition than does any other aspect of American marketing. In agricultural marketing, we find a large number of atomistic producers, a standardized product (after it is graded), reasonably complete market information, and in many instances a large number of buyers. Three factors destroy this classical model: often there is a limited number of buyers in a given market—especially local markets; there is not complete mobility of supply from one market to another; and, probably most important of all, governmental influences often completely upset price determination based upon the forces of supply and demand.

By individual producers

In some commodity fields, individual sellers have been able to exert some influence on the prices of their products by banding together in growers' cooperatives through which they control a larger segment of the total supply. In some instances, cooperatives have succeeded in differentiating their products to the point where they can engage in nonprice competition to some extent and thus have a bit more influence in price determination. These cooperative activities are discussed later in this chapter.

When a processor of fruits and vegetables contracts in advance of the growing season for the entire output of a farmer, prices are determined to a limited extent by the individual bargaining powers of the processor and the grower. For the bulk of such products as grains, fiber crops, and livestock, where the factor of perishability is not so critical, the real pricemaking forces are found in the organized commodity exchanges in the central markets. Even here, however, governmental influences on price determination are paramount.

Governmental influences on pricing of agricultural products

On and off over a period of several decades, the United States has had what is called a "farm problem." The problem may be manifested in various ways. For example, total farm income may be less than the rates in other major industries. Another aspect of the problem is that farm prices and farm income fluctuate violently at times. These fluctuations reflect the fact that periodically we produce a greater supply than the market is able to absorb. Usually a farmer can sell his entire output. His income is related directly and solely to price—either to the price he receives for his output or to the price he pays for input factors such as land, machinery, and fertilizer. When the free forces of supply and demand are allowed to work in an agricultural market, a farmer has virtually no control over the prices he receives for his product. Over a period of time, the general instability of these prices can be devastating to an individual producer and to the agricultural industry in general. Consequently, it has been considered in the national interest for the Federal government to step in.

Throughout the years, the Federal government has employed several different methods and programs in an effort to stabilize prices of agricultural products at a level high enough to ensure a favorable farm income and a healthy agricultural industry. One of the oldest of the governmental influences is the tariff industry. Tariffs exist on several agricultural products, thus tending to keep prices from being depressed by imports of low-cost, foreign-grown commodities. Another early, indirect governmental influence on pricing was a law (the Capper-Volstead Act of 1922) which allowed farmers to band together and operate a marketing cooperative association without being held in violation of the antitrust laws. In 1930 the Federal Farm Board was established, and one of its functions was to buy up surplus output—particularly wheat and cotton—in an attempt to hold prices at an adequately high level. This program failed for several reasons, one of which was that there were no controls over the amount which farmers could grow.

Another Federal farm program, started in 1933 under the Agricultural Adjustment Act (AAA), established the concept of production controls. Farmers were paid for *not* growing certain crops or raising some types of livestock. Another important government action with respect to pricing and production controls was the establishment of the Commodity Credit Corporation (CCC) in 1933. This agency has rather broad powers to buy, sell, and store many different commodities and to make loans to growers of these products.

The concept of parity was introduced in 1933 in the Agricultural Adjustment Act. Since that time, this concept has permeated many of the government programs designed to influence and stabilize farm prices. With respect to agricultural marketing, *parity* may be defined as the price-level relationship whereby the prices which farmers receive give them a purchasing power equal to that which they had during a stated base period. Thus if a perfect, or 100 per cent, parity relationship exists, a farmer today, with the price he receives from the sale of 100 bushels of wheat, can buy as much fertilizer, seed, clothing, land, and other items as a farmer during the base period. If the price of what he purchases goes up, then the price for his crop must also go up if parity is to be maintained. Parity pricing refers to prices of units of output (bushels, bales, etc.) and not to total income. Therefore, even if 100 per cent parity were maintained, a farmer's purchasing power could still decline if his total output declined.

In the legislation on this matter, the years from 1909 to 1914 were selected as the base period. Many critics feel that these years do not represent a period of "normal" relationships between farm prices and general price levels. These were halcyon days for farmers in that the prices they received were extraordinarily high in relation to the cost of the items they purchased. It seems unrealistic and possibly unfair to the economy in general to base a parity relationship on a period of abnormal prosperity for one segment of the economy.

Various Federal laws have been passed to support prices at a certain percentage of parity. Price supports are mandatory for six basic commodities (wheat, corn, tobacco, cotton, rice, and peanuts) plus a few others. In addition, price supports may be established for another small group of products if certain conditions are met. The number of commodities supported by parity pricing is smaller today than in the 1940s, when encouragement was needed to expand output. From about 1941 to 1954, the prescribed level of support for the basic commodities was, in general, set rigidly at 90 per cent of parity. Since 1954, prices have been supported on a more flexible basis, with levels ranging from 75 to 90 per cent of parity. Usually price support measures are accompanied by requirements for acreage reductions.

The practical implementation of parity pricing is effected through the loaning powers of the Commodity Credit Corporation. If the market price is *above* the prescribed support level—say 85 per cent of parity—the grower will sell on the open market. If the market price is *below* the support level, then the grower can get a nonrecourse loan on his crop from the Commodity Credit Corporation. The loan will be for an amount equivalent to the support price times the number of units of output. As collateral, the farmer turns over his crop to the CCC for storage. If the market price later rises above the support level, the farmer can redeem his crop, sell it, and pay off his loan. Ordinarily the price does not rise enough to induce the farmer to redeem his crop. The CCC-stored surpluses just continue to mount.

Besides parity pricing, other noteworthy measures are used by the government to support prices on agricultural commodities. One such method is the outright purchase of certain perishable items such as butter, eggs, cheese, and beef when the market price drops below a certain level. Purchases are made from processors or middlemen, not directly from growers. The CCC disposes of these surpluses through welfare agencies, school lunch programs, foreign aid programs, and similar ventures. If the domestic open-market price rises sufficiently, the surpluses are sold through regular marketing channels. Another price-control measure is illustrated by the Federal marketing agreement for fluid milk. In a market where interstate commerce is involved, if two-thirds of the milk producers request it, the Department of Agriculture will intercede and fix the prices which farmers will receive when they sell their milk in this market. Many such Federal milk-marketing agreements are already in effect, and they account for a substantial share of the milk sold in this country. Another set of governmental influences limits production by reducing the number of acres planted. A "soil bank" plan was put into effect in 1956 in order to conserve agricultural land and to curtail acreage planted in certain crops.

In this section we have simply described some of the measures designed to handle the "farm problem." It is not within the scope of this book to evaluate these measures in detail from a social, political, or marketing point of view.[3]

---

[3] For a careful analysis of the problem with some suggestions for the future, see *Toward a Realistic Farm Program,* Committee for Economic Development, New York, 1958. This report was prepared by the Program Committee of the Research and Policy Committee of the CED.

PROMOTIONAL PROGRAM

In general, the promotional efforts discussed in Chapters 21 to 23 are not relevant to individual producers of agricultural goods. Owing to the nature of the product (it is not differentiated) and the nature of the seller (he is small and is essentially a producer, not a marketer), very little personal selling or advertising is done in agricultural marketing.

What little promotion there is applies almost wholly to consumer products. In some instances, producers of industrial raw materials, such as wool, which are used to manufacture consumer products will advertise to consumers urging them to buy products made from the raw material. This type of industrial promotion is ordinarily best used when the derived demand for the raw materials can be increased within a short-run period. For instance, if there were a major increase in the sale of woolen products, the wool growers would feel the pleasant effects within a year.

In the field of agricultural consumer products, there have been some notably successful efforts in product differentiation and, consequently, in advertising and other forms of nonprice competition. Usually the work is done by an organization representing a group of producers. In some cases the organization is an individual farmer-owned cooperative. First, the group differentiates its product by establishing a brand name for it. High standards are set, and the products are carefully graded. The cooperative usually insists that only the part of the output which meets these high standards will be allowed to carry the brand. Then, through an excellent advertising program, the brand is promoted. Some well-known examples are Sunkist oranges and lemons, Land O' Lakes dairy products, Tillamook cheese, Diamond walnuts, Calavo avocados, and Eatmor cranberries.

In order to stimulate primary demand—the demand for a class of agricultural products rather than one brand—products may be advertised by state government commissions (Washington State Apple Commission), by groups of cooperatives (National Wool Growers Association), or by processors of the raw materials (American Meat Institute).[4]

---

[4] For reports on some recent experiences with agricultural promotion programs, see Joel Wolfson, "Planning and Executing an Effective Agricultural Promotion Program," *Journal of Marketing*, January, 1965, pp. 33–36; and in William S. Decker (ed.), *Emerging Concepts in Marketing,* American Marketing Association, Chicago, 1963, see S. Watson Dunn, "Product and Market Characteristics Conducive to Successful [Agricultural] Promotion," pp. 491–501; Gerald C. Quackenbush, "Responsiveness of Dairy Product Sales to Promotional Effort," pp. 505–513; and Peter L. Henderson, "Response of Lamb Sales to Promotion," pp. 517–531.

For an example of controlled experiments conducted by the U.S. Department of Agriculture to measure the sales effects of advertising, see William S. Hoofnagle, "The Effectiveness of Advertising for Farm Products," *Journal of Advertising Research,* December, 1963, pp. 2–6.

AGRICULTURAL PRODUCERS' COOPERATIVES

Farmers have long recognized the problems and limitations they face when operating as individual enterprises. They have discovered that they can improve their competitive position by joining together in organizations through which they can market or process their combined output and purchase their equipment and supplies. These farmer organizations are known as farmer cooperatives, agricultural marketing cooperatives, or cooperative marketing associations. Sometimes they replace existing private middlemen or processors who have been doing the job; in other cases they provide facilities where none had previously existed. Agricultural cooperatives are member-owned, but they are usually managed and operated by hired executive specialists and office help.

In general, modern-day agricultural cooperatives operate according to the basic principles of cooperation formally established and developed over one hundred years ago by a group of weavers in Rochdale, England. Agricultural cooperatives are established to benefit the producers, however, whereas the Rochdale plan was designed to further the interests of consumers. Some of these principles of cooperation are as follows:

1. Membership is open to any interested party. From a practical standpoint, in a producers' cooperative a member ordinarily is a grower of the commodity being marketed or processed by the cooperative.
2. Each member gets one vote regardless of how many shares of stock he owns in the organization.
3. The products are sold at market prices.
4. Profits are distributed according to the amount of business a member does with or through the cooperative. Profits are *not* distributed in relation to the number of shares of stock owned. Instead, the interest paid on invested capital is limited by the rules of the organization. The rate is nominal, usually about 5 per cent.
5. A considerable amount of time, money, and manpower is spent in educational effort and missionary work to "spread the cooperative gospel."

Producers' cooperatives are found in the insurance, irrigation, electric power, and telephone industries, as well as in others, but they are particularly important in agriculture. Agricultural cooperatives exist throughout the country, but they tend to be more heavily concentrated in the North Central and Pacific Coast states. In terms of sales volume by types of commodities, cooperatives play a significant role in the marketing of grains, dairy products, livestock, and various fruits and vegetables.

Primary objective and paths to that goal

The primary goal of a producers' association is to maximize the income of its members. The fine growth of the agricultural cooperative movement, as measured by the increases in sales volume over the past thirty years or so, is indicative of the extent to which this goal has been reached successfully. An analysis of the paths used by the cooperatives to reach this main target will give some insight into the operating methods and philosophies of these associations.

Orderly marketing   This concept involves the gradual distribution of an association's combined output to carefully selected markets on a planned basis. The entire output is not dumped at random into various markets at harvesttime. Carried on properly and with some degree of social conscience, orderly marketing can benefit both producers and consumers. Its value becomes doubtful, however, when it is used to secure control over the seasonal supply of a product and then to market it at a monopoly price. This seldom happens because it is virtually impossible to control the entire supply.

Improved bargaining position of seller   Ordinarily, if a great number of producers of a certain product join together to market their output, their combined forces place them in a much better bargaining position with respect to price determination than if each grower had marketed his output independently.

Pooling   The process of pooling is an adjunct to orderly marketing and improved bargaining. Pooling is the system by which the cooperative determines the unit price to be received by its members for their crops. Each member brings his crop to the cooperative as soon as it is harvested. Thus the association will be receiving the output of various members throughout a harvest season. During this same period the cooperative will be selling the output through regular channels on an orderly basis. A part of the total output may be sold each day, and conceivably a different price may be received for each sale. The cooperative pools the receipts from all the sales. By dividing the total receipts by the total number of units shipped, it determines the unit selling price. Each member is credited with that unit price times the number of units sold through the association. Usually adjustments are made for differences in the grades of the product sold.

Elimination of trade abuses   Another by-product of the large-scale operation and bargaining strength of cooperatives has been the elimination of various trade abuses formerly suffered by individual farmers at the hands of middlemen and processors who were able to control the bargaining process.

Improved standardization and grading   Cooperatives generally are credited with improving the standards for the products they handle. Strict adherence to a set of standards and improvements in grading have enabled the associations to sell a better quality of products and thus to receive higher prices. One reason associations have been able to upgrade product quality is that they have helped to improve production methods and to make production more efficient.

Demand stimulation   As noted earlier in connection with promotion, agricultural cooperatives are largely responsible for what little product differentiation and accompanying advertising there are in the field of agricultural marketing.

Provision for vertical integration   By assuming roles formerly held by middlemen in local and central markets, cooperatives have eliminated the profits of these firms. The functions of these middlemen have not been eliminated, but the cooperatives have been able to do the total job more efficiently and more economically. In dairy products, food freezing, food canning, and other fields, cooperatives operate their own processing plants.

Purchasing supplies and equipment   The marketing cooperative itself may purchase supplies and equipment directly, or a purchasing association may be formed in connection with a marketing cooperative. In still other instances, the grower, as a member of a cooperative, is able to buy his machinery, seed, fertilizer, and other production equipment and supplies at a much lower price than if he dealt individually and directly with local retail outlets.

Organizational structure

It is customary to classify producers' cooperatives as local, federated, or centralized associations. The *local* associations were the earliest cooperatives, and today they account for about 90 per cent of the total. Local organizations usually operate in local wholesaling markets and perform functions associated with these markets. Some examples of local cooperatives are grain elevator companies, creameries, livestock shipping associations, and fruit growers' associations.

A *federated* cooperative is an association of local cooperatives. By banding together, they control a larger share of the crop in a region. A federated cooperative can provide many services, such as advertising, better grading and packing facilities, transportation arrangements, settlement of freight claims, orderly marketing over a wider area, marketing research, finding new markets, finding new uses for products, etc. The organizational control rests with the local associations. The authority moves from the bottom up, so to speak. Some well-known examples of federated cooperatives are Sunkist, Inc., Land O' Lakes Creameries, Inc., and Diamond Walnut Growers, Inc.

A *centralized* cooperative is a large organization, sometimes covering regions in more than one state. The authority and control rest in a central group, not at the local level. A centralized association may result from a consolidation of existing local groups. In other cases, the entire centralized association may have been aggressively organized by a small group of producers. Centralized and federated cooperatives provide essentially the same services. The Sun Maid Raisin Growers Association, the Washington Farmers Cooperative, and the California Almond Exchange are a few examples of centralized groups.

Management problems

Probably the greatest problem or competitive limitation faced by agricultural cooperatives has been their traditional inability to recognize the importance of good management. They have been unable to attract and keep good executives largely because they are unwilling to pay enough or grant sufficient authority to the managers. Apparently, the farmer is unable to feel that anyone can perform a service or be worth a high salary unless he creates form utility. Also, 8 A.M. to 5 P.M. office hours seem to run counter to the farmer's concept of a day's work.

Another basic problem in agricultural cooperative associations is the traditional independence of farmers in the United States. They seem not to be imbued with the true spirit of cooperation that apparently is found in Scandinavia and in other countries. In fact, it is interesting to note that in one region where cooperatives have thrived in the North Central states, there are concentrations of farmers of Scandinavian descent.

Many farmers are in a cooperative only for economic gain; there are no social or cultural attachments. If a farmer does not do as well financially as he thinks he should, he is likely to drop out. Also, many growers are not happy with the system of pooling receipts. Those who sell their crops early in the season when prices are high are especially inclined to feel that they suffer from the pooling system. On balance, a cooperative's chance for continued success lies in its ability to justify its existence on an economic basis. It will survive only so long as its members believe they are doing better by working through the cooperative than they could individually.

Fundamentally, the marketing of agricultural products is not different from the marketing of manufactured goods. In the past, however, people in the agricultural industry devoted their attention almost entirely to problems of pricing and channels of distribution. In fact it often appeared as if they equated marketing with the physical flow of commodities. Little attention was given to product-planning and promotional activities. Let us hope that in the future the people concerned with marketing agricultural goods will come to appreciate the full scope of marketing and recognize its applications to their field. Instead of simply urging people to "eat more beef" or "drink more milk —it's good for you," they should base their promotional efforts on market studies of buying motives, usage patterns, opportunities for innovation, etc. Consumers must be shown specifically *how* and *why* they should eat more beef or drink more milk.

The traditional attitude toward marketing in agricultural production may be overcome by *group* activity. The successful efforts of Sunkist, Inc., formerly the California Fruit Growers Exchange, show what can be done by groups which are truly marketing-oriented. This cooperative took the orange—a non-differentiated product which was once considered a Christmas luxury item—and made it an everyday household necessity by developing new uses, branding the product, maintaining consistent quality standards for the brand, developing packaging, improving physical distribution, and using good advertising and sales promotion.

QUESTIONS AND PROBLEMS

1. As far as the marketing implications are concerned, in what respects does agricultural production differ from manufacturing activity?

2. In which of the subclassifications of industrial products would you categorize agricultural products?

3. Name some brands of agricultural products. What other agricultural products offer real possibilities for product differentiation?

4. Cite some examples of good and poor packaging of agricultural products. What agricultural consumer products now ordinarily sold in bulk form offer real possibilities for packaging?

5. How do you reconcile (a) the trend toward packaging of agricultural consumer goods and (b) the buying habit of squeezing, pinching, or just generally feeling the product?

6. Why are local markets so important in the marketing of agricultural products?

7. Select one or two types of fresh produce sold in a local store and trace the channels for these products. If necessary, interview local retailers and, if possible, a nearby wholesaler.

8. "Central markets are used almost entirely for the distribution of agricultural consumer goods. Industrial products from the farms tend to bypass these markets." Do you agree? Explain, using examples of specific commodities.

9. Explain some of the changes which have occurred in the channels for agricultural products and point out the reasons for the changes.

10. What factors should a fruit grower consider when trying to decide whether to market his crop through a local cash buyer or a local cooperative association?

11. To what extent are governmental influences operative in the pricing of agricultural products grown in your part of the country?

12. Describe the role of the Commodity Credit Corporation in the pricing of farm commodities.

13. How is the pricing of farm products related to warehousing activities?

14. "Some people criticize the efforts to promote farm goods on the ground that the programs have been conducted by agriculturalists rather than marketing men. The program should be based on an analysis of buying habits, consumer motivation, possibilities for product innovation, and new uses for present products. Product benefits should be stressed more." Comment on this opinion; if possible, relate it to specific farm commodities.

15 In what respects does a producers' cooperative differ from a corporation?

16 "Orderly marketing is just another term for monopolistic control of the product's supply." Discuss.

17 Why is it that members of a manufacturers' trade association do not get together and engage in orderly marketing? Is it socially desirable to allow farmers to engage in practices which are considered in restraint of trade when done by a group of manufacturers?

18 Why do some of the members of a cooperative object to the practice of pooling?

26

INTERNATIONAL MARKETING

"More than ever before the economic future of the United States is vested in the marketing process—and future American progress will be determined largely by marketing management's success on the new frontier —the world market."[1] The president of a large manufacturer of business machines (Burroughs) concluded these remarks on our future economic growth with the observation that ". . . international marketing is the number-one problem of our time, the number-one challenge, and the number-one opportunity." While some people may believe that these are overstatements of the position of international marketing, we cannot deny the fact that multinational companies are evolving in our socioeconomic system, as firms integrate their domestic and foreign operations into world enterprises.

Basically, marketing fundamentals are universally applicable. Whether a firm sells

[1] Ray R. Eppert, "Passport for Marketing Overseas," *Journal of Marketing,* April, 1965, p. 6.

in Toledo or Timbuktu, its marketing program should be built around a good product or service properly priced, promoted, and distributed to a market which has been carefully analyzed. We devote a separate chapter to international marketing, however, because there are considerable differences in the strategic and tactical implementation of marketing programs for foreign as against domestic markets. These modifications become necessary because of the environmental differences which exist among and within the many nations. This diversity of environments intensifies the risks, complexities, and uncertainties in the tasks facing the marketing executives of a world enterprise.

A company operates its marketing program within the economic, political, and cultural environment of each of its markets—foreign and domestic—and none of these environments is controllable by the firm. Consequently, an executive should try to understand this environment and anticipate its effect on his marketing program. What complicates this task in international marketing is the fact that the environment—particularly the cultural environment—often consists of elements very unfamiliar to, and perhaps not even recognized by, the marketing executives.[2] Further complicating the situation is the tendency for a person unconsciously to use his own cultural values as a frame of reference for solving problems centered in a foreign environment. This "self-reference criterion" has been called the root cause of many international business problems.[3]

IMPORTANCE OF INTERNATIONAL MARKETING

Among companies in the United States, there seems to be a growing awareness of international marketing opportunities and an increasing willingness to enter foreign markets. As domestic markets become saturated, American producers —even those with no previous international experience—now look to foreign markets as outlets for surplus productive capacity and as sources of wider profit margins and higher returns on investments.

The world market—huge and expanding—often offers greater growth and profit opportunities than the domestic market. The indication of continued increases in population, buying power, gross national product, and capital investment in many foreign nations makes it almost inevitable that these countries will constitute profitable growth markets (as well as strong competition) for many consumer and industrial products. Let us consider just a few examples. The gross national product in Western Europe increased 77 per cent between 1958 (the year the Common Market was created) and 1965, while that of the

---

[2] For an expansion of this thesis and a more complete treatment of international marketing using the environmental approach, see John M. Hess and Philip R. Cateora, *International Marketing,* Richard D. Irwin, Inc., Homewood, Ill., 1966.

[3] James A. Lee, "Cultural Analysis in Overseas Operations," *Harvard Business Review,* March–April, 1966, pp. 106–114. This article proposes a systematic four-step framework designed to reduce the influence of the self-reference criterion.

table   26–1

Value of some leading commodity-group exports as percentage of domestic output, 1963

Percentage of domestic output (by value) exported			
30 per cent or more		*20 to 29 per cent*	
Leaf tobacco	30	Pulp mill products	20
Construction and mining equipment	31	Cotton farm products	21
Sulfur	34	Machine tools	22
Sewing machines	34	Textile machinery	22
Milled rice	43	Cash grains	24
Molybdenum	43	Metalworking machinery	24
Grease and tallow	46	Carbon black	24
		Oil field machinery	25
		Refined copper	28
		Anthracite coal	28
		Phosphate rock	28

SOURCE: *U.S. Commodity Exports and Imports as Related to Output: 1963 and 1962,* U.S. Bureau of the Census, 1966, p. 120.

United States rose only 51 per cent during the same period. During the decade of the 1960s, the population of Western Europe is expected to increase only 9 per cent, while the overall gross national product should rise 70 per cent. The net result will be rising living standards and a larger potential market for consumer and industrial goods. Japan and Latin America present the same general picture. Africa is largely an emerging market with real growth prospects.

Sales in foreign markets are a significant part of the lifeblood of many American industries. For example, 31 per cent (by value) of the domestic output of construction and mining equipment is sold outside the United States. A comparable percentage for leaf tobacco is 30; for molybdenum, 43; and for textile machinery, 22. Table 26–1 lists these and other products where 20 per cent or more of the domestic output is exported. A much longer list would be needed to itemize the industries where 10 to 19 per cent of the domestic output is marketed outside the United States.

Generally speaking, the foreign assets, the foreign sales volume, and often the foreign profits of United States companies are rising more rapidly than their domestic counterparts. These are some of the conclusions arrived at in a research study covering the international activities of 100 large American corporations from 1950 to 1960.[4] In 1950, one half of these companies had more than 5 per cent of their total capital in foreign assets. By 1960, this ratio had doubled; that is, the median firm had 10 per cent of its assets invested abroad (Fig. 26–1). In 1950, only one out of ten companies in this study had

[4] See *International Enterprise: A New Dimension of American Business,* McKinsey and Company, Inc., New York, 1962.

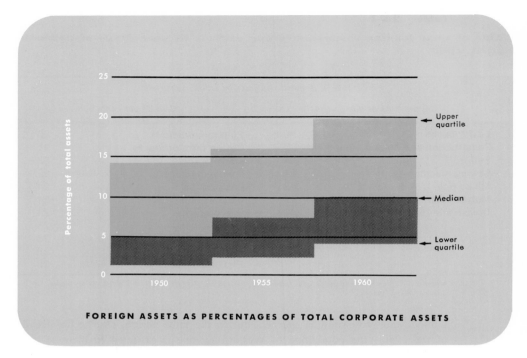

FOREIGN ASSETS AS PERCENTAGES OF TOTAL CORPORATE ASSETS

fig. 26–1

Between 1950 and 1960, the median firm doubled the percentage of its foreign assets as related to its total investment. In 1960, one-quarter of these firms had more than 20 per cent of their assets invested abroad.

SOURCE: McKinsey and Company, Inc., New York.

as much as 20 per cent of its assets committed to foreign operations; by 1960, the foreign assets in one out of four companies had passed the 20 per cent level (Fig. 26–2).

The picture is much the same when foreign sales are compared with domestic sales; foreign sales are growing at a much more rapid rate. In 1950, half the companies were getting less than 7 per cent of total sales from foreign sources; by 1960, this median figure had risen to 12 per cent (Fig. 26–3). In 1950, only one out of five firms derived at least 20 per cent of its sales revenues from foreign markets. By 1960, however, one out of three firms was in the over–20 per cent bracket (Fig. 26–4).

International marketing is a two-way street, however. The same expanding foreign markets which offer fine growth opportunities for American firms also have their own producers who, in turn, are providing substantial and intensive competition both in the United States and abroad. American consumers have responded favorably, for example, to Japanese radio-TV products (Sony) and

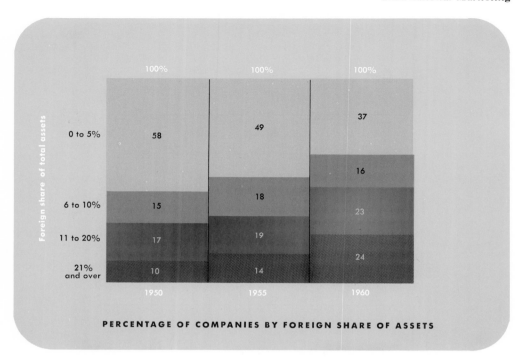

fig. 26–2

In 1960, only 37 per cent of the companies had less than 5 per cent of their assets invested abroad. Note the rise (from 10 to 24 per cent) in firms where foreign assets account for at least one-fifth of the total.

SOURCE: McKinsey and Company, Inc., New York.

motorcycles (Honda), to Italian clothes and sewing machines (Necchi), to German cameras (Leica) and autos (Volkswagen), and to Dutch petroleum products (Shell) and electric razors (Norelco). Especially strong competition is coming from Japan and the countries in the European Economic Community (EEC), more popularly known as the European Common Market. This is a group of six Western European nations (Belgium, France, Italy, Luxembourg, the Netherlands, and West Germany) which have banded together in a multinational economic union. Ultimately, tariffs and other trade barriers will be erected around it. Competitive challenges are also being encountered from the member units of other multinational economic organizations such as the European Free Trade Association (EFTA—Austria, Denmark, Norway, Portugal, Sweden, Switzerland, and the United Kingdom), the Latin American Free Trade Association (LAFTA), and even the Council for Mutual Economic Assistance (COMECON—Russia and other Communist European nations).

In summary, it seems likely that the factors of surplus productive capacity,

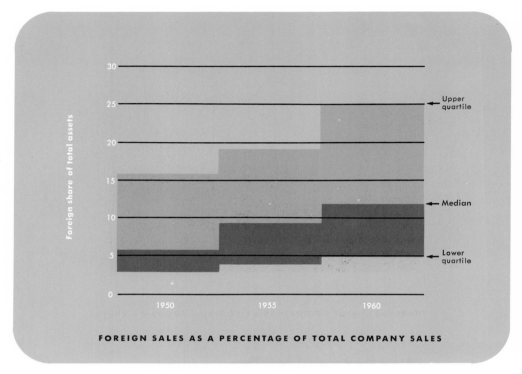

FOREIGN SALES AS A PERCENTAGE OF TOTAL COMPANY SALES

fig. 26–3

In the median firm in one out of four companies foreign sales as a share of the total rose from 7 to 12 per cent. In 1960, foreign sales exceeded 25 per cent of total revenues.
SOURCE: McKinsey and Company, Inc., New York.

shrinking domestic profit margins, and intensified foreign competition—added to the lure of rapidly expanding, attractive foreign markets—are combining to encourage (and even force) American firms to devote more effort to the vigorous development of their international marketing programs.

STRUCTURE AND EVOLUTION OF MULTINATIONAL OPERATIONS

Once a company has elected to market part of its output in a foreign country, management must soon decide which organizational structure will be employed to implement this international venture. Any of several alternative structures, each with its relative merits and limitations, may be used.[5] In part, the choice

[5] For an analysis of five such structures, with the advantages and disadvantages of each, see "Which Way to the Common Market, Please?" *Sales Management*, May 18, 1962, p. 56.

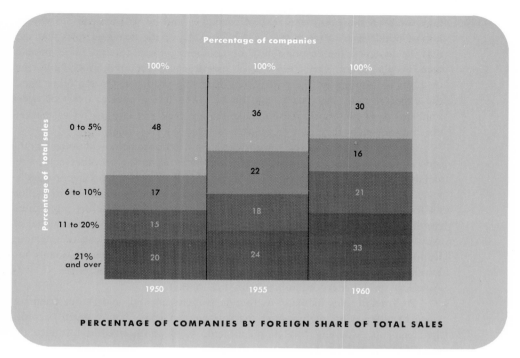

Percentage of companies

PERCENTAGE OF COMPANIES BY FOREIGN SHARE OF TOTAL SALES

fig. 26—1

Note the increase in what we may call "international companies," that is, firms in which more than 20 per cent of sales revenues come from foreign sources.

SOURCE: McKinsey and Company, Inc., New York.

depends upon whether the international arm is intended to remain as a secondary appendage to the domestic body of the business, or whether management is interested eventually in developing a fully integrated world marketing enterprise. A company may go through five reasonably well-defined stages as it evolves into a truly multinational firm.

A company may progress in an orderly manner through one evolutionary stage at a time, or management may bypass some stages. The same firm may be in any or all stages at the same time. Depending upon the company's familiarity with a given foreign market, the maturity of economic development in the foreign nation, and the country's political stability, a company may export products to one country, establish a licensing arrangement in another, and build a manufacturing plant in a third.

In the first stage, the company *exports through foreign trade agent middlemen.* Management's effort in the exporting venture may be somewhat sporadic —up when there are excess inventory stocks to be marketed, and down when the domestic market can assimilate the manufacturing output. The company may establish the position of export manager, and he will use various export-import middlemen to reach the foreign markets; or the domestic sales manager may be assigned the responsibility of contacting these foreign trade middlemen. At this point, very little risk or investment is required. Also, little time or effort is required on the part of the exporting producer. On the other hand, the exporter must pay tariffs, and he has little or no control over his agent middlemen. Furthermore, these middlemen are generally not aggressive marketers, and normally they do not generate a large sales volume.

To counteract some of these deficiencies, management will move to the second stage—*exporting through company sales branches* or other sales subsidiaries located in foreign markets. Bypassing the export-import agent middlemen enables a company to promote its products more aggressively, to exploit its foreign markets more effectively, and to control its sales effort more completely. Of course, the firm is still exporting, with the attendant drawbacks. Also, management now has the time- and money-consuming task of selecting, training, and otherwise managing a sales force of (1) foreign nationals unfamiliar with the product and the company's marketing practices or (2) American middlemen unfamiliar with the market.

As foreign sales increase, as foreign markets expand, and as our company gains experience in international marketing, management may enter *licensing* arrangements, whereby foreign manufacturers are authorized to produce the articles. In this third stage, the company's major effort is usually still domestic production for the domestic market. The foreign licensing, however, does commit productive capacity and technical know-how on a regular basis to the foreign markets. To distribute this foreign-produced output, the company may still rely on foreign trade middlemen, or the company's own sales branches or subsidiaries may be established in major foreign markets.

Licensing offers a manufacturer a flexible arrangement with a minimum investment whereby he can still enjoy the advantages of his patents, research, and know-how. Through licensing, he can enter a market which might otherwise be closed to him as an exporter because of exchange restrictions, import quotas, or prohibitive tariffs. At the same time, by licensing, a manufacturer may be building a future competitor who will learn all he can from the manufacturer and then proceed independently when the licensing agreement expires.

In the fourth stage, the company moves to build or otherwise acquire its own production facilities in foreign countries. The structure may be a *joint venture or a wholly owned foreign subsidiary*. A joint venture is a partnership arrangement wherein the foreign manufacturing or marketing operation is owned in part by the American company and in part by the local foreign nationals (company or individuals) of the country involved. Share of foreign ownership may be any percentage—more than, less than, or exactly 50 per cent. Obviously, when controlling interest in a joint venture is owned by the foreign nationals, the American firm has no real control over any of the marketing or production activities; decision-making authority accompanies ownership control. At the same time, a joint venture may be the only structure (other than licensing) through which an American firm can enter a given foreign market. Nationalistic tendencies in the form of exchange restrictions, tariffs, or plain political exclusion of foreign-owned companies may preclude any operation other than a joint venture or one in which there is a licensing arrangement.

Wholly owned manufacturing and marketing subsidiaries in foreign markets are commonly found in companies which have evolved to an advanced stage of international business. Even then, however, this international division is typically still separate from, and second in importance to, the domestic operations. With a wholly owned foreign subsidiary, a company has maximum control over its marketing program and production operations. Some countries offer tax holidays or other incentives to attract American subsidiaries. This type of international structure, however, requires a substantial investment of money, manpower, and managerial attention. Thus, a large-volume operation is usually needed to justify the investment. As noted earlier, nationalistic tendencies on the part of foreign governments may preclude this type of structure. Also, organizational and personnel problems may arise when there is an attempt to coordinate the international and domestic divisions.

This leads us to the final evolutionary stage—and one reached by very few companies as yet—the emergence of the truly *world enterprise*. Both foreign and domestic operations are integrated and no longer separately identified. In this type of multinational venture, one plant may be in Bombay, a second in Brussels, and a third in Boston. The regional sales office in Atlanta is basically the same as the one in Athens (Greece, not Georgia).

While only a few companies may be world enterprises, certainly the bulk of the international business is done by firms which have progressed beyond the export stage. In 1960, about two-thirds of all foreign sales by United States firms came from products manufactured abroad; by 1970, it is forecasted that over three-quarters of our total foreign sales will come from operations in foreign countries.[6]

PROBLEMS IN DEVELOPING AN INTERNATIONAL COMPANY

A company interested in setting up an international marketing organization should recognize that it faces significantly greater risks and uncertainties than it does when this task is performed at home. In the domestic market, company management is usually more familiar with the environment—and politically and economically this environment is usually more stable. Executives are acquainted with the institutional structure for distribution; their experience is an aid in forecasting competitive strategies; and their marketing intelligence provides a relatively high level of knowledge concerning consumer motives and habits.

[6] *The Emerging World Enterprise*, Booz, Allen & Hamilton, Inc., New York, 1962, p. 5.

The problems confronting executives who are developing an international marketing enterprise come from two sources: conditions external to the firm and conditions arising from internal management situations.

External problem conditions

Aspects of *exchange controls and other currency regulations* constitute a major problem to consider when expanding into a foreign market.[7] Many nations set limits on the amount of earned or invested funds which may be withdrawn from the country. These exchange controls may be established because the country has a balance-of-payments problem or a shortage of foreign exchange. Limits may also be set in order to prevent the flight of domestic capital, to protect local industry, or to aid in the socialization of the economy.

Tariffs, import quotas, and other import restrictions are a problem area hindering international business. While these limits are established to stimulate national self-sufficiency and to encourage the development of domestic enterprise, the net result is still a significant obstacle to transnational operations. In some countries, the *political uncertainty* occasioned by social unrest, forthcoming elections, recent or impending independence, extreme programs, and even armed conflict is a deterrent. Sometimes high tax levels, tax discrimination, or other *unsatisfactory tax conditions* in a country will discourage foreign business activity. Another impediment is some form of *restriction on foreign companies and/or personnel.* Perhaps a nation requires that executives and other personnel of a foreign firm operating within the country be local citizens or that majority ownership be held by nationals of the country. *Labor problems* —strong unions, shortages of qualified personnel, required profit sharing, limits on a firm's authority to reduce the work force by layoffs—all act as an obstacle to foreign expansion.

Internal management problems

Notwithstanding the substantial external roadblocks just reviewed, it was the consensus from one study that companies experience a greater incidence of *internal,* rather than external, problems in the management of an international business.[8] The major internal problem reported was *orientation,* that is, the problem of getting the top executives to manage the firm as a single, integrated world enterprise rather than thinking and acting in terms of a domestic company with a separate international division. *Organization* was a second, and perhaps corollary, problem area. Organizational difficulties arise when the international division is appended to the domestic operations, instead of the two being integrated. When established separately, the international operation

[7] For a report on this and other problems experienced by companies from twelve nations which invested in eighty-eight countries, see *Obstacles and Incentives to Private Foreign Investment: 1962–1964,* National Industrial Conference Board, Inc., Studies in Business Policy, no. 115, New York, 1965.

[8] This section is adapted from *The Emerging World Enterprise,* pp. 13–15.

tends to be isolated and top management accords it stepchild status. This leads to another problem—*staffing*. Failure to organize as an integrated world company leads to a failure to develop truly international executives. Another staffing consideration is the difficulty of selecting and training foreign nationals for executive and lower-level jobs. Companies reported problems in *coordinating* the various foreign and domestic departments. Finally, in the area of managerial control, questions arise as to whether *control* of operations should be centralized in corporate headquarters or whether, and to what extent, it should be vested in decentralized foreign locations. There seems to be a tendency to centralize the control of financial, legal, and research activities, while permitting local control of marketing, production, personnel, and purchasing functions.

DEVELOPING AN INTERNATIONAL MARKETING PROGRAM

Firms which have been eminently successful in marketing in the United States have no assurance whatsoever that the same pattern will be duplicated in foreign markets. Some companies, successful at home, have been able to repeat these results abroad; other equally successful domestic marketers, however, have had the opposite experience in international marketing. A key to satisfactory performance overseas lies in gauging which aspects of American marketing techniques and know-how should be retained, which ones adapted, and which ones abandoned in foreign markets.

One analysis of the experiences of American firms successful in multinational marketing identified some basic concepts around which these companies built their marketing programs.[9] First, outstanding marketers have learned to export their approach to decision making—their analytical marketing techniques—rather than their domestic marketing practices. The ability to identify a problem, analyze it, and select the best alternative is the American firm's differential advantage. A specific marketing practice may be useless abroad, but the analytical technique for developing this practice is universally exportable. The successful marketer also realizes that each foreign country, and even sections within a country, usually have environmental and cultural differences which can affect virtually every aspect of his marketing program. Finally, a successful company is sensitive to the differences in its competitive position at home and abroad, and will change its marketing policies and strategies accordingly. A company which enjoys 30 per cent of the American market for a product will need a different marketing program in a foreign country where it is fighting for a 3 per cent share of market.

International marketing research

As important as a continuing marketing-intelligence system may be in the domestic market, it would seem to be even more essential in foreign markets

---

[9] *International Enterprise: A New Dimension of American Business,* McKinsey and Company, Inc., New York, 1962, pp. 18–19.

because the risks and uncertainties are so much greater. Actual practice is to the contrary, however. Only limited facilities and modest funds are invested in marketing research in foreign countries as compared with expenditures in the United States. The several reasons advanced to account for this disparity can perhaps be distilled into one basic point. Because of the differences in the problems encountered in foreign as against domestic marketing research, the costs relative to the value received are greater abroad than at home. Consider just two illustrations of this point.[10] Each of the many heterogeneous foreign markets is usually quite a bit smaller than the domestic market. Yet, when conducting a research study which involves sampling in these smaller markets, the sample size needed to ensure statistical validity and reliability does not decrease in proportion to the market size. Consequently, the cost of the research project, relative to market size, is greater for the smaller markets. As another example, consider the many types of market information (population, buying power, government regulations, weather data, etc.) which are readily and inexpensively available in the United States, but which must be collected at some cost in each foreign market. Consequently, less research funds are available for sample surveys and other more sophisticated research projects considered quite commonplace in domestic marketing research.

The extent of use of foreign marketing research and the nature of the facilities seem to vary somewhat in relation to the level of economic development achieved in the country. Apparently, marketing research is not used to any extent in underdeveloped countries, whereas considerable and sometimes very sophisticated use is made of this tool in countries with advanced economies.[11]

To understand the nature and problems of research in international marketing, an executive should try to understand how the environmental conditions in each foreign market affect the following four basic elements of research: systematic analysis, customer information, statistical data, and operational economy.[12] Fundamental to marketing research is the idea that problems should be solved and decisions made in a *systematic, analytical manner.* Unfortunately, an orderly, rational approach runs counter to the instincts of most people throughout the world. In many parts of the world, the cultural personality—

---

[10] See *Researching Foreign Markets*, National Industrial Conference Board, Inc., Studies in Business Policy, no. 75, New York, 1955.

[11] For some of the environmental obstacles and technical difficulties in applying research techniques in underdeveloped countries, see Harper W. Boyd, Jr., Ronald E. Frank, William F. Massy, and Mostafa Zoheir, "On the Use of Marketing Research in the Emerging Economies," *Journal of Marketing Research*, November, 1964, pp. 20–23. For a picture at the other end of the scale, see Edward L. Brink, "The State of Marketing Intelligence in the United Kingdom," in Peter D. Bennett (ed.), *Marketing and Economic Development*, American Marketing Association, Chicago, 1965, pp. 72–78; and Charles K. Ramond, "Operations Research in Foreign Marketing," *Journal of Marketing Research*, February, 1964, pp. 17–24.

[12] John Fayerweather, *International Marketing*, Prentice-Hall, Inc., Englewood Cliffs, N.J., 1965, pp. 93–96.

tempered by aspects of religion and education—is such that people are guided by intuition, emotional reaction, or tradition. None of these is particularly conducive to the scientific approach. A second and related element in marketing research—*customer information*—is dependent upon the ability and willingness of people to respond accurately and completely when researchers pose questions involving attitudes, opinions, buying habits, motives, etc. In many foreign societies, the suspicion of strangers, the distrust of government, and the individualistic personality which believes these things are "none of your business" all serve to compound the problems of gathering information.

The scarcity of *reliable statistical data* may be the single biggest problem in some foreign markets. Figures on population, personal income, and production may be only crude estimates. Few studies have been made on such things as buying habits or media coverage. In the design of a research project, the lack of reliable data makes it very difficult to set up a meaningful sample. Lack of uniformity makes intercountry comparisons very unreliable.[13] The element of *operational economy* was mentioned earlier as a partial explanation of why less money is spent on foreign than domestic marketing research.

The procedure followed in a foreign marketing research project is basically the same as that used in domestic marketing. Thus, the scientific research process outlined in Chapter 3 is equally pertinent here. Only the implementation will be different, country by country.[14]

Analysis of foreign markets

Nowhere in a company's total marketing program is the influence of the cultural and economic environment seen more clearly than in the analysis of consumer and industrial market demand. Market demand in all countries is determined by population, economic ability to buy, and buying behavior—motives and habits. Also, human wants and needs have a basic universal similarity. People need food, clothing, and shelter; they seek a better life in terms of lighter work loads, more leisure time, social recognition and acceptance, etc. But at about this point, the similarities in foreign and domestic markets end. Furthermore, significant differences exist between and within foreign countries, thus forcing us to segment and define each market carefully.[15]

A cosmetics firm selling in a Latin American country, for example, may segment its market by upper-, lower-, and middle-income groups and by urban

[13] For an excellent list of sources of secondary data on foreign markets, see John M. Hess and Philip R. Cateora, *International Marketing*, Richard D. Irwin, Inc., Homewood, Ill., 1966, pp. 400–404.

[14] For a step-by-step procedure followed by the Hoover Company (vacuum cleaners) in planning a foreign marketing study preparatory to investing in overseas production facilities, see Victor P. Buell, "How to Study Foreign Markets," *Journal of Marketing*, July, 1958, pp. 9–16.

[15] See Ernest Dichter, "The World Customer," *Harvard Business Review*, July–August, 1962, pp. 113–122; and Yves Fournis, "The Markets of Europe or the European Market?" *Business Horizons*, Winter, 1962, pp. 77–83.

and rural areas. The same marketing program will not reach each segment because these markets have different potentials and characteristics. The upper-income class wants high-grade products sold through exclusive stores and advertised in high-quality newspapers. In rural markets, the products must be inexpensive; there may even be a need to promote primary demand because cosmetics are not fully accepted in this market.[16]

When analyzing the economic ability to buy on the part of consumers in a given foreign market, management may first study the broad measures such as gross national product or per capita national income. Three other economic factors which perhaps are more meaningful in each market are (1) distribution of income, (2) rate of growth in buying power, and (3) extent of available consumer financing.[17] Large portions of the population in the emerging economies have very low incomes. A much different income-distribution pattern—with resulting differences in marketing programs—is found in the industrialized markets of Western Europe, where there are large groups of working classes and a burgeoning middle-income market. Thus, many of the products commonly in demand in Belgium or the Netherlands would find very small markets in some African or Asian countries where consumers often cannot afford more than the basic necessities. In Japan and West Germany, the economic growth has greatly outstripped the population increases since 1950, so the net effect is a substantial increase in per capita buying power. In these countries, the marketing opportunities and requirements are different from those in countries such as India (or even the United States), where there has been a relatively slow rate of per capita economic growth.

An understanding of the cultural environment in a given market will, in turn, help in understanding the buying motives and habits of consumers in that market. Some of the cultural elements to identify and to analyze for their effect on a firm's marketing program include (1) the family system, (2) other social groups and institutions, (3) the educational system, (4) the language, and (5) the religious system.[18] A country where the family is a close-knit unit will attract a different type of advertising campaign from the one appropriate in a society where the family members more frequently come and go independently, and it will constitute a market for different products. In Japan, India, and other cultures where parents typically arrange the marriages of their children, marketing programs are different from those in the United States and other countries where the youths are free to find and select their own mates. The educational system affects the literacy rate, which in turn influences advertising, branding, and labeling. The brand may become all important if the potential consumers cannot read and so must recognize the article by the picture on the label. Language differences, too, pose problems.

[16] This example is taken from John Fayerweather, *Management of International Operations: Text and Cases,* McGraw-Hill Book Company, New York, 1960, p. 65.

[17] See Fayerweather, *International Marketing*, pp. 31–35.

[18] See Hess and Cateora, *op. cit.,* chap. 4, "Cultural Dynamics in Assessing World Markets"; see also Fayerweather, *ibid.,* pp. 35–47.

Literal translations of American advertising copy or brand names may result in ridicule of, or even enmity toward, American products. Even some English words have different meanings in England, Australia, and the United States. The religion in a country has a tremendous influence on the value systems and behavioral patterns of consumers. In countries where the Protestant ethic (hard work and frugal living) is prevalent, we find less of a market for labor-saving devices and prepared cake mixes. Moslems disapprove of liquor, and Hindus deemphasize material goods.

A few examples may illustrate how buying habits are influenced by cultural elements. One-stop shopping is unknown in most parts of the world. In many foreign markets people buy in small units, sometimes literally on a meal-to-meal basis. Also, they buy in small specialty stores. To buy food for a week-end, a housewife in West Germany will visit the chocolate store, the dairy store, the meat market, the fish market, a dry grocery store, the greengrocer, the bakery, the coffee market, and possibly some other specialty food stores. While this may seem to be an inefficient use of time, we must recognize that a shopping trip to that housewife is more than just a chore to be done as fast as possible. To her it is a major part of her social life. She will visit with her friends and neighbors in these shops. Shopping in this fashion is simply a foreign version of the American woman's bridge club or neighborhood coffee break. Only in recent years in some Western European countries have we seen the advent of the supermarket. Another buying habit to contend with in many foreign markets is the absence of the one-price system. Consumers expect to haggle and bargain over each purchase; it is a way of life which must be acknowledged in a marketing program.

Often the question of "who buys" is related to the cultural factors in a market. In many Moslem countries, wives are kept in seclusion, yet they play a major role in managing the family's economic life. In other countries where women enjoy freedom and liberties not available to Moslem women, the men of the house may make the buying decisions. In still other foreign markets the buying is done by servants. Each situation requires a different type of promotional program and a different approach to the person who buys.

In this chapter, we have stressed the point that significant environmental differences exist between and within foreign countries and that these differences should be recognized when building a marketing program. Perhaps we have overstressed this point or at least have neglected to note a countervailing development. On the horizon we can see a trend toward standardization of tastes, wants, and habits, especially in the Western European countries. Travel, television, and trade are proving to be effective homogenizers of European culture.[19] Signs indicate that the European consumers are developing into a

[19] "Three Europes, One Boom," *Business Week*, Sept. 10, 1966, p. 116. Also see Erik Elinder, "How International Can European Advertising Be?" *Journal of Marketing,* April, 1965, pp. 7–11; Ilmar Roostal, "Standardization of Advertising for Western Europe," *Journal of Marketing,* October, 1963, pp. 15–20; "Europe Goes Shopping," *Business Week,* May 18, 1963, p. 58.

mass market. Now let us be sure we understand this situation. A German is still a German, a Swede knows he is still a Swede, etc. We do not have a European consumer or a common European market—yet. The cultural differences are still very much present, but the old order is changing, and we can see increasingly cosmopolitan demands. Pizzerias do business in Germany, lasagna is sold in a Stockholm supermarket, British fish-and-chips are wanted on the Continent, and whisky sales are large in France. People from many countries have a common demand for better housing, cars, appliances, and opportunities to travel. An alert marketing executive should certainly watch this developing "Americanization of tastes."

Product planning for international markets

Most companies would not think of entering a domestic market without careful and often extensive product planning. Yet typically an American firm enters a foreign market with essentially the same product it sells in the United States. Even when a product is changed expressly for an international market, the modification is apt to be minor—converting an appliance to 220-volt electrical systems or painting and packaging the product to protect it against the destructive tropical climate and insects, for example. The absence of foreign-market product planning by United States firms is one reason that foreign manufacturers have moved successfully into international markets. An illustration of this point is found in the European markets for automatic washing machines after World War II.[20] American firms exported, or manufactured in Europe, the same models which were popular sellers in the United States. In Europe, they were market failures because of their design. They had the wrong temperature, they were the wrong shape and size, and they had the wrong action; what appealed to a French housewife was wrong for the German market, and so on. Because the potential sales in these markets seemed small, the United States firms did not redesign the product; instead, they yielded the market to upcoming European manufacturers. Today, the European market for washers is about as big as the market in the United States.

One key to success in product planning thus has a familiar ring—that is, adapt to the cultural tastes and economic characteristics of the particular foreign market, rather than try to sell the American-market product abroad.[21] In Europe, a six-cubic-foot refrigerator is the most popular size, in contrast

[20] E. J. Tangerman, "Where Mass Design Failed," *Product Engineering*, Dec. 6, 1965, pp. 78–82. For a report on one United States company—the Philco Corp.—which is marketing a broad line of refrigerators, washers, and other appliances designed extensively and specifically for various European markets, see "To Succeed in Europe, Philco Goes European," *Business Week*, Oct. 2, 1965, p. 132.

[21] See Fayerweather, *International Marketing*, pp. 51–61; and Robert D. Stuart, *Penetrating the International Market*, American Management Association, Management Report no. 84, New York, 1965, chap. 4, "Fitting the Product to the Market," pp. 40–45.

to the larger units preferred in the United States. While the cost difference is a factor, the basic reasons for the Europeans' choice lie in the cultural behavioral patterns of the consumers. As noted earlier, to many European housewives a food-shopping trip is a social event. They go daily and thus do not buy large quantities which must be stored for a few days in a refrigerator. Also, if they have no car, they walk to the store and cannot carry large quantities. As yet, frozen foods are not purchased to any extent, so large freezer space for storage is not needed.

Management should examine the quality-durability features of its product in relation to its price and the value systems in the market. One firm may lower its product's quality or durability in order to reduce the price and thus reach a larger segment of the market. Another firm may maintain its traditionally high quality (and correspondingly high price) because its product is a status symbol in that market or because management wants to capitalize on the reputation for high quality which United States firms often enjoy, as compared with local manufacturers.

Often in a foreign-market product-planning situation, a company is faced with this problem: Can we afford to modify the design, quality, or some other feature of our product; that is, will the existing or future demand offset the additional costs of producing, inventorying, and marketing the modified products? Answers to these questions are not easy to come by. Sometimes management can compromise by making a relatively inexpensive change, such as selling pharmaceuticals by the individual capsule or packaging razor blades singly rather than in multiple units. In other instances, the foreign market may simply not offer a large enough sales potential to warrant extensive product design changes.

Branding is especially important in foreign marketing. As suggested above, the brand picture may be the only part of the product that a consumer can recognize. Foreign consumers' preference for American products often overcomes their nationalistic feelings, so in many instances a company can use the same brand that is used in the domestic market. In one case an American pharmaceutical firm built a plant in a Southeast Asian country. This was a nationalistic country fostering local industry. The product was labeled as a local product and its American origin concealed. The product was a market failure because people did not trust the purity and quality of local drugs. In other cases a literal translation may be harmful, so a different name must be selected. The legal aspects of brand registration and ownership in foreign countries may create problems. In some nations, a local firm or person may "pirate" an American brand name and thus block its use by the American company in the foreign country.

Packaging must often be altered to meet foreign marketing requirements. One firm was unsuccessful in introducing its mayonnaise in Germany because the product was packaged in jars, and Germans usually buy salad dressing in tubes. Labels must be changed to identify the quantity of the contents in the metric system. Colors have different meanings in foreign nations. Red is popular in China, but not in some African countries. White indicates mourning in China and Korea. Such information must be considered in product development.

International distribution systems

Perhaps nowhere else in the marketing program do we find it as difficult to generalize or categorize international marketing patterns as in the area of distribution systems. The conglomerate nature of *domestic* middlemen and their functions is found to an even greater degree when we examine *international* distribution patterns. Yet it is imperative that companies which market internationally be able to thread their way intelligently through the maze, for obviously a product must be *distributed* effectively, as well as planned, priced, and promoted. We must be concerned with the physical distribution system, the transfer-of-title negotiations, and the accompanying activities such as pre-sale and postsale service, promotion, and risk taking.[22]

Understanding the environment in a foreign market helps in understanding the middlemen and the distribution system because these marketing institutions are a product of their environment. In foreign markets, just as in the United States, consumer buying habits are a major factor in shaping distribution channels and middlemen's activities. The perceptive, and thus usually successful, retailers, for example, will capitalize on environmental change by introducing innovations which anticipate trends in the environment. Thus, when supermarkets were introduced in some Western European countries, they were accepted enthusiastically because enough of the market was ready to change from the practice of shopping at several small, limited-line stores.[23]

Middlemen used in foreign marketing   Four groups of middlemen to be recognized in foreign trade include (1) American foreign trade middlemen, (2) foreign trade middlemen located abroad, (3) wholesalers and retailers operating within foreign markets, and (4) manufacturers' sales branches and offices located in foreign countries.[24]

[22] A useful framework for generalizing about retail operating methods in different marketing systems is found in Edward W. Cundiff, "Concepts in Comparative Retailing," *Journal of Marketing*, January, 1965, pp. 59–63. For another approach to analyzing patterns of distribution, see Hess and Cateora, *op. cit.*, pp. 463–472; and Fayerweather, *ibid.*, chap. 6.

[23] For just a few of the changes in foreign institutions and distribution patterns which reflect environmental change, see "Discounting: Mexico's Newest Revolution," *Business Week*, July 6, 1965, p. 52; "Spaniards Say 'Si' to Department Stores," *Business Week*, May 28, 1966, p. 176; Thomas J. Murray, "The Overseas Boom in Door-to-door Selling," *Dun's Review and Modern Industry*, November, 1964, p. 35; Gianfranco Molinari, "Latest Developments in Automatic Retailing in Europe," *Journal of Marketing*, October, 1964, pp. 5–9.

[24] See Roland L. Kramer, *International Marketing*, 2d ed., South-Western Publishing Company, Cincinnati, 1964, chaps. 9–11.

AMERICAN FOREIGN TRADE MIDDLEMEN   A five-way classification is useful in describing middlemen who specialize in foreign trade and who are located in the United States. Actually, through the years it has become difficult to place a given firm in any one of these categories. One company may fill the role of a commission house, export merchant, manufacturers' agent, or broker, depending upon the individual transaction. Thus this classification is often one of functional activity rather than of separately identifiable specializations. Among these middlemen, specialization is found in other forms, however. Some companies operate only in certain geographic regions, such as Asia, Latin America, or Europe. There is also specialization by line of products handled.

An *export and/or import commission house* acts as an agent for the *buyers* and is paid a commission by the buyers. An export commission house is a resident buyer or an American-based representative acting for foreign buyers. As a separately identifiable institution, the commission house is disappearing, although the function—buyers' representative—is still performed by various firms.

An *export and/or import merchant* is a merchant wholesaler buying products in his own name and then reselling either abroad or at home. Import merchants are found in several fields, such as food products, some raw materials (wool), and some manufactured products (linen, china). The name "export merchant" today describes a function in foreign trade rather than a type of institution.

Manufacturers' export agents represent several noncompeting American manufacturers in foreign markets and are paid a commission by these sellers. Export agents perform functions similar to those of manufacturers' representatives operating in the domestic market. The operations of *export and import brokers* are much the same as those of brokers in domestic marketing. In foreign trade these middlemen are especially active in the marketing of staple commodities such as grain, cotton, wool, sugar, and coffee.

The "export house" is probably the most popular term used to describe all American foreign trade middlemen, with the possible exception of brokers. The term is even used to include those firms which import products into the United States. Many foreign trade middlemen engage in such a wide variety of activities that they defy accurate titling. They simply are American middlemen engaged in foreign marketing. Any narrower descriptive title may be misleading or erroneous. One company may do both importing and exporting as an independent merchant and at the same time act as an export agent for a manufacturer. Another importer-exporter may also own and operate sugar plantations, manufacturing plants, a bank, or a steamship line.

FOREIGN TRADE MIDDLEMEN LOCATED ABROAD   In most foreign countries there are independent middlemen (importers, exporters, brokers, and some wholesalers) who are engaged in foreign trade and who operate in essentially the same way as American-based foreign trade firms. From the standpoint of an American producer, however, the main outlets abroad for manufactured goods are *agents and distributors*. These are firms which act as sales representatives for the American firms in foreign markets. Agents and distributors differ primarily in two respects: agents do not take title to the goods and normally do not carry inventory stocks. These middlemen are so important in the distribution system that often a manufacturer will grant exclusive territorial rights to a firm. They perform a wide variety of services, including personal selling, advertising, providing market and credit information, repairs, billing, settling disputes, and collecting invoices; in addition, distributors perform the functions of warehousing and bulk breaking.

Channels of distribution   When selecting the channel of distribution to be used in foreign marketing, an executive probably will use one of the following five alternatives. Two of these are indirect, involving the use of middlemen all the way, and the other three involve direct selling to some extent, along with the establishment of foreign sales offices or branches by the manufacturer.

1.   Manufacturer—foreign trade middlemen (exporters) in the United States —foreign trade middlemen (importers) abroad—wholesalers and/or retailers in foreign countries—consumer or industrial users

2.   Manufacturer—foreign trade middlemen in the United States—wholesalers and/or retailers in foreign countries—consumers or industrial users

3.   Manufacturer—foreign trade middlemen in foreign countries—wholesalers and/or retailers—consumers or industrial users

4.   Manufacturer—wholesalers and/or retailers abroad—consumers or industrial users

5.   Manufacturer—industrial user

The main problem at this point is to decide whether or not to engage in direct selling and, if so, to what extent. The middlemen who operate *within* foreign countries are, in general, less aggressive and perform fewer marketing services than their American counterparts. The foreign marketing situation, however, usually argues against direct selling. Often the demand is too small to warrant the establishment of a sales office or branch. Also, the wage structure and selling methods tend to give foreign middlemen an advantage. Government controls frequently preclude the use of an American sales organization abroad. In some foreign countries, for instance, controlling stock interest in a corporation must be held by citizens of the foreign country. Consequently, middlemen in foreign countries are usually used in the channel structure, whether the American seller exports directly to sales offices abroad or uses American exporting middlemen.

When foreign middlemen are used, the American seller usually advertises extensively and furnishes point-of-purchase display materials to strengthen the efforts of the middlemen. Missionary salesmen are sometimes employed. If the product requires mechanical servicing or installation, the American manufacturer must provide reliable repair service. This means training local middlemen or sending in American service representatives or both. The firm may decide to establish a foreign sales office, even though foreign middlemen are used extensively. Local middlemen often require financial assistance. If retailers cannot get bank credit, the manufacturer must supply this need. Frequently the interest rates on installment loans in foreign countries are high enough to make the financing function rather attractive.

Selection of individual middlemen   Because of their wide variation in intelligence, aggressiveness, and dependability, selecting individual native middlemen in foreign countries is a real task. Exporting firms should consider many of the same criteria used in selecting middlemen in domestic markets. Important factors include a middleman's reputation, intelligence, management ability, and financial status, as well as the usual product lines he carries, his location, the geographic scope of his market, and in some cases his nationality and political affiliations. Often a manufacturer must decide whether an efficient operator is more desirable than an aggressive seller. Many local middlemen fit only one of these requirements. In the final analysis, the manufacturer must select his middlemen in light of the selling job needed. Some jobs demand good service; others require skill and personal contacts; still others necessitate middlemen who can educate potential buyers and stimulate primary demand.

Physical distribution   In foreign marketing, various aspects of physical distribution are quite different from anything found on the domestic scene, and they require careful attention from marketing executives. In general, the total cost of physical distribution is a much larger share of the final selling price in foreign markets than in domestic markets. Packing requirements, for example, are more exacting for foreign shipment. Problems caused by humidity, pilferage, breakage, and inadequate marking of shipments must be considered. Requirements of commercial shipping documents and governmental documents increase and complicate the paper work in foreign shipping. Marine insurance and the traffic management of international shipments are specialized fields involving facilitating agencies ordinarily not used in domestic marketing. In conclusion, the new capabilities in logistics control plus the faster rates of change in international marketing point up the need for an enlarged, higher-level physical distribution activity.[25]

Pricing in international markets

In earlier chapters, we recognized that determining a basic price and establishing various pricing policies are complex tasks, often involving trial-and-error decision making. These tasks become even more complex in international marketing because management must contend with additional variables such as

[25] Robert E. McGarrah, "Logistics for the International Manufacturer," *Harvard Business Review*, March–April, 1966, p. 154.

currency conversion problems, a myriad of possible bases for price quotations, and often a lack of knowledge or control of middlemen's pricing. The principles and methods of price determination in multinational marketing are quite similar to those discussed in Chapters 17 to 20.

Cost-plus pricing is probably used to a greater extent in export marketing than at home, although there are some notable exceptions to this generalization. The cost-plus approach, coupled with additional cost factors not found in the domestic market (tariffs, special taxes, international shipping costs, larger margins for middlemen, etc.), can result in some startling differences between foreign and domestic prices on the same article. An example of this "price escalation" is shown in Table 26–2. Some manufacturers try to reduce these differentials by (1) accepting a lower net price on exported goods, (2) establishing overseas manufacturing operations to escape tariffs, (3) modifying the product to get it into a lower tariff classification, or (4) eliminating some of the middlemen in the trade channels.[26]

Sometimes a firm's foreign price may be *lower* than its domestic price. The price may be lowered in order to meet foreign competition, to dispose of outmoded products or distress merchandise, to broaden the market by tapping low-income segments, or to remove supply from the home market and thus preserve the home-market structure. Sometimes governments engage in the practice of "dumping." That is, government action supports the domestic price at a level above the international market price; when products are exported, they are sold below the domestic price. Through the years the surplus production of several raw materials has led to government control of world market prices. Individual governments have tried to stabilize the prices of coffee, nitrates, sugar, and rubber. Also, governments of several countries have established joint agreements covering the price of such commodities as tin, potash, cocoa, and wheat.

Foreign middlemen often are not aggressive in their pricing policies and strategies. Only a very few have adopted supermarket or discount-selling methods. They prefer to maintain high unit margins at the expense of low sales volume, rather than develop large sales volume by means of lower prices and smaller margins per unit sold. In fact, there is considerable rigidity in price structures in many foreign markets. In some cases, inflexibility stems from the presence of cartels and other combinations of firms which tend to restrain independent action in pricing and other marketing activities. The rigidity is sometimes engendered by price-control legislation whch prevents retailers from cutting prices substantially and at their own discretion. American producers should be aware that combinations among manufacturers and middlemen are tolerated to a far greater extent in many foreign countries than in the United States, even when the avowed purpose of the combinations is to restrain trade and reduce competition. Recognizing this, Congress passed the Webb-Pomerene Act in 1918, allowing American firms to join in a trade combination in a for-

[26] Hess and Cateora, *op. cit.,* pp. 565–567.

table 26-2

Causes and effects of price escalation

The price paid by the foreign consumer at retail can greatly exceed the manufacturer's net when we use cost-plus pricing and include the many extra costs to be covered in international marketing. Why is the retail price in example 4 ($4.79) so much higher than the $2.58 price in example 2?

	Domestic example	Foreign example 1: assuming the same channels with wholesaler importing directly	Foreign example 2: importer and same margins and channels	Foreign example 3: same as 2, but with 10 per cent cumulative turnover tax	Foreign example 4: long channels, larger retail margins, no turnover tax
Mfg. net	$ .95	$ .95	$ .95	$ .95	$ .95
Transport, c.i.f.		.15	.15	.15	.15
Tariff (20%)	x	.19	.19	.19	.19
Importer pays	x	x	1.29	1.29	1.29
Importer margin when sold to wholesaler (25% on cost)	x	x	.32	.32 +.13 turnover tax	.32
Wholesaler pays landed cost	.95	1.29	1.61	1.74	1.61
Wholesaler margin (33⅓% on cost)	.32	.43	.54	.58 +.17 turnover tax	.54
Local foreign jobber pays	x	x	x	x	2.15
Jobber margin (33⅓ on cost)	x	x	x		.72
Retailer pays	1.27	1.72	2.15	2.49	2.87
Retail margin (50% on cost)	.63	.86	1.08	1.25 +.25 turnover tax	1.92 (66⅔% on cost)
Retail price	$1.90	$2.58	$3.23	$3.99	$4.79

NOTE: (1) All figures in United States dollars; (2) x means this cost is not applicable in this example; (3) the exhibit assumes that all domestic transportation is absorbed by the middlemen; (4) transportation, tariffs, and middleman margins vary from country to country, but for purposes of comparison only a few of the possible variations are shown.

SOURCE: John M. Hess and Philip R. Cateora, *International Marketing*, Richard D. Irwin, Inc., Homewood, Ill., 1966, p. 564.

eign country without being charged with a violation of the American antitrust laws. Probably the best known of these international marketing combinations is the cartel. A *cartel* is a group of companies which produce similar products and which have combined to restrain competition in manufacturing and marketing. Cartels exist to varying degrees in the production and marketing of steel, aluminum, fertilizers, electrical products, petroleum products, rayon, dyes, and sulfur. Originally they were formed to regulate competition in industries faced with conditions of chronic overproduction. Later they expanded their activities to include maintaining prices, setting up sales territories, establishing uniform documents, and even doing centralized selling.

Another area of pricing practices peculiar to foreign trade relates to aspects of price quotations. With respect to shipping, insurance, and related export activities and charges, three bases of price quotations used extensively in foreign trade are f.o.b., f.a.s., and c.i.f. When a shipment is priced f.o.b. (free on board), the f.o.b. point is usually the inland point of departure or the port of shipment. When a shipment is priced f.a.s. (free alongside ship, at port of export), the seller pays all charges to deliver the goods to the dock alongside the vessel but not on board. All shipping activities, costs, and risks from that point are the responsibility of the buyer. Under a price quotation of c.i.f. (cost, insurance, freight) at a given point of destination, the seller pays all costs up to the arrival of the shipment at the foreign port.[27]

Prices may be quoted in United States dollars or in the currency of the foreign buyer. Here we become involved in problems of foreign exchange and conversion of currencies. When prices are quoted in United States dollars, exchange controls and restrictions by foreign governments may impede the conversion of foreign currency to dollars, thus delaying the collection of invoices. As a general rule, a firm engaged in foreign trade—whether it is buying or selling, exporting or importing—prefers to have the price quoted in its own national currency. Risks from fluctuations in foreign exchange—that is, devaluation of the currency of the other country—then are shifted to the other party in the transaction. In addition, an importer can readily determine his resale price, compute his profits, and compare offerings from sellers in different countries. Sometimes a foreign importer will prefer to have the price quoted in the currency of the exporting nation if he sees an opportunity to speculate profitably in exchange fluctuations or if he thinks that he can buy at a lower price by assuming the risks of fluctuations. The decision on whether to quote prices in the national currency of the importer or the exporter depends on the relative bargaining power of each and on how badly each wants the sale to be made.

Advertising in foreign markets

Any analysis of international promotional programs should encompass the management of international sales forces, sales-promotional techniques, and adver-

[27] For an expanded discussion of international price quotations and terms, see Kramer, *op. cit.*, pp. 388–404.

tising programs. Because of space limitations, however, our brief discussion is confined only to advertising as illustrative of the managerial problems in international promotion. Advertising is selected because it is probably used by more firms in international marketing than either a company sales force or some of the sales-promotional techniques. Many companies without their own international sales force—they use foreign trade middlemen—will advertise internationally. In years to come, the management of an international sales force will undoubtedly command more attention. As foreign sales and investments become a significant share of a company's total, management often discontinues the use of export-import middlemen and establishes its own international sales force. In this way, the firm can increase its control and aggressiveness in both its distribution and its promotion.

In international advertising, one controversial issue is the extent to which advertising can be standardized in foreign markets. In years gone by, the consensus was that a separate program (copy, appeals, media, etc.) had to be tailored for each country or even regions within a country. While nobody is recommending complete uniformity, today we are finding much support for the idea that a commonality can exist successfully in international campaigns. Many companies are using basically the same theme, slogan, colors, copy, layout, etc., in all their international advertising.[28] Perhaps the situation abroad is the same as that in the United States—the more similar we find the customers' motivations, buying habits, and environment (cultural, economic, and political) the more similar our advertising can be in these markets.

An American producer marketing in foreign countries will find the advertising situation quite different from that which he faces at home. This generalization applies to the consumer and governmental attitudes toward advertising media, the copy requirements, and the organizational structure employed to manage advertising.

Attitude of foreign markets and governments toward advertising   In many countries the traditionally negative attitude toward marketing in general and toward advertising in particular is a hardship for American firms. The "build a better mousetrap" theory still prevails to a great extent throughout Europe and the rest of the world. Some foreign consumers feel that a product is of dubious value if it has to be advertised. People in many foreign countries object particularly to American "hard sell" advertising. Many countries have stringent laws regulating advertising copy and media. In West Germany, for example, a seller cannot make product comparisons in his advertising. In West Germany, the Scandinavian countries, and other European markets, the use of exaggerated claims is severely restricted. As a general rule, advertising must be factual and must employ a "soft sell" approach. On the other hand, some mar-

[28] For an advocate of increased standardization of advertising in Western Europe, see Elinder, *op. cit.* For a more cautionary point of view which recognizes still-existing diversities in language, media, and government regulations, but which also recognizes that standardization is bound to grow, see Roostal, *op. cit.*

kets—Latin America, for example—treat and accept advertising much as we in the United States do. Where the government regulates the use of radio and television for advertising and where newspapers are government-controlled, this, too, affects their use as advertising media.

Choice of media   Essentially the same types of advertising media are available in foreign countries as in the United States, with the exception of television in some markets. Some print media, such as *Time, Life,* and *Reader's Digest,* which are published in the United States are also published abroad in foreign languages. Other magazines are published in the United States but are circulated primarily in foreign markets. There are also the print media published and circulated in particular foreign markets; for these there is no American connection at all.

In foreign markets American exporters encounter problems related to media selection which are not normally met in the United States.[29] One factor peculiar to foreign marketing is the low rate of literacy in many areas. A seller might ordinarily prefer print media to show a colored picture of his product and explain its merits. If he is selling in a market where 90 per cent of the people cannot read and do not buy magazines or newspapers, however, he may be forced to use radio, which on other counts may be a far less effective medium for his product. Another major problem is the unavailability of accurate information regarding the quantitative and qualitative nature of media circulation. Sometimes the rates paid for media space are determined on a bargaining basis; sometimes the rates for American sellers are higher than for native firms. Political and religious considerations are more important determinants of newspaper circulation and readership in many foreign markets than in the United States.

Preparation of advertisements   Most of the mistakes in writing copy and preparing individual advertisements may be traced to lack of intimate knowledge of the foreign market. As we have said, the wrong use of color or a poor choice of words can completely nullify an otherwise good ad. Illustrations are of prime importance in many markets because of the illiteracy factor. They are, of course, effective in all markets, but they must be accurate, believable, and in accord with local cultures. If agencies and advertisers could have qualified people from the individual foreign markets check every advertisement before it reaches the public, many mistakes could be eliminated. The translation of the advertising copy into the appropriate foreign language is a major problem. Usually, the American must first be translated into English, and then again translated into the individual foreign tongues. Here the advertiser especially needs someone both adept and current (an expatriate often will not do) in the idioms, dialects, and other nuances of the foreign language.

[29] See "Europe's Media Morass," *Sales Management,* May 4, 1962, p. 44.

Management of foreign advertising   The advertising program in foreign markets can be coordinated and controlled in three general ways. Control may be centralized in the home office of the American seller; it may be exercised jointly by the home office and the foreign representatives; or it may be delegated entirely to the seller's foreign representatives. On balance, the best arrangement seems to be centralized management and control. It is difficult to exert budgetary control over an internationally decentralized operation. Better advertising talent and more advertising specialists are available in the home office than in any single foreign market. The home office can work with American advertising agencies who have foreign offices; thus it can have some of the advantages of local market contacts but still retain basic control. Economies can be realized through centralized creation and production of the individual advertisements. Also, when international media are used, some centralized control is necessary. Finally, centralized management of the advertising program makes it easier to coordinate advertising with other aspects of the company's promotional and marketing programs. Of course, centralized management means that the American seller loses the tremendous advantage of having personnel closely acquainted with local cultures, languages, and buying habits.[30]

Even when the program is centrally managed, administrators must still decide which kinds of advertising agencies to use: purely domestic firms, American agencies with overseas branches, or foreign agencies. To reach most foreign markets, the most desirable compromise is probably an American agency with overseas branches.

THE FUTURE: A WORLD MARKETING ENTERPRISE

For countless American companies, the marketing opportunities and challenges of the future lie in international marketing. This conclusion seems inevitable as management views its home markets being saturated, its excess productive capacity, its shrinking profit margins, and the intensified competition in the United States coming from both domestic and foreign firms. This broadening of marketing horizons, however, will be a new experience in most cases. When exports are measured as a percentage of gross national product, the United States ranks last among the major trading nations in the world, although we do rank first in dollar volume of trading. Most companies in the United States have never felt that export markets provided them with an opportunity to increase sales volume and profits significantly. Even the increasing competition from foreign imports has usually served only to intensify the American sellers' competitive efforts at home, rather than turning their interest to international markets.

[30] For the ways in which a variety of firms have organized for international advertising, see Gordon E. Miracle, "Organization for International Advertising," in Peter D. Bennett (ed.), *Marketing and Economic Development,* American Marketing Association, Chicago, 1965, pp. 163–177.

But the winds of change are awakening American executives to the opportunities in multinational marketing. To make the most of these opportunities a company is urged to think big and plan ahead—clichés, yes, and perhaps trite, but useful admonitions nevertheless. A country-by-country market analysis is becoming increasingly common and is certainly better than going abroad with a one-shot, unplanned approach because some random opportunity has presented itself. Better than a country-by-country analysis, however, is a global planning approach. By taking a total global systems approach, a company is not apt to be blocked later on by some decision made earlier in another country.[31]

Experienced international marketing men also caution prospective entrants into this field that ". . . you can't dabble or 'take a little flyer' into international marketing. It's strictly a total commitment effort. If your company can't afford the effort, money, or time, don't try it!"[32] Unfortunately, even though it is illogical, too often a company will use the "dabble" method to enter a foreign market where the environment is totally strange, and yet will attack a new domestic market with full vigor and resources.

It is commonly alleged that products manufactured in the United States are being priced out of world markets because of our high cost structure. The facts, however, do not fully support this allegation. One study of 249 items produced in both the United States and foreign markets showed the comparative cost position of United States–made products.[33] In Fig. 26–5, we see that the United States is in about an equal cost position with foreign producers. The other part of Fig. 26–5 shows the total costs by segments. Here we see that the United States manufacturer enjoys a significant advantage in material costs, which counterbalances his severe cost disadvantages in plant overhead, selling, and especially direct labor.

Often our labor costs and prices are offered as excuses, when the truth of the matter is that we have failed to apply our know-how of modern marketing management in foreign countries.[34] While marketing skills, facilities, and aggressiveness are increasing among foreign firms, American sellers too often seem complacent and static. Part of the difficulty is that many American firms do not have a marketing orientation in their export business. In the past, much emphasis has been placed on production and financial problems in foreign markets. Textbooks on foreign trade have stressed export mechanics such as rates of exchange, credit transactions, and shipping methods and terms.

Permeating this chapter has been the theme that marketing management in American firms must become more internationally minded. We conclude with

[31] For a step-by-step case example of how one firm went about global planning, plus an evaluation of this approach, see *International Enterprise: A New Dimension of American Business,* McKinsey and Company, Inc., New York, 1962, pp. 21–24.

[32] "In Marketing Abroad, Go All Out," *Printers' Ink,* July 31, 1964, p. 42.

[33] *The Emerging World Enterprise,* Booz, Allen & Hamilton, Inc., New York, 1962, pp. 5–6.

[34] Laurence P. Dowd, "Is the United States Being Priced out of World Markets?" *Journal of Marketing,* July, 1960, pp. 1–8.

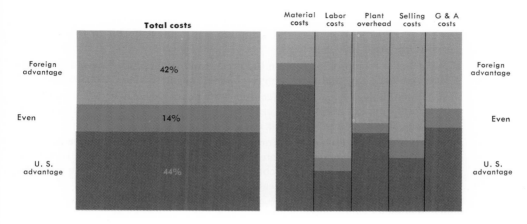

COMPARISON OF U.S. AND FOREIGN COSTS ON 249 PRODUCTS, 1960.

fig. 26–5

United States firms and foreign producers ended about even, each having a cost advantage in a little over 40 per cent of the cases. American firms enjoyed a big differential advantage in material costs. Do you think the labor cost gap between American and foreign producers will soon close?

SOURCE: Booz, Allen & Hamilton, Inc., from National Industrial Conference Board data.

a statement from the same executive who was quoted at the beginning of the chapter. He notes the following five reasons why it is mandatory that the United States be successful in world marketing.[35]

1. We cannot adequately expand our economy at home without meeting competition abroad.

2. We cannot eliminate large-scale unemployment in this country unless we do smaller-scale employing in other countries.

3. To achieve a higher tide of prosperity here, we must be willing to develop trade with those whose prosperity is still at very low ebb.

4. Balancing our international payment books at home requires filling many more order books abroad.

5. If we are to remain dominant and competitive in the United States market, we must compete successfully in the world market.

QUESTIONS AND PROBLEMS

1 In what fundamental respects is international marketing different from domestic marketing?

2 Report on *export* marketing activities of companies in the state where your school is located. Consider such topics as the following: What products are ex-

[35] Ray R. Eppert, "Passport for Marketing Overseas," *Journal of Marketing*, April, 1965, p. 6.

ported? How many jobs are created by export marketing? What is the dollar value of exports? How does this figure compare with the value of foreign-made goods imported into the state?

3   What is the relationship between the organizational structure selected for international marketing and a company's channels of international distribution?

4   A United States luggage manufacturer with annual sales over $20 million has decided to market his products in Western Europe. Evaluate the alternative organizational structures which this company should consider.

5   Select three countries—one in Europe, one in South America, and one in Africa—and assume that a United States manufacturer of auto and truck tires plans to market his products in these countries. What problems will this manufacturer face in each of the following areas?
    a. Exchange controls
    b. Tariffs on tires
    c. Restrictions on foreign companies or personnel

6   From a management standpoint, what are the differences between a company organized and operating truly as a world enterprise and a firm in which the international division is separate from the domestic organization?

7   Select one product—manufactured or nonmanufactured—for export and the country to which you would like to export it. Then prepare an analysis of the market for this product in the selected country. Be sure to include the sources of information which you used.

8   If there are foreign students on your campus, interview some of them to determine how cultural factors would influence the marketing of American products in their countries.

9   In your interviews with foreign students, determine how their native buying habits differ from ours. Consider such patterns as when, where, and how people in their country buy. Who makes the family buying decisions?

10   Many countries unfortunately have a low literacy rate. In what ways might a company adjust aspects of its marketing program to overcome this problem?

11   Why should special attention be devoted to labeling and branding when selling United States products in foreign markets?

12   Describe the role of the export house in foreign marketing.

13   An American manufacturer wished to market his products in some Western European countries. What services could he expect to receive from an agent or a distributor in these markets?

14   If an American manufacturer uses foreign middlemen, he must usually stand ready to supply them with additional financial, technical, and promotional help. If this is the case, why is it not customary to bypass these middlemen and deal directly with foreign buyers?

15   Why does an American exporter normally prefer to have prices quoted in United States dollars? Why should the foreign importer prefer that the quotation be in the currency of his country?

16   "Prices of American products are always higher in foreign countries than at home because of the additional risks, expenses of physical distribution, and extra middlemen involved." Discuss.

17   Carefully distinguish among f.o.b., f.a.s., and c.i.f. as bases for price quotations in foreign marketing.

18   To what extent do you think international advertising can be standardized?

19   Study the advertisements in the foreign newspapers and magazines available in your college or city library. Particularly note the advertisements of American products, and compare these ads with the advertisements for the same products in American newspapers and magazines. In what respects do the foreign ads differ from the domestic ads? Are there significant similarities?

20   What are some of the media selection problems faced by American exporters in foreign markets?

21   Is the United States manufacturer being priced out of world markets because of his high cost structure?

case 22. CASCADE-COLUMBIA FRUIT GROWERS'
ASSOCIATION

Branding and promoting agricultural products

The Cascade-Columbia Fruit Growers' Association is a large federated agricultural cooperative with headquarters in Yakima, Washington. Packing plants and cold-storage warehouses are maintained in Wenatchee and Sunnyside, Washington, as well as in Yakima. During the apple harvest season, the cooperative operates assembling centers at other locations throughout the Yakima and Wenatchee Valleys in the rich fruit-growing country east of the Cascade Mountains in the state of Washington. This particular federated cooperative has a membership of approximately seven hundred growers, who belong to the six local associations which together comprise the Cascade-Columbia federated unit.

The cooperative offers an extensive assortment of services to its members including assembling, grading, packing, warehousing, and selling the fresh fruit. The members may also buy their production supplies such as fertilizers, insecticides, and spraying equipment from the association. Virtually all the members patronize their association. In addition, Cascade-Columbia offers its services and supplies to about sixty nonmember growers. Members and nonmembers alike receive the same treatment from Cascade-Columbia in that both groups pay the same price for marketing services and production supplies. The non-members, however, do not share in patronage refunds.

A five-man board of directors elected by the membership has the responsibility for top policy making and long-range planning in the association. The operational management authority and responsibility are in the hands of a full-time manager who is hired by the board of directors and who reports to the board. For the past twelve years, Mr. Ray Ferris has been the manager of the Cascade-Columbia Association. His family still operates an orchard near Yakima, and Ray himself is a graduate of Washington State University in Pullman, where he majored in business administration. Currently his salary is $15,000 a year. Through the efforts of Mr. Ferris, Cascade-Columbia has been a well-operated and well-managed cooperative. For each of the past two years, its net profit margin on sales was 4.2 per cent, which is well above the average net profit for cooperative fruit growers' associations in Washington.

While pears, cherries, apricots, and peaches are marketed by the association, by far the largest source of revenue is the sale of apples. Of the total annual sales volume of $11.0 million, apples account for $8.0 million, pears represent $1.2 million, other fruits total $700,000, and the sale of supplies and services brings in $1.1 million. The cooperative ships from 2 to 2½ million bushels of apples each year, and about two-thirds of these shipments are the Red Delicious variety. In addition, the association packs and markets five other varieties of apples—Jonathan, Golden Delicious, Winesaps, McIntosh, and Rome. While it is risky to speak of an "average" price received by the cooperative for its apples, typically a bushel of the Red Delicious variety is sold at a price which is substantially above the sales price of the other varieties. This premium for Red Delicious may range from 20 per cent above the price of Golden Delicious to 45 per cent above the price for Jonathans.

For some time, Mr. Ferris has considered that his main problem is to develop a more effective program for identifying and promoting the Cascade-Columbia fruits, especially the apples which are packed and sold by the cooperative. He would like to differentiate his products in some way so as to remove the Cascade-Columbia apples from the obscurity and anonymity of being just another "Washington apple."

In the past, the Cascade-Columbia cooperative has not engaged in any promotional efforts in its own name. Instead, it has relied on the advertising and sales-promotional programs of the Washington State Apple Commission. This commission is a state governmental agency formed many years ago after a majority vote of the apple growers in the state. The growers are assessed 5 cents on each box of apples produced. This assessment provides the operational and promotional funds for the commission. The efforts of the commission throughout the years in magazine, newspaper, and outdoor advertising campaigns have been effective (along with the fine quality of the fruit) in broadening the market and in developing consumer recognition and acceptance of, as well as preference for, Washington apples.

At this point, Mr. Ferris is considering recommending to his board of directors that they establish a brand for Cascade-Columbia apples and market them under this brand name. As possible brand names he has considered Yakima, Cascade, Indian Chief, Columbia-Cascade, and Wenakima (a combination of Wenatchee and Yakima). He has analyzed the successful history of Sunkist, Inc. (formerly the California Fruit Growers' Exchange), in its cooperative marketing of oranges and lemons under its own brand. Mr. Ferris has also investigated other Western agricultural cooperatives which have successfully differentiated their products by branding and promoting them. Included in his study are the cooperative associations marketing Diamond walnuts, Tillamook cheese, Sun-Maid raisins, and Darigold dairy products. Currently he is trying to get some information about another Washington fruit-marketing cooperative, which for some time has been marketing apples under its own brand, concerning its promotional programs, its degree of success, the problems it has encountered, and its future plans. The name of this cooperative is Wenoka, a combination of Wenatchee and Okanogan, the river valleys where the cooperative is located.

QUESTIONS

1   Should the Cascade-Columbia Association market its apples under its own brand name?

2   If so, outline a promotional program which you would recommend, attaching cost estimates to your program.

case 23. KOHL OIL CORPORATION: PETROSEAL*
Entering the international market

In the nations with developing economies, there is a growing need for adequately surfaced streets and highways to accommodate the intensified transportation requirements. Most areas of the United States are adequately serviced by paved, all-weather highways, but even the most advanced foreign countries still rely mainly on unsurfaced or poorly surfaced roadways. Thus, the Kohl Oil Corporation of Harrisburg, Pennsylvania, is faced with the gloomy prospect of declining domestic markets but a rapidly growing foreign market potential for its penetrating road-surfacing material called Petroseal.

In three production facilities in Pennsylvania, Texas, and California, Kohl produces a full range of petroleum products ranging from gasoline to asphalt. Petroseal, which accounts for $2 million of the company's $9 million sales, is considered to be the only major product with a significant foreign market potential. Petroseal is distributed and applied in the United States and Canada by licensed distributors who use their own equipment to spray the heated compound directly onto cement-treated or untreated road soils. Domestic distributors receive factory training and have access to company engineers for help in dealing with wide variations in application situations. Petroseal results in a hard, high-compression, uniform layer of deeply penetrating, asphalt-stabilized material. The product requires no mechanical mixing or blending and can be stored in ordinary (uninsulated) tanks. It can be pumped at low temperatures, requires no special handling equipment, and can easily be heated to the low application temperature (150°F). A road can be surfaced with Petroseal for about one-third the cost of hot-mix asphalt and requires equipment costing only about one-fifteenth as much as that needed for hot mix. Although the end product is not quite so durable as hot mix, Petroseal has been widely used in the United States on medium-traffic roads and in areas where roads are needed, but road-building funds are scarce. Relatively easy application and low initial cost indicate that the product is ideal for nations desiring to develop roads at a minimum cost.

Information and advertisements have been disseminated in technical periodicals, and in a two-year period have resulted in some $200,000 of Petroseal exports to a variety of countries throughout the world. The initiative for export sales in all cases has come from customers, exporters, or importers. Kohl Oil has been willing to sell to any purchasers who could pay the domestic price (f.o.b. plant) in advance in U.S. dollars, and who would purchase a minimum of 5,000 barrels (210,000 U.S. gallons). The small-volume foreign shipments and the company's lack of preparedness for international marketing have caused such inefficiency that there has been little or no profit on the present volume.

The rapid growth in volume has indicated to Kohl Oil officials that they should consider direct action to develop world markets before other petroleum companies enter the burgeoning market. Petroseal is one of three similar products dominating the domestic market, but any major producer could enter the market at any time if volume and profits seemed to warrant such action. The company is also concerned that its product's reputation may be damaged by unsupervised application. Sales to date have been made directly to American contractors operating abroad, to foreign governments, to American exporters, and to a variety of foreign agents and importers.

* Case written by Prof. John M. Hess, University of Colorado.

Summary evaluation of international market opportunities for Petroseal

Market area or region	Advantages	Problems
European Common Market	Rapid growth	Potential competition
	Ample dollars	Well-developed hard roads
		Tariff
European Free Trade Association	Good growth	Few miles of roads
	Some dollars	Most roads hard-surfaced
Eastern Europe	Great need	Political situation
North Africa and Middle East	Great need	Domestic oil interests
	Road-building emphasis	Mandatory local production
Latin America	Great need	Dollar shortage
	Road-building emphasis	Government instability
	Alliance for Progress	Profit and ownership controls
	Seasons reverse of U.S.	
Far East	Growing need	Distance

Preliminary research and executive hunch indicate wide variation in foreign markets and problems. Some of this information is summarized in the above table.

Because the company has failed to profit on its overseas business, Mr. Kohl, the president, has established a task force to determine whether the company should enter an international market or markets. The group is also expected to come up with recommendations relative to production and distribution and other marketing policies.

QUESTIONS

1   What marketing mistakes has the company made so far?

2   What market information should the task force seek to aid it in its decisions?

3   Which countries or regions seem to offer the most favorable marketing opportunities?

PART EIGHT

PLANNING AND
EVALUATING THE
MARKETING EFFORT

27

MARKET PLANNING

In Chapter 2 we noted that the management process involves several functions, three of which are planning, operating-directing, and analyzing-evaluating. Parts 3 to 6 were devoted to the directing and operating of the marketing program; this and the following chapter will emphasize planning and evaluation. Conscious or unconscious planning permeates all aspects of a firm's marketing program. Earlier, for example, we spoke of planning the product and planning the promotional campaign. Throughout both the planning and the analysis-evaluation activities, management can make extensive and profitable use of marketing research as an aid in decision making. Much of the methodology discussed in Chapter 3 has practical value in our present discussion.

PLANNING IN THEORY AND PRACTICE

A careful student of marketing has referred to planning in marketing as "the exercise of analysis and foresight to increase the effectiveness of marketing activities."[1] Another writer states that ". . . the purpose of planning is to manipulate the present systematically in order to be prepared for the future."[2] In Chapter 2, planning was discussed as a management function separate from that of establishing objectives. Actually market planning, broadly viewed, starts with the determination of marketing goals; it then involves a determination of how the goals will be reached. Several alternative courses of action may be followed, and management must apply problem-solving and decision-making processes to select the best of the alternatives. Thus planning is also concerned with the operating system—the strategies and tactics—through which the goals are reached, the quantity and quality of effort needed to attain the goals, and, finally, the firm's ability to generate this effort.

Planning may also be viewed as an extension of the input-output theory developed by Prof. Wassily Leontief, of Harvard. "Most planning is the attempt to exercise such foresight with respect to the anticipated outputs of an organization so that the inputs can be utilized with maximum efficiency."[3] Once management forecasts its desired output—that is, sets a goal—then through careful planning it can determine what input factors will be needed to attain the output goal. To illustrate, assume that management wants to enter a new geographic market and attain a sales volume of $2 million in this market by the end of the second year. Through input-output analysis, management can estimate what inputs are necessary in the form of advertising, personal selling, production facilities, financial aid, and personnel to reach the goal. Of course, management may find that the required inputs are beyond the firm's capacity. Then the output goal must be altered along more modest lines. Thus availability of inputs may actually set limits on output. In essence, planning involves a matching of means and ends, or inputs and outputs.[4]

Importance of planning

Planning may be done formally or informally—in a simple, crude fashion or in a scientific, sophisticated manner—but, nevertheless, planning is inevitable when a firm is confronted with alternative courses of action. The concept of planning is not new, but the growing importance of the marketing concept in our economy has resulted in an increased recognition of the value of formal, organized planning. As one writer said, "The hard core of the so-called market-

[1] Wendell R. Smith, "The Role of Planning in Marketing," *Business Horizons,* Fall, 1959, p. 54.

[2] Mark E. Stern, *Marketing Planning,* McGraw-Hill Book Company, New York, 1966, p. xi.

[3] Wroe Alderson, *Marketing Behavior and Executive Action,* Richard D. Irwin, Inc., Homewood, Ill., 1957, p. 414.

[4] For a report on one of the newer input-output models as developed by the Office of Business Economics of the U.S. Department of Commerce, see "Input-Output: What It Is; How to Use It; What It Will Do," *Sales Management,* Nov. 5, 1965, pp. 37–44.

ing concept . . . is effective and scientific use of market planning."[5] Truly, any success which marketing management has in increasing the productivity and profitability of marketing operations depends in large part upon the nature of the market planning. Formal market planning is one of the most effective *management tools* available to the businessman for risk reduction.

The dynamic nature of our economy, its increasing complexity, the growing fierceness of competition, and the shrinking profit margins are all combining to force management to focus more attention on scientific market planning. In an age when forward-looking competitors are employing such managerial aids as operations research, motivation research, and electronic data-processing equipment, a company may be committing economic suicide if it relies on haphazard, informal planning based on executive hunches, uninformed guesses, and personal biases. Many other advantages accrue from organized, long-range planning based on careful marketing research. In the first place, it can save a considerable amount of executive time and effort. With a formal staff group assigned to planning tasks, line executives can be freed for other revenue-producing work. Also, internal coordination and communication can be improved, and executives can be provided with some framework for day-to-day decisions. Formal planning should also elicit disciplined thinking because executives must put their thoughts in writing before acting. Good planning forces a firm to do advanced scheduling.[6] As a result, management by crisis and expediency can be reduced to a minimum, and short-term disturbances can be placed in a proper perspective. Furthermore, planning forces the company to establish goals and consequently reduces the amount of aimless activity.

Objections to formal planning

Despite the many benefits to be gained, many companies still do not employ scientific market planning. In a firm that has enjoyed a favorable rate of growth, the executives may see no need for organized planning. Planning is often absent also in a small firm where one man—frequently the founder—has dominated. Actually, if such a company is successful, often the guiding executive is fundamentally a good planner. He just does not recognize planning as a formal activity.

In both of these nonplanning situations, executives will claim that their operations change so frequently and so quickly that advance planning is not feasible; the situation does not remain stable long enough for the plan to be effective. Usually this argument is only a mask for the real reason, which is that the executives prefer to trust their own spur-of-the-moment judgment. Other objections to formal planning are often voiced. Many top-level executives claim they do not have time to engage in formal planning activities.

[5] Smith, *op. cit.*, p. 57; see also Eugene J. Benge, "The 'Expanded' Sales Manager and Long-range Planning," *Sales Management*, Nov. 10, 1960, p. 54.

[6] Hector Lazo and Arnold Corbin, *Management in Marketing*, McGraw-Hill Book Company, New York, 1961, pp. 68–70.

Possibly this could be alleviated if these executives were more willing to delegate the authority for planning. Another objection is the common cry that "our business is different." Time and again this point has been disproved. Most companies have common business problems which lend themselves to planning. Planning is almost always not only possible but also profitable. Other executives claim that their markets are made up of consumers whose uncertain motivation and behavior cannot be forecast. Motivation research, studies matching consumer buying intentions with actual purchases, and other research refinements are tending to remove this obstacle. Some executives object to planning because they feel it cannot be done scientifically. Others feel that it is too expensive or that there is no point in planning if they cannot control the operations of their suppliers.

Regardless of how substantial these objections may seem, they cannot negate the proved value of sound planning. Ordinarily these objections are an attempt to cover up weaknesses which exist elsewhere in the managerial structure.

Scope of market-planning activities

The length of time for which planning is done serves as one basis for classifying market planning. Long-range planning, for three, five, ten, or twenty-five years, is probably more important than short-range planning. Top management and special planning staffs are involved in long-range planning, and the resultant policy decisions cover broad, far-reaching topics, such as plant, market, or product expansion. Short-term planning usually covers periods of three months, six months, or a year. It is done at the operational level by lower- and middle-echelon executives and is concerned with such things as adjusting prices to meet current competition, buying for the coming season, handling the day-to-day problems of a sales force and the specifics of the current advertising campaign, and selecting middlemen in a new market.

Some goals call for continual planning, whereas others require special, or *ad hoc*, planning.[7] Planning to reach the goal of profit maximization or a target share of the market is a continual process. On the other hand, the development of a plan to be used when a patent expires or the anticipation of what effect a change in sales territories will have on other marketing activities is *ad hoc* planning.

One of the most important jobs in marketing planning is to integrate the four major ingredients in the marketing mix—the product policies, the distribution structure, the pricing system, and the promotional programs. In Parts 3 to 6, these elements were discussed separately and in consecutive order. In a realistic business situation, they interact upon one another, and their planning must be conducted concurrently.

Finding the best combination of marketing mix would be an ideal problem for a computer if all the elements could be quantified. Several models

[7] Smith, *op. cit.*, p. 55.

could be established, and through quantitative analysis, management could select the one best suited for its purposes. The fact of the matter is that all factors cannot be assigned quantitative values. *Qualitative* considerations with respect to customers, middlemen, and other factors affect the marketing mix to a major extent. Marketing executives, of course, are not totally helpless in this matter of integrating the marketing mix. Many research tools are available, and a scientific approach can be employed to some extent in determining the mix. Also, management is getting an increasing amount of help from other disciplines, such as psychology, sociology, mathematics, and statistics.

Some people distinguish between *market* planning and *marketing* planning, with the former being considered only one phase of the latter. The remainder of this chapter is devoted to market planning in a narrow sense. That is, we shall consider the determination of market and sales potentials, sales forecasting, and budgeting.

DETERMINATION OF MARKET POTENTIAL AND MARKET SHARE

Market planning in a firm should begin with a quantitative measurement of the total market potential for the product in question and a measurement of the share of this market which the firm is getting. These measurements form the basis of the sales forecast for the product. The sales forecast in turn is the basis for all budgeting in a firm, and budgeting itself is an essential tool for market planning and managerial control. Even for various types of operational planning, such as establishing sales territories or setting sales quotas for salesmen or middlemen, management should consider the market potential in each segment of the market.[8]

Some of the terms used in this section should be defined because often in business they are used loosely and interchangeably. This is particularly true of such concepts as "market potential," "market share," "sales potential," and "sales forecast." In addition, it will be helpful to understand the meaning and use of a "market factor" and a "market index." The definitions of all but the last two terms are based on those set forth by the American Marketing Association.[9]

Market potential is the maximum combined sales opportunities for all sellers of a good or service during a stated period of time in a stated market. This is an industry-wide potential.

Market share (synonymous with sales potential or market penetration) is "the ratio of a company's sales to the total industry sales on either an actual or potential basis." Thus we may speak of the "market potential" for automatic washing machines but the "market share" (or sales potential) for one com-

[8] See Alfred R. Oxenfeldt, "How to Use Market-share Measurement," *Harvard Business Review*, January–February, 1959, pp. 59–68.

[9] Committee on Definitions, Ralph S. Alexander, Chairman, *Marketing Definitions: A Glossary of Marketing Terms*, American Marketing Association, Chicago, 1960, p. 15.

pany's brand. In the case of either market potential or market share, the market may encompass the entire United States, or even the world, or it may be limited to some part segmented by income, by geographic area, or on some other basis. For example, we may speak of the market potential for washing machines on the Pacific Coast or the market share for General Electric washers in homes with incomes of $7,000 to $10,000. The market potential and market share will be the same when a firm has a monopoly in its market as in the case of a telephone company or some other public utility. A firm marketing a unique, highly differentiated product may find the market potential and market share coextensive, at least until effective competition enters the market.

Sales forecast is defined later in this chapter.

A *market factor* is an item or element which exists in a market, which may be measured quantitatively, and which is related to the demand for product or service. To illustrate, the number of cars three years old and older is a market factor underlying the demand for replacement tires or affecting the market potential for replacement tires. In Chapter 4 we spoke of population and income factors which affect the market for consumer products. In Chapter 7 we mentioned some of the market factors which affect the demand for industrial goods.

A *market index* is simply a market factor expressed in percentages or in some other mathematical term. Sometimes more than one market factor is combined into a single index number. A market factor or market index may be developed for the entire national market or for any segment of it. To illustrate, in 1965 the index representing expenditures for personal services in the United States was close to 180, with the year 1950 serving as the base period of 100. The index was computed in constant dollars, so increases in the price level did not affect the index numbers. Thus, from 1950 to 1965 there was a real increase of 80 per cent in expenditures for services. If sales of our product are related directly to expenditures for personal services, then our 1965 sales (in constant dollars) should be about 80 per cent above the 1950 level.

Techniques for determining market potential

Ordinarily a company will determine the market potential for its product in a predetermined market and then from this figure determine its market share or sales potential. If a company's sales are a minor segment of the industry total, it may start directly with a determination of sales potential and not compute the total industry market potential at all. In some industries the trade association gathers data from all member firms, and, from this information, a firm can rather easily determine the market potential. When a business must determine the market potential and market share all by itself, however, then one or more of four basic techniques may be employed. The computations involved in the four techniques are described briefly at this point.

Since each product is different, firms with multiple products should prepare a separate analysis for each article or each product line. Furthermore, it is frequently advisable to use as many of the techniques as is economically feasible; one can serve as a check against the result found by another. A final guiding principle for management to keep in mind is the value of using the minimum-maximum technique. This is a system by which management determines a range of possible potentials, first by estimating potentials under the *least* favorable circumstances, and then by assuming the *most* favorable market conditions.

Market factor derivation   This technique consists, first, in selecting one or more appropriate market factors which directly influence or are related to the demand for the product in question. Then the market factor is measured, various market segments are eliminated, and, finally, the net measurements are translated into estimates of the market potential for the product.

A manufacturer of automobile tires, for example, wants to know the market potential for replacement tires in the United States in 1969. The main market factor is the number of automobiles on the road. The first delimitation is the estimate of how many cars are likely prospects. Assume that the seller's studies show that the average passenger car is driven about ten thousand miles a year and the average driver gets about twenty-five thousand miles from a set of four tires. This means that all cars which become 2½ years old during 1969 can be considered a part of the potential market for replacement tires during that year. Reasonably detailed information regarding the number of cars sold between July 1, 1966, and June 30, 1967, is readily available from state and county licensing agencies and also has been compiled by private organizations. In addition, a similar count must be established for cars reaching 5, 7½, and 10 years of age during 1969. These ages are multiples of 2½; that is, a five-year-old car presumably would be ready for its second set of replacement tires. The number of cars in these age brackets times four should give a fair approximation of the market potential for replacement tires in 1969. We are, of course, dealing in averages. Not all drivers will get 25,000 miles from a set of tires, and not all cars will be driven exactly 10,000 miles a year.

The seller then must determine his share of this market. Here the analysis becomes more subjective. He must consider the quality of his product in relation to competitive products, the strength of his distribution system and promotional program, the extent of competition, his market share in past years, his plans for market expansion, and many other factors.

The market-factor-derivation method has much to recommend it. It is relatively simple and inexpensive to use, and it requires relatively little statistical analysis. It is reasonably easy to understand, so that non-statistics-oriented executives can follow the method and interpret the results. Usually the factors selected are those for which detailed, reliable data are available.

The key to the successful use of this method lies in the selection of the proper market factors. Management must be able to prove that a relationship does exist between the selected factor and the market for the product. It is also important that the researcher minimize the number of market factors used. The greater the number of factors, the greater the chance for erroneous estimates, and the more difficult it is to tell the extent to which each influences the demand for the article.

Correlation analysis   This technique is simply a mathematical refinement of the market-factor-derivation method. When correlation analysis is used, the variations in the potential sales of the product are mathematically correlated with the variations in the measurements of the market factor. In effect, the correlation measures the variations in two series of historical data. Consequently, this method can be used only when a lengthy sales history of the industry or the firm is available, as well as a history of the market factor's measurement.

Probably the major advantage of correlation analysis is the exactness of the estimate of market demand, assuming, of course, that the elements in the statistical estimating equation are accurate. By placing the measure of the market factor into the estimating equation, the researcher can come up with an accurate estimate of the market or sales potential. This is a more precise measure than the one developed through direct derivation, where the correlation analysis is implicitly assumed to be a perfect +1.00. Rarely does this perfect relationship exist between a market factor and the sales of a product. Also, correlation analysis allows a researcher to incorporate more than one factor into the formula.

There are at least two major limitations to this method. First, as suggested above, a lengthy sales history must be available. To do a really good job, a researcher needs about twenty years of sales records. Also, he is assuming that approximately the same relationships have existed among the variables during this entire period and, furthermore, that this relationship will continue throughout the period for which potentials are being estimated. This may be a highly unrealistic assumption. In contrast, the direct-derivation method does not require this lengthy sales history. The other major drawback is that very few marketing executives understand correlation analysis and can actually do the necessary computations. Thus a statistical staff may be necessary; even then, because of their lack of comprehension, the executives may suspect the results.

Consumer surveys   Another commonly used method of determining market potentials is to survey a sample of potential customers, asking them whether they would buy the product at the stated price. Aside from the extremely high cost and large amount of time needed in this method, there is another very serious limitation. It is one thing for a consumer to say he *intends to buy* a product, but quite another for him *actually to buy it*. Surveys of buying intentions inevitably show an inflated measure of market potential. They are widely used, however, particularly where there are inadequate data for a market-factor-derivation or a correlation analysis.

Test markets In using this technique, a firm markets its product in a limited geographic area and, from this sample, projects the company's sales potential (market share) over a larger area. Thus management determines how many people actually *buy* the article and not how many *say* they will buy. If a company can afford the money and time required for the test-market method, it will find that this is the best way of measuring the full potential for its particular product. Unlike the other techniques for determining market potential, management estimates and judgment do not play such a key role here. Great care is needed, however, to set up and control a test-market experiment.[10]

Determining territorial potentials

After a company has determined the market potential or its market share of the entire market, the executives may want to establish market or sales potentials for each territory assigned to its salesmen or its middlemen. These territorial potentials may be used for several purposes, such as setting sales quotas, determining territorial boundaries, evaluating performance of sales units, or allocating advertising effort.

Once the potentials are calculated for the total market, it is ordinarily easy to compute territorial potentials. Management simply uses a pertinent market factor or market index which has been determined for small geographic areas such as counties or cities. For example, assume that a manufacturer of machine tools estimates his market share for a given year to be $12 million; the market factor he uses is the number of employees in manufacturing establishments. Referring to his information sources, he can get the number of manufacturing employees in each county. He determines that 9 per cent of the total manufacturing employees are located in his western region and 6 per cent in his southern territory. The potential in these territories is then calculated at $1,080,000 and $720,000, respectively.

SALES FORECASTING

While a sales forecast ordinarily can be made more intelligently if the company first determines its market and/or sales potentials, actually many firms start their market planning directly with the sales forecast.

The American Marketing Association gives the following definition:[11]

Sales Forecast. An estimate of sales, in dollars or physical units for a specified future period under a proposed marketing plan or program and under an assumed set of economic and other forces outside the unit for which the forecast

---

[10] For a comprehensive series of twelve articles which report on trends, ideas, intrigues, and case histories in test marketing, see "Management Guide to Test Marketing," *Sales Management*, Aug. 27, 1965, p. 21. See also Cameron Day, "New Stature, New Dimensions for Test Marketing," *Sales Management*, Nov. 10, 1964, p. 79.

[11] Committee on Definitions, *op. cit.*, p. 20.

is made. The forecast may be for a specified item of merchandise or for an entire line.

Comment. Two sets of factors are involved in making a Sales Forecast; (1) those forces outside the control of the firm for which the forecast is made that are likely to influence its sales, and (2) changes in the marketing methods or practices of the firm that are likely to affect its sales. In the course of planning future activities, the management of a given firm may make several sales forecasts each consisting of an estimate of probable sales if a given marketing plan is adopted or a given set of outside forces prevails. The estimated effects that several marketing plans may have on Sales and Profits may be compared in the process of arriving at that marketing program which will, in the opinion of the officials of the company, be best designed to promote its welfare.

It may be noted that a sales forecast is influenced by a company's proposed marketing program and by an assumed set of external influences. The forecast is *not* an estimate of sales under ideal conditions; this would be more like the calculation of sales potential. In some cases a sales forecast and a sales potential may be the same, but usually a sales forecast is less. The company's existing production facilities may limit its opportunity to sell more units during the coming year, or the sales force and distribution system may prevent the company from realizing its full sales potential. The company might be able to bring its forecast nearer to its full sales potential if more funds were available to devote to market expansion and a more intensive promotional campaign.

A good sales forecast is undoubtedly the most important single planning tool. It is the basis of sound budgeting; in fact, as noted earlier, all budgeting starts with the sales forecast. Financial planning for working capital requirements, plant expansion, and other needs is based on anticipated sales. Scheduling of all production resources and facilities, such as setting manpower needs, purchasing raw-material requirements, and determining the rate of production output, depends upon the sales forecast.[12]

Sales-forecasting periods

One year is probably the most widely used period for sales forecasting, although many firms prepare forecasts for periods of three or six months. Also, many firms review or revise their annual forecasts monthly or quarterly. Annual sales forecasts tie in with annual financial planning and reporting and are often based on estimates of the coming year's business activity.

Short-run forecasts of less than a year may be desirable when activity in the firm's industry is so dynamic or volatile that it is not feasible to look ahead a full year. As a case in point, many firms engaged in fashion merchandising,

---

[12] For a review of the sales forecast's importance to nonmarketing executives, see John D. Louth, "Management's 'Forgotten' Sales Forecast," *Dun's Review and Modern Industry*, October, 1965, p. 65.

producers and retailers alike, prepare a forecast which covers only one fashion season.[13]

In some instances, long-range forecasts (more than one year) are helpful in financial planning and in planning for long-term plant, equipment, and materials needs. These long-range estimates are really estimates of sales potentials rather than sales forecasts. They usually indicate maximum sales opportunity and are in no way related to the firm's marketing program.

Factors influencing future sales volume

The many factors which can influence future sales volume may be grouped into four categories: (1) conditions within the company, (2) conditions within the industry, (3) conditions in customers' industries, and (4) general socio-economic factors. Each element within each category will have varying effects on the forecast, depending upon the differences in products, company situations, etc. Also, while the company has partial or total control over some variables, it may have absolutely no control over many external factors. Nevertheless, in preparing a forecast, a marketing administrator should gather and analyze as much information as possible regarding the effect of these factors on future sales volume.

Methods of sales forecasting

Sales forecasts may be based on intuition, hunches, and uninformed guesses or on highly detailed statistical correlation and trend analysis techniques. The methods of arriving at a forecast fall into two general groups. One is based on a "buildup" technique. Estimates are accumulated for various segments of the market or from various organizational units in the company, and the composite figure is the sales forecast. The other major category includes all methods whereby the forecaster seeks a relationship between one or more variables and the future sales volume. Some of these methods are identical to those used in determining market and sales potentials.[14]

---

[13] As an example of short-run forecasting done by one such company—a manufacturer of seasonal, fashion sportswear—see Carl Vreeland, "The Jantzen Method of Short-range Forecasting," *Journal of Marketing*, April, 1963, pp. 66–70.

[14] For a more detailed description, explanation, and evaluation of five major methods of sales forecasting, see William J. Stanton and Richard H. Buskirk, *Management of the Sales Force*, rev. ed., Richard D. Irwin, Inc., Homewood, Ill., 1964, pp. 554–569. The five methods are executive opinion, sales force composite, trend projection, market factor derivation, and correlation analysis. A case example illustrates the use of three of these techniques. For an excellent source, see *Forecasting Sales*, National Industrial Conference Board, Inc., Studies in Business Policy, no. 106, New York, 1964; see also Robert Reichard, "What's New in Sales Forecasting: A Survey of Current Company Practices," *Management Review*, September, 1965, pp. 34–45.

Once the total forecast is determined, it should be subdivided in as much detail as possible. That is, a forecast should be prepared in dollars and/or units for each territory, product line, customer group, or other meaningful sales unit. The itemized forecast can then be used in detailed operational levels of planning, such as setting sales quotas or allocating the advertising appropriation.

The computer and other electronic data-processing equipment offer an opportunity for a breakthrough in sales forecasting; firms can assimilate and analyze data more quickly with this equipment. Both executives and staff researchers can use the more complex methods of forecasting, once they become aware of the forecasting potential of a computer.[15]

Past sales and trend analysis   A favorite method of forecasting is to base the estimate *entirely* on past sales. This technique is used frequently by retailers whose main goal is to "beat last year's figures." The method consists simply in applying a flat percentage increase to the volume achieved last year or to the average volume of the past few years. The same rate of increase is anticipated for every product in the company's line.

This technique is simple, inexpensive, and easy to apply. For firms operating in a reasonably stable market situation, where their market shares have remained constant for a period of years, it is possible that past sales can be depended upon as the sole indicator of future volume. On balance, however, the method is highly unreliable. Most firms operate in a dynamic market. Also, it is unrealistic to assume that each article in the product mix will enjoy the same rate of growth. Finally, changes in the marketing program can have varying effects on future sales and destroy the relationship with past sales activity. In some of the other sales-forecasting methods, management considers past sales as one of several influencing factors.

Trend analysis is a variation of the forecasting method based on past sales, but it is a bit more complicated. It involves either a long-run projection of sales trends computed by the statistical technique known as the least-squares method, or a short-run projection (forecasting for only a few months ahead) based upon a seasonal index of sales. Adding the statistical sophistication in long-run trend analysis does not really remove the inherent weakness of basing future estimates only on past sales activity. Short-run trend analysis may be acceptable if the firm's sales follow a reliable seasonal pattern. Thus if sales reach 10,000 units in the first quarter (January–March) and, historically, the second quarter is always about 50 per cent better, then we can forecast sales of 15,000 units in the April–June period.

Sales force composite   This is a buildup method. It consists in collecting from each salesman or each middleman an estimate of sales of various products in his territory during the period to be covered by the forecast. The total

---

[15] See "The Computer in Marketing," part 4, "Sales Forecasting," *Sales Management,* Jan. 7, 1966, pp. 45–52; see also Robert L. McLaughlin, "The Breakthrough in Sales Forecasting," *Journal of Marketing,* April, 1963, pp. 46–54.

composite of these separate estimates is the company's sales forecast. This method may be used advantageously if the firm has competent, intelligent, high-caliber salesmen and if it is selling to a market composed of relatively few but large customers. Thus a sales forecast based on this method would be more applicable to large electrical generators than to small general-use motors.

The sales-force-composite method has the merit of placing responsibility for forecasting upon the shoulders of the men who must meet their own target. Also, it takes advantage of the salesmen's specialized knowledge of their own market, and it should make them more willing to accept their assigned sales quota. On the other hand, it takes salesmen away from their main task—selling. Furthermore, salesmen are not trained or qualified to do the research needed in forecasting; they are in no position to see the "big picture," that is, the total company operations and the domestic and international socioeconomic conditions which influence future sales volume.

Analysis of market factors   This method is identical to the market-factor-derivation technique explained earlier in connection with the determination of market potentials and market share. For most companies the analysis of market factors is probably the best forecasting method to use because it is the most reliable and valid. The fundamental thesis underlying the validity of this method is that the future sales of a given product depend upon the behavior of certain factors related to the market demand for the product. Thus if we can determine what these factors are and can measure their relationship to sales activity, then we can forecast future sales simply by studying the behavior of the factors. If the market-factor behavior occurs prior to the period covered by the forecast, there is a lead-lag situation. The two procedures used to translate the market-factor behavior into an estimate of future sales are the direct-derivation method and the correlation-analysis technique.

The direct-derivation procedure consists in selecting the market factors which are directly related to the company's future sales volume, obtaining a quantitative measurement of these market factors, and then deriving directly from the measure of the market factor an estimate of the sales during the period covered by the forecast. Let us refer to our earlier illustration of determining the market potential for replacement tires on automobiles. Assume that we have determined through past analysis that we can sell about 400,000 tires for every million cars which become 2½, 5, 7½, and 10 years old during 1969. (That is, we have 10 per cent of the market because 1 million cars equals 4 million tires.) Now all we have to do is determine the total number of cars reaching these four ages in 1969 and then make our forecast accordingly. If there are 20 million cars, our sales forecast will be for 8 million tires.

The entire discussion of correlation analysis presented in the earlier coverage of potentials is also pertinent here.

Executive judgment   This method covers a wide range of possibilities. Basically it consists of obtaining opinions regarding future sales volume from one or more executives. If these are really informed opinions, based on other valid factual measures such as market-factor analysis, then this type of executive judgment is desirable. Certainly all the previously discussed forecasting methods should be tempered with sound executive judgment. Forecasting should not be done solely by slide rule, computer, or mathematical model. On the other hand, forecasting by executive opinion alone is a risky technique. In some instances, it is simply intuition or guesswork.

BUDGETING

After a firm has determined the market and sales potential for its products and has established a sales forecast, it is in a position to prepare its various budgets. A budget is a fundamental tool for planning and evaluation; it is the written expression of a plan.

Types of budgets

Many different budgets and subbudgets should be established within a firm. In the marketing department alone, at least four should be used—a sales budget, a selling expense budget, an advertising budget, and a departmental administrative budget. Other departments, particularly production, also should prepare several detailed budgets. In a retail or wholesale operation, separate budgets ordinarily will be prepared for each department or product grouping.

The key budget in a firm is the sales budget; it should be prepared in as much detail as possible. Anticipated sales should be stated for each product, territory, customer group, and any other meaningful sales unit. Income estimates, of course, stem from the sales forecasts.

Benefits from budgets

A budget offers a guide to management in its quest for a proper balance between income and outgo. In fact, a budget may be viewed as a reflection of planned expenditures and the revenues anticipated by the management. The budget also serves as a control mechanism to help ensure that the planned expenditures go for the originally intended purposes.

Another value stemming from a budget is that it helps to coordinate activities of the various operating units in a company. For instance, the plan should prevent a production or purchasing department from manufacturing or buying several years' supply of some item at one time; conversely, proper budgeting should ensure that the sales department will not be faced with periodic out-of-stock conditions. Financial executives can keep track of money needs in production, sales, and other departments.

A budget also sets a standard for the performance of organizational units. After a budget is set up, additional planning activities can be conducted in order to implement the plan that the budget represents. Each department or unit covered by a given budget strives to match the standards set by this plan.

A corollary benefit of budgetary control is that it offers a basis for performance review and evaluation. When actual performance does not meet budgetary standards, analysis can be undertaken to explain why. Meeting these standards is usually deemed satisfactory performance, and when standards are not met, the burden of proof is on the organizational unit which varies.

Budget preparation

Budgets usually cover a quarterly, semiannual, or annual period. In some cases monthly budgets are developed; rarely is a budget prepared for a period of more than one year. In some fields, such as the manufacturing and retailing of wearing apparel, budget periods coincide with certain seasons. Whatever length of time is covered, budget periods should strike a balance between the amount of control desired and the cost of preparing the budgets.

It is difficult to generalize on the subject of who has the responsibility for preparing budgets. Normally no common pattern is discernible for the major budgets in a company. In large firms, there is sometimes a budget director who is responsible for preparing the budget; in other cases, a budget committee may prepare the sales budget as well as the general company budget. Departmental sales and operating budgets are usually the responsibility of departmental managers.

Problems in budget management

One major criticism of budgets is that often they are inflexible. Executives who are overzealous about staying within their budgets may fail to take advantage of opportunities provided by changed conditions in the market or in other areas affecting company welfare. Such executives may be compared to the quarterback who moved the ball 70 yards in three plays from his own 20-yard line and then kicked because he was told to punt on the fourth down. Some budgets are enforced so strictly that management punts no matter what.

Flexibility is certainly to be desired in a budget. The problem, however, is to set a proper limit on flexibility. Marketing executives need freedom to meet the exigencies that crop up in the dynamic market situation, but unrestricted freedom of action can remove all semblance of planning and control from the budget.

Budget administrators also need to control waste stemming from budgetary procedure and history. Some firms force a department to spend all its allotted funds within the budgetary period; no carry-over is allowed. In other cases, department executives must spend the money only for narrowly specified purposes. After reaching the budgeted limit for an article, they cannot buy more of the article with funds budgeted to another account, even though it may contain a surplus. Another related problem is that executives feel that they must spend all of their budgeted funds or face the prospect of having future allotments cut. The philosophy "let's ask for twice what we really need in the hope of getting enough" stems from budget inflexibility and leads to waste.

Most of these problems can be solved fairly easily with a judicious amount of flexibility in the budget, with careful budgetary supervision, and with a fair and realistic attitude on the part of the budget officer and other executives. A budget is a tool to help executives; it should not be allowed to degenerate into an obstacle or a challenge.

QUESTIONS AND PROBLEMS

1 "Planning involves the matching of means and ends—of matching inputs and outputs." Explain how this concept may be applied in a practical fashion to the promotional program in a firm. To new-product development.

2 Explain some of the ways in which formal marketing planning serves as an effective form of risk management in marketing.

3 "There is no sound reason why marketing executives should not engage in formal planning." Discuss.

4 Using examples of consumer or industrial products, carefully distinguish between market potential and sales forecast. Why is the sales forecast usually smaller than the sales potential?

5 What are some logical market factors which you might use in estimating the market potential for each of the following products?
   a. Central home air conditioners   d. Sterling flatware
   b. Milking machines   e. Safety goggles
   c. Golf clubs

6 How would you determine the market potential for a textbook in a beginning course in marketing?

7 What are some of the problems a researcher faces when using the test-market method for determining market or sales potentials?

8 A grocery products manufacturer estimates that sales of his new cereal will reach $15 million next year. How much should he expect to sell in the state in which your school is located?

9 What effect would each of the following occurrences have on the market potential for furniture? For a manufactured grocery product?
   a. Establishment of a 10 per cent Federal sales tax accompanied by a major cut in Federal income tax rates
   b. Increase in minimum wages to $2 per hour

10 "No company should forecast its sales without making some use of the executive-judgment method, yet this method never should be used to the exclusion of other methods." Discuss.

11 What companies—manufacturers or middlemen—might be interested in forecasting sales on a weekly or a monthly basis?

12 If a firm bases its sales forecasts on estimates compiled by its salesmen, should a salesman be rewarded financially for correctly forecasting the sales in his territory during the coming year?

13 What is the managerial relationship between budgeting and planning? Between budgeting and evaluation?

14 "Budgeting is a managerial tool particularly suited for use by large firms. It is not suitable for use by small manufacturers or middlemen." Discuss.

15 How can management introduce an adequate amount of flexibility into its budget?

16 "If a department within the marketing division of a company fails to spend its allotted funds during the budget period, the department should be allowed to carry over the surplus to the next period and still get its full budgeted amount for the next period." Discuss.

17 How can individual executives be persuaded to stop asking the budget officer for more funds than they really need?

28

ANALYSIS OF SALES VOLUME AND MARKETING COSTS

After a firm's plans have been set in operation, the results should be analyzed and evaluated as promptly as possible. Without an evaluation, management is in no position to tell whether its plan worked, to what degree it was successful, and what the reasons were for success or failure. At various points earlier in this book, we have reviewed and appraised separate parts of our marketing program—the product-planning process, the performance of our salesmen and middlemen, and the effectiveness of our advertising program, for instance. Our analysis and evaluation have been continuing activities. At this point, we want to study the results of our total marketing effort in the form of an analysis of our sales volume and our marketing costs.

In many respects, planning and evaluation are interrelated activities. Evaluation logically follows planning in that planning sets forth what should be done, and evaluation shows what really was done. Sometimes a circular relationship exists: plans are made, the operational results are evaluated, and new plans are prepared on the basis of this appraisal. Marketing-related information about past activities stems from a review and appraisal, and it forms a basis for future planning. Information about the future involves forecasting and estimating, and yet predictive techniques are applied to historical data.

THE MARKETING AUDIT: A TOTAL EVALUATION PROGRAM

To appreciate fully the managerial activities of analysis and evaluation, we shall first consider the concept of a marketing audit as a total evaluation program.[1] Audits are not new to business management. Traditionally, they have carried the connotation of a review and evaluation of some business activity. They have long been used in accounting and financial operations, and we are also accustomed to manpower or personnel audits. Really all we are doing here is applying the concept of an audit to our marketing operations and the marketing program.

A *marketing audit* may be defined as *"a systematic, critical, and unbiased review and appraisal of the basic objectives and policies of the marketing function and of the organization, methods, procedures, and personnel employed to implement the policies and achieve the objectives."*[2] In this definition six areas in marketing are identified for appraisal—objectives, policies, organization, methods, procedures, and personnel. To qualify as a marketing audit, any appraisal must include all six, along with the underlying philosophies upon which the activities are based, because the audit has the connotation of a *total* evaluation program. A fragmented appraisal of some marketing methods or activities may be useful and pertinent, but it is not a marketing audit; it is only one part of an audit. Furthermore, to be classed as a marketing audit, the review and appraisal must be done systematically. The audit must be a coordinated, integrated study of the total program, and it should be done at one time.

Although an audit suggests an after-the-fact review and a search for weaknesses in a business structure, a marketing audit includes an evaluation of the effects of alternatives *before* a decision is reached. Thus the audit becomes an aid in decision making. In addition to identifying weaknesses in a company's program and suggesting means to eliminate them, marketing audits should include reviews of successful operations so that management may capitalize on its strong points. Furthermore, an audit should anticipate future

[1] The "marketing audit" concept and case studies from three companies are presented in *Analyzing and Improving Marketing Performance: "Marketing Audits" in Theory and Practice*, American Management Association, Management Report no. 32, New York, 1959. Much of this section is based on this source. See especially Abe Schuchman, "The Marketing Audit: Its Nature, Purposes, and Problems," pp. 11–19; and Alfred R. Oxenfeldt, "The Marketing Audit as a Total Evaluation Program," pp. 25–36.

[2] Oxenfeldt, *op. cit.*, p. 26.

situations. An audit is intended for "prognosis as well as diagnosis. . . . It is the practice of preventive as well as curative marketing medicine."[3]

SCOPE OF EVALUATION ACTIVITIES

A complete marketing audit as explained above is something of an ideal. Rarely does a firm conduct a full audit of the total marketing program—the marketing mix, that is—because the cost and difficulty of the task are great. Instead, management usually appraises individual components of the marketing mix. Such an evaluation is desirable if a full-scale audit is impossible. A major shortcoming, however, is the possible lack of integration among the several areas studied. For instance, a recommendation stemming from a review of the distribution system may have serious implications in pricing or promotion.

The analytical process is essentially the same three-stage task regardless of which area is the subject of management's attention. First, management must gather and analyze the facts and compare the actual results with the budgeted figures in order to determine the extent of the variations. Next, it must determine what specific factors in the market or in the marketing program are responsible for the program's results. Finally, it must develop plans, policies, and procedures with the intent of improving unsatisfactory conditions and capitalizing on favorable ones. To summarize, the administrator's job is to find out *what* happened, *why* it happened, and then decide *what to do* about it.

MISDIRECTED MARKETING EFFORT

One of the primary benefits of analysis and evaluation activities is that they can help correct misdirected or misplaced marketing effort.[4]

The "80-20" principle

A company does not enjoy the same rate of net profit on every individual sale. The rate of profit on one segment of the company's sales volume is usually above or below the company's average rate. In most firms a large proportion of the orders, customers, territories, or products accounts for a small share of the profits. This relationship between selling units and profits has been characterized as the "80-20" principle; that is, 80 per cent of the orders, customers, territories, or products contributes only 20 per cent of the net sales,

---

[3] Schuchman, *op. cit.*, p. 14.

[4] The term "misdirected marketing effort" was first noted in Charles H. Sevin's writings on distribution cost analysis. Some of the remarks in this section are based on Sevin's publications. See Charles H. Sevin, *Distribution Cost Analysis,* U.S. Dept. of Commerce, Economic Series, no. 50, U.S. Government Printing Office, Washington, D.C., 1946; and *How Manufacturers Reduce Their Distribution Costs,* U.S. Dept. of Commerce, Economic Series, no. 72, U.S. Government Printing Office, Washington, D.C., 1948.

gross margin, or net profit. Conversely, 20 per cent of these selling units accounts for 80 per cent of the volume or profit. The 80-20 figure is used simply to epitomize the misplacement of marketing efforts; actually, of course, the percentage split varies from one situation to another.

The basic reason for the 80-20 situation is that some misdirected or misplaced efforts are found in most marketing programs. Marketing efforts and costs follow the *number* of territories, customers, products, or other selling units rather than the actual or potential sales volume or profit. In a retail sale which is to be charged and delivered, approximately the same order-filling, billing, and delivery expenses are involved, whether the sale is a mink coat or a necktie. Manufacturers may assign one salesman or one branch office to each territory, and yet there may be substantial differences in the volume and profit returns from various districts.

Reasons for misdirected marketing effort

Many businessmen are unaware of the misdirected marketing effort in their firms. They do not know what percentage of total sales and profits comes from a given product line or customer group. Ordinarily they do little or nothing about analyzing and appraising their marketing operations. Also, in the past, administrators have been volume-conscious rather than profit-conscious. They have relied upon sales volume as the sole criterion for measuring the success of a marketing program. The increasing acceptance of the marketing concept should blunt this emphasis on sales volume. It still exists, however, among manufacturers who set sales volume quotas for their salesmen, among wholesalers who pay their salesmen a commission on net sales, and among retailers who base their sales goals on the preceding year's sales volume figures.

Frequently executives cannot uncover their misdirection of effort because they lack sufficiently detailed information. The analogy of an iceberg in an open sea has been used to illustrate this stituation. Only a small part of an iceberg is visible above the surface of the water, and the submerged 90 per cent is the dangerous part. The figures representing total sales or total costs on an operating statement are like the visible part of an iceberg. The detailed figures representing sales, costs, and other performance measures for each territory, product, or salesman correspond to the important submerged segment.

Total sales or costs on an operating statement or other figures representing total performance are too general for a marketing executive interested in analysis and evaluation. In fact, the total figures are often inconclusive and misleading. More than one company has shown satisfactory overall sales and profit figures, but when these totals were subdivided by territory, products, or some other basis, serious weaknesses were discovered. A manufacturer of rubber products showed an overall annual increase of 12 per cent in sales and 9 per cent in net profit on one of his product lines one year, but when he analyzed his figures more closely, he found that the sales change within each territory ranged from an increase of 19 per cent to a decrease of 3 per cent. In some territories, profits increased as much as 14 per cent, and in others they were down 20 per cent. This is a practical example of the "iceberg principle."[5]

An even more important cause of misplaced marketing effort is that marketing executives must make decisions even though their knowledge of the exact nature of marketing costs, as well as the managerial tools controlling these costs, is woefully inadequate. In other words, management lacks (1) knowledge of the disproportionate spread of marketing effort and (2) reliable standards for determining what should be spent on marketing and what results should be obtained from the expenditures.

As an illustration, a marketing executive really does not know how much to spend on advertising, marketing research, or sales training. Even more troublesome is the fact that, after the money is spent, there is no satisfactory yardstick to determine whether the results are satisfactory. If a company spends $250,000 more on advertising this year than last year, management ordinarily cannot state what the resultant increase in sales volume or profits should be, nor do the executives know what the results would have been if an equivalent sum had been devoted to new-product development, management training institutes for middlemen, or some other aspect of the marketing program.

ANALYSIS OF SALES VOLUME

An *analysis of sales volume* is a careful study of the internal records of a firm as they are summarized in the net-sales section of the operating statement. A researcher studies the dollar and/or unit sales in total and analyzes these sales on the basis of such subdivisions as territories, product lines, time periods, customer groups, and order sizes. A sales volume analysis may be extended to include a study of the cost of goods sold and the resultant gross margin, also divided into various product and market bases. A *marketing cost analysis* is a detailed study of the operating expense section of the profit and loss statement in an attempt to determine the relative profitability of each product line and various market segments. A sales volume analysis and a marketing cost analysis are thus closely related activities. Together they constitute a detailed study of a company's operating statement.

Limitations of volume analysis

Two major limitations face the marketing administrator who wishes to use a sales volume analysis as a basis for his decision making. The first is that the necessary detailed data are usually not readily available in a form useful to the analyst. Accumulating and processing these essential facts can be a tedious, expensive task. Fortunately, the advent of the computer and other electronic

---

[5] The term "iceberg principle" was first suggested to the author in the writings of Richard D. Crisp. For example, see Richard D. Crisp, *How to Reduce Distribution Costs,* Funk & Wagnalls Company, in association with *Modern Industry* magazine, New York, 1948.

data-processing equipment has greatly facilitated the information-gathering step and has opened tremendous new opportunities for management to analyze sales data.[6]

The second limitation is that even a completely reliable sales volume analysis may, if used alone, be misleading. A volume analysis alone may show that sales of a certain product or sales in a given region are steadily increasing as a percentage of market potential. A study of gross margin or marketing costs, however, may show that the firm is enjoying a "profitless prosperity." Nevertheless, we hasten to point out that while a full marketing cost analysis is more desirable than a volume analysis alone, certainly a volume analysis is better than nothing.

Bases for analyzing volume

There are many bases upon which a company may analyze its sales volume. These include total sales volume, territories, product lines, customer groups, and size of orders. To illustrate some aspects of a volume analysis and show what can be done with the results, we shall build our discussion around a hypothetical firm—the Great Western Office Furniture Company. This firm sells in thirteen Western states, including Alaska and Hawaii. The market is divided into four territories. The company's product mix is divided into four broad categories: desks, chairs, filing and safekeeping equipment, and accessories (wastebaskets, desk sets, desk pads, clothes trees). Some of these products are manufactured by the Great Western Company, and others are purchased from outside sources but sold under Great Western's brand.

Total sales volume   There are two trend figures related to total sales volume that we should study. The first is the trend in the company's total sales volume over a period of years, and the second is the trend in the company's share of the market. As we know, a company's sales may increase steadily while its share of the market actually decreases.

An analysis of total sales volume is probably the easiest of all the usual types of marketing analyses made by management. Figures on the company's total volume ordinarily are readily available from the firm's accounting records. All an executive needs in addition is an accurate estimate of total industry sales in the geographic market covered by the company. Trade associations and government agencies are excellent sources for industry volume statistics in many fields.

Table 28–1 shows the information necessary to start an analysis of total sales volume in the Great Western Office Furniture Company. The company's annual sales doubled (from $18 million to $36 million) during the ten-year period ending in 1966. Furthermore, they increased each year over the pre-

---

[6] See "The Computer in Marketing," part 5, "Sales Analysis," *Sales Management,* Mar. 4, 1966, pp. 49–56.

ceding year, with the exception of 1963. Thus far the company situation is very encouraging. When industry figures are introduced for comparison, however, the picture changes. During this decade, the industry's annual sales have increased from $120 million to $300 million (a 250 per cent increase), with the result that the company's share of market declined from 15 to 12 per cent. In summary, the company's annual sales increased 200 per cent, but its market share declined 20 per cent. We have now concluded the first of the three steps in the analytical procedure—we know *what* happened.

The next step is to determine *why* Great Western's market position declined. The number of possible causes is almost limitless, and this is what makes management's task so difficult. A weakness in almost any aspect of Great Western's product line, distribution system, pricing structure, or promotional program may have contributed to the loss of market share. It may be that the real culprit is competition. There may be more strong competitors in the market, who were attracted by rapid growth rates in market potentials, or competitors' marketing programs may be more effective than Great Western's own excellent program.

Sales by territories   While a study of total sales volume may be a good place to start a sales analysis, it is usually insufficient because of the workings of the iceberg principle. To uncover activity in the submerged segments of the market, administrators will analyze sales volume by territories. This type of

table   28–1

Annual sales volume of Great Western Office Furniture Company, industry volume, and company's share in thirteen-state market

This table gives the basic data needed for a sales volume analysis in a single firm. In this case, the company's volume doubled in ten years, but its share of the market declined from 15 to 12 per cent. What factors might account for this decreasing market share? Is a sales volume analysis sufficient to detect situations characterized as "80–20" or "iceberg"?

Year	Company volume in millions of dollars	Industry volume in company's market, in millions of dollars	Company's percentage share of market
1966	36.0	300	12.0
1965	34.7	275	12.6
1964	33.1	255	13.0
1963	30.4	220	13.8
1962	31.7	235	13.5
1961	28.0	200	14.0
1960	24.5	170	14.4
1959	22.5	155	14.5
1958	21.8	150	14.8
1957	18.0	120	15.0

analysis may also bring to light the existence of the 80-20 principle in that a large share of volume may be coming from a small number of territories.

It may be helpful to explain briefly one four-step territorial sales analysis procedure which is reasonably simple and need not be expensive or time-consuming. The first step is to determine what share of the company's total sales volume should come from each territory. This involves selecting a market index which can be used to establish territorial potentials. (The use of market indices to determine territorial potentials was discussed in the preceding chapter.) For instance, one firm used an index of residential building permits issued. If 15 per cent of the total residential building permits issued in the nation during one year were issued in the company's Midwestern region, then 15 per cent of the company's sales volume should be obtained from that area. If the firm's total market covers only part of the country, then the total annual building permits issued in that limited area would be equated to 100 per cent. Thus if a company operated only in the six New England states and if 28 per cent of the building permits issued in that six-state area were issued in Massachusetts, then management should expect 28 per cent of its total sales volume from that state.

The next step is to determine the actual total sales made during the period under review. The third step is to multiply each territorial index by the actual total sales in order to establish the goal or par for each district. Finally, the actual sales figure in each territory is compared with the predetermined stand-ard of performance for the region, and any variation is tabulated.

This procedure is illustrated in Table 28–2. The company has set up four sales territories to cover its thirteen-state market. By applying a pertinent market index chosen by management, we find that 30 per cent of the total sales should have been obtained from territory A, 25 per cent from territory B, etc. Applying these percentages to the total annual volume of $36 million, we find that

table   28–2

Territorial sales volume in four territories of Great Western Office Furniture Company, 1966

Here the iceberg principle is at work. Territory D is $2.4 million below its sales goal, while the performances in the other three regions are above par. How did management derive the figures in the market-index column?

Territory	Market index, per cent	Sales goals, in millions of dollars	Actual sales, in millions of dollars	Performance percentage	Dollar variation, in millions
A	30	10.8	12.5	116	+1.7
B	25	9.0	9.6	107	+ .6
C	21	7.6	7.7	101	+ .1
D	24	8.6	6.2	72	−2.4
Total	100	36.0	36.0		

the dollar goal was $10.8 million in region A, $9.0 million in B, etc. The actual territorial sales are tabulated in column 4, and the dollar variation is listed in column 6.

The critical column is the one entitled Performance Percentage. The percentages are derived by dividing the actual sales by the territorial goal. A performance percentage of 100 means that the territory did exactly what was expected of it. Thus from the table we see that territories B and C did just a little better than was expected, territory A passed its goal by a wide margin, and territory D was quite a disappointment.

When management knows what has occurred in each territory, it must find the reasons for the performances and then take constructive action based upon the findings. Consequently, a careful study should be undertaken to find out why area D did so poorly. The fault may lie in one or more aspects of the marketing program in that area, or competition may be particularly strong there. An attempt should be made to determine what accounts for A's success and whether this information can be helpful in the other regions. Also, the executives should analyze territorial volume by products and customer groups. Even though area A did well, the iceberg principle may be at work within the region. The fine total performance within A may be covering up weaknesses in separate product lines.

Sales by products   Management may use any of several types of volume analyses by product lines. One type is simply a tabulation of the annual sales by individual products or related groups of products for the past several years. This tabulation shows the percentage of total volume obtained from each line. From it, management can ascertain any trend in sales by products.

table   28–3

Sales volume in two territories of Great Western Office Furniture Company, 1966

In Table 28–2, we saw that territory A exceeded its sales goal by $1.7 million (16 per cent), while territory D was 28 per cent below par. Now we can see more of our iceberg by determining which products accounted for these variations. Sales of desks were $1,150,000 above the goal in territory A and $1,400,000 below the forecast in territory D. Note also that A was well above its market target in filing equipment, while D fell off considerably in sales of chairs.

Product line	Territory A ($000)			Territory D ($000)		
	Goal	*Actual*	*Variation*	*Goal*	*Actual*	*Variation*
Desks	$ 4,500	$ 5,650	+$1,150	$3,800	$2,400	−$1,400
Chairs	3,400	3,300	− 100	2,400	1,420	− 980
Filing equipment	2,100	2,700	+ 600	1,800	1,900	+ 100
Accessories	800	850	+ 50	600	480	− 120
Total	$10,800	$12,500	$1,700	$8,600	$6,200	−$2,400

It is particularly helpful if industry figures are available for each product line. Then the executives can compare the firm's record of sales with industry figures, as was done in Table 28–1 for total sales. If the company's sales in one product line are decreasing, this is not so bad if industry sales for this article are also declining. If one product accounts for a very small part of the company volume, management can evaluate this situation better if industry figures are available for comparison.

Another type of product sales analysis is made by studying the sales of each product *in each territory* over a period of years. Through such a study, management can determine in what geographical market each product is relatively strong or weak. Great Western may find, for instance, that its total sales of desks increased 14 per cent last year but that sales of this product declined 2 per cent in territory B.

To study product sales in each territory, we can use the method illustrated in Table 28–2 in connection with the territorial analysis. That is, through the application of appropriate market indexes, management can establish sales goals for each product line in each territory. Then actual sales can be compared with these goals. In Table 28–2, we saw that territory A reached 116 per cent of its goal, or an excess of $1.7 million; territory D was short of its goal by 28 per cent, or $2.4 million. What actually occurred in these two districts is identified more specifically by the type of product sales analysis illustrated in Table 28–3. Selected market indexes were applied to each product line to establish product sales goals in each territory. Thus in A, the total goal was $10.8 million, with $4.5 million expected from sales of desks, $3.4 million from sales of chairs, etc. In district A, almost two-thirds of the $1.7 million excess over quota came from sales of desks, and one-third was contributed by the line of filing equipment. While the region as a whole surpassed its goal by 16 per cent, the sales of chairs declined about 3 per cent ($100,000). In fact, sales of chairs were below par in both territories.

MARKETING COST ANALYSIS

An analysis of sales volume on the several bases discussed earlier in the chapter can be quite helpful in appraising a company's marketing efforts. A volume analysis, however, does not tell us anything about the *profitability* of a territory, product line, salesman, or group of customers. In order to determine the relative profitability of the various selling units, management may conduct a marketing or distribution cost analysis.[7] In the literature, the term "distribution cost analysis" seems to be preferred. "*Marketing* cost analysis" is more representative of the full scope of the analytical activity and is more in line with the

[7] Several fine books and journal articles cover the more technical phases of marketing cost analysis. For example, see Donald R. Longman and Michael Schiff, *Practical Distribution Cost Analysis*, Richard D. Irwin, Inc., Homewood, Ill., 1955; or J. Brooks Heckert and Robert B. Miner, *Distribution Costs,* 2d ed., The Ronald Press Company, New York, 1955.

concept of marketing management. The two terms are used synonymously in this chapter.

Nature and scope of marketing cost analysis

A marketing cost analysis is a detailed study of a firm's entire distribution cost structure. For the various cost items, management may establish a budgetary goal or a standard of performance and then analyze the extent and cause of variations between the actual and the budgeted expenses.

Marketing cost analysis can be used by the individual business firms to determine the cost of performing marketing activities such as outside selling, billing, advertising, and warehousing. It can be used to determine the expenses and profits of the company's various products, customer classes, territories, and order sizes. This is an extremely important use in relation to the Robinson-Patman Act, because this law requires firms to justify their discount schedules on the basis of cost differentials. Marketing cost analysis may also be used to establish and appraise various marketing policies and operating procedures.

Like a sales volume analysis, a marketing cost analysis is more concerned with analysis than with bookkeeping or accounting practices. Furthermore, cost analysis is frequently performed on a sporadic or sampling basis, whereas the accounting system is maintained on a routine, continuing basis. We may analyze territorial costs in only half the districts or study the cost of selling various products for only a six-month period. The cost analysis, however, is closely related to the accounting system in one very important way. A detailed system of ledger accounts is a virtual necessity if management wishes to do a thorough cost analysis because much of the raw data for a cost analysis comes from the accounting records.

Some significant differences exist between marketing cost analysis and production cost accounting. First, their scope or coverage differs. In production cost accounting, management is interested in determining the costs per unit of product; in marketing cost analysis, the administrators are interested not only in marketing costs for each product, but also in the marketing expenses attached to geographic market segments, separate customer classes, and various order sizes.

Most production expenses are related to the operation of machines or to men who are subject to constant personal observation and supervision. Consequently, it is possible to measure rather accurately the cost of producing a unit of the product. On the other hand, marketing expenses are incurred by salesmen whose job is not completely repetitious and whose activities are not constantly observed by a supervisor. Therefore, usually it is not possible to determine the time, effort, and resultant costs related to individual marketing activities.

A third, and probably more important, difference exists. With respect to production activities, the costs are a function of volume $(C = fV)$; that is, the costs react to a change in volume. To illustrate, if the factory output is increased 15 per cent, then *as a result* there is an accurately measurable change in costs. In marketing, on the other hand, volume is a function of costs $(V = fC)$; that is, the sales volume output reacts to a change in input cost factors. Volume will ordinarily increase, for example, *as a result* of adding more salesmen or spending money for advertising.

In these relationships, management can foretell quite accurately what will happen to production expenses when there is, say, an increase of 10 per cent in the volume produced. A marketing executive is not in a correspondingly advantageous position. He cannot say, for instance, exactly how much increase in volume should be expected when the advertising budget is increased 10 per cent or when two new salesmen are added in territory A.

Problems involved in cost analysis

One practical general limitation to marketing cost analysis is that some type of specialization of personnel or variety in products must exist in a company; otherwise, costs will be incurred in lumps which cannot be subdivided satisfactorily. Also, management must realize the need for, and benefits of, marketing cost analysis. It must have some understanding of the techniques involved in cost analysis and be able to interpret the results of the analysis. From the start, management should recognize that cost study will require a considerable amount of manpower, time, and money. Even if the company has a machine accounting system and uses other forms of data-processing equipment, the cost may still be high.

Classifying marketing expenses   Once management decides which of its costs can be categorized as marketing expenses, it must organize the costs into useful classifications. In the accounting systems of most companies, the operating expenses are classified according to the direct object of the expenditures. Thus we find ledger accounts for rent, salesmen's commissions, taxes, postage, salaries, office supplies, etc. These are often called "natural" expenses. For purposes of a marketing cost analysis, administrators usually find it necessary to reclassify these expenses according to the marketing functions involved. Then all costs pertaining to one activity, such as advertising or warehousing, are grouped together.

To regroup the various natural (ledger) expenses, management must first determine which functional classifications will be most useful and then allocate the natural expenses to the appropriate function. There is no standard list of functional classifications; each firm should tailor-make its own. The following groupings, however, can apply to many firms:

1.   Selling—direct costs (salesmen's compensation, travel, etc.)

2.   Selling—indirect costs (sales training, sales supervision, marketing research, sales statistics, etc.)

3.   Advertising and sales promotion

4.   Warehousing
5.   Transportation and shipping, including order filling and packing
6.   Credits and collection (bad-debt losses, credit office expenses)
7.   Order processing and billing
8.   Marketing administrative expenses

Allocating costs   Undoubtedly one of the most difficult problems in cost analysis, whether it is an analysis of marketing or of production expenses, is that of cost allocation. In a marketing cost analysis, this problem occurs in two places. First, the ledger expenses must be allocated to appropriate activity cost groupings. Then these resultant functional cost totals must be allocated to individual territories, products, or some other market segment. The value and success of a marketing cost study depends to a considerable extent upon the selection of cost allocation bases. The choice of illogical or unreasonable bases can distort the results and mislead management.

Operating expenses can be divided into direct and indirect expenses. (These are sometimes called "separable" and "common" expenses.) Direct, or separable, expenses are those which are incurred totally in connection with one market segment or one unit of the sales organization. Thus the salary, commission, and travel expenses of the salesman in territory A are a direct expense for that territory. The cost of media, time, or space to advertise product C is a direct cost of marketing that product. The task of allocating direct expenses is easy. They can be apportioned in their entirety to the marketing unit, such as a product or territory, for which they were incurred.

The allocation problem really arises in connection with indirect, or common, costs. These are expenses which are incurred jointly by more than one marketing unit and, therefore, cannot be apportioned totally to one product, territory, or other market segment.

A given cost does not remain permanently in either the direct or the indirect category. Its classification depends upon the type of cost analysis being made. If a firm is analyzing costs by territories, then salesmen's salaries are direct expenses chargeable entirely to the territory in which they work. If the company conducts a cost analysis by products, however, and each salesman sells the entire line of products, then salaries are indirect, or common, expenses and should be prorated according to the estimated time salesmen devote to each product.

Within the category of indirect expenses, some costs are more indirect than others. That is, some of the activity cost groupings are directly related, at least to some extent, to the territories, products, or other marketing units being studied. For instance, the total cost for advertising, direct selling, order filling, or shipping would decrease if some of the products or territories were eliminated. By the same token, they would increase if some territories or product lines were added. These functional costs might be called *partially* indirect.

On the other hand, activity cost groups covering marketing administrative expenses and general administrative costs are *totally* indirect. Total expenses for maintaining the chief marketing executive, his staff, and his office would remain about the same, whether or not the number of territories or product lines was changed.

A study of business management today will disclose that different companies follow fundamentally different principles or philosophies in allocating totally indirect costs such as administrative overhead expenses. One approach is to allocate these expenses equally among all territories, products, or other units being studied. This is an easy method, but it is obviously inadequate and in no way related to actuality.

Another approach is to allocate these expenses in proportion to the sales volume obtained from each segment being analyzed. This method is also sometimes used to apportion partially indirect expenses, such as billing, shipping, and order filling. The philosophy is that the expense burden should be placed where it can best be borne. The large-volume territories or products are thus charged with the bulk of these expenses. Although this philosophy has some merit, it does not accurately reflect the real situation.

A third allocation system is simply to prorate the indirect costs in the same proportion as the direct expenses. If one territory has been charged with 20 per cent of the total direct expenses, it is also assigned 20 per cent of the indirect costs. Sometimes partially indirect expenses such as billing and shipping are allocated to the marketing unit on some reasonable basis. Then the totally indirect expenses of administrative overhead are prorated in the same proportion as the sum of the direct plus partially indirect costs.

In Table 28–5, which we shall discuss later, we shall see some of the better, more precise bases which are suggested for allocating a specific functional cost to various product groups or sales territories.

Full-cost versus contribution-margin controversy   One approach to the allocation of indirect costs is known as the "contribution-to-overhead" or the "contribution-margin" method. Under this system, management determines the gross margin of each marketing unit being studied. Then the direct expenses which have been allocated to each unit are deducted from the gross margin. These are the costs which presumably would be eliminated if the corresponding marketing unit were eliminated. After deducting these separable costs, the remainder is the amount which that unit is contributing to cover total overhead or indirect expenses.[8]

There is a basic point of conflict between the contribution-margin approach and the full-cost approach to the allocation of costs. In the full-cost approach,

[8] For an example of a practical application of this method, see *McKinsey–General Foods Study: The Economics of Food Distribution*, General Foods Corporation, White Plains, N.Y., 1963; and *McKinsey–Birds Eye Study: The Economics of Frozen Foods*, General Foods Corporation, White Plains, N.Y., 1964.

all indirect expenses are allocated among the marketing units being analyzed. Proponents of the full-cost approach contend that the purpose of a marketing cost study is to determine the *net* profitability of the units being studied. They feel that the contribution-margin approach does not fulfill this purpose.

Under the contribution-margin system no attempt is made to allocate indirect costs, especially the totally indirect ones such as administrative expenses. Advocates of this approach contend that it is not reasonably possible to make an accurate apportionment of these items among organizational units or market segments. Furthermore, items such as administrative costs are not at all related to any one territory or product, and there the unit should not bear any of the costs. Contribution-margin supporters also state that management is not concerned with fixed, indirect costs when making decisions affecting short-run situations. They suggest that management is then concerned only with alternative courses of action where cost structures are variable. Finally, they point out that a full-cost analysis may show a product or territory with a net loss, whereas this unit may be contributing something to overhead. Some executives might recommend that the losing department be eliminated, overlooking the fact that the unit's contribution to overhead would then have to be borne by other units. Under the contribution-margin approach, there would be no question about keeping this unit so long as no better alternative could be discovered. On balance, it seems that both methods, contribution margin and full cost, merit a place in marketing cost analysis.[9]

Types of marketing cost analyses

Three types of marketing cost analyses are commonly used by business. One is an analysis of costs as they appear in ledger accounts; another is a study of marketing expenses grouped into functional classifications; and the third is an analysis of marketing costs after they have been allocated to territories, products, or other marketing units.

Analysis of ledger expenses The simplest, quickest, and least expensive way to make a marketing cost analysis is to study the object-of-expenditure costs as they appear in the accounting ledgers. The researcher simply lists expense totals for delivery salaries, salesmen's travel expenses, advertising salaries, telephone and telegraph, etc. These costs may be compared with similar totals for past years, and each expense may be expressed as a percentage of net sales. If at all possible, the company's expense ratios should be compared with industry figures. Many trade associations publish median figures and other measures of central tendency for the industry as a whole.

---

[9] For an excellent evaluation of the two methods, see Longman and Schiff, *op. cit.*, pp. 358ff.; and Heckert and Miner, *op. cit.*, pp. 31, 34, 197–204. Also, in support of partial allocation but not necessarily the contribution-margin method alone, see Charles H. Sevin, *Distribution Cost Analysis*, U.S. Dept. of Commerce, Economic Series, no. 50, U.S. Government Printing Office, Washington, D.C., 1946, p. 18.

table 28-4

Expense distribution sheet, Great Western Office Furniture Company, 1966

The worksheet is a useful tool when allocating ledger-account expenses among the various groups of activity costs. Why is the salesmen's travel expense allocated entirely to direct selling, while the office supplies expense is prorated among all activity groups? What is a good basis for allocating the property tax expense among the functional cost groups?

Ledger expenses	Totals	Selling— direct costs	Selling— indirect costs	Advertising and sales promotion	Activity cost groups Ware- housing	Transportation and shipping	Credits and collections	Order processing and billing	Marketing adminis- trative
Salesmen's salaries	$ 2,500,000	$2,500,000							
Salesmen's travel	570,000	570,000							
Salesmen's commissions	2,400,000	2,400,000							
Media space	1,200,000			$1,200,000					
Dealer displays	200,000			200,000					
Advertising salaries	175,000			175,000					
Office supplies	180,000	25,000	$ 18,500	25,500	$ 15,000	$ 19,500	$ 15,000	$ 52,500	$ 9,000
Telephone	90,000	42,000	9,000	6,750	1,500	5,250	9,000	6,000	10,500
Administrative salaries	615,000	150,000	100,000		55,000	40,000	60,000	110,000	100,000
Property taxes	240,000	8,000	20,500	12,500	128,500	18,000	13,500	23,500	15,500
Bad debts	30,000						30,000		
Freight out	1,500,000					1,500,000			
Total	$11,700,000	$5,900,000	$875,000	$1,800,000	$425,000	$1,800,000	$225,000	$400,000	$275,000

Analysis of functional expenses   When a marketing executive wants additional information in order to help him control the cost of various marketing activities, such as advertising or warehousing, he should make an analysis of marketing expenses classified into groups representing these activities.

The procedure in a functional cost analysis is to decide what activity groups will be used and then allocate each ledger expense among the appropriate activities. An expense distribution sheet is often useful in this procedure (Table 28–4). The ledger expenses listed in the left-hand column are prorated among the appropriate columns which represent the functional groups. Some items such as the cost of advertising media space (newspapers) or time (television) can be apportioned directly to one activity (advertising and sales promotion). For other expenses, the cost can be prorated only after management has established some reasonable basis for allocation. Rent or property taxes, for instance, may be allocated according to the proportionate amount of floor space occupied by each department. Thus, if the warehouse accounts for 30 per cent of the total square feet of floor space in the firm, the warehousing function would be charged with 30 per cent of the rent or property taxes. A columnar total represents the full cost of each function. In Great Western's case, advertising and sales promotion cost $1,800,000, and warehousing costs $425,000.

A functional cost analysis gives an executive more helpful information than he can get from an analysis of ledger accounts alone. By comparing expense distribution sheets for several periods, management can ascertain which particular ledger expenses are responsible for significant changes in the cost of an activity. Finally, an analysis of activity expenses in total provides an excellent starting point for management to analyze these expenses by territories, products, or other marketing units.

Analysis of functional costs by market segments   The third and most beneficial type of marketing cost analysis is a study of the costs and profitability of each segment of the market. Common practice in this type of analysis is to divide the market by territories, products, customer groups, or order sizes. Cost analysis by market segment will enable management to pinpoint trouble spots or areas of satisfactory performance much more effectively than can be done with an analysis of either ledger account expenses or activity costs.

The procedure for making a cost analysis by market segments is quite similar to the method used to analyze functional expenses. The total of each functional cost is prorated on some appropriate basis to each product or market segment being studied. By combining a sales volume analysis with a marketing cost study, a researcher can, in effect, prepare a profit and loss statement for each of the product or market segments. In a territorial analysis, for example, all he needs to do is classify sales by territories and then determine the cost of purchasing or making the merchandise which was sold in each region. The difference between the sales and cost figures is the territorial gross margin. The third step is to allocate each activity expense among the territories. If only the

table   28–5

Bases of allocating functional cost groups to sales territories and to product groups

A given functional cost group may be distributed among territories or products on the basis of some measurable characteristic which bears a "causative" relationship to the total amount of that functional cost group. Explain, using numbers, how advertising media costs would be allocated to territories.

Functional cost group	Basis of allocation	
	To sales territories	To product groups
1. Selling—direct costs: sales salaries, incentive compensation, travel, and other expenses	Direct	Selling time devoted to each product, as shown by special sales-call reports or other special studies
2. Selling—indirect costs: field sales-office expense, sales-administration expense, sales-personnel training, marketing research, new-product development, sales statistics	Equal charge for each salesman	In proportion to direct selling time or time records by projects
3. Advertising: media costs such as TV, radio, billboards, newspaper, magazine, etc.; advertising production costs; advertising department salaries	Direct; or analysis of media circulation records	Direct; or analysis of space and time by media; other costs in proportion to media costs
4. Sales promotion: consumer promotions such as coupons, premiums, etc.; trade promotions such as price allowances, point-of-purchase displays, co-operative advertising, etc.	Direct; or analysis of source records	Direct; or analysis of source records
5. Transportation: railroad, truck, barge, etc.; payments to carriers for delivery of finished goods from plants to warehouses and from warehouses to customers; traffic department costs	Applicable rates times tonnages	Applicable rates times tonnages
6. Storage and shipping: rent or equivalent costs for storage of inventories in warehouses; insurance and taxes on finished goods inventories; labor and equipment for physical handling, loading, etc.	Number of shipping units	Warehouse space occupied by average inventory. Number of shipping units

table   28–5—Continued

Functional cost group	Basis of allocation	
	To sales territories	*To product groups*
7. **Order processing: preparation of customer invoices; freight accounting; credit and collection; handling cash receipts; provision for bad debts; salary, supplies, space and equipment costs**	Number of order lines	Number of order lines

SOURCE: Adapted from Charles H. Sevin, *Marketing Productivity Analysis*, McGraw-Hill Book Company, New York, 1965, pp. 13–15.

direct expenses are allocated, then the figure arrived at by subtracting expenses from gross margin is the territory's contribution to overhead. If all expenses are allocated and then subtracted from gross margin, the final result is the territory's net profit.

Table 28–5 presents examples of some reasonable bases for allocating groups of functional costs among sales territories and among product groups.

Use of findings from combined volume and cost analysis

The findings of a combined volume and cost analysis may be used by management in making decisions on many aspects of the marketing program.

Territorial decisions   Once marketing administrators know the net profit (or contribution to overhead) and sales volume of the territories in relation to potential, they should throw their major effort into the weakest district because the greatest opportunity for improvement lies there.

Changes in other districts may be called for, too. Territorial boundaries may need to be adjusted to bring them into line with current potential. Often a company lets its territorial limits remain untouched long after shifts have occurred in market potential. As a result, some districts have more potential business than one salesman can effectively develop, whereas others have insufficient potential to support a salesman.

Territorial problems stem from weaknesses in the distribution system, and changes in channels of distribution may be needed. Some firms which have been using manufacturers' agents may find it advisable to establish their own sales forces in growing markets. Other businesses may try to bypass wholesalers in some districts and sell directly to retailers or industrial users. Territorial problems may call for changes in selling methods. A company might use mail or telephone selling rather than personal salesmen in unprofitable districts. Intensive competition may be the cause of unprofitable or declining volume in some districts, and changes in the promotional program may be advisable.

Of course, a losing territory might be abandoned completely. After World War II many firms discontinued selling in districts when military bases or defense plants were closed down. If an abandoned region has been contributing anything to overhead, even though a net loss was shown, management must recognize that this contribution must now be carried by the remaining districts.

Product decisions When the relative profitability of each product or group of products is known, management may take action in several areas to improve the situation. A product line may be simplified by eliminating slow-moving, unprofitable styles, sizes, and colors. The salesmen's compensation plan may be altered to encourage the sale of high-margin items. Conversely, commissions may be reduced on low-margin items to deter the men from devoting an inordinate amount of time and effort to them. Channels of distribution may be altered. Instead of selling his complete group of products directly to industrial users, for example, a machine tools manufacturer shifted to industrial distributors for standard products of low unit value. Advertising appropriations may be altered in order to develop more effective advertising for some line of merchandise. Changes in product policies themselves may be effective. For instance, multiple packaging may increase unit sales and thereby reduce the unit cost of order filling, billing, and shipping. Changes in handling and physical distribution methods may enable a company to employ less expensive packaging materials and processes.

Pricing policies and practices with respect to each product should be reviewed carefully to determine whether price changes upward or downward may increase total revenue and net profit.

In the final analysis, management may decide to discontinue handling a product entirely. Before this is done, however, careful consideration must be given to the effect this decision will have on other items in the line. Often a low-volume or unprofitable product must be carried simply to round out the line. Customers expect the seller to carry the article, and if he does not, then he may lose business in his other products.

Decisions on customer classes and order sizes By combining a volume analysis with a cost study, the executives can determine the relative profitability of each group of customers. If a substandard rate of net profit is coming from one group, changes in the pricing structure used for these accounts may be required. The prices may be raised to cover costs more effectively; or if competition is severe and there is an elastic demand, the prices may be reduced. Perhaps accounts which have been approached directly should be turned over to middlemen.

Marketing cost analysis by *size of order* is often helpful in connection with customer classification cost studies. Management can determine its break-even point with respect to order size and can ascertain the amount of sales volume and net profit obtained from each order-size classification. A common problem plaguing many firms today is that of the small order.[10] Many orders are below the break-even point. The revenue from each of these is actually less than the allocated expenses because several costs, such as billing, accounting, or direct selling, are the same whether the order amounts to $10 or $10,000.

Small-order accounts create a difficult decision-making situation. Management's immediate reaction may be that no order below the break-even point should be accepted and that small-volume accounts should be dropped from the customer list. Actually, such a decision may be erroneous and harmful. Management should determine first why certain accounts are small-order problems and then adopt procedures to correct the situation. Careful study and proper handling can very often turn a losing account into a satisfactory one.

There are several reasons why a customer may be a small-order problem. He may be new and growing (however, eventually he may become a highly profitable account). He may be buying a sufficient total volume of merchandise, but on a hand-to-mouth basis; that is, he may send in many small orders instead of a few large ones. He may be spreading his purchases among many different suppliers, thus creating small-order problems for all of them. Sometimes the accounting method determines whether a customer or order is profitable or not. If a customer is charged only with the appropriate *marginal* costs required to do business with him, he may be a profitable customer, but if he is charged with his share of all costs—that is, if an average cost basis is used—his account may show up as a net loss.

A multitude of practical suggestions may be made to aid management in reducing the costs of small orders or increasing the size of the order. Management may initiate customer education, establish minimum order sizes, change the price structure, use multiple packaging, turn to direct-mail or telephone selling, or use wholesalers instead of direct selling.

Future of cost analysis

The use of marketing cost analysis has increased considerably in the past thirty years; refinements in technique and methodology have come rapidly, and the future is highly promising. Management is appreciating more and more the importance of measuring and controlling costs. If there is any real problem in the area of cost analysis, it is the shortage of skilled personnel. This shortage will undoubtedly be alleviated as college instruction in the field is increased and as trade and professional associations in business administration place added emphasis on marketing cost studies. The situation will also be helped as marketing and accounting people come to realize that they have mutual problems in this area and can benefit from more closely coordinated efforts.

[10] For a report on the pressures, costs, and complications of small orders, see Carl Reiser, "The Short-order Economy," *Fortune,* August, 1962, p. 90.

QUESTIONS AND PROBLEMS

1 The iceberg principle has been likened to a medical diagnosis where the patient's complaint is different from the real problem. Is the analogy appropriate? Explain.

2 "A sales volume analysis is of very little value unless it is accompanied by a marketing cost analysis." Discuss.

3 A sales volume analysis by territories indicates that the sales of a manufacturer of roofing materials have increased 12 per cent a year for the past three years in the territory comprising South Carolina, Georgia, and Florida. Does this indicate conclusively that the company's sales volume performance is satisfactory in that region?

4 A manufacturer found that one of his products accounted for 35 to 45 per cent of the company's total sales in all but two of the eighteen territories. In each of those two districts, this product accounted for only 15 per cent of the company's volume. What factors might account for the relatively low sales of this article in the two districts?

5 What are some bases upon which retailers may profitably analyze their sales volume?

6 Explain how the results of a territorial sales volume analysis may influence a firm's promotional program.

7 What effects may a sales analysis by products have on training, supervising, and compensating the salesmen?

8 "Products, territories, or customers which are found in a sales volume analysis to be substantially below par should be dropped from the company's marketing program." Discuss.

9 "In production, costs are a function of volume; in marketing, volume is a function of costs." Explain.

10 "The Robinson-Patman Act served as the greatest stimulus ever for the development and widespread use of marketing cost analysis." Explain.

11 Are the following expenses properly classified as marketing or production costs? Does the nature of the company or the nature of the product influence your decision?

a. Credit   e. Repair service
b. Shipping   f. Styling and designing
c. Packaging   g. Engineering
d. Labeling   h. Inventory control

12 What is an unprofitable sale? Explain carefully, keeping in mind the various kinds of costs such as total, marginal, average, etc. Should a company ever intentionally accept unprofitable business? Explain.

13 A national manufacturer of luggage and other leather products, such as briefcases, wallets, attaché cases, and pocket notebooks, employs thirty salesmen. Each salesman has his own territory, and each man sells the entire group of products. The company calls directly on department stores and specialty luggage stores. The marketing department wishes to make a territorial cost analysis. What bases do you recommend they use for allocating each of the following costs?

a. Salesmen's salaries

b. Salesmen's commissions paid on net sales
c. Sales training expenses
d. Newspaper advertising
e. National magazine advertising
f. Marketing research
g. Shipping
h. Billing
i. Manager of the sales force and his office expenses
j. Marketing manager's salary and office expenses

14 Do you recommend that a firm adopt the full-cost or the contribution-margin approach when allocating indirect marketing costs?

15 Of what value is an analysis of ledger expenses? What are some marketing policies which might be based on this type of analysis?

16 "Firms should discontinue handling losing products." Discuss.

17 Do you agree with the following statements?
a. "Customers whose annual purchases are large never present a small-order problem."
b. "Small-order problems are always created by small-annual-volume customers."

18 Should a company discontinue selling to an unprofitable customer?

29

MARKETING: APPRAISAL AND PROSPECT

Throughout this book, using a micro approach, we have examined the problems facing an individual manufacturer or middleman in the management of his marketing activities. In the development of a marketing program, we have employed the systems concept of marketing, that is, the view that marketing is a total system of interacting business activities designed to plan, price, promote, and distribute want-satisfying goods and services to consumers and industrial users. Within this context, we have seen the importance of the marketing concept as a guiding business philosophy for top management. To have a reasonable chance for long-run success, executives should fully accept and implement the idea that a market orientation must pervade the management of all business activities.

We have also studied the role of marketing in the total economy. Using a macro approach, we have seen marketing as a system which creates and delivers a standard of living to the people in an economy of abundance. There is an inextricable involvement of marketing in our annual gross national product of over $800 billion. We have studied the structure, composition, and behavior of consumer and industrial markets, and we have studied the institutional structure of retailing and wholesaling middlemen and the functions they perform. Physical distribution has been treated as a total system rather than a series of fragmented, unrelated activities. Price-making and promotional programs have been analyzed in detail.

In this concluding chapter we shall develop in summary form a marriage of three topics—an appraisal of (1) marketing in the American economy, (2) the government's role in marketing, and (3) the outlook for the future of marketing.

It is necessary to keep in mind that our frame of reference is the present-day economic system of the United States: a free-enterprise but *imperfect* economic system. Price is the prime determinant of resource allocation. We call our system imperfect, however, because the market is not composed of elements basic to the theoretical model of perfect competition—elements such as great numbers of well-informed, always rationally acting buyers and sellers, each so small that his individual activity has no appreciable influence on total supply, demand, or price. Another imperfection is the structural rigidity of our system. There is probably greater freedom of exit and entry in the retailing part of our market structure than in any other segment, but even here some rigidities exist. In the interests of the general welfare, the various levels of government often act so as to affect the free play of market forces.

Another point to keep in mind is that the American economic system contains many freedoms, but for every freedom—whether it is political, economic, religious, or social—we pay a price. For example, one economic privilege we have is freedom of choice; we are offered a wide variety of products and often a considerable number of brands of each product. The price we pay for this freedom is the burden of making up our minds—of making a market decision about which products and brands we will buy with our limited resources.

EVALUATION OF MARKETING SYSTEM

Anything so important and all-pervasive as marketing is bound to draw a share of censure. In some cases, criticism is leveled at marketing in the individual firms, while in other situations the target is the role of marketing in the economy. We can summarize the major charges at this point, but it will not be possible within the scope of this book to discuss and evaluate them in detail. Separate chapters in other books and, in some instances, entire texts have been devoted to this task.

In order to appraise our marketing system, we need some yardsticks for measurement. First, what is the objective or goal of the system? Throughout this book we have stressed the philosophy of the marketing concept. The goal of the marketing concept is to develop a customer orientation on the part of management. In line with this philosophy, it seems reasonable to establish as a goal the satisfaction of consumers' wants, as they are expressed by the consumers themselves. Then marketing should be appraised on the basis of how well it achieves this goal, that is, how effectively it satisfies consumers' wants. We grant that this goal is a questionable one in the minds of many people. Some feel that the consumer does not know what is good for him—that some group (usually the government) should take over the responsibility for setting standards. Others believe that the social and economic goals should be to build a country's military strength, to promote the growth of its underdeveloped segments, or to perpetuate the large wealth and high social position of a favored few. Regardless of these other possible goals, however noteworthy some people think they are, *we shall evaluate marketing in light of its ability to satisfy consumers' wants, as the consumers themselves define or express these wants.*

Next we must try to establish objective, quantitative yardsticks for measuring the extent to which marketing has achieved this goal. In *an individual company*, the effectiveness of marketing can be measured generally by the company's financial status. This is measured on the bases of operating costs, net profits, operating ratios, comparisons with similar firms, and so on. Tools have been developed to measure the profitability of various products, territories, channels, salesmen, and advertising media within a given firm.

A different situation prevails when we attempt to measure quantitatively marketing's contribution to consumer want satisfaction in *our economy*. Input-output analysis may be employed, although it is difficult to assign objective values to the various factors in input and output unless we use the market value of these factors. For instance, in the marketing system we can measure quantitatively the value of such inputs as newspaper space used in advertising, time and program costs for television advertising, freight carloadings, marketing research costs in developing the brand and package, salesmen's compensation and expenses, and others. The output factors may be summarized as consumer want satisfaction. But, of course, so far no one has been able satisfactorily to impute objective values to this output. Market price indicates what consumers are willing to pay, but it does not accurately measure satisfaction received. Consequently, much of our evaluation of marketing's contribution to consumer want satisfaction in our economy must be done on a subjective basis.

Criticisms of marketing

Critics of our marketing system have raised many thought-provoking questions and generated many lively discussions. In order to summarize the major charges of the critics, we shall group them according to their relationships to the four components of the marketing mix—the product, the distribution structure, the price system, and the promotional activities.

With respect to *the product*, critics allege that many products are of poor quality; for the price the seller charges, the products and services could or should be better. Furthermore, heavily promoted product improvements are often trivial. Planned style obsolescence encourages consumers to get rid of products before they are physically worn out. Besides, there are too many different types of goods and too many different brands of each type. As a result, the buyer is confused; he is unable to make accurate buying decisions.

Probably the main objection to the *distribution structure* is that it is unnecessarily complex and includes too many middlemen. This is a two-part charge: there are too many different types of middlemen and too many of each type. Regarding the *price system,* we hear that prices are too high or too inflexible or that they are controlled by the large firms in an industry. Some people feel that price competition has largely been replaced by nonprice competition.

The strongest and most bitter indictments leveled against marketing are in the area of *promotional activities*—especially in personal selling and advertising. Most of the complaints about personal selling are at the retail level, where we find both consumers and businessmen disenchanted with the poor quality of retail salesmanship. Objections are also voiced against the poor services offered by many retailers, even by stores whose high prices would seem to reflect a service-oriented policy.

The general criticisms against advertising may be divided into two groups —social and economic. From a *social* point of view, advertising is charged with overemphasizing our material standard of living and underemphasizing our cultural, spiritual, ethical, and moral values. Advertising also is charged with making people want and buy things they should not have, cannot afford, and do not need.

A major social criticism of advertising today, and one that has some justification and should be considered by marketing men throughout our economy, is that advertising is often false, misleading, deceptive, or in bad taste.[1] Exaggerations, conflicting claims, overuse of sex and fear appeals, jarring commercials, inane claims, excessive numbers of commercials on radio and television, and poor choice of the placement of commercials are some examples of this general point of censure. As with most criticisms in marketing, this one applies to a small segment of advertising. The main offenders are advertisers of a limited number of consumer goods, and the advertising medium causing most of the furor is television. The charge of false, misleading, and offensive advertising is rarely made against advertisers of industrial products or companies which advertise consumer products in trade journals. Most of our retail department store display advertising is not subject to this charge, nor is most of the newspaper classified advertising.

[1] An excellent four-part report entitled "Truth and Taste in Advertising" has been published in *Printers' Ink.* See part 1, "Crisis in Advertising: What Caused It, Who's to Blame, What Needs to Be Done," Nov. 27, 1959, p. 23; part 2, "Advertising vs. Government: Why Some Laws Help, Others Pose a Great Threat," Dec. 4, 1959, p. 21; part 3, "Advertising Control from Within: Why Self-regulation Isn't Working Today," Dec. 11, 1959, p. 29; part 4, "A Program to Restore Truth and Taste, and Public Confidence, in Advertising," Dec. 18, 1959, p. 19.

One of the *economic* criticisms of advertising is that it costs too much; it increases the cost of marketing and therefore the price of products. Some people feel that advertising restricts the total quantity of goods produced. Others feel that advertising leads to restraint of competition and the concentration of supply in a very limited number of firms in an industry. Finally, advertising is charged with causing a misallocation of our resources. This criticism is related to the assertion by John K. Galbraith and others that advertising has contributed significantly to an imbalance of expenditures between the private and public sectors of our economy. For instance, these people believe that American business promotes frills on automobiles when it should be concerned with clearing slums, improving our schools, and eliminating air and water pollution. Furthermore, these critics believe that more of our national output should be diverted from the private to the public sector.[2]

Importance of understanding true nature of criticisms

When evaluating the charges against marketing, we should be careful to recognize the differences in the nature of the various charges. For example, we should understand what fundamentally is being criticized. In a company, is it the marketing department or some other department which is the cause of the complaints? In the economy, is it the marketing system or the general economic system itself which is being criticized? It is also helpful to sort out the points wherein the critics (1) are misinformed, (2) are unaware of the services performed by the marketing system, or (3) are trying to impose their own objective value judgments on consumers; that is, the critics do not agree that the goal of the marketing system should be consumer want satisfaction as the consumers *themselves* define and express their wants.

In some cases the criticisms of marketing are fully warranted; they point out weaknesses and inefficiencies in the system and call for improvement. By most people's standards, there are instances of deceptive packaging and of misleading and objectionable advertising. There are weaknesses in marketing just as there are in any system developed and operated by human beings. The real key to the evaluation of our marketing system lies in the answers to two fundamental questions. First, is the present system of marketing achieving its goal (that is, satisfying consumers' wants as the consumers themselves express these wants) better than any other known alternative could? The answer is an unqualified "yes." Second, are constant attention and effort being devoted to improving the system and increasing its productivity and efficiency? Generally speaking, the answer to this question also is a strong "yes."

Progress sometimes may seem slow. Companies that operate in a socially

---

[2] See John K. Galbraith, *The Affluent Society*, Houghton Mifflin Company, Boston, 1958; for a different point of view, see, for example, John W. Lowe, "An Economist Defends Advertising," *Journal of Marketing*, July, 1963, pp. 16–19; and V. E. Boyd, *Advertising and Public Service: Not-so-strange Bedfellows*, American Association of Advertising Agencies, Nov. 19, 1964.

undesirable manner even over a short-run period of time are harmful. Price-fixing and objectionable advertising are intolerable and inexcusable. Instances of this nature, though widely publicized, are in a small minority, however, when the total picture of marketing is viewed. In essence, we are saying that weaknesses exist in marketing and that a continuing effort must be devoted to their elimination. However, at the same time, we should not overlook the improvements in marketing and consumer want satisfaction over the years. The way to correct existing weaknesses is not to destroy or seriously restrict and regulate the existing system.

Does marketing cost too much?

Many of the censures of marketing may be summarized in the general criticism that marketing costs too much. It is estimated that the total cost of marketing for all products is about 50 per cent of the final price paid by ultimate consumers. Admittedly, total marketing costs are a substantial proportion of total sales value of all products. However, the question of whether marketing costs too much is in many respects somewhat academic because we do not have sufficient information to make comparisons. We do not know how the costs of marketing compare with the costs of manufacturing, mining, and other activities which create form utility. Even if we had accurate data on marketing costs, we would still have no objective criteria for determining whether these expenses were too high or not high enough. As we said in Chapter 28, we have not yet developed adequate tools for measuring the return (output) that is derived from a given marketing expenditure (input). To say that marketing costs are too high implies that one or more of the following situations prevail: marketing institutions are enjoying abnormally high profits; more services are being provided than the consumers and businessmen demand; marketing activities are performed in a grossly inefficient manner; consumption is declining; total costs (production plus marketing) are increasing. Actually, there is no reasonable evidence that any of these conditions exists.

It is granted that total marketing costs have risen substantially both absolutely and relatively over the past 100 years. At the same time, careful studies indicate that these costs have been leveling off for the past two or three decades.[3] Nevertheless, it is important that we understand the reasons for this increase in marketing expenses. Certainly it would be a mistake simply to jump to the conclusion that the cost increase indicates growing inefficiencies in marketing. Actually, the rise in marketing expense is traceable to several factors, some of which are external environmental influences. As an example, there has been an increase in the number of people employed in marketing relative to the number employed in production simply because the workweek in marketing has been shortened relative to that in production. In the latter part of the nineteenth

---

[3] Harold Barger, *Distribution's Place in the American Economy since 1869*, Princeton University Press, Princeton, N.J., 1955.

century, people employed in wholesaling and retailing worked about sixty-six hours a week; those employed in production worked about fifty-two. Today, both groups work about forty, and this shift toward equality has meant that relatively more employees were added in marketing.

Another reason that the number of marketing workers and the costs of marketing have increased is that consumers are demanding more services and more marketing refinements today than in the past. Consumers today demand credit, delivery, free parking, attractive stores, merchandise return privileges, and other services. A related point is the rise in consumer demand for products emphasizing style and for merchandise assortments covering considerable breadth and depth. Certainly we could cut marketing costs, problems, and risks substantially if consumers would buy on a cash-and-carry, no-returns-permitted basis in stores displaying small quantities of standardized merchandise on pipe racks or in wooden boxes.

Sometimes the seeming increase in distribution costs is really the result of a more careful classification of business expenses. If a small businessman or farmer produces his goods and sells them himself, all his operating expenses are classed as production expenses (creation of form utility) because he is classified as a producer. Once this businessman or farmer employs the advantages of specialization of labor, however, or once his markets expand, he will probably use independent middlemen to help in the marketing process. Immediately the costs are separated into production and marketing classifications. Marketing expenses seem to have increased substantially, even though there may have been no real change in the total cost picture. In a large company which adopts the marketing concept, many expenses (such as new-product development, inventory control, transportation, and warehousing) which formerly were classified as production costs will now be shown as marketing expenses simply because the expense-generating activity is now the organizational responsibility of the marketing manager.

It is a mistake to study the trend in marketing costs alone. A total cost approach should be adopted. In many instances, a firm can reduce its total costs by increasing its marketing costs. To illustrate, an increase in advertising and personal selling expenditures may so expand a firm's market that the unit production cost can be reduced more than the marketing costs have increased. Thus the net effect is to reduce the total expenses. Production economies are also made possible by improvements in sales-forecasting techniques—a marketing expense. In another situation, production economies can result when a company locates near sources of raw materials or low-cost power, yet marketing costs (transportation) may be increased in the new location. Production economies can also be effected by operating one large factory rather than having several small plants in several regions. Yet the centralization will increase physical distribution costs and will require added expenses for demand-stimulation activities in order to reach all parts of the wide market.

One approach to a better understanding of the role of marketing in the economy is to apply the concept of "value added by marketing" as a counterpart of the already-accepted concept of "value added by manufacturing." "Value added by marketing" is a much more accurate term than "cost of marketing" to describe the output or utilities created by marketing.[4]

It is understandable that productivity in marketing may never match the level attained in manufacturing or agriculture. Marketing offers far fewer opportunities for mechanization. It is one thing to control and measure the input and output value of machines, but it is quite another problem when the activity largely involves dealing with people. To the extent that the marketing system is not perfect and that marketing costs have not reached a theoretical minimum, we may say that marketing does cost too much. Until we can define objectively this perfect system, however, and until a better system for satisfying consumer wants is proposed, we shall continue with the existing system. Its benefits in both the private and public sectors of our economy are bounteous by almost any measure used. American business will continue to work to improve the efficiency of marketing, to measure accurately its cost, and most important of all, to explain to the American public the essential role marketing plays in our economy.

GOVERNMENT'S ROLE IN MARKETING

In many situations the government probably rates second to the consumer in importance as an external environmental influence on marketing. Anything that is so much a part of our economic system as marketing is bound to be influenced directly by governmental action. Throughout this book, major legislation and other governmental actions were discussed when pertinent to particular areas of marketing policies and strategies. At this point we shall draw a few summary observations regarding the role our government plays in marketing.

At all times a marketing executive must be aware of the impact which his internal decisions have on the external environment of his firm. Particularly should he consider the political or governmental appraisal of his internal policy making. In most companies, the marketing department, more than any other, feels the intervention of the government—Federal, state, or local. This in no way suggests that regulation of nonmarketing activities is unimportant.

Governmental intervention takes two forms. First, the government offers aid on a voluntary basis to businesses in an effort to foster and preserve competition and to increase business efficiency. Countless examples of such aid could be cited. Federal agencies such as the U.S. Department of Commerce and the U.S. Department of Agriculture gather and publish many different sorts of information of considerable value to marketing men. The Small Busi-

---

[4] Prof. Theodore N. Beckman, of the Ohio State University, developed the "value-added" concept in marketing. See his "The Value Added Concept as Applied to Marketing and Its Implications," in Stewart H. Rewoldt (ed.), *Frontiers in Marketing Thought*, Indiana University, Bureau of Business Research, Bloomington, Ind., 1955, pp. 83–99; or his "Value Added by Distribution," *Twenty-eighth Boston Conference on Distribution*, Boston Chamber of Commerce, Boston, 1956, pp. 43–47.

ness Administration has published many marketing aids for small businesses. At the state level, many states offer programs in distributive education (retailing) with Federal support through the George-Dean Act.

The second form of governmental intervention involves regulation and control. A study of our business history shows rather clearly that governmental regulations come about because (1) private industry is either unable or unwilling to accept its responsibility for acting in the public interest or (2) special-interest groups foster the legislation.

As examples of governmental action resulting from the inability or refusal of private business to accept its responsibilities, we have the various antitrust laws, the laws prohibiting unfair competition, and the legal restrictions on advertising. In the late nineteenth century, society felt that monopolistic practices were contrary to the public interest, so the Sherman Antitrust Act was passed. Later, when private industry did not accept its responsibilities in matters of labeling and selling food and drugs—when it sold adulterated products and used deceptive labels—Congress passed the Pure Food and Drug Act (1906). In years following, shortsighted businessmen found ways to circumvent this law, and it was strengthened by further restrictive amendments in 1938.

In some areas, government engages in business itself, directly competing with private enterprise. Often the original reason for such government activity was that private enterprise could not or would not meet consumer demand. This reason lies behind the government's development of water resources and its activity in financing home mortgages.

In some cases, a private business group seeks government intervention to support the group's self-interest. We see the results of this form of activity in such legislation as the state fair-trade laws, unfair-practices acts, laws restricting interstate trade, chain store taxes, and municipal Green River ordinances regulating door-to-door selling. The stated purpose of these laws is to protect competition. In effect, however, they protect *competitors* rather than *competition,* and there is a substantial difference between the two. Some of these legal measures actually penalize the low-cost, low-selling-price, generally efficient operations of chain stores and large-scale independents, while at the same time protecting the high-cost, inefficient retailers. In such cases these laws tend to injure competition.

Often a marketing executive who seeks legislation favoring his own special interest will profess to be an advocate of free competition, when in actual fact he is attempting to combat strong, but entirely fair, competition. Sometimes it seems that a marketing man's only criterion of fair competition is whether it allows him to beat a competitor. Unfair competition is, of course, any situation in which he loses. Marketing management must realize that it is not possible to regulate one part of a segment of the economy and let other parts go unrestrained. Regulation usually begets more regulation.

In many public regulations affecting marketing, emphasis has been placed primarily upon the protection of competition, allowing the protection of consumers to occur (if it does occur) as a by-product. Marketing legislation in general is business-oriented rather than consumer-oriented. (Of course, there are exceptions, such as the Federal Pure Food, Drug, and Cosmetics Act, the various labeling laws, and some of the provisions of the Wheeler-Lea amendment.) Another weakness (from the consumers' viewpoint) in our marketing legislation is the absence of Federal "watchdogs." That is, suit must be brought, under most laws, by an injured party—usually not an injured consumer. A corollary weakness is the absence of speedy, inexpensive means for the redress of consumer grievances.

PROSPECTS FOR THE FUTURE

The executives responsible for managing firms engaged in manufacturing, wholesaling, or retailing may well ask the question, "What does the future hold for marketing?" In general, businessmen will continue to experience evolutionary change throughout the entire marketing process and structure. The crystal ball seems quite clear regarding many major developments which may be expected during the late 1960s and the 1970s. Some of the prospects are actually a continuation of significant trends which have been in evidence for some years now. The final sections of Chapter 12 could be reread profitably at this point in order to review some of the major trends in retailing.

Scientific marketing and consumer research

In the coming years we can expect to see continued emphasis on scientific marketing. There should be increased use of careful marketing planning, including the determination of objectives and the development of long-range and short-range strategies. Marketing research, both quantitative and qualitative, will improve and will be used extensively. Marketing cost analyses will also be improved and their use expanded. Particularly can we hope for refinements and improvements in the analysis of consumer motivation and behavior. In their enthusiasm for planning, marketing leaders will look for more efficiency in the execution and evaluation of their plans. Increasingly we can expect companies to adopt and implement the concept of marketing intelligence as a continuing, total system of information management to aid in problem solving and decision making.[5]

Interdisciplinary contributions to marketing

Marketing as a separate field of study evolved from the general discipline of economics. To an increasing extent, however, marketing men are coming to recognize that they can draw heavily and profitably from many other disciplines. The behavioral sciences—psychology, sociology, anthropology—have contributed much to an understanding of consumer motivation and behavior. Statistics and mathematics, as well, have contributed to quantitative measurement in

[5] See Kenneth P. Uhl, "Better Management of Market Information," *Business Horizons*, Spring, 1966, pp. 75–82.

marketing. Demography, geography, and ecology have contributed to an understanding of markets and market movements. Looking to the future, we can expect marketing men to become better trained in the use of the tools of other disciplines and more cognizant of their value to our field. The interdisciplinary tools such as operations research, linear programming, PERT (Program Evaluation Review Technique), CPM (Critical Path Method), and queuing theory will probably be used to an increasing extent in solving the problems connected with physical distribution, the measurement of advertising effectiveness, product policies, and other marketing activities.

The computer and marketing management

The development of computers and other electronic data-processing equipment is a boon to marketing. The use of this equipment increases a firm's marketing efficiency tremendously because marketing executives are able to analyze and evaluate the marketing effort and conduct many other types of marketing research projects in greater detail, at less expense, and with more speed than has been possible heretofore. There seems to be hardly any limit to the potential for computer use in making detailed analyses of sales, consumers, industries, and salesmen's performances; in making sales forecasts; in doing short-range and long-range planning; in determining product mix, media selection, and physical distribution programs; and in participating in a myriad of other marketing activities.

Growth of multinational marketing

To an increasing extent, we may expect the marketing programs in many firms to acquire an international perspective. The major opportunities for growth markets in many companies lie in their foreign markets, so we shall see marketing executives directing their attention to the international aspects of their businesses.

Development of professional marketing personnel

As students become aware of the increased economic and social importance of marketing, and as they become aware of the opportunities in the field, greater numbers of qualified personnel will be attracted to a professional career in marketing. As has been stated directly and indirectly so often throughout this book, staffing, or selection of personnel, is the most important of all management activities. Successful planning and execution of marketing programs depend ultimately upon the people who do the work.[6]

[6] For examples of what some top marketing executives were earning in 1965, see "Executive Compensation: A Good Case for Cash," *Sales Management,* July 16, 1965, pp. 39–44; gross income, not including stock appreciation and fringe benefits, ranged from $31,000 to $125,000 in this sample of some 115 medium- and large-sized firms.

Marketing management's recognition of its social responsibility

Marketing administrators have long since understood their responsibilities to their company, its customers, and its stockholders. It is also vital that they recognize their accountability to society in general. In return for the privilege of existing and operating in our economic system, marketing management must conduct itself and its affairs in an efficient, ethical, and socially desirable manner. If management does not accept its social responsibilities, society will eventually restrict or entirely withdraw its freedom of operation. Certainly most of the governmental restrictions placed upon marketing activities have been the result of management's failure to recognize and live up to its responsibilities.

There are two other reasons why marketing management must fulfill its social responsibilities. First, the marketing department in a firm represents the company to the public. If the advertising department produces misleading ads or if the salesmen resort to unacceptable, high-pressure tactics, these actions help to create an unfavorable public image of the firm. On the other hand, when the salesmen, marketing researchers, or other marketing people conduct themselves in a socially desirable manner, their actions reflect favorably on the entire firm. Ordinarily the public does not meet the production and office workers in a company. Consequently, a firm is rarely judged by the actions of these employee groups. In fact, the marketing department is often blamed for mistakes (such as a defective product or an incorrect bill) made by these other groups simply because the marketing personnel are the only employees who have contact with the public.

The necessity of fulfilling our social responsibility is also highlighted by the fact that our entire economic system is sometimes judged by the impression left by marketing people. Earlier in the chapter we observed several of the criticisms of marketing. Invariably the public's reaction to these criticisms is a demand for restrictive and regulatory legislation. This type of legislation, if enacted in sufficient measure, might substantially modify the freedoms we now enjoy. Consequently, anything a marketing executive does to develop a socially desirable operation in his company will also help to strengthen and perpetuate the economic structure within which he works.

If it is true that the basic moral fiber of the entire population is looser today than in the past and that the pursuit of the "fast buck" is something of a national illness, marketing executives can at least act to improve business standards in their own not-so-small sphere. For example, by increasing the efficiency of marketing operations, they can minimize distribution costs and selling prices and thus enable consumers to maximize their purchasing power. By properly interpreting and anticipating consumer demand, whether it is an active or a latent demand, marketing management can better supply want-satisfying products and services. If management refuses to accept this responsibility for interpreting and satisfying consumer demand, the public will look elsewhere for want satisfaction, and the institution they will be most likely to seek out is the government. Management can refuse to do business with unethical suppliers or customers, even though temporary advantages may accrue from such relationships. Top marketing executives can increase their control over operating personnel—particularly salesmen and advertising people —to ensure higher standards of operation. Administrators can cooperate with trade associations, better business bureaus, and other business groups interested in raising ethical business standards.

This appeal for increased social responsibility on the part of marketing executives is in no way inconsistent with the primary goal of business, namely, long-run profit maximization. The hope is that management will avoid "marketing myopia" and adopt a long-run point of view. Too many marketing executives are shortsighted; they do not see the possible repercussions from their activities. To them, the end justifies the means, and the end is often simply a single sale. If the consumer is misled or if an industrial buyer is overstocked, this is all right, so long as a sale is made. Myopic managers do not see that, in the long run, a continuation of these or similar socially undesirable practices can result in lost business and invite governmental regulations. On the other hand, socially responsible attitudes and actions are more likely to result in profit maximization and to ensure a "better tomorrow."[7]

Growing recognition of importance of marketing

If the 1950s are considered the decade during which modern marketing management was born, then the 1960s and 1970s should be the years during which it comes of age. After seeing the splendid accomplishments and progress made in marketing during the past decade, we can anticipate that the marketing concept will be adopted and put into practice by increasing numbers of firms. Little doubt will be left regarding the absolute need for an attitude, philosophy, and practice of customer orientation throughout all departments of a business. In fact, it will not be at all surprising to see many enterprises move into the stage characterized by an executive of the Pillsbury Company as one in which "marketing will become the basic motivating force for the entire corporation."[8] Marketing already influences short-range operating policies in many firms. In the foreseeable future, it will come to influence long-range policy to an increasing extent.

In the first chapter of this book, marketing was defined as a total interacting system of business activity designed to plan, price, promote, and distribute want-satisfying products and services to markets. Undoubtedly, more and more administrators will come to appreciate the full scope and significance of what is involved in this definition. One writer observed that there are three essential conditions which must prevail in order for marketing leadership to

---

[7] See Thomas F. Schutte, "Marketing Implications of Executive Perceptions of Business Ethics," in Stephen A. Greyser (ed.), *Toward Scientific Marketing*, American Marketing Association, Chicago, 1964, pp. 186–199.

[8] Robert J. Keith, "The Marketing Revolution," *Journal of Marketing*, January, 1960, p. 38.

evidence itself.[9] First, top management must recognize that marketing problems are fundamentally different from production problems. This carries major implications regarding executive selection, marketing strategies, and the sales organization. Second, management must recognize the dynamic quality of the marketing problem—change is constantly occurring. This means that the firm must make long-range plans. An executive must really know his market today and be able to forecast what it will be like five to ten years from now; in addition, he must understand the shifting channel structures. Third, management must develop and improve its conceptual skill and its ability to see the entire organization as a whole and the interrelationships among parts of this whole.

Both within the individual firm and within the socioeconomic system, modern marketing is the key to successful economic expansion. This fact will be recognized by increasing numbers of businessmen and consumers. In fact, one of the most significant achievements anticipated over the next several years is greater public understanding and appreciation of the social and economic values of marketing.

QUESTIONS AND PROBLEMS

1   What specific recommendations do you have for reducing the costs of marketing?

2   Some people feel that too much power is concentrated in big business in the United States and that large firms should be broken up. Yet these same people will drive a General Motors car, buy groceries at a large chain supermarket, buy home appliances made by a giant in the industry, wash with a brand of Procter & Gamble soap, and brush their teeth with the leading brand of toothpaste. How do you reconcile the behavior of these people with their opinion concerning big business?

3   "Middlemen make unfairly high profits." Do you agree?

4   Name some products which you feel are marketed under too many different brand names. About how many should be eliminated? How should we go about the elimination process?

5   Some people believe that there are too many gasoline service stations in their communities. Suggest a method for reducing the number of stations. Are there too many in your college community? How many should be eliminated?

6   Does marketing result in a misallocation of resources?

7   Evaluate the following criticisms of advertising:
    a.   Advertising creates a false sense of values.
    b.   Advertising costs too much.
    c.   Advertising is in bad taste.
    d.   Advertising is false, misleading, and deceptive.
    e.   Advertising tends to create monopolies.

8   What proposals do you have for regulating advertising?

[9] Arthur P. Felton, "Conditions of Marketing Leadership," *Harvard Business Review*, March–April, 1956, pp. 117–127.

9   List the major Federal laws affecting marketing. Indicate in each case whether the law's principal purpose is to aid business or regulate it. Briefly describe the intent and provisions of each measure.

10   Should the Federal government establish a "department of the consumer" to aid and protect the consumer?

11   Explain the ways in which the Federal Trade Commission helps the consumer. Refer to specific laws where appropriate.

12   If there is a better business bureau in the city where you go to school, interview the manager and prepare a report covering the following topics:
a.   The bureau's procedure for handling a complaint
b.   Some of the bureau's recent activities
c.   Examples of various types of complaints
d.   The annual budget and the source of funds
If there is no better business bureau in your community, what, if any, organization fills essentially the same role?

13   Besides the examples in this chapter, can you name some fields of business which the government entered because private enterprise was unable to meet, or refused to meet, consumer demand?

14   What criteria might be used to determine whether a marketing executive is fulfilling his social responsibility?

15   Is it ethical to hire a competitor's salesman, marketing researcher, or advertising man?

16   Discuss the relationship between illegal and unethical marketing practices. For instance, are illegal acts always unethical? Are unethical marketing activities always illegal? Give examples in each case.

case 24. HILLCREST PRODUCTS, INC. (C)
Determination of market potential and sales potential

The executives of Hillcrest Products, Inc., are trying to arrive at an estimate of how many 16-ounce bottles of their new glass cleaner they can expect to sell in the first year the product is marketed. Before they can determine the company's sales potential, these men realize they first must estimate the industry's market potential. Hillcrest Products, Inc., is a small company recently formed to manufacture and market a line of cleaning products. The sales mainstay of the line is an all-purpose liquid glass cleaner to be sold through food brokers to supermarkets. Initially the company will sell in markets centered in Denver, Salt Lake City, Kansas City, Omaha, Oklahoma City, Albuquerque, and El Paso. These are food brokerage markets and are also the locations of chain-store buying offices which purchase for member stores in the surrounding areas. As an example, the Denver buying offices supply stores in Colorado, Wyoming, and northern New Mexico and parts of South Dakota, Nebraska, Kansas, and Oklahoma. The glass cleaner is sold in two packages: (1) a Duo-Pak, which consists of a 16-ounce glass bottle of the liquid cleaner plus an 8-ounce plastic bottle with a plunger-type spray dispenser and (2) a 16-ounce bottle intended for refill purposes. The product has significant differential advantages over competitive brands. Also, the company intends to support the product with a substantial advertising campaign.

Mr. Grady, who is the vice-president in charge of marketing and also one of the company's founders, feels that the number of households is a reasonably good market factor to use as a basis for estimating potential. He does not know, however, what percentage of households use commercial glass cleaners. He also wonders whether the percentage of households using the product varies among the several geographic segments of the company's market. Is glass cleaner used as widely in Omaha as in El Paso? Is there the same market acceptance of this product in large metropolitan centers as in small towns or rural communities? Do climatic differences play a significant role in the consumption of this product? The answer to the last question depends to a great extent upon whether the cleaner is used to any considerable degree outside the house. When some people think of glass cleaner, they think primarily of washing windows. This suggests outside use of the product; thus it would be subject to climatic factors. Market tests show, however, that the product is used mainly on interior glass surfaces; consequently, climate may not be such a controlling factor as was originally thought.

Another key consideration is the rate of use per household, that is, the number of bottles or ounces used each year in an average home. There are two possible market situations. The rate of usage may vary from city to city, or it may vary according to the size of the city or town. Thus in Kansas City, households may use an average of four 16-ounce bottles a year, while in a small town in western Kansas, the rate of consumption may be only two or three bottles a year. The alternative possibility is that the rate of usage *per household* may be the same regardless of size of city or location, but the percentage of total households using the product may vary among geographic market segments. That is, those families which do use a commercial glass cleaner may use about the same number of bottles a year, but 80 per cent of the households in region A may use the product, and only 60 per cent in area B.

One market factor which may prove helpful was uncovered in an annual survey of consumer preferences conducted by the *Denver Post*. Respondents were asked whether they bought a glass cleaner for use in their homes and, if so, what brand they had bought last. This annual brand study is participated in by a number of newspapers throughout the country; it was started many years ago by the *Milwaukee Journal*. So that the results may be comparable, the same research and sampling methods are used by all participating newspapers. The *Denver Post* survey showed that 75 per cent of the households in metropolitan Denver use a commercial glass cleaner. Of this group, 70 per cent buy Windex, 10 per cent use Glass Wax, and 6 per cent purchase Bon Ami. The remaining 14 per cent of the market is split among ten or more brands, each of which has a market share of less than 3 per cent.

QUESTIONS

1   What is the market potential for this glass cleaner in units (16-ounce bottles) in the following wholesale trading areas for grocery products?

    a.   Denver (includes Colorado, Wyoming, and northern New Mexico and parts of South Dakota, Nebraska, Kansas, and Oklahoma)

    b.   Omaha (all of Nebraska except the panhandle area, western Iowa, southeastern South Dakota, and southwestern Minnesota)

    c.   Kansas City (Kansas, except for the extreme western part, and western Missouri); Wichita is a self-contained food brokerage area, but for Hillcrest's purposes it is included in the Kansas City market

    d.   Oklahoma City (Oklahoma)

    e.   Albuquerque, El Paso (New Mexico, except for the northern tier of counties, and some forty to fifty counties in West Texas); Albuquerque and El Paso actually are two separate wholesale markets, but for the purposes of determining a total potential, Hillcrest grouped the two cities

    f.   Salt Lake City (Utah, eastern Idaho, eastern Nevada)

2   Estimate the market share (sales potential) for Hillcrest's glass cleaner.

case 25.   CONTINENTAL GYPSUM COMPANY (B)

Determination of market potential for industrial products

In the course of deciding what plant capacity and other production facilities to construct, the executives of the Continental Gypsum Company have come to realize that they should estimate the present and future market for their products. The Continental Gypsum Company is a new firm capitalized at $20 million for the purposes of manufacturing and marketing gypsum products. Geological exploration parties connected with the company have discovered a deposit of gypsum which is one of the largest ever found in the world. A ton of the ore has been rated exceptionally high in pure gypsum content.

Preliminary marketing studies have shown that the industry consists of a relatively limited number of firms. Some of the better-known competitors include the United States Gypsum Company, the National Gypsum Company, the Kaiser Gypsum Company, the Pabco Division of Fiberboard Products, and the Flintkote Co. The product is generally not differentiated, and price competition is usually more important and more prevalent than nonprice competition. Because the product is bulky and of low unit value, freight is a substantial part of the final selling price. Consequently, firms tend to sell in markets where they enjoy a locational advantage or where they can afford to absorb some of the freight expense. On the basis of these factors, Continental has defined two market areas—a primary area and a secondary area—where it plans to compete. The primary market area consists of the states of Colorado, Wyoming, Utah, and Idaho. The secondary area includes Washington, Oregon, Arizona, New Mexico, Montana, Nebraska, and North and South Dakota.

These initial marketing studies have also shown that gypsum is used primarily in building products. In recent years, gypsum building products have accounted for approximately 75 per cent of the tonnage and 94 per cent of the dollar value of all gypsum products sold annually. This building products group consists almost entirely of wallboard, lath, and plaster. In fact, wallboard alone accounts for about one-third of the total tonnage sold annually and for over one-half of the gypsum industry's annual dollar sales volume.

As a result of these market studies, the Continental Company wants to estimate the market potential for gypsum building products in both its primary and secondary market areas. The executives have agreed that some aspect of residential housing seems to be a reasonable market factor to use for this estimate. The number of building permits issued, the number of new housing starts, or some similar quantitative measure of housing seems appropriate. Management understands that this information regarding housing would be available from the F. W. Dodge Corporation. *Construction Review*, a monthly publication of the U.S. Department of Labor, is another reasonably available source of excellent housing statistics. Anthony Francisco, the chief sales executive, has called attention to the fact that the company should be conservative in its estimates. Of course, using residential housing as a market index would tend to understate the full market potential for gypsum building products because not all housing is of the residential type.

If housing is to be used as the market factor, it will be necessary to estimate the amount of gypsum used per house. This, in turn, depends upon the size of the house and the products used for interior walls and ceilings. The estimate of the size of the house would have to take into consideration the fact that 15 to 25 per cent of residences are multifamily units. In the company's proposed marketing areas, probably over 90 per cent of the houses use wallboard. (In the region east of the Mississippi River, it is estimated that only about 50 per cent of the houses use wallboard.)

Houses using wallboard normally use the ½-inch thickness on interior walls and ceilings and possibly the ⅝-inch thickness in the garage. Lath and plaster usually total ¾ of an inch in thickness, with each product being ⅜ of an inch thick. Therefore, if the estimate of market potential were based on all houses using wallboard, the figure would be low. Lath and plaster homes use 25 to 50 per cent more gypsum products than homes built with wallboard.

To determine how much wallboard is used per house, one gypsum company uses the following formula: number of 4- by 8-foot sheets $= \dfrac{\text{square footage of house}}{10} + 5$. Thus a 1,300-square-foot house uses 4,320 square feet of board ($\frac{1,300}{10}$ + 5 = 135 4- by 8-foot sheets = 135 × 32 = 4,320). To convert square feet of wallboard into tons, one gypsum company figured that 1,000 square feet of ½-inch board weighs one ton. Thus a 1,300-square-foot home would take about 4⅓ tons of wallboard.

QUESTION

1   What is the annual market potential in tons for gypsum building products used in residential housing in the company's primary market area? In the secondary market area?

APPENDIX

MARKETING ARITHMETIC

Marketing involves people—customers, middlemen, and producers. Much of the business activity of these people, however, is quantified in some manner. Consequently, mathematical figures are used as tools for the analysis of their quantitative relationships. Some knowledge of the rudiments of business arithmetic is essential for decision making in many areas of marketing. Since most students taking this course have already had a beginning course in accounting, this appendix is intended as a review. In marketing, we frequently use the following accounting or business arithmetic concepts: (1) the operating statement, (2) markups, and (3) analytical ratios. Another useful concept—discounts and terms of sale—is reviewed in Chapter 19 in connection with price policies.

THE OPERATING STATEMENT

An operating statement—often called a profit and loss statement or an income and expense statement—is one of the two main financial statements prepared by a company. The other is the balance sheet. An *operating statement* is a summary picture of the firm's income and expenses—its operations—over a period of time. In contrast, a *balance sheet* shows the assets, liabilities, and net worth of a company at a given time, for example, at the close of business on December 31, 1968.

The operating statement shows whether the business earned a net profit or suffered a net loss during the period covered. It arranges in orderly fashion a summary of the income and expense items which resulted in this net profit or loss. The information in a profit and loss statement also serves as a basis for computing several ratios useful in a financial analysis or a marketing analysis of the company's operations.

An operating statement may cover any selected period of time. Because of income tax requirements, virtually all firms prepare a statement covering operations during the calendar or fiscal year. In addition, it is common for businesses to prepare monthly, quarterly, or semiannual operating statements.

Figure A–1 is an example of an operating statement for a wholesaler or retailer. The main difference between the operating statements of a middleman and a manufacturer is in the cost-of-goods-sold section. A manufacturer shows a net figure for cost of goods *manufactured,* whereas the middleman's statement shows net *purchases.* There is no standard form for presenting an operating statement; some statements are far more detailed than others. The main idea is to present the information in a clear, understandable fashion. If additional detail is desired, one can look to the accounting records and other supporting data upon which the operating statement was based.

Major sections

From one point of view, the essence of business is very simple. A company buys or makes a product and then sells it for a higher price. Out of his sales revenue, the seller hopes to cover the cost of the merchandise and his own expenses and have something left over which he calls net profit. These relationships form the skeleton parts of an operating statement. Sales minus cost of goods sold equals gross margin; gross margin minus expenses equals net profit. An example based on fig. A–1 is as follows:

Sales	$80,000
Cost of goods sold	48,000
Gross margin	32,000
Expenses	27,000
Net profit	$ 4,800

Sales   The first line in an operating statement records the gross sales—the total amount sold by the company. From this figure, the company deducts its sales returns and sales allowances. In virtually every firm at some time during an operating period, customers will want to return or exchange merchandise. In a sales return, the customer is refunded the full purchase price in cash or credit. In a sales allowance, the customer keeps the merchandise but is given a reduction from selling because of some dissatisfaction. The income from the sale of returned merchandise is included in a company's gross sales.

After sales returns and allowances are deducted from gross sales, the resulting amount is net sales. This is the most important figure in the sales

fig.   A–1

Alpha-Beta Company, operating statement, for year ending December 31, 1963

Gross sales			$87,000
Less: Sales returns and allowances	$ 5,500		
Cash discounts allowed	1,500	7,000	
Net sales			$80,000
Cost of goods sold:			
Beginning inventory, January 1 (at cost)		18,000	
Gross purchases	49,300		
Less: Cash discounts taken on purchases	900		
Net purchases	48,400		
Plus: Freight in	1,600		
Net purchases (at delivered cost)		50,000	
Cost of goods available for sale		68,000	
Less: Ending inventory, December 31 (at cost)		20,000	
Cost of goods sold			48,000
Gross Margin			32,000
Expenses:			
Salesmen's salaries and commissions		$11,000	
Advertising		2,400	
Office supplies		250	
Taxes (except income tax)		125	
Telephone and telegraph		250	
Delivery expenses		175	
Rent		800	
Heat, light, and power		300	
Depreciation		100	
Insurance		150	
Interest		150	
Bad debts		300	
Administrative salaries		7,500	
Office salaries		3,500	
Miscellaneous expenses		200	
Total expenses			27,200
Net profit			$ 4,800

section of the statement. It represents the net amount of sales revenue out of which the company will pay for the products and all its expenses. The net sales figure is also the one upon which many operating ratios are based. It is set at 100 per cent, and other items are then expressed as a percentage of net sales.

Cost of goods sold   From net sales, we must deduct the cost of the merchandise which was sold as we work toward discovering the firm's final net profit. In determining cost of goods sold in a retail or wholesale operation, we start with the value of any merchandise on hand at the beginning of the period. To this we add the net cost of what was purchased during the period. From this total we deduct the value of whatever remains unsold at the end of the period. In Figure A–1 the firm started with an inventory worth $18,000; purchases were made which cost $50,000. Then the firm had a total of $68,000 worth of goods available for sale. If all were sold, the cost of goods sold would have been $68,000. At the end of the year, however, there is still $20,000 worth of merchandise on hand. Thus during the year, the company sold goods which cost $48,000.

In the preceding paragraph, we blithely spoke of merchandise "valued at" a certain figure or "worth" a stated amount. Actually the problem of inventory valuation is complicated and sometimes controversial. The usual rule of thumb is to value inventories at cost or market, whichever is lower. The actual application of this rule may be difficult. Assume that a store buys six footballs at $2 each and the next week buys six more at $2.50 each and then places them, jumbled, in a basket display for sale. Then one is sold, but there is no marking to indicate whether the cost of goods sold was $2 or $2.50, and the inventory value of the remaining eleven balls may be $27.50 or $28. If we multiply this situation by thousands of items and thousands of purchases and sales, we may begin to see the depth of the problem.

Another figure which deserves some comment is the net cost of delivered purchases. A company starts with its gross purchases at billed cost. Then it must deduct any purchases which were returned or any purchase allowances received. The company should also deduct any discounts taken for payment of the bill within a specified period of time. Deducting purchase returns and allowances and purchase discounts gives the net cost of the purchases. Then freight charges paid by the buyer (called "freight in") are added to net purchases to determine the net cost of *delivered* purchases. In some accounting systems, firms place their purchase discounts near the bottom of the operating statement in a section called "other income," thus treating these discounts as a reflection of financial ability to pay bills promptly. The preferred location of this income item in retail and wholesale operations today is in the cost-of-goods-sold section, so that management may see the net cost of its purchases.

In a manufacturing concern, the cost-of-goods-sold section takes on a slightly different form. Instead of determining the cost of goods *purchased*, the company determines the cost of goods *manufactured*. Cost of goods manufactured is added to the beginning inventory to ascertain the total goods available for sale. Then after the ending inventory of finished goods is deducted, the answer is cost of goods sold. To find the cost of goods *manufactured*, a company starts with the value of goods partially completed (beginning inventory of goods in process) and then adds the cost of raw materials and parts, direct and indirect labor, and factory overhead expenses incurred during the period. By deducting the value of goods still in process at the end of the period, management knows the cost of goods manufactured during that span of time.

Gross margin　　Gross margin is determined simply by subtracting cost of goods sold from net sales. Gross margin, sometimes called gross profit, is one of the key figures in the entire marketing program. When we say that a certain store has a "margin" of 30 per cent, or a salesman's compensation plan is set up to encourage the man to push the "high-margin" products, we are referring to the gross margin.

Expenses　　Operating expenses are deducted from gross margin to determine the net profit. The operating-expense-section includes marketing, administrative, and possibly some miscellaneous expense items. It does not include cost of goods purchased or manufactured; these expenses have already been deducted. Expenses may be itemized in several different ways.

MARKUPS

It is common practice for retailers and wholesalers to use the concept of markup when determining the selling price for an article. Normally the selling price must exceed the cost of the merchandise by an amount sufficient to cover the operating expenses and still leave the desired profit. The difference between the selling price and the cost of the item is the markup; sometimes it is termed the "mark-on."

The markup is closely related to the gross margin. It will be recalled that gross margin is equal to net sales minus cost of goods sold. Looking below the gross margin on an operating statement, we find that gross margin equals operating expenses plus net profit. Normally the initial markup in a company, department, or product line must be set a little higher than the overall gross margin desired for the selling unit because ordinarily some reductions will be incurred before all of the articles are sold. For one reason or another, some items will not sell at the original price. They will have to be marked down, that is, reduced in price from the original level. Some pilferage and other shortages may also occur.

Typically, for convenience in computation and for other reasons, markups are expressed in percentages rather than dollars. The first problem is to determine the base for the percentage. That is, when we speak of a 40 per cent markup, what do we mean, 40 per cent of what? Markups may be expressed as a percentage of either the cost price or the selling price. To determine markup percentage when it is based on cost, the formula is:

$$\text{Markup percentage} = \frac{\text{dollar markup}}{\text{cost}}$$

when the markup is based on selling price, the formula is:

$$\text{Markup percentage} = \frac{\text{dollar markup}}{\text{selling price}}$$

It is important that all interested parties understand which base is being used in a given situation; otherwise the results can differ considerably. To illustrate, Mr. A runs a clothing store and claims he needs a 66⅔ per cent markup to make a small net profit. Mr. B, who runs a competitive store, says he needs only a 40 per cent markup and that A must be wasteful, inefficient, or a big profiteer. Actually, both merchants are using identical markups, but they are using different bases. Each man buys hats at $6 apiece and sets the selling price at $10. This is a markup of $4 per hat. Mr. A is expressing his markup as a percentage of cost, thus the 66⅔ per cent figure ($\frac{4}{6}$ = 66⅔ per cent). Mr. B, in quoting a 40 per cent markup, bases his on the selling price ($\frac{4}{10}$ = 40 per cent). It would be a mistake for Mr. A to try to get by on B's 40 per cent markup, so long as A uses cost as his base. After buying the hats at $6, Mr. A would end up with a selling price of $8.40 if he used B's markup but his own (A's) cost basis; that is, 40 per cent over $6 equals $2.40. This $2.40 markup on the average over the entire hat department would *not* enable A to cover his usual expenses and make a profit. Unless otherwise indicated, markup percentages are always stated as a percentage of selling price.

The computation of selling price is simple if we know dollar cost and the desired percentage markup. The following diagram, along with some examples, should help the student to understand the various relationships among selling price, cost, and markup, whether the markup is stated in percentages or dollars and whether the percentages are based on selling price or cost.

	$	$
Selling price		
− Cost		
Markup	$	$

In these examples, the markups are based on selling price. A merchant buys an article for $90 and knows he must get a markup of 40 per cent. What is his selling price? By filling in the known information in the diagram, we see the following picture:

	$	
Selling price		100%
— Cost	90	
Markup	$	40%

It is easy to see that the percentage figure representing cost is 60 per cent. Thus the $90 cost equals 60 per cent of the selling price. The selling price is then $150 ($90 equals 60 per cent times selling price; then $90 is divided by .6 or 60 per cent to get the answer of $150).

Another common situation facing a merchant is to have competition set a ceiling on selling price, or possibly he must buy an item to fit into one of his price lines. Then he wants to know the maximum amount he can pay for the item and still get his normal markup. For instance, assume that the selling price of an article is set at $60 (by competition or by the $59.95 price line). The retailer's normal markup is 35 per cent. What is the most he should pay for this article? Again, let us fill in what we know in the diagram. The dollar

Selling price	$60	100%
— Cost		
Markup		35%

markup is $21 (35 per cent of $60), so by a simple subtraction we find that the maximum cost the merchant will want to pay is $39.

It should be clearly understood that markups are figured on the selling price *at each level of business* in a channel of distribution. A manufacturer applies a markup to determine his selling price. The manufacturer's selling price then becomes the wholesaler's cost. Then the wholesaler must determine his own selling price by applying his usual markup percentage based on his—the wholesaler's—selling price. The same procedure is carried on by the retailer whose cost figure is the wholesaler's selling price. The following computations should illustrate this point:

Retailer's selling price	$20 ⎫	Retailer's markup equals $8 equals
Retailer's cost	$12 ⎭	40 per cent
Wholesaler's selling price	$12 ⎫	Wholesaler's markup equals $2
Wholesaler's cost	$10 ⎭	equals 16⅔ per cent
Producer's selling price	$10 ⎫	Producer's markup equals $3 equals
Producer's cost	$7 ⎭	30 per cent

If a firm is used to dealing in markups based on cost—and sometimes this is done among wholesalers—the same diagrammatic approach may be employed that was used above in the examples of markup based on selling price. The only change is that cost will equal 100 per cent, and the selling price will be

100 per cent plus the markup based on cost. As an example, assume that a firm bought an article for $70 and wanted a 20 per cent markup based on cost. The markup in dollars is $14 (20 per cent of $70) and the selling price is $84 ($70 plus $14).

Even though it is customary to compute markups on the basis of selling price, a marketing executive should understand the relationships between markups on cost and markups on selling price. For instance, if a product costs $6 and sells for $10, there is a $4 markup. This is a 40 per cent markup when based on selling price, but a 66⅔ per cent markup when based on cost. An executive should also be able to convert from one base to another. The following diagram may be helpful in understanding these relationships:

Selling price = 100%   Cost = 100%

	40%	Markup = $4.00	66⅔ %	
$10 = 100%				$10 = 166⅔ %
	60%	Cost = $6.00	100%	

These convertible relationships may be expressed in the following formulas:

(1) Percentage markup on selling price = $\dfrac{\text{percentage markup on cost}}{100\% + \text{percentage markup on cost}}$

(2) Percentage markup on cost = $\dfrac{\text{percentage markup on selling price}}{100\% - \text{percentage markup on selling price}}$

To illustrate the use of these formulas, let us assume that a retailer has a markup of 25 per cent on cost and wants to know what the corresponding figure is, based on selling price. In formula (1) we get

$$\frac{25\%}{100\% + 25\%} = \frac{25\%}{125\%} = 20\%$$

A markup of 33⅓ % based on selling price converts to 50 per cent based on price, by using formula (2) as follows:

$$\frac{33\tfrac{1}{3}\%}{100\% - 33\tfrac{1}{3}\%} = \frac{33\tfrac{1}{3}\%}{66\tfrac{2}{3}\%} = 50\%$$

ANALYTICAL RATIOS

From a study of the operating statement, management can develop several ratios which will be useful tools in analyzing and evaluating the results of its marketing program. In most of these cases, net sales is used as the base of 100 per cent. In fact, unless it is specifically mentioned to the contrary, all ratios reflecting gross margin, net profit, or any operating expense are stated as a percentage of net sales.

Gross margin percentage

This is the ratio between gross margin and net sales. Referring to fig. A–1, the gross margin percentage is $\dfrac{\$32,000}{\$80,000}$, or 40 percent.

Net profit percentage

This ratio is computed by dividing net profits by net sales. In fig. A–1 the ratio is $\dfrac{\$4,800}{\$80,000}$, or 6 per cent. This percentage may be computed either before or after Federal income taxes are deducted, but the answer should be labeled adequately to reflect which it is.

Operating expense percentage

When total operating expenses are divided by net sales, the result is the operating expense ratio or percentage. In fig. A–1 the ratio is 34 per cent ($\dfrac{\$27,200}{80,000}$). In similar fashion, we may determine the expense ratio for any given cost. Thus we note in fig. A–1 that the rent expense was 1 per cent, advertising was 3 per cent, and salesmen's salaries and commissions, 13.75 per cent. Frequently in its operating statement, a company will add a percentage column at the right. This column will start with net sales being 100 per cent and will show for each item on the statement its percentage in relation to net sales.

Rate of return on investment

A commonly used measure of the operating success of a company is its rate of earnings or rate of return on investment. Here we use both the balance sheet and the profit and loss statement as sources of information. The earnings rate is obtained by dividing the net profit by the total capital investment.

Rate of stockturn

Management often measures the efficiency of its marketing operations by means of the stockturn ratio. This figure represents the number of times the average inventory is "turned over" or sold during the period under study. The ratio is computed on either a cost or a selling-price basis. That is, both the numerator and the denominator of the ratio fraction must be expressed in the same terms, either cost or selling price.

On a cost basis, the formula is as follows:

$$\text{Rate of stockturn} = \frac{\text{cost of goods sold}}{\text{average inventory at cost}}$$

The average inventory is determined by adding the beginning and ending inventory and dividing this answer by two. In fig. A–1 the average inventory is $\dfrac{\$18,000 + \$20,000}{2} = \$19,000$. The stockturn rate is $\dfrac{\$48,000}{\$19,000}$, or 2.5. Because inventories usually are abnormally low at the first of the year in anticipation of taking physical inventory, this average may not be representative. Consequently, some companies add the book inventories at the beginning of each month and divide this sum by twelve.

If the inventory is kept on a retail basis, as is done in most large retail organizations, the stockturn rate equals net sales divided by average inventory at selling price. Sometimes the stockturn rate is computed by dividing the number of *units* sold by the average inventory expressed in units.

Wholesale and retail trade associations in many types of businesses compile and publish figures showing the average rate of stockturn for their members. A firm with a low rate of stockturn is apt to be spending too much on storage and inventory expenses. Also, the company has a higher risk of obsolescence or spoilage. If the stockturn rate gets too high, this may indicate the company maintains too low an average inventory. Often a firm in this situation is operating on a hand-to-mouth buying system. In addition to incurring high handling and billing costs per order, the company is apt to be out of stock on some items.

Markdown percentage

Sometimes a retailer is unable to sell an article at the originally posted price, and he reduces this price in order to move the goods. A *markdown* is the reduction from original selling price. Management frequently finds it very helpful to determine the markdown percentage and to analyze the size and number of markdowns and the reasons for them. Retailers, particularly, make extensive use of markdown analysis.

Markdowns are expressed as a percentage of net sales and *not* as a percentage of original selling price. To illustrate, assume that a retailer purchased a hat for $6 and marked it up 40 per cent to sell for $10. The hat did not sell at that price, so he marked it down to $8. Now it is true that his advertisement or display sign may advertise a price cut of 20 per cent. Yet in our calculations, his markdown is stated at $2 or 25 per cent of the $8 selling price.

Markdowns in a department or in an entire company are computed for a given period of time by dividing total dollar markdowns by total net sales during that period. The important points should be noted here. The markdown percentage is computed in this fashion, regardless of whether the markdown items were sold or are still in the store. Also, the percentage is computed with respect to total net sales and not only in connection with sales of marked-down articles. As an example, assume that a retailer buys ten hats at $6 each and prices them to sell at $10. He sells five hats at $10, marks the other five down to $8, and sells three at the lower price. His total sales are $74, and his markdowns are $10; he has a markdown ratio of 13.5 per cent.

Markdowns do not appear on the profit and loss statement because they occur before an article is sold. The first item on an operating statement is gross sales. That figure reflects the actual selling price, which may be the selling price after a markdown has been taken.

A refinement in the computation of the markdown percentage involves sales allowances. Actually, these allowances are added to markdowns in determining the markdown percentage. The formula is

$$\text{Markdown percentage} = \frac{\text{dollar markdown} + \text{dollar sales allowances}}{\text{total net sales in dollars}}$$

The reasoning here is that, in effect, an allowance is simply a markdown taken after the sale was made. In the hat example above, if the retailer saw that a hat was soiled, he would mark it down $2. Assume that he did not notice the defect and that he sold the hat for $10. The customer later saw that the hat was soiled and voiced his dissatisfaction. He kept the hat, but was given a $2 allowance. Allowances here should not be confused with sales returns where the customer returns the article and is refunded the full purchase price.

SELECTED READINGS

PART 1. MODERN MARKETING

Alderson, Wroe: *Dynamic Marketing Behavior,* Richard D. Irwin, Inc., Homewood, Ill., 1965

Anderson, R. Clifton, and Philip R. Cateora (eds.): *Marketing Insights: Selected Readings,* Appleton-Century-Crofts, Inc., New York, 1963.

Barger, Harold: *Distribution's Place in the American Economy since 1869,* Princeton University Press, Princeton, N.J., 1955.

Bartels, Robert: *The Development of Marketing Thought,* Richard D. Irwin, Inc., Homewood, Ill., 1962.

Bliss, Perry (ed.): *Marketing and the Behavioral Sciences,* Allyn and Bacon, Inc., Englewood Cliffs, N.J., 1963.

Boyd, Harper W., Jr., and Richard M. Clewett (eds.): *Contemporary American Marketing,* rev. ed., Richard D. Irwin, Inc., Homewood, Ill., 1962.

———— and Ralph Westfall: *Marketing Research: Text and Cases,* rev. ed., Richard D. Irwin, Inc., Homewood, Ill., 1964.

Britt, Steuart H., and Harper W. Boyd, Jr. (eds.): *Marketing and Administrative Action,* McGraw-Hill Book Company, New York, 1964.

Brown, Lyndon O.: *Marketing and Distribution Research,* 3d ed., The Ronald Press Company, New York, 1955.

Charvat, Frank J., and W. Tate Whitman: *Marketing Management: A Quantitative Approach,* Simmons-Boardman Publishing Corporation, New York, 1964.

Converse, Paul D.: *The Beginning of Marketing Thought in the United States,* University of Texas, Bureau of Business Research, Austin, Tex., 1959.

Cox, Reavis: *Distribution in a High-level Economy,* Prentice-Hall, Inc., Englewood Cliffs, N.J., 1965.

Davis, Kenneth R.: *Marketing Management,* 2d ed., The Ronald Press Company, New York, 1966.

Dirksen, Charles J., Arthur Kroeger, and Lawrence J. Lockley (eds.): *Readings in Marketing,* Richard D. Irwin, Inc., Homewood, Ill., 1963.

Ferber, Rober , Donald F. Blankertz, and Sidney Hollander, Jr.: *Marketing Research,* The Ronald Press Company, New York, 1964.

Field, George A., John Douglas, and Lawrence X. Tarpey: *Marketing Management,* Charles E. Merrill, Inc., Englewood Cliffs, N.J., 1965.

Frey, Albert W., and Gerald Albaum (eds.): *Marketing Handbook,* 2d ed., The Ronald Press Company, New York, 1965.

Green, Paul E., and Donald S. Tull: *Research for Marketing Decisions,* Prentice-Hall, Inc., Englewood Cliffs, N.J., 1966.

Heidingsfield, Myron S., and Frank H. Eby, Jr.: *Marketing and Business Research,* Holt, Rinehart and Winston, Inc., New York, 1962.

Holloway, Robert J., and Robert S. Hancock (eds.): *The Environment of Marketing Behavior,* John Wiley & Sons, Inc., New York, 1964.

Holmes, Parker (ed.): *Marketing Research: Principles and Readings,* 2d ed., South-Western Publishing Company, Cincinnati, 1966.

Howard, John A.: *Marketing Management: Analysis and Planning,* rev. ed., Richard D. Irwin, Inc., Homewood, Ill., 1963.

Kelley, Eugene J.: *Marketing: Strategy and Functions,* Prentice-Hall, Inc., Englewood Cliffs, N.J., 1965.

————, Hector Lazo, Arnold Corbin, and Edward Kahn (eds.): *Marketing Management: An Annotated Bibliography,* American Marketing Association, Chicago, Bibliography Series, no. 8, 1963.

Koontz, Harold, and Cyril J. O'Donnell: *Principles of Management,* 3d ed., McGraw-Hill Book Company, New York, 1964.

Lazer, William, and Eugene J. Kelley (eds.): *Managerial Marketing: Perspectives and Viewpoints,* rev. ed., Richard D. Irwin, Inc., Homewood, Ill., 1962.

Luck, David J., Donald Taylor, and Hugh Wales: *Marketing Research,* 2d ed., Prentice-Hall, Inc., Englewood Cliffs, N.J., 1961.

McFarland, Dalton E.: *Management Principles and Practices,* The Macmillan Company, New York, 1958.

Oxenfeldt, Alfred R.: *Executive Action in Marketing,* Wadsworth Publishing Company, Inc., Belmont, Calif., 1966.

Phelps, D. Maynard, and J. Howard Westing: *Marketing Management,* rev. ed., Richard D. Irwin, Inc., Homewood, Ill., 1960.

Schreier, Frederick T.: *Modern Marketing Research,* Wadsworth Publishing Company, Inc., Belmont, Calif., 1964.

Shaw, Steven J., and C. McFerron Gittinger (eds.): *Marketing in Business Management,* The Macmillan Company, New York, 1963.

Walters, S. George, Max D. Snider, and Morris L. Sweet (eds.): *Readings in Marketing,* South-Western Publishing Company, Cincinnati, 1962.

Wasson, Chester R.: *The Strategy of Marketing Research,* Appleton-Century-Crofts, Inc., New York, 1964.

Westing, J. Howard, and Gerald Albaum (eds.): *Modern Marketing Thought,* The Macmillan Company, New York, 1964.

Zober, Martin: *Marketing Management,* John Wiley & Sons, Inc., New York, 1964.

PART 2. THE MARKET

Alexander, Ralph S., James S. Cross, and Ross M. Cunningham: *Industrial Marketing,* rev. ed., Richard D. Irwin, Inc., Homewood, Ill., 1961.

American Management Association: *Trade Relations Defined,* Management Bulletin no. 19, New York, 1962.

Britt, Steuart Henderson (ed.): *Consumer Behavior and the Behavioral Sciences,* John Wiley & Sons, Inc., New York, 1966.

Corey, E. Raymond: *Industrial Marketing: Cases and Concepts,* Prentice-Hall, Inc., Englewood Cliffs, N.J., 1962.

Dewhurst, J. F., and associates: *America's Needs and Resources: A New Survey,* The Twentieth Century Fund, New York, 1955.

Ferber, Robert, and Hugh G. Wales (eds.): *Motivation and Market Behavior,* Richard D. Irwin, Inc., Homewood, Ill., 1958.

Katona, George: *The Powerful Consumer,* McGraw-Hill Book Company, New York, 1960.

Katz, Elihu, and Paul Lazarsfeld: *Personal Influence,* The Free Press of Glencoe, New York, 1955.

McNeal, James U. (ed.): *Dimensions of Consumer Behavior,* Appleton-Century-Crofts, Inc., New York, 1965.

Martineau, Pierre: *Motivation in Advertising,* McGraw-Hill Book Company, New York, 1957.

Mazur, Paul: *The Standards We Raise: The Dynamics of Consumption,* Harper & Row, Publishers, Incorporated, New York, 1953.

National Industrial Conference Board, Inc.: *Use of Motivation Research in Marketing,* Studies in Business Policy, no. 97, New York, 1960.

Newman, Joseph W.: *Motivation Research and Marketing Management,* Harvard Graduate School of Business Administration, Cambridge, Mass., 1957.

Rich, Stuart U.: *Shopping Behavior of Department Store Customers,* Harvard University Press, Cambridge, Mass., 1963.

Smith, George H.: *Motivation Research in Advertising and Marketing,* McGraw-Hill Book Company, New York, 1954.

Tucker, W. T. (ed.): *Foundations for a Theory of Consumer Behavior,* Holt, Rinehart and Winston, Inc., New York, 1966.

Warner, W. Lloyd, and Paul Lunt: *The Social Life of a Modern Community,* Yale University Press, New Haven, Conn., 1941.

———, Marchia Meeker, and Kenneth Eells: *Social Class in America,* Science Research Associates, Inc., Chicago, 1949.

PART 3. THE PRODUCT

American Management Association: *Developing a Product Strategy,* New York, 1959.

———: *Establishing a New-product Program: Guides for Effective Planning,* Management Report no. 8, New York, 1958.

———: *How to Plan Products That Sell: Guides for Development and Commercialization,* Management Report no. 13, New York, 1958.

———: *The Integrated Approach to Product Planning,* Marketing Series, no. 101, New York, 1957.

———: *New Products: New Profits,* New York, 1964.

———: *Product Development in Small and Medium-size Companies,* Research and Development Series, no. 4, New York, 1957.

———: Any of several reports in the Packaging Series.

Berg, Thomas L., and Abe Schuchman (eds.): *Product Strategy and Management,* Holt, Rinehart and Winston, Inc., New York, 1963.

Cole, Robert H., Lloyd M. Deboer, Richard D. Millican, and Nugent Wedding: *Manufacturer and Distributor Brands,* University of Illinois, Bureau of Economic and Business Research, Bulletin Series, no. 8, Urbana, Ill., 1955.

Coles, Jessie V.: *Standards and Labels for Consumers' Goods,* The Ronald Press Company, New York, 1949.

Dreyfuss, Henry: *Designing for People,* Simon and Schuster, Inc., New York, 1955.

National Industrial Conference Board, Inc.: *The Product Manager System,* Experiences in Marketing Management, no. 8, New York, 1965.

Pessemier, Edgar A.: *New-product Decisions,* McGraw-Hill Book Company, New York, 1966.

PART 4. DISTRIBUTION STRUCTURE

Beckman, Theodore N., Nathaniel H. Engle, and Robert D. Buzzell: *Wholesaling,* 3d ed., The Ronald Press Company, New York, 1959.

Charvat, Frank S.: *Supermarketing,* The Macmillan Company, New York, 1961.

Clewett, Richard M. (ed.): *Marketing Channels for Manufactured Products,* Richard D. Irwin, Inc., Homewood, Ill., 1954.

Constantin, James A.: *Principles of Logistics Management,* Appleton-Century-Crofts, Inc., New York, 1966.

Davidson, William R., and Alton F. Doody: *Retailing Management,* 3d ed., The Ronald Press Company, New York, 1966.

Dorr, W. C.: "Direct vs. Jobber Distribution: An Appraisal of the Pros and Cons," *Sales Management* (three-part article), Feb. 1, 1949, p. 37; Feb. 15, 1949, p. 56; Mar. 1, 1949, p. 92. (This is an older reference, but it is still a fine, pertinent appraisal.)

Duncan, Delbert J., and Charles F. Phillips: *Retailing: Principles and Methods,* 7th ed., Richard D. Irwin, Inc., Homewood, Ill., 1967.

Entenberg, Robert D.: *The Changing Competitive Position of Department Stores in the United States by Merchandise Lines,* rev. ed., The University of Pittsburgh Press, Pittsburgh, Pa., 1961.

Frederick, John H.: *Using Public Warehouses,* Chilton Company—Book Division, Philadelphia, 1957.

Goeldner, Charles R.: *Automatic Merchandising,* American Marketing Association, Bibliography Series, no. 9, Chicago, 1963.

Heskett, J. L., Robert M. Ivie, and Nicholas A. Glaskowsky, Jr.: *Business Logistics,* The Ronald Press Company, New York, 1964.

Hill, Richard M.: *Wholesaling Management: Text and Cases,* Richard D. Irwin, Inc., Homewood, Ill., 1963.

Hollander, Stanley C., and Gary A. Marple: *Henry Ford: Inventor of the Supermarket?* Michigan State University, Bureau of Business and Economic Research, Marketing and Transportation Paper no. 9, East Lansing, Mich., 1960.

Lebhar, Godfrey M.: *Chain Stores in America: 1859–1950,* Chain Store Publishing Co., New York, 1952.

Lewis, Edwin H., and Robert S. Hancock: *The Franchise System of Distribution,* The University of Minnesota Press, Minneapolis, 1963.

Lewis, Howard T., James W. Culliton, and Jack D. Steele: *The Role of Air Freight in Physical Distribution,* Harvard Graduate School of Business Administration, Cambridge, Mass., 1956.

McNair, Malcolm P., and Eleanor G. May: *The American Department Store: 1920–1962,* Harvard University Press, Cambridge, Mass., 1963.

Mossman, Frank H., and Newton Morton: *Logistics of Distribution Systems,* Allyn and Bacon, Inc., Englewood Cliffs, N.J., 1964.

National Industrial Conference Board, Inc.: *Building a Strong Distributor Organization,* Experiences in Marketing Management, no. 6, New York, 1964.

————: *Selecting and Evaluating Distributors,* Studies in Business Policy, no. 116, New York, 1965.

Palamountain, Joseph C.: *The Politics of Distribution,* Harvard University Press, Cambridge, Mass., 1955.

Preston, Lee E.: "Restrictive Distribution Arrangements: Economic Analysis and Public Policy Standards," *Law and Contemporary Problems,* Summer, 1965, pp. 506–529.

Revzan, David A.: *Wholesaling in Marketing Organization,* John Wiley & Sons, Inc., New York, 1961.

Schreiber, G. R.: *A Concise History of Vending in the U.S.A.,* Vend Magazine, Chicago, 1961.

Smykay, Edward W., Donald J. Bowersox, and Frank H. Mossman: *Physical Distribution Management,* The Macmillan Company, New York, 1961.

Staudt, Thomas A.: *The Manufacturers' Agent as a Marketing Institution,* U.S. Government Printing Office, Washington, D.C., 1952.

Warshaw, Martin A.: *Effective Selling through Wholesalers,* University of Michigan, Bureau of Business Research, Ann Arbor, Mich., 1961.

PART 5. THE PRICE SYSTEM

Bachman, Jules: *Pricing: Policies and Practices,* National Industrial Conference Board, Inc., Studies in Business Economics, no. 71, New York, 1961.

Cassady, Ralph, Jr.: *Price Warfare in Business Competition,* Michigan State University, Bureau of Business and Economic Research, Occasional Paper no. 11, East Lansing, Mich., 1963.

Dean, Joel: *Managerial Economics,* Prentice-Hall, Inc., Englewood Cliffs, N.J., 1951.

Dixon, Brian: *Price Discrimination and Marketing Management,* University of Michigan, Bureau of Business Research, Ann Arbor, Mich., 1960.

Edwards, Corwin D.: *The Price Discrimination Law: A Review of Experience,* The Brookings Institution, Washington, D.C., 1959.

Hollander, Stanley C.: *Restraints upon Retail Competition,* Michigan State University, Marketing and Transportation Paper no. 14, East Lansing, Mich., 1965.

————: *Retail Price Policies,* Michigan State University, Bureau of Business and Economic Research, Occasional Paper no. 1, East Lansing, Mich., 1958.

Kaplan, A. D. H., Joel B. Dirlam, and Robert F. Lanzillotti: *Pricing in Big Business,* The Brookings Institution, Washington, D.C., 1958.

Machlup, Fritz: *The Basing-point System,* McGraw-Hill Book Company, New York, 1949.

National Wholesale Druggists Association: *The Basis and Development of Fair Trade,* 3d ed., New York, 1955.

Oxenfeldt, Alfred R.: *Pricing for Marketing Executives,* Wadsworth Publishing Company, Inc., Belmont, Calif., 1961.

Rowe, Frederick M.: *Price Discrimination under the Robinson-Patman Act,* Little, Brown and Company, Boston, 1962.

Taggart, Herbert F.: *Cost Justification,* University of Michigan, School of Business Administration, Ann Arbor, Mich., 1959.

PART 6. PROMOTIONAL ACTIVITIES

Aspley, John C., and John C. Harkness: *Sales Manager's Handbook,* 10th ed., Dartnell Corp., Chicago, 1966.

Baker, Richard M., Jr., and Gregg Phifer: *Salesmanship: Communication, Persuasion, Perception,* Allyn and Bacon, Inc., Englewood Cliffs, N.J., 1966.

Barton, Roger: *Media in Advertising,* McGraw-Hill Book Company, New York, 1964.

Borden, Neil H.: *Advertising in Our Economy,* Richard D. Irwin, Inc., Homewood, Ill., 1945. This is a summary of Neil H. Borden, *The Economic Effects of Advertising,* Richard D. Irwin, Inc., Homewood, Ill., 1942.

Boyd, Harper W., Jr., and Joseph W. Newman (eds.): *Advertising Management: Selected Readings,* Richard D. Irwin, Inc., Homewood, Ill., 1965.

Brink, Edward L., and William T. Kelley: *The Management of Promotion,* Prentice-Hall, Inc., Englewood Cliffs, N.J., 1963.

Crawford, John W.: *Advertising,* 2d ed., Allyn and Bacon, Inc., Englewood Cliffs, N.J., 1965.

Dirksen, Charles J., and Arthur Kroeger: *Advertising Principles and Problems,* rev. ed., Richard D. Irwin, Inc., Homewood, Ill., 1964.

Frey, Albert W.: *Advertising,* 3d ed., The Ronald Press Company, New York, 1961.

——— and Kenneth R. Davis: *The Advertising Industry: Agency Services, Working Relationships, Compensation Methods,* Association of National Advertisers, New York, 1958.

Gross, Alfred: *Sales Promotion,* 2d ed., The Ronald Press Company, New York, 1961.

Kirkpatrick, C. A.: *Advertising: Mass Communication in Marketing,* Houghton Mifflin Company, Boston, 1964.

Kleppner, Otto: *Advertising Procedure,* 5th ed., Prentice-Hall, Inc., Englewood Cliffs, N.J., 1966.

Lucas, Darrell, and Steuart Henderson Britt: *Measuring Advertising Effectiveness,* McGraw-Hill Book Company, New York, 1964.

McNeal, James U. (ed.): *Readings in Promotion Management,* Appleton-Century-Crofts, Inc., New York, 1966.

National Industrial Conference Board, Inc.: *Measuring Advertising Results,* Studies in Business Policy, no. 102, New York, 1962.

———: *Pretesting Advertising,* Studies in Business Policy, no. 109, New York, 1963.

Pederson, Carlton A., and Milburn D. Wright: *Salesmanship: Principles and Methods,* 4th ed., Richard D. Irwin, Inc., Homewood, Ill., 1966.

Robinson, Patrick J., and David J. Luck: *Promotional Decision Making,* McGraw-Hill Book Company, New York, 1964.

Russell, Frederic A., Frank H. Beach, and Richard H. Buskirk: *Textbook of Salesmanship,* 7th ed., McGraw-Hill Book Company, New York, 1963.

Sandage, Charles H., and Vernon Fryburger: *Advertising Theory and Practice,* 6th ed., Richard D. Irwin, Inc., Homewood, Ill., 1963.

Seehafer, Gene F., and J. W. Laemmar: *Successful Television and Radio Advertising,* rev. ed., McGraw-Hill Book Company, New York, 1959.

Stanton, William J., and Richard H. Buskirk: *Management of the Sales Force,* rev. ed., Richard D. Irwin, Inc., Homewood, Ill., 1964.

Stroh, Thomas F.: *Salesmanship: Personal Communication and Persuasion in Marketing,* Richard D. Irwin, Inc., Homewood, Ill., 1966.

Thompson, Joseph W.: *Selling: A Behavioral Science Approach,* McGraw-Hill Book Company, New York, 1966.

Thompson, Willard M.: *Salesmanship: Concepts, Management, and Strategy,* John Wiley & Sons, Inc., New York, 1963.

Wedding, Nugent, and Richard S. Lessler: *Advertising Management,* The Ronald Press Company, New York, 1962.

Wright, John S., and Daniel S. Warner: *Advertising,* 2d ed., McGraw-Hill Book Company, New York, 1966.

———— (eds.): *Speaking of Advertising,* McGraw-Hill Book Company, New York, 1963.

Zacher, Robert V.: *Advertising Techniques and Management,* Richard D. Irwin, Inc., Homewood, Ill., 1961.

PART 7.   *MARKETING IN SPECIAL FIELDS*

A. Agricultural marketing

Abrahamsen, M. A., and C. L. Scroggs (eds.): *Agricultural Cooperation: Selected Readings,* The University of Minnesota Press, Minneapolis, 1957.

American Institute of Cooperation: *American Co-operation,* Washington, D.C., published annually.

Bakken, Henry H., and Marvin A. Schaars: *The Economics of Cooperative Marketing,* McGraw-Hill Book Company, New York, 1957.

Bowring, J. R., H. M. Southworth, and F. V. Waugh: *Marketing Policies for Agriculture,* Prentice-Hall, Inc., Englewood Cliffs, N.J., 1960

Committee for Economic Development: *Toward a Realistic Farm Program,* New York, 1958

Fowler, S. H.: *The Marketing of Livestock and Meat,* Interstate Printers and Publishers, Danville, Ill., 1961.

Knapp, Joseph G. (ed.): *Farmers in Business,* American Institute of Cooperation, Washington, D.C., 1963.

Kohls, Richard L.: *Agricultural Marketing,* rev. ed., The Macmillan Company, New York, 1961.

Shepherd, Geoffrey S.: *Marketing Farm Products: Economic Analysis,* 3d ed., Iowa State College Press, Ames, Iowa, 1955.

Waugh, Frederick V. (ed.): *Readings on Agricultural Marketing,* Iowa State College Press, Ames, Iowa, 1954.

B. International marketing

Bartels, Robert (ed.): *Comparative Marketing: Wholesaling in Fifteen Countries,* Richard D. Irwin, Inc., Homewood, Ill., 1963.

Bennett, Peter D. (ed.): *Marketing and Economic Development,* American Marketing Association, Chicago, 1965, pp. 49–183.

Coyle, John J., and Edward J. Mock (eds.): *Readings in International Business,* International Textbook Company, Scranton, Pa., 1965.

Dewhurst, J. Frederic, and others: *Europe's Needs and Resources,* The Twentieth Century Fund, New York, 1961.

Dowd, Laurence P.: *Principles of World Business,* rev. ed., Allyn and Bacon, Inc., Englewood Cliffs, N.J., 1964.

Dunn, S. Watson: *International Handbook of Advertising,* McGraw-Hill Book Company, New York, 1964.

Ewing, John S., and Frank Meissner: *International Business Management: Readings and Cases,* Wadsworth Publishing Company, Inc., Belmont, Calif., 1964.

Fayerweather, John: *International Marketing,* Prentice-Hall, Inc., Englewood Cliffs, N.J., 1965.

————: *Management of International Operations: Text and Cases,* McGraw-Hill Book Company, New York, 1960.

Hess, John M., and Philip R. Cateora: *International Marketing,* Richard D. Irwin, Inc., Homewood, Ill., 1966.

Kramer, Roland L.: *International Marketing,* 2d ed., South-Western Publishing Company, Cincinnati, 1965.

Leighton, David S. R.: *International Marketing: Text and Cases,* McGraw-Hill Book Company, New York, 1966.

Stanley, Alexander O.: *Handbook of International Marketing: How to Export, Import, and Invest Overseas,* McGraw-Hill Book Company, New York, 1963.

Stuart, Robert D.: *Penetrating the International Market,* American Management Association, Management Report no. 84, New York, 1965.

PART 8. PLANNING AND EVALUATING THE MARKETING EFFORT

Bass, Frank M., Robert D. Buzzell, Mark R. Greene, William Lazer, Edgar A. Pessemier, Donald L. Shawver, Abraham Schuchman, Chris A. Theodore, and George W. Wilson (eds.): *Mathematical Models and Methods in Marketing,* Richard D. Irwin, Inc., Homewood, Ill., 1961.

Buzzell, Robert D. (ed.): *A Basic Bibliography on Mathematical Methods in Marketing,* American Marketing Association, Bibliography Series, no. 7, Chicago, 1962.

————: *Mathematical Models and Marketing Management,* Harvard Business School, Division of Research, Cambridge, Mass., 1964.

Commerce Clearing House: *Trade Regulation Reporter,* New York. (Looseleaf reporting service.)

Cox, Reavis, Wroe Alderson, and Stanley J. Shapiro (eds.): *Theory in Marketing,* 2d ser., Richard D. Irwin, Inc., Homewood, Ill., 1964.

Crisp, Richard D.: *Sales Planning and Control,* McGraw-Hill Book Company, New York, 1961.

Day, Ralph L. (ed.): *Marketing Models: Quantitative and Behavioral,* International Textbook Company, Scranton, Pa., 1964.

Edwards, Corwin D.: *Big Business and the Policy of Competition,* Western Reserve University Press, Cleveland, Ohio, 1956.

————: *Maintaining Competition: Requisites of a Government Policy,* McGraw-Hill Book Company, New York, 1949.

Grether, E. T.: *Marketing and Public Policy,* Prentice-Hall, Inc., Englewood Cliffs, N.J., 1966.

Halbert, Michael H.: *The Meaning and Sources of Marketing Theory,* McGraw-Hill Book Company, New York, 1965.

Heckert, J. Brooks, and Robert E. Miner: *Distribution Costs,* 2d. ed., The Ronald Press Company, New York, 1953.

Howard, John A.: *Marketing Theory,* Allyn and Bacon, Inc., Englewood Cliffs, N.J., 1965.

Howard, Marshall C.: *Legal Aspects of Marketing,* McGraw-Hill Book Company, New York, 1964.

Lazer, William, and Eugene J. Kelley: *Interdisciplinary Contributions to Marketing Management,* Michigan State University, Bureau of Business and Economic Research, Marketing and Transportation Paper no. 5, East Lansing, Mich., 1959.

Longman, Donald E., and Michael Schiff: *Practical Distribution Cost Analysis,* Richard D. Irwin, Inc., Homewood, Ill., 1955.

Mulvihill, Donald F. (ed.): *Guide to the Quantitative Age,* Holt, Rinehart and Winston, Inc., New York, 1966.

Mund, Vernon: *Government and Business,* 3d ed., Harper & Row, Publishers, Incorporated, New York, 1960.

National Industrial Conference Board, Inc.: *Development of Marketing Objectives and Plans,* Experiences in Marketing Management, no. 3, New York, 1963.

————: *Sales Analysis,* Studies in Business Policy, no. 113, New York, 1965.

————: *Sales Forecasting,* Studies in Business Policy, no. 106, New York, 1964.

————: *Small Orders: Problems and Solutions,* Studies in Business Policy, no. 94, New York, 1960.

Schwartz, George (ed.): *Science in Marketing,* John Wiley & Sons, Inc., New York, 1965.

Sevin, Charles H.: *Distribution Cost Analysis,* U.S. Department of Commerce, Economic Series, no. 50, 1946.

————: *How Manufacturers Reduce Their Distribution Costs,* U.S. Department of Commerce, Economic Series, no. 72, 1948.

————: *Marketing Productivity Analysis,* McGraw-Hill Book Company, New York, 1965.

Stern, Mark E.: *Marketing Planning,* McGraw-Hill Book Company, New York, 1966.

Zaltman, Gerald: *Marketing: Contributions from the Behavioral Sciences,* Harcourt, Brace & World, Inc., New York, 1965.

INDEXES

NAME INDEX